Psalms

INTERPRETATION
A Bible Commentary for Teaching and Preaching

INTERPRETATION

A BIBLE COMMENTARY FOR TEACHING AND PREACHING

James Luther Mays, *Editor*
Patrick D. Miller, Jr., *Old Testament Editor*
Paul J. Achtemeier, *New Testament Editor*

JAMES LUTHER MAYS

Psalms

INTERPRETATION

A Bible Commentary
for Teaching and Preaching

John Knox Press
LOUISVILLE

Library of Congress Cataloging-in-Publication Data

Mays, James Luther.
   Psalms / James Luther Mays.
       p.   cm. — (Interpretation, a Bible commentary for
teaching and preaching)
   Includes bibliographical references and indexes.
   ISBN 0-8042-3115-X

   1. Bible. O.T. Psalms—Commentaries. I. Bible. O.T. Psalms.
English. New Revised Standard. 1994. II. Title. III. Series.
BS1430.3.M33   1994
223′.207—dc20   93-32887

© copyright John Knox Press 1994
This book is printed on acid-free paper that meets the American
National Standards Institute Z39.48 standard. ∞
10 9 8 7 6 5 4 3 2 1
Printed in the United States of America
John Knox Press
Louisville, Kentucky 40202-1396

For
The Conclave
and all the others who sat and studied together
in the annual Seminar on Psalms
at Union Theological Seminary in Virginia,
1957–1994

"How good and pleasant it is when covenant kin
sit together in unity . . .
for there the LORD *has ordained*
the blessing of enduring life."
(Psalm 133)

SERIES PREFACE

This series of commentaries offers an interpretation of the books of the Bible. It is designed to meet the needs of students, teachers, ministers, and priests for a contemporary expository commentary. These volumes will not replace the historical critical commentary or homiletical aids to preaching. The purpose of this series is rather to provide a third kind of resource, a commentary which presents the integrated result of historical and theological work with the biblical text.

An interpretation in the full sense of the term involves a text, an interpreter, and someone for whom the interpretation is made. Here, the text is what stands written in the Bible in its full identity as literature from the time of "the prophets and apostles," the literature which is read to inform, inspire, and guide the life of faith. The interpreters are scholars who seek to create an interpretation which is both faithful to the text and useful to the church. The series is written for those who teach, preach, and study the Bible in the community of faith.

The comment generally takes the form of expository essays. It is planned and written in the light of the needs and questions which arise in the use of the Bible as Holy Scripture. The insights and results of contemporary scholarly research are used for the sake of the exposition. The commentators write as exegetes and theologians. The task which they undertake is both to deal with what the texts say and to discern their meaning for faith and life. The exposition is the unified work of one interpreter.

The text on which the comment is based is the Revised Standard Version of the Bible and, since its appearance, the New Revised Standard Version. The general availability of these translations makes the printing of a text in the commentary unnecessary. The commentators have also had other current versions in view as they worked and refer to their readings where it is helpful. The text is divided into sections appropriate to the particular book; comment deals with passages as a whole, rather than proceeding word by word, or verse by verse.

Writers have planned their volumes in light of the requirements set by the exposition of the book assigned to them. Biblical books differ in character, content, and arrangement. They also differ in the way they have been and are used in the liturgy, thought, and devotion of the church. The distinctiveness and use of particular books have been taken into account in decisions about the approach, emphasis, and use of space in the commentaries. The goal has been to allow writers to develop the format which provides for the best presentation of their interpretation.

The result, writers and editors hope, is a commentary which both explains and applies, an interpretation which deals with both the meaning and the significance of biblical texts. Each commentary reflects, of course, the writer's own approach and perception of the church and world. It could and should not be otherwise. Every interpretation of any kind is individual in that sense; it is one reading of the text. But all who work at the interpretation of Scripture in the church need the help and stimulation of a colleague's reading and understanding of the text. If these volumes serve and encourage interpretation in that way, their preparation and publication will realize their purpose.

The Editors

PREFACE

The psalms have a double identity. They are Scripture and liturgy. They compose a book of the Bible and are found in our hymnals and books of worship and prayer. When we think of them in historical perspective, another identity emerges. They are the liturgical poetry of ancient Israel, texts with a history of composition and use before they became Scripture.

A commentary in this Interpretation series needs to keep all three identities in view. That puts some strain on the commentator's task. The attempt to interpret the psalms in awareness of the depth in their identity explains some things about the commentary and its writing.

The comment on particular psalms pays more attention to the language and literary shape than to questions about their original social and historical context. The language and the literary shape constitute the text that has been preserved, and it is this text that has been used, reread, and translated as a psalm. Form-critical and historical questions are subordinate rather than primary agenda. I have tended to construe the language as part of the vocabulary of the Book of Psalms and then of the Old Testament in general. The first goal of comment has been to ask what this Old Testament text, read in its literary and canonical context, says about God and God's way with human beings and the predicament and promise of human life before the reality of God.

I have frequently consulted the Midrash Tehillim, Augustine, Neale and Littledale, Luther, Calvin, Spurgeon, and Barth while working on particular psalms. While I have not regularly quoted or cited these sources, they have been immensely useful in enabling me to maintain a sense of historic psalmody. At times they gave guidance to dimensions of a psalm whose meaning has been recurrently significant.

Readers will find that the commentary is uneven. Some psalms receive sustained attention; others are dealt with briefly. The unevenness is intentional, the result of two concerns about the use and usefulness of the commentary. The first concern has been that of keeping the comment within the limits of one volume. Because of the length and complexity of the Book of

ix

Psalms, commentaries of several volumes have become customary. But the accessibility and convenience of a one-volume work for those for whom this series is designed are evident.

The second concern has been that of creating a commentary written in the light of priorities derived from the use and study of the Psalms in the church. Guided by these priorities, I have written expository essays on many of the psalms; others are treated in a concise descriptive fashion. The psalms that receive more attention fall into these overlapping groups: (*a*) psalms that have an important place in liturgical tradition and practice; (*b*) psalms that are used in the New Testament, especially in its Christology; (*c*) psalms that have had a special place in the theological work of the church; (*d*) psalms that are significant witnesses to the theology of the Psalter and those whose interpretation can contribute to a theology of praise and prayer and piety; (*e*) psalms that illustrate the types and functions of psalms in general; and (*f*) psalms whose location and character help in understanding the shaping and shape of the Book of Psalms as an interpretive context.

Because of its orientation to the use of psalms as Scripture and liturgy, the comment has been written in an attempted empathy with the texts and in gratitude for them. The practice of a hermeneutic of suspicion and ideological criticism is left to others. Whatever failures do mark this commentary are not, I hope, caused by lack of awe before the role the Psalms have played in the life of Judaism and Christianity.

When Scripture is quoted, the translation is that of New Revised Standard Version (NRSV). If the quotation varies from the NRSV and is not identified, the translation is my own. I have regularly looked at the Jewish Publication Society's new version (NJPS), the Revised English Bible (REB), and, after it appeared, the Revised Psalms of the New American Bible (RNAB). They have often provided useful options for construing and translating the Hebrew text.

Mary Will Mays has tested the clarity and accuracy of the manuscript through several revisions with unflagging support and interest. Sally Hicks has turned the manuscript into a typescript with persistent professional skill; consultations about its production have been mingled with memorable talk about Redskins, gardens, and fishing. My colleague and coeditor Patrick Miller has supported my work not only with editorial advice but even more by his own work as an interpreter of the Psalms.

Finally, I record my gratitude to the students whose participation in the annual class in Psalms at Union Theological Seminary in Virginia has created a continuing festival of joy and illumination. This volume is dedicated to some of them as representatives of all of them.

CONTENTS

INTRODUCTION

COMMENTARY

BOOK ONE
Psalms 1—41

BOOK TWO
Psalms 42—72

BOOK THREE
Psalms 73—89

BOOK FOUR
Psalms 90—106

BOOK FIVE
Psalms 107—150

Introduction

1. The Importance of the Psalms

"It is my view that in the words of this book the whole human life, its basic spiritual conduct and as well its occasional movements and thoughts, is comprehended and contained. Nothing to be found in human life is omitted" (Athanasius, *Ad Marcellinum*).

The Psalter "might well be called a little Bible. In it is comprehended most beautifully and briefly everything that is in the entire Bible. It is really a fine enchiridion or handbook" (Luther, *Luther's Works*, 35:254).

In the Book of Psalms, "there is nothing wanting which relates to the knowledge of eternal salvation" (Calvin, *Commentary*, p. xxxix).

"The Psalter occupies a unique place in the Holy Scriptures. It is God's Word and, with a few exceptions, the prayer of men as well" (Bonhoeffer, *Life Together*, p. 44).

1.1. These testimonies make imposing claims for the psalms. They all see in the Psalter a comprehensiveness that is the basis for its importance. The psalms, they say, comprehend the complexity of human life, the variety in the Bible, the elements of the doctrine of salvation, and the two dimensions of divine-human communication. Such quotations from sources spread across history testify to the immense significance of the psalms for Christian thought, worship, and conduct. The influence of the psalms cannot possibly be reduced to a summary that does them justice. One can only sketch the roles the psalms have played in some important areas of Christian faith and life.

1.2. *The psalms and the Old Testament.* The Book of Psalms is a virtual compendium of themes and topics found in the rest of the Old Testament. The marvelous works of God in creation, judgment, and salvation, Israel's story, the law of life, the Holy City and the Presence there, the once and future Davidic messiah, warning against wickedness and exhortation to righteousness, the majesty and tragedy of the human condi-

1

tion, the everlasting and present and coming kingdom of God—all belong to the agenda of the psalms. Here we find a summary of the rest of the first part of the Christian canon and perspectives that open up on all its parts. The psalms in their common and constant use constitute one of the most important ways in which the Old Testament is known in the church.

1.3. *The psalms and the New Testament.* Psalms and its prophetic companion, Isaiah, are the two Old Testament books most quoted in the New Testament. The frequency of the use of the psalms is evidence of the essential role the Psalter plays in New Testament literature and thought. The psalms are especially crucial in Christology. They are the primary scriptural context for the titles by which Jesus is identified. In the Gospel accounts he is recognized at his baptism with a quotation from Psalm 2 ("You are my son") and the narrative of his passion is woven with quotations and motifs from Psalms 22; 31; and 69, putting the Gospel story, as it were, in interpretive psalmic parentheses.

1.4. *The psalms and corporate worship.* The Book of Psalms has always been the scriptural book of prayer and praise for synagogue and church. Psalms have been recited and sung in a variety of ways in services of worship—as responsorials, chants, and metrical hymns. Sentences and sequences from them are employed as invocations, adorations, and confessions in liturgy. Hymns have been composed as Christian renditions of their text. Their language and functions are foundation and resource for what is said and done in the service. Their influence and effect are present in the corporate worship of Christians even where a conscious intention to use the psalms is absent.

1.5. *The psalms and spiritual discipline.* The psalms have been used widely and continuously to nurture and guide personal meditations and devotions. Christians have said them as their own prayers, as guides to learning to pray, and as texts through which they came to know themselves and God more surely. Through them, individuals connect themselves with a chain of prayer that binds the saints across the ages and frees them from isolation and arbitrary autonomy in prayer.

1.6. *The psalms and theology.* Because of their character and content, the psalms have always played a special role in reflection and thought on the Christian faith. The Book of Psalms is composed of the poetry of praise, prayer, and instruc-

2

tion in piety, the fundamental elements of religion in which authentic faith comes to expression. Religion is essentially composed of the praise of God and prayer to God and the practice of a life of trust and obedience before God. Reflection on the Christian religion must turn on the pivots of these psalmic functions. The foci of the psalms are God and the human being— God in God's way with the world and all who live in it, and human beings in their individual and historical existence under God. The psalms speak of God's work of creation, judgment, and salvation. They speak of the glory, mystery, and misery of the human condition. They proclaim the sovereignty of Israel's God, the LORD, as the eternal, all-encompassing one central truth of reality. Because they deal with the principal functions of religion and the basic tenets of God's way with us, the psalms are crucial texts for theological work.

1.7. Each of the ways in which the psalms have been important for the community of faith points to a use and purpose of their current interpretation. The last section of this introduction will illustrate the possibilities by identifying the comment on psalms that can serve such purposes.

A book of such significant value is bound to be a work that is comprehensive and complex. One of the primary problems that afflict the interpretation of the psalms is the tendency to be reductionistic in approach, that is, to assume there is a simple and single answer to the question of the identity of the psalm. The basic assumption that guides the interpretation of any text is an explicit or implicit answer to the question, What is it? An interpreter's understanding of the identity of a psalm will go a long way toward guiding study and conclusions. If one works with too restricted an answer, the richness and levels of meaning that can belong to the identity of a psalm may go unnoticed. Some reflection on the question, What is a psalm? is in order. This introduction considers the question in the light of the primary factors that constitute the identity of a psalm. The character of a psalm as text, the history of the composition of psalms and the Book of Psalms, a psalm as part of a book, the psalms as a kind of literature, and the theological thought that informs the psalms are all related dimensions that contribute to a working answer to the question.

3

2. The Anatomy of a Psalm

What is a psalm? The first way to answer the question is to identify the features that make up a psalm as a text. What elements constitute its identity? What basic and given dimensions of a psalmic text must the interpreter recognize as the foundation and point of departure for understanding? Since we are asking about what is typical of all the psalms, one psalm can be chosen as an illustration. An analysis of Psalm 3 can serve as a case study.

2.1. *The heading.* The text of Psalm 3 is composed of a heading and the psalm itself. In most versions of the Bible, the heading is printed in a different type to distinguish it from the psalm. The heading, or superscription, gives information about the psalm. The following text, it says, is a psalm that belongs to David and was used when he fled from his son Absalom. Two-thirds of the psalms are introduced by headings; the other psalms are sometimes called orphan psalms because they don't "belong to anybody." On the headings and their significance for interpretation, see sec. 3.5.

2.2. *Translation.* The psalms we read and interpret are translations of a particular Hebrew text into English. The translation involves decisions about which text to translate, how to construe its grammar, and what English words and phrases best render the meaning of its words. It is to be expected that the current English versions will sometimes make different decisions about these matters. The NRSV warns us that it follows the Syriac instead of the Hebrew in Ps. 3:2, making a sentence into a statement *to* the psalmist instead of *about* him. The translations of Psalm 3 in NRSV, NJPS, and REB differ at many other points. When they are compared closely, it is apparent that all the differences are simply different ways of saying the same thing in English. Comparing translations helps the interpreter find different ways to talk about a text, and it also can increase the precision with which the text is understood. Sometimes the comparison identifies crucial issues of meaning. The word in verse 8 that NRSV and NJPS translate "deliverance" is rendered as "victory" in REB and "safety" in RNAB. The differences here are sufficient to lead understanding in different directions. Comparison will also often turn up different decisions about the tense and mood of Hebrew verbs that will affect the interpreta-

4

tion of the text. This commentary is based on the NRSV tested by the Hebrew. Where issues of vocabulary and grammar have crucial implications for interpretation, they are discussed in the comment. Citations of NJPS and REB are often used. The revised edition of the NAB Psalms was available too late for extensive use. For detailed help with these matters, the interpreter can use the exegetical commentaries on the Hebrew text. The volumes by Hans-Joachim Kraus and those by Peter C. Craigie, Marvin E. Tate, and Leslie C. Allen in the Word Biblical Commentary will be particularly helpful.

2.3. *Poetry.* Psalm 3, like all the other psalms, is poetry. Sometimes, in the prophetic books, for instance, it is difficult to determine whether a text is poetry or prose. But there is no doubt about the psalms. They are Hebrew poetry at its best. That they are poetry should never be forgotten by the interpreter. They require an imaginative, open, evocative reading that involves feeling as well as thought.

Hebrew poetry is written in units that can be called *lines* and *measures*. Lines are usually composed of two or three measures (cola). In the printed text, lines begin at the left-hand margin and the following measure or measures are indented. In Psalm 3, each verse is a line of two measures except for verse 7, which contains two lines. In Hebrew, the lines were composed so that they could be chanted or sung in a *rhythm*. Obviously the rhythm cannot be reproduced in translations, but it is the rhythmic quality of the original text that makes it so possible to turn psalms into metrical hymns and chants in English. *Parallelism* is another formal feature of Hebrew poetry that can be observed in English, and it is far more important for the interpreter. The sense or content of the measures in a line is parallel. In one way or another, the sense of the second measure and the third, if there is one, corresponds to that of the first. Sometimes there is parallelism even between lines. The ways in which the parallels work cannot be reduced to a few categories. The parallels are as varied as the ingenuity of the psalmist allows. In verse 1, the second measure repeats the first in other words. In verse 2, the first measure introduces a quotation and the second gives it. The first two lines are bound also. The first tells what the enemies do and the second, what they say. As one tracks the parallels through the rest of the psalm, one uncovers a typical variety of the relationships. Reading a psalm according to the parallels in measures and lines is important. The parallels

5

make up one dimension of the artistic form and structure of thought in a psalm.

Besides the formal features of lines, measures, rhythm, and parallelism, psalmic poetry is characterized by some semantic features. The psalms contain a high density of rhetorical devices. Similes, metaphors, idiomatic expressions, and hyperbole particularly are frequent. Psalm 3 illustrates several of the devices: metaphor, "God is a shield" (v. 3); idiom, "strike the cheek and break the teeth" (v. 7); hyperbole, the portrayal of the enemies as innumerable (vv. 1, 2, 6); and similes, all the "like" phrases in Psalm 1. The density of these rhetorical devices in the psalms says something important to the interpreter. Psalms are not to be read in a literal way, as if the reference of their language were denotative on a flat level. As with poetry in general, their language is that of indirection and evocation. One has to read with a patient tentativeness and an awareness of the intentional, multivalent quality of the language. Is verse 5 a direct reference to a cultic practice of incubation at a shrine, or is it an evocation of trust in terms of hypothetical conduct?

Detailed comment on the poetic dimensions of the psalm requires a lot of analytical description and often turns out to be reductionistic. Little is attempted in this commentary, but the intention has been to interpret in a way that is constantly sensitive to the poetic quality of the psalms. For specific help with the appreciation and analysis of poetry, see Petersen and Richards, *Interpreting Hebrew Poetry*; and Miller, *Interpreting the Psalms*, chapter 3.

2.4. Psalm 3, like all the other psalms, is a composition. That is, it is a piece of literature written as a coherent unit to serve a specific purpose or function. The sentences of the psalm, its lines and measures, are related to each other as parts of a whole. Its thought or content is arranged in a structure. The style and the content indicate the function that the psalm is designed to serve. What a psalm does and how it does it are important matters for the interpreter.

Psalm 3 is composed to serve as a prayer. It uses vocatives to call on the LORD (vv. 1, 3, 7). It addresses the LORD directly in most of its lines. It is the voice of a person in trouble calling upon the LORD for help. As a prayer, Psalm 3 is a case of one of the three general functions of psalmic poetry: prayer, praise, and instruction. Most of the psalms serve one function or another, sometimes more than one. The first measure in verse 8

6

can be read as a sentence of praise. Prayer, praise, and instruction are often held together in psalms in significant ways. In this respect of serving a specific social function for community and individuals, the psalms are different from much modern poetry. Psalmic poetry never serves purely aesthetic purposes or fulfills its purpose by simply being poetry. It was, and is, there to be used in and for the religious community to serve the purpose for which it was composed.

The coherence of Psalm 3, its unity as a unit, is composed of functional and rhetorical elements. It hangs together as a prayer. Its lines, individually and in groups, play a role as part of its prayer. Verses 1–2 describe the trouble that is the reason and need for prayer. Verses 3–6 are statements of the trust on which the prayer is based. Verse 7 is the petition for help supported by another statement of confidence in the LORD. Verse 8 concludes with a sentence of praise and a wish for the LORD's blessing on his people. The coherence of this arrangement of functions is strengthened by integrating rhetorical devices of repetition, internal reference, and movement. The repetition of the motif "many" binds the first three measures together (vv. 1–2) and is echoed in the "ten thousands" and "all my enemies" of verses 6–7. The statement of the enemies that there is no help for the psalmist in God (v. 2) is opposed by the statement that deliverance belongs to the LORD (v. 8; in Hebrew, "help" and "deliverance" are the same word). The assertion of trust moves from statements about God to statements about the psalmist to hold together the one trusted and the one who trusts. Such rhetorical devices are widely used in psalmic composition to implement the coherence of the functional elements and give the whole literary effect.

Obviously a major dimension of understanding and interpreting is the recognition of the parts of a psalm, their role and relations in the whole, and the presence of integrating and embellishing elements. This commentary tries to be helpful in this respect. The analysis of the composition of a psalm that usually comes early in the comment is intended to be a proposal for a way to read it that turns attention back to the psalm. The users of this commentary should keep the text of the psalm constantly before them.

3. The History of the Psalms

3.1. Part of the answer to the question, What is a psalm? lies in the history of the composition, transmission, and collection of the psalms as a book. We must admit right off that precious little is known for certain about the who, when, and why of the composer of particular psalms. Psalms are notoriously difficult to date and at best can be placed in broad eras, like the monarchy or the postexilic period. The use of the psalms down through the ages as Scripture and liturgy shows that we do not have to depend on precise answers to historical questions.

On the other hand, the psalms were in fact written by somebody in Hebrew in circumstances and for purposes that belonged to the history of Israel. They are, in the first instance, the religious poetry of a particular community. They come to us as tradition. They are given to us as a means of standing in identity and continuity with the faith of that community. If we read and use them so as to dissolve them completely into our sensibilities and consciousness, they become merely empty vessels of language that we fill with our own meanings. Their value as tradition is lost. They do not lead us and convert us to think and pray and praise as they do.

It is difficult in any case to dehistoricize the psalms always and completely. In them we encounter the voices of individuals and communities speaking of predicaments and possibilities that belong to their experiences. The style and the content of the psalms invite us to ask who it is that speaks. In many cases, the headings of the psalms seem to give an answer. The voice is identified as that of David or Solomon or Moses or the Korahites or the Asaphites, but mostly of David. If we take these attributions as information that these people were the authors and assume that the psalms contain direct data about them, then we are giving the psalms a kind of historical reading.

In kind, the psalms are not history, nor are they directly about history, but they have a history. Attention to what we can reliably infer about their composition and preservation may save us from wrong historical thinking about them and uncover ways of understanding them that are truer to their character and helpful in their use as Scripture and liturgy. The following are important facets of the story of the psalms.

3.2. The Book of Psalms is obviously collection literature. It

8

is composed of independent pieces assembled to compose the book. The individual psalms come from different times and backgrounds that range across the course of Israel's career. The book is in this respect like a contemporary hymnal that includes hymns from the early church, the Reformation, and the decade of the hymnal's publication.

The composition of psalms began with the beginning of corporate worship in Israel and continued beyond the closure of the Book of Psalms. Psalm writing in Israel was part of a broad and imposing religious culture of the ancient Near East. The psalmists in Israel used genres and compositional matter common to that culture. Not a few of the psalms speak of God and Zion and God's chosen king in idioms that are adaptations of common religious tradition (e.g., 2; 24; 48). Some of the psalms are revealing illustrations of Israel's engagement with and struggle against Canaanite religion during the early monarchy (e.g., 29; 82; 93). In other psalms, the theology of the law as the central theologumenon points to the postexilic period (e.g., 1; 19; 119). In a sense, the historical setting of the psalms can be said to be the entire history of Israel's religion.

The composition, transmission, and collection of the psalms and the formation of the book were a very long process that stretched across eras of change. The preservation of the psalms was not a neutral archival process but involved the selection, reuse, revision, and grouping of the psalms that went with their constant use in Israel's worship, the devotion of circles of the faithful, and the emergence of Scripture. The Book of Psalms is the deposit of that long process.

3.3. The quest for the origin of individual psalms leads to occasions in Israel's public exercise of religion, not to their authors. The psalms were composed by persons of brilliant poetic skills and religious learning; that much is evident from the text. But the personal identity of the authors is unknown, and commentators in referring to them are left to speak repeatedly of the ubiquitous "psalmist." In this respect, the conclusion that David did not write the psalms attributed to him (discussed below) has meant a decline in the style and actuality of interpretive writing. After the loss of David's life as interpretive setting, psalm study tried for a while to locate them in historical settings suggested by data in the books of Kings, Chronicles, and Maccabees, but the connections made between psalm and event were so contrived that the approach was largely unconvincing. It was

9

replaced by the approach of form criticism that has dominated psalms study for most of this century. Hermann Gunkel, its pioneering practitioner in psalms study, concluded that the psalms could be sorted out into groups based on similarity of elements, vocabulary, and purpose (sec. 5.1–7). The groups comprise types or genres of psalms that are designed for use as the verbal expression of various ongoing religious functions or settings in life. These repeated occasions generated the types, and particular psalms were expressions of the types.

The settings inferred from the types include occasions that focus on the entire community and those that focus on the life and needs of individuals in the community. Psalms were written for the annual national festivals and their celebration of the LORD's providence in the world and Israel's destiny. The psalms would be used for processions, entrance ceremonies, pilgrimage songs, and liturgical agenda as well as for general praise. They were used also in times of disaster and danger that affected the entire community and brought it together for lament and appeal to God for help. The occasions that focused on the individual included the presentation of appeals to God for help in various kinds of predicaments, ceremonies of thanksgiving for relief from trouble, and confessions of trust and commitment. The place of the Davidic king in Israel's life and the rituals that interpreted and celebrated his importance were another generative source of psalm composition.

3.4. The relation between types and occasions in Israel's religious life does not, however, determine alone the context in which a particular psalm should be interpreted. The identification of the literary form of a psalm with one of the types does not bind the psalm to the corresponding setting in life. During the long course of the composition and transmission of psalms, Israel's religion passed through times of significant transition. The movements from early to late monarchy, from independence to exile, from a society organized as a national state to one constituted as a religious community, changed the circumstances and outlook of the community in which the psalms were composed. Inevitably, there were shifts in the way types were understood and used. The effects of the shifts are constitutive dimensions of the psalms collected in the Psalter. Some of the more important shifts are the following. The cited psalms are illustrative.

Existing psalms were revised and expanded to adapt them

10

to different contexts, much as hymns have been adapted from time to time (18; 51; 68; 102).

Psalms written for ceremonies centering on individuals came to be used by the community. The community understood itself and spoke as the individual in the psalm; the "we" became an "I." The first person style then became a literary convention of composition (25; 56; 66; 77; 135).

When there were no longer reigning kings in Israel, the psalms written for use in royal ceremonies were reread as divine promises and prophecies of a future messiah (see the comment on Psalms 2; 89; 110).

Types were loosed from the settings from which they derived to be used as literary conventions in psalm composition. The so-called mixed types are a result (9—10; 19; 25; 75; 77; 90; 91; 92; 94; 115).

The function of psalms shifted from a focus on performance in ritual proceedings toward instruction. The intention to propagate and preserve the piety of the righteous became increasingly important (15; 33; 34; 90; 135).

Interpretation must be aware of the potential depth and variety that can belong to the identity of a psalm. Classification according to type provides only one perspective. The psalm participates in the history of transmission that produced the Book of Psalms. Though this commentary is concerned with the psalms as a present unit, it attempts to be aware of the depth in each psalm. Illustrative attention is paid to shifts in settings and uses where it is especially important. The interpretation of the psalms as Old Testament texts is already a listening to the psalm in different contexts.

What all of this means is that the psalms incorporate in their own story a rather precise anticipation of the way they have been and are used in the liturgical and devotional life of Judaism and Christianity. The process of rereading and revising and relocating that goes with their use today is not a violation of their identity; it is, instead, a continuation of just what took place in the production of the book we now have.

3.5. Headings or superscriptions introduce one hundred and one of the psalms. These headings contain clues about the transmission and the use of the psalms, although the exact meaning of the terms in the headings is quite obscure. The headings belong to individual psalms, were not part of the original text, and were probably built up rather than prefixed in toto.

11

The components vary from psalm to psalm. As a whole, the headings are composed of technical terms concerning performance and composition (e.g., to the leader, with stringed instruments, Psalm 4), classifications (e.g., psalm, Psalm 3; *shiggaion*, Psalm 7), liturgical designation (e.g., for the dedication of the temple, Psalm 30; for the memorial offering, Psalm 38), attributions (e.g., David, Korahites, Moses), and cross-references to David's story in the Books of Samuel (e.g., 3; 7; 18—thirteen in all).

The technical terms and classifications point to the use of the psalms as a musical repertoire for performance at worship, a use for which hymns were obviously composed. But other pieces, such as prayers, agenda for royal rituals, and didactic speeches have been adopted for musical performance. They have all become, in our sense of the word, psalms.

The liturgical designations reflect the beginning of the process of selecting certain psalms during their transmission for particular purposes and occasions (e.g., Psalm 92, for the Sabbath Day; Psalm 38, for the memorial offering). Only a few psalms have these designations, but the process of assigning psalms to specific uses continued in Judaism and Christianity in the selection of psalms for services on each day of the week, for high days of the year, for cycles of lections, and so forth.

The attributions probably came about in different ways for different purposes. None of them identify authors in the current sense of the term. The Korahites and the Asaphites were guilds of temple musicians (II Chron. 20:19; I Chron. 16:7), and the psalms attributed to them (Asaph, Psalms 50; 73—83; Korah, Psalms 42—49; 84—85; 87—88) must have belonged to their repertoire or were associated with them in some traditional way. The earliest attributions of some psalms to David may have been based on the tradition that honored him as patron and founder of temple music (I Chronicles 15—16). That may be the result of the need to find in established tradition a significant and appropriate identification for the individual voice in the psalms. Certainly the attributions of psalms to Solomon (Psalms 72; 127) and to Moses (Psalm 90) are based on connections between these psalms and the Scriptures about them. In any case, the attributions were understood in the late Old Testament period to identify the psalms as prayers prayed by David. The cross-references to the story of David in thirteen psalms are midrashic comments based on that conviction (3; 7;

12

18; 34; 51; 52; 54; 56; 57; 59; 60; 63; 142). They come from the period when the composition, transmission, and study of the psalms were influenced by the Scriptures that had already established themselves as authoritative. The result of attributions and cross-references was to make David the patron and prototypical case of the piety of dependence and trust represented by the psalms, especially the prayers. David became the example and teacher of psalmic piety, as Solomon did of proverbial wisdom. See the comment on Psalm 3; and Mays, "The David of the Psalms."

3.6. At some stage in their history, the psalms were assembled in collections or groups that are still visible in the present book. The book was formed by arranging these existing collections in sequences and interlocking blocks supplemented by yet other psalms. The primary, though not the only, basis for the collections was the attribution.

There are two Davidic collections, Psalms 3—41 and 51—72. The end of the second is marked by a note that "the prayers of David son of Jesse are ended" (72:20). The last psalm in each collection has a concluding doxology (41:13; 72:19), a feature that set a pattern for marking the end of other groups as the book grew. The psalms in these groups are predominantly individual prayers and songs of dependence and trust featuring the theme of the LORD as refuge. They may have been the earliest form of prayer books. They provided a literature of devotion authorized by David as a resource for learning and practicing faith and obedience. The earliest stage of the formation of the Psalter points to a use that continues to this day.

There are two collections attributed to the guilds of temple musicians, one for the Asaphites (50; 73—83) and one for the Korahites (42—49). They are composed primarily of corporate prayers, hymns, and speeches that feature the classical theological traditions of the people of the LORD. It is thought that they incorporate the contribution of the northern centers of worship to the psalmic repertoire of the Jerusalem temple. Through them the great themes of Israel's worship as a community are heard in the Psalter.

The second Davidic group was inserted in the Asaphite, and the Korahite was prefixed to form a larger block (42—83) that underwent an editorial revision to replace many instances of the name LORD (Heb. *yhwh*) with God (Heb. *'elohim*). This revision may have been a monotheizing procedure to empha-

13

size that Israel's God is the God of all the earth, a central claim of psalmic theology. This "Elohist Psalter" was extended by the addition of other Korahite psalms (84—89), the last of which concludes in a doxology (89:52). This conflation of Davidic, Asaphite, and Korahite psalms, along with the first Davidic group, seems to have been the first form of the Book of Psalms. With the addition of Psalms 1 and 2 as an introduction, the first three books were complete.

The rest of the Book of Psalms appears to have been assembled in a more ad hoc manner. Some of the manuscripts of the psalms found at Qumran arrange Psalms 90—150 in ways different from the canonical Psalter, suggesting that the order was subject to variation at the time the Qumran copies were made. This final section does contain a large group of songs of ascents, an anthology of songs for pilgrims (120—134), and a notable sequence of hymns celebrating the kingship of God (93; 95—99). A doxology at the end of Psalm 106:48 provides a marker that separates the sequence into the final two books of the Psalter. Two sequences of psalms introduced and/or concluded by the liturgical cry "Hallelujah" proceed and follow the songs of ascents (111—113; 115—117; and 146—150), giving the fifth book a tone of joyous praise.

The process of assembling the psalms into groups and merging the groups in a book created the literary context for the interpretation of particular psalms. The process must have been selective. The songs preserved are a harvest chosen because they best satisfied the purposes of the collectors. The process says to the interpreter, "Here is the literature in whose light you can and may read and construe a psalm." We are given just these psalms, but we are given all of these. The resulting book is the consummate anthology. In its formation it was crafted by the twin impulses of worship and Scripture making. It combines many different times and settings and acts of Israel's worship. It endows the whole with the several identities of its contents. It is all praise and prayer and instruction. It is at the same time liturgy and Scripture. The making of the book was in truth the creation of what we know as a "psalm."

4. The Book of Psalms

14

4.1. The history or formation of the Book of Psalms provides one approach to the question, What is a psalm? A psalm is what is found in the Book of Psalms, an answer that seems all too simple but turns out to be quite complex when its implications are pursued. The present form, the shape of the book that resulted from the process of formation, also provides a way to think about the question. True, the book is a collection of individual pieces. Psalms are usually read and interpreted one by one. But the order of the book is not haphazard. The psalms are arranged in an order that gives form to the whole. The form of the book as well as its formation tells us something about a psalm. It gives some directives concerning their interpretation and use.

The more important features of the book's form as a whole are the following. There is an introduction (Psalm 1 combined with Psalm 2) and a conclusion (Psalm 150). The book is divided into five sections by psalms with concluding doxologies (Psalms 41; 72; 89; 106), with Psalm 150 serving to conclude the final section and the whole book. There is a movement within the book from an emphasis on one function of psalmody, prayer, to that of praise. Certain psalms are located in the book in such a way as to prompt a reading of the psalm and the book. These features say at least three important things about the purpose and use of Psalms as a book, and perhaps a fourth.

4.2. Psalm 1 as introduction opens up one approach. It elevates *torah* as a medium through which God gives and human beings may receive life. *Torah* in Psalm 1 means instruction in the broadest sense, written tradition that is authoritative for the people of God. Specifically, Psalm 1 introduces the psalms as *torah*, as Scripture to be studied, heeded, and absorbed. This definition of the psalms as instruction is confirmed in the book in several ways. The term, along with the vocabulary of its word field, occurs repeatedly in the psalms. A number of psalms are composed in the style of teaching (e.g., 1; 37; 49; 78; 112). In others the voice of a teacher speaks in the styles of prayer, thanksgiving, and praise (e.g., 25; 32; 92; 94; 111). The fivefold division of the book may be a way of making it correspond to the five books of the Mosaic Torah. At least the Midrash Tehillim thought so: "Moses gave Israel the five books, and David gave Israel the five books of Psalms" (Midrash Tehillim on Psalm 1).

In the psalms, says this directive, you may find instruction about what God is like and how God deals with people and the world. You can learn about the human predicament and human

15

possibilities in a world populated by the powerful and the lowly, the wicked and the righteous. You can learn about the conduct of life and how that affects its outcome. You will be taught trust and the language of trust, prayer and praise. Through this book God will give you strength in adversity and gratitude in success, penitence in guilt and thanksgiving in forgiveness. The psalms compose a book of Torah. In all their styles and types they give instruction. So they can be used. And so they have been used, all of them, to this day. (See Mays, "The Place of the Torah Psalms in the Psalter"; and McCann, *A Theological Introduction to the Book of Psalms: The Psalms as Torah*.)

4.3. Psalm 3, the first psalm after the double introduction of Psalms 1 and 2, opens a second approach. The third psalm is a prayer. It is the voice of one of the people of the LORD surrounded by myriad forces who contradict his trust in the LORD for salvation. In the face of such opposition, the prayer holds to trust and asks for the help of the LORD. From the third psalm on through the first three books of the Psalter (3—89), psalms of need and thanksgiving and confidence predominate. Most are composed as the voice of an individual; others are in corporate style. Their constant social context is the adversarial pressure of arrogance, deceit, and cynicism. Salvation is the persistent theme: salvation needed, received, and enjoyed. It is all called taking refuge in the LORD repeatedly, with the clear implication that the prayers themselves are the means of taking refuge. After book III, these prayers punctuate the rest of the Psalter until the last is heard in Psalm 144.

At the end of Psalm 72 is a note that says, "The prayers of David son of Jesse are ended." Apparently the note once marked the end of a collection of prayers attributed to David that has been incorporated into the Psalter, since other prayers of David come after the note (sec. 3.6). The gathering of Davidic prayer books began the process that led to the Book of Psalms. These prayer books were not created as archives but as living liturgy. They were a resource of meditation and devotion through which the scriptural David could nurture and guide the spiritual life of the pious in Israel. The Psalter had its origin with prayer books. Under their influence, all the psalms have been read and used as prayer. The psalms have been the prayer book of the faithful for individual devotion and corporate worship to this day.

4.4. Psalm 150 as conclusion points to a third answer to the

16

question, What is a psalm? Psalm 150 begins and ends with a call to "praise the LORD," and every one of its measures in between is a variation of this basic sentence of praise. Its final line invokes the praise of everything that breathes. Psalm 150 stands at the end of the Psalter like an enthusiastic hallelujah chorus that defines the whole. Its call to praise is at the same time an offer of the Book of Psalms as the repertoire of praise.

The book's conclusion is anticipated within the book in a number of ways. "Hallelujah" appears in the last three psalms of book IV (104—106). Book V opens with the great "O give thanks" psalm, Psalm 107, and is dominated by panels composed of "Hallelujah" and "O give thanks" psalms (111—118; 135—136; 146—150). At the beginning of book IV is a group of psalms that celebrate the reign of the LORD (93; 95—100). This massive concentration of psalms of praise in the last third of the Psalter creates the movement from the dominant tone of prayer in the first two-thirds to praise as climax and consummation. Most of the prayers also contain elements of praise (sec. 5.2.1), and psalms of praise are scattered through the first three books. The title given to the Hebrew Psalter is "Praises" (Heb. *tehillim*, a nominal form of the call, *hallelu*).

The title puts the whole book into the category of praise. The move discloses that even psalms of prayer and instruction are, in effect, praise of the LORD. The one witnesses that the LORD alone is God and savior of those who pray; prayers are testimony that "help comes from the LORD." The other witnesses that the LORD is the pathway of life; instruction is a testimony that the determination of good and evil in every sense these terms can have belongs to the sovereignty of the LORD. The book leads those who use it to find the principal purpose of existence in the orientation and joy of praise. So the book and all its psalms can be understood and used. To this day its verses are chanted and sung, its individual pieces turned into metrical psalms and recast as hymns, and its words used to express the praise and thanksgiving of individuals and congregations.

4.5. Psalm 2 as part of the book's double introduction opens up yet another perspective (on the ways in which Psalms 1 and 2 are bound literarily, see the comment). Psalm 2 lets us hear the voice of the anointed king whom the king of heaven has put in Zion as the response by the kingdom of God to the kings and rulers of earth. The king represents the kingdom of heaven on earth and will extend the reign of God over the unruly, rebellious kings of the world. In the book there are at intervals psalms that feature God's anointed king in various ways (sec. 6.11). But at the end of book III there is a great psalm of lament (Psalm 89) that God's covenant promise to the king has been contradicted by the humiliating, devastating victory of his enemies. Then, in Psalm 110, the promise that the king will represent the kingdom of God to the nations of earth is renewed, and in Psalm 132 the voice of pilgrims is heard, recalling God's promise to the anointed king. Because the sequence moves from promise through disaster to renewed promise and expectation, and because these psalms about the anointed king are included in the Psalter formed long after the kings of Judah had vanished, they must have been read and preserved and included as a form of prophecy. The position and the content of Psalm 2 call them to our attention and signal their importance.

In these psalms the only name given to the anointed king is that of David. In them the entire history of kingship in Judah has been collapsed into the question of God's steadfast love to David as the secret of God's coming rule in the world. The attribution of so many psalms to David brings them all into the context of this question with a surprising effect on the presentation of the anointed king in the Psalter. In the psalms about the anointed king, his figure is constituted largely by the election of God and the scope of his destiny. But in the prayers, David is one of the lowly, beset by all of the predicaments that belong to common humanity, vulnerable and needy. He is the messiah, son of God, enactor of the reign of God; and, yet, he is only an Israelite and a human being. The prayers even imply that it is in the travail of his human nature that this David mysteriously will carry out his vocation (e.g., see the comment on Psalm 22).

Approached from this perspective, the Psalter can be read as a Davidic, messianic book of prayer and praise. In it we hear the messiah speak about the kingdom of God and pray for the vindication of the reign of God in the messiah's salvation. By the existence of the book as Scripture and liturgy we are invited to enter into and join in this messianic prayer and praise. We are given a way to find our place in the coming reign of God through the messiah's solidarity with our humanity. Of course, it is the Psalms, read from this perspective, that uncovers their relation to Jesus and the Christology of the New Testament. See

Mays, " 'In a Vision': The Portrayal of the Messiah in the Psalms."

4.6. These four features of the Book of Psalms are the initial and major ways in which its shape is interpretive. Within these book-spanning characteristics, many other instances of shaping immediate contexts have been recognized. The joyous declaration of the reign of the LORD in Psalms 93—99 can be read as an answer to the lament over the messiah's humiliation in Psalm 89. At the beginning and the end of Psalm 145 is a resolve to praise the LORD forever, and the Hallelujah psalms in 146—150 provide the repertoire for that praise. Psalms are sometimes set in pairs intended to compose a more comprehensive completeness than one psalm allows. Psalm 103 praises the LORD as the savior who forgives sin, and Psalm 104 praises the LORD as the creator who provides for all life. See also Psalms 9 and 10, 111 and 112. Catchwords seem often to bind one psalm to the next. Some of these matters are noted in the comment on particular psalms. One could attempt a commentary based on the book itself as setting for the psalms. Indeed, the form of the book is a subject of great interest currently, and eventually it may be possible to compose a commentary based on the book itself as the interpretive context of the psalms. For further reading on the shape of the book and interpretation, one may begin with the articles in the issue of *Interpretation* devoted to "The Book of the Psalms" (April 1992, 46/2) and move to Gerald Wilson's *The Editing of the Hebrew Psalter.*

5. Types of Psalms

5.1. In contemporary psalms study, the dominant approach to the question, What is a psalm? is the method of form criticism. It answers the question by identifying the genre or type of literature to which a particular psalm belongs and the setting in life in which the genre functioned. For instance, one might determine that Psalm 38 is a lament of an individual (genre/ type), designed for use in the rituals for a sick person (setting in life). Or one might conclude that Psalm 24 is an entrance liturgy (type) designed for the processional of the ark and its company into the sanctuary (setting in life). Type is identified by the presence in a psalm of a set of features (elements of composition, expressions, intentions) common to the genre.

Setting in life is inferred by connecting the features with what is known about religious practices in Israel and, more broadly, in the ancient Near East.

This description of form criticism in psalms study is an all-too-simple account of a complex matter. The approach has made an enormous contribution. Contemporary critical interpretation of the psalms is founded on the work of Hermann Gunkel and Sigmund Mowinckel, its pioneer practitioners. The approach has rescued psalms study from the dead end of anchoring psalms in biography and events of history and clarified their connections with Israel's religious life and its traditions and conventions. An extensive discussion of the types found in the Psalter and proposals about their settings are regular parts of every introduction to the Old Testament and to commentaries on the psalms. There are excellent books on the subject; among the best are those of Claus Westermann, listed in the bibliography. It is not necessary, nor would it be useful, to discuss the matter at length here. What is offered below is a succinct description of the major types in the Psalter for reference in the comment on particular psalms. Types of less frequent occurrence are discussed in the comment. The question of setting in life is dealt with below and in the comment lightly. There is less agreement on this question, understandably. The more precise proposals are, the more tenuous and controvertible they become. It is wished, moreover, in this commentary not to bind the interpretation of a psalm to a defining setting. For that reason also, no complete list of psalms according to classification by type is undertaken in the following discussion. Such lists are a temptation to take form-critical identification as the final and decisive goal and guide of interpretation.

Because form criticism looms so large in contemporary psalms study, some observations about its use, and possible abuse, by the interpreter are in order. A type or genre is constituted of standard elements and features that can be arranged, developed, and related in various ways. Knowing what the typical elements are can help in the analysis of a particular psalm. One can see what the composer has done in this case and can follow better the movement of meaning through the psalm. Reading a psalm in terms of its typical elements, however, does not account for all the aspects of a psalm's composition. A literary analysis is crucial in discerning the individuality of a psalm. Form criticism looks for the typical. It is important to ask also

20

what constitutes a psalm's individuality. After all, each psalm has been included on its own right in the book, not on the basis of its genre. One also needs to remember that, in the history of psalm writing, types became literary conventions used by the psalmists independently of settings in life that generated the type. Identifying a psalm by type does not necessarily determine a context of composition and use in which it is to be interpreted (see sec. 3.4). 10-11

5.2. The Prayer for Help of an Individual

5.2.1. This type is by far the most numerous in the Psalter. The typical character is: An individual in serious trouble cries out to the LORD for salvation. These prayers are usually called "laments" in introductory literature, but that classification does not identify their central character and has a negative meaning for many.

The typical elements may be summarized as follows.

a. They are composed in first person style as direct address to God, and they frequently open with a vocative "LORD."

b. The basic and constituting component is the petition. The petition typically asks to be heard and to be helped (one or both).

c. There is a description of trouble that presents the needs of the petitioner. The trouble is typically described in terms of a relation to God, to others, and to self. A particular psalm may include all three, two, or only one.

d. The petitions are often supported by attached statements of reasons why the petition should be heard. The reasons typically appeal to the character of God, the petitioner's relation to God, and the dimensions and implications of the petitioner's predicament.

e. Statements of confidence in God, confessions of trust, are usually made.

f. A promise of sacrifice and/or praise may round out the prayer.

There is no standard order or arrangement of these elements in the prayers. Their composers combined the elements in quite different and creative ways that make up the distinctiveness of a particular psalm. Different elements come to the fore as the dominant tone of a prayer. For a psalm that is a virtual paradigm of the type, see Psalm 13. For variations, follow the analysis of Psalms 3—7 in the comment. For sharp

21

contrast, compare Psalms 88 and 16. In some of the prayers, the confession of confidence in God is so extensive that it shifts the emphasis in tone away from desperate need to trusting reliance (e.g., 4; 16; 23; 27; 56; 62).

5.2.2. These prayers are not only the most numerous; they present the most difficult problems of explanation and appropriation of any group in the Psalter. The important problems of explanation can be largely gathered up under the question of the identity of the individual. Who is the "I" in the psalms?

For many of these prayers, of course, an answer is given in their heading. The prayers are attributed to David. But the heading is not part of the type and stands outside the data considered by form criticism (sec. 3.5). There is a respectable minority position in psalms study that assigns most of these prayers to royal literature and concludes that they were written for the Davidic kings of Judah and belong to David in that sense. The matter remains at issue. What we can do is observe the ways in which the petitioners speak of themselves. The two most characteristic ways are the descriptions of trouble and self-identifications in terms of roles and character.

The descriptions of trouble use language that belongs to three kinds of experience: sickness in the sense of the whole range of physical and psychological abnormalities; accusation, including everything from formal proceedings of the community to the betrayal of neighbors and family; and armed conflict, from local fights to national warfare. For psalms whose language seems to refer rather clearly to one kind of experience, see Psalm 38 on sickness, Psalm 26 on accusation, and Psalm 3 on armed conflict. It seems reasonable to assume that various examples of the type reflect the use of such prayers and rituals for the sick and accused and attacked. But it is also the case that language from different spheres can be used in the same psalm. The impression grows as the psalms are studied that though the language was generated by these different areas of experience and rituals connected with them, it has become in many cases a more general vocabulary of need, a rhetoric of affliction, a rich traditional convention used to depict the one who prays as a sufferer. It is less calculated to identify a particular predicament and more to characterize neediness and helplessness in the liturgy of prayer.

22

The individuals who pray the prayers address the LORD as "your servant." They speak of their identity with the righteous,

the faithful, the lowly and poor and needy. They count themselves among those who take refuge in the LORD, seek the
LORD, love the LORD. None of these terms and categories concerns clues to the identity of a particular individual. No person
is any one of these on his or her own. The terms and categories
are one and all theological liturgical identifications. Indeed, it
is through the prayer and the devotion, dependence, and trust
enacted by the prayer that these roles and terms of identity
have their actuality.

The prayers regularly speak of an environment of hostility
that is part and parcel of the trouble described. That is expected
with accusation and attack, but it also occurs with the language
of sickness. The protagonists of this hostility correspond to the
roles and terms of the individual's identity. The enemies of
God oppose the servant of God. The wicked are adversaries of
the righteous. The lowly-poor-needy are beset by the strong-
arrogant-ruthless. Nowhere are the adversaries named or
given a recognizable identity. These roles, like those of the individual and his group, are theological liturgical terms (see the
discussion under sec. 6.16–19).

Who, then, is the individual in the prayer psalm? It seems
the question is correctly put. There is an individual *in* each
psalm, known through the first person voice and its self-descriptions and self-designations. But the individual *in* the psalm is
not the same as the individual for whom the prayer was composed. The connection is not autobiographical or historical. The
individual in the psalm is an instance of a type, just as the
particular psalm is. The composition of a prayer undoubtedly
reflects in certain ways the person and circumstances for which
it was composed. But the reflection is a modulation of a paradigm of the one who in trouble cries out to God for deliverance.
The identity in the psalm is given to and assumed by the one
who prays the prayer. The language of the prayer is disclosive.
It brings to light who one must be and who one is in crying out
to the LORD from the depths of existence.

It is this vagueness that frustrates explanatory questions,
but it is also just this paradigmatic openness of the individual in
the prayers that has made them so accessible for the praying of
any and many. Down through the ages many have said they
found themselves and their feelings and circumstances *in* these
prayers. The closer truth is that one finds oneself *through* these
prayers. One comes to know liturgically and theologically who

The Lord Reigns, 46

34 ✓

we are and what we need and one finds language to say it all to God. See Mays, "A Question of Identity"; and Miller, *Interpreting the Psalms,* chapter 4.

5.3 Thanksgiving Song of an Individual

5.3.1. "This poor soul cried, and was heard by the LORD, and was saved from every trouble" (34:6). This sentence of three clauses summarizes the central theme of a song of thanksgiving. The song says it in direct address to the LORD and repeats it as testimony to a worshiping fellowship. The song is the liturgical counterpart of the prayer for help. The prayers typically conclude with a promise of praise and sacrifice. The song fulfills the promise in a liturgy of gratitude. The song is the praise and usually provides a context for the presentation of a sacrifice of thanksgiving. Psalm 107 provides an excellent orientation to the liturgical practice of gratitude by individuals (see the comment on Psalm 107).

The typical elements of the song are these:

a. Praise addressed to the LORD that rehearses the cry for help in trouble and reports the LORD's response of hearing and help.

b. Summons to a community of worship to join the praise and testimony to them about the meaning of the deliverance for God's way and for the life of the saved.

c. Presentation of praise and/or sacrifice to keep promises made in a prayer for help.

Psalms that represent this type are few compared to the number of prayers for help. For illustrative examples, see the comment on Psalms 30 and 116. The type is sometimes combined with others in one psalm; see the comment on Psalms 40 and 118. It is not likely that their scarcity in the Psalter reflects the situation in Israel's liturgical life. The dominance of prayers in the book more likely is a result of the needs of the community for which the prayer books of David were assembled. The presence of the thanksgiving songs in the Psalter is nonetheless a canonical witness that the cycle of trouble, prayer, and help is not complete without specific and public acts of gratitude. The regular reference to a company of worshipers shows how important the experience of grace in the individual's life is for the community. The statements in the songs about the new meaning that salvation has brought to the life of the one helped is a testimony to the transforming power of grace.

24

5.4. The Corporate Prayer for Help

5.4.1. When disaster threatened the existence of the entire national community, urgent prayer was offered on behalf of the people of God. Some of these corporate prayers are preserved in the Psalter. Most of them belong to the Asaphite collection; one is a Korahite psalm. Clear examples are Psalms 44; 74; 79; 80; and 83. All of these psalms describe circumstances created by the superior military power of other nations. The destruction of Jerusalem and its temple seems to be the occasion for at least two (74 and 79).

The elements of the type are the same as those of the individual's prayer for help, with two exceptions. These prayers are composed primarily as the voice of the community, we instead of I. The corporate prayers feature recollections of God's way and work in the past.

a. Petitions to hear and help are the defining element.

b. Descriptions of trouble speak of God's absence or wrath, the community's humiliation and suffering, the power and arrogance of enemies.

c. Appeals to the community's identification with God, and to God's honor and glory, support the petitions.

d. Assertions of trust in the LORD appear in some of the prayers.

e. The prayer rehearses what God has done in the past in the history of the community and even in the creation of the world. These recollections are ways of making the suffering of the community an issue of the LORD's sovereignty in the world.

f. Praise is promised in gratitude for the sought help.

5.4.2. Though they are few in number, these corporate prayers have immense theological importance. The recollections contain some of the most important statements in the Psalter about God's way with Israel and the world. The prayers are the voice of a community that knows that its last and best hope lies in the sovereignty of its God.

5.4.3. It is puzzling that no convincing examples of songs of corporate thanksgiving are preserved in the Psalter. Whether there are any is a matter of disagreement. It is possible that other types take their place in the collection. The heading of Psalm 30 is evidence that the individual songs were appropriated for corporate use. Hymns like Psalm 98 praise the LORD for saving help to the entire community. The basic thanksgiving formula, "I/we give thanks to you, O LORD," has been.revised to become an introductory summons to general hymns of praise that speak of the marvelous works of the LORD (e.g., 105; 106; 107; 136). In all these ways the function of corporate thanksgiving is represented in the Psalter.

5.5. The Hymn

5.5.1. "Great is the LORD, and greatly to be praised" (145:3). The function of praise in the Psalter belongs first of all to the hymn. There are elements of praise in the prayers. Songs of thanksgiving praise the LORD for a specific experience of deliverance. But the primary genre of praise is the hymn. Praise is the exaltation of that which makes one exult. The hymn is a song of praise of which God is the sole subject. In language of exuberant joy, the hymn says what God is like and has done and characteristically does. The ark represented the immanent presence of the LORD in Zion's temple. The hymns gave the invisible presence audible representation in the space and place of worship. They are by reason of their character and function intensely theological.

We can assume that most of the hymns in the Psalter were composed for performance at the seasonal festivals and on other high occasions of corporate worship. The texts of the hymns offer little specific guidance for more certain conclusions.

5.5.2. The liturgical cry "Hallelujah" is a hymn condensed to one terse Hebrew sentence. Its syntactic components are the basic elements of the hymn. It is composed of a plural imperative summons to praise (*hallelu*) and the short form of the LORD's name (*jah*, abbreviated from Yahweh). This is the primary pattern of hymns of praise. They are composed of an invocation of praise addressed to variously identified groups, from the righteous to all the earth, and a statement of the basis of the summons in the content of praise. The content elaborates the name of the LORD by proclaiming the predicates of which the LORD is subject. The imperative says that praise is necessary and right and open to all whom it addresses. The predications state the meaning of the name. "From the rising of the sun to its setting the name of the LORD is to be praised" (113:3).

5.5.3. Another liturgical formula represents the elements of the hymn in more detail. "O give thanks to the LORD, for he is good; his steadfast love endures forever." The formula is also composed of the two elements of call to praise and basis of praise. The latter is joined to the former by the conjunction "for," the standard connective in the hymns. The formula is used in the Psalter as an introduction to psalms (106; 107; 118) and as a rubric for the composition of psalms (see the comment on Psalms 136 and 100). In its second part, this little hymn exhibits the crystallization of a choice of the preferred predicate for the characterization of the LORD. The focus is put, not on might or holiness or any of the other attributes so commonly given God in the psalms; the formula emphasizes the goodness of the LORD as the attribute beyond all others that calls for and calls forth praise. The goodness of the LORD is further defined as steadfast love, the active helpfulness of the LORD to all whose God and king the LORD is (see sec. 6.8 below).

5.5.4. Of the some thirty-five hymns in the Psalter, twenty-two are composed on this pattern of summons plus proclamation (invocation and praise). This simple scheme is used by composers in a wide spectrum of ingenious variations. As illustrations, see Psalms 29; 47; 98; 113; and 145. In Psalm 150, the imperative element takes over completely. For examples of the way the pattern is used for theological purposes, see the comment on Psalms 117; 113; 100; and 98.

5.5.5. There are hymns that do not follow the pattern. Some employ only the second part, the proclamatory body of praise. They tend to be hymns with specialized topics, hymns whose subject is Zion as the city of God (46; 48; 84; 87) and two on the kingship of God (93; 99; and perhaps 97). There is a small group of hymns composed as the praise of an individual, the harvest of a late development in hymnody when the psalmists composed praise poetry as votive offerings to the LORD (e.g., 8; 103; 104). For other rather individual patterns of composition, look at the prayer style of Psalm 65, the blessing hymn Psalm 67, and the theophany hymn Psalm 114.

5.6. Psalms of Instruction

5.6.1. The function of instruction, unlike prayer and praise, is not served by a primary type. But psalms composed out of a concern to guide and encourage the trust and obedience of worshipers do play a major role in the composition of the Book of Psalms. The prayer, "Lead me in your truth, and teach me" (25:5), is given at least a partial answer in the voice of teaching,

27

exhortation, warning, and testimony found in the psalms. The category "wisdom psalms" is often used as a classification of a varying selection of psalms because they contain formal and thematic features characteristic of Proverbs, Ecclesiastes, and Job. The classification should not be understood to mean that such psalms had a setting in life in the "school" rather than corporate and individual worship and have been brought into the Book of Psalms as a kind of body of foreign material. They are, rather, the harvest of a phase in the history of psalmody when the strategies and styles of the literature of teaching were combined with those of prayer and praise to teach a people at worship.

5.6.2. There is a great deal of variety in the formal strategies of composition used to implement the purpose of teaching. The following are illustrations of some of the most frequent.

a. Didactic sentences that exhort, warn, and assert. Psalm 37 is composed completely of such sentences. They are found in the composition of hymns (e.g., 33:16–17) and prayers (e.g., 25:8–10).

b. Acrostic or alphabetic poems that are organized by the letters of the Hebrew alphabet (9—10; 25; 33; 34; 37; 111—112; 119; 145). Psalms composed on the pattern of the alphabet intend a kind of completeness and have a clear structure that guides the listener or reader. They are all good hunting grounds for other formal devices of pedagogy.

c. Beatitudes (*'ashre* sayings) are scattered through the psalms. They commend a kind of conduct. See the comment on Psalm 1, an expanded beatitude.

d. Instruction is validated and commended by the convention of narrating an individual experience (32; 34; 37; 73; 94).

Psalms composed with a concern to instruct are often anthological in several ways. Some are composed of a medley of features of different types conflated in a single poem (see the comment on Psalms 33; 19; 119). Some seem to be using the material of other extant psalms or Scriptures (see the comment on Psalms 145 and 103).

5.6.3. The concern for teaching is also reflected in the emphasis on certain topics. Three psalms are devoted to *torah* as the crucial medium of relationship between God and the faithful (see the comment on Psalms 1; 19; 119). There are also psalms that specifically address the problem for faith set by the well-being of the wicked (see the comment on Psalms 37; 49;

73). Contrasting the way and destiny of the wicked and the righteous is an amazingly pervasive feature of psalmic instruction (1; 9—10; 11; 12; 14; 32; 34; 37; 49; 52; 58; 73; 75; 91; 92; 94; 111—112; 119).

The boundaries of the group of psalms that serve the function of instruction are obviously difficult to draw. Psalm 78 shows how Israel's foundation story can be used for teaching. Psalm 50 is a covenant address composed in the style of prophetic speech, but it clearly gives instruction about righteousness and wickedness. Psalm 15 may have been composed as a qualification liturgy at the temple gates, but its *torah* style of question and answer makes it possible to read it simply as teaching. The concern to instruct has in effect drawn the entire Psalter toward the role of "a lamp to my feet and a light to my path" (119:105).

5.7. Other Literary Types

Beyond these major literary genres there are psalms composed on other literary forms scattered through the Psalter. A few reflect ceremonies of procession and entrance (118; 24; 15). Psalms 50 and 82 have the form of speeches made in legal proceedings. Ceremonies that centered on the Davidic king provided the setting for inaugural declarations (2; 101; 110), prayers for success and war (20; 21), thanksgiving after victory (Psalm 18) and lament over defeat (Psalm 89), as well as a wedding song (Psalm 45). The songs of ascents (Psalms 120—134) contain a potpourri of kinds of material used apparently in connection with the visits of pilgrims to Zion. For recent assessments of the form-critical classification of psalms, see chapter 5 in the introductions by Klaus Seybold and chapter 1 in that of John Day.

6. The Theology of the Psalms

6.1. What is a psalm? A crucial way to answer the question is to consider the theology of the psalms. What understanding of God informs and shapes their language? Given the long history of psalm writing, and the variety collected in the book, one might expect to find different answers in different groups of psalms. Given their poetic and liturgical character, one will certainly not expect to find systematic and rationalistic thinking about God in them. Granted such cautions and qualifications, is there a way of thinking about God and God's way with world and humankind that characterizes the entire Psalter and contributes to the identity of every psalm?

The first and most obvious answer lies in the name of God. The psalms all praise and pray to the God whose name is YHWH, the name transcribed in Hebrew manuscripts and translated in our versions as LORD (printed in caps and small caps to distinguish the name from the title, Lord). The importance of the *name* as identity and representation of the God of the psalms cannot be overbid (e.g., 8; 66; 68; 69; 92; 113; 145). The LORD is the one whose deeds and words made the people who praise and pray in the psalms and made God known to them. The LORD is the God of Abraham and Sarah, Moses and Deborah, David and Ruth, and the prophets, God of the sojourn and exodus and the land and exile and return. By the name, the psalms point to the God of Israel and the rest of the Old Testament. In the psalms, God is never just god, but always One whose identity is as particular as that of an individual person.

In the psalms the name is frequently combined with a metaphor. The first presentation of the LORD in the Psalms portrays God as the one throned in the heavens who has set "my king on Zion, my holy hill" (2:4–6). The first appellation of the LORD by title is "my king and my God" (5:2). The metaphor is that of kingship. In the psalms the metaphor is carried explicitly by verbs for ruling and nouns for king and kingship. Beyond these explicit terms is a network of interconnected roles and actions and attributes that the psalms employ to speak of the LORD's way with the world and its people and the relation of human beings to the LORD. At the center of the network stands the liturgical cry, "The LORD reigns," with all that the cry denotes and connotes (NRSV translates the sentence, "The LORD is king"). Joined to the name, reigning and kingship constitute the root metaphor that gives coherence and definition to the other aspects of the theology of the psalms. The proclamation of the LORD's reign is the theme of Psalms 24; 29; 47; 93; 96; 97; 98; and 99. These psalms furnish the context for learning all that the psalmic understanding of the LORD's reign involves.

What is a psalm? When viewed as limbs and branches dependent on the substance of this root metaphor, the psalms are the poetry of the reign of the LORD. They are the praise and proclamation and prayer of those who believe that the confes-

30

sion "The LORD reigns" states the basic truth about the world
and life lived in it.

6.2. A condensed overview can perhaps suggest the inter-
relatedness of the topics and roles that are of principal importance in the theology of the psalms.

The LORD's rule is first of all the double work of creation
and salvation. The divine king is a warrior who has overcome
the unruly chaos to establish the world and has subdued the
hostile powers of the world to gain a place and a people in the
world. The marvelous deeds of creation and salvation make
the LORD the judge of gods, nations, his people, and every life
in the world. In these marvelous deeds, the holiness, power,
justice and righteousness, and steadfast love and faithfulness
of the LORD's kingship are made known. Israel is the people
in whom the LORD's dominion takes shape in the world. The
place that represents the LORD's kingship in the world is Zion,
the city of God. As regent to represent the divine rule to the
people of God and the nations of the world, the LORD has
chosen David and made him messiah. As means of obedience
and gift of life, the LORD has given the people of God the law
as instruction.

The campaign to consummate the reign of God in the world
continues. Nations rage against it; people ignore and subvert it.
Opposition and conflict, enemies and adversaries are part and
parcel of its present and prospect. All who seek to live in the
reign of the LORD are caught in the conflict and endure the
incompleteness. The people of God are afflicted. The messiah
is humiliated and rejected. The faithful are undone by hostility
and done in by the powers of death. The voices and roles in the
psalms are defined by the situation of the conflicted reign of the
LORD. The *servants* of God are those who acquire their identity
in having the LORD as Lord. The *enemies* are their counterpart.
The *righteous* are those who live and speak in ways that affirm
the reign. The *wicked* are the opposite. The *lowly* (poor, needy,
humble) are those who know that they are dependent on the
LORD for deliverance from alienation, sin, and death. Their
counterpart is composed of the arrogant, the ruthless, and the
proud.

The time of the psalms is the interim. The hymns proclaim
among the nations, "The LORD reigns." The prayers of the
people of God are based on the confidence that the proclamation is true. The instruction lights the darkness of the before-

31

times with the assurance that life and experience will ultimately vindicate the proclamation.

For a fuller discussion of "the LORD rules" as the organizing confession of the Psalter, see Mays, "The Center of the Psalms"; and idem, "The Language of the Reign of God." For an expanded treatment of the theology of the psalms, one can turn to Kraus, *Theology*. In a commentary, the topics and roles that compose the agenda of the psalms' theology are best explored in the context of specific psalms. The psalms cited in the following overview identify the contexts where the comment gives particular attention to their exposition.

6.3. *The LORD reigns.* Psalms 47; 93; and 95—99 offer expositions of the proclamation, "The LORD reigns." They show how the sentence is understood and what it includes and connotes in psalmic contexts. Its principal dimensions are establishing the earth and judging the peoples, that is, sovereignty over world and history (96:10).

6.4. *Creation.* The reign of the LORD is depicted in terms of cosmic combat with the primeval chaos by which the earth-world is established (93; 104; 29). Heaven and earth exist because the LORD reigns, and all live in God's reign and are dependent on it for life.

6.5. *Salvation.* The reign of the LORD is depicted in terms of combat with historical powers (at times given cosmic identities) by which a people and a place are gained in the world (47; 68; 98; 114; the Song of the Sea in Exodus 15 is the canonical prolegomenon).

6.6. *The Warrior.* The LORD of hosts is the king of glory because he is mighty in battle (24:7–10). For portrayals of the LORD as the divine warrior, see the comment on Psalm 18:7–15 and the texts cited there.

6.7. *The Judge.* The LORD "has established his throne for judgment" (9:7). "His judgments are in all the earth" (105:7). The judgments are the providential interventions of the LORD to maintain his sovereignty. They are salvific as well as punitive acts to set things right. Psalms 9—10 are a virtual anthology on the LORD's judgment of nations and individuals. The LORD is judge of the gods (Psalm 82), of peoples and nations (Psalm 96), of the people of the LORD (Psalm 50), and of individual lives (Psalm 94).

6.8. *The Attributes.* The psalms repeatedly attribute certain principal characteristics to "the great king over all the

32

earth." "His greatness is unsearchable" (Psalm 145) and includes his awesome majesty (Psalm 97), irresistible power
(Psalm 76), and holiness (Psalm 99). Two pairs of attributes
receive special emphasis; righteousness-justice is the foundation of his rule, and his actions are accompanied by steadfast
love–faithfulness (97:2; 89:14). Steadfast love (Heb. *hesed*) is
indeed the characteristic of the LORD that informs all the others
and constitutes the goodness of the LORD (136; 103; *hesed* is
translated in different ways in various versions. To be brief and
simple, one may say that *hesed* means the reliable helpfulness
of the LORD to any and all that are dependent on him; see
107; 36).

6.9. *The People of God*. The community who speak in the
psalms call themselves "the people of his pasture, and the sheep
of his hand" (95:7). The LORD redeemed them to be the tribe
of his heritage (74:2). Their prayers for help are the best place
to learn how they understand their existence in terms of the
LORD's way with them in the past (44; 74; 77; 80). Psalms 78;
105; and 106 use the story of God's way with them and theirs
with God in the past as lessons to the present.

6.10. *The City of God*. Mount Zion is "the city of the great
king" because the LORD chose it as the place of his presence,
the earthly counterpart to the heavenly throne and palace. Its
meaning and importance are celebrated in Psalms 46; 48; 84;
and 87. Its value to worshipers and pilgrims is evident in Psalms
42—43; 120—134; and 137.

6.11. *The King of God*. The regent on earth of the LORD's
reign is the Davidic king, designated as the Anointed by the
LORD's covenant (89; 132). His kingship is given the vocation to
represent the divine rule to the people of the LORD and to the
nations. See Psalms 2; 18; 20; 21; 45; 72; and 110.

6.12. *The Law of the LORD*. To distinguish, bless, and govern his people, the LORD has given them his *torah* in word,
decrees, commandments, and statutes. The LORD's law is destiny and mark of his people (105:45; 147:19–20) and norm of
their faithfulness (25:10; 103:17–18; 112:1; 50:16). The anointed
king and other leaders know the will of their sovereign by the
commandments (18:21–22; 89:30–33; 99:7). The law is even an
instrument of salvation (94:12–15; 119 passim). Its permanence
and authority are based in the creation itself (93:5; 33:4–7;
111:7; 148:6). For psalms devoted to the law, see Psalms 1; 19;
and 119.

33

6.13. *The Human Response*. The psalms are not only informed by a theology of the reign of the LORD. They are the primary form that language takes in response to the reign of the LORD. In their three principal functions, they define the ways in which human beings live by and in the kingdom. Because "the LORD reigns," human beings may and must praise in wonder and joy, pray in dependence and gratitude, and practice the piety of trust and obedience. The psalms are in the canon of Scripture to be used. They are to be interpreted in the service of their use.

6.14. *The Conflict*. The reign of the LORD by its very nature and purpose involves conflict. The reign is not only manifest in the LORD's victory over cosmic and historical chaos. Because it is the reign of one God whose way in the world is being worked out through one people and one presence and one king and a particular kind of human conduct, the rule encounters the opposition of nations and rulers and people whose gods and power and autonomy are denied by the reign of the LORD. There is not a psalm that does not in some way or other reflect some dimension of this fundamental conflict. Psalms 9–10 give a good overview.

6.15. *The Human Predicament*. The conflict turns upon and brings to light the predicament that belongs to corporate and individual existence. The people in the psalms are structured by finitude and fallibility, by mortality and vulnerability and sinfulness. The people in the psalms are identified by roles and characterizations that locate their identity in the context of the conflict of the LORD's reign.

6.16. *The Servants and the Enemies*. Those who say the psalms are called servants of the LORD. In the Old Testament vocabulary, a servant is one whose identity and conduct are defined by relationship to a lord (16:2; 116:16). The LORD "delights in the welfare (*shalom*) of his servant" (35:27). *Shalom* is the comprehensive term for the theological, social, and personal well-being given by creation and blessing and restored by salvation. It is the wholeness, goodness, and integrity of relational existence to God, self, and others. Whatever and whoever disturbs and destroys the *shalom* of the servants touches the will and way of their Lord. The omnipresent enemies in the psalms are those who have done so. All the harm attributed to enemies in the psalms is in one way or another destructive of the *shalom* of the world. Their attitudes and conduct oppose the sovereign pleasure and purpose of the LORD. The enemies of the community and of the individual in the community are never just national or personal foes. Their hostility is set within the context of the reign of the LORD.

6.17. *The Righteous and the Wicked*. The servants and the enemies are frequently called the righteous and the wicked to characterize them in terms of conduct. The terms are the antonyms of the morality of the reign of the LORD. In the vocabulary of the psalms, "the faithful" (Heb. *hasid*; e.g., 85:8; 86:2; 116:15) and "those who fear the LORD" (e.g., 85:9; 135:20) are used as virtual synonyms of "the righteous." The rightness of the righteous is character and conduct shaped and guided by trust in and loyalty to the LORD as God and king. The righteous think and speak and act in a way that makes for *shalom* in the community and the world. The wicked are the polar opposite. Their conduct is depicted as autonomous, arrogant, deceitful, violent; Psalm 10 contains a comprehensive typical description. For instruction about the righteousness required by the Presence of the LORD, see Psalms 15 and 24. Typical prayers of the righteous are Psalms 5; 7; 17; and 26. Psalms 11; 12; and 14 draw sharp contrasts between the two roles. The temporary well-being and success of the wicked set a painful problem for the faithful righteous, which they could endure only by trust in the reign of the LORD (34; 37; 49; 73).

6.18. *The Weak and the Strong*. "You deliver the weak (*'ani*) from those too strong for them" (35:10). The weak and the strong are another pair of roles for the servants and the enemy. The weak are the needy, poor, lowly, humble, afflicted (all variant translations and synonyms of *'ani*), who know they cannot save themselves and depend on the LORD for help against forces with which they cannot cope. The category includes physical, economic, and social factors but is primarily defined by stance in any neediness. It belongs to the office of the king to support the helpless and restrain the strong (see Psalm 74 on the Davidic king). Those who present themselves as helpless before the threat of strong enemies lay claim on that royal responsibility when they say, "I am poor and needy." The LORD fulfills that responsibility perfectly (12; 14; 68; 69; 82; 102; 140).

6.19. *The Sinner*. The servants of the LORD as community and individuals fail to trust and obey. They have lived, and can and do live, lives that are not ruled by the reign of the LORD. The story of the people of the LORD can be told as a narrative of their sinfulness and the LORD's wrath and steadfast love (78; 106). They have learned that the LORD does not tolerate their sinfulness (Psalm 90), but also that the LORD in sovereign freedom does not deal with them according to their sins (103; 130). So they pray corporately and individually, "Do not enter into judgment with your servant, for no one living is righteous before you" (143:2). See the prayers in Psalms 25; 32; 36; 39; and 51; and see the excursus on sickness and sin in the comment on Psalm 38.

6.20. *My King and My God*. The way in which the servants speak of "my king and my God" transcends any simple meaning of these rubrics. The knowledge of the divine sovereignty is deepened and enriched. Here and there the psalms uncover the truth for which no words are ever quite adequate: The reign of God is God. It is not just the control of God, the help of God, the blessing of God. To say "my king and my God" with the psalms is to know that the very self of the LORD is all this. The reign of God is the need for God. "You are my God, I seek you, my soul thirsts for you" (63:1; see 42—43; 62; 63; 130; 139). The reign of God is God as salvation. "Say to my soul, 'I am your salvation'" (35:3; see 27; 31; 40; 59; 142). The reign of God is God as life. "Whom have I in heaven but you? And there is nothing on earth that I desire other than you" (73:25). "You are my Lord; I have no good apart from you" (16:2). "The LORD is my shepherd; I shall not want" (23:1).

7. Using the Psalms and the Commentary

What is a psalm? With respect to their use of the psalms, the answer must be twofold. The psalms have a double identity. They are Scripture, one book in the canon of writings that make up the Bible. The psalms may and should be used in all the ways in which Scripture is used. They are also liturgy, texts that are used in the church's service of God through worship. The use of psalms has been most effective when the two identities have been held together. When the interpretation of the psalms as Scripture has informed, corrected, and enriched their use as liturgy, and their use as liturgy has given interpretation a vital context and living purpose, then psalmody has been and will be at its best.

The long tradition of psalmody in the church creates a variety of opportunities and needs for the interpretation of psalms.

The opinion sometimes expressed that the psalms are appropriate for prayer and praise but not as texts for preaching is simply contradicted by the practice of great preachers and theologians from earliest Christian times to the present. The psalms also offer rich possibilities for teaching and Bible study in a number of contexts important to the life of faith. Interpreting the psalms through preaching and teaching is probably most effective when it is planned in relation to some use of the psalms in the round of practices established in the interpreter's community. The plans listed below identify some of the possibilities. With each plan a group of psalms is proposed as texts for its implementation. The selection is, of course, guided by tradition in the case of psalms for Sundays and for seasons and days in the Christian year. Other selections are the suggestion of the commentator. The comment on many of the recommended psalms has been written with the intention of making it useful for such purposes. An especially valuable resource for the preaching and teaching of the psalms is McCann, *A Theological Introduction to the Book of Psalms: The Psalms as Torah*.

7.1. *Psalms for Seasons and Days in the Christian Year.* In the liturgical tradition, there are psalms that are designated for use every year on certain days and at certain times. Some of these psalms are more closely identified with their designated occasion than any other Scripture. The interpreter can seek out the meaning of the relation between text and time. How does the psalm speak of and to the time? How does the time as context interpret the psalm? Psalms 96; 97; and 98 for Christmas Eve and Christmas Day; Psalm 72 for Epiphany; Psalm 29 for the Baptism of Jesus, Epiphany I; Psalm 51 for the beginning of Lent; Psalms 22 and 31 for Palm Sunday and Good Friday; Psalm 116 for Maundy Thursday; Psalm 118 for Easter Day; Psalm 110 for Ascension Day; and Psalm 104 for Pentecost.

7.2. *The Psalms for Sunday.* The triennial cycle of psalms set for the Sunday service provides an opportunity for Bible study and preaching that informs and deepens their use, whether as hymns, lections, or responsorials. Congregations, classes, and choirs need assistance in an authentic use of the psalms. The cycle covers most of the psalms. Interpreters can well use the cycle themselves to learn the Psalter better through study and devotional reading during the week. The psalms for Sunday are identified in liturgical resources and calendars.

37

7.3. *Psalms and Hymns.* Psalms play a significant role in the sung praise and prayer of the church. They are used as metrical songs and chants with antiphons. Their motifs and themes are present in virtually every hymn. One way by which to heighten knowledge and appreciation of psalms and hymns is by studying the appropriation of psalms in the composition of Christian hymns. One will need to ask what process of rereading and resaying enters into the composition. Important things about the general appropriation of the psalms as Christian liturgy can be learned. Possibilities are Psalm 46 in Luther's "A Mighty Fortress Is Our God," Psalm 98 in Isaac Watts's "Joy to the World!" Psalm 72 in Watts's "Jesus Shall Reign," Psalm 103 in Henry Lyte's "Praise, My Soul, the King of Heaven," and Psalm 148 in Francis of Assisi's "All Creatures of Our God and King." Through the indexes in hymnals one can discover other hymns composed from psalms.

7.4. *Psalms and a Theology of Praise.* There is hardly any reflection on the action and meaning of praise itself in the psalms, but the material of theological reflection on praise is incorporated into the psalms themselves. Begin with the comment on Psalms 117; 113; 100; and 33. Use that orientation to study other hymns of praise in the Psalter. See the sequence from Psalms 145 to 150 and the hymns that praise the LORD as sovereign (47; 93; 95—99).

7.5. *Psalms and a Theology of Prayer.* An understanding of prayer and guidance in the practice of prayer can be found in the structure and content of the prayers in the Psalter. See the comment on Psalm 13; 86; 25; 34; 39; 130; 30; and 116. Reflection on the experience of saying a prayer psalm as one's own prayer can lead to insights and consideration of the practice of prayer. Another approach used throughout the history of Christian interpretation is that of comparing a prayer psalm with the Lord's Prayer and asking which petitions in the latter are present in the psalm and how they are expressed.

7.6. *Psalms and Spiritual Discipline.* The psalms have always been a primary resource in the nurture of the spirit. The faithful find themselves in and through the psalms, claim language for their neediness and gratitude in their words, and receive support and encouragement for living from them. For learning to read them for such uses, the comment on the following psalms may be helpful: For meditation on who and what we are before God, Psalms 8; 49; 90; 139. On God as creator-provider and savior, Psalms 104 and 103. For psalms of trust in God as our need and our help, Psalms 16; 23; 27; 36; 42—43; 62; 63; 73. Practice in using and learning the psalms in this way is good preparation for their use in pastoral care.

BOOK ONE
Psalms 1—41

Psalm 1: Delight in the Law

The Book of Psalms begins with a beatitude. Not a prayer or a hymn, but a statement about human existence. Here at the threshold of the Psalter we are asked to consider the teaching that the way life is lived is decisive for how it turns out. This opening beatitude also serves as an introduction to the book. Its location as the first psalm is not accidental; the psalm is there to invite us to read and use the entire book as a guide to a blessed life. It introduces an agenda of themes that recur frequently in the book and play a fundamental role in its theology. So the psalm needs to be interpreted at two levels: first as a psalm in its own right and then in its relation to the whole book.

1. Psalm 1 has the form of a complex beatitude. The form is composed of the formula, "Blessed (is) the one . . . ," followed by a word or a clause that identifies a kind of character or conduct: for instance, "Blessed the one who takes refuge in him" (34:8). Here in Psalm 1 the basic beatitude is "Blessed the one whose delight is in the law of the LORD." One way to analyze the elaboration of this central statement is to note the pattern of contrast in the psalm. Verse 1 says what the blessed do not do, and verse 2 says what they do do. Verse 3 uses a long simile and a short statement to describe the good outcome of the life of the blessed. Verse 4 uses a brief contrasting simile, and verses 5–6 use a long concluding statement to describe the failed life of the wicked. Behind this pattern in the literary structure is the antithetical pair of righteous/wicked, though the righteous are not specifically mentioned until the concluding statement, because the psalm is designed to emphasize one thing as fundamental to the righteous—engagement with the

40

law of the LORD. That is the central purpose of the psalm, to commend joyous and continuous concern with the law of the LORD. "Blessed" is the traditional translation of the saying's formulaic word; contemporary translations prefer "happy" in order to distinguish these sayings from pronouncements of blessing that invoke the beneficent work of God on persons and groups. In blessings, the formulaic Hebrew term is *baruk*; in beatitudes, *'ashre*. The primary difference is that the blessing invokes God's beneficent support of life, while the beatitude points to and commends the conduct and character that enjoy it.

This opening beatitude is followed by others scattered through the Psalter. The next one comes at the end of Psalm 2, and with this one it forms an inclusion that binds the two psalms together as a double introduction to the book. In all, there are twenty-five such sayings in the Psalms, compared to eight in Proverbs. The beatitude seems to have been a favored literary form in post-exilic psalm composition. The subject of the psalmic beatitudes is the religious life, piety as enacted or enjoyed. They commend both obedience and trust. Their presence in the psalms is one evidence of the instructional purpose that informs psalmody in its later history. This first beatitude prompts the reader to think of the entire book as instruction for life and commends a kind of conduct that uses the Psalter in that way.

2. The commended conduct is constant reflective meditation on the "law" (*torah*) of the LORD that grows out of delight in it and concern for it. The basic meaning of the term *torah* is instruction, not legal rules and stipulations. Commandments and ordinances are called *torah* because they instruct. The term is used variously in the Old Testament for material that directs belief and conduct ranging from prophetic oracles (Isa. 1:10) to a version of the Book of Deuteronomy (Deut. 31:24). Here "*torah* of the LORD" is used in a comprehensive sense to refer to the whole body of tradition through which instruction in the way and the will of the LORD is given to Israel. This psalmist knows *torah* in the written form, Scripture that one can read and absorb (see Josh. 1:8). It is from this written *torah* that wisdom for the living of life can be gained. It is the medium from which one can learn the way and the will of the LORD and store up that learning in one's heart so that it shapes the structure of consciousness (40:9; 37:31). This is the reason why *torah*

41

is the cause of delight, not because it is an available instrument of self-righteousness, material for a program of self-justification, but because the LORD reaches, touches, and shapes the human soul through it. For this psalm, *torah* is a means of grace. Jeremiah 17:7–8 says, "Blessed is the one who trusts in the LORD. . . . That one is like a tree planted by water." When Psalm 1 replaces "trust in the LORD" with "delight in the LORD's *torah*," it is not to substitute confidence in the law and self. The psalmist trusts himself to *torah* as a discipline of entrusting life to the LORD. The psalm represents the prototype of Scripture piety that is part of the heritage of Judaism and Christianity.

As introduction to the book, Psalm 1 invites us to expect and receive *torah* from the psalms, that is, to read them as Scripture. The reader will come upon two other great witnesses to *torah* piety in Psalms 19 and 119. Scattered through the psalms are recurrent references to *torah* and its constituent elements and forms that show how fundamental it is to the religion the Psalter represents and nurtures. Indeed, Psalm 1 wants the whole to be read as instruction—instruction in prayer, in praise, in God's way with us and our way under God. The division of the Book of Psalms into its five component books doubtless expresses the same view of the Psalter by giving it an analogous shape to that of the first five books of the biblical canon, which came to be called "the Torah" in Jewish tradition (Mays, "The Place of the Torah Psalms in the Psalter," pp. 3–12).

3. The counterparts of those whose life is directed by the LORD's instruction are the wicked. The psalm uses the opposing word pair "wicked/righteous" for pedagogical purposes. The terms are categories of discrimination that function as simple opposites, with no grading between the two and no ambiguity in either. But the categorical character of the terms does not imply that their use reckons with absolute moral righteousness or wickedness. The discrimen that determines which applies is theological. The issue is the relation of a pattern of living to the LORD, and in the psalm's theology, life either is in the right with God or it is not. No partly righteous, no a-little-bit-wicked. Do life purpose and life performance confirm or deny the sovereign deity of the LORD? For the *torah* piety of this psalm, the central question is what directs life. If concern with and searching the revelation of the LORD informs and guides living, then one is in the right on this question. The wrong in the wicked lies in the fact that they offer another possibility. Their advice and

The Lord Reigns
p. 128

42

path and position are their own. The direction given life by
them expresses their sinfulness and cynicism. In their very autonomy they are wrong, and those who are guided by their
torah are in the wrong with respect to the LORD's *torah* (see
Job 21:14). The psalm does not call those devoted to the LORD's
torah to withdraw from society into a defensive ghetto. What
is to be avoided is not the wicked but their influence and effect
on life. Jesus ate with sinners, but he did not follow their way.
The psalmist does know about the power of socialization, so he
warns against this corrupting effect.

The terms "wicked" and "righteous" are important elements of the psalmic vocabulary. They are used to characterize
individuals and groups. The particular discrimen in question
will differ, but always the basic criterion is the rightness or
wrongness of one's response to the reality and revelation of the
LORD's sovereign rule over human affairs. In the psalms the
wicked play three principal roles. Their character and actions
are described to warn against living that conflicts with the will
of the LORD and to provide a background of contrast that sets
the identity of the righteous in profile (e.g., 5:4–6, 9–10). They
afflict the lowly, accuse the innocent, and undermine the trust
of the faithful, and so constitute the distress from which the
psalmists cry for deliverance (e.g., 3:7; 10:2; 11:2). In corporate
form, they threaten the people of the LORD and put the course
of the LORD's providence in question (e.g., 9:5–6, 17). In all their
roles the wicked represent the incongruence in the human
world between the will of God and the will of human beings.
Psalmic speech about them seems to simplify what could be
understood as complex and ambiguous matters, but the necessity for faith to recognize the disastrous and tragic disparity
between God and human beings gives this speech a significant
grounding in God's relation to the world.

4. Psalm 1 teaches that life is a journey through time; living
chooses a particular route for existence. It uses the great biblical
metaphor of the "way," a road or path that one follows. Within
all the individuality that particular lives express, there are ultimately only two ways for the journey to take, the way of the
righteous and the way of the wicked (v. 6). The first way leads
to the fulfillment of life, depicted by the favorite simile of a tree
that bears fruit (v. 3). That way is incorporated in the providence of God (v. 6*a*), because it follows the direction given
through the *torah* of the LORD. The fulfillment is not so much

43

a reward as a result of life's connection with the source of life. The second way is really an illusion. It has no more substance than chaff that the wind drives away (v. 4) and no future among the righteous who are vindicated by the judging of God, who watches over human life. The wicked are grounded and guided within themselves, a way that has no connection with the source of life. That way will perish. Let the readers understand and ask in what way their feet are set.

The first psalm teaches without qualification that each way has its distinctive destiny. The claim is the claim of faith, not experience. It will be reiterated at other points in the psalms (e.g., Psalm 37). But it will also be qualified in many ways. The prayers testify that the righteous meet affliction rather than fulfillment in life. Some psalms wrestle with the enigma of the prosperity and power of the wicked (e.g., Psalm 73). A few perceive that only the forgiveness of God can sustain life because of the sinfulness of the human condition (e.g., Psalm 130). Almost certainly verse 5 came to be understood in the light of apocalyptic eschatology like that of Daniel (see Daniel 7; 12) as a reference to a vindicating judgment beyond this life. Nevertheless, qualified in all these ways, the doctrine endures and is heard again in the New Testament from another teacher who uses beatitudes and warns that the outcome of life depends on one's guidance by his *torah* (Matthew 5—7). "Blessed," he says, "are those who hear the word of God and keep it" (Luke 11:28).

Psalm 2: This Is My Son

The second psalm is paired with the first as a double introduction to the Psalter. Psalm 1 addresses the question of individual life faced with the problem of wickedness in society; its answer for faith is the instruction of the LORD as the guide to the fulfilled life. Psalm 2 addresses the question of the community of faith faced with the problems of a history made by nations contending for power; its word to faith is the announcement of the messiah into whose power God will deliver the nations. The second psalm is a poetic speech by the messiah. It is the only text in the Old Testament that speaks of God's king, messiah, and son in one place, the titles so important for the presentation of Jesus in the Gospels. Its exposition can serve as an introduction to the other psalms whose subject is God's king (18; 20; 21; 45; 72; 89; 110; 144). After we look at the psalm itself,

44

we will consider its setting and use in Israel's religion, its theology, its role and meaning in the context of the Book of Psalms, and its use as Scripture in the New Testament.

1. *The structure.* Psalm 2 is composed of four easily recognizable parts. The first part, verses 1–3, is an exclamation in the form of a long rhetorical question. It expresses astonishment at the rebellion of the nations and their kings against the dominion of the LORD and his anointed. A quotation dramatizes their purpose. The second part, verses 4–6, describes the scorn and wrath with which the LORD, the heavenly king, responds. A quotation announces the action the king of heaven has taken to meet the revolt of the kings of earth; the LORD has installed his own king on his holy mount. In the third part, verses 7–9, the king reports the content of a decree that records the identity and dominion that the LORD has granted him. He has been made son of the LORD by the LORD's fathering that very day and has been promised universal dominion and power to achieve it. Then, in the fourth part, verses 10–12, the rulers of earth are exhorted to submit to the LORD's kingship. They are offered an alternative to his punishing wrath against all who defy his rule. The psalm is concluded by a beatitude that commends those who take refuge in the LORD.

The subject of the psalm is apparent in its structure. It is concerned in all four parts with the relation between the kingdom of the LORD and the kingdoms of the earth and their rulers. The psalm deals with the question of power. Where does power to control the powers at work in world history ultimately reside? The thesis of the psalm is that the answer is given in the messiah, the son of God to whom the sovereign of heaven has given the right and power to rule the world.

2. *The context of Israel's religion.* The stupendous and sweeping thesis of the psalm poses a question about its central figure. Who in Israel was the son of God to whom world dominion is given by the LORD of the universe? How was the psalm used and who spoke in it? The conclusion of Old Testament scholarship is that the psalm was composed for use by a Davidic king of Judah on the occasion of his installation. Psalm 2 is one of the royal psalms, so called because their text clearly indicates that they concern rituals and ceremonies for the king. It is the first of a number that belong to the proceedings of the inauguration of a king, or perhaps to a festival celebrating that inauguration (110; 72; 101). We know something of the importance and

45

proceedings of putting a person in a position of power from the installation of officials in our time—presidents, bishops, judges, and others. Such occasions and their ceremonies are historical descendants of the inauguration of kings in the ancient world. In that world and culture, the king was the preeminent person. He had a special relation to the gods, and it was through their relation to the king that the gods dealt with the nation or people in certain ways. He was the agent of defense, justice, and welfare (see Psalm 72). Power was mediated through him. The language and the rituals of installation were based on and expressed this view of the king. They were adopted and adapted for the sacral ceremony centering on the king in the Jerusalem temple along with the rise and development of monarchy in Israel. Many of the elements of Psalm 2 correspond to features of royal ritual and liturgy in the surrounding nations, especially that of Egypt. The notions that the king was created or selected by the deity, was given special names, titles, and identities in sacred actions, was granted universal dominion, and was endowed with the prowess to establish it over nations and defend it against enemies are common to ancient Near Eastern royal literature (see Keel, pp. 243f.).

In interpreting Psalm 2 and its companion royal psalms, we must remember that this way of believing and speaking about the king had a specific social location where it had its meaning and function. Its subject is the relation between God and king. It is really more about God than about the king. It is confessional, formulaic, poetic, and ideal. It transcends human existence and human history. It is not the language of actual or practical politics or government, nor is it individual or biographical. Israel had other ways of talking and believing about kings and kingship that are present in narrative, law, and prophecy. The idiom found in the psalms was used to express faith in what the LORD, the God of Israel, was working out through the office of the Davidic kingship. The office, not the individual or the particular historical situation, was its theme.

3. *The theology of office.* Psalm 2 seems designed to serve as the public proclamation of the king before the audience gathered for his installation. In it he declared the significance of his kingship for the other nations and their rulers. Though it is at its conclusion rhetorically addressed to these other rulers, it was an interpretation of his office for his own court and people.

46

The basic assertion is that the king's installation is a divine act. The entire process of his designation and inauguration was a sacred enactment of the choice of the LORD who had installed him on the holy mount. On the double election of the king as the LORD's earthly regent and the holy hill of Zion as God's capitol, see the comment on Psalm 132. The two titles, "his anointed" and "my son," are symbols of the divine choice. Anointing was a ritual of designation and endowment. Consecrated oil was poured from a sacred horn onto the head by a representative of God. The importance of the rite in selecting a king seems to have been unique in Israel. The representative of God was traditionally a prophet. The designated one was called "the anointed" (Heb. *mashiach*; Gr. *messias, christos*). "The anointed" was the principal royal title in Judah; it is found in narrative as well as psalms (e.g., I Sam. 10:1; 12:3; Ps. 18:50; 20:6).

"You are my son" (v. 7) is the only appearance of "son" as title of the Davidic king in the psalms. It is the ritual counterpart to the prophetic promise, "I will be his father, and he shall be my son," given to David in II Samuel 7:14 (see its echoes in I Chron. 17:13; 22:10; 28:6). In Psalm 2 the king is reporting the content of a decree or protocol that presumably has been given or read to him earlier in the proceedings. The decree interprets the rituals of installation as a divine "begetting" of the king as son of God. "In what is done this day I have become your father and you my son." Sonship is created by sacral-legal action. Its reality is an identity and status of special right and special responsibility to God in analogy to the special right and responsibilities a son has in relation to a father in Israel's culture.

The divine decree also offers the king the grant of universal dominion. The promise that the Davidic king can break and smash the nations is conventional royal language for the power to rule. Obviously the divine grant of worldwide rule to the kings of Judah stands in great contrast to historical reality. The Davidic empire at its height might have been thought to be an initial realization of the grant, but it was hardly the equal of other empires at its time. The logic of the psalm is not historical but theological. The issue that informs the psalm is the question of the ultimate power in the universe. The psalm is based on the faith that the LORD throned in heaven is the ultimate power. The dominion of the son must correspond to the sovereignty of the father. Correspondence between the heavenly king and the

47

anointed king is an important feature of the royal psalms. The human king is not equal to or identical with, but in certain respects corresponds to, the divine sovereign. So the inaugural of the anointed is a declaration that "the LORD reigns" in the midst of a history whose powers deny it.

4. *The context of the book.* As the second panel of the Psalter's introduction, Psalm 2 identifies and orients the reader to themes that run through the entire book. We see and hear God in the persona that he is given in the psalms, the sovereign enthroned in the heavens. Kingship is the comprehensive theological metaphor. A mount made holy by his choice and an anointed regent represent his rule in the world. All nations and people with their rulers belong to his dominion. The prayers and praise and poetry of the book are all psalms of the kingdom of God.

The nations appear as opponents, the guise they frequently wear in the psalms. Their rebellion against the LORD and his anointed transcends some cultic or historical occasion and becomes an interpretation of all history short of the coming of the reign of God in the world. Every nation, people, group, and organization that possesses and uses power autonomously independent of the rule of the LORD is theologically in rebellion. They are under the wrath of God, the divine zeal for his own rule. They are offered the service of the LORD as the better way.

The final line of Psalm 2 instructs the readers who have to live with the tension of the "not yet" in the midst of the perils and threats of the powers at work in the world. They are tempted to be afraid and discouraged, tempted to believe that the powers are the only reality, even in danger of submitting and trusting life to the purposes of the powers. The word to them is, "Blessed are all who take refuge in him." To take refuge in the LORD is one of the most important expressions for the piety nurtured by the psalms. Literally, it means to seek shelter or protected space. Used as a metaphor, it belongs to the psalmic vocabulary of trust, the act of turning to and relying on the LORD's salvation (see the comment on Ps. 7:1). Here in the introduction it points forward to all the following prayers, beginning with Psalm 3, and was probably added to Psalm 2 to do just that. The prayers are the liturgy of those who take refuge in the LORD, in the midst of all the powers in the world that threaten the way of those who seek to live in the rule of God. On the form of the beatitude, see Psalm 1, sec. 1.

The distance between the ideal of the psalm and the reality of experience for those who formed and used the Psalter is apparent. The kings of Judah had not fulfilled their office by ruling in a way that corresponded to the kingship of the LORD. Prophets had hammered that lesson home. Instead of claiming the nations for the reign of the LORD, they had repeatedly been defeated. Finally a time came when there was no king, no Davidide, no anointed. The psalm could be read in the light of the prophets' foretelling of a descendant of David yet to come, that is, as eschatological promise, not as royal ritual. The genre of Psalm 2 and its companion royal psalms was revised by their inclusion in a book of Scripture. They were kept because the divine promise in them was still believed and the revelation in them of God's way in the world was still trusted.

It is also possible that these psalms were read in a corporate and democratizing way. That is, God's commitment and promises to David were believed to hold good for the faithful community. After all, the welfare and the destiny of the people were always bound up with the career of the king. There are strong hints in literature from the exile and later of a belief that the faithful in Israel had replaced the absent king in God's way with the nations and history (e.g., the servant figure in Isaiah 40—55, the transfer of the Davidic promise and vocation in Isaiah 55, the saints of the Most High in Daniel 7, the faithful who win the victory over the nations in Psalm 149, the crowning of humanity in Psalm 8). Possibly the two readings were not absolute alternatives for those who read the psalms. Neither the Psalter nor the Old Testament gives directives for a final choice between the views.

5. *Psalm 2 in the New Testament.* Two features of Psalm 2, the designation of the king as the son of God by God and the opposition of the nations and their kings to the reign of the LORD and his anointed, play important roles in the Christology, ecclesiology, and eschatology of the New Testament.

The declaration of God to the king, "You are my son," becomes the central assertion about the relation of Jesus to God. In the Old Testament, "king" and "anointed" are more frequent and important titles, but in the New Testament, "son" moves to the fore as the identification of the One whom God has chosen to represent his kingdom in the world. More than the other titles, it emphasizes the correspondence between the heavenly sovereign and the person of his human regent. The

49

setting of the declaration in the New Testament is the disclosure event, moments when the relation of Jesus to God is revealed. The declaration is heard in the baptism of Jesus (Mark
1:11 and parallels) and his transfiguration (Mark 9:7 and parallels; II Peter 1:17). It is proclaimed as the meaning of his resurrection (Acts 13:33; Rom. 1:4). It is God's central word to and
about Jesus (Heb. 1:5; 5:5). The psalm does not tell us how Jesus
of Nazareth will fulfill this office. That is a surprise of the Gospels. The political and military idiom of the psalm is transformed in his life into an evangelical mode, but the psalm insists
that it is precisely this person, in his preaching and teaching and
healing, and in his death and resurrection, who is God's sovereign response to every seat of power and use of power that is
independent of God's rule. The psalm insists on the universal
significance of the sonship of Jesus for human history.

In Acts 4:23–31, the first stanza of Psalm 2 is used to interpret the opposition of rulers and peoples to God's anointed,
Jesus, and as a basis for courage in the face of threats against the
infant church by the authorities. The psalm showed the apostles
that the hostility of the powers was no cause for despair. Instead, the hostility was the right and proper setting for their
preaching, because the declaration of the Son of God is God's
answer to the opposition of the world's powers. So they "spoke
the word of God with boldness." Preaching the Son of God is
a mission designed for the situation of conflict. (See the comment of Luther, 12:5ff.)

In Revelation, the scenario of the psalm as a whole is read
as eschatological prophecy whose fulfillment belongs to the end
of history. Then the warfare of the powers of earth against God
and his anointed will reach its climax (Rev. 11:18; 19:19), in
which the one who is King of kings and LORD of lords will gain
the victory and rule the nations with a rod of iron (Rev. 19:11,
16). Then, heaven will announce that history has reached its
goal, for "the kingdom of the world has become the kingdom
of our Lord and of his Christ, and he shall reign forever and
ever" (Rev. 11:15). The early Christians lived between the "already" of the Messiah and the "not yet" of his rule over the
kings and nations who persecuted them. The psalm assured
them of the coming dominion of the Christ in a victory that
would also be theirs (Rev. 2:26–29) and gave them a reason to
be faithful.

When the risen Jesus announced to his assembled court,

"All authority in heaven and on earth has been given to me. Go therefore and make disciples of all nations" (Matt. 28:18f.), we are hearing the Christian version of the grant to the Old Testament messianic king: "Ask of me, and I will make the nations your heritage" (Ps. 2:8).

Psalm 3: Many Are My Foes

After the double introduction provided by Psalms 1 and 2, the voice of prayer is heard. That voice will dominate the first two-thirds of the Psalter; it is first of all a book of prayer. Most of these prayers are prayers for help composed in first person style (Introduction, sec. 5.2). The third psalm is a brief and typical example of such prayers.

1. The prayer begins by calling on the name of the LORD and describing the trouble that occasions the prayer (vv. 1–2). It asserts trust in the LORD as the protector of the one who prays, the source of his dignity and confidence (v. 3), and as the one who does answer his prayers (v. 4). That trust is expressed in conduct, the prayer says, by restful sleep (v. 5) and the absence of fear in the midst of trouble (v. 6). A double petition seeks the LORD's response and saving help (v. 7a). The petition is supported by praise of the LORD as the one who rebukes and disempowers the wicked enemies (v. 7b). The prayer concludes with a brief theological sentence proclaiming that salvation belongs to the LORD and with an invocation of the LORD's blessing upon the people of the LORD (v. 8).

2. For whom was the prayer composed? All of the elements of its structure and many of its expressions are typical of this kind of prayer. Its individuality lies in the way the elements are arranged and the motifs are developed. The description of trouble depicts a person surrounded by overwhelming hostility. The threefold repetition of the motif "many" in the first two lines sets the scene. The language does not require a military crisis, an interpretation suggested by the superscription. Calling the LORD "a shield" is a conventional way of speaking of God as one's protector (e.g., 7:10; 18:2; 28:7). The reference to "ten thousands of people" (the translation is uncertain) is hyperbole used to profess confidence in the LORD. The identity of the petitioner is simply a believer in the LORD who faces threatening hostility in trust; the prayer is the voice of that trust. The prayer was composed to give that identity and its language to

51

any of the religious community who find themselves beleaguered by enmity.

3. The central theological issue of the prayer is what many are saying about the petitioner: "There is no salvation for him in God" (v. 2). This devastating appraisal organizes the whole prayer. It discloses the true significance of the hostility. The assertions of trust deny its validity. The petitions are an appeal to God to disprove it. The confession, "Salvation belongs to the LORD," contradicts it. Ordinary life is accompanied by experiences of the antagonism of others. The experience of hostility runs across the gamut of spheres in which life is lived. Opposition arises in the family, in the neighborhood, in earning a living, in political and national and religious communities. That was true in Israel and in all societies. Whatever threatens or damages the support of life or the joy of life or living space or right to life is foe, enemy. But this prayer is not designed to serve the human inclination to complain, to feel sorry for oneself, and to blame others. It is not written as a litany of paranoia. Hostility takes many forms, but the hostility with which this prayer is concerned transcends hostility understood as conflict between human beings. At root it concerns an assault on God. The assumption or intimation or claim that there is no help for another in God is not only an attack on a fellow human being; it is a limiting, arrogant presumption against God. That is why the enemies of the psalmist are also called "wicked" (see Psalm 1, sec. 3). The specific meaning of the enemies' accusation is not explained. "No salvation for him in God" may simply be an estimate that the psalmist's situation is hopeless; there is no escape from his distress. It could be the scornful judgment of a cynical scoffer that the God of this pious person is of no use in the situation. Or it could be an accusation that the psalmist has no right to appeal to God and expect God's help; God could help, but somehow the psalmist is disqualified and God won't help. Whatever the particular point of the sentence, its final implication is that the one who prays is without God and therefore without hope. That is the real trouble beneath the tangible trouble, opened up and brought to light by the hostility. In the religious world of the Old Testament, in such a situation there were only two possibilities: either the enemies were right or the psalmist had a right to hope. Only God could decide and disclose the truth.

"No salvation for him in God" is a mortally dangerous

weapon against the soul. It has an ally in every crevice of doubt, anxiety, and guilt in the heart. No reasoning or counsel or procedure is a sure defense against it. One can either believe it or believe in God. The psalm is composed to encourage faith and to give it language. The prayer calls out the name of the LORD and puts the one who uses it in the situation of personal address. It falls back on the petitioner's membership in the chosen community and calls the LORD "my God." It speaks of the experience of God's provident protection and care in the past (v. 3). It points to the calm that comes from trusting God instead of fearing human enmity (vv. 6–7). It recites the doctrine that "salvation belongs to the LORD" to remind the distressed that no trouble is beyond help and no human hostility can limit God's help. In all these ways the psalm encourages and supports faith and invites the distressed to pray, the ultimate act of faith in the face of the assault on the soul.

4. The prayer has a heading or superscription that does identify the person and situation. The heading classifies the prayer as a "psalm," the first of many David psalms and one of the thirteen that are given a setting in the biblical story of David (see Introduction, secs. 3.5, 6; 4.5). The psalm is assigned to the time when David fled from his son Absalom. The story of the time is told in II Samuel 15. The learned sage who made the connection between psalm and story found a number of similarities in them. David was beset by multitudes (II Sam. 15:13), spent a night of danger (II Sam. 17:22), and through all was concerned about the welfare of the people (II Sam. 15:14). Perhaps the sage saw in Shimei's curses upon David (II Sam. 16:5–14) a form of the hostile taunt, "No salvation for him in God." The sage had before him a psalm assigned to David, and these similarities persuaded him that it was here in David's story that the psalm fitted. There are incongruences between psalm and story. The tenor of the prayer is not in accord with David's attitude toward Absalom and his allies. Nothing in the story suggests that David believed that there was no help in God for him. Jerusalem was not known as the elect "holy mount" of the LORD in David's time before the temple was built. These differences argue against taking the connection between prayer and story as historical. The modern notion of critical history did not belong to the sage's intellectual world. He was working at a kind of inner-biblical exegesis, a process of interpreting Scripture by Scripture. He worked in a time when

the psalms had come to be regarded as Scripture, and thus the proper place to find answers about questions like, "When did David pray this prayer?" was in the scriptural account of David. Instead of giving us historical information, the sage's answer invites us to search the story of Absalom's revolt as a heuristic context for the psalm. In David's betrayal by a beloved member of his family, in his humiliation before a watching public, and in his agonizing concern to practice "damage control" in the situation, the interpreter may discover narrative illustrations of the kind of predicament in which the psalm works as prayer. Such discoveries open the psalm to other connections with personal and corporate experience. Heuristic reflection leads to theological, pastoral, and homiletical intimations, not to historical conclusions. It encourages us to search for the connections between our own story and the psalm. Early Christian interpreters of the psalm noticed that David's path of sorrow led him across the brook Kidron (II Sam. 15:23) to ascend the Mount of Olives (II Sam. 15:30). That reminded them of the one of whom King David was the Old Testament type whose path of affliction also passed that way in the midst of many enemies (Neale and Littledale, 1:104ff.). They saw in the psalm the expression of his passion, the language of his own betrayal and humiliation. They were led to reflection on the way he dealt with his enemies and were helped to understand the intention they could bring to the psalm as their own prayer. The other narrative headings in the psalms are like this one in kind and function. Mistaken as historical notices, they lead to puzzlement. Taken as permission and encouragement to heuristic reflection, they lead to discoveries that lend concreteness and use to the liturgical language of the psalm.

5. The location of the third psalm with its heading, after the introductory psalms and at the beginning of a long sequence of prayer psalms, prompts the reader of the book in certain ways. The prayers are the response that faith is led to make to the beatitude, "Blessed are all who take refuge in him" (2:11); the theme of refuge will be struck repeatedly in the prayers as their favorite metaphor for trust (see 7:1). The "David" who in Psalm 2 is called "son of God" and who here in Psalm 3 is offered the nations as his possession flees before the hostility of his own son in humiliation; the contrast points to the unconditional humanity of this "son of God" whose way is beset by hostility and questioning of God's revelation to him. Finally, all who commit

54

their lives to the direction of *torah* and hope in the Son of God are shown that they must make their way through prayer.

Psalm 4: When Honor Is Lost

Psalm 4 is an individual prayer for help (see Introduction, sec. 5.2). Its occasion is the trouble caused by falsehood. The honor of the one who prays has been damaged by a lie (v. 2). In spite of distress, the prayer's dominant mood is confidence. In that confidence the prayer petitions God to hear and help (v. 1), rebukes those who cause humiliation (vv. 2–5), and declares trust in God (vv. 6–8). In the culture of ancient Israel, honor was of the greatest value; it is in most societies. Honor is the dignity and respect that belong to a person's position in relation to family, friends, and the community. It is an essential part of the identity that others recognize and regard in dealing with a man or a woman. In Israel its loss had tragic consequences for self-esteem and social competence. Shaming and humiliating a person was violence against them worse than physical harm. Job's lament over his lost honor (Job 29) is eloquent testimony to the suffering caused. The fourth commandment shows the importance of the notion in the family. Though the term and the notion are not prominent in our culture, the reality and experience of it are inherent in the roles and expectations that belong to all social relations.

The prayerful and theological significance of this psalm is that God is the ultimate basis of the "honor" of the faithful. The psalmist has a basis of identity that transcends the judgments of others—the relation to God. He calls the LORD "God of my right," that is, the one on whom his "rightness" as a person depends. One's righteousness is finally a matter of God's judgment. See Isaiah 50:8f. and Romans 8:31.

Indeed, the language of the psalm suggests a situation in which the psalmist has already appealed to God and been answered, probably in sacral proceedings, by a word or sign that God has identified and claimed the psalmist as one of the faithful (v. 3) and by doing so has freed the one who prays from the constraints of distress (second line of v. 1). That would explain the exhortation addressed to the detractors (vv. 2–5) calling on them to be in trembling awe before this evidence of divine acceptance and to desist from the sin of their falsehood. Instead, they should bring sacrifices to express their own devotion to righteousness, trust themselves to God, and forsake their malicious intentions.

The prayer concludes with a declaration of the psalmist's experience of grace (vv. 6–8). It contrasts the mood of some in the time with that of the one who prays. Many in restless dissatisfaction with what they have pray a version of the ancient prayer of Numbers 6:25, "Let the light of your face shine on us, O LORD!" (v. 6), hoping for an increase of corn and wine. But the one who prays has been given more joy by the sign of God's acceptance than would be gained from an abundance of meat and drink. The gift of trusting God transcends the value of any material good. That gift brings with it *shalom*, a sense of completeness in relation to God, self, and others. No sleepless anxiety erodes the night. The psalmist is content to find security in God.

Verse 8 has prompted believers through the ages to use Psalm 4 as an evening prayer or hymn. Whether or not one's honor has been injured by misunderstanding, lack of appreciation, scorn, or lie, it is good at the close of the day to repair to the marvelous vindication given to faith in the sign of Jesus Christ and to know with Paul that "the peace of God, which surpasses all understanding, will guard your hearts and your minds in Christ Jesus" (Phil. 4:7).

Psalm 5: My King and My God

In Romans 3:13, Paul quotes verse 9 of Psalm 5 in a catena of descriptions of the conduct of the wicked taken from the Psalms. He uses the quotations to argue that "all, both Jews and Greeks, are under the power of sin." Such was not the point and purpose of these descriptions of conduct in the Old Testament. But Paul's point and purpose are pertinent to the use of Psalm 5 and other similar psalms in devotion and liturgy, for we can never hear the declaration that wickedness contradicts the will and way of God without trembling at our own need of repentance and dependence on grace, nor can we ever pray in the midst of the conflicts of life as though we could distinguish in an ultimate and final way between the righteous and the wicked. The point and the purpose of Psalm 5, however, belong to a quite particular predicament in which the power of the lie threatens the life of the faithful. The psalm does permit and encourage believers to repair to prayer, when they and others suffer from falsehood, in confidence that their prayer is in accord with the royal pleasure of the heavenly king.

1. The structure of Psalm 5 is composed of a sequence of petitions and assertions, each followed by supporting subordinate clauses attached by the conjunction "for." Verses 1–2 open the prayer with petitions in the form of an appeal to a king to be heard. The opening vocative, "LORD," calls upon the God of Israel, who is addressed in the role of king and God of the one who prays (Introduction, sec. 6.1). The form of the appeal introduces the prayer as the suit of a subject about a matter that belongs to a king's office and concerns the king's rule and realm. Verses 3–7 state the royal policy on the basis of which the appeal is made. The appeal is brought at the time for morning prayer in confidence that it is in accord with the king's will. The royal policy is stated in the first clause of verse 4: The king is not pleased with wickedness. Then five traditional categories of wickedness are added to elaborate the concept: an evil person, the boastful, evildoers, liars, and people who shed blood and deceive. The last two anticipate the specific case at issue (see v. 9). In verse 7 the petitioner claims his own fealty to the king as the second basis for the appeal. The psalmist comes before the royal presence in the holy temple depending on God's steadfast love (*hesed*) and in reverent awe submitting to God's will and power. The general grounds having been laid, the specific appeal for help is made in verse 8, and a motive to support it is given in verse 9. The language of the petition is not so much moral as salvific. "Lead me . . . , make your way straight before me" is a request for the protecting providence of God, a prayer that life be kept within the sphere and course of God's own way, safe from the destructive ways of others. The petition seeks an action of God's "righteousness," which, as so often in the psalms, means the divine purpose and power to make people and affairs right for life. God's help is needed because of "enemies" (so NRSV), referred to by a Hebrew word that characterizes them as "watchers" who lie in wait for the life of the psalmist with the concentration that a carnivore gives its intended prey. Verse 9 describes their conduct as a use of language: mouth, heart, throat, tongue. What they say about the psalmist is empty of facts, destructive, bears the stench of death, and is deceptively slick. They lie with murderous intent.

The second petition for help (v. 10) is made against the adversaries because as liars they willfully oppose the good pleasure of the divine king. The petition is an appeal to the LORD to disclose who the real guilty party is and to bring upon the liars the very exclusion from a place in God's kingdom that they deceitfully planned for the psalmist.

The third petition for help (vv. 11–12) appeals to another policy of the divine king; he blesses the righteous and grants them the protection of royal favor. Therefore, when the innocent are protected and liars are disclosed and rebuked, the LORD's rule is revealed, and those who love the LORD and depend on the LORD are given a new reason for joyful praise of their God and king.

2. This prayer is one of the biblical witnesses that the lie is one of the most dangerous and detestable forms that evil takes, especially when a falsehood is used to harm another. The psalm may have been written for a person who was falsely accused or slandered in a way that destroyed standing or rights in the community. The psalm would be prayed in the temple as a last resort to appeal to God as the final administrator of justice, looking for a vindicating answer through oracle or sign or event. Used as liturgy, the psalm became a prayer of the community and of individuals in it for divine protection against the misrepresentations or slanders used within and against the community. We have only to remember Jeremiah and Jesus, the postexilic community and the earliest Christians, as illustrations of the predicament described in the psalm.

3. Speech is the distinctively human capacity, the interpreter of others and of all around us. It is also the cheapest, most common and inhumane means of causing trouble and anguish for others. There is a profound and essential relation between truth telling and God. To use speech that is empty of truth about another is to practice the opposite of God's will. "You shall not bear false witness." So this psalm asks us whether we take the opposition between truth and lie seriously enough as a matter of faith, whether we are ready to stand with those damaged by falsehood and propaganda, and whether we are alert to the lies to us and about us told by the powers and opinions of our culture.

The style and the arrangement of the psalm instruct us to pray according to the reign of God. The prayer is based on God's way as sovereign over humanity: Wickedness is rejected, righteousness favored. Remember that in the theology of the psalmist, the righteous are those who love, trust, and depend on

God and want to be led in God's way. The psalm sees the predicament as a question placed against the reign of God and prays in an Old Testament way, "Thy kingdom come—now," and in this particular situation. The prayer against the enemies is a way of saying that in the time and experience of the one who prays, there seems to be no other course for the righteousness of God to take. At other places in the Old Testament, and clearly in the career of Messiah Jesus, God reveals that there are other courses to take, and that makes a difference in the way one prays for the manifestation of God's reign against threatening evil. But the essential understanding of God's royal policy against wickedness is never, ever, at any place in Scripture, revised or revoked. Prayer that loses its context in the theological morality of the psalms is no longer authentic prayer for the kingdom of God.

Psalm 6: O LORD, Heal Me

This prayer for help is a passionate, agonized appeal to the grace of God against the wrath of God. It sees the LORD as the cause of death and as the giver of life. It is based on a severe concentration on the LORD as the one meaning of experience, of what is and can be, and so sees everything in terms of God's sovereign freedom. The vocabulary used in the psalm suggests that it was written as a prayer by a sick person for healing (Introduction, sec. 5.2.2). The vocabulary of sickness and healing was used metaphorically in the Old Testament for social and theological conditions, so the psalm probably came to be used as a general prayer for the restoration of the community. By the fifth century of the Christian era, the psalm was established as one of the traditional prayers of penitence used particularly during Lent.

1. The language of the prayer describes a person who is seriously ill. Physical vigor wanes, body and life are disturbed, unbalanced, groaning and grief have gone on and on, and vitality seems to leak away with the outpouring of sighs and tears. Death is an imminent probability. No specific terms for particular diseases are used; the description is not clinical in any sense. But illness in the Old Testament thought world is not comprehended in a diagnostic way; it is not sickness as an objective phenomenon that is spoken about but the experience of being sick, what a person can express in words of feeling, emotion,

and meaning. Anyone who has been seriously ill senses what is finding its way to language in this anguished poetry. Often in the concentration of modern medical treatment on strictly physical causes and procedures, the need for suffering to find words and be heard is overlooked or suppressed. This and similar psalms bring that dimension of serious illness to light and give it its necessary place. (See the comment and the excursus on Psalm 38.)

But for this prayer the theological meaning of serious illness is even more important than the psychological. At the very beginning the affliction is interpreted as God's action in wrath to punish, and at the same time God is held to be the one "who heals all your diseases" (103:3). The entire span of sickness and health is understood in relation to the LORD. Life and death of a person are in God's hands. No other cause is contemplated, and no other relief is sought. There is no mention of sin or sinfulness, or any explicit prayer for forgiveness. The suffering is simply so intense and prolonged that it is taken to be the work of God's wrath. Yet the affliction is not mutely accepted or borne with an "It is the LORD; let him do what is right in his own eyes." It is opposed by the very means of the prayer. "Don't . . . heal . . . turn . . . save," the prayer pleads, as though it were certain that God's usual and preferred way with human beings favored health and life. This prayerful undertaking to comprehend affliction and healing in relation to one divine will is at once one of the profoundest efforts to fulfill in the realities of life the first commandment and at the same time an undertaking full of theological tensions.

2. The prayer supports the petitions with three reasons or motives. The first is the intensity and length of the suffering (vv. 2f., 6f.). The psalmist believes that God is moved by human anguish and responds to helplessness. The LORD is compassionate. The second is the steadfast love of God (v. 4). The psalmist knows that God's characteristic of doing the best by those who are related to him and who depend upon him is stronger than God's way of letting people suffer the consequence of what they choose to be or do. The third is the finality of death (v. 5). For the psalmist, there was beyond death only the shadowy nonexistence of the underworld in Sheol. But it is not the bare fact and terror of the psalmist's own end that is offered as an appeal to God. That would have been to set an overweening valuation on one's mere existence. The instinct to survive prompts one to

See Ps 161 p. 88

60

pray and think that way, but the psalmists never do. Instead, the appeal is based on the loss of the praise of God in which God's ways and works are remembered and expressed. In the view of life and death behind this prayer, the praise of God is possible and actual only within the sphere of salvation history and in response to it. One must be a corporate and individual participant in God's way with the people of God for praise to occur. Sheol lay beyond and outside God's way with his people. There praise did not occur. The point in the appeal is not so much that God loses the praise of the psalmist but that the psalmist loses God. In the understanding of the psalms, life and praise are very closely related. Where life is perceived and lived as a gift of God, praise must break forth. Where praise and prayer are missing, there is no relation to God. To be without them is to be without God. From the viewpoint of this prayer, that is, the true terror and reality of death. At the end of verse 7, "all my foes" are cited as one of the sources of distress and then addressed directly in verse 8 as troublemakers. They are not the cause of the psalmist's affliction; rather, they are its exploiters and exacerbators. Perhaps in the very face of the psalmist's appeal to God they have publicly and willingly given him up for dead, reckoned him deserving of his misfortune, and even intended to profit from his demise. His healing and return to life will shame their hostility and expose their perfidy (v. 10).

The troublemakers are rebuked on the basis of a confidence proclaimed three times: The LORD has heard/accepts my appeal (vv. 8f.). The praying concludes in certainty that it has been heard. To what does "the LORD has heard" point? It could be a claim upon the promise that the LORD hears those who call on him, or it could point to a word of salvation spoken by a prophet in the temple as a liturgical answer to verses 1–7. In either case, the psalmist in his distress trusts the word of God rather than the discouraging words of human beings. Ultimately it is in such trust that all prayer must be concluded.

3. The psalm's understanding of suffering as the effect of God's wrath is a theological act of faith in the God of Israel. It is the choice of the believer that flows from obedience to the first commandment to have no other god, to recognize no other divine power and no other power as divine. It is a choice against other options offered in the culture: another god, demonic powers, magical spells of enemies, sheer fate beyond the sphere of God's sovereignty. It is not a choice as such to believe in an

angry God; rather, it is a choice to understand experience through belief in one God and to encompass all experience within the relation to that God.

The prayer reminds us of choices we have to make. Living in a scientific culture, we will think out the experience of physical suffering in a different way. What was a life crisis for an Israelite is not for us. We know about immediate and proximate causes and remedies. But choices remain. Crises of health that threaten life do come. Situations arise when little is certain. Do we bracket God out of what happens to us? Does experience bear no meaning about our condition in relation to God? Do we see our exposed mortality at all as a condition of our disturbed relation to God? The experience of serious illness can always be a lesson to our finitude and fallibility, an occasion for reflection and repentance, and a summons to dependence on God through prayer. It would be an unbiblical religion to see meaning for faith only in positive experiences that can be interpreted as the blessing and favor of God. The God of the Bible works upon our historical and personal experiences through, as the Bible says in its metaphors, "wrath as well as grace."

4. When Psalm 6 became a penitential prayer, it was moved to a different hermeneutical situation. The words of the text were a score played with a new emphasis and purpose. As a cultic prayer in Israel, it was language prepared for a particular person who was understood to be sick because of God's wrath. As a penitential, it became the general prayer of all who as sinners confessed the "sickness" of sin. The shift in the function of the psalm would have begun when it was used as congregational liturgy in Israel and was included in a book of Scripture. The prophets' use of the vocabulary of sickness (e.g., Isa. 1:5f.) to portray the condition of the whole people under judgment may have prepared the way for the use of Psalm 6 and other similar language in the prayers in congregational penitence. When Genesis 3 is taken as canonical context, all the faithful understand that their mortality and its symptoms are generic conditions of the disturbed relation of humanity to God.

Death places a question against the existence of every person. It closes the books on life and the possibilities of repairing its faults and failures. It confronts us with the alternatives of final alienation from God or final acceptance by God. As liturgical and personal prayer, Psalm 6 provides words for sinners who face the meaning of their own mortality to rest their lives on

God's grace for salvation and to declare that from the gospel they take confidence that they are heard.

Psalm 7: In You I Take Refuge

1. Psalm 7 is a prayer for deliverance from enemies (Introduction, secs. 5.2; 6.17). The prayer begins with the declaration, "O LORD, my God, in you I take refuge." Taking refuge in the LORD or making the LORD one's refuge is a favorite and frequent metaphor in the psalms for the religious act of trusting one's life to the care of God in uncertain or threatening situations (11:1; 16:1; 25:20; 31:1; 46:1; 61:3; 62:7–8; 71:1, 7; 94:22; 141:8; 142:5; see the metaphor and its word field in 91:1–2, 9). In ordinary usage, the Hebrew verb meant to take shelter from bad weather or to seek a refuge from enemies. As a metaphor it belongs to the vocabulary of trust. The opening declaration, then, tells us what the intention of the whole prayer is. The prayer itself is a way of taking shelter in the providence and salvation of God. See the comment on Psalm 2, sec. 4.

2. The prayer's defining petition is the formulaic appeal, "Judge me, O LORD, according to my righteousness" (v. 8; see Introduction, sec. 6.7). The accusation is typically left unspecified. The accusers are persecutors whose hostility is compared to the ferocity of a lion (vv. 1–2). In support of his innocence, the accused invokes a curse upon his life if he is guilty of wickedness (vv. 3–5). Verse 4 may suggest that the psalmist has been involved in an injury against one with whom he should have lived in *shalom* (NRSV, "my ally") and who is now his antagonist. The prayer seeks from the LORD, who knows what is right, a decision that will uphold the righteous (innocent) and bring the persecution by the wicked (guilty) to an end (v. 9). Verses 10–11 express confidence in God as righteous and relentless judge, and verses 12–16 express belief that those who plot harm against others only prepare their own hurt. The prayer concludes with a vow of praise (v. 17).

3. A prayer made on the basis of one's own righteousness and integrity poses a serious question. How can anyone possibly ground prayer on such a basis with honesty? Part of the answer comes from recognizing the purpose for which this prayer and others like it were composed. They are not intended to be a litany of self-righteousness before God. The psalms know that there is no autonomous independent righteousness on the basis

63

referred p.89
on (95:17)

of which human beings can deal with God (130:3; 143:2). Such prayers were composed for a person who was in the right in comparison with an antagonist. They are the expressions of a good conscience before hostility and opposition. They are a profession of faithfulness to the LORD. In the matter at hand, the psalmist had clung to the LORD and the LORD's ways. The wrong lies in the hostility that puts faithfulness in question. Faithfulness is a possibility for those who know the LORD as "my God," and this prayer is the voice of that faithfulness.

But the situation and the intention of the psalm are not the whole answer. They must not be isolated from the other bases identified in the prayer. The first is the righteousness of the LORD (v. 17). Apart from the righteousness of the LORD this prayer could not even be thought, let alone said. By election and covenant the LORD has become the personal God of the psalmist (note "my God" in vv. 1, 3, and 6) and has given the psalmist the right to take refuge with him in time of trouble. Based on that relationship, the psalmist appeals to the LORD as the judge of the peoples (vv. 6–8) who tests the mind and conscience of every person so that he may act as righteous judge and save the upright in heart (vv. 9–11). The righteousness of the LORD is this electing, judging, and saving activity. It is the righteousness of the LORD that has called forth the righteousness and integrity of the psalmist, and in it he takes shelter in his trouble. It is the true basis of the prayer on which all else depends (see the comment on Psalm 26).

In verses 12–16 the psalm confesses the belief that the evil that the wicked do turns back on them, so that they prepare their own punishment. They fall into the pit they have dug for others (see 9:16; 35:7–8; 57:6; 141:10; Prov. 26:27). These observations about the way things work seem strange in such a prayer, but in the context of the psalm they serve as another of its bases. In a world where wickedness is its own punishment, the innocent may face its threats and pray with more confidence. The psalmist surely understood this belief in the light of the work of the LORD as judge. Things work that way because God stands in the shadows keeping watch over his own.

4. The heading appears to be one of the thirteen that refer a psalm to an incident in the biblical story of David (Introduction, sec. 3.5). Its form, however, is different from the other such headings, and no Benjamite named Cush can be found in the story of David or anywhere else. Did the sage who added the

reference know of a story about David and Cush that was not included in the biblical account? Or, as seems more likely, is the apparent reference a garbled instruction about how the psalm was to be performed (so Childs, p. 138)? The reference remains mysterious.

Psalm 8: You Have Given Them Dominion

P+T
the Psalms
p. 97

Psalm 8 is the first hymn of praise in the Psalter. It interrupts the sequence of prayers for salvation to say something very important about the God to whom the prayers are made: The LORD is the cosmic sovereign whose majesty is visible in the whole world. The psalm also discloses why the salvation of those who pray is so important for the reign of God: As human beings, they have an office in God's kingdom.

1. Psalm 8 is clearly a hymn of praise, but it is unlike any other in structure and style. It is the only hymn in the Old Testament composed completely as direct address to God. It begins and concludes with an exclamation of adoration. The body of the hymn is composed of two unequal sections (vv. 1b–2 and vv. 3–8). The exclamations set the theme of the whole: "O LORD, our Sovereign, how majestic is your name in all the earth!" (vv. 1a, 9). The LORD who is sovereign over the congregation that sings the hymn possesses a cosmic majesty evident in all the earth. The psalm does not imply that the sovereign self of God is apparent in the visible world. There is no pantheism here. The majesty to be seen is that of the name of the LORD. The content of "name" is the works and words of the one whose identity and will are expressed through them. The psalm sees in all the earth the work of the word of the LORD and views the work of the LORD as the word of the LORD's sovereignty. The body of the hymn praises the LORD as creator, but there and here the language distinguishes between creator and creation while marveling at the majesty of the one discernible in the other.

The meaning of the first part of the body of the hymn is uncertain because of problems with the text of verse 1b and with the reference of the language in verse 2. The two lines could be translated this way:

65

> Your splendor above the heavens is praised
> from the mouth of babes and infants.

> You have established power because of your foes,
> to quell enemy and avenger.

The phrase "above the heavens" is the clue. The picture is that of the LORD as cosmic ruler who established sovereignty by subjecting the hostile powers of chaos. For other uses of the picture to portray the LORD as creator-king, see the comment on Psalms 89:5-14; 104:1-9; and 29:10. The claim that God's royal splendor in heaven is praised by infants is probably poetic hyperbole. Every human sound, says the poet, is response to this universal reign.

The second section of the hymn is spoken in an individual voice because the experience it describes belongs more to the individual than to the community. This section continues the focus on "your heavens" as the sphere of cosmic sovereignty, and it reports the wondering reflection that arises when a mortal looks at the heavenly bodies as the result of the LORD's creation and control. The reflection marvels at the attention and importance that God gives to the human being in such a universe. Though this section turns on the question of a human about the human species, the whole is composed of statements about what the LORD does. That is very important. The hymnic function of praise is not deserted for a moment. The reflection is voiced in the idiom of worship.

2. The entire hymn, the thematic exclamations and both parts of the body, is an expression of the sovereignty theology that is a hallmark of the Psalter (Introduction, sec. 6.1, 2). The LORD is the divine cosmic monarch to whom the earth and all that is in it belong because the LORD mastered chaos and founded the world (e.g., 24:1-2). What is distinctive in Psalm 8 is the way this theology is used to define humankind. "The son of man" (generic term for a member of the human species; NRSV, "mortals") has been invested with a rank just below that of God (the term may mean "divine beings" here), has been endowed with the royal traits of glory and honor, and has been given dominion over all living things (vv. 5-8). This is the psalm's answer to what philosophy and science have called "the man question." The generic human being is an official in the administrative arrangement of the kingdom of God. The species is under God's dominion and has been given dominion. Its nature is constituted in relations, and humankind is known for what it is when it is understood in terms of this pattern of

66

relationships. The psalmist who composed this hymn was thinking about the human being in the same way as Genesis 1:26–28 and 2:19–20 do. The language of the psalm is closest to the first, and it is likely that the poet had this text in mind and was composing a hymn on a text of Scripture. What the psalmist has added is the description of the human in terms of royal rank, visualizing the concept "dominion" in terms of royal theology and interpreting the notion of the "image of God" by the process of ordination and enthronement. The likeness lies in a correspondence in the sovereignty system. God has established dominion over chaos and brought forth creation; humankind is given capacity and vocation to master other animals and bring forth civilization. There is a background for this thinking in the royal culture of the ancient Mideast. A number of Egyptian and Mesopotamian royal inscriptions speak of the king as the "image" of the deity in order to represent the correspondence between the rule of the two and the closeness of their relation (Levenson, *Creation*, pp. 112ff.). On the authority of the Genesis passages, the psalmist has put the entire race in the status of a king. "The human race is YHWH's plenipotentiary, his stand-in" (Levenson, *Creation*, p. 114).

This raises a question about another figure in the psalms who is given a royal status in the divine sovereignty system, the anointed Davidic king who is so close to God that he is called "son of God" (see the comment on Psalm 2). The epithets of royalty (splendor, glory, honor) are used in the psalms for God, king, and humanity to indicate royal identity. The Davidic king is given dominion over the nations; humankind, over living creatures. The problem for the one is the chaos of history; for the other, the chaos of wildness. The two are side by side in the Psalter. How is their relation to be understood? The theory of "democratization" suggests that the office was transferred to all people when there was no longer a king in Israel. That does not do justice to the prominence of the anointed king in the Psalter. Is the question only taken up in the New Testament?

3. Definition of the human being as the earthly regent of the heavenly rule is accompanied and preceded by a question whose formulation is very important. The psalm does not frame the question absolutely and ask, "What is man?" The question is qualified: "What is the human being that you, LORD, remember and visit them?" "Remember" and "visit" are biblical verbs used to speak of the divine response to human finitude and

67

fallibility, the necessary attention God pays to mortals. The human about whom the psalm asks is the God-remembered and God-visited mortal. The psalmist knows about that mortal existence as an Israelite, a member of the covenant people. But his question is not about Israel alone; it is about the entire race. He believes and assumes that God remembers and visits every human, that Israel's experience with God is the truth about God's way with all. Finitude, fallibility, and ultimate dependence are structural to human existence and in some form, whether explicitly religious or not, emerge into an experience that is in some way an intimation of the Other. The psalmist qualifies the "man question" to show that it rises out of the knowledge of God's relation to man that was given to Israel. "Man is made an object of theological knowledge by the fact that his relationship to God is revealed to us in the Word of God" (Barth, III/2, p. 19).

Actually, no one asks the man question in an unqualified form. Philosophy and the sciences qualify the question in the light of their interests and data. What is the human species that it has the capacity to reason, has physical structures similar to certain other animals, creates its own habitat, and so on? These are important forms of the question and lead to significant knowledge. But the psalmist would insist that the human being is not fully and finally understood apart from the psalm's form of the question.

In the psalm, the question is not an invitation to philosophical reasoning or scientific research. In all the appearances of Psalm 8 in the Old Testament, including this one, the psalm's purpose is to acknowledge the finiteness of a human being, his unimportance and limits (144:3–4; Job 7:17; 15:14). The recognition is evoked here by contemplation of the vast depth of the night sky with its moon and myriad mysterious stars, an experience to which people of many times and places have testified. The experience is not, however, that of being "lost in the cosmos"; rather, it is of awe and wonder at the marvelous majesty of God, who can make and has made a royal regent of this mere mortal. The question is asked in the psalm to serve the purpose of the hymn, praise of the LORD.

4. Defining the human species by using the office of royal regent as a metaphor means that the vocation and role are constitutive of its theological identity. This view has significant implications and raises difficult problems.

68

a. The *administration* of the LORD's reign in the world extends beyond messianic king and covenant people to include humanity as a whole. Everybody is involved in the kingdom of God. Being human means being ordained and installed in a right and responsibility within the divine sovereignty. God didn't just make us; God made us both a representation and representatives of the reign of the LORD to the other creatures. The status belongs to the role per se, not to individuals or groups. It can be carried out only in identity with the whole and ultimately fulfilled only by the entire species.

b. Human dominion extends over domestic and wild animals, birds, and fish. The list is meant to include all living creatures. This designation of the sphere of human dominion reflects the struggles of early humans to domesticate and control, to live with and by the use of the wildness of the world. It represents the entire human undertaking to do what the other animals cannot and do not do, order and shape what is already there into a habitat. Animals are dependent on a habitat; humans depend on their capacity to craft one. The power and responsibility that belong to that capacity are interpreted by the psalm as a regency given to humankind in the world. The psalm invites us to see all the civilizing work of the human species as honor and glory conferred on it by God and, therefore, as cause and content for praise of God.

c. In the psalm's world of thought, kingship had an ideal and normative dimension. Dominion involved a pattern of responsibility. Glory belonged to the ruler, but the ruling was to be for the benefit of the ruled (see especially the comment on Psalm 72). In the psalm, moreover, the dominion of the human corresponds to and is subordinate to the reign of the creator. Human beings are to use their power over creatures in a way that serves the purposes and practices of their own sovereign. Its legitimacy depends on that correspondence and subordination. In the vision of the psalm, civilization is meant to be a vast project of stewardship.

d. The psalm does not consider whether or how the race has carried out its ordination. Like the psalms about the anointed king, it has the office in view but not the character of those who occupy it. The psalm speaks its praise of God from the primeval vantage of the original purpose of God, in this like Genesis 1 and 2. This gives the psalm a protological dimension and therefore an eschatological potential. Its vision of the royal office of the human race is completely theocentric, but humanity in its career has performed the office in an anthropocentric mode. Dominion has become domination; rule has become ruin; subordination in the divine purpose has become subjection to human sinfulness. The creatures suffer. Those who read and sing this psalm must remember that along with this word about their vocation as humans there are other words in the Bible about their character and work. They are to share the wonder and exuberance of the psalm at the majesty of God but know fear and trembling at the disparity between the vision of humanity and the reality of human culture. For a full discussion of human dominance over animals and a probing reflection on its problems, see Barth, III/4, pp. 348–356.

5. The understanding of the human being in the New Testament is Christocentric. Its view is formed by the fact that Jesus Christ, the new Adam, who identified himself with the race and represents it in his person, has risen from the dead to an exaltation of glory and honor. Psalm 8 was interpreted in the light of Christ. The eschatological potential of the psalm was brought to clear expression. The question of the relation between the office of the anointed king and the royal rule of the human race was given an answer. "We do not yet see everything in subjection to him [man]," says the Letter to the Hebrews, "but we do see Jesus" (Heb. 2:5–9). It is by the reign of God in and through Christ that all things will be finally made subject to the sovereignty of God. Through Christ the perfect correspondence of human dominion to God is fulfilled (I Cor. 15:20–28; Eph. 1:16–23). So Christians, as they praise the LORD with this psalm, will do so in penitence and hope, remembering that "the creation waits with eager longing for the revealing of the children of God" (Rom. 8:19).

Psalms 9 and 10: Let Not Mortals Prevail

Psalms 9 and 10 are together a song of the people of God who live in faith in the reign of God in the midst of the afflictions of history. Though the song is divided into two parts in Hebrew manuscripts and in most English versions, it appears as one psalm in the Septuagint and in translations dependent on it. A number of features unify the two. Together they compose an acrostic psalm; every second poetic line begins with a successive letter of the Hebrew alphabet (Introduction, sec. 5.6.2).

70

Though the pattern of letters is broken in the middle of the alphabet, with some letters missing, it is nonetheless quite clear for most of the lines. There are also motifs and phrases common to the two, and a plan of composition for the whole.

1. *Type and setting.* The poem is somewhat bewildering if one comes to it expecting one of the regular types of psalms. It appears to be a rather formless sequence of lines with shifting topics and functions, perhaps determined in an arbitrary and external way by the requirements of the alphabet. Some have assessed it in this way. But the composer had an overall plan of composition that carries out his purpose. He used the forms and language of the individual prayers of help and the song of thanksgiving, and, less prominently, the hymn of praise. The primary clue to the design is the recognition that the composer has personified the congregation as an individual and given them the role of the "lowly" (*'ani*; NRSV, poor, afflicted; see Introduction, sec. 6.18). The role of the wicked enemy is assigned to the nations. The comparison of the forms and themes and roles in Psalm 7, an individual prayer for help, with Psalms 9 and 10 will help one to see what is happening here. It is liturgical dramatization. The situation reflected in the composition is that of the postexilic congregation of the faithful whose life is beset and threatened by conditions and incidents caused by the succession of peoples who held power over them. The acrostic pattern is used, as it seems to be in all its appearances in the psalms, as a device of synthesis and comprehensiveness.

2. *Structure and language.* Psalm 9 begins in the idiom of the song of thanksgiving with the basic sentence of thanks for deliverance (138:1). As an offering, the singer brings praise of the LORD's wonderful deeds—not just one saving event but all of them (9:1–2). The report of the wonderful deeds begins as an account of personal deliverance from enemies through the action of the LORD as judge (9:3–4). But suddenly the enemies are the wicked nations, and the account of their judgment recalls the LORD's action in the past against the nations who threatened Israel and have passed from history; the prophets and their oracles against the nations are in the background (9:5–6). In contrast to the vanished nations, the permanence of the kingship of the LORD who rules and judges the peoples is cited, drawing on hymns of the LORD's kingship (9:7–8; cf. 98:9; 96:10). On the basis of the reign of the LORD, the psalm affirms confidence in the LORD as a stronghold for the oppressed in

71

times of trouble (9:9–10) and raises a hymn of praise to the
LORD who hears the cry of the lowly (9:11–12). But next the
idiom shifts to the prayer for help with a cry for the grace of
the LORD and a promise of praise for deliverance (9:13–14).
Confidence is affirmed in God's judgment of the wicked nations
and its method and in the prospects of the lowly for deliverance
(9:15–18). Then a fervent petition for the nations to be judged
prepares for the following prayer (9:19–20).

In Psalm 10, the idiom of the individual prayer for help
takes over. The opening complaint describes a general ongoing
problem; the LORD is absent "in times of trouble" when the
wicked persecute the lowly (10:1–2, the opposite of 9:9–10). A
long and traditional description of the wicked (10:3–11) portrays conduct that denies accountability to God (10:3–4, 10–11;
see Psalm 14), prospers in arrogant iniquity (10:5–8), and op-
presses the lowly (10:9). The petition "Arise, O God" is repeated
(10:12; 9:19), supported by a complaint over the rejection of
God's relevance by the wicked (10:13). An assertion of confidence (10:14), an imprecation against the wicked (10:15), and
another assertion of confidence that the LORD helps the lowly
conclude the prayer. One might think of Psalm 10 as an individual prayer for help against the wicked, a kind of counterpart to
the thanks and prayer in Psalm 9 about the nations. But in 10:16
the personification and problem of Psalm 9 is restated: The issue
is still the contradiction between the everlasting reign of the
LORD and the conduct of the nations.

The whole, then, is a prayer. It begins with thanksgiving for
the history and salvation in which the LORD has disclosed his
reign by his judgment of the nations. It laments the present
situation in which nations act with impunity and call the kingship of God into question. It asks for the intervention of the
LORD to judge the nations and deliver the lowly. The portrayal
of the congregation and the nations in terms of the prayer and
thanksgiving of the individual interprets both in a highly theological way and creates prayer that is designed for the new
situation of the congregation. The composition undoubtedly
reflects the practice in its time of using the individual genres of
psalms for corporate purposes.

3. *The role of God.* The LORD appears in the psalm as the
king enthroned in Zion, whose realm includes all nations and
whose rule will last forever (9:4, 7–8, 11, 19; 10:16). This kingship is precisely the one portrayed in the psalms whose theme

72

is the kingship of the LORD (e.g., 47; 93; 96; 98; 99). The feature of the LORD's rule emphasized here is the role of acting as judge of the nations (7:6–8; 58:11; 82:8; 94:2; 96:10, 13; 98:9). God has assumed kingship to judge the nations (9:7). He has acted in the past against wicked nations; the ruins of history bear evidence (9:5–6). He has made himself known in judgment; it has been a medium of self-disclosure (9:16). His judgments have been made with righteousness and equity; their purpose is to set things right (9:8). It was the duty of the king to hear the cry of the helpless, and it is to that responsibility that the individual prayers for help are directed. That feature of the theology of the LORD as king is also called upon in this prayer (9:9–10, 12, 18; 10:17–18). The portrayal of the LORD's kingship draws on the theology of the kingship psalms and on that of prayers for help and thanksgiving songs. The psalmist even calls the LORD "the one who holds those who shed blood accountable" (NRSV, "he who avenges blood," 9:12, a characterization that appears elsewhere only in the postdiluvian instruction of Noah as universal humanity, Gen. 9:5; cf. Ezek. 33:6). The prayer builds up a quite comprehensive vision of the LORD as the one who has the power and responsibility to set things right in the human world.

4. *The role of the congregation.* The only direct self-description in the prayer depicts one who has been delivered from enemies in the past by the righteous judgment of God (9:3–4) and who now suffers from the hostility of adversaries (9:13). But the concern of the prayer is for a type, the lowly, a category that appears as a singular and plural noun in the Hebrew ('ani, 10:2, 9; 'aniyim, 'aniwim, 9:12, 18; 10:12, 17). A word field of related notions is used to fill out and expound the basic category (oppressed, 9:9; 10:18; needy, 9:18; innocent, 10:8; helpless, 10:8, 14; orphan, 10:14, 18). Persons of this kind are the ones who have a claim on the king's justice. The congregation casts itself in this role as a confession about its own helpless dependence and as the basis of its appeal. They do not pray as the elect; they claim no special rights. In the midst of history and life, they know themselves as the "poor." And the prayer is formulated primarily as an appeal for God to act in judgment on behalf of all who belong to this category. It is, so to say, a class action appeal. "Blessed are you poor, for yours is the kingdom of God" (Luke 6:20); it is the lowly who by dependence and anticipation already live in the rule of God.

5. *The role of the nations.* The prayer contains one of the interpretations of the nations given in the Bible. The nations/peoples are cast as the wicked and play the role given the enemy in the individual prayers for help. The descriptions of the conduct of the wicked are not employed in a merely formal way; they are meant as serious analysis of what nations are like. First, nations pursue what they call "national self-interest." They are set "on the desires of their heart" and are zealous for their own advantage (10:3). Second, in the pursuit of their goal, they are possessed with a sense of achievement and invulnerability (10:5–6). Third, when nations pursue their vision of their manifest destiny, they deal oppressively with poorer nations and the weak in their own nation (10:2, 7–10). Fourth, in all of this, they are secular in the ultimate sense. They do not think in terms of accountability to God (9:17; 10:3–4, 11, 13). The only judgments they are concerned with are the judgments worked out in pursuit of their own policy. Fifth, the nations are only "mortal." Twice the psalmist at crucial points in the prayer uses a word for the nations that connotes the mortality, fallibility, and frailty of the human (*'enosh*, 9:19–20; 10:18). As *'enosh*, nations are "of the earth," created, part of the creation, totally human, divine in no respect. Like humans, nations pass away and are forgotten (9:5–6). This is what they do not know, so they strut in the earth as if they own the permanence that belongs alone to the reign of the LORD (10:5–6 and 10:16).

Israel had learned from the prophets and from the exile that all of this was true of them as a nation. When the LORD made himself known in judgment, they came to know themselves and to recognize the wickedness of nations that forget God.

6. *The petition.* On behalf of themselves as the lowly and on behalf of the lowly with whom they have been taught to identify, the congregation voices the plea, "Arise, O LORD" (9:19–20; 10:12). The cry is an ancient rubric that in early Israel was addressed to the ark when it was brought out to lead the army in battle against the enemies of the people. Now the congregation uses it to pray for God's intervention in the world. They want the nations to learn that they are only *'enosh*, to experience the fear of the LORD. They want to be freed from the tyrannizing of "the man who is of earth." They want the nations to discover that their schemes and strategies and practices are self-destructive (10:2 and 9:15–16). They want to live

74

in a land and world from which arrogant nationalism has vanished (9:17; 10:16). They want to live in a world determined by the justice of God's reign. "Let not *'enosh* prevail!" "Thy kingdom come, thy will be done." Let all the nations live as the lowly, in identity with the lowly.

Psalm 11: Flight or Faith

When the righteous are threatened by the power of the wicked, what course will conduct take: flight or faith? Psalm 11 is a song of trust that answers that question (see Introduction, sec. 5.2.1 on songs of confidence and sec. 6.17 on the topic of the righteous and the wicked). The opening declaration, "In the LORD I take refuge" (v. 1*a*) is the theme of the whole. The God of the psalmist is taken as protection and help. The rest of the psalm is a particular exposition of that confession of faith. (On the declaration, see the comment on Ps. 7:1.)

1. The circumstances in which the psalm is to be sung are sketched in lines that are typically woven of metaphors and images (vv. 1*b*–3). A group is addressed who has assessed the situation and what can be done about it. How the Hebrew of these verses is to be read and how far the quotation of the group's words extends are uncertain, but we may take the translation of NRSV and NJV as reliable bases for interpretation. We need not linger over the question who the group is. The purpose of the quote is rhetorical; it poses an option that is not acceptable to those who take refuge in the LORD. The danger of the wicked to the righteous is portrayed by the image of a skulking archer who, unseen, aims his arrow at the upright in heart from the shadows. Then, moving to another image, the quotation assesses the situation as hopeless: the foundations are destroyed. "Foundations" translates a Hebrew word that occurs only in this psalm; analogous texts like Ezekiel 30:4 suggest that the term is a metaphor for the bases of common life and social order. It is characteristic of the wicked in the psalms to oppose and subvert the practice of righteousness, the conduct that creates *shalom*. When there is no generally accepted ethos at the foundation of a society, violence and injustice prevail (v. 5), and those who seek to be faithful to the ways of *shalom* are helpless. "What can the righteous do" but "flee like a flushed bird that flutters away to the shelter of highland thickets." The

75

quotation as a whole poses an option for conduct in troubled and anarchistic times: to desert public space and abandon social action responsible to the rules of righteousness.

2. The rest of the psalm states another answer to the question. What can the righteous do when the wicked are powerful and the bases of life are undercut? They can hold to the vision of the LORD as righteous judge and make the LORD the foundation of their life. (On the LORD as righteous judge, see Introduction, sec. 6.7.) Verses 4–7 delineate the principal points of the doctrine.

   a. The LORD reigns over all from the heavenly temple-palace, and from that transcendent position assays and assesses the outward conduct and inner thought of all human beings (7:6–8, 11; 9:7–8; I Thess. 2:4; Rev. 2:23).

   b. The LORD is righteous. Righteousness is not an accidental or external characteristic or simply a norm for human life. It belongs to the very person of the LORD as an essential of God's identity.

   c. The LORD opposes the wicked and favors the righteous. This policy expresses God's very identity. As the policy of the sovereign of the universe, it is the ultimate basis for the conduct and outcome of life. (See the comment on Ps. 5:4–7.)

   d. The LORD will act to punish wickedness and vindicate the righteous with the favor of his presence. It is for this vindication that many of the psalms pray and on which others, like this one, set their hope. "Coals of fire and brimstone" (v. 6) as instruments of judgment recall the story of Sodom and Gomorrah (Genesis 19).

When there is no action for the righteous to take that has promise of succeeding in the face of the power and danger of wickedness, they can testify to the righteous judge of all, in whose hands rests the estimate and outcome of every life. That confession is action and often leads to action that otherwise would never be taken. Jeremiah is a case study (Jer. 11:20; 12:3; 17:10; 20:12).

Psalm 12: The Faithful Have Disappeared

Psalm 12 is a prayer for the LORD's saving help (v. 1) in a time when wickedness is dominant in society. The world seems to be populated only with the wicked, who are everywhere (v. 8). The psalm begins with a lament that the faithful have van-

76

ished from the human race (v. 1) and concludes with the lament that baseness is exalted in the human race (v. 8), statements of hyperbole about the character of the general population.

The prevalent wickedness is characterized in terms of what has happened to language in the society; the themes are lips, tongue, and heart (vv. 2–4). Language expresses character. Hypocrites, people with a double heart, lie and deceive (v. 2). The arrogant put trust in their speech as the instrument of their power; their talk about their own deeds is like the praise of God's great acts, and they pervert the confession of faith, "The LORD is with us," into "Our lips are with us" (vv. 3–4). Deceptive and self-confident speech is the advertisement of a conduct and character that ignore God and subject the neighbor to the inexorable purposes of selfishness. When faithfulness wanes and wickedness waxes, the poor and needy suffer; they are left without support or advocate (v. 5).

In verse 5, prayer becomes prophecy and a word from the LORD is cited as a confession of trust that the LORD will act to deliver the poor and needy. The word expresses the character and conduct of the LORD just as surely as the talk of the wicked expresses their character. The LORD is a God who hears the poor and needy when they cry to him. Israel learned that when they were oppressed in Egypt. The law taught it (e.g., Exod. 22:21–24), and the prophets proclaimed it (e.g., Isa. 3:13–15). The psalmist puts that word in contrast to the language of the wicked; the word of the LORD is pure, that is, true and reliable (v. 6).

From time to time the prophets lamented the general wickedness of their society (Micah 7:1–7; Isa. 57:1–13; 59:1–21; Hos. 4:1–3). Jesus grieved over the wicked and adulterous generation in whose midst his life was set (Mark 8:38; 9:19). In such times the faithful repair to the LORD in prayer and trust the LORD's promises. In contrast to all around, they make prayer and prophecy the mode of their speech.

Psalm 13: How Long, O LORD?

Psalm 13 is the shortest of the prayers for help in the Psalter. In spite of its brevity, the psalm is virtually a paradigm of the essential features of such prayers (Introduction, 5.2.1). Hermann Gunkel called it a parade example of the laments of an individual. Because of its typicality, Psalm 13 has often been

The Lord
Reigns,
chap. 6
✝
77
P ✝ T the
Psalms
p. 167

used to illustrate the elements of these prayers. It can also provide an introduction to their basic theological dimensions.

1. "LORD!" says the prayer and calls on the name of the LORD. The prayer is not interior reflection or meditative musing but direct address. The psalm speaks *to* God, using the name that God has given the people of God as self-revelation. The name bestows the possibility and the promise of prayer. Prayer is already response, based on the grace of the knowledge of God given through words and works. Nothing in the troubles of life and the experience of the absence of God cancels the privilege of faith to speak directly to God in confidence of being heard. Prayer arises because God has first taken the initiative to call forth faith.

2. The description of trouble (vv. 1–2) is composed of lines of decreasing length and rising intensity, held together by the repetition of "How long?" These exclaiming interrogatives give the description the tone of protest. The questions do not seek information; they present distress. Urgent neediness finds its voice in them. The agenda of distress is threefold: trouble with God, with self, and with others. God does not help; there is no evidence of God's attention and care. Anxiety tortures the mind with painful questions. An enemy dominates the situation. Though the three are distinct, they are not separable. Together they compose the full account of trouble that comes upon faith. It is theological, personal, and social. In the order of experience, helplessness causes anxiety and anxiety protests to God. But in the order of prayer, the trouble with God comes first, because that is what matters most to faith. The psalm does not say specifically what the trouble is; it is concerned rather with a structure of neediness that brings to light the full character of the predicament of existence. Real trouble is rarely simple. What attacks our existence exposes weakness and makes us wonder about world and God. It is risky to think of human problems too easily in terms of God's forgetting and turning away, to involve God in real and imagined threats, but it is more dangerous for faith to consent to isolation and believe that the experience of alienation cannot be turned into prayer.

3. The petition is typically double: "Hear me" and "Help me" (v. 3). In the psalm's understanding of prayer, both are important, but the distinction between the two is more formal than real. Any word that faith can hear as answer from God breaks the isolation of suffering and renews the strength of

hope. Any help that comes may be read by faith as answering word and trust is revived. The petitions seek the revival of life, appealing to God who alone is the giver and protector of life. Without the salvation of the LORD there will be death. Life is at stake, and the enemy is the foe of life, the adversary of existence. Who the enemy is and how the enemy works is not important; what matters in the prayer is that the enemy wears the mask of death. The prayer is based on the belief that the lives of those who belong to God matter to God. So the prayer calls the LORD "*my* God." This trusting claim can be made because the one who prays belongs to the people who have by election and covenant been given the right to say "our God." Just as all the children in a family each say "my mother" in an intimate and personal way without in any sense losing their sense of the family, the psalmist says "my God" as part of the people of God. On the other hand, God is no less the personal God of each individual because he is such as the God of the whole family of God. "My God" can be and has been said in selfishness and arrogance, but it is a greater error not to confess that one belongs to God in answer to the grace of election.

4. The prayer concludes in trust and hope, the trust expressed in a confession of confidence in God's steadfast love (v. 5) and the hope affirmed in a promise of praise to come because the LORD has dealt with the psalmist according to need (v. 6). The protest and the petition lead to joyous praise in celebration of God's salvation. How is this shift to be understood? Is it biography, an account of a movement from discouragement to reassurance that accompanies and redirects the course of the prayer? Is it liturgy, the change being the response to an unrecorded answer given by a priest between petition and praise? As it stands in Scripture, the psalm is without a narrative setting or liturgical instruction. It is based neither in psychology nor cult; it makes the shift and connection as text. The psalm leads those who read and pray it from protest and petition to praise; it holds all three together as if to teach that they cohere in the unity of prayer. There is a coherence that holds the apparently separate moments together. God is so much a God of blessing and salvation that one must speak of tribulation and terror as the absence of God. Yet God is so much the God of *hesed* that one must speak to God in the midst of tribulation and terror as the God of "my salvation." The psalm's composition is guided by the radical knowledge of faith that

cannot separate God from any experience of life and perseveres in construing all, including life's worst, in terms of a relation to God. It is shaped by such a persuasion of graciousness that it refuses to see the present apart from God and cannot imagine the future apart from God's salvation. Luther called the stance of this prayer the "state in which Hope despairs, and yet Despair hopes at the same time; and all that lives is 'the groaning that cannot be uttered' wherewith the Holy Spirit makes intercession for us, brooding over the waters shrouded in darkness. . . . This no one understands who has not tasted it" (quoted by Perowne, 1:156).

5. The psalm in its succinct representative character is there to teach us how to pray. But it also shows us who we are when we pray. We are given our true identity as mortals who stand on the earth and speak to God who is ours but never owned. Agony and adoration hung together by a cry for life— that is the truth about us as people of faith. As the elect of God, we are not one but two. We are simultaneously the anxious, fearful, dying, historical person who cannot find God where we want God to be, and the elect with a second history, a salvation history, a life hid with Christ in God. "How long, LORD?" we lament into empty space. We also say, "You have dealt bountifully with me." All the while we pray for life in our dying, pray because through the gospel we bear already in us a foretaste of the life to come. "For while we live, we are always being given up to death for Jesus' sake, so that the life of Jesus may be manifest in our mortal flesh" (II Cor. 4:11).

Psalm 14: There Is No One Who Does Good

Psalm 14 instructs and encourages the lowly righteous in the face of prevalent and dominant wickedness. In this purpose it is like Psalm 12. It develops a theme heard repeatedly in Psalm 10 (see 10:3–4, 11, 13). Psalm 53 is a slightly different version of Psalm 14. The translation in the Greek Bible offers yet another expanded version of the psalm, important because it is the one quoted by Paul in Romans 3:13–18.

Things are not what they seem, says this psalm, drawing on the analysis of wisdom and on prophecy's vision of reality to redescribe the situation of the lowly righteous. What seems smart to the wicked is really foolish, and the apparent foolishness of depending on the LORD is true wisdom. The psalm is

80

concerned, not with the plight of an individual, but with the state of society as a whole. Verses 1–4 describe the conduct of those whose character sets the tone of the whole, people whose private confession of faith is, "There is no God." The description is given irony by portraying the LORD as a divine Diogenes (the man who searched Athens with a lantern in the daytime looking in vain for an honest man) who surveys humanity to see whether there are any who are wise enough to seek God (vv. 2–4). Verses 5–6 give encouragement to the lowly righteous for such a time, and the psalm concludes with a wish prayer for the salvation of the people of the LORD.

It would be easy to get off on the wrong foot in reading this psalm. The psalm could be taken as the self-serving lament over the evil of the world by those who polish their own piety in contrast; but the lament is authentic and bears the hurt of those who suffer from things as they are. The psalm could be dismissed as an exaggerated pessimism to be put down with the counsel that things are never really that bad, but the psalm brings the findings of God into the picture to urge its seriousness. Fair interpretation of the psalm would deal with at least three principal problems.

1. The first problem is the opening sentence: "The fool (*nabal*) says in his heart, 'There is no God.'" The sentence seems to say that atheists are silly and atheism is frivolous. We know that in our culture that is not so. The denial of the existence of God is made by serious and honest people. In the society that this psalm describes, however, *nabal* does not mean things like dumb, inept, silly, clown, buffoon. Rather, the term designates a person who decides and acts on the basis of the wrong assumption. The story of the man named Nabal (I Samuel 25) is the classic portrayal of a *nabal*. Nabal was prosperous and prominent, but he made the wrong assumption about David, while his wife Abigail discerned the danger and destiny of David. A *nabal* is a person who, whether shrewd or powerful, makes a mistake about reality.

The "foolishness" with which the psalm is concerned is to say in one's heart there is no God. That may sound as though the psalmist lived in a secular society and endured atheists who denied the existence of God. But the rest of the psalm makes it clear that the problem is not a reasoned intellectual argument against the existence of God but conduct based on the private assumption that human beings are not held accountable by God

(10:13). The psalmist reasons from the way people act to the way they think. If people enact life in corrupt and perverse ways (vv. 1–3), do not pray to God in their need but live by preying on others (v. 4), then they are denying the reality of the LORD, the God of exodus and the covenant and the prophets. (For other expressions of God's irrelevance, see Jer. 5:12; Zeph. 1:12; I Cor. 15:34.) The setting of the psalm is a society in which corruption is "eating up" the people of the LORD, and it discloses the meaning of that situation. It does not address, therefore, the phenomenon of modern atheism directly. But the "atheism" it does uncover is more dangerous, insidious, and general because it is a reasoning that can be found, as the prophets and Jesus insisted, in the hearts of the religious as well as the secular. The psalm is not concerned with the question of whether people accept the existence of a supreme being. It is concerned with whether people acknowledge the reality of the LORD, the God of Israel, by calling on the LORD in need and seeking the LORD in the decisions of life. That is the prudent conduct the LORD looks for among human beings (v. 2; on "to seek the LORD" as obedient conduct, see Amos 5:4, 6, 14). Patrick D. Miller, Jr. (*Interpreting the Psalms*, pp. 94–99), offers an excellent discussion of the point.

2. The second problem is the total scope of the psalm's indictment. Verses 1–3 seem to say that all have played the fool by thinking of life as though it were not accountable to the LORD. The sentence "There is no God" is echoed twice by the similar sentence "There is no one doing good." The two sentences go together, the second being the interpretation of the first. The second also applies the description to everybody. In Hebrew, the "all" of verse 3 is "the all," the whole, and the verse drives the point home with "There is not even one" who does good.

On the other hand, verses 4–6 seem to distinguish between "the evildoers who consume my people" and the lowly righteous who take the LORD as their refuge. What is to be made of this apparent contradiction of inclusive and distinguishing language? It helps to recognize that the psalmist with his "all" was not making a doctrinal statement about the human condition; rather, he was speaking of the society in which he lived as a whole by describing the conduct that marked its character. He is more the prophet doing social analysis than the theologian discussing anthropology. Speaking differently of the corporate whole and of individuals and groups within it is a common feature of prophecy and psalms. But for our purposes, theologically we would do well to let the tensions stand unresolved. Who would claim exemption from the psalmist's "all" by pretending always to live as if life were accountable to the LORD? Yet precisely for those who know they have come short, the LORD opens up by grace the way of taking refuge in the LORD and seeking the LORD. When Paul quoted the Greek Bible's version of the psalm in Romans 3, he maintained the tension: "All have sinned, but those who believe in Jesus Christ are justified by grace."

3. Third, how are verses 5–6 to be understood? In spite of some problems in the textual tradition, it is clear that here encouragement is offered to the lowly righteous. The evildoers will be gripped with the dread of the divine, the experience that comes from overwhelming confrontation with the presence and power of the LORD. The somewhat mysterious "there" suggests that this will happen precisely in their oppression of "my people." Somehow it will be disclosed that the LORD is with the company of the righteous, who in the poverty of their powerlessness make the LORD their refuge. Their weakness and trust, such a perfect contradiction, of the power and autonomy of the evildoers will be the means of revealing the true reality which their oppressors do not know and cannot understand. Just how this will happen is not said, but the notion points to the power of the witness of martyrs and especially to the cross of Jesus.

The wish prayer with which the psalm ends (v. 7) shifts the focus from oppressors and oppressed in the society to the whole people and its future. The prayer yearns for a salvation that would change the present time of distress to one of rejoicing in the LORD, a time that includes oppressor and oppressed alike.

Psalm 15: Who May Be Present Before the Presence?

What is at issue when we come into the presence of the LORD? Who are we, and what should we be, as we come? This brief psalm begins with this question (v. 1) and gives one answer to it (vv. 2–5). The question is a serious one for all who gather as the congregation constituted by the promised presence of

83

God. The answer should keep them from ever entering the presence routinely or casually.

1. In the psalms, the place of the presence is the mountain made holy by the LORD's choice and designation of it to represent the divine sovereignty in the geography of the world and to be the site where God is "there," available to the praise and prayers of human beings (see 2:6; 48:1–3; 132:13; I Kings 8). To speak about being in this sacred space, the psalm uses language from Israel's social life that referred to the resident alien, the outsider who was permitted to live along with those to whom tents and territory belonged. Those who enter the presence are like resident aliens, because they have no inherent right to be there; the privilege must be granted. The psalm's opening question is put in the style of direct address to the LORD, perhaps as recognition that only the LORD has the authority to determine who may be there.

2. The answer to the question "Who?" is not given by naming names or designating groups or classes but by a sketch of the character of the righteous (see 24:4–5; Ezek. 18:5–9; Micah 6:8). The sketch is composed of positive (vv. 2, 4a) and negative (vv. 3, 4b–5a) features of conduct. Verse 2 lists general traits; verses 3–5a cite specific acts. The list of general traits is introductory; living with integrity, doing what is right, and speaking faithfully what one is thinking are primary virtues in Old Testament ethical thought. The specific acts are illustrative examples of the virtues. The first set of examples concern the neighborhood (v. 3), the second the religious community (v. 4a; see the comment on Psalm 1, sec. 3), and the third the larger society (vv. 4b–5a). The examples listed by the psalm appear in proverbial, prophetic, and legal material. They belong to the established tradition of right and wrong in Israel's religion. All of them are cases of conduct that effect the well-being or *shalom* of various levels of the community. The form of the answer as a whole is something like the response we would make to a question about someone's character; the answer would be composed of general traits illustrated by what the person usually does or does not do. The genre is characterization. Because the characterization in the psalm serves serious liturgical and theological purposes, it has been composed with poetic proportion and careful selection. It is a picture, not prescription.

3. The answer concludes with a sentence that could be read either as an observation of how life works or as a promise: Those

whose conduct fits the characterization will not be shaken forever (v. 5*b*). To be shaken or moved is a way of speaking about
the unsettling undermining effect of the chaotic dimension of
reality. God has overcome the cosmic chaos and founded the
earth so that it cannot be shaken (24:1; 93:1; 96:10; 104:5). God's
presence keeps his holy dwelling Zion from being shaken by the
chaotic powers of history (46:5; 125:1). And the righteous,
whose life is based in the way of God, are secured against any
ultimate undoing by the troubles that buffet life (10:6; 13:4;
16:8; 17:5; 21:7; 30:6; 62:2, 6; especially 112:6). The implication
is that the life of the righteous, like the world and the holy
mountain, has foundations in God's dominion over the chaotic
forces of reality.

4. Was Psalm 15 composed to be used as a liturgy for entering the courts of the temple (see 118:19–21)? There are two
other texts with the same form of question about who may be
in the presence of God, characterization, and concluding statement (24:3–6; Isa. 33:13–16; see also Micah 6:6–8). The form
itself would be suitable for such an occasion. There are hints in
the Old Testament and from other religions of the period that
lists of qualifications for entering sanctuaries were used (Deut.
23:1–8; II Chron. 23:19; see Gerstenberger, 14/1, pp. 86–88).
Both of the psalmic texts and the one from Isaiah, however,
seem to be uses of the form to compose a poem for instructional
purposes to teach the congregation about the character of its
relation to the LORD. They contain no cultic qualifications and
conclude with statements about life rather than admission to
the sanctuary. The heading of Psalm 15 identifies it as a text for
musical performance in religious gatherings, and that is the use
to which it has been put as part of the Psalter.

5. Is it a surprise to find among the psalms a piece of liturgy
that insists on the same relation between temple and conduct,
worship and life, holy place and righteous person, that the
prophets demand (Isa. 1:12–17; Amos 5:21–24; Jer. 7:1–15;
Micah 6:6–8)? It should not be, because the psalms witness to a
vision of God that lies at the basis of prophetic proclamation.
The LORD is a God with whom the evil may not sojourn (5:4–6),
the divine judge who tests the righteous and the wicked in the
holy temple (11:4–7). The insistence on the correlation between
righteous God and righteous people in the psalms is unrelenting
in its pervasiveness.

The psalm is liturgy, not law. It is not a text for some sort of judicial procedure to exclude the unqualified; rather, it is the rehearsal of a purpose and a possibility. This kind of person, says the psalm, is what the Presence intends. This Presence, says the psalm, is the power that makes this kind of person possible. The Presence calls and commands, judges and redeems. To be in the place of the Presence means to be at the point where the purpose and power of God come to bear on a person's identity and formation.

The psalm, then, transcends the actual performance of the lives of those who come to the place of the Presence. But it does ask them whether this is what they want to be like and whether they are trying to be like this and whether they come to this place in the hope of being like this. Christians come to worship in the confidence that God has made Jesus Christ our righteousness (I Cor. 1:30). We may be tempted to take the righteousness given by grace to faith as an excuse for the failure of our lives, but the psalm insists that it is rather the purpose and the power of God to regenerate them.

Psalm 16: You Show Me the Path of Life

Psalm 16 is a prayer of unusual proportions. It begins with a brief petition for the protection of God (v. 1). The psalmist asks that "the keeper of Israel" watch over his life (Psalm 121). The petition is supported by a motive clause, a declaration that the psalmist has made the LORD his refuge. "In you I take refuge" is a formula for trusting one's life to the care of God (see the comment on Pss. 7:1 and 2:12). The rest of the prayer is an exposition of that trust. The psalm teaches that trust is not merely a warm feeling or a passing impulse in a time of trouble; it is a structure of acts and experiences that open one's consciousness to the LORD as the supreme reality of life.

1. Trust is first of all the relationship that determines all else about a person. The psalmist confesses, "You (YHWH) are my lord ('adon)." The reverse of that confession is, "I am your servant ('ebed)." The psalmist knows himself as a person who belongs to another. As servant of the LORD, he receives the goodness that comes to him in life as coming from no other source than his lord (on the lord-servant relation, see Introduction, sec. 6.16). Because he belongs to the LORD, he is confident that his needs will be met.

Trust is monotheistic, not pluralistic. The psalmist's commitment to the LORD is exclusive (vv. 3–4). He enacts the first commandment in his life. For him, there is no other God. The holy and mighty deities whom others in the land worship are a source of troubles, not joy, and he does not recognize them or participate in their worship. The text of verses 2*b*–4*a* is uncertain. The comment understands "the holy" and "mighty" (NRSV, "noble") to be references to other gods. See the translation of NJPS.

Trust takes the very relation to God itself as the greatest benefit of the LORD's way with the servants of God (vv. 5–6). When the psalmist calls the LORD his "portion and cup" and speaks of lot and lines and heritage in describing the goodness of his destiny, he is using the vocabulary and concepts that are employed in the Book of Joshua to describe Israel's occupation of the promised land as the outcome of God's salvation of Israel. Tribes, clans, and individuals were given a portion as their heritage that was laid off by lines determined by casting the sacred lot. The psalmist sees the LORD as the benefit that has come to him through God's way with Israel. See the comment on Psalm 142:5.

Trust concentrates the mind on the LORD (vv. 7–8). Through praise the psalmist keeps the LORD in the center of his attention, practices the presence of the LORD. In this way he is open to the instruction of the LORD that comes to him through the guidance of his conscience in the still hours of the night. The conscience (literally, "kidneys" as organ where the conscience has its seat; NRSV, "heart") is an instrument of the LORD's instruction when the consciousness is informed and guided by the praise of the LORD. And praise makes the psalmist so conscious of the power and loving-kindness of the LORD that he is not threatened and unsettled by lesser things.

Trust is confidence of life in the face of death (vv. 9–11). All three dimensions of the psalmist's being—heart, soul, and body—participate in this joyous security. It infuses his entire being. The exuberance of his confidence arises from the knowledge that the LORD will not surrender his faithful one to Sheol and the Pit, the realm of death. Death in the thought world of the psalms is not only the polar opposite of life, the loss of one's own vital existence. It is also the loss of the presence of God and the pleasures of that presence. It is God that is lost in death. When God's providence keeps the faithful in the path of life, they receive far more than a continued existence. They receive

87

the joys and pleasures of the presence of God. For the psalmist, life means being able to enjoy the presence of God. See the discussion of this view of death in the comment on Psalm 6.

2. Two features about this psalm have always impressed its readers. The first is the way in which the LORD fills the personal horizon of the psalmist. Every one of the prayer's lines in all their variety says in one way or another, "The LORD is everything to me." The LORD is my lord, my God, my destiny, my counsel, my vis-à-vis, my security. The whole confesses, "The LORD is my life." That is why the psalmist is confident of life. It is this focus on God, absorption in God, identity with God, the LORD who is the source of life, that gives faith a confident hold on life.

The second is the way the confession "I have no good apart from you" (v. 2) echoes through the song in its references to pleasant places, goodly heritage, complete joy, and pleasures forevermore. The psalm is full of joy in the LORD. Life and joy go together. Life is consummated in joy. Where death is removed as threat, life is finally free for complete joy in the presence of God, who alone can deliver from Sheol.

Both features turn on the theme of life. It is understandable that the point in the psalm that has drawn the most attention of its interpreters is the psalmist's unqualified statement of confidence that the LORD will not abandon him to Sheol but will show him the path of life. What does that claim mean? It depends on who says the psalm and in what situation. It can be understood as the prayer of an Israelite who, threatened by an untimely death, takes refuge with the LORD at the sanctuary. It could be the prayer of corporate Israel after the exile was over, when they had learned that the LORD would not abandon the people to death (Ezekiel 37); note the representative Israelite of Lamentations 3, who in the midst of the loss of everything learns to say, "The LORD is my portion" (Lam. 3:24). It can be read as the general prayer of the faithful who, without any doctrine of resurrection or eternal life to explain just how, nonetheless trust the LORD to keep them with such total confidence that they cannot imagine a future apart from life in God's presence. The language of the psalm presses toward an unbroken relation between LORD and life. Other places in the psalms where this happens are Psalms 41:12 and 73:24; see also Psalms 36:9 and 63:3.

In the apostolic church, Psalm 16 was read in the light of the

88

resurrection of Jesus. In sermons, both Peter and Paul (Acts 2:24–32; 13:34) cite verse 10 as a hope fulfilled for the first time when God raised Jesus from the dead. In the resurrection of Jesus Christ, the last limitation on the connection between the LORD and life was transcended. Now it is possible to say the psalm in the midst of life and in the face of inevitable death with a trust that matches the language of the prayer. The LORD has made known the path of life.

Psalm 17: I Shall Behold Your Face

Psalm 17 is a prayer in which a person who trusts in God and has been faithful to God in his conduct appeals for deliverance from wicked, hostile adversaries. The psalm is one of the prayers for help in first person singular style (see Introduction, sec. 5.2). It is composed of petitions for deliverance (vv. 1–2, 6–9), a plea of innocence (vv. 3–5), a description of the adversaries and a petition for their defeat (vv. 10–12, 13–14), and a concluding assertion of trust (v. 15).

The prayer typically uses language that draws on different spheres of experience and culture in Israel. The opening petition employs legal language and appeals to the LORD as judge. The second petition employs the imagery of asylum or sanctuary in which the persecuted takes refuge at a shrine. The enemies are described as predatory animals. God is asked to overthrow the enemies, acting as the divine warrior who intervenes on behalf of his own. (On the formulaic petition "Rise up, O LORD," see 9:19 and 10:12. On the theological problems of claims to innocence and righteousness, see the comment on Psalms 7 and 26.)

The concluding statement of confidence (v. 15) makes it clear how important the relation to God is in the theology of these prayers. Their purpose is not simply to gain relief from dangers and difficulty. The real trouble with the trouble reflected in these prayers is that one's relation to God is troubled. Deliverance not only brings relief but restores a sense of acceptance and communion. Acceptance bestows righteousness. Communion occurs in the experience of the presence. The prayer anticipates an answer given as a vision of the form of the presence (face) of the LORD. The vision will convey justification; it will be a sign of the acceptance that makes the relation to God right. "The upright shall behold his face" (11:7; see Matt. 5:8).

89

Just how the vision of the presence occurred is not known. Israel was forbidden to make any likeness of the LORD in the form of an image (Exod. 20:4; Deut. 5:8). But Moses and the elders "saw the God of Israel" in the ritual meal that concluded the Sinai covenant. Moses as officiant in the tent-tabernacle "beheld the form of the LORD" (Num. 12:8). In the psalms there are references to seeing God or the face of God in the temple (e.g., 42:2; 63:2; 36:7–9). There is a seeing that comes with prayer and waiting that transcends what eye can behold.

In Christian interpretation there is a long tradition that sees a reference to the resurrection in verse 15. "When I awake from the sleep of death, my life will be finally fulfilled when I see God." In the context of Israel's religion, "when I awake" may have referred to a ritual of spending the night at the holy place after prayer for help waiting for the propitious time of the morning. But the verse can be read with a second sense, because it is only the resurrection to be with the LORD that brings the final and full justification of the life of the faithful.

Psalm 18: You Made Me Head of the Nations

"The LORD lives!" That exultant, thankful cry can be taken as the theological climax of Psalm 18 (v. 46). When Israel spoke of the living God, the epithet did not mean alive as opposed to dead but active in contrast to ineffective or passive. The entire psalm is praise of the God who acts. The action of God is not an abstract notion in the psalm. The LORD acts specifically on behalf of the anointed king, who is threatened by death and enemies in a deliverance that is at the same time the LORD's own vindication as God of history (vv. 50, 30–31). The action of God is what the LORD does to vindicate the reign of God. Psalm 18 is a sequel to Psalm 2, where the LORD ordains the anointed king as regent representative of the reign of God and promises him dominion over the nations. Psalm 18 is testimony by the anointed that the LORD has kept the promise in a time of direst need. Psalms 20 and 21 also witness to God's support of the king.

The organizing structure of the psalm is composed of the elements of a song of praise for deliverance (Introduction, sec. 5.3). After introductory praise (vv. 1–3), the psalm gives a report of distress in the past (vv. 4–5) and of appeal to the LORD (v. 6) that was answered by God's deliverance (vv. 16–19), for which

the psalm praises the LORD (vv. 31–42). This basic structure has
been elaborated by other elements to make the psalm one of
the very longest in the Psalter. A theophany description dramatizes the response of God (vv. 7–15); descriptions of the righteousness of the king (vv. 20–24) and the perfection of God
(vv. 25–30) fill out the praise and thanks for salvation as a victory
that established dominion over the nations (vv. 43–48). A vow
to praise the LORD among the nations (vv. 49–50) concludes the
long section of praise. This complexity is probably the result of
several phases of elaboration behind the psalm's present form.
Its ponderous character points to the importance of its subject;
God's salvation of the Davidic line as vindication of the reign
of God was a crucial topic for the faith of the psalmists. It is
important to search out the function and connection of the
many parts that constitute the whole.

1. *Introductory praise (vv. 1–3).* The first line states the
theme and purpose of the whole in direct address: "I exalt you,
O LORD, my strength" (translating a likely emendation of the
Hebrew verb). Calling the LORD "my strength" anticipates
verses 31–42, where the messiah attributes his prowess in battle
to divine preparation and endowment (note "strength" in
vv. 32, 39). Verse 2 extends "my strength" into confessional
praise that recites the longest series of predicates for God found
in the Psalter. Most are metaphors identifying the LORD as
provider of protection. All are qualified by the possessive pronoun "my" so that their repetition emphasizes the dependence
of the person of the psalmist on the person of God. The metaphor "my rock" (represented by two Hebrew words) is the most
frequent in Psalms and in poetry elsewhere. The metaphorical
sense seems to lie in the firm and strong character of rock as
support. A god is called "rock" as the deity who provides refuge
for those who belong to the deity, as the references in Deuteronomy 32:4, 30–31, and 37 show. Verse 3 identifies the human
situation in which the confession is made, the call to the LORD
in need of salvation from enemies. The enemy is given no historical or social identification in the song itself. What matters is
that they are forces threatening the existence of one who calls
the LORD "my God." The psalm moves at a mythopoeic theological level; it unfolds a narrative plot and prospect that could
interpret many historical occasions.

2. *The report of salvation (vv. 4–19).* The report depicts
salvation as a cosmic drama, not as a subjective personal experi-

91

ence. The enemies are the agents of death and Sheol, the under-world realm of unbeing that is the antithesis of the realm of the living God (see the comment on Ps. 116:3; cf. Jonah 2:6–7). Death's entrapment of the LORD's king is an assault on the cosmic and historical reign of the LORD. The messiah must be delivered from "the great waters," the chaos that threatens the ordered world established by the LORD's reign (v. 16; see the comment on Psalm 93). The LORD heard from his heavenly palace-temple, to which the temple on Zion is an earthly corre-spondent, reached down from on high, and delivered him.

A theophany description (vv. 7–15) stands after the hearing in heaven and prepares for God's reaching down. Its function is to portray God's coming down (v. 9) to assert sovereignty in the world. The description of an appearance of the deity is a literary genre on its own. The typical features of the genre are a depiction of God's appearance in awesome meteorological and geological phenomena and a description of the effect of God's coming on the world. Elements of description were adopted and adapted from those of the activities of gods that belonged to the religions of the nations surrounding Israel (Keel, pp. 209–230). In Israel's development of the genre, there are memories of the LORD's victories on behalf of his people at the Red Sea (Exodus 15) and in the settlement of the land (Judges 5). The genre is used in different kinds of psalms to speak of and present the irresistible power and the passionate active zeal of the LORD in defending his people and advancing his rule in the world (Psalms 29; 50:2–3; 68:7–8; 77:16–20; 97:2–5; 144:5–8). In Psalm 18 the theophany is opened and closed by descriptions of the cosmic effect of God's coming down (vv. 7, 15) which enclose the portrayal of the appearance (vv. 8–14). God is angry because the assault on his messiah is a revolt against his rule. The divine anger is portrayed in fire and smoke imagery, the divine appearance in thunderstorm imag-ery. We must be clear that the referent of the images for Israel was not simply volcanoes and earthquakes and thunderstorms. The montage of images served to represent a transcendent and marvelous dimension of Israel's experience of God's response to human history. The genre is not at home in the thanksgiving psalm of an individual. Its presence here emphasizes that the individual who speaks this psalm bears in his existence and destiny the claim of God's sovereignty in history.

3. *Praise of the LORD (vv. 20–30).* The report of salvation

92

is typically followed by praise of the LORD that draws implications from the experience and bears testimony to what it discloses about the LORD. That happens in this section, but in a strange way. The king begins with a recitation of his own righteousness. The explanation lies in the last line of the preceding section: "He delivered me, because he delighted in me" (see 22:8; 47:11–12). Verses 20–24 are an exposition of that sentence, a section marked off by the theme, "The LORD dealt with me according to my righteousness" (vv. 20, 24). God's deliverance was evidence of his favor, his pleasure in the king. The claim is not a crass assertion of self-righteousness by the king but a confession that he had been true to the righteousness in which the divine choice to be king had set him. He had not created the righteousness but had lived within it and according to it. He had fulfilled the vocation given the king to embody the law of the divine king. The ideal is particularly important in the deuteronomic tradition (see Josh. 1:7; 23:6; Deut. 17:19–20).

In the next section of praise the king testifies to the general theological truth of which his salvation was an instance (vv. 25–27) and confesses what it means for his own vocation (vv. 28–29). The concluding exclamation (v. 30) states the theme of the whole: "This God—his way is perfect." (The same theological sentence is the theme of the great song at the end of Deuteronomy, chap. 32, see v. 4.) The term "perfect" (Heb. *tamim*) means "whole, of a piece, integral." *Tamim* marks the character of one whose conduct is coherent, consistent, reliable. God is perfect because what God says is proven by what he does; he is the shield of those who take refuge in him, who hold to him and his ways (see Prov. 30:5). The perfectness of the LORD is manifest by his dealing with human beings in a way that is coherent with the revelation of himself. The LORD is loyal to the loyal, delivers the lowly (*'ani*) who trust in him, while he undoes the perverse and brings down the haughty. He is the light and strength of the king, who is himself *tamim* ("blameless," vv. 23, 25) in obedience and trust. It is important to understand that in the theology of this reflective praise, obedience and trust are not separated but thought of as a single feature of human conduct in relation to God. Obedience is trust and trust is obedience, both one as a holding to the LORD in loyalty.

4. *The victory of the messiah (vv. 31–50).* The second part of the psalm follows the form of a song of victory that praises the LORD who gives triumphs to his king (v. 50). It begins with

an exclamation over the incomparability of the LORD as savior-deity (v. 31), confesses how the LORD endowed the king with prowess and support (vv. 32–36) that enabled him to defeat his enemies in battle (vv. 37–42). The king's victories have put the nations in awe of him and made them submit to his rule (vv. 43–45). So the king praises the LORD as the living God who does all these things (vv. 46–48) and vows to exalt the LORD among the nations (vv. 49–50). The song is based on a theology of "messiah-victor" that involves the following related features.

a. The strength by which the messiah gains the victory comes from God. Twice he says that God "girded me with strength" (vv. 32, 39). The God whose way is perfect (v. 30) has made the messiah's way perfect, that is, God whose conduct corresponds to his character has made the messianic king able to act in a way that corresponds to his vocation. A king must win the battle. Defeat by his enemies means the dissolution of his reign.

b. The portrayal of the king as actor against the enemies, instead of God, is quite unusual in the Old Testament. The king pursues his enemies and completely defeats them. They are helpless before him. They are terrified and surrender when they even hear of him. No army is mentioned; the king in his God-given prowess is completely in focus (vv. 37–38, 42, 44–45). It is in these features that the picture of the king seems so militaristic and exaggerated. The picture is common in royal iconography and inscriptions of monarchies of the time, especially in Egypt (see Keel, pp. 291–308). The picture was based on the belief and the concentration of invincible power in the person of the king. The use of the picture in the self-description of the Davidic king serves to emphasize the role of the chosen messiah in the warfare between the rule of the LORD and the kingdoms of the world. It prevents the figure of the messiah from being completely obscured by the action of God. It also reflects the historical fact that human kingship arose in early Israel in the crisis brought on by the attacks of other nations (Judges I; Samuel).

c. The victory of the king over his enemies establishes him as "head of the nations." Its effect reaches beyond his enemies to establish his rule over unknown and foreign peoples. Word of him brings them to submission (vv. 43–45). In the ancient Near East the ideal hegemony of a king extended to the limits of the sphere of power of the deity whose regent and agent he

94

polytheism to monotheism

was. Accordingly and polemically, the psalm sees in the victories of the Davidic king the manifestation of the LORD's sovereignty over the nations. The messiah's victory is believed to be the establishment of the reign of God in the world. Indeed, the opening couplet of the song of victory states the theme in a claim of exclusive deity for the LORD because the God of Israel is alone the Rock, the only God who saves his people and his king. The claim is one that the great prophet of the exile raises to his chief theological argument for the exclusive sovereignty of Israel's God in history (Isa. 44:8; 45:21).

5. It is impossible to find a definitive historical setting for this psalm, some victory by a king of Judah that would account for its language. The psalm is not about just any one victory; it tells about a climactic triumph in which the one who has been selected and prepared to be the LORD's own warrior overcomes his enemies in such a decisive way that the nations turn to him as their head and the chaos of history is overcome (see 2:1–3). Like the other psalms about the anointed, it speaks in terms of the ideal and the ultimate (but note the agonizing exception in Psalm 89). If the psalm in its present or earlier form was used from time to time to praise God for battles won, then it identified those particular occasions as provisional installments of a transcendent and ultimate consummation. It made the limited transient triumphs significant because of what they represented and anticipated.

This "mythic" character of the psalm makes it inherently prophetic. When there was no longer any king in Judah, the psalm would have been read as prophecy of a victory to come. The concluding reference "to David and his descendants forever" (v. 50) meant that God's promise to David of an everlasting kingship was part of the psalmic purchase on the future. The prophet of the exile announced that God's commitments to David were given to the community of the faithful; he seems to have cited verse 43 of this psalm (see Isa. 55:3–5). Psalm 149 is based on the belief that the assignment to be God's instrument in overcoming the hostility of the nations belongs to the whole people of God. On these matters, see the comment on Psalm 2, sec. 4.

6. This song of praise for deliverance and victory has another location in the Old Testament. A slightly different version appears in the story of David at the conclusion of his career (II Samuel 22). In that location this thanksgiving for one deliver-

ance becomes a theological interpretation of all the escapes and battles in David's career. The transcendent character of the song is given voice in a narrative context. There was, says the song's narrative introduction, a day when the LORD had delivered David from the hand of all his enemies. Deliverance from all enemies is an eschatological hope of the people of God. This hope was fulfilled one day in David's life; the song reads David's career of deliverance as a paradigm and type of what God will one day accomplish through David's seed for all the servants of the LORD. The heading of Psalm 18, except for the typical terms "to the leader, to the servant of the LORD, to David," was composed to incorporate the song in II Samuel. It is a narrative introduction of the same type as Deuteronomy 31:30; Exodus 15:1; and Numbers 21:27, and in form unlike the other narrative references that head eleven other psalms. Where the latter use events in David's story to illustrate the setting of these psalms, this one uses the achievements of David's career as a type and sign of the consummation about which Psalm 18 speaks. (On the headings, see Psalm 3, sec. 4.)

In traditional Christian interpretation of Psalm 18, David is understood as a type of Christ. The psalm is the voice of a person in the power of death crying out to God, who delivers him. In the deliverance, God vindicates his own righteousness and reveals the perfection of his own way. The deliverance is a victory that makes the person the ruler of all nations. Christians have seen the scenario as one fulfilled in the death, resurrection, and ascension of Jesus Christ. The military idiom of the psalm becomes medium of a testimony to Christus Victor, who triumphed over death, sin, and Satan. In Christ, descendant of David, the ultimate triumph of salvation is enacted.

Psalm 19: Meditation of My Heart

"LORD, my rock and my redeemer" are the last words of Psalm 19. On the way to that confessional conclusion the psalm speaks of the creation's testimony to the creator (vv. 1–6), the incomparable value of the law of the LORD (vv. 7–10), and the human need for divine forgiveness and protection (vv. 11–13). One must meditate on all three parts and make the whole the words of the heart in order to understand the devotion and trust expressed in the concluding confession. The psalm is often used as two separate texts in liturgy and hymns (vv. 1–6 and 7–14).

The unity of the psalm has been questioned by some scholars, but the three quite different topics and styles have a unity in the intention of the psalmist to compose a psalm that would be an acceptable offering to "my rock and my redeemer."

1. The sum of the first part of the psalm can be stated quite simply. The world witnesses to God. The creation manifests the glory of its creator. But the writer is a poet who does not deal in propositions. The psalm offers us instead a vision of poetic imaginative personification. It is based on the notion, not uncommon in biblical thinking, that every created thing has the capacity of a creature to acknowledge its originator. The notion is explicit, for instance, in the creation account in Genesis when all things are ordered by the word of God and in the prophecies of Isaiah 40–55. The heavens, says the psalm, do what the congregation does in its praise. The congregation enumerates the mighty works of God and proclaims them as the glory of God (see Psalm 29). The heavens by being the work of God's hand do the same. In their marvelous beauty and expanse, they are the praise of God. Day and night are the creation of God (Genesis 1). Day speaks to day; night gives knowledge to night, all in ringing choral antiphony. There is no speech, no words, no voice that is heard. Yet their voice goes out into the whole world. It is all very mysterious and marvelous. The visible becomes vocal. Seeing is experienced as hearing. The imagination is in the midst of an unending concert sung by the universe to the glory of God.

The sun is an example of this glory. God has put the sun under the canopy of the sky. It rises like a bridegroom emerging from the bridal chamber after his wedding night and follows its track across the sky like a mighty man running his course with joy. Its warmth reaches everything in the world, stirring, calling forth, and supporting life.

A danger and a question arise at this point in the psalm. The danger is that the poet be misunderstood and the glory be taken for the self of God, the world viewed as divine. The aesthetic consciousness and nature piety want to stop at this point and recognize God in nature. But there is no pantheism here, no nature religion. There is some evidence that the poet knew and drew on hymnic traditions from other ancient Near Eastern religions that praised the sun as god. But the poet keeps creator and creation separate. The creation is moved from the side of the divine to that of the congregation; it is not divine but praises

the divine. The psalm is a witness against nature worship and
finding God in nature.

The question is, and theologians usually raise it in connection with the psalm, whether the psalm speaks of "natural revelation." Is this voice of the universe that can be seen but not
heard visible to all? Do and can all hear the music of the spheres
praising God? Does one have to know of the creator first to
perceive God's praise in the creation? Paul said, "Ever since the
creation of the world, God's invisible nature, namely, his eternal power and deity, has been clearly perceived in the things
that have been made" (Rom. 1:20). Joseph Addison's hymnic
version of this psalm says that though the radiant orbs of heaven
have no voice, "In reason's ear they all rejoice, And utter forth
a glorious voice; Forever singing, as they shine, 'The hand that
made us is divine.' " The psalm does not answer the question
explicitly. Perhaps there is a clue in the Hebrew name *El* given
to God in verse 1. *El* is the designation for God as father creator
of all. It is in that identity of "eternal power and deity" that the
one praised by the creation can be known.

What the psalm does do explicitly is to follow this first section with the next one and thereby ask us to think about them
together. Connections are made. The creator of the universe is
the LORD who gives *torah*; the creator's authority is behind the
law (93:5). The covenant instruction to the people of the LORD
is set within a universal context; it concerns everyone. Just as
the sun's warmth benefits all life, the *torah* is life-giving and
enhancing. The heavens have no voice, but the *torah* of the
LORD is word in many forms. The creation does not speak, but
the LORD has spoken in *torah*. For other creation-law sequences, note Psalms 119:89–96 and 147:15–20.

2. The second part of the psalm is a precisely constructed
poetic passage exalting the virtues, benefits, and desirability of
the *torah* of the LORD (usually "law"; better "instruction"; see
the discussion at Psalm 1, sec. 2). Here we learn why the first
psalm speaks of "delight in the *torah*." There are six similar
lines, all composed of a sentence whose subject is a term for
torah and whose predicate names a quality of *torah*; to each
sentence is appended a phrase that adds a benefit or another
quality. Two comparative sentences commending the desirability of *torah* over wealth and the sweetest food round out the
section. The style of the whole is like that of the poetry in
Proverbs composed to exalt and commend the wisdom that

begins with the fear of the LORD; note the common features that occur in Proverbs 1—4. The theological basis of this description of *torah* is the identification of the Sinai covenant and its teaching as the wisdom by which Israel is to live and find life (Deut. 4:1–8). The terms for *torah* are an eclectic list referring to whatever the poet viewed as a medium of the LORD's instruction. Four of the six are single, two are plural, indicating that the poet thinks of *torah* as a comprehensive entity that is present also in particular precepts and legal sentences. The predicates as a group are those used for the qualities of what is righteous, right in relation to the LORD; note the way verse 9 concludes with the statement, "They are altogether righteous." Righteousness inheres in the *torah*, and the righteousness of persons depends on it. The first four appended phrases recite the benefits of *torah*; it bestows life, wisdom, and joy.

It is not too much to say that the psalm understands the *torah* of the LORD as revelation by which the LORD revives, enhances, and guides human life; it is the divine medium of righteousness for human beings. Clearly the poet does not think of *torah* as the letter that kills (II Cor. 3:6) or the law that condemns (Rom. 3:19f.). Calvin observed that "these titles and commendations by which he [the psalmist] exalts the dignity and excellence of the Law would not agree with the Ten Commandments alone." And Calvin concluded that the psalm speaks of "the whole body of doctrine of which true religion and godliness consists" (Calvin, 1:318). The psalm has regularly been understood in Christian interpretation to refer to the content and function of Scripture. Again a question arises. Can righteousness come through *torah* alone, even if the term refers to the whole teaching of Scripture? The third part of the psalm must be read to consider that question.

3. The third part of the psalm is a prayer for God's help. In the prayer the psalmist acknowledges that he cannot be righteous through *torah* alone. Now he speaks to the LORD directly and calls himself "your servant," the liturgical designation of one who belongs to the LORD and is dependent on the LORD. The teachings given through *torah* are, he says, both warning and promise (v. 11). The word "warn" has a special provenance in the passages in Ezekiel where the prophet is commissioned as a watchman to warn against wickedness so that the LORD may give life instead of death (Ezek. 3:15–21; 33:1–9). *Torah* plays the role of the prophet for the psalmist. The reward prom-

ised to those who observe *torah* is recorded in the benefits listed in verses 7–8. The poet has heard the warning and knows the promise, but he also knows the human condition and the society in which he lives. Mortals make unintended errors, unconscious mistakes (see Leviticus 4—5; Numbers 15). So he asks God to acquit him, to clear him of guilt. The social environment of life does not encourage the observance of *torah*; insolent people scorn *torah* piety. So the psalmist prays that God protect him from domination by their prestige and power (the language of v. 13 is reminiscent of Gen. 4:7). Only by God's pardon and preservation can the psalmist be blameless (in the sense of complete and whole in life under God) and innocent of much transgression. The prayers in the Psalter customarily open with vocative address and call on the name of the LORD at the beginning. Here the poet saves the cry "LORD" to the very end and joins to it the confessional appeal "my rock and my redeemer" (on such terms, see 18:1–2). By the progress and unity of the psalm, those who read it and sing it are taught that it is only by the salvation of God that joy in the creation and observance of *torah* are possible.

4. In a rare identification, the composer tells us what this psalm is and what it is for (v. 14). The psalmist calls it "words of my mouth and meditation of my heart." It is composed for oral recitation in an act of worship. The words express the musing of the heart, the seat of consciousness in which thoughts are formed. Through the words the heart finds voice and the self is presented to God. The prayer serves the purpose of a sacrifice; "be acceptable" is a technical term for qualified offerings to God at the sanctuary. In the temple service, sacrifices were offered to seek God's pardon and restoration (Leviticus 4—5; Num. 15:22–31). In the intention of the psalmist, this prayer poem is such an offering.

Psalm 20: Save the King, O LORD

The practice of praying for rulers, presidents, and governors is an ancient and enduring tradition. These prayers express the deep awareness of a people that their destiny is bound up with the success of the one who has been invested with power for the sake of the whole. Psalm 20 is such a prayer. It concludes with the petition, "O LORD, save the king" (v. 9; NRSV, "give victory to"). Like Psalms 18 and 21, it was composed for the

ceremonies and services concerned with the king's office as a
military leader and defender of the nation (see the comment on
Psalm 2).

1. The theme of the whole is set in the first measure, "The
LORD answer you," and is repeated in the psalm's last measure,
"answer us." The first part is an extended bidding prayer in
which the congregation expresses its wish that the king's prayers made in Zion's sanctuary and accompanied by sacrifices be
answered (vv. 1–5). Then a representative individual proclaims
confidence that, the king having prayed and the people having
joined their prayers to his, the LORD will answer with mighty
saving help for his anointed (vv. 6–8). The psalm concludes with
the congregation's direct prayer for the king and appeal to be
heard (v. 9). The king and the people who call the LORD "my
God" have the right to call upon the LORD in a time of trouble
and have the promised privilege of the LORD's answer. The
psalm is a liturgy in which the people support the prayers of the
king and add their intercession for him.

2. The basic theology of the psalm is the confessional cry,
"Salvation belongs to the LORD" (3:8). Every line assumes, expresses, and confesses this belief that the LORD will deliver
those who call on him. That confidence is particularly focused
on the theologumenon of "the name of the LORD" (vv. 1, 5, 7;
see the comment on Ps. 8:1, 9). The "name" is appealed to,
confessed, and praised as the manifestation of the God who
bears the name. The name not only identifies but becomes the
identity of God. The name bears the presence, power, and
person of God. Jacob characterized the LORD as "the God who
answered me in the day of trouble" (Gen. 35:3). That character
is the reality present in the name to which the congregation of
Israel entrusts the king and itself.

The importance of the king in the psalm is clear. He is the
LORD's anointed (see Psalm 2). He is the central person on
whom the intercession of his people is concentrated and for
whose prayers they seek a divine answer. It is his salvation from
and victory over threatening danger that will bring them joy.
They are bound into the hope of his salvation. But in the theology of the psalm, the king is not the savior but the saved. The
saving victory will be God's work. This way of praying was a
liturgical antidote against a way of believing to which any people are tempted who vest power in a person to provide for their
security and success. When the Israelites insisted on having a

king because of their fear of the Philistines, they told Samuel that they needed a king to govern them and go before them and fight their battles (I Sam. 8:20). But in Israel's primary tradition, those were precisely the roles of the LORD. Centuries later, when the Babylonians had razed Jerusalem and carried its king into exile, the singer of Lamentations mourned the loss of "the breath of our nostrils, the LORD's anointed, he of whom we said, 'Under his shadow we shall all live among the nations' " (Lam. 4:20). But in the theology of the psalms, the LORD is the life of Israel in the protection of whose shadow they lived. The king could not in any separated and independent way be the basis or content of trust. What happened in and through him had to be the will and work of God and should confirm the people in their trust in the LORD alone.

the use of is not the source of dependence

The disavowal of dependence on chariots and horses and the avowal of calling on the name of the LORD is another expression of this theology. In Israel's world, horse and chariot were the supreme weapons of royal military might. Egyptian and Mesopotamian rulers had themselves portrayed in chariots and on horses to glorify their power in war (Keel, pp. 237–240). From the time David and Solomon introduced professional troops and chariotry, the kings of Israel and Judah were tempted to take the destiny of the nation into their own hands by building up military strength. But Israel's primary tradition of faith remembered that Israel had gained their land without chariots and horses. David even slew Goliath in the name of the LORD with a sling (I Sam. 17:45–47)! The theology was hardly pacifist, but it was antimilitaristic. It was intended to have real implications for national policy, as Isaiah insisted to King Hezekiah (Isa. 31:1–3; 30:15f.; see Zech. 4:6). In the name of this theology, the deuteronomic law restrained military buildups (Deut. 17:16). The psalms reiterate that trust in weapons is a contradiction to faith in the LORD (33:16–19; 44:3, 6–7; 147:10–11).

3. It is interesting to note that the psalm has shifted toward a purely congregational prayer by the punctuation of verse 9 in the Masoretic text. The Hebrew reads, "O LORD, grant victory! May the king [i.e., God] answer us when we call" (so NJPS). This reading emphasizes that the LORD is the true king. It may represent a democratizing understanding that claims the right and privileges of the anointed for the people (see Psalm 2, sec. 4).

102

As Scripture the psalm teaches the church to pray for those who hold the power of office, because they, like us, are dependent on the LORD. It warns against ever letting our dependence on their service turn into the trust we owe to God alone. It warns against allowing their fascination with military strength to make us support policies based on trust in military might.

As liturgy, the psalm leads us into the strange position of praying for the saving victory of our Messiah, who has already been given the victory over sin and death for our sake. But we worship and pray while the end has not yet come, "when he delivers the kingdom to God the Father after destroying every rule and every authority and power" (I Cor. 15:24). Through the psalm we may join our prayers to the intercessions of Christ for us in hope and anticipation of the consummation of his victory.

Psalm 21: The King Trusts in the LORD

Psalm 21 is the third in a sequence of psalms that in different ways celebrate the dependence of the king on the strength of the LORD (see Psalms 18 and 20). This theme is set in its opening and closing lines, forming an inclusion around the whole (vv. 1, 13). The first part praises the LORD for all the benefits the king derives from the strength of the LORD (vv. 1–6) and concludes with a statement of the basis of the relation between God and king (v. 7). The second part is addressed to the king; it expresses confidence that the LORD's wrath will be joined to his struggle with his enemies so that he can overpower them (vv. 8–12). It concludes with a congregational exclamation of praise for the strength and might of the LORD (v. 13).

The psalm may have been composed for recital in the ceremonies of enthronement (see v. 3) or for rituals celebrating and renewing the reign of a king (on the role of the king, see Introduction, sec. 6.11). As in the other psalms for the king, the theological purpose of Psalm 21 is to subordinate the human king to the divine king. Everything the king is, has, and does comes from God. The royal person is cause and reason for praise, trust, and hope in God.

According to the ideal of kingship in the psalms, the king was given the privilege and power of prayer in a preeminent way. As the one who was son in relation to God, he could ask and hope to be answered. But what he received from God he

103

must request. None of his gifts and endowments were inherent in his person. He was the model of the indispensable place of prayer in the human relation to God. The Old Testament basis for "Our Father in heaven" was laid in him (2:7–8; 18:6; 20:4–5; see Mark 11:23–34; Luke 11:5–13).

The summary terms for the benefits bestowed on the king are blessings (vv. 3, 6) and saving help (vv. 1, 5). Blessing is the life-enhancing effect of the LORD's presence and favor. Saving help is the deliverance from enemies. The specific benefits listed here are the crown, a full complete life, and the glorious majesty that belongs to a ruler whose God is with him when his enemies threaten. It is interesting to reflect on this list in the light of the story of Solomon in I Kings 3:3–15. When Solomon was given the right of petition, he passed over long life, riches, honor, and power over enemies to choose an understanding mind to govern, the ability to discern between good and evil. The story sets the higher value on a gift that was directly a service to God and the people (see Psalms 72 and 101).

Verse 7 teaches that the king's relation to the Most High is based on trust in the divine loving-kindness (*hesed*). It is through trust that the king prays for and acts in the strength of the LORD. He must rely on the LORD to stand by his choice of and promises to the king. The crucial importance of trust on the king's part is vividly illustrated in Isaiah's confrontation with King Ahaz, who was terrified because of the plan by Israel and Syria to displace him as king. Isaiah said, "If you will not believe, you will not be established." Ahaz had to trust himself to the God who elected and installed him; else he severed his relation to the strength of God (Isa. 7:1–17, see vv. 2, 4, 9, and 12). Ahaz, the anointed king, said to the prophet, "I will not ask," the final failure of trust.

In the postmonarchical period, faithful Israelites would have found in this psalm, read as Scripture, instruction that blessing and salvation come through the prayer of those who trust in the loving-kindness of the LORD. The church has seen in the portrayal of the king a model and type fulfilled in the Christ, who lived in perfect dependence and trust and whose prayers were answered with victory over sin and death.

Psalm 22: My God, My God, Why Have You Forsaken Me?

When the Gospels tell the story of the passion of Jesus, prayers are used to weave the fabric of the narrative. Specifically, Psalm 22 is the principal Old Testament resource employed by the evangelists to portray, and so interpret, the climax of Jesus' career.

The facts are these: Thirteen (perhaps seventeen) Old Testament texts appear in the passion narrative of the Gospels. Some are quotations, some allusions. Of the thirteen, eight come from the Psalms. Five come from Psalm 22, two from Psalm 69, and one from Psalm 31. All of these three psalms are prayers for help on the part of one who suffers, the kind of psalm usually classified as "the lament of an individual" in generic analysis.

The best-known connection between Psalm 22 and the passion narrative is Jesus' great cry, "Eloi, Eloi, lema sabachthani," a quotation of the prayer's first sentence (Mark 15:34; Matt. 27:46). But it is not just the opening words that are involved. Citing the first words of a text was, in the tradition of the time, a way of identifying an entire passage. Moreover, features of the psalm's description of the psalmist's experience appear in the Gospel narrative (v. 7 in Mark 15:29; Matt. 27:39; v. 8 in Matt. 27:43; v. 15 in John 19:28; and v. 18 in Mark 15:24; Matt. 27:35; Luke 23:34; and John 19:24). The very experiences of the one who prays in the psalm become part of the scenario of the passion. So the Gospels draw a connection not only between the prayers of Jesus and the psalm but as well between the person of Jesus and the person portrayed in the self-description of the psalm. In the intellectual world of Judaism, one of the most important ways of understanding the meaning of present experience was to make sense of the contemporary by perceiving and describing it in terms of an established tradition. That seems to be happening in the connection between psalm and passion story.

Because of the close connection of Psalm 22 with Jesus, the custom developed in the early church of taking the psalm as Jesus' words and relocating it completely in a christological context. This results in understanding the psalm in terms of

105

Jesus. But the canonical relation between passion narrative and psalm invites us also to understand Jesus in terms of the psalm, that is, to view him through the form and language of this prayer. That would be to follow the example of the apostles and the evangelists by using the psalm as a hermeneutical context. It may be that in this way we glimpse something about the Christ and prayer and the relation between the two that might not be clear from other perspectives.

The Genre of the Psalm. We can begin by recognizing that Psalm 22 is a "prayer for help" and shares many characteristics with prayers of this kind (Introduction, sec. 5.2). Its basic purpose appears in petitions to God for deliverance from life-threatening trouble (vv. 11, 19–21). The trouble is described, as in some of these prayers, in terms of three relations: to God, others, and self. God's providential care is missing (vv. 1–2); others reject (vv. 6–8) and attack him (vv. 12–13, 16–18); and the needy one experiences the loss of life power (vv. 14–15). The prayer asserts trust in the LORD (vv. 3–5, 9–10). In place of the usual vow of praise or prospective praise, this psalm concludes with a long hymnic section (vv. 22–31). Psalm 22 shares words and motifs with other prayers for help as well as structural features. Like the other psalms of its genre, Psalm 22 was composed for liturgical use. What one hears through it is not the voice of a particular historical person at a certain time but one individual case of the typical. Its language was designed to give individuals a poetic and liturgical location, to provide a prayer that is paradigmatic for particular suffering and needs. To use it was to set oneself in its paradigm.

That is first of all what Jesus does in his anguished cry to God when he begins to recite the psalm. He joins the multitudinous company of the afflicted and becomes one with them in their suffering. In praying as they do, he expounds his total identification with them. He gives all his followers who are afflicted permission and encouragement to pray for help. He shows that faith includes holding the worst of life up to God. "In the days of his flesh, Jesus offered up prayers and supplications, with loud cries and tears, to him who was able to save him from death, and he was heard for his godly fear" (Heb. 5:7).

But to classify Psalm 22 as one of the prayers for help is only a first step in recognizing the character of this psalm. One senses in simply reading the text a difference, a development of the type that raises it to its very limits and begins to transcend

106

them. There is an intensity and a comprehensiveness about the psalm that presses toward the ultimate possibilities that lie in the event sketched in the psalm: an afflicted person appealing in helplessness to God and then praising God for help. This magnification of the typical event has been noticed by interpreters through the centuries. Calvin saw how largely the psalm outruns any experience in David's life: "From the tenor of the whole composition, it appears that David does not here refer merely to one persecution, but comprehends all the persecutions which he suffered under Saul" (Calvin, 1:357). And Franz Delitzsch agrees that in this psalm "David descends, with his complaint, into a depth that lies beyond the depth of his affliction, and rises, with his hopes, to a height that lies far beyond the height of the reward of his affliction" (Delitzsch, 1:306). There is, of course, the possibility that this feeling about the scope of the psalm is prompted by its association with the death of Jesus. Yet when one carefully examines the psalm in the context of other prayers for help, it becomes clear that the intensity and the comprehensiveness are a fact of the psalm's composition; it is there in the text itself.

The Structure of the Psalm. The psalm is composed by using the device of repetition or doubling. There is a twiceness in the arrangement from the opening vocative to the total structure itself. The whole is composed of a prayer for help (vv. 1–21) and a song of praise for help (vv. 22–31). These two types and the acts they express are distinct, as would be expected from the different situations that gave rise to them. But here the two are joined in a unity as though the two acts of prayer and praise and the two situations of affliction and salvation must be comprehended in one arc of meaning to express what is happening.

The prayer moves through two cycles (vv. 1–11 and 12–19), each concluding in the petition, "be not far" (vv. 11, 19). Each of the cycles is composed of a twofold alternation of elements. The first cycle is made up of two laments over the psalmist's trouble (vv. 1–2 and 6–8), each followed by appropriately corresponding assertions of confidence in God (vv. 3–5 and 9–10). The second cycle is made up also of two laments (vv. 12–15 and 16–18), each composed of a description of surrounding bestial forces (vv. 12–13 and 16), followed by descriptions of the nearness of encroaching death (vv. 14–15 and 17–18). The second petition (vv. 19–21) intensifies the first (v. 11) by threefold repetitions.

107

The song of praise is also composed of two sections (vv. 22–26 and 27–31). The first section is a hymn in first person style whose focus is on the congregation who celebrate with the psalmist his deliverance and is made up of a summons to praise (vv. 22–23) and the subject or reason for praise (vv. 24–26). The second section widens the circle of praise from congregation to humanity itself, all nations (v. 27), the strong and the dying (v. 29), and even people yet unborn (vv. 30–31).

To hear or read the psalm is to be confronted with a testimony that comprehends the absence and the action of God in a configuration of affliction unto death and salvation to life. The figure whose prayer and praise are heard undergoes a reversal of relations: before, mocked and rejected because of his dependence on God; after, joined by a company who celebrate with him because of it; before, surrounded by forces of evil whose threat replaces the present power of God; after, the occasion for the universal eternal celebration of the sovereignty of God. What happens in this psalm is, in its basic plot, a case of the experience through which the believing Israelite passed in praying in tribulation, using prayers for help and then later, when delivered, praising God with a company of friends. Here the two are joined, intensified, and magnified in a scenario that identifies the combination as the way in which God manifests and discloses his universal eternal reign.

The "Identity" in the Psalm. In this finely wrought compositional design, each of the four parts (the two of the prayer and the two of praise) makes an important contribution to the identity of the figure who is known only through the poetic liturgical typical language of the psalm. Again, he comes through as generic, one of the faithful in trouble who cries out to God, one of a multitude for whom the prayers for help were written. But the figure also comes through as a special case of the type. Each of the parts builds up this prototypical identity in typical and particular ways.

Verses 1–11. The first part is as a whole an elaboration of the opening cry, an exposition of the misery and mystery contained in "My God, my God, why have you forsaken me?" What it means to say "my God" comes clear in verses 3–5 and verses 9–10. Having God as "my God" rests first of all on belonging to a community for whom the center of all reality is "the holy one" who is enthroned as king in heavenly and earthly temple (see Psalm 99) and whose acts of salvation are the content of Israel's

108

hymns of praise. It is to share the meaning and tradition of "our ancestors," who in times of trouble trusted and cried and were delivered; it is to believe that experience is the truth about God for me. It is important for the identity of this figure that the kingdom of God and the corporate context are so quickly established as features of his situation; in reverse order they will be the themes of the praise that describe the significance of his salvation.

Saying "my God" is based as well on quite personal experience. This individual relationship is described by the use of a metaphor that portrays God in the role of a human father who takes the child as it comes from the womb, lays it on its mother's breast to be nursed, and thereafter furnishes the environment of provision and security in which life is lived. It is the testimony of a whole life lived in dependence on God. Notice that in declaring his right to say "my God," the figure speaks not of his own acts or character or status but only of God and what God has done.

Therein lies the pain. His statements about God are confessions of faith, of confidence in God. But in the prayer they serve also as complaints, as panels of contrast to the figure's present situation. The ancestors cried out and were saved, but he cries day and night, with no answer (v. 2). All of his life has been an experience of the "delight" of the LORD, but now he has lost the value of a person in the eyes of others who scorn him in his troubles and mock him with his dependence on his God (vv. 6–8). God's way in salvation history with his people and in providence with his saints is not working in the life of this figure. God is his central problem, the focus of his pain. The alternation in the psalm between descriptions of trouble and statements about God's way expresses the contradiction that rends the soul when the unity of faith and experience is broken. The figure can speak of that rupture theologically only as forsakenness, as the distance of God. The figure is a person in whose trouble the salvation history of God with his people and the providence of God for his faithful are at issue.

Verses 12–21. The second part of the psalm develops the theme, "Trouble is near," which is heard at the end of the first part (v. 11). Using the motif "surrounds" (vv. 12, 16), the psalm describes what is "near" to fill the space left vacant by the "farness" of God. The figure is identified as a person surrounded and being done to death by a company of evildoers, a social

109

group whose unity lies in their common consent to evil. Animal metaphors are used to convey the viciousness and danger. (The extended metaphor is unique in the Psalms; the simile "like a lion" is used to characterize foes in 7:2 and 10:9–10.) Lion and ox are conventional pairs to represent the epitome of power. Hounds and hunters (vv. 16, 20) evoke the helpless prey. The identity of these evildoers is hidden behind the animal masks they wear. Perhaps the metaphors give these enemies a demonic cast; in the ancient Near Eastern religions, demons and divine figures often appear as animals. The metaphors render them as bestial, powerful, dramatizing intensely the mortal overwhelming plight of the figure.

In alternation with the lament over the evildoers, the figure describes his own condition in two panels whose common point is the approach of death; its signs are in his body (vv. 14–15) and its expectation in those who watch him (vv. 17–18). Paradoxically, he experiences the activity of his distant God in his descent into the realm of death (v. 15); God's sovereign power is mysteriously mingled with the forces that drive him from the sphere of the living. The unusually extended petition in verses 19–20 concludes the prayer. Verse 19 repeats the thematic petition for God to end his absence and pleads for deliverance from the surrounding powers, listing them in reverse order—hunters, hounds, lion, and ox (vv. 20–21). The effect of the whole is to create a shifting montage of images evoking violence and dying that never comes into focus so that the horror could be identified and confined to some specific kind of suffering. Instead, one is given the impression of the terror of cosmic anarchy brought to bear on one figure, a vision of what happens when evil breaks through the normal restraints of humanity because the restraining, correcting salvation and providence of God are absent.

NOTE: There are two places in the text of this part of the psalm where uncertainties have played important roles in its interpretation and so need to be noted. The last clause of verse 16 in the Masoretic text reads "like a lion my hands and feet," which NJPS follows in translating, "like lions [they maul] my hands and feet," making the clause a continuation of the hunting image of the previous two clauses. The RSV follows the Septuagint in rendering, "They have pierced my hands and feet," a reading that early Christian interpreters connected with the crucifixion of Jesus. The fact that this reading is not

110

reflected in the Gospel's use of the psalm may mean that it was unknown to those who formed the tradition of the passion of Jesus. The NRSV translates, "My hands and feet have shriveled." The second place is a puzzling affixed verb at the end of verse 21 that would normally mean "you (have) answer(ed) me." Again, the RSV follows the Septuagint with "my afflicted (soul)," which the context supports. Others find in the Hebrew text a liturgical signal that an oracle of salvation intervenes between verses 21 and 22. Neither of these problems is subject to any certain solution.

Verses 22-26. With its third part the psalm moves from prayer for help to praise for help, from one genre to another. The setting assumed by the language now is the service of thanksgiving in which a person whose prayer for deliverance has been answered goes to the sanctuary with those who rejoice at his restoration, does what is necessary to keep the vows made in the prayer for help, and provides a sacrificial meal for the company of family and friends who are with him, and sings a song of praise and thanksgiving for his salvation. What we hear in verses 22-26 is the song, whose references to the service and its rituals are transparent (see the comment on Psalms 30 and 118). Now all has changed for the figure. Instead of forsakenness, an answer has come to his cry (v. 24). Instead of the scorn of his fellows and the threat of evildoers, he is surrounded now by a company of brothers in praise and faith. Instead of laments at the encroachment of death, he can offer his brothers a wish for enduring life (v. 26).

As we listen to the hymn, we learn two things about the figure. First, the group who celebrate his deliverance with him have a theological spiritual identity. They are not simply family, friends, and neighbors, a company constituted by natural and accidental relations. They are brothers (v. 22) in a religious sense. All the different designations refer to this fraternal company: "fearers of the LORD" (vv. 23, 25), "seekers of the LORD" (v. 26), "the lowly" (v. 26; Heb., *'aniwim*; NRSV, "afflicted" or "poor"), "descendants of Jacob/Israel" (v. 23). This last designation does not mean that Israel as a nation is the lowly; rather, that the lowly, seekers, fearers are the true Israel, the real congregation who live by the praise of the LORD. The language of the hymn reflects a group who without separating themselves from the national society in a social way are thinking and speaking about themselves and their relation to God in a way

111

that is beginning to redefine what it means to be Israel. They are the people who in an intentional and public manner "commit their way to the LORD," the stance for which the figure was scorned and mocked (vv. 7–8). The figure is by self-understanding and confession one of the lowly, an 'ani. It is not his affliction that has made him a lowly one; rather, he has undergone his affliction as one of the lowly. This leads to the second thing that is learned about the figure. His deliverance is an event that exemplifies and demonstrates the profoundest faith of the group. The LORD does not despise the affliction of the lowly but hears his cry for help (v. 24; see the similar declaration in 69:33 and 102:17; Psalms 9—10 and 34 develop the theme at length). People despise the lowly in his affliction. They take his affliction as a reason to scorn dependence on the LORD (vv. 6–8). But the LORD makes the affliction an occasion for giving a signal that it is the lowly in whom he delights. So the company of brothers in faith celebrate not only the salvation of the figure but the good news for them in his deliverance. The satisfaction they find in the thanksgiving meal is far more than physical; it nourishes their spirit. (Note the connections with Isa. 55:1ff.) The salvation of the figure is the ground for faith for all the lowly.

Verses 27–31. The fourth part connects the fate of this afflicted one with the future of the kingdom of the LORD. The significance of his salvation is now proclaimed for the entire world and its many families of peoples (v. 27), for all conditions of human existence from the "vigorous" (so NJPS; NRSV, "all who sleep") to the dying (v. 29), for future generations yet unborn (vv. 30–31). Everyone—everywhere, of every condition, in every time—will join in the worship of those who recognize and rejoice that universal sovereignty belongs to the LORD. This will all take place through the proclamation of the salvation of the afflicted one as the righteousness (v. 31, *sedaqa*; NRSV, "deliverance") of God. That deed of righteousness will become the basis and content of the nations' worship; they will "remember" (Heb. *zkr*), that is, evoke an event of the past as the significant reality of the present. This last panel of the psalm identifies the figure as the one whose suffering and salvation are proclaimed to the world as a call to repent (notice *shub* in v. 27; NRSV, "turn") and believe in the kingdom of God, the dominion of the LORD.

That even the dying are caught up in the response of worship is a surprise. In the thought world of the psalm, the dead do not praise the LORD. (See the discussion on 6:5.) Verse 29 does not seem to include those already dead (the Hebrew text is quite difficult to read at the end of the verse and the beginning of v. 30). Yet to praise the LORD in the throes of death means that some profound change has taken place because of the salvation of the afflicted one that brings dying itself within the sphere of the LORD's reign. The reach of the LORD's righteousness is pressing on the limits of Israel's view of the possible.

The vision of this hymn is prophetic in character and eschatological in scope. Its place at the conclusion of Psalm 22 connects a vision of the universal, comprehensive, everlasting kingdom of God to what the LORD has wrought in the life of this afflicted one whose prayer and praise the psalm expresses. The connection sharpens the question about the identity portrayed in the psalm, and the question is not so much about particular historical or cultic identity as a theological one. In the Old Testament, God deals with the nations through the corporate entity of his people. The only individual *through whose person* God deals with the nations is the Davidic king, the messiah, the son of God, and, one must add, the unidentified servant of the "songs" in Isaiah 42:1–4; 49:1–6; and 52:13—53:12. Psalm 22 cannot be the prayer and praise of just any afflicted Israelite. Though we cannot know for certain for whom it was written and through what revisions it may have passed in the history of its use, in its present form the figure in the psalm shares in the corporate vocation of Israel and the messianic role of David.

Uses and Meanings. The use of Psalm 22 in the New Testament and in the liturgy of Holy Week gives hermeneutical directions about the way believers are to understand it. We are given a role in the scenario of the psalm. We do not identify, either as individual or community, with the person who prays and praises, as in the use of many other psalms. That role is claimed for and explicated by Jesus alone. We are, rather, the congregation on Passion Sunday and Good Friday who listen to the psalm as hearing the words of our Lord and strain to understand what his performance of his psalm means. And the psalm points us to the places and roles given to us—the table fellowship gathered by the celebration of his eucharist (rendering of thanks) and the people, whether vigorous or dying, who have the gospel of the kingdom of God preached to them. Heard

113

from these places and roles, the psalm may bring us a new and renewed realization of what Jesus' performance of the psalm means for him and for us.

1. That Jesus as Son of God uses the prayer and undergoes the experience described in it does something to suffering that changes its face for those who believe in him. It becomes something he has been through at its typical worst. The change is not something empirical but experiential. We can grasp the dimensions of the change if we can imagine ourselves thinking of suffering only as something from which God is absent or which God inflicts on people. Knowing "he has been through it" does not give us a final explanation or metaphysic. It does give us a new perspective, experience, and stance.

2. The psalm combines prayer and praise, language of suffering and celebration, in one arc of unity so as to say the one is not to be understood apart from the other. The possibilities in this dying are not seen apart from the celebration, and the celebration has its basis and cause in the identity and conduct of the dying one. The psalm as a unit reminds us that neither in faith nor liturgy are the moments of the passion story and Holy Week to be isolated. The periods are, rather, perspectives from which to view the whole. The mystery and meaning are that it is the living Lord who tells of his dying and it is the crucified One who lives.

3. In its unity the psalm provides a scenario for reflection on the significance of Jesus' death and resurrection that is different from the traditional models of sacrifice, trial, and combat.

a. The psalm interprets Jesus' passion and resurrection as a theodicy for those who commit their way to the LORD. The Gospel accounts make it very clear that Jesus suffered and died as one of the "lowly." In the psalm it is the dying of one who trusts in the LORD that raises the question about God, and it is his salvation that leads to the knowledge that God "has not despised or abhorred the affliction of the afflicted" (a very real possibility to Old Testament people and to moderns). Jesus' enactment of the scenario includes the affliction to death and is ground for knowledge that whatever the anguish caused by the conflict of faith and experience may mean, it does not mean that God has failed those who cry to him. For the lowly, the passion and resurrection of Jesus are a justification of God in whom they trust and a vindication of their trust.

b. The psalm interprets Jesus' passion and resurrection as

114

a summons to the world (in the most inclusive sense of that term) to believe in the reign of the LORD. In the psalm, all the people of every nation, condition, and time are expected to turn to the LORD in praise of his sovereignty because he acted to deliver the dying afflicted one. How the psalmist understood that expectation is not clear. Second Isaiah proclaimed that the LORD's deliverance of the exiled dying Israel would be a revelation of the LORD's reign to all the nations. In the psalm, dying is portrayed as the experience of a threefold loss: of vitality, of social support, and of God. It was clear that where death set the final seal on that threefold experience for those who identified themselves with the LORD, a line was drawn against his sovereignty. Life and its loss are what bind all people in every nation, culture, and time. All face and finally experience the threefold loss: of physical vitality, of the possibility that family and friends can sustain and relieve, of a conscious relation to the cosmic power that creates and maintains existence. In the passion of Jesus, that threefold loss is undergone and he dies. But his resurrection is the signal to all who dread and undergo the threefold loss that death itself has been brought within the rule of the God of Jesus Messiah. It is the news that is of ultimate concern for all humanity.

4. The psalm suggests that we think of the Lord's Supper as a thanksgiving of the lowly. It is the *eucharist* instituted and defined by a lowly one and shared by the lowly. This raises a question about the self-understanding we bring to the Lord's table, and whether we come as one of the lowly. The term refers to those who conduct life in dependence on God. It is an identity constituted by a personal stance of mind and will toward the "world." It is not defined economically or ritually or institutionally. Its features may be seen in Jesus' human life: a centering on God, prayer, gratitude, obedience, empathy, and patience with others. The beatitudes are relevant here, and the psalm reveals that they are instruction to us about our identity in coming to the table of the Lord.

Psalm 23: The LORD Is My Shepherd

1. Psalm 23 begins with a metaphor: The LORD is my shepherd. In a metaphor something is said to be something else that it obviously and literally is not. A word used as a metaphor brings all that it denotes and connotes in ordinary language to

the explication of that to which it is related. A metaphor used for theological purposes is very serious business. It does not simply describe by comparison; it identifies by equation. A metaphor becomes the image as which and through which something or someone is known and understood. It conveys more, and it speaks more powerfully than is possible to do in discursive speech. A metaphor is not as precise and limited as discursive speech. It draws on varied experience and evokes imagination. It is therefore plastic in meaning, capable of polysemy.

The opening metaphorical statement is a signal that the whole psalm is composed in a metaphorical idiom. That is one of the reasons for its poetic power and perdurance as a poem of faith. It is also the reason why interpreters who look for the original meaning or for the correct explanation or pose interpretive questions in terms of either/or receive ambiguous answers from the text. Are the Hebrew verbs to be translated in the present tense, making the psalm a statement of present experience, or in the future, making it a statement of hope? Does the shepherd image govern the whole, or is the image of host introduced in verses 5–6, or is the image of guide also introduced in verses 3b–4? Does the poem refer in verses 5–6 to an institutional setting, and was it composed for liturgical use there, or is the whole a matter of imagery and the true setting the spiritual life of the psalmist? Is the person who speaks through the psalm an individual or corporate personality? It is the genius of the metaphorical idiom that it permits these questions without allowing any one answer to control the reading of the psalm.

2. The psalm has been composed as the exposition of its opening line. The line makes a positive and a negative statement. The positive statement relates the LORD and the psalmist through the metaphor "shepherd." That metaphorical statement, broadly enough understood, controls the imagery of the whole. The negative statement is a self-description of the psalmist. It uses the word "lack" (NRSV, "want") in an absolute sense; the transitive verb is given no object. The psalmist lists what he does not lack in the rest of the psalm.

"Shepherd" was a rich and complex notion in Israel's culture. Of course, the ways of sheep and their shepherd were familiar to all. The primary duties of the shepherd's vocation were provision and protection for the flock. The shepherd pastured the flock, led them in the right way when they had to

116

move, fended off predators—pastoral activities described in the psalm. The sheep were his responsibility, and he was accountable for their welfare and safety. But the notion of being shepherd of persons opens up a background of tradition that is far broader than animal husbandry.

In the ancient Near East the role and title of shepherd were used for leaders as a designation of their relation to the people in their charge. As a title, "shepherd" came to have specific royal connotation. Gods and kings were called the shepherd of their people. Both are described and portrayed with mace (rod) and shepherd's crook (staff) as siglia of office. In narrative, song, and prophecy the LORD is called the shepherd of Israel, his flock (Gen. 49:24; Pss. 28:9; 74:1; 95:7; 100:3; Jer. 31:10; Micah 7:14). The LORD made David his undershepherd (Ps. 78:70–72), and the kings of Israel were judged as shepherds (Jer. 23:1–4; 49:20; Micah 5:4). The title had special associations with the LORD's leading and protecting in the wilderness (Pss. 77:20; 78:52–53; 80:1) and in the return from the exile (Isa. 40:11; 49:9–10).

To say "The LORD is my shepherd" invokes all the richness of this theological and political background as well as the pastoral. The metaphor is not restricted to associations with what actual shepherds did; it is informed by what the LORD has done and what kings were supposed to do. One does not have to shift to images of guide and host to account for the whole poem. "Shepherd" understood against its usage in Israel accounts for the whole. The statement is a confession. It declares commitment and trust. It also has a polemical thrust against human rulers and divine powers. The psalm entrusts the support, guidance, and protection of life only and alone to the one whose name is the LORD.

3. The body of the psalm completes the sentence, "I do not lack . . . ." It does not leave those who say it to fill it out with what they want out of their own subjective wills. It has its own agenda of what the LORD does to fulfill one's needs. The very personal syntax of the opening confession is maintained in the recitation of "what the LORD (he/you) does for me." The items in the recitation can be read and understood in relation to three areas. First, what the LORD does draws on what is prayed for in the prayers for help. Second, it reflects the song of thanksgiving with its report of salvation and accompanying festivities, except here the account tells what the LORD does, not what the LORD has done in the past. Third, the recitation is at points

connected with the language of Israel's testimony to its salvation in the exodus. Here are illustrations of points of contact with these areas.

    a. "I do not lack . . . ." During forty years in the wilderness, Israel lacked nothing (Deut. 2:7). This specific declaration is generalized in Psalm 34:10.

    b. "He restores my soul/life." The restoration of life is asked for and thanks is given for it in individual and corporate prayers and psalms (Pss. 30:3; 116:7; 80:3, 7; 44:25; Lam. 1:11, 16–19).

    c. "He leads me in the paths of righteousness" (Pss. 5:8; 27:11; 77:20). Exodus 15:13 describes the LORD leading the people like a flock to holy pastures (Craigie, p. 207).

    d. "You are with me." The word of salvation addressed to those in danger and given in answer to prayers is, "Fear not, I am with you" (Gen. 15:1; 26:24; Deut. 20:1; 31:8; Isa. 41:10, 13; 43:5). Those delivered sang, "The LORD is for me; I do not fear" (Ps. 118:6). Indeed, "shepherd" could be read as metaphor for the reality, "I am with you."

    e. "You prepare a table before me." This is an image dependent on the feast that was part of the rituals of thanksgiving (Pss. 22:22–26; 116:13). God "prepared a table" for Israel in the wilderness (Ps. 78:19).

    f. "Goodness [the benefit of blessing] and loving-kindness [*hesed*, basis of deliverance] shall pursue me." In the prayers for help, it is the enemies who pursue. "All the days of my life" is a phrase that is counterpart to the life threatened by death in the prayers. On dwelling in the house of the LORD continually as a figure of constant protection, see Psalms 27:4–5; 52:8; 61:4; and 63:2–4.

All who know the prayers and thanksgiving songs and stories of salvation will say Psalm 23 hearing the resonances and allusions to these other areas. This protects the psalm from too individualistic and subjective a reading. The psalm's confession is based on the salvation history of the people and expresses the individual's participation in God's ongoing salvific activity. The trust expressed is not just a matter of mood. Strength must be found, a way must be walked, harm and evil threatened. Enemies persist. That is the environment of trust. Trust is not a rosy, romantic, optimistic view of things. Its foundations are prayer and thanksgiving and the story of salvation. "There is a great

118

difference between this sleep of stupidity and the repose which faith produces" (Calvin, 1:395).

4. Although the use of shepherd as an image of God as sovereign over the people was well established in Israel, its use in a first person singular confession is unparalleled. It is the focus of the shepherd's care on one person that gives the psalm such intimate force. The individual dimension of trust and the experience of grace are lifted up. Perhaps in an indirect way the psalm prepares for the story of the shepherd who does leave the flock to go on a search for one lost sheep (Luke 15:4).

The earliest Christians said, "The Lord is my shepherd" and understood Lord to be also the title of Jesus. In John 10:11, Jesus says directly, "I am the good shepherd." They found him to be "shepherd and guardian" of their souls (I Peter 2:25; 5:4). In the Christian rereading of the psalm, Jesus, as the shepherd in David's place, is the one who restores our souls, leads us in the paths of righteousness, accompanies us through danger, spreads the holy supper before us in the presence of sin and death, and pursues us in his gracious love all the days of our lives.

Psalm 23 has had a regular place in the liturgy of funeral services. That is a proper setting for its use. It gives the congregation poignant words of trust to say in the face of the enemy who is not yet destroyed (I Cor. 15:26). The recitation of the psalm prepares for the eschatological picture in which it is echoed, the picture of the Lamb who has become king and shepherd and guides the redeemed to living water. Here the absolute sense of "I do not lack" is completely fulfilled (Rev. 7:15–17).

Psalm 24: The King of Glory

The subject of Psalm 24 is the kingship of the LORD. The psalm is composed of three distinct parts, each with its own particular topic and literary genre. But all three parts speak about the LORD's sovereign rule and each is the text for a liturgical act of identification. The identifications are all theological assertions of central importance.

1. The first part of the psalm (vv. 1–2) identifies the "owner" of the world. In form it is a confessional declaration of the sovereignty of Israel's God. In the Hebrew text the psalm's first word is a prepositional phrase that designates possession: "The LORD's is the earth." For the faith of the psalm, that

119

simple sentence asserts the most important fact about reality. The declaration concerns everything in the world and everyone who lives in it. Because the inhabitants of the world depend on it for existence, they are included in the ownership of the LORD. The LORD owns the world, says the confession, because it is his work. His work is described as a founding and establishing on seas and rivers. The description is creation language that speaks of the world as the product of an ordering power who provides stable and reliable existence out of formless and unstable chaos. In this view, the world is the result of an overpowering, an achievement that is finished but never simply an accomplished fact. Seas and rivers are names for the unstable chaos in the cosmology of the ancient Near East. The chaos is always there, hostile to the ordered world. The world exists because the LORD is and remains sovereign. To see the world is to behold the evidence of the reign of the LORD. To live in the world is to be a dependent on the reign of the LORD.

The confession has a polemical function. The declaration that the LORD is owner is an intentional denial that anyone else is. In Israel's culture the denial was directed against any deity, such as Marduk, for whom similar claims of sovereign possession were made in Babylon. It relativized the claims of human rulers and entrepreneurs whose ownership of parts of the world always tended to absolutize itself. What the confession excludes in the modern world must be made clear by the congregation who profess it. It excludes any scientism that takes the world to be merely the result of inexplicable and purposeless causes. It raises questions about every tendency of human beings to absolutize ownership. To whom do we think practically and operationally the world belongs? To a roster of nations? To the state? To corporations? To whoever has money to get title to pieces of it? The confession qualifies every conceivable answer to such questions.

2. The second part of the psalm (vv. 3–6) identifies the congregation who make the confession. They are the company of those who seek the presence of the owner of the world (v. 6; see NJPS). The form of an instruction on entrance to a sanctuary is used to make clear what it means to be the people who seek the Owner. The instruction is composed of a question (v. 3), an answer (v. 4), a promise (v. 5), and confirmation (v. 6). Psalm 15 is a case of the instruction used as the form of an independent

120

unit; the comment on it should be read and will be assumed here. see p. 85

The hill of the LORD is Mount Zion, on which the temple stands. It is holy because the LORD chose it as the place where the presence of the Owner would be accessible to those who live in it (Introduction, sec. 6.10 and the comment on Psalms 48 and 132). But the holiness of the place poses a question in the midst of the world. What has been made holy is marked off from everything else by its identification with God. It must be kept separate from whatever is inimical to God and contradicts God. So the question about those who stand in the holy place must be asked. In Israel's religious culture, it could be answered in terms of clean and unclean, and the performance of purification rituals to deal with the problem of cultic uncleanness (Leviticus 11—15). Instead, the psalm answers in terms of a description of character.

The adjectives "clean" and "pure" do not belong to the Old Testament vocabulary of ritual purification; they are ethical terms. Clean hands are those innocent of wrong against others. The pure heart thinks and wills only fealty to the LORD (73:1; Matt. 5:8). Those who do not lift up their soul to what is false are faithful to the true God and to truth (so NRSV, following Septuagint; NJPS translates "who has not taken a false oath by My life," probably understanding the sentence in terms of the third commandment). The "one who does not swear deceitfully" is faithful to the neighbor. The four items in two pairs characterize a person who is faithful to God and neighbor. These qualifications did not make up a checklist to be applied to worshipers in a legalistic fashion as they enter the sanctuary; they are, rather, instruction to be read as part of the liturgy of worship. As such, they set forth the theology of the congregation. They sketch a paradigm of the "righteous," that is, one who is right for the relationship at hand. They portray the rendered life, a life disciplined by the confession that the LORD is owner of all, including self and neighbor, and oriented toward the coming of the king of glory.

In Israel the purpose of coming to the sanctuary was to seek blessing and righteousness. So verse 5 continues instruction by emphasizing that it is the righteous who receive blessing and righteousness (NRSV, "vindication") from God. Blessing is the divine gift of provision for and support of life. Righteousness is

121

the divine gift of acceptance into and renewal of a relation with God that enables and encourages human righteousness in living. There is an important circle involved. The creator gives life and relationship in the first place, but it is those who respond by practicing rightness in living who receive a renewal and confirmation from God. They keep the circular movement initiated by God unbroken. Verse 6 simply emphasizes the same point; only those who come to the holy place as the righteous are truly seeking the presence of God; worship is otherwise vain and void. The prophets and Jesus, of course, say "Amen" to this (e.g., Amos 5:21–24; Matt. 5:21).

3. The third part of the psalm (vv. 7–10) identifies the king of glory. The identification is made in the form of an entrance liturgy composed of a demand for admission, a question about who is admitted, and proclamation of the name of the entrant (cf. 118:19–21). The liturgy is repeated in order to emphasize and elaborate the identity of the entrant, the obvious purpose of its recitation. What the liturgy affirms is that the king of glory is the mighty warrior, the LORD of hosts. The significance of this identification made as an entrance ceremony depends on understanding the names and titles and their relationship.

Entrance is demanded for "the king of glory," a title that appears nowhere else in the Old Testament. But its meaning is clear from Psalm 29, where the equivalent "God of glory" is used (29:3) and "glory" is the thematic word. Psalm 29 describes the LORD as the divine warrior who has gained everlasting kingship over the primeval ocean by the might he manifests in the thunderstorm. The response of the heavenly host to the proclamation of his kingship and power is the liturgical cry of "Glory" (29:1–2, 9). In Psalm 24 the liturgy at the gates assumes the proclamation of the LORD's reign based on his foundation of earth by his might over seas and rivers. The LORD arrives at the gates that are both the everlasting doors to his heavenly palace and the entrance to the precincts of the temple on Zion. Entrance is demanded as recognition of his glory.

The inquiry about the identity of the king of glory is a liturgical provision to connect this general title with a name and title that belong specifically and exclusively to Israel's God. The first answer claims the role and rights of the divine warrior for the LORD. Creation was a battle, and the LORD's victory revealed his glorious kingship. The second answer claims the rank of king of glory for the LORD of hosts. The title "LORD of hosts"

122

or "God of hosts" is the throne name of Israel's God (Isa. 6:5). It is the title the LORD bears as royal resident in Zion (84:1, 3), the one whose power makes the city of God invulnerable against its enemies (46:7, 11; 48:4–8). The title refers to the hosts who surround the LORD's heavenly throne and who praise and consult him and carry out his decisions as sovereign of the world (e.g., 29:1–2; 82:1; 89:6–7). In Psalm 89:5–14 there is a long description of the LORD of hosts in which all the theological features of Psalm 24 appear. It is especially important for verses 3–6 that righteousness, justice, steadfast love, and faithfulness are said to be features of the reign of the LORD of hosts. That explains the necessity of the character of the righteous for those who go to stand in his royal presence. (On the above, see especially Mettinger, pp. 123–157.)

The occasion for the performance of this entrance liturgy in Israel's religious life may have been a procession that brought the ark into the temple precincts as part of a festival celebrating the reign of the LORD. The name LORD of hosts was closely associated with the ark as a symbol of the LORD's identity and presence. When the ark entered the temple gates, the entrance reenacted the final movement of a narrative pattern of great significance in the religious culture of the ancient world. In both Mesopotamia and Canaan, the god who was victorious over the primeval sea gained kingship and the right to a temple-palace that represented his sovereignty. Creation, kingship, and temple were closely connected. The entrance of the ark was the dramatic representation of the LORD's identity as sovereign of the world. The entrance liturgy of verses 7–10 is the dramatic version of the confession of verses 1–2 (see Cross, pp. 91–111).

4. The three parts of the psalm concern the central elements of faith, life, and worship. The psalm gives the inhabitants of the world a confession with which we may acknowledge how the world came to exist and whose we are. Existence in the world is possible because of the existence of the world. The world exists because the will and the work of the LORD have prevailed against the chaos of nonexistence to bring forth a benevolent and life-sustaining order. Creation is a victory of our God of which we are the constant beneficiaries. The confession calls for a life that is itself ordered by the sovereignty on which it depends.

The psalm teaches us what that life is like in the simplest

123

terms. It is a life that in thought and deed in relation to God and others is faithful. Only a life lived like that fits into and reflects the character of the sovereign to which it belongs. Like the creation, it is ordered by the will and the work of the LORD so as itself to be a part of the ordering that makes for the life of all. It is a life founded and established by the blessing and righteousness of the LORD in the midst of the chaos of evil.

The psalm also announces that the LORD "comes" to us. The LORD stands at the door and knocks (Rev. 3:20). He has come to be present with us and for us. He comes as the victor who has prevailed against the chaos of unbeing and so is able to prevail against the chaos of evil. That is good news. Unless he were there for us with his blessing and righteousness, we would have nowhere to go to find help to sustain and set right our lives. Our existence depends on his creation; our blessing and righteousness depend on his coming.

This theme of advent has prompted the location and use of the psalm in the Christian year. The psalm has long association with the celebration of the ascension of Jesus. Used in this connection, it portrays Jesus as the victor over sin and death who enters the heavenly realm through the eternal doors to reign at the right hand of God as the king of glory. In contemporary lectionaries the psalm is used in the season of Advent and on the Sunday of Jesus' entry into Jerusalem. On these occasions the psalm discloses the mystery of Mary's child. The babe born in a stable is the king of glory. The man who enters the holy city only to be rejected and executed is the hidden king of glory. In him God comes to us and for us to bring blessing and righteousness.

Psalm 25: Teach Me

The beginning, end, and arrangement of Psalm 25 are major clues to understanding its character. It begins with a line that is a profound description of prayer: "To you, LORD, I lift up my soul" (v. 1; 86:4; 143:8). In Israel, lifting up one's hands in a stretched-out position was a gesture of entreaty used in prayer. To lift up the soul to God is a metaphor for what the gesture means. The metaphor portrays prayer as an act in which individuals hold their conscious identity, their life, in hands stretched out to God as a way of saying that their life depends completely and only on the help of God. The expres-

124

sion is a psalmic synonym for "In you I trust" (v. 2), "I take refuge in you" (v. 20), and "I wait for you" (vv. 3–5, 21). The psalm's dominant style is that of the individual prayer for help (see Introduction, sec. 5.2). It is primarily composed of petitions (vv. 2–7, 11, 16–22) and assertions of trust (vv. 1–2*a*, 15). The introductory metaphor characterizes the whole as a lifting up of the soul to God. The psalm is a prayer that says, "In the midst of all the troubles of life [vv. 17, 18, 22] I place my hope in you, and you alone, O God."

The psalm ends with a petition that concerns Israel, the whole people of God, and their redemption from all their troubles. The corporate reference of the conclusion calls attention to other points in the prayer where a concern transcends the situation of an individual. The psalmist's plea to be spared humiliation by enemies is followed directly by the same plea on behalf of "all who wait" on the LORD (vv. 2–3). The hope that those who wait on the LORD would not be put to shame is a feature of exilic prophecy and lament (e.g., Isa. 42:23; 40:31; Lam. 3:25), and "waiting for the LORD" became a stance of faith encouraged by psalmic prayer (e.g., 27:13–14; 37:34; see the comment on Ps. 130:5–6). The picture of salvation includes a life in the "good" that God gives through the land and the possession of the land by the next generation, features of the deuteronomistic picture of the blessings of covenant faithfulness (vv. 13, 10; see the comment on possessing the land in Psalm 37). The psalm is among those in which first person singular style has a corporate dimension. The prayer is the voice of an individual whose troubles and hopes are those of the whole people. It leads individuals to pray in solidarity with the whole people of God, and the congregation to pray in the unity of an individual identity.

The arrangement of the psalm's lines follows the order of the Hebrew alphabet. The psalm is composed as an acrostic poem. Though the prevailing style is that of an individual prayer, the form is that of an instructional poem that goes through the agenda of prayer in a comprehensive way (Introduction, sec. 5.4). The purpose of the psalm is apparent in the pronounced interest in the topic of instruction (vv. 4–5, 8–10, 12, 14). The agenda of the prayer for help is dealt with in a generalizing and inclusive fashion. The petitions for the LORD to be the teacher of the one who prays use virtually every available verb in the vocabulary of instruction. Petitions are made for deliverance from general troubles, from enemies whose threat is never stated, from sins past and present, from guilt, and from affliction. This is all doubtless brought about by the poet's need to compose a poetic line for each letter of the alphabet. But the resulting prayer is not an artificial conceit. The device has been used to the poet's purpose to create a genuine and poignant prayer that gathers up the needs and hopes of the people who live in the midst of opposition to their faith, fearing the dangers of history, aware of their sinfulness, but trusting in the LORD and living out of hope in the LORD's salvation. It is this "universal character and harmony with the plan of redemption" that led Delitzsch to say of this psalm that "it contains nothing but what is common to the believing consciousness of the church in every age" (Delitzsch, 1:341).

Undoubtedly the distinctive theological feature of the psalm is its emphasis on the topic of instruction. It is the subject of petitions (vv. 4–5), of hymnic description of the LORD (vv. 8–10), and of wisdom teaching (vv. 12–14). The way instruction is thought about here has important theological implications for the practice of prayer and the doctrine of salvation.

1. First of all, and quite simply, learning is the subject of prayer. There is a being-taught not to be gained from human teachers and sources. It does not come from the work of reason, the compiling of information, the distillation of general experience. It must come from God, because what this instruction does to and for human life only God can do. The need of it is part of our dependence on God, so it must be the subject of prayer, as it is in the psalm. The life of prayer is incomplete unless there are supplications that say, "Teach me, instruct me, guide me, let me know."

2. The subject of the instruction prayed for is identified in different ways as though no one way defined it adequately. Verse 10 speaks of the LORD's covenant and testimonies which are its content (see II Kings 17:15), but it is not information about covenant requirements that is sought here. Rather, knowledge of the LORD's covenant itself is sought, and that knowledge is the *sod* of the LORD, a word that means the "counsel" of the divine sovereignty or, even better, the secret or mystery of the decision of God's kingship (translating v. 14 with NJPS, see Amos 3:7; NRSV, "the friendship of the LORD"). It is guidance that makes it possible to live in and according to the rule of God. Or, the psalm says, it is the ways and paths of

126

the LORD which are covenant love and faithfulness, and into which the LORD as their savior guides the afflicted and sinners (vv. 10, 4–5). Those who walk according to God's way with the world and human beings walk in the way that is right (v. 9). The LORD reveals his mystery to those who fear him (v. 14) and shows covenant love to those who keep the covenant (v. 10). But fearing the LORD and keeping the covenant is what the prayer seeks to be taught. This dialectical relation between what God teaches and what human beings do is created by the necessity of holding together all that the prayer says about the learning it seeks. The dialectic is intentional, a way to the truth of the prayer. What is required is also given. What is needed is already known, but in the asking the knowledge is realized.

3. Instruction is sought as a gift of salvation. Along with supplication for deliverance from the traps the world sets for the believer (v. 15) and the forgiveness of sin, the prayer seeks the guidance of life into the way of the LORD. This is one of the psalms that sees clearly that the *torah* of the LORD, his instruction of those who fear him, is part of God's saving work and completes the salvation of liberation and justification with sanctification (see the comment on Psalms 1; 19; 119). Those who are freed from affliction and pardoned of their sin need guidance for life. The psalm taught Israel to seek the grace and salvation given in the *torah*. It teaches the church to pray for the Spirit to bring into our lives not only the power and mercy of God but as well a being-taught the way we are to live through the knowledge of God's ways with us.

Psalm 26: Judge Me, O LORD

referred to on p. 89 (Ps 17)

"Vindicate me, LORD, for I am righteous." That is the theme. The prayer is written for people who need the "judgment" of God. That is the existential occasion of the prayer. The theme sounds theologically wrong and the occasion unlikely. To pray for vindication on the basis of one's own righteousness contradicts what we have learned from Jesus and Paul. It sounds like the prayer of the Pharisee (Luke 18:11f.). It conflicts with Paul's doctrine that "all have sinned" (Rom. 3:23). Surely it is incredibly presumptuous to pray that God investigate and vindicate us. Perhaps the only use we can make of Psalm 26 is to take it as a negative example, an Old Testament contrast to proper prayer and faith.

127

Before we relegate the psalm to that use, we need to be sure we have understood the language and purpose of the psalm in its own terms. It may be that there are positive things to be learned about the project of living and the uses of prayer.

1. First, what is prayed for? The petitions come in verses 1, 2, 9–10, and 11. The thematic supplication that all the others develop is the opening appeal that in Hebrew says literally, "judge me" (NRSV, "vindicate"; REB, "uphold my cause"). In Israel's social life, this appeal would have been made by an innocent party who had been unjustly accused or had been injured by another and sought a decision to set things right, to order the matter justly. The situation assumed is like that of the widow in Jesus' story who kept petitioning a judge to right a wrong done to her by an adversary (Luke 18:3). Naturally, the innocent party would make the appeal and a relieving decision would be redemptive (v. 11). The prayer turns to God as the supremely authoritative judge of nations and individuals because he is the arbiter who knows not only the facts but what lies in heart and mind, what is felt and intended (v. 2). The decision sought is put in the plea of verse 9; "Don't withdraw my life, don't deal with me as though I deserved to die." God is asked to order the situation of the one who prays so that things work out for life instead of death.

2. When would such a prayer be made? The petitions assume a situation in which one needs the ordering decision of God to restore the circumstances of life. But as usual in the Psalms, the language is so formulaic and traditional that it is open rather than restrictive about the setting of such a prayer. There is a series of texts that describe a procedure that could be followed by people falsely accused or involved in cases where evidence was inconclusive; they could come to shrine or temple to seek a clarifying verdict from God given through an oracle or an ordeal or by lot (I Kings 8:31–32; Deut. 17:8; Exod. 22:6–8; Num. 5:11ff.). Perhaps prayers like Psalm 26 were composed for use in these proceedings. Jeremiah, accused and attacked by opponents of his prophetic activity, prayed like this for God's providence to vindicate his mission and message. So such prayers could be used outside formal proceedings in hope of an answer that would take shape in the course of experience. In any case, this psalm and others like it are not concerned with the final judgment and the ultimate destiny of the soul but with proximate and specific problems of life in which justice and

128

right are not created by what human beings know and do but seem to depend on what God knows and can do. Then one prays, "Judge me, give me justice."

3. But one prays to be judged only if one is *saddiq*—a word that means "right, righteous" in the broadest sense and in judicial contexts means "innocent" in the case to be decided. A large part of Psalm 26 is self-description of the one who prays (vv. 1, 3–8, 11). The term "righteous" is not used in this description, but that is what the description comes to. The self-description is not individual, the identification of a particular person; it is, rather, the portrait of a type, the recitation of what is typical and characteristic of a manner of living; the description is composed of features drawn from the traditional language used to identify and characterize the type. (It is instructive at this point to compare Psalms 1; 15; 24.)

Here the primary motif, stated at the beginning (v. 1) and at the end (v. 11), is "walk in integrity (*tom*)." Hebrew *tom* and English "integrity" denote something that is whole, of a piece, as we say. *Tom* means to have essential coherence, to be one thing. When the remainder of the description is examined, it is apparent what gives the life described its integrity: a devotion to the LORD that governs all of life. Everything else in the self-description is an aspect of the devoted relation: unwavering trust (v. 1), living in the light of the LORD's steadfast love and faithfulness (v. 3). The love of the psalmist's life is the temple, because that is the place and space where God lets his glory be known (v. 8). He keeps his hands free of acts inimical to God's will and way (v. 6), so that when he praises God by reciting what God has done, the deeds of his life will be coherent with his praise (v. 7). As an act of devotion he has refused to let his thinking and doing be formed and guided by the falsity, hypocrisy, and wickedness prevalent among some in the society (vv. 4–5). Finding the nurturing social context in the great congregation is a matter of faith for him (v. 12). In this description the areas of what we call religion and morality are regarded as one, believing and doing are understood as an undivided whole. Integrity is a quality of life lived out of that understanding where the love of God orders will and work.

Such an integrity is not self-righteousness, a conviction of autonomous moral superiority based on one's independent achievements. It is not legalism, conduct based simply on a checklist of requirements. It is, rather, the offer to God in prayer of a wholeness of religion that was demanded by the prophets (e.g., Amos 5:21–24) and taught by Jesus (e.g., Matthew 23). Perhaps what gives us pause before the psalm is a serious hesitancy about describing ourselves favorably to God. But we need to remember what the prayer seeks—the vindicating decision of God in circumstances where life or vocation is accused or suspected by others. Jeremiah prayed like this on occasion. Paul, suspected and challenged in his mission and faith, claimed a good conscience before God (II Cor. 4:2; 1:12; Acts 23:1; 24:16). Luther interpreted this psalm personally in the context of accusations against him of disloyalty to the church and perversion of doctrine. Times may and do come when we need the help of remembering that God knows the mind and heart, even if others don't, and of believing that God will vindicate faithfulness even if the world does not.

In the ordinary round of life, one can take this prayer as a challenge and goal of integrity. The description of integrity in the psalm is formulaic and ideal, but in the thinking of the psalm it is the necessary and achievable integrity—if we trust in the LORD "without wavering."

Psalm 27: My Light and My Salvation

Psalm 27 is a favorite of many because it expresses the central impulse of biblical religion, trust in the LORD, in such eloquent and poignant words. In this it is like Psalm 23. It teaches what real trust is like, and it leads those who follow its lines in liturgy or meditation toward that trust.

The psalm is one of the prayers for help (Introduction, sec. 5.2). Its form is unusual in the extended confession of trust made to others (vv. 1–6) which precedes the prayer addressed directly to the LORD (vv. 7–14). Because of the difference in style and function of these two parts, some have concluded that two separate psalms have been joined to create Psalm 27. This feature of the structure has led to its division into two portions in liturgical use. But the psalm is a unity. A number of motifs bind the whole together (salvation in vv. 1, 9; adversary in vv. 2, 12; heart in vv. 3, 8, 14; rise in vv. 3, 12; seek in vv. 4, 8; life in vv. 4, 13. See Craigie, pp. 230f.).

The prayer begins with alternating interdependent declarations about God and self: God is light, salvation, refuge to the psalmist—the psalmist fears no human being (v. 1). The declaration would hold, the psalmist continues, even for situations like the slander of evildoers (v. 2) and the attack of a hostile army (v. 3). He so trusts the LORD that his one request "in the day of trouble" is to be in the sanctuary where the LORD is present (v. 4), where he will be protected by the holy space of the shrine (v. 5) and in safety from enemies may worship the LORD (v. 6). This sustained confession of confidence in the LORD declares in the midst of the human world the trust on which the following prayer is based.

The prayer is composed of petitions that the LORD hear and help. There are four, each followed by a statement about the reason for the petition. The first two reasons base the prayer for help in the LORD. First, the prayer is made in obedience to one of the principles of Israel's religion; in times of trouble one is to go to the shrine where the LORD is present and appeal for favor and help, that is, "seek the face of the LORD" (v. 8; see 24:6; II Sam. 12:16; 21:1; Hos. 5:15; etc.). Second, the prayer is made in trust that the LORD's relation to his servant (v. 9) is more reliable and enduring than even that of father and mother; trouble may drive father and mother to forsake their role as parents, but it moves God all the more to respond to his servant (v. 10). The second two reasons base the prayer in the situation of the psalmist. He is in danger because of enemies (v. 11*b*) who are false witnesses against him (v. 12*b*). The reference to enemies who are false witnesses that intend violence may be a clue to the situation for which the prayer was composed; the motif is introduced in verse 2. In Israel's society, the courts had no attorney to prosecute or defend, or judges to ensure fair procedures. The witness played a dominant role, bringing accusations and evidence. The testimony of a witness put one's status in the community and in relation to God in question. A false witness violated one of the ten words of God (Exod. 20:16; see Deut. 19:18; Prov. 6:19; 14:5). They left the innocent no recourse but to appeal to God at the shrine or to claim sanctuary at the shrine.

The way the psalm concludes, however, argues against restricting its meaning and use to this one situation in Israel's social system. Verse 13 in Hebrew is the first clause of an unfinished conditional sentence: "Unless I believed to see the goodness of the LORD in the land of the living . . ." (see NJPS). The psalmist is confident that he will experience the favor and help of the LORD in his life. The implication of the unfinished condi-

131

tional clause is that otherwise he could not pray as he has. The horizons of expectation stretch out beyond some particular crisis to the course of life during which the psalmist relies on the LORD to "teach me your way" (v. 11). Verse 14 is an exhortation in imperative singular style. To whom is it addressed? As a word to a person appealing false accusation at the shrine, it makes little sense to say "Wait on the LORD," because that is precisely what this combination of trust and prayer expresses—waiting on the LORD. (On the notion, see the discussion of Psalm 130.) The exhortation seems to be a concluding commendation of the stance of trust expressed in the psalm addressed to whoever uses it and to a personified congregation.

These last two verses and some other touches in the psalm (e.g., the line from 23:6 in v. 4) suggest that in the development of this prayer the situation of false accusation has been generalized as a metaphor for the typical opposition that the faithful as individuals and as community experience. Verbal assaults, slander, malicious reports, and evaluations mark the course of life of the faithful and the history of the people of the LORD. Think of Joseph, Moses, David, Jeremiah, the exiles, Nehemiah. Beyond the Old Testament, there will be Jesus, the infant church, Paul, the martyrs. The psalm in its present form is a text to teach and express trust for a way of life whose living will again and again be misrepresented, misunderstood, and put in question in the cultures in which it is undertaken.

The psalm is a profound and beautiful text on trusting the LORD. Among the points it makes are these:

1. The two parts of the psalm are one more way in which the Psalter teaches how closely related are trust and need. The urgent prayer of the second part is the complement of the confident confession of the first part. Trust is active and real precisely when one is aware of one's vulnerability, of one's ultimate helplessness before the threats of life, "in the day of trouble," as the psalmist puts it. On the other hand, the voice of neediness speaking urgent pleas for help arises from trust, which transforms mere anxiety to prayer.

2. Trust is possible for those who know the LORD as the savior of their life. The psalm articulates that knowledge at the very beginning where it calls the LORD "my light, my salvation, the stronghold of my life" (v. 1). Salvation concerns life; life is in question in some way where salvation is needed. Salvation is intervention that makes life possible in the face of all that

threatens, weakens, and corrupts life. The LORD is called "light" because light drives darkness away. It is in the light that life revives and flourishes; it is in the light that one can see the way. Israel came to know the LORD as "God of my salvation" (v. 9) at the beginning of their history when they sang, after their deliverance at the Red Sea, "The LORD has become my salvation" (Exod. 15:2). Christians called the LORD light and salvation and stronghold of life because of the deliverance from sin and death given in Jesus Christ. Trust is the practice of the knowledge of God as savior in all our living.

3. Trust is nurtured and strengthened by the exercise and discipline of religion. In his time of trouble the psalmist asks one thing: to be in the temple, where he can visualize the beauty of the LORD and seek the direction for his life that comes with the instruction given there through oracle and precept (v. 4). To make his prayer, he goes to the place of the presence of God, obeying the exhortation of Israel's religion, "Seek ye my face" (v. 8). When trust is kept a private matter, unspoken and unshared, it becomes a personal project and may decay into no more than our own resolution and willpower. Trust needs the stimulus and renewal that come from confronting and contemplating religion's representation of the revelation of God in liturgy, architecture, and proclamation.

4. In this psalm the opposite and counterpart of trust in the LORD is fear of human beings. They are dangerous because of what they do through language. By slander and lies they can place the self and life of the faithful in an environment of falsehood. The psalm is a refusal to let falsehood become the language world of existence. In its praise and prayer it evokes the reality in whose life faith chooses to live—the salvation of the LORD.

Psalm 28: If You Are Silent to Me

Psalm 28 is a prayer for help in first person singular style, with some features that are not typical of the genre (see Introduction, sec. 5.2). It begins with a petition to be heard (vv. 1–2). If the LORD does not respond, it would make the petitioner like those who are on the way to the Pit, to Sheol, the realm of death. In the psalms, Sheol is a place of silence where neither God's word nor human praise is heard (see the comment on Ps. 30:9). To experience the silence of God is a foretaste of death, a visit to Sheol. Verse 2 describes the act of prayer, the cry for help with hands lifted up toward the inner chamber of the temple (I Kings 6:19), as a way of giving the petition added reality.

The petition to be helped (vv. 3–5) combines a plea not to be dealt with as one of the wicked with a request that the LORD give the wicked what their conduct deserves. Indeed, in this combined petition the conduct and reward of the wicked are the subject of every line after the wicked are named in the first line of verse 3. The petition sounds like a general profession of innocence; in effect, it is a request to be dealt with as one who is righteous and not wicked (see the comment on Psalm 26). The prayer against the wicked is simply a reiteration of the theology that in the world as the LORD has created and orders it, wickedness invokes its own destruction. The conduct of the wicked is described in two formulaic ways; no particular adversaries seem to be in view. The wicked are those who talk about *shalom* with their fellows while thinking about how to do them in (v. 3; see Jer. 9:8; Ps. 5:9). The wicked do not pay attention to the way the LORD works out the downfall of those who do wrong (Pss. 10:3–4; 14:1–2; 54:3; 64:8–9; and note Isa. 5:12). By a repetition of terms, the psalm sets the "work" and "deeds of the hands" of the wicked in opposition to the "work" and "deeds of the hand" of the LORD. Because those who "work evil" do not consider "the work of the LORD," he will tear down and not build them up (the language used in Jer. 20:4–6; 42:10; 45:4; 1:10).

After the petitions to be heard and helped, the psalm blesses the LORD with a hymn of thanksgiving, praising the LORD for hearing (v. 6) and helping (v. 7). The praise seems to assume that an answer has been heard and help has been given.

In verses 8 and 9 the concern of the prayer is broadened to include the people of the LORD and the anointed king of the LORD. The LORD is praised as the one whose sovereignty is the strength available to his people (see 29:10–11) and whose saving acts are the refuge of the Davidic king who rules as the elected messiah and representative of that sovereignty. (On the anointed, see Psalm 2, sec. 3.) Then intercession is made for the salvation of the people of the LORD, who is asked always to tend and sustain them as a shepherd cares for his flock; the imagery resembles that of Psalm 23 and Isaiah 40:9–11. The deliverance of the individual who prays the psalm seems to be connected with the safety and blessing of king and people. Possibly the

134

psalm was composed for recitation by the king or his representative, but it is just as likely that an individual includes concern
for king and people in this thankful praise for being heard, or
that an individual prayer has been developed for corporate use.
In any case, the psalm holds the individual, the anointed, and
the people of the LORD together in that inseparable unity
which belongs to the purpose of God.

Psalm 29: The God of Glory

Psalm 29 is an Old Testament doxology in praise of the
LORD as sovereign of the universe. The kingdom, power, and
glory are its themes.

1. The psalm is a hymn of praise composed of the usual
elements of a summons to praise (vv. 1–2) and the body or
content of praise (vv. 3–10); the concluding line is a prayer
based on the praise (v. 11). There is little else, however, that is
usual about the hymn (Introduction, sec. 5.5.4). The summons
is addressed to divine rather than human beings. They are to
ascribe to the LORD the glory and the power that the LORD's
name represents. The glory is ascribed in a sevenfold proclamation of the power (vv. 3–4) and the powerful effect (vv. 5–9) of
"the voice of the LORD." The proclamation takes the form of a
description of a thunderstorm (vv. 3, 7) that comes from the sea
to crash against the coastal mountains and their forests, and
even to shake the wilderness beyond them. The proclamation
reaches its climax in a declaration that the LORD is throned over
the flood as king forever (v. 10). The declaration states the
meaning of the proclamation; the thunderstorm is the glory, the
display of the powerful rule of the LORD. The concluding
prayer invokes that power as a divine blessing that creates
peace for the people of the LORD. There is much here that
needs explaining.

2. The hymn was presumably composed for performance
by or for the congregation assembled at the temple. But, except
for the last verse, it looks to the heavenly realm and imagines
the cosmic palace of God. There the LORD is enthroned as
sovereign of the universe. His throne is above the flood, the
cosmic ocean that was thought in the cosmology of the ancient
east to surround the world. Around the throne are the heavenly
host, the divine beings who make up the heavenly court and
council (89:7; 103:19–21; 148:1–2). The hymn envisions the

135

scene described more fully in such passages as Psalms 89:5–14; 97:1–5; Isaiah 6; and Revelation 4:1–11. The opening call for the heavenly host to glorify the LORD is a liturgical way for the congregation to equate its own praise with what is right and required in the heavenly palace-temple. The congregation's doxologies correspond to the doxologies of heaven. Note that in the version of verses 1–2 used in Psalm 96:7–9, the summons is directed to the families of earth.

3. The hymn is a doxology. The organizing motif is the term "glory." The summons features the term (vv. 1–2), and the term occurs at the beginning and at the end of the proclamation of the voice of the LORD (vv. 3, 9). Glory is used in two related senses. First, it is a summary term for the attributes of the LORD as king. The LORD is called the "God of glory" (v. 3), a unique title that is a variant of "king of glory" (see 24:7–10). The strength and power, holy splendor and majesty of the LORD are his glory. Second, glory is a term for the manifestation, the display of the LORD's divine royalty in the world. The sevenfold proclamation of the voice of the LORD depicts and evokes the manifestation of the God of glory (cf. Rev. 10:3–4). The hymn makes this very clear by reporting at the proclamation's conclusion that everyone in the temple, both the heavenly palace and the earthly sanctuary, is saying "Glory" in recognition of what the proclamation means (v. 9).

4. The phenomena used to portray the voice of the LORD are those of the thunderstorm—thunder, lightning, and wind. The voice is more a sounding than a speaking, but it is not only sound. The voice of the LORD is the active agent that produces every effect described in the proclamation; it is heard, seen, and felt. The psalm uses the notion as a medium of the person and power of the LORD; it is the thematic subject of a description of a theophany, an appearance of God in the world. Descriptions of theophanies are usually used in the psalms and the prophets to speak of the LORD's appearance and intervention in human affairs to save and judge (see the comment on Psalm 18, sec. 2). Here its purpose is simply to evoke the power and majesty of the LORD as ruler of the universe. There was a reason in Israel's world for using the thunderstorm in portrayals of the LORD's appearance (for other cases, see 18:7–15; 68:4, 8, 33; 77:16–18; 97:1–5; 104:3–4). In the religious myth of the time, the thunderstorm was an established medium of theophany, especially the appearance of the warrior God who won kingship

over other gods and the world. It had a special association with the Canaanite god Baal, whose voice was said to be heard in the thunder (see Cross, pp. 147ff.; and Day, pp. 57ff.). So the proclamation of the voice of the LORD had a polemical function. The name of Israel's God appears in eighteen of the psalm's twenty-three measures, as if to say by its constant repetition that it is the LORD, not any other deity, whose power rules the world. Where in Canaan's myth sea and river were the opponents of Baal in his battle to gain kingship, in the psalm the mighty waters and the flood are simply subject to the LORD's power as symbols of his everlasting reign (see the similar Psalm 93).

The proclamation of the voice of the LORD, then, is a literary and theological strategy designed as a doxology. The psalm does not point readers and hearers to some meteorological display and say, "Go and be overwhelmed by lightning and thunder." The poetic evocation of a storm composed on the theme of the voice of the LORD in the hymn itself fulfills the opening call to doxologize and prepares the worshiper for the prayer at the end. It is a witness to the urgent importance of the doxological experience for the human condition. Existence is subconsciously moved by the need for a kind of ecstasy—not the ecstasy of possession, of being invaded, taken over and used by another, but the ecstasy of the disclosure of another who is what we are not, confrontation by another in the aura of whose power we find possibilities not ours. It is a dangerous need, because in the world of entertainment and politics it can lead us to occupy our spirits with vacuous excitement or to trust ourselves to posturing zealots or to idolize whatever powers are operative in our society. But it is an unquenchable need. The marvelous possibility in worship is a use of time and space and sound to create the doxological situation in which "Glory!" is uttered in response to the one true God.

5. Psalm 29 is the only text in the Old Testament in which the glory of the LORD is so extensively and directly said to be manifested in what we moderns call natural phenomena. In the religious culture of Israel's time, the quarters were too close to the gods who were identified with parts of the natural world. Confusion between deity and world was always possible. It required a long struggle to clarify the relation between creator and creation. The psalmists were careful—persistent but careful. The defining themes in Israel's praise were events in the LORD's way with his people and in the processes of history. In

137

the New Testament the subject of doxology undergoes a surprising personal concentration. With few exceptions, the subject is Jesus, the Son of God. For John, the deeds of Jesus were signs, a disclosure of his participation in the majesty of God (John 2:11; 11:4, 40), and to know Jesus by faith as Son of God was to behold his glory (John 1:14). For Paul, the crucified Christ is the LORD in whom glory is manifest (I Cor. 2:8); the light of the knowledge of the glory of God is seen in the face of Jesus Christ (II Cor. 4:6). It was the gospel in song and proclamation that re-created the medium and provided the doxological moment. Psalm 29 has often been used as the psalm for the first Sunday after Epiphany, when the focus is on the baptism of Jesus. The choice is a profound interpretation of the occasion. The liturgical setting connects the psalm's mighty theophany with the quiet epiphany in the waters of the Jordan. The voice of the LORD in the thunderstorm is paired with the voice from heaven saying, "This is my Son." The storm says, "This is my cosmos"; the baptism, "This is my Christ." The two go inseparably together. The Christology is not adequate unless its setting in cosmology is maintained. The Old Testament doxology is necessary to the gospel.

6. Though the doxological orientation of the Bible is not toward "nature," the psalm does call for attention to the significance of the thunderstorm. In the psalm it is a "sign" in the Johannine sense of God's sovereignty over the cosmos. True, Israel had to be careful because it had to lean against the merging of natural and divine. But at certain other points signals are also given of an understanding that the creation contains signs of the creator, notably Psalms 19; 24; 8; and Genesis 1:26 (cf. I Cor. 11:7). We need to attend those signals because we live in an era in which consciousness of and thought about the natural world are shaped in a quite different way by the science and technology of modern culture. Our tendency is to see the world as a complex to be explained and exploited, to take the unnecessary step beyond science of reducing the world to the dimensions of our reason and needs. Our view is captive to economics and research; the poetic and mythological vision is dimmed. Calvin already saw the looming displacement: "It is a diabolical science," he said, "which fixes our contemplations on the works of nature, and turns them away from God. . . . Nothing is more preposterous than, when we meet with mediate causes, however many, to be stopped and retarded by them, as by so many

138

obstacles, from approaching God" (Calvin, 1:479–480). Where physics and biology are allowed to empty the mythopoeic vision, our lives are cramped within horizons of our own making. Religion and theology are increasingly dominated by psychology and existentialism because they have retreated to inner space to contemplate the human psyche and consciousness. The thunderstorm as theophany is a sign that the LORD is God also of outer space. Perhaps Psalm 29 is in the canon of Scripture to call us to see the world afresh as creation—and say "Glory!" before "the LORD, maker of heaven and earth."

Psalm 30: You Have Turned My Mourning Into Dancing

Psalm 30 is a prayer of thanksgiving for deliverance. On the type, see Introduction, sec. 5.3. In it a person whose prayer for help has been answered brings an offering of praise and proclamation in gratitude.

1. The opening declaration, "I extol you, LORD," identifies the purpose of the song. The declaration is supported by an acknowledgment of the LORD's deliverance (v. 1*a* plus 1*b*–3); the basic report of prayer and deliverance in verse 2 anticipates the longer narrative in verses 6–12. An invitation in the form of an imperative hymn calls the faithful to join in the praise because God's anger and human weeping are so quickly replaced by God's sovereign pleasure and human joy (vv. 4–5). Then an extended narration of deliverance tells of previous distress (vv. 6–7), quotes the prayer for help made because of the distress (vv. 8–10), and confesses that it is the LORD who has turned mourning to celebration and silence to praise (vv. 11–12).

The composer has woven a pattern of alternation and reversal through the entire poem. "I cried out—you healed" (v. 2) sets the basic pattern; the other alternations are variations on this basic theme. The movement from divine anger to sovereign pleasure in verse 5*a* is correlated with the opposite movement from divine pleasure to displeasure in verse 7. The alternation of weeping and joy in verse 5*b* anticipates the move from mourning to gladness in verse 11. The danger of the silencing of praise by death (v. 9) is resolved when the soul breaks silence with praise (v. 12). The repeated and complex use of the

139

pattern of alternation is a way of making the psalm's theological subject heard again and again. The psalm is a cantillation of the change wrought by the salvation of God (Col. 1:11–14).

2. Psalm 30 has many verbal connections with the prayer of King Hezekiah when he was sick (Isaiah 38) and with Psalm 6. It reads as if it were a prayer of thanks to be said after a prayer for help like Psalm 6 had been answered. Verse 2 suggests that recovery from serious illness is the deliverance reported here. The title, however, in one of the few cases of the identification of the use of a psalm, says it is "a song for the dedication (*hanukkah*) of the house." According to the Talmud, Psalm 30 was used in the festival of dedication inaugurated by Judas Maccabeus in 165 B.C. to celebrate the purification of the temple after its desecration by Antiochus Epiphanes (I Macc. 4:52; II Macc. 10:1ff.; John 10:22). Possibly the psalm was used even earlier in connection with the dedication of the second temple (Ezra 6:16–18; Neh. 12:27–43). Whatever the precise historical reference of the title, it is one more indication of the use of first person style to speak of corporate experience. The formulaic poetry of salvation can be and was read as a rendering of individual or national experience. It is this openness of its language that has led to the use of the psalm by individuals to speak of the God-given changes in their lives and by the whole community to speak of the drama of salvation, especially in reference to Christ.

Whether read as the prayer of one person or of the entire community, the psalm makes important points about the relation between prayer and praise.

3. Psalm 30 is a prayer that is wholly praise; it is also praise that comes out of prayer. The prayers for help typically contain elements of praise in their statements of trust and particularly in the promises of praise to be offered in gratitude for God's help. In these ways the prayers for help anticipate the prayer of thanksgiving. Its praise completes and consummates what was begun in supplication. Without it, there would be no human answer to the divine answer (Luke 17:18; 18:43). The subject of praise here is the deliverance prayed for. The verb for praise is *hodah,* which has as its object a quite specific action in God's past and is therefore thanksgiving in the form of acknowledgment (Westermann, *Praise and Lament,* pp. 26ff.). Our engagement with God is truncated and aborted unless the help we receive in answer to our supplications is made the

140

subject of praising thanksgiving. Nor is our corporate or individual relation to God perfected except as we learn and say in prayerful praise how the LORD has met our neediness with his grace.

4. In Psalm 30 the importance of praise to God is the basis (v. 9) and the goal of prayer (v. 12). Death was the danger from which the psalmist has been rescued. Death is spoken of as descent into Sheol, going down into the Pit (vv. 3, 9). The terms and the view they represent are determined by the grave as the place of the dead (see Keel, pp. 62ff.). Deliverance is called a "drawing up," as though the psalmist were already going down into the realm of death (v. 1). In the thought world of Israel, death was viewed as sphere and power that affected and threatened the living (see the comment on Psalm 116). The psalms' constant association of the enemies with death (v. 1) laid the groundwork for the personification and eschatologizing of death as the ultimate foe in the New Testament (I Cor. 15:26; Eph. 6:10ff.). Death and resurrection are not yet in view in the New Testament sense, but the language of the psalm only awaits the Christ event for reinterpretation. What is most threatening about death here is its character as a realm of silence. Death means the loss of praise (on this motif, see 6:5; 88:10–12; 115:17; Isa. 38:18–19). The psalmist had made the loss of praise the very basis of his supplication and thereby dared to make one of the most important statements in the Bible about the theological value of praise. At issue is there being someone to proclaim the faithfulness of the LORD. Praise has a theological basis as well as an anthropological one. Praise is the way the faithfulness of the LORD becomes word and is heard in the LORD's world (v. 9). For people, it is the language of joy and gladness that goes with life and is life in contrast to the silence of death (vv. 11–12). And salvation is here understood as reaching its goal, not just in the restoration of the needy, but finally in the praise of God.

5. The psalm shows how prayer and praise can together become a rubric for holding the experiences of life in relation to God. It makes a simple direct reading of experience in terms of the context of the LORD's sovereign reality. The psalmist's earlier untroubled life is attributed to the royal pleasure of God (v. 7a). His distress comes when the LORD hides his face (v. 7b). His restoration is a change worked by the LORD (v. 11). He sees his previous attitude as a mistaken reading of God's favor, for

141

he said in his self-confidence what should be said only in complete dependence on God: "I shall never be moved" (v. 6 and 10:6; 16:8; 62:2). Now he sees his life as a vocation of thanksgiving to the LORD. Correlating the course of life so directly with the sovereignty of God is, of course, risky. All sorts of distortions and misreadings are possible. But there is a strong faith in the providence of God here. Prayer and praise, if they are to be authentic and vigorous, must have actual life as their subject and not hover carefully in generalities above the earth. Life must be experienced in relation to God, sought and received as from the LORD's hand.

Psalm 31: Into Your Hand I Commit My Spirit

Psalm 31 gained a special place in Christian devotion and liturgy when Jesus in Luke's Gospel used verse 5 as the final prayer of his life: "Into your hand I commit my spirit" (Luke 23:46). Like Psalms 22 and 69, Psalm 31 became a kind of commentary on the passion of Jesus; Christians read in its description of affliction a witness to the suffering he endured (read the comment on Psalm 22). In liturgical tradition it is inseparably connected with the celebration of Holy Week; currently, Psalm 31:9–16 is the psalm selection for Passion Sunday in all three years of the lectionary cycle.

1. Like its companions, Psalm 31 is an individual prayer for help from distress (see Introduction, sec. 5.2). The theme of the whole is stated in the formulaic sentence: "In you, LORD, I take refuge" (on the formula, see the comment on Ps. 7:1). The motif of refuge is continued in metaphors like rock, stronghold, fortress, and crag and is resumed at the end in verses 19–24. Indeed, the prayer as a whole is a "taking refuge in the LORD."

Psalm 31 has three parts. The first part is formally a complete prayer (vv. 1–8) and has often been used separately as a reading in liturgy. It opens with the formulaic declaration for putting one's self under the protection of the LORD and becoming a refugee in the LORD's sphere. Verses 1–4 are petitions for deliverance punctuated by statements of trust (vv. 3a, 4b) anticipating the assertions of confidence in verses 5–6 (in v. 6 read "I hate" with Masoretic text for NRSV "You hate"). The first movement is rounded off with a promise of praise anticipating deliverance (vv. 7–8).

The second part (vv. 9–18) opens with the formulaic "Be

142

gracious to me, LORD" and continues with a twofold description of trouble: with self (vv. 9–10) and with others (vv. 11–13: in v. 11, translate "Because of all my adversaries, I have become a disgrace to my neighbors"; see NJPS). After more assertions of trust (vv. 14–15), the psalm appeals for deliverance from persecuting enemies; the wicked threaten the righteous one and the LORD must intervene lest the trust of the righteous be made ridiculous in the face of the arrogance of persecutors (vv. 15–18).

The psalm concludes with praise and exhortation. There is first praise for the goodness of the LORD who protects those who take refuge with him (vv. 19–20). Then there is praise, introduced by the "Blessed be the LORD" formula, because the LORD answered the psalmist's prayer for help (vv. 21–22). The psalm ends with a call to the faithful *hasidim* to love and rely on the LORD in need (vv. 23–24). The deliverance of the one who prays this prayer is a revelation of the way God deals with those who rely on him and the basis for summoning them to a life of enduring trust.

2. The psalm has been called a model of a prayer that is confident of being heard. This confidence informs the prayer from start to finish; to pray this psalm is to be led into and instructed in this confidence. But the confidence of the prayer is not in any respect a virtue of the one who prays. It is, rather, a possibility that is based on the character of the one to whom the prayer is made. The psalm speaks to the LORD as the *'el 'emet* (v. 5), the God who can be relied on and believed in because he is true to himself and continues always to be what he has shown himself. In speaking to the faithful God, the psalm recurrently speaks of him to evoke the right vision of the one addressed. The LORD is "my God, my rock, my fortress, my stronghold, my refuge" (vv. 14, 3–4) because he has claimed me by election and covenant in the initiative of his grace. He shows his righteousness (v. 1) in the redemption of his chosen (v. 5—as the prophet of Isaiah 40–55 and the apostle Paul also knew) and his loving-kindness (*hesed* in vv. 7, 16, 21) in faithfulness to his own. He enfolds those who entrust their lives to him in the abundant goodness of his providence (vv. 19–20). The faithfulness of God creates a faithful people (v. 23)—the one goes with and is dependent on the other—who may pray and live in the confidence of faith. The writer of II Timothy understood this when he wrote, "I know whom I have believed and am sure that

143

he is able to guard until that day what I have entrusted to him" (II Tim. 1:12).

3. Among all the familiar expressions of trust used in the psalm are two that are unique to this prayer. One is the sentence, already mentioned above, "Into your hand I commit my spirit" (v. 5). Because the sentence in Luke's Gospel was the dying word of Jesus and because of similar words of the dying Stephen (Acts 7:59), it has been used by believers across the ages as the prayer with which to take leave of this life in faith; among their numbers were Polycarp, Bernard, and Luther (see the index in Prothero). The sentence became a poignant personal liturgy of the dying for consenting in trust to the return of the spirit to the God who gave it. But in Hebrew and in the context of the psalm the sentence means something like "I entrust my life to your sovereign disposition"; it is an existential confession of ultimate helplessness, dependence, and trust, a way of saying in the midst of affliction, "It is up to you, God, what becomes of me, and I am willing to have it so."

The other unique sentence is a different way of saying the same. "My times are in your hand" (v. 15) does not mean it depends on God how long I live, but my destiny (the occasions when things happen that determine my life) is in the hand of God. These are sentences that belong to living as well as dying. Indeed, it is a question whether they can be said at the end in authenticity unless they have been our confession all along the way. In the mouth of Jesus the sentence is surely a profound interpretation of his entire life. Calvin said that unless a person practices such a reliance on the providence of God in the living of life, "he has not yet learned aright what it is to live" (Calvin, 1:503).

4. For whom and for what occasion was this prayer composed? On the whole, the language seems to have been generated by the custom of seeking sanctuary at holy places from foes. Typically, it is difficult to give a specific historical answer, and the use of formulaic language in Psalm 31 is more extensive than in the average psalm (Craigie, p. 259). But we can give a canonical and then a liturgical answer. From the text we learn that Psalm 31 is the prayer of a "servant of the LORD" (v. 15) who undergoes affliction and alienation because of opponents. The canonical connections run first of all to Jeremiah. The similarities between the language of psalm and prophet are impressive (among others, compare v. 11 with 20:18; v. 13 with

144

20:10; v. 18 with 17:18). And they run also, of course, to Jesus.
Prophet and Messiah are both scriptural illustrations of the
identity of the servant who in the face of opposition commits
his life to the LORD. Their examples show how even through
failure and death the providence of the faithful God determines
the "times" of his servants. And they encourage and exhort us
through the words of verses 23–24 to find love, strength, and
courage in life and death through making their commitment of
trust.

Psalm 32: I Will Confess My Transgressions

Psalm 32 is the second of the seven traditional penitential
psalms (see Psalms 6; 38; 51; 102; 130; 143). It is not itself a
penitential prayer in which confession of sin is made. It is instead a psalm in which the practice of penitence is taught as a
lesson. In Proverbs 28:13 the lesson is formulated as general
instruction using the same terms as the psalm: "He who con-
ceals his transgressions will not prosper; he who confesses and
forsakes them will obtain mercy." In Psalm 32 the lesson is
based on a case of experience reported in verses 3–5 where the
psalmist tells about the torment he suffered when he was silent
and the forgiveness he received when he acknowledged his sin
to the LORD.

The report takes the form of prayer of thanks for help (see
Introduction, sec. 5.3), with its typical narration of trouble, appeal to the LORD, and deliverance. The profession of confidence (v. 7) and the summons to the righteous to take the
deliverance as an occasion for praise (v. 11) also belong to the
type. Such a prayer was itself a public testimony offered to
others. But here the testimonial function has become outright
instruction given in the form of sayings of congratulation as
beatitudes (vv. 1–2; on the type, see Psalm 1, sec. 1), exhortation
(vv. 6, 8–9), and proverbial saying (v. 10). The psalm is a prayer
that advocates penitence. The instructional function accompanies and is as important as the function of praise.

The psalm, then, probably belongs to the late phase of psalmody when the pedagogical role of worship became more significant. In its concern to teach the practice of penitence as the
mode of prayer that all those devoted to the covenant should
use (v. 6), it supports the preeminence of penitential prayer in
the postexilic period (Ezra 9; Nehemiah 9; Daniel 9). The per-

145

son whose experience is cited as the basis of instruction is far more than a single private individual; the psalmist is a paradigmatic figure whose example incorporates and expresses Israel's experience of God's way through judgment to restoration. After Paul quoted verses 1–2 in his exposition of God's justification of the sinner (Rom. 4:6–8), the church read and used the psalm in the light of the pardon offered to faith in Jesus Christ. It has become a text that fulfills the promise of verse 8: "I will instruct you and teach you the way you should go." It is a summons and a guide to the confession of sin.

1. The psalm lifts up the blessedness of the forgiven sinner. There are many beatitudes in the psalms, more than in any other book of the bible. Nothing in the text of the psalms gives a reason for ranking one above the rest. They together form a composite picture of the well-being of the life lived according to the established ways and orders of God; each commends a feature of that well-being as desirable and attainable. But Psalm 32 gives the impression of having learned from the prophets that the pardon of God is the first and principal basis of the life of the people of God (e.g., Isa. 40:2; 55:6–7). The intensity and insistence of the double beatitude and the triple synonymous categories (those whose transgression is forgiven, whose sin is covered, to whom the LORD does not reckon guilt) lift up the forgiveness of sin in a very special way. Calvin observed that all that the Scripture says about blessedness in other beatitudes depends on the blessedness commended here, "the free favour of God, by which he reconciles us to himself" (Calvin, 1:526). That is, of course, an estimate of what is of value to life that contradicts current opinion about what makes for happiness. Only those will believe it who are taught what the psalmist and the apostle have learned from the judgment and grace of God.

2. The psalm points to the crucial importance of the confession of sin. It is the human way to the forgiveness of sin. God's way is to forgive sinners, and we do not acknowledge his grace unless we present ourselves to him as sinners.

a. The psalm makes it explicit within the Old Testament that confession of sin belongs to prayer in particular and to one's relation to God in general. The old pattern of crying out to God in trouble (e.g., 107:17–22), the notion of repentance as a simple return to God from unfaithfulness, is here amended. There must be a confession of sin. The cry to God when one is in trouble must begin with penitence; that is the way all who are

146

devoted to the covenant are to pray (v. 8); that is the way those who feel the affliction of God's judgment are to pray (vv. 3–4).

b. The psalm contrasts "I kept silent" (v. 3) with "I said" (v. 5). The contrast between silence and speaking has a correlation with general human experience. When one has wronged a wife, a parent, a friend, a neighbor—someone with whom there is a conscious relationship—and refuses to acknowledge it, to put the wrong into words so that it is there in speech available to be dealt with, then the wrong retained and sheltered begins to become part of one's identity. It harms and hardens and diminishes. This experience belongs to the life of corporate identities as well as to individuals. Where God is the other, silence is the performance of stubborn pride or of a spirit struck dumb for fear of being found out. It is the way of Adam hiding from the presence. In the silence every affliction and problem takes the form of the judgment of God: "Thy hand was heavy upon me." Worst of all, the silence is the rejection of grace.

c. Confession of sin must be said to God. Secret remorse, counseling with the self, or intimations of guilt are not confession. The silence must be broken in the presence of the other. Again by triple synonymous statements the psalm emphasizes that confession happens only when it is spoken to the other: "I acknowledged to you . . . I did not hide . . . I said, I will confess to the LORD" (v. 5). The indivisible unity is "I confess—you forgive." The basis of this necessary sequence is the role of faith. Confession is the knocking to which the door opens, the seeking that finds, the asking that receives. Confession of sin to God is confession of faith in God. It is the action of trust that God is a God who keeps covenant (v. 10*b*). It is language about God as well as self. If we say we have no sin, we not only deceive ourselves but we make him a liar, who is faithful and just and will forgive our sins (I John 1:8–10). Faith is not like the horse and mule without understanding (v. 9); faith understands that we are sinners and God is gracious.

3. The psalm warns that confession of sin must be made with integrity. Its second beatitude adds the qualification "in whose spirit there is no deceit" (v. 2). Because the confession of sin is the act of a sinner, it can be sinful. God is not deceived, but the sinner may deceive himself. Three times in his comment on this psalm Augustine warns "Do not claim the right to the kingdom on the grounds of your own justice, nor the right to sin on the grounds of God's mercy" (30/62-4). That is, do not

let the confession of sin become a work of your rightness, nor
an easy presumption on God's forgiveness. Both ways are deceit. Augustine and Luther and Calvin and Barth all take their
cue from Paul (Rom. 4:7–8) and in their interpretation of the
psalm do not tire of insisting that confession of sin is in no
respect a work of our righteousness; it is faith, pure faith, that
brings no righteousness of its own. The righteousness received
in forgiveness comes because "The LORD imputes no iniquity"
(v. 2). On the other hand, the practice of repentance can
become so routine, inconsequential, shallow, lacking in real
seriousness, wanting no sanctification that it is a presumption on
the mercy of God and a belief in cheap grace. "The sacrifice
acceptable to God is a broken spirit" (51:17). For the Christian,
the cure for deceit comes by keeping the crucified Christ in
view as God's judgment on and pardon of our sin.

Psalm 33: Rejoice in the LORD, O You Righteous

Psalm 33 is a hymn of praise with a specific purpose. It
proclaims the LORD as the one in whom the righteous may
place their trust and hope. The purpose is evident in the rather
didactic style of most of the hymn (vv. 6–19) and in its concluding profession of trust (vv. 20–21) and prayer (v. 22). It praises
the God whom the righteous trust—therein lies their rightness,
that they trust the LORD. At the same time, it teaches and
encourages trust and hope by describing the LORD as the one
who can be trusted.

1. The psalm begins following the form of the imperative
hymn (Introduction, sec. 5.5.4). Verses 1–3 are a prolonged call
to praise, and verses 4–5 state the basis and content of the
praise. In verses 6–19 the praise is developed and expanded by
the use of a variety of styles and topics. The LORD is praised as
God of heaven and earth (vv. 6–9), of nations and peoples
(vv. 10–12), of human beings (vv. 13–15), and finally of those
who fear him (vv. 16–19). Then in conclusion the righteous who
fear the LORD assert their trust (vv. 20–21) and pray that the
LORD's steadfast love will vindicate their hope (v. 22).

The number of poetic lines is the same as the number of
letters in the Hebrew alphabet. That is undoubtedly intentional
on the part of the poet. It is a clue that the psalm is meant to
be as complete and comprehensive in covering its subject as the
alphabet is in listing the letters. This concern about comprehen-

148

siveness is apparent in other ways, for example, in the way in which terms are compiled in verses 1–5 and the delineation of the four spheres over which the LORD rules in the body of the hymn. This is a hymn composed for use as praise and for teaching about the God who is praised.

2. In the call to praise (vv. 1–3), the vocabulary for worship with music is nearly exhausted. This is the first reference to the use of instruments in the canonical order of the psalms, and so it has been the textual occasion in traditional commentary for a discussion of the propriety and validity of the use of instruments in worship. In the history of culture, music was originally a sacred performance. In our time, the problem of deciding whether certain kinds of music created outside the religious sphere are appropriate for worship often vexes those who plan liturgy. For the psalmist and his world, it was praise that gave rise to music and formed it and controlled it. Where that can authentically be the case, music of all kinds is the most exquisite and complete form of praise. For those who are right with the LORD, a hymn of praise is "seemly" (NRSV, "befits"; NJPS "fits," so v. 1; see 147:1). There is an implicit theology of music here; it must be authentically the praise of the LORD and offered by those who are right with the LORD. The why and the who are crucial.

In the basis for praise, terms are again piled up, five of the most-used words to describe the way of the LORD: upright, faithfulness, righteousness, justice, and steadfast love (see Introduction, sec. 6.8). Here these terms are applied to the word and work of the LORD; the two go together, as verse 6 shows. The work is accomplished by the word. The psalmist thinks with a theology of the word as the consummate instrument of the LORD in his works. In the arrangement of the characteristics of the LORD's word and work, steadfast love comes last. The earth, says the hymn, is full (not of the glory of the LORD, as in Isa. 6:3) of the *hesed* of the LORD!

3. This statement is the pivot on which the psalm turns. The rest of the psalm will expound its meaning. The LORD is God over all, the sole sovereign of every sphere of reality— world, nations, humanity, and the community of those who fear the LORD. So the righteous who live in the world in the midst of the nations as a community in need of salvation trust in and pray for the *hesed* of the LORD.

The LORD is God of the world, creator of the heavens (v. 6)

149

and the earth (v. 9). Both are the work of his word, the result of his command. He put the primeval oceans in their place (v. 7; see 24:2). The poet thinks with Genesis 1. To dwell in the world is to live and move and have being in the sphere of the word of God. The only way truly to know the world is to fear the LORD, that is, to have the LORD as God. The psalm does not consider the world in and of itself to be a revelation of the LORD; the psalm is not an expression of a natural theology (see Psalm 19). Rather, it summons all to fear the LORD as God in the light of God's revelation to Israel (v. 8).

The LORD is God over the nations (vv. 10–12). Nations and peoples act out policies and plans that guide their participation in what we moderns call history. Their designs are the expression of their sense of their identity, destiny, and power. The question of whose "counsel" prevails is at root the question of whose sovereignty is to govern the world. Isaiah and others in the Isaiah tradition declared in specific crises of Israel's history that the LORD's counsel and plans will prevail (Isa. 8:10; 46:10). The psalmist says that it belongs to the way of the LORD to frustrate the design of nations who set out to make themselves the center of the world and to order its peoples to their design. The clue to what is going on in history is to be found in that "nation" whose God is the LORD, because the LORD has chosen it as his own possession. Such a nation does not have its own counsel and designs but lives out a plan that serves the sovereignty of the LORD. No nation can itself decide to play that role based on its own sense of destiny or character. The role itself must depend on the election of God to be the social group possessed in their purposes and plans by the LORD. The question for Israel was whether "the LORD is our God in truth." That is the question for every elect community in history.

The LORD is God over human beings (vv. 13–15). He created their minds and understands what they do. From the vantage of the heavenly throne he "sees" all human beings, a mythopoeic way of saying that the consciousness of the LORD comprehends every person (11:4; 14:2; 102:20). In other texts, this all-knowing surveillance by God implies accountability, warning, and comfort. Here it is stated simply as a fact of the godship of the LORD. That God is means that every human life is known. There is ultimately no isolation or secrecy. The LORD is praised as the one to whom our lives are ever present.

The LORD is God of salvation (vv. 16–19). When death

150

threatens and life is at stake the question about help arises. The psalmist knows the proclamation of Isaiah 45:20–25 that only the LORD saves, because he alone is God. He makes the point by contrasting the vanity of depending on the very strongest of human resources with the care of the LORD for those who fear him. The issue is not whether one does whatever one can to face threats but, rather, in what one places ultimate trust and hope. The psalmist's term for having the LORD as God is "to fear the LORD," and that means to make his steadfast love one's ultimate hope.

4. The reflection on hope and salvation leads into the concluding assertion of hope and prayer for the LORD's *hesed* (vv. 20–22). The psalm thus leads those who praise the LORD as God to the confession and petition that confirm that praise in a stance of life composed of trust and hope.

The psalm as a whole expresses in language the theological vision of reality that belongs to the worshiping community. Our normal way of thinking is to divide the world into distinct spheres, each with its own separate features and laws. We think in terms of nature, history, individual psychology, and religion. The psalm sees behind the various dimensions of reality the comprehending actuality of the sovereign LORD whose being as God comprehends and controls them all.

Psalm 34: O Taste and See

Psalm 34 is in many respects a companion of Psalm 25. Both are acrostic poems whose poetic lines begin with letters of the Hebrew alphabet in order. In both, the letter *waw* is omitted and a final line beyond the alphabetic sequence is added to make twenty-two lines. Psalm 25 employs the liturgical form of a prayer for help and Psalm 34 the form of thanksgiving for help, but in both the instructional function dominates. In Psalm 34 the element of witness to others in the song of thanksgiving has developed into a teaching mode. The psalm is a general thanksgiving that gives instruction in the theology of both phases of psalmic prayer: the cry for help and thankful praise for help. It gives the impression of a song composed "as an institutionalized, regular act of offering thanks to the LORD (Gerstenberger, p. 147). On the song of thanksgiving and the acrostic poem, see Introduction, secs. 5.3; 5.6.2, respectively).

The learned scribe who searched the Books of Samuel for

151

connections between David's life and the psalms found a relation between verse 8 and a word in I Samuel 21:13 that is not apparent in translation. The king in the story in Samuel is named Achish, while the title calls him Abimelech. See Psalm 3, sec. 4.

The psalm begins with an invocation of praise from the singer and the congregation who are named the lowly, the people who live in trust and dependence on the LORD (vv. 1–3). The report of deliverance is given in verse 4, and its implications are drawn in the form of exhortations, statements, and a beatitude in verses 4–10. Then an outright invitation to learn the fear of the LORD (v. 11) is followed by instruction about it (vv. 12–14) and about the relation between the fear of the LORD and prayer and deliverance (vv. 15–22).

The liturgical and instructional spheres and functions are brought together in this psalm in a way that affects both. Important qualifications of the understanding of prayer are made through the introduction of themes and concerns that belong to teachers of wisdom and prophets. These themes and concerns are in turn affected by the liturgical setting in which they are placed.

1. In verse 11 a teacher exhorts "sons," that is, students, to listen to his teaching, and he names a subject, "the fear of the LORD." Then he proceeds to give the instruction in verses 12–14. His topic is ethics. The question addressed is how to fulfill the desire for life. The answer is the practice of the fear of the LORD by the avoidance of evil in speech and deed and the doing of good in pursuit of the peace or welfare of others. The outcome, only implied here, will be a long and satisfying life. The style, topic, question, instruction, and promise are all characteristic of the Book of Proverbs and the instruction given there (e.g., Prov. 1:7, 8, 29; 3:1–2; 4:1). Here the psalm is setting forth the wisdom about the way things work that those who desire life need to know.

2. This instruction is set alongside another way of speaking about the fear of the LORD, using verb and participle instead of noun (vv. 7, 9). Those who fear the LORD are identified by other designations that are principally at home in the liturgical sphere: the righteous (vv. 15, 17, 19, 21), the lowly (v. 6), the one who takes refuge in the LORD (vv. 8, 22). In all these verses the topic is prayer. The question addressed is set by the troubles that beset life (vv. 6, 17, 19). The answer is the cry to the LORD,

modeled in the report in verse 4, and commended repeatedly
(vv. 5–6, 10, 15, 17–18). The promised outcome is the deliverance of the LORD (vv. 17–20). Here the psalm is setting forth
faith in the efficaciousness of prayer and in the God who guarantees its efficaciousness (especially vv. 15, 17, 6).

3. The hermeneutical interaction between the two forms
of instruction gives an ethical dimension to liturgical practice.
It is not enough simply to be the needy who cry to the LORD
when they are in trouble. It is the God-fearers who have already
made the LORD the basis and guide for the conduct of life
around whom the angel of the LORD sets up a protecting camp
(v. 7). The psalm is in this way making the same point that the
prophets have made about Israel's cult. Seeking the LORD in
supplication is not to be separated from loving good, hating evil,
and seeking *shalom* (cf. v. 14 and Amos 5:15). "Not everyone
who says to me, 'Lord, Lord' . . . but he who does the will of my
Father" (Matt. 7:21).

4. On the other hand, the interaction keeps the truth of
ethical instruction from being understood in simplistic, me-
chanical, and dogmatic fashion. It is not the case that those who
do good live good, not in any immediate and uncomplicated
sense. The psalm says it plainly: "Many are the afflictions of the
righteous" (v. 19a). Those who have learned the fear of the
LORD are not exempt from overwhelming troubles. The ethical
life must be lived as the prayerful life. It is to the broken of heart
and the crushed of spirit, to those who know that they cannot
help themselves or base their lives on how they live, that the
LORD is near (v. 18; cf. 51:17; Isa. 57:15; 61:1).

5. The psalm holds the two dimensions together as essen-
tials of biblical faith. Neither can be surrendered, because God
is holy and loving. It is true that avoidance of evil and love of
good makes for life. It is true that the LORD delivers the righteous who call on him in all of their troubles. Merit and need,
reward and salvation are structures of the relation between
God and human beings. Faith lives in terms of both without
ever reaching an easy equivalence and leaves the working out
of it all to God.

The line in the psalm that has drawn the most attention
through the years is the exhortation to "Taste and see that the
LORD is good." "Taste" is used here in the sense of "find out by
experience." What does this unusual and daring admonition
mean? In the context of the psalm it can only be a proposal that

one try out the pursuit of peace and the practice of prayer as the way to open living to the LORD's gift of life through his reward and his salvation.

Psalm 35: You Deliver the Weak

1. Psalm 35 is a long complex prayer for help in first person singular style. On the type, see Introduction, sec. 5.2. The principal elements of the type are repeated in cycles. Petition for the LORD's help and prayer against enemies are combined in a way that shows how closely related the two are (vv. 1–8, 17–21, 22–26). Where the hostility of adversaries was the reason for prayer, the disqualification and removal of the hostility seemed the only possible resolution in the religious and social world of Israel. Here the adversaries are the trouble (vv. 11–16, 7, 20). The prayer makes vows of praise to be given when the adversaries are put to shame (vv. 9–10, 18). It concludes with a request that the petitioner's deliverance be the basis of praise for his supporters and himself (vv. 27–28).

2. The prayer was composed for the typical situation in which a person needed vindication because of the damaging hostility of others. Its language draws on a variety of social settings and images. The enemies, for instance, are portrayed as armed foes (v. 1), hunters (vv. 7–8), malicious witnesses in a court trial (v. 11; is this a real clue to the trouble?), a mocking mob (vv. 15–16), and lions (v. 17). There seems to be a plea of innocence in the report that the petitioner has in the past shown solidarity with these adversaries when they were in grievous trouble (vv. 12–16). Not only is their hostility without cause (v. 7); they pay him back evil for good. The petitioner is in the right and appeals to the righteousness of God for vindication (v. 24), perhaps in the form of a verdict given as an oracle to the petitioner: "I am your salvation" (quoted in v. 3). In one of the narratives about David (I Samuel 24), Saul is the "pursuer" (see v. 3 of the psalm) and David prays in Saul's presence for the LORD to judge between them, to plead his cause, and deliver him, using the language of the petitions in the psalm (compare I Sam. 24:14–15 with Ps. 35:1, 3, 23–24). The narrative setting is a clue to the kind of situation for which the psalm is composed; the psalm is a formal version of David's impromptu prayer designed for rituals at a shrine.

3. Whatever the uncertainty about the cultic setting of the

154

prayer, there are two points at which its theological setting is clearly declared. Both declarations are hymnic portions of praise anticipating the response the petitioner will make to God's deliverance. The first is the praise of the LORD's incomparability as the God who rescues the lowly and needy (*'ani* and *'ebyon*) from the stronger one who uses his superiority to rob the lowly of the justice due them (v. 10). On the motif of incomparability, see Psalm 113:5; on the strong who rob the lowly of their right, cf. Isa. 10:2; Prov. 22:22. That is the scenario enacted in the prayer. The enemies are the strong; the petitioner is the lowly one; it is up to the LORD to intervene to restore the right (*mishpat*) of the petitioner (v. 23). The second declaration is the praise of the greatness of the LORD whose sovereign good pleasure is the *shalom* of his servant (v. 27). The adversaries have destroyed the *shalom* of the petitioner, that wholeness of self with others and God which belongs to the good and normal state of life. The petitioner makes his plea in the role of the servant of a king whose interest and responsibility it is to protect and provide for the *shalom* of his servants. These declarations have an importance beyond the context of Psalm 35. They are nuclear statements of the theology that informs all of the prayers in the Psalter (see Introduction, secs. 6.16, 19).

Psalm 36: In Your Light We See Light

"These are some of the most wonderful words in the Old Testament. Their fulness of meaning no commentary can ever exhaust" (Perowne, 1:282). Similar remarks about Psalm 36 are scattered through the history of psalm interpretation. These wondering estimates of the psalm's profundity are based primarily on the praise of the LORD in verses 5–8 and particularly on the declaration of verse 9 on which the praise is based: "With you is the source of life; in your light we see light."

As verses 10–11 show, the psalm is a prayer for help. The prayer has three parts: a description of the wicked (vv. 1–4), praise of the LORD (vv. 5–9), and petitions (vv. 10–12).

1. The wicked are described by portrayal of their character as a type. The portrayal functions as the description of trouble from which the petitions seek deliverance. The trouble does not come from some one evil person or group who threatens the one who prays. The trouble lies, rather, in the very brave and bold reality and character of the wicked. At the center of their

155

character is a basic orientation. In their secret hearts they listen to the oracle of rebellion. As a consequence it is on the self and its deceitful autonomy rather than on the fear of God that their attention is fixed. From a consciousness oriented to self instead of to God come deceiving words and evil deeds. Wrong becomes a habit and a commitment. Character is set. It is not surprising that Paul draws on this description in arguing the power of sin; in Romans 3:18 he quotes verse 1, in which "transgression" seems to be personified. But in the psalm it is the character of the wicked that drives one to prayer. For the psalmist, evil is not an abstraction, or only one judgment about things, or merely a value rooted in one way of viewing things. It is the very shape that the character of the wicked assumes. That the wicked are, and are what they are, is a threatening reality in the world in which the faithful live. To ignore that reality would mean blindness to the situation of faith.

2. To the character of the wicked the psalm contrasts the character of the LORD. The section of praise describes the LORD's character in the direct address of prayer. The description functions in the prayer as the confession of trust. The praise speaks first of the greatness of God (vv. 5–6) and then of human dependence on God (vv. 7–9). The two principal pairs of attributes of the LORD are said to be cosmic in dimension. Heavens and clouds mark the upper limit of the world; mountains of God and the great deep are terms of immensity. The attributes are loving-kindness and faithfulness (the LORD's firm reliability in his care for those to whom he is related) and righteousness and justice (the LORD's vindication of those who depend on him and follow his way). Israel had come to know these attributes in its history with the LORD (Introduction, sec. 6.8). They were manifest most of all in his saving activity. But here the psalmist speaks of them as manifest in God's salvation of all living things—man and beast—and by salvation means God's ongoing providential care by which he preserves life; verse 9 is anticipated; the life of man and beast depends on the LORD. The thought is quite similar to Psalm 104. This is the first part of the psalm's answer to the character of the wicked—the knowledge of the God who holds the whole world in his hand. The irony of it! The wicked who has no fear of God is himself incorporated in the great system of divine providential care.

156

In verses 7–9 the praise is concentrated on the loving-kindness, the *hesed,* of God, the characteristic above all others to which the prayer psalms appeal (note v. 10). God's *hesed* is manifest in the way in which humankind depend on God's saving help: he provides shelter (v. 7*b*), food (v. 8*a*), and drink (v. 8*b*), and so is the source of life (v. 9). The language of these verses is highly allusive and symbolic, carrying several levels of reference held together in a rich interplay of meaning that outruns any one explanation. On one level the language refers to the ministry provided through the worship of the temple— the house of the LORD, the sanctuary provided for those who take refuge there, the food and drink of sacrificial rituals. On another level the language refers to shelter, food, and drink, the necessities that support physical and social life. The psalmist is describing a provision for all humankind, not just Israel. On yet another level the language connotes a communion with God that transcends the experience of liturgy and providence. "The shade of your wings," "the richness of your house," and "your river of delights" (is the name "Eden" hidden in the word for delights, *'adanim*?) are symbolic of a personal proximity to God that relates fragile finite human beings to the divine. It is this receiving from God that occurs in complex and related ways— through common life, liturgy, and the inner world of the spirit—that the psalm seeks to describe. The language expresses the profound perception of the one who sees the inner unity of all the ways life is received from God. The effect is very much like that of the complex images of Psalm 23, especially verses 5–6.

Verse 9 sums up the account of human dependence on God in two related sentences: "For with you is the source of life; in your light we see light." The first sentence confesses the faith that founds all of Israel's prayers. Life as existence, as full and good living, as community, as restoration—life in every sense is the gift of the LORD. The source of life is "with him" (on the sense of this prepositional phrase, see the comment on Psalm 130). Wherever there is life, there is a receiving from the source. Again the irony! The wicked are related to the source. God sends his rain on the just and on the unjust (Matt. 5:45). The mysteriously redundant second sentence plays with two meanings of the metaphor "light." It can be reworded as "By your favor [the light of your face] we experience salvation [light as opposite of dark times]." But the rewording is less than the original whose redundancy contains mysteries that will be contemplated again and again by those who use the psalm.

3. The plural "we" shows that a community speaks, not some one individual about a private mystic revelation. They "see" what the wicked do not, and it is their prayer, corporately (v. 10) and individually (v. 11), that concludes the psalm. As those who know the LORD and whose hearts are upright in confessing their dependence on the LORD, they ask that the LORD's *hesed* rather than the power of the wicked determine their present and future. The prayer concludes in the confidence that "there," that is, where the *hesed* of the LORD continues, the wicked will in the end be impotent and of no importance.

This psalm, then, is a prayer that may be prayed by those who have seen light in the light of the LORD and know him through the revelation of his loving-kindness. In the face of the threatening shape that evil takes in the character of the wicked, this prayer rehearses and renews the vision of existence as a great system of grace. The light shines in darkness and the darkness does not put it out. The illumination of faith is itself a gift of life, because faith understands that life comes from God and how God gives life.

4. In the New Testament the symbols of light and food and drink are used to speak of the life that comes in and through Jesus Christ. "In him was life, and the life was the light of men" (John 1:4). "I am the bread of life" (John 6:35). "The water that I give him will become in him a spring of water welling up to eternal life" (John 4:14). Because of that witness Christians understand that the "source of life" that is "with God" is Jesus Christ and they think of the service and sacraments as presence and participation represented by the symbols of verses 7–8. It is in this way that the psalm is read when it is used as the proper psalm for Monday of Holy Week.

Psalm 37: The Meek Shall Inherit the Earth

This is a pastoral psalm. It offers counsel about a perennial question. What will the members of the religious community take as the decisive clue to the way life should be lived? Will it be the prosperity and power of the wicked or the providence of God? The choice is between the pressures of the present and the promise of the future. The choice is between faith and no faith. It is important to describe the fundamental point of the

158

psalm in this way. The psalm has often been read as advocacy of a doctrinaire moralism that believes evil is punished and good rewarded in some kind of deterministic, simplicistic way. There are lines in the psalm that, taken by themselves, may seem to invite such a reading. The whole and all that is said must be considered (Introduction, sec. 5.6).

1. The psalm is an acrostic poem, that is, a poem composed of the scheme of the Hebrew alphabet. In Psalm 37 there are two poetic lines to a letter, the first line beginning with the appropriate letter of the alphabet. The alphabet provides the primary structure of the psalm. When one reads it in Hebrew, one can notice at places how the poet has had to work to find a word that begins with the needed letter. The poem does begin in the imperative mood (vv. 1–9) and then shifts to the indicative for the rest of the psalm predominantly. Exhortation about the wrong way and the right way to respond to the success of the wicked is given in verses 1–9; in this imperative section all the related themes of the poem are stated and repeated. The rest of the poem is a sequence of variations on the themes. The indicative section introduces further statements to elaborate the themes. The poem is composed of negative and positive exhortations (e.g., vv. 1, 3), proverbial sentences of different styles (e.g., vv. 16, 12–13), and reflective observations (e.g., vv. 35–36), types of material collected in the Book of Proverbs. The psalm uses the forms and substance of theological wisdom to instruct the congregation. The contrast and conflict between the wicked and the righteous form its basic rubric. See the comment on Psalm 1, sec. 3; and compare Psalms 11 and 12.

2. The psalm addresses a specific spiritual predicament. It is not a sequence of abstract general statements. It reaches out to offer nurture in a situation in which keeping the faith is difficult. The addressees of the imperatives at the psalm's beginning are not spoken to as the self-confident righteous. They are people who are in danger of falling into frustrated envious vexation and even destructive anger (vv. 1, 7, 8). They are bewildered by the incongruence between faith and experience. Their consciousness has been captured by the success of people who do not follow the way of the LORD. If they dwell on this provocation, their whole mood of life will become bitter and uncertain. The teacher knows that this is a real possibility for the religious. In the exhortations he warns them and invites

them to another way. In the descriptions of the LORD's way with the righteous and the wicked, he seeks to persuade them to hold to this other way.

3. The problem people are the wicked. In the vocabulary of the psalms and wisdom, the term is a theological-moral category. Its necessity derives from faith in God and knowledge of the way of God. The wickedness of the wicked lies first of all in their enmity toward God (v. 20), which is evident in their autonomous way of life. They follow a way that is their own and pursue their own schemes (vv. 7, 16, 35). That puts them in opposition to the righteous (v. 12). If they have to afflict the poor and needy to achieve their goals, they do it (vv. 14, 32). They are not wicked because they are wealthy but wealthy because they are wicked. The scandal to the spirit of the faithful is that the wicked enjoy success. Power and prosperity are generated better by autonomy than discipleship. The teacher of this psalm recognizes that God's sovereignty allows for the wicked and their success. They are very real, and the problem they pose is very searching. On the category "wicked," see the comment on Psalm 1, sec. 3.

4. The teacher's counsel to the perplexed is based on the belief in God that lies at the foundation of the law and the prophets. The LORD is sovereign. His power is not put in question by those who go their own way; "The LORD laughs at the wicked" (v. 13; cf. 2:4). "The LORD loves justice" (v. 28), so ways of life that contradict justice and righteousness are founded alone on the finitude of human beings who live for themselves. The LORD is faithful to his faithful (vv. 28, 17, 18, 33); their life is founded in the one whose way is the foundation of the universe.

5. It is on the basis of this certain belief that the teacher gives his counsel. He gives it in two ways, by exhortation and description of the righteous. Together these two forms of counsel sketch a piety of the righteous. Righteousness is first of all trust, delighting in the LORD as the prime source of joy and peace in living, committing one's way to the LORD, making faith a refuge against the threats and problems of life (vv. 3–5, 39–40). Trust issues in conduct that follows the way of the LORD (vv. 3, 27). Trust structures the consciousness with wisdom and justice in the law of the LORD (vv. 30–31). Faced with the problems that the present time poses, trust "waits in the stillness of patience for the LORD"; the righteous live in hope

(vv. 7, 34) in the time of trouble (v. 39); notice that the teacher gives his listeners the same counsel that the prophet gave the community of exiles in Babylon (Isa. 40:31; 42:23). The teacher proposes no explanations based on psychology or sociology. He commends only the stance that is based on the knowledge of God.

6. Instead of explanations, the teacher gives reassurances and promises unfolded out of his theology. Faith must "wait on the LORD" who disposes of time and what happens in it. The sovereignty of God is not contained within a person's contemporaneity. Instead, time is contained within the divine sovereignty. Note the references to time and statements about the destiny of the wicked (vv. 2, 10, 13, 36). In time the wicked will have "their day" of reckoning. The teacher seems to have thought of that day as being as near as early Christians thought the Parousia was. His estimate of the schedule may be incomplete, but his ultimate judgment is as true as his theology. Repeatedly the teacher assures the perplexed that the wicked are temporary and unsubstantial (vv. 2, 10, 20, 35–36; see 1:4). They are no more real and permanent than the finite self on which their way is based. They have no future; only the "peaceable" have a future (vv. 37–38; "future" with NJPS instead of "posterity" with NRSV). The teacher's testimony to what he has observed himself about the destiny of the righteous (v. 25) and the wicked (vv. 35–36) is a conventional way of saying what he believes. Both statements may have been empirically correct for him, but they can't be meant as generalizations for everybody's experience. The whole poem assumes that the faithful know trouble and need. When the teacher speaks of the future of the righteous, he uses one theme repeatedly. The righteous (those who wait for the LORD, the meek, the blessed) "shall inherit/possess the land" (vv. 3, 9, 11, 18, 22, 29, 34). They will realize the promise to Abraham (Gen. 15:7; see the comment on Psalm 105). Inheriting the land as the sphere and possibility for a life of blessing and peace is not so much a reward; rather, the purpose of God is fulfilled in the life of the righteous in the land. The theme has risen to the level of the symbolic. It is not the nation Israel but the Israel of faith that has a future in the reign of God. The ground is laid for the teacher of the beatitudes, who will say, "The meek shall inherit the earth" (Matt. 5:5).

161

Psalm 38: No Soundness in My Flesh

Psalm 38 is a prayer for help composed for use by the sick. On the type, see Introduction, sec. 5.2. Like Psalm 6, it begins with the petition, "LORD, do not rebuke me in your anger, nor chastise me in your wrath." Like Psalm 6, it is one of the traditional penitential psalms used during Lent and Holy Week. On sickness as the occasion for prayer; see the following excursus, and on the theological interpretation of prayers of the sick, see the comment on Psalm 6.

Psalm 38 has twenty-two lines, the number of letters in the Hebrew alphabet. Its language and agenda are formulaic and typical. These features show that the psalm is a carefully composed prayer rather than an impromptu utterance. But the composer's skill has captured and expressed the anguished predicament of those for whom it was prepared. The prayer is a compelling illustration of the way sickness is viewed in the psalms—not as a clinical phenomenon but as a personal experience. The subject is not sickness but being sick.

1. First, being sick has a theological dimension. Here being sick is understood as correcting chastisement brought by the LORD in wrath because of the folly of sins committed by the one who prays (vv. 1–5). No particular sin is named; general terms are used to leave the prayer open to whoever uses it. Confession of sin is made in the form of a declaration of guilt (v. 18); the confession justifies God's wrath and at the same time moves from the human side toward reconciliation. On the importance of confession of sin, see Psalms 39:1–3 and 32:5.

2. Second, being sick has physical and psychological dimensions. Verses 3–10 compile a comprehensive list of bodily and mental afflictions all experienced as a loss of soundness or wholeness and health in the body (vv. 3, 7). Existence is threatened; the powers of life are nearly exhausted (vv. 10, 17). Being sick reduces one to the identity of the lowly ('ani) who is helpless in the face of greater hostile powers and dependent on the salvation of God (vv. 21–22; see the comment on the title of Psalm 102).

3. Third, being sick has consequences in both groups who make up the pattern of social relationships. The inner circle of kin and friends withdraw from the afflicted (v. 11). The outer circle of the hostile take the illness as an opportunity to prevail

(v. 12). Because he is smitten by God the afflicted makes no response to his detractors (vv. 13–14; see 39:9). Bereft of any human support, he waits on the answer of the LORD to his prayer (vv. 15–16). But any guilt or wrong against the adversaries is specifically denied; their hostility is unjustified. The confessed sin is against the LORD alone (cf. the comment on Ps. 51:4). The two responses of withdrawal and hostility remind us of the enduring instinct for avoiding the afflicted and blaming them for their suffering.

4. How did this prayer for salvation from sin and sickness come to be used as an individual and corporate penitential prayer in the church? The shift to this use undoubtedly began in Old Testament times. The prophets used the language of sickness to describe the condition of Israel suffering judgment for its sin (e.g., Isa. 1:5–6). The individual who laments the affliction of Judah under judgment in Lamentations 3 employs motifs found in Psalm 38 (cf. Lam. 3:1–15). As part of a book of Scripture the psalm was used for reading and liturgy in the early synagogues. The title specifies a use for the psalm with a word the meaning of which is uncertain. The Greek version identifies it as a psalm for the Sabbath, showing that it was in regular liturgical use. Christians continued this corporate liturgical use, understanding its language of bodily affliction as a metaphorical depiction of our condition as sinners.

EXCURSUS

Sickness and Sin in the Psalms

Psalm 38 makes a direct connection between sin and sickness and understands the sickness as the effect of God's wrath. Because the language of corporal suffering is used to describe a variety of troubles, we cannot be sure whether certain psalms that use the language were written for the sick. But the connection seems to be drawn in a number of other places in the psalms (6:1; 32:3–5; 39:10–11; 41:4; 88:7, 16; 107:17–22; perhaps in the sequence in 103:3). The connection raises troubling pastoral and theological problems. Perhaps that is why Psalms 6; 38; 39; and 88 are not selections in the Common Lectionary for

p. 60

Sunday use. Here are some matters that may be considered in the interpretation and use of these psalms.

1. The connection between sin and sickness is made in prayers prepared for particular people under certain kinds of conditions. The prayers do not make general universal statements that all sickness is punishment for specific sins. Those who used these prayers would do so out of their own sense of need or would be guided to their use by prophet or priest or other official counselor.

2. The faith of the psalmists concentrated on the LORD as the one divine power with which life had to reckon. Nothing in life was left outside the scope of the LORD's providence, and no other God or superhuman power or demon (Psalm 91) was considered. The divine purpose in affliction might be correction, instruction, purification, or vicarious suffering as well as punishment. These psalms reflect that concentration and treat sickness as a religious as well as a clinical matter.

3. The belief that God's wrath at human sin takes effect in negative ways on human life is common to Old Testament and New Testament. But these psalms as a particular expression of that belief are appealing to God's prior will that human beings be healthy and whole. Psalm 38 offers no other reason than the confession of sin and the loss of wholeness and health as a basis for appeal to "my God."

4. When these prayers are read and understood in the context of the whole of Scripture the confession of sin may refer to the sinful condition of every human being. Sickness is not correlated with some specific sin of the person who prays; rather, it is the condition that brings to light in a special way our sinfulness and need of grace. "The one aspect which dominates the field in the Old and New Testament Scriptures . . . is the one in which sickness is a forerunner and messenger of death, and indeed of death as the judgment of God and the merited subjection of man to the power of nothingness in virtue of his sin" (Barth, III/4, p. 366).

5. The Book of Job is an eloquent protest against the dogma of a necessary connection between the affliction of a particular person and guilt.

6. In the Gospels, Jesus' acts of healing the sick are signs of the kingdom of God in which Satan and death are defeated. Jesus distinguished forgiveness and healing but held them together as part of being made whole (Mark 2:1–12). Jesus carries

out the will of the LORD that the sick be forgiven and restored. The prayers of the sinful sick may be read as appeals to God in his name.

7. These psalms must not be interpreted and used in such a way as to cause despair in the conscience of those who are afflicted or self-righteousness in those who are well. The psalms combat and deny despair. "For thee, O LORD, do I wait; it is thou, O LORD my God, who will answer" (38:15). And they accuse all who withdraw and lack compassion and all who find any self-satisfaction in the affliction of another (38:4–12). See Seybold and Mueller; and Barth, III/4, pp. 356ff.

Psalm 39: I Am Your Passing Guest

Psalm 39 is a strange prayer. It has the principal features of the prayer for help in first person singular style. It includes petitions to be heard and helped (vv. 12–13 and 8, 10) and descriptions of the trouble that is the occasion of the prayer (in vv. 8–13). The one who prays suffers from an affliction that is understood as a "blow" from the LORD to chastise for transgression (vv. 8, 10, 11). The death of the one who prays is in prospect (vv. 10, 13). The prayer seems to be a penitential supplication of one who is grievously ill. See Introduction, sec. 5.2; and "Excursus on Sickness and Sin" in the comment on Psalm 38. But the suffering is portrayed less as a case of personal and social affliction (contrast Psalm 38) and more as a matter of the general human predicament of transience and futility. The whole prayer is pervaded with a melancholy about the human condition. This is not the prayer of one who has lost the health and joy of life lived in the blessing of the LORD and asks to be returned to that good life. Rather, it sees human existence itself as a predicament of which the present suffering is an intensification.

The prayer begins with a report that the sufferer has passed through a period when he observed the discipline of silence (vv. 1–3). He had tried the way of patiently bearing affliction as the chastisement of the LORD (see v. 9, which should be translated in the past tense). During that time he had not given the wicked any encouragement by impious questioning of the LORD's righteousness or ability to help (37:7). The report introduces the prayer by giving a reason why it should be heard.

After this introduction the theme of the brevity and in-

165

security of life is sounded and repeated in all three parts of the lament (the beginning of each part is marked by a vocative LORD, vv. 4, 7, 12). The request to learn how long he has to live is hardly a request for information; it is, rather, a rhetorical form of lament that he senses his time is up (vv. 4–5a). This lament about God's abbreviation of his own life is followed by a lament over the transience and futility of all human life in the form of a sequence of observations introduced by "surely" that sound like Job and Ecclesiastes. The general lament seems intended to reinforce the personal one as the basis for the petitions to be heard and helped. See the transience motif as the topic of lament in Psalm 90; Job 7:7–10; 14:1–12; and Isa. 40:6–8. Notice that the transience common to all the ancestors is also basis for the petition in verse 12. The only statement of confidence in the prayer (v. 7) is introduced by the protesting question, "And now, Lord, what is there for me to wait on," seeing that life is short and you have made mine shorter? His hope is in the God who has made human existence finite and futile and his own existence tortured and tenuous. The concluding petition is not "Save, draw near, be with me," but "Look away from me" (v. 13; so Job in 10:20–21; 14:1–6). Please leave me alone, that I may have some relief and a bit more of life. The occupation with the general and particular transience of human existence is so pervasive that it seems to overshadow and absorb the problem of sin. The prayer never, in fact, makes an explicit declaration of sin; rather, it simply assents to the understanding that sin is the cause of the "stroke" that has affected life. Compare Psalm 90.

Who is it that prays like this? It is the person who sees his own predicament only in the context of the general human predicament and thinks of God only as the ultimate reality who sets limits against sin and life. The mood and the view of this prayer are always a possibility for us; it has its partial truth and corresponds to a way we may see self and world and God. The psalmist in a marvelous and telling phrase identifies himself to God as "your resident alien and sojourner" (v. 12), originally the term for a social category, the alien allowed to reside in another people's territory without the rights that belong to permanent residents (Gen. 23:4). In a divine saying given in Levitical instruction the term is used as a metaphor to characterize Israel's residence in the land: "You are alien residents and sojourners with me" (Lev. 25:23). The psalmist in yet one more move has applied the metaphor to life in the world. In the prayer made at the end of his life David uses the very words of Psalm 39:12 and shows how differently the identity of "resident alien with God" is structured when all the blessings of the salvation history are in view (I Chron. 29:15). In Hebrews 11:13 and I Peter 2:11 the metaphor is used for Christians, and in the contexts the difference made by the hope of resurrection to eternal life transforms the prospects of those who know that they, like the fathers, are no more than passing guests and sojourners in this world.

Psalm 40: I Delight to Do Your Will

Psalm 40 contains a number of striking literary and theological features. Verses 13–17 reappear as Psalm 70. A complex song of praise for help (vv. 1–11) precedes a prayer for help (vv. 12–17). Sacrifice, the usual ritual of thanksgiving, is rejected. The psalmist claims to have the LORD's instruction inside him. A written scroll is used in the ritual that the psalm accompanies.

The first two features pose related problems. Can part of a composition be detached and used as an independent psalm, or can a psalm be composed by using existing pieces? The evidence argues that both procedures were followed in psalm composition. Can praise for help precede prayer for help in psalmic liturgy? Probably; compare Psalms 9—10; 27; 44; and 89.

1. It is important to note that the first part of the psalm tells about the past (vv. 1–10). It begins with a report of deliverance (vv. 1–3). The singer was in death-threatening trouble. He prayed for help. The LORD delivered him. The deliverance was the subject of a "new song," a hymn of praise that is a witness and summons to others to fear and trust the LORD. The witness continues in a "beatitude" (v. 4) that teaches that trust in the LORD is a better course of life than resorting to other gods (so the NRSV; or does the unusual language mean "arrogant self-confident men," as in NJPS?). The psalmist sees his deliverance as one more example of the innumerable wonders by which the LORD has preserved his people; the salvation of the psalmist is set within the continuity of salvation history of Israel (v. 5).

Now the difficult verses 6–8. When a person came to a shrine or temple to perform the public rituals of thanksgiving for deliverance, the rituals included the offering of a sacrifice of

167

thanksgiving along with the song of praise for help (see 50:23; 56:12; 107:22; 116:14, 18; etc.). But in verse 6 a surprising thing happens. The psalmist praises the LORD because the LORD did not desire or require any kind of sacrificial offering! The psalmist knew this because "you bored ears for me," that is, the LORD had given him the capacity to hear the LORD (hearing always involves responding and obeying; note Isa. 50:4–5 and the similar gift of hearing to the servant of the LORD). If sacrifice were not to be brought, what was the alternative? Verses 7–8 can be understood in this way. The psalmist came to the temple with a scroll on which was written an account of his trouble, prayer, and deliverance, and his praise of the LORD for his salvation. The content may have been more or less what is said in verses 1–5. The writing would have been recited and deposited in the temple as witness and praise to the LORD (on the practice of displaying written tributes to deities in sanctuaries, see Keel, pp. 326ff.). Besides the document, the psalmist brought himself—a person whose desire is to do what pleases his God and in whose inmost parts is the LORD's instruction (v. 8). He presents himself as a person who wants what the LORD wants and who feels and thinks with and through the *torah* of the LORD. It is important to remember what the function of this statement about the self is. It is not the self-righteous claim of a confident legalist. It is an offering of praise for salvation, and what is even more important, it is the confession of a transformation of the self worked by salvation. Where human desire and will are conformed to divine pleasure and instruction, the purpose of praise through sacrifice and song has been incorporated into the very processes of the self. The true thanksgiving for salvation is witness and will.

In verses 9–10 the psalmist tells his God that he has been a faithful witness. The theme of the telling is stated in the first sentence: "I brought tidings (*bisser*) of your setting-right-deed (*sedeq*) in public assembly." One way to do that was through singing praise to the LORD (96:1; Isa. 60:6). In the rest of the statement the whole vocabulary used to speak of God's saving action is used to expand on the theme: righteousness, salvation, loving-kindness, and faithfulness. The psalmist has done what the saved are supposed to do—proclaim the good news of God's salvation to others, that they may be led to trust in the righteousness of God. Verse 11 is best read as a statement of trust (with NJPS) rather than as a petition (with NRSV). The psalmist

168

trusts himself to the gospel he has proclaimed in the situation
in which he now is. He does what is usually so difficult to do—
live by the gospel you preach.

2. That situation comes to light for the first time in verse 12
and is described there in a way that makes it clear how difficult
trust is. The psalmist is surrounded and caught by misfortunes
and iniquities as if trapped by a hostile army. His present troubles and failures seem as numerous as the LORD's past wondrous
deeds (cf. v. 5). Though many could see how the LORD saved in
the past (v. 3), now the psalmist cannot see beyond all his problems. God's saving righteousness was in the psalmist's heart
(v. 10), but now his heart fails him. The psalm teaches that the
torah in the heart does not prevent sin, nor does the experience
of salvation spare us from the need of God's help.

So with his testimony to his relation to God's salvation in the
past and confession of his present need, the psalmist turns to
prayer for help (vv. 13–17); this is where Psalm 70 begins. The
whole is composed in the idiom of petition. The psalmist seeks
the LORD's help urgently (v. 13) from threats to his life (vv.
14–15). He prays for the time when all who seek the LORD and
love his salvation can praise his greatness with joy (v. 16). But
for now he must speak as one who is "poor and needy" (on the
rubric, see Introduction, sec. 6.18) in dependence on the LORD
as his help (v. 17).

This prayer psalm gives, as they all do, a liturgical theological profile of those who use it. It is a rather complex picture. (On
the question of who speaks in vv. 6–8, see Barth, II/2, pp. 604f.;
and Kraus, *Theology*, p. 162.) The psalm reflects a person who
had been in danger of death, had cried to the LORD, was delivered, found himself responsive to the LORD in a new way, had
offered witness and self as thanksgiving instead of sacrifice, but
now in trouble, conscious of failings, appeals in weakness to the
LORD for deliverance. This profile and the language in which
it is sketched have important connections with exilic prophecy.
In the prophecies of Jeremiah and Ezekiel there are promises
of a people of the LORD who have the LORD's *torah* in their
heart (Jer. 31:31–34; Ezek. 36:25–28). The prophet of Isaiah
40—55 was called to bring tidings (*bisser*) of the LORD's saving
righteousness (*sedeq*; compare Isa. 40:9; 41:27; 52:7 with Ps.
40:9). He describes one group he addressed as a people who   169
know the LORD's saving righteousness and in whose heart was
his *torah* (Isa. 51:7). *Torah* always means the instruction or

teaching of the LORD, but what its particular content is can be as varied as the ways Israel was instructed by its God. In Second Isaiah, *torah* is the tidings of the reign of the LORD that will be revealed in his saving righteousness as a ground for trust (Isa. 42:4; 51:4). After the exile, there were those who continued the vocation of Second Isaiah and applied his basic message to the disappointing times of the reconstruction of the people of the LORD (Isa. 61:1). And there were psalmists who experienced the fulfillment of the promise of *torah* in the heart (Pss. 37:31; 40:8; 119:11). It was in these circles of temple singers and prophets in the Isaiah tradition that sacrifice was relativized in favor of praise and proclamation of the LORD's saving righteousness (Pss. 40:6; 50:7-15; 69:30-33; cf. Isa. 66:1-4). The eighth- and seventh-century prophets had rejected the sacrifices of Israel because they were offered by a disobedient people whom sacrifice could not make acceptable (e.g., Amos 5:22; Isa. 1:11; Jer. 7:22). These postexilic psalmists take a somewhat different approach. Because the experience of God's saving righteousness was so important in their understanding of God and of their relation to him, they concentrated liturgical and theological attention on its proclamation in praise and its practice in piety. Praise and piety were for them the true responses to the salvation of the LORD. Psalm 40 is shaped by this theology. It lays it all out in verses 1-11 as the identity in which the "poor and needy," whose strength and own righteousness are not enough, pray for the LORD's help.

3. Verses 6-8 have always had special importance in the use of the psalm in liturgy and theology because the Letter to the Hebrews uses these verses as the words of Christ (Heb. 10:5-7) and thereby gives a new answer to the question of who speaks. Once the earliest Christians had understood the life and death of Jesus as perfect obedience to the will of God, it would have been impossible for them to read verse 8 without thinking of him. The author of the letter quotes a version of verses 6-8 that differs from the Hebrew psalm and in some respects from its translation in the Septuagint. That means the relation of psalm to letter is indirect. But in one major respect the letter follows the psalm precisely. The psalmist, who knows that the conformation of his mind and desire to the will and revelation of God takes the place of sacrifice, is a type for Jesus, whose obedience unto death replaced all cultic sacrifice and accomplished once for all the perfect sacrifice. The psalmist with his

170

praise and piety still must pray for salvation from suffering and
sin. That is where we all are. But our prayers are made in hope,
because the sacrifice for sin has been made for us once for all.

Psalm 41: Happy Are Those Who Consider the Weak

Psalm 41 is composed of four distinct elements. There is an
extended beatitude describing the LORD's approval of and help
for those who are concerned about the weak (vv. 1–3). A frequent purpose of a beatitude is to instruct (on the beatitude, see
Psalm 1, sec. 1); here it introduces a prayer and shifts to the
prayer's style of direct address to God in the final measures of
verses 2 and 3. The prayer that begins at verse 4 is a prayer for
help in first person singular style. Petitions for the gracious
mercy of the LORD (vv. 4, 10) open and conclude a lament over
hostility shown to the one who prays (vv. 5–9). The prayer
begins with a quotation formula that identifies the prayer as one
said in the past. The third element is thankful praise that the
prayer just quoted has been answered (vv. 11–12; this classification depends on translating the verbs in these verses in the past
tense). The fourth element is the doxology of verse 13, which
marks the conclusion of book I of the Psalms (Introduction, secs.
3.6; 4.1).

The psalm appears to be a prayer of thanksgiving said when
the prayer for help had been answered (Introduction, sec. 5.3).
The occasion of offering praise for the LORD's help is used to
teach a lesson to the congregation. The LORD's help against the
enemies of the psalmist is taken as a judgment against their
conduct and as a validation of the opening beatitude about
those who, in contrast, show concern for the weak. The psalm
belongs to the period in the history of psalmody when instruction has become more important as a function of prayer and
praise. The psalm gives God the praise and builds up the faith
of the congregation.

The language of the psalm identifies sickness as the occasion
of the quoted prayer. Sickness is connected with sin against the
LORD, as is often the case in such prayers (v. 4; see the excursus
in the comment on Psalm 38). But the connection is not developed here in any way; the petition in verse 4 seems to make the
connection as if saying "Heal me, LORD, for I have sinned

171

against you" were simply the right way to pray for restoration. Indeed, the beatitude speaks of the illness of those who are concerned about the weak and in this respect are righteous (v. 3). The thanksgiving takes healing as a sign that the LORD is pleased with the one who prays and has supported that one because of his integrity (vv. 11–12). The confession of sin does not exclude the integrity of the one who makes it, nor does illness imply that those afflicted are simply and only sinful. The relation between sin and sickness is dealt with here in a complex way, as theologically it must be.

The lesson taught by the psalm is that concern for the poor and needy, the helpless and the weak, is righteousness. God is like that. The LORD's people should be like that. The enemies are not like that; their conduct toward the sick is wrong. This lesson is taught by the law, prophets, and wisdom in the Old Testament. In the New Testament it is reiterated in "Blessed are the merciful, for they shall obtain mercy" (Matt. 5:7; see 25:31–46). According to John 13:8, Judas' betrayal of Jesus was a fulfillment of the psalmist's rejection by a member of his most intimate circle (v. 9). The psalm helps us to see how Jesus identified himself with the weak and helpless and suffered the rejection they experienced. Judas becomes the name of all those described by the psalm as enemies of the weak.

BOOK TWO
Psalms 42—72

see
Ps 84

Psalms 42 and 43: My Soul Thirsts for God

1. *"My soul thirsts for the living God . . . the God of my life" (42:2, 8).* The prayer is about the need of human life for the life that the living God bestows, revives, and preserves. Here it is understood and said very clearly that life depends on God. The need is spoken about in the beginning by the use of the powerful image of thirst. His prayer, the psalmist says, is like the braying of a deer over watercourses gone dry. The comparison may be strange to our cultural and religious sensibilities, but it expresses the frustrated and compelling demand of unslaked thirst. The body cannot live without water. Its lack, quicker than anything else except breath itself, is felt as desperate desire. The soul cannot survive without God. That is true of every human soul, not just the deeply pious. Many or most may not understand the thirst that disturbs and drives their living, but it is there because God created the human soul to correspond to God. Where that correspondence is weakened, disturbed, or interrupted, the experience of its lack becomes like the thirst and hunger that is the opposite of being satisfied. The advantage of the psalmist is that he knows what is missing (42:4). He understands that the dissatisfaction of life is the thirst for God. (For other uses of thirst as metaphor for the need of God's presence, see Pss. 63:1–2; 143:6; Isa. 41:17; 55:1.)

Psalms 42 and 43 together compose the prayer in which that need is brought to the only one who can meet it. The two psalms are held together by a continuity of language themes and type to compose a prayer for help in first person singular style. There are three parts, each concluded by the same refrain (42:5, 11; 43:5). The first two parts describe the trouble that is

173

the setting of the prayer, and the third presents the petition for help.

2. The language with which the trouble afflicting the psalmist is described is typically conventional, poetic, and metaphoric. As is usually the case with these prayers, it is impossible to tie composition and use to a particular historical or biographical occasion. Psalm 42:6–7, with its reference to "the land of Jordan," "Hermon," and "Mount Mizar," seems to locate the performance of the prayer on the slopes of Hermon, where the Jordan River rises beyond the northeast boundaries of Israel. But it is apparent that the deeps, floods, and waves of 42:7 are metaphors for overwhelming trouble, as often is the case in biblical poetry. The psalmist knew something about the headwaters of the Jordan and used the location in an exaggerated way as a poetic device. If these verses were a reference to a particular location, it would be the only such case in the prayers of the Psalter.

The best clue to the social and theological setting is the taunting question that the singer puts in the mouth of his adversaries: "Where is your God?" (42:3, 10). In all its occurrences in the Old Testament, the question appears in liturgical material (Pss. 79:10; 115:2; Joel 2:17; Micah 7:10), where it is a feature of the description of trouble. The question is a formulaic motif used to characterize the situation in which those who trust in the LORD are put to shame in the presence of others because of some trouble that calls their faith into question. In its other occurrences, the question comes from the nations and is addressed to the cultic community. In Psalm 43:1 the enemies are named "an ungodly people." The taunt and the social conduct that it represents are "the oppression of the enemy" (42:9; 43:2), the cause of the lament (42:3, 9; 43:2). The enemies' oppression is understood as a sign that God has "forgotten" and "cast off" the singer (42:9; 43:2). The social, personal, and theological experience of the absence of God is the soul's thirst. These matters, along with the clear liturgical character of Psalms 42—43, and some connections between these psalms and Psalm 44, suggest that the psalm was composed for a representative individual who speaks with and for a group in the troubled times of the postexilic period when the faithful were at the mercy of other peoples in whose midst they had to live.

3. The psalm appears to be a prayer song sung in preparation for pilgrimage to the temple in Jerusalem. Being in the

174

temple before the altar, part of a festival congregation, joining
in the shouts and songs of praise is what the psalm remembers
and anticipates (42:3, 4, 5, 11; 43:3, 4, 5). Its goal and hope are
to praise the LORD once again in his dwelling on the holy hill
of Zion. The help for which the psalm appeals is divine guidance and protection on the way (43:3). Two characteristics of
God, light and faithfulness, are thought of as powers that can be
dispatched in response to the prayer (see 85:10–13). Pilgrimage,
going to God, is not merely a human project; God must aid from
the beginning. One comes to God with the help of God.

The pair of divine characteristics to which the prayers for
help usually appeal are steadfast love and faithfulness. Here the
first is replaced by light because light is what emanates from the
face or presence of God (4:6; 44:3; 89:15; see the comment on
Ps. 36:9) It is the presence of God for which the psalmist longs
(42:2). It is the presence of God that will slake the thirst of the
soul, fill the void of the absence of God. For the psalm, the
presence of God on the consecrated hill at the appointed dwelling place is absolutely real. The presence is not empirically
tangible. Yet in and through the holy space filled with the faithful and their liturgies, the soul "sees the face of God." That
encounter is the answer to the question set by the society and
the solution to the troubles that challenge faith. The theological
foundations of this prayer are expressed in the songs about the
City of God, the Zion psalms (see Introduction, sec. 6.10). It is
one of the psalms that reveals the spiritual character of the
doctrinal and theological dimensions of that theology. (See also
Psalms 36; 63.)

4. The "spirituality" of this prayer for help is especially
evident in the refrain unique to such prayers. Its repetition
colors the entire prayer functioning as an antiphon for its recitation. In the refrain, the ego addresses the soul. Calvin remarked
that "David here represents himself as if he formed two opposing parties" (Calvin, 2:139). What is to be made of this unusual
feature? The modern inclination may be to read the refrain as
an expression of a completely subjective transaction, the effort
of a courageous soul to change its mood by its own spiritual
courage. That would overlook the fact that the refrain is liturgy,
not autobiography. In it the ego who speaks to the downcast
soul is the liturgical and confessional ego speaking to the con-   175
sciousness shaped by a society and circumstances that do not
support faith. The liturgy and the confession refocus conscious-

ness on God known and experienced in the praise of the community at the place where God condescends to be present for them.

When facing the suffering of his passion, Jesus echoed the language of these psalms in speaking of his own downcast, disquieted soul (compare 42:5 and 6 with Matt. 26:38 and John 12:27). None of us escapes the need that is the subject of this prayer. Jesus teaches us also that those who have and understand the thirst are indeed blessed, because it is the thirst that brings us to the justifying presence of God (Matt. 5:6). In the Gospel of John, he reveals himself as the source of the water that satisfies the thirst of the soul (John 4:14; 6:35; also Rev. 21:6). For Christians who live in a world that constantly raises the question, "Where is your God?" these psalms are indispensable liturgy and Scripture. They disclose the real nature of our souls' disquiet as thirst for God. They turn us toward the worship of praise, sacraments, and preaching in and through which our Lord wills to be present for the congregation.

Psalm 44: For Your Sake We Are Slain

Psalm 44 is the first of the corporate prayers for help in the present arrangement of the Book of Psalms. On the type, see Introduction, sec. 5.4. This one differs from the others in one remarkable feature that has always drawn the attention of interpreters, its firm profession of innocence under the covenant (vv. 17–22). "In this respect Ps. xliv stands perfectly alone: it is likely the national mirroring of the Book of Job, and by reason of this takes a unique position in the range of Old Testament literature side by side with Lam. ch. iii and the deutero-Isaiah. . . . In this psalm, Israel stands in exactly the same relation to God as Job and 'the servant of Jahve' in Isaiah" (Delitzsch, 2:66f.).

1. The prayer begins with a recollection of salvation history (vv. 1–3) followed by a confession of faith (v. 4) and a statement of trust (vv. 5–8). Then in sharp contrast a present situation of defeat (vv. 9–12) and humiliation (vv. 13–16) is described. Responsibility for the disaster is disclaimed in an assertion of faithfulness (vv. 17–22). Petitions (vv. 23, 26) and complaints against the LORD (vv. 24–25) conclude the prayer. The prayer is composed in corporate style; the shift to individual style at points (vv. 4, 6, 15) could reflect the voice of the performer of the

176

prayer for the congregation, or, more likely, it simply represents a customary personification of the congregation.

2. The recollection of salvation history is authenticated as the personal knowledge of the congregation gained from accounts by the fathers, the authorities on tradition in the community (78:3; Judg. 6:13; Deut. 6:20–25). The recollection concerns Israel's coming into possession of the land, the event that gave them a place and continuity in history. The event is described as a "work" of God and is recounted in such a way as to emphasize that it was God's doing and not that of Israel. God's reason for giving them the land was a free sovereign decision to favor them (v. 3). Nations were dispossessed and Israel planted to spread out like a vine in the land (Exod. 15:17; Ps. 80:9–12). Vocabulary and theology are similar to those found in Deuteronomy (e.g., Deuteronomy 7 and 9).

The congregation's assertion of trust is formulated as a personal appropriation of the recalled event. The congregation acts and lives in terms of its confidence that the recollection is the truth about God. In its confrontation with the nations, the congregation relies on and praises the LORD. They identify themselves as the LORD's servants and trust themselves to God's saving help. "You are my king and my God, ordaining saving events for Jacob," they confess (v. 4, following Septuagint with NRSV; 5:2; 68:24; 74:12; 84:3). Behind this confession is probably the ancient theology that the LORD assumed the role of king over Israel through the victories by which the land was gained (see 68; 114; 47). The recollection of the past and the confession in the present are ways of actualizing and activating the reality of their content, a liturgical invocation of the work of God that is in such bitter and bewildering contrast with the present.

3. The prayer describes the present also as the work of Israel's God (vv. 9–16). Through six poetic lines the "you" of God is the first word and subject of the verbs. The prayer does not doubt that the LORD is in control of history, but his work is strange. The basic sentence of which the rest of the description of trouble is an elaboration is: "You have rejected us [vv. 10–12] and humiliated us [vv. 13–16]." The operational side of the congregation's trouble is, "You do not go out with our armies" (cf. v. 9 and 60:10). The outcome is a military disaster that brings a physical, political, and psychological loss of identity.

There is an important perspective on "the enemy" in the

177

transition from the confession to the complaint. The enemies are created by God's action in salvation history; in assuming kingship over a particular people and giving them a place and destiny in history as his people, God's action provokes a hostility from those who oppose them (vv. 5–7). "The enemies" are the national and social forces of history that oppose the manifestation of the kingship of God in history. It is to these enemies, the nations playing this role, that God has abandoned and subjected his own people as though they were of no significance (v. 12).

The prayer gives no reason for this devastating reversal. No motive or emotion is attributed to God. The brutal fact of defeat and humiliation that threatens the death of the people (vv. 11, 22, 25) is simply construed as the work of God; the confession is applied to experience. All that the prayer can offer is a protest of faithfulness (vv. 17–22) that expresses bewilderment rather than understanding. According to the covenant theology laid out in Deuteronomy, such disasters as the prayer describes would be visited on the people of God for breach of the covenant (Deut. 28:15–69; Craigie, p. 333). But, says the congregation, we have not betrayed the covenant. Specifically, we have not turned to another God, even in secret (the central concern of Deuteronomy's theology of covenant). This protest does not claim perfect sinlessness or total innocence under the covenant; that would be too much in the light of Israel's history. But the protest does claim basic loyalty. The confession of verses 4–8 is the truth about this congregation.

4. The concluding petition (v. 26) uses ancient and traditional imperatives for invoking the intervention of a deity. "Rouse yourself from sleep, awake" is simply an idiom for going into action (7:6; 35:23; 59:5). Psalm 121 asserts the trust that Israel's God is never inactive. The trouble here is that the LORD has been active through the agency of the nations (vv. 9–14). "Arise, O Lord" was the ancient ritual cry chanted as the ark of the LORD was lifted to lead the procession of Israel's host into battle. The petitions are based on an appeal to the steadfast love (*hesed*) of God. The last hope of a faithful people is the faithfulness of God.

5. The attempt to find a time and a people for whom this prayer was appropriate, a people firm in faithfulness to Israel's God, yet suffering military disaster and oppression, has led to many different proposals, none certain. The psalm has been

located in the time of David and in exilic and postexilic periods. There is an old and venerable opinion that it expresses the prayers of Jews who at great cost refused apostasy in the time of the persecution by Antiochus Epiphanes (I Maccabees 1—2). The psalm belongs to the collection of Korahite psalms (see Introduction, sec. 3.6) and reflects the traditions that are present in Hosea, Jeremiah, and Deuteronomy. More than that, it is impossible to say with certainty. The psalm is certainly there as a textual testimony that at some time the people of God have prayed in this way, and may at times pray this way. In liturgical use, only verses 1–8 are sometimes said, an abbreviation that may be touched with triumphalism.

6. The theological pathos of this prayer lies in the continuity and discontinuity between recollection on the one hand and complaint on the other. Both construe the history through which the congregation has lived and lives as the work of God. That is the continuity, and the prayer holds to that continuity with unyielding commitment. But the work of God to make a place in the midst of the nations for the people of God has turned into a dissolution of the congregation and a discrediting of their faith by the nations. That is the discontinuity. The congregation can speak of it only as inexplicable mystery that has no discernible basis in God's way or theirs. The psalm is a prayer of faith in the face of the inexplicable.

At the end of the protest of its faithfulness, the congregation who prayed this prayer make an assessment of their affliction that is of great portent. "For your sake we are slain," they say (v. 22; cf. 69:7). In the psalm this "for your sake" refers to the taunts of their foes described in verses 13–16. In that polytheistic age the taunt that was flung at those overwhelmed by their enemy was the derisive insult, "Where is your God?" (See the comment on Psalm 42, sec. 2.) Those who prayed this psalm had faced their foes in the name of the LORD and in trust in him. "For your sake" meant they could see no other meaning and purpose in their confession and trust than that they were accounted as sheep for slaughter. But that minimal and doleful interpretation of their suffering opens on the prospect of an understanding of suffering as a service to the kingdom of God. The prospect leads to the suffering servant of Isaiah 53, to Jewish martyrs, and to the cross of Calvary. The apostle Paul will later quote verse 22 to a persecuted congregation of early

179

Christians (Rom. 8:36) to persuade them to understand their suffering in the light of the death and resurrection of Jesus Christ.

Psalm 45: At Your Right Hand Stands the Queen

1. In societies ruled by monarchs, a royal wedding was a grand and important event. It was a religious as well as a political occasion; the king played the central role in both spheres of national life. The celebration was attended by members of the ruling families from allied and subject states; often the wedding was a form of diplomacy and the bride a princess from another country (see Keel, pp. 283–285).

Psalm 45 was composed for the proceedings of such an occasion and reflects its magnificence. The king is clothed in robes made fragrant by the richest spices of the east. His bride is dressed in robes woven with gold and dyed in many colors. A company of royal princesses surround the king, and the queen is accompanied by her court of virgins. Music enlivens the ivory-inlaid rooms of the palace. The groom is praised in an extravagant manner (vv. 2–9). Then the royal bride is given a charge to recognize the king both as husband and monarch, the one as wife, the other as subject (vv. 10–12). She is led into the palace for presentation to the king and consummation of the union (vv. 14–15). The king is promised progeny through whom his rule will be extended in all the earth and throughout generations to come (vv. 16–17).

2. The themes of the praise of the king are largely those found in other psalms about the royal figure (see Introduction, sec. 6.11). But more than in any of the others, the king himself is the subject of praise here. The king's beautiful appearance and gracious speech are said to be the basis and result of God's unending blessing (v. 2); that leaders should possess presence and eloquence is an ancient, as well as modern, expectation (I Sam. 9:2; 16:12). The king is a mighty warrior who defends the cause of truth and right and defeats his enemies (vv. 3–5; cf. 2:9; 18:31–48; 21:8–12; 89:20–22). In his reign, throne and scepter are dedicated to the support of righteousness and opposition to wickedness so that his elevation by God to be the anointed is justified (vv. 6–7; 72; 101).

180

All these compliments are features of the ideal of kingship and describe the persona that is appropriate to the office (see the comment on Psalm 2). But the psalm is not only unusual and extravagant compliment; it is unique in addressing the king with the title "god" (*'elohim*). Whether this happens in verse 6 depends on how the Hebrew text is understood. The simplest translation is "Your throne, O God, is everlasting" (so NRSV and Septuagint). Other readings are advocated that avoid the vocative "God" as an appellation for the human king (so NJPS, REB). Such a designation of a king does occur in the royal literature of other contemporary nations. If this is a unique case in the Old Testament, the term *'elohim* need not indicate belief in a king who is divine by nature but rather a divinely chosen and gifted person (see the comment on Psalm 2:7). The throne names for a Davidic king in Isaiah 9:6 may be an analogy: "Mighty God, Everlasting Father." But *'elohim* does seem to press the limits of adoration of a human king in a religion ruled by the principle of "no other god." Immediately the psalm goes on to subordinate the king to "God, your God" (v. 7).

3. In yet another respect Psalm 45 is unique. It opens and closes in the voice of its composer, who introduces the psalm with a reference to himself. Verse 1 provides an unparalleled glimpse of the persons who composed and often, as in this case, spoke the psalms. He is an "expert scribe" trained for his task; the term also identifies Ezra's profession (Ezra 7:6). Scribes were important officials of royal courts in the ancient Mideast who were responsible for a broad range of activities and were learned in the literature, traditions, and practices of their people. Scribe does not sound as though it is the right vocation for a psalmist, but that is because we have a too limited and later notion of the office. The scribe served in the royal court and temple to make appropriate language available for all kinds of needs. This scribe calls the psalm "a good word/saying" and names it "my work that I say to/for the king." His tongue is his pen; that is, he has composed the psalm orally and speaks it himself. It would have been committed to writing later, probably to commemorate the occasion (see v. 17). It is to such as this scribe that we owe a great many of the psalms. The intellectual environment and subjects and styles of these composers changed with historical shifts in their social context. But the office and its practitioners were there from monarchical times right on into the New Testament period.

181

4. In the postmonarchical period this "good saying" for a king's wedding was read by some as a messianic text. The Tar-

gum of verse 2 reads, "Thy beauty, O king Messiah, is greater than that of the children of men" (Delitzsch, p. 73). Others likely found in it an allegory of the relation between God and the people of God. Marriage had been well established as a representation of the LORD's election of and covenant with Israel in classical prophecy (Hosea 1—3; Jeremiah 2; Ezekiel 16; 23; Isa. 62:1–5). The allegorical figure was used broadly in the New Testament for Christ as bridegroom and the church as bride (Matt. 9:15; John 3:29; Eph. 5:22–33; Rev. 19:7–9; 21:2; 22:17). The writer of the Letter to the Hebrews found in the worrisome lines of verses 6–7 precisely the language to speak of the person and office of the Son of God (Heb. 1:8–9). Guided by these directives, Christians have traditionally understood the psalm as a song of the love between Christ and his church. This interpretation is also a safeguard against attributing the divine right of rule to any other save Christ, in whose hands it is utterly safe.

Psalm 46: A Mighty Fortress Is Our God

Psalm 46 is the first of the songs of Zion, hymns that feature the importance and meaning of Jerusalem in the LORD's relation to his people and world (Introduction, sec. 6.10). It is the biblical text for Martin Luther's famous hymn, "A Mighty Fortress Is Our God." Both psalm and hymn celebrate the confidence that the people of God may have in his help because of his choice to be with them: in the psalm through his presence in the City of God, in the hymn through his presence in Christ.

1. The theme of the psalm is the LORD of hosts as refuge. The theme is stated in an introductory declaration (v. 1) and then repeated twice (vv. 7, 11) as refrain, dividing the song into three parts. The first part declares that even the ultimate threat of the dissolution of the earth by the cosmic sea would not turn the congregation's trust into fear. The second speaks of the City of God. Because of God's relation to the city, it will not be shaken. There are subtle wordplays in the Hebrew text between the first and second parts that heighten the contrast between secure city and insecure cosmos and history. The waters of the sea and the nations both "roar," and mountains and kingdoms both "totter," but the City of God is not made to "totter." God's presence in the midst of the city means "the LORD of hosts is with us." It is through God's help for the city

182

that the LORD provides refuge for his people. The third part is an exhortation that desolations brought about by warfare be ◁—— seen as the work of the LORD. The exhortation is supported by a divine word that calls for acknowledgment that the LORD is God because of his exaltation among the nations of the earth. It would appear that the LORD's defense of the city is a battle of worldwide significance and consequence; "earth" appears in all three verses of the third part, resuming its appearance in verses 2 and 6. Much of the song employs language that is cryptic in its allusiveness. The language is drawn from a vision of cosmos and history that turns on the faith that the LORD as king of the universe has chosen Jerusalem as his capital to represent his reign in the world.

2. The introductory verse and the two refrains state the controlling theme of the song. All three are confessional statements, declarations of the congregation's trust. They are liturgical sentences with which worshipers trust their lives to the helping protection of their God. The titles given to God and the predicates attributed to him all serve that purpose. LORD of hosts identifies the LORD as the divine warrior who leads the heavenly hosts against cosmic and human foes to maintain his rule. The divine voice that makes the earth melt (v. 6b) is the central motif of evocations of the divine warrior (see 29; 18:7–15; 24:8 and 10). God of Jacob emphasizes the LORD's relation to Israel from the time of the ancestors; as Israel's God, the LORD has been "with us," the presence in Israel's historical way to bless and protect wherever he led them. During all that time, the LORD "proved to be a help in trouble" (cf. 48:3). When the confession calls God "refuge" and "fortress," it takes up a frequent term of psalmic language, heard first in Psalm 2:12 and repeated again and again. The term is usually found in psalms in individual voice (see the comment on Ps. 7:1). It is a figure for trusting life to God's saving help in the presence of dangers (e.g., 61; 62; 91). Here the entire community makes the confession. "Therefore we will not fear" (v. 2) states the marvelous prospect that trust opens up. Faith makes one unafraid. Concern and caution may persist, but for those who make the confession, trust prevails.

3. The song declares confidence in the face of two dangers, the sea and the nations. In the worldview of the time, the sea threatened the earth's security, and in the experience of that era, the nations were a threat to corporate life. The psalm be-

gins with the dangers of an unstable world. In ancient cosmology, earth rested on the foundations of mountains that went deep into the cosmic ocean. Signs of its instability were seen in earthquakes, volcanoes, floods, and droughts. In the worldview of Canaan, sea and river were hostile gods whose threat to earth was constant. But for the psalmist, the LORD is so much the sovereign of the universe that cosmic instability need not be feared. The earth is the LORD's because he has founded it on the seas (24:1). The question of its ultimate reliability is a question about the rule of God (see the comment on Psalm 93).

The danger with which the psalmist is really concerned comes from the nations, and he moves on to that one in the second and third stanzas. The nations in their raging and kingdoms in their instability produce a historical chaos more dangerous than the cosmic one. Indeed, historical insecurity seems to replace cosmic instability in Israel's vision of reality; note that the same language is used about seas and nations: seas and nations "rage," mountains and kingdoms "totter." But the congregation knows that the LORD of hosts is also sovereign over national powers as well as cosmic.

4. In that knowledge the psalm issues an invitation as the climactic expression of confidence in the LORD (vv. 8–11). The invitation is best understood as addressed to the nations themselves; note the similar exhortation to the nations in Psalms 2:10–12 and 66:5. In a daring interpretation of world history, the psalm points to the desolation brought about by war and calls on the nations to recognize in it the work of the LORD. War is self-defeating; it brings about the destruction of those who practice it. In its terrible futility it is a revelation of the power of the LORD who seeks order and opposes chaos. In a prophetic word from God, the psalm concludes by turning the vision into exhortation to the nations: "Cease your warring! Stop your attacks! Leave off your vain attempts to subject history to your power. There is but one power exalted over the earth and nations. Only one is God—the one whose work is the destruction of weapons and whose help is the refuge of those who recognize that he is God."

5. The psalmist's confidence that "the LORD of hosts is with us" is based on the LORD's relation to Zion. Verses 4–5 speak of that relation. Zion is the City of God, which the Most High has made holy by choosing it as his dwelling, the place on earth that represents his divine rule as symbol of capitol and palace. (On

184

Zion as the City of God, see the comment on Psalm 48.) The somewhat mysterious reference to "the river whose channels bring joy to the City of God" comes from the symbolic language used in the ancient Near East to imagine and speak about the dwelling place of the gods. A stream was said to issue from the cosmic mountain where this dwelling was; it was a symbol that interpreted the mountain as center of the universe and source of life (Gen. 2:10–14; Ezek. 47:1–12; Joel 3:18; Rev. 22:1–2). The symbol is a way of speaking about the cosmic and theological role of Jerusalem created by the choice of God. Because the LORD of hosts was "in" the city, it was removed from the instability of earth and history. The city would not totter. Yet, in every line, the song is true to its theme. It never says, "Zion is our refuge." The City of God, even in its temporal local manifestation, remains a transcendental reality. It exists in temporal, local dimension purely and simply in that God chooses to dwell with mortals.

6. Psalm 46 is not a song about an impregnable city of God, a metropolis of security founded in the world to exempt its inhabitants from the dangers of history. Its true subject is the God who will help the people in whose midst he has chosen to be and who for a time chose Jerusalem and its temple as the locale of his "dwelling." The song does not invite trust in a place but in a Presence who wills to dwell with people. In the Old Testament, God's dwelling in time and space was never fixed and final. The locale was a movable tabernacle, a shrine at Shiloh, the temple in Jerusalem. The dwelling was always both real and relative. Isaiah lamented that Judah did not take its reality seriously enough (Isaiah 28—29). Jeremiah accused his contemporaries of misunderstanding how relative it was (Jeremiah 7). Jerusalem did "totter"; it fell to the Babylonians; the psalms themselves record the dismay and pain (e.g., Psalm 74). Joel articulated the eschatological dimension of God's dwelling with humankind (Joel 3:16–21). In the New Testament, the dwelling of God with mortals took the form of a person (John 1:14) and was inseparably linked to Jesus Christ. It became fixed, though not final. Its eschatological reach rises to a new importance; the texts are Hebrews 11:10; 12:18–24; 13:14; and Revelation 21. For a theological reflection on "the dwelling of God," see Barth, II/1, pp. 478–483.

Ascension (handwritten)

Psalm 47: King Over All the Earth

1. Psalm 47 is a hymn that praises the LORD as king. Its literary structure is composed of a summons to praise followed by the content of praise (see Introduction, sec. 5.5.4). The sequence is used twice. A first summons (v. 1) is supported by an account of one way in which the LORD gained his rule (vv. 2–5). The second summons (v. 6) is followed by a description of the LORD throned in the midst of his court (vv. 7–10). A "selah" concludes verse 4; it may separate verse 5 as the climax and center of the whole. The theme of the whole is: The LORD is king over all the earth (vv. 2, 7 specifically). One way to describe the logic of the hymn is: The LORD has made a place for his people among the nations so that the nations may be included among his people. (On the kingship of God, see Introduction, sec. 6.1–5.)

inclusive of all nations (handwritten)

2. The occasion for the hymn is an event. Something has happened to which the psalm is a response. The LORD has "gone up" (v. 5) and has assumed his throne (v. 8). In the liturgical drama of the temple the event may have been portrayed by a procession bearing the ark (24:7–10). In the royal ceremonies of the ancient Near East, when a king had mounted the dais and assumed the throne, whether on the day of his coronation or on a great state occasion, the surrounding court would acclaim the king's rule. Assuming the throne was always a symbolic assumption of rule. Representatives of his subjects would acclaim his royal identity and acknowledge his authority. The psalm provides a way for the congregation to acclaim the LORD as the sovereign above all other sovereignties.

3. The hymn combines two traditions. One is the memory and interpretation of the way Israel gained its land (vv. 3–4). The land is a heritage that the LORD himself chose and gave to Jacob/Israel by helping them to overwhelm the nations and peoples who were already there. The LORD did it as an expression of his love for Jacob. "Love" is to be understood in the sense the term had in ancient Near Eastern suzerainty covenants, the favor shown vassals dependent on the great king. The other tradition is the narrative plot of ancient Near Eastern myth about the way one god acquired sovereignty. The pattern involved subduing and defeating chaos, the assumption of kingship, and acquiring a royal place, a palace for a throne. (See the

comment on Psalms 29; 68; 77.) In the psalm the two are merged. The conquest of Palestine's peoples becomes the basis for the LORD's kingship, and in turn the LORD's kingship becomes the basis for his claim on all nations and peoples of the earth. The particular is the basis for the universal, and the universal draws out the meaning of the particular. The myth interprets the meaning of history.

4. The psalmic vision of the kingship of God is multidimensional. It involves history, liturgy, and myth, and so memory of the past, experience of the present, and hope for the future. Remembering the conquest as the initiative of God is the tangible point of reference. Viewing that point as a revelation that the LORD is the king of all the earth gives cosmic and eschatological meaning to it. It becomes a manifestation of what is going on behind and above the chaos of history. Celebrating the LORD's assumption of a universal rule in liturgy actualizes memory and meaning for present experience. In these respects, this hymn is a paradigm for authentic understanding and celebration of the reign of God. The reign of God is never there apart from an event in the human world, but never fully there in any event. It is not purely eschatological, and yet it will be fully there only in final fulfillment. It cannot be perfectly represented by any human proceedings, but it can be experienced by human beings as actuality only in praise and prayer of liturgy.

5. Notice the implicit understanding of "the people of God" in verse 9. The people of God are constituted, not by ethnic or national identity, but by recognition of the rule of the LORD. The notion goes back behind Sinai to Abraham and to the promise that in and through his seed all nations of the earth would be blessed (Gen. 12:1–4). The theology of God's universal kingship in the psalm reaches back and makes contact with the universal purpose of God in the election of the ancestors. The extension of the reign of God becomes the mode of fulfilling the promise.

6. The exilic Isaiah connected the return of the Babylonian exiles to Zion to the announcement of the reign of the LORD (52:7–10). Jesus of Nazareth connected his career with the announcement of the reign of God (Mark 1:14–15). Both show how the celebration of God's rule can acquire and has acquired new historic points of reference to inform hope and liturgy. According to Jewish tradition, Psalm 47 was sung in the temple seven

187

Ascension

times before the trumpet blast inaugurating the new year. The early church used the psalm to celebrate the ascension of Jesus, a practice that is commonly followed still in the liturgy of many churches. In these liturgical contexts, the psalm declares that the reign of God is the transcendent truth about what is inaugurated in the new year and in the new era.

Psalm 48: The City of the Great King

The LORD is the great king who is sovereign over the world and all the nations in it; Zion, the city and the hill on which it stands, is the great king's capital and site of his temple-palace. That is the theology on which Psalm 48 is based. It is one of the songs of Zion (Introduction, sec. 6.10), hymns whose subject is the importance and meaning of Jerusalem in the LORD's relation to his people and the world. The song speaks of Jerusalem under the sacred name of Zion and portrays Israel's small and unimposing capital as the city of God. Its purpose was to lead the congregation to see what only the eyes of faith could perceive.

heavenly counterpart

1. The unifying theme of the song is the LORD as defender (stated in v. 3). The song begins with the praise of the greatness of the LORD whose city is the center of the earth and who has revealed himself as a refuge in its citadels (vv. 1–3). The second part (vv. 4–8) ranges the kings of earth (cf. 2:1–2) against the great king in his city and reports that on seeing it (i.e., city and citadels), the kings were thrown in panic. The congregation testifies that what they have seen confirms what they have heard. (What they had heard about and now have seen presumably is the imposing citadel of the city as representation of the LORD as stronghold; see vv. 12–14 and Psalm 46.) In the third part (vv. 9–11), the congregation confesses what God's role as defender of the city gives them to think about as they worship in the temple—God's steadfast love and righteousness (NRSV, "victory") displayed in his judgments (i.e., saving acts to maintain his rule and defend his realm). The psalm concludes with a general call for a procession that circles the city, all the while viewing its defenses as representation of the God who will be their guide forever (as in Psalm 23). The song seems designed for use by pilgrims, probably to the fall festival, as they stood before the temple and prepared for a procession around the

188

city. The psalm would help those who sang it see Jerusalem in a way they could not without its faith and vision.

2. The psalm discloses the human town as the city of God. The geographic site is of course Jerusalem, the old Jebusite citadel that David captured and made his capital, so that it was called "the city of David." But for the psalm, the political place is the theological place, and it is of that identity that it speaks by using a vocabulary that does not correspond to the physical and political reality of Jerusalem. The low ridge on which Jerusalem sits is called a holy mountain, beautiful in its towering height that makes it visible and central to the whole earth. It is called, not Jerusalem, but Mount Zion. It is located, not in the Judean hill country, but on the "summit of Zaphon" (so NJPS correctly instead of NRSV "in the far north"; Zaphon is the name of the cosmic mountain where El and Baal exercised their kingship in the mythology of Canaanite religion). It is not the town of David but the capital of "the great king," the most high God who rules over all other kings, gods, and human beings; and he it is who has established and now maintains the city. In all this contradictory language the psalm is disclosing that other identity which Jerusalem acquired when the ark of the LORD was brought into its walls (see Psalm 132). In the religions of Israel's world, "the place" of the gods where they assembled and from where the high god ruled was such a cosmic mountain thought of in terms used in this psalm. Because the LORD had chosen Jerusalem as the place for ark and name to be, the worshiping congregation knows that this place has acquired the identity and role of "the city of the great king."

3. The psalm views the city as a medium through which God can be known. The temple-palace of the holy city is the place where pilgrims are led to "imagine" (v. 9; NRSV, "ponder") God's acts as the great king. There they are confronted by signs and symbols of God's reign. They see the temple, its architecture and furnishings, as representation of God's way in his rule—God's steadfast love (v. 9), righteousness and judgments (v. 11). The visible is transparent to the invisible and focuses mind and spirit on what cannot be seen. The city is also a visible witness to God. What the pilgrims can see of Zion, with its towers, ramparts, and citadels, furnishes them the material to tell a later generation about God (vv. 12–14). As the content of confession and testimony, Zion provides two themes of instruc-

189

tion and nurture. First, the city is one of the ways by which God has specific identity and through which people know and respond to God in his particularity. Our God is the God, says verse 14, to whom this city belongs, who is worshiped in its temple, and whose reign is symbolized by its royal plan. Second, the city is a visible sign of God's commitment to the people whose life is guided by his way. It is tangible evidence that the LORD has taken them as flock to which he is shepherd. The pilgrims are to go home and tell of Zion in such a way that others will know better who God is and that God is our God.

4. The psalm interprets the city as the symbol of God who is the refuge of those who trust in him. "By her citadels God has made himself known as refuge" (v. 3). Note that it is not the fortifications of Jerusalem but God himself who is haven; the citadels represent to the eye the refuge created by the rule of the LORD. Verses 4–7 describe the effect of seeing the defenses of Jerusalem as manifestation of the LORD on other kings who assault the city. Reports of the defeat of unnamed kings and enemies occur in other Zion songs (46:8–9; 76:1–12). The reports do not seem to refer to some specific historical occasion, but they do reflect Israel's past experiences of the help of the LORD (48:3; 46:1). The reports are dramatic combinations for liturgical purposes of these memories and confidence in the certainty of the great king's defense of his city. In Zion's role as city of God, its citadels become the medium of theophany. The notion of the impregnability of the city arises from its identity as city of God and depends on God's relation to the city. In verse 8 the worshiping congregation reports that they also "see" in the city of God. What they had known only as a report becomes visible to the pilgrims by the medium of the city.

5. The way in which the psalm speaks of Jerusalem as Zion, the city of David as the city of God, is a way of envisioning the earthly in terms of the heavenly, the temporal in terms of the everlasting. It is language that uncovers the transcendent dimension of the immanent created by the relation of God's rule to the world. The psalm uncovers what modern Christians can easily lose, the discernment of the church as a society created in the finite and temporal by the infinite and everlasting. The church is not just a human society that can be analyzed by sociological description. A vocabulary is needed that is not congruent with buildings we build, organizations we devise, and rolls of conglomerate persons. Faith must also say of the church,

190

"Holy . . . catholic . . . body of Christ," because, whether humble or imposing in its social form, it is constituted in its theological reality by the Spirit and the name of God. It is the city of God, a society that represents and anticipates the coming reign of God.

Psalm 49: The Ransom of Life

At a turning point in their relationship, Jesus asked his disciples and the crowd what profit there is in gaining the whole world if one forfeits one's life, since there is nothing anyone can give in exchange for one's life (Mark 8:36–37). His subject was losing and saving one's life. That is also the subject of Psalm 49. Indeed, it forms the background of Jesus' teaching.

1. The literary structure of the psalm has three parts. There is an introduction in which the psalmist invites the widest possible audience (vv. 1–2) and identifies the character of the speech he is about to deliver (vv. 3–4). The speech is divided into two sections each marked by a refrain (vv. 5–12 and 13–20). The opening summons to an audience claims that the speech concerns every human being. What the psalm says is of the widest application. It offers "wisdom" and "understanding," guidance for living in the way life can be lived to fulfill it. The wisdom will come from listening to and meditating on a "proverb" as a way to unravel a "riddle" of life. The proverb may be stated in the refrain that compares human beings to animals (vv. 12, 20). The essence of the riddle lies in what the similarity of human beings to animals means. The psalm lets us hear the voice of the teacher, who gives instruction to the congregation in their identity as general humanity. The teacher speaks first of himself and the way he has learned to deal with one of life's sorest problems (vv. 5–15) and then he exhorts the congregation to emulate the wisdom he has been given (vv. 16–20). Use of the first person style is not a way to report personal individual experience. The style is, rather, a convention of teaching in Israel to convey convictions that belong to the teacher's theological tradition. For a similar introduction to a speech, see Psalm 78:1–4 and the comment there. On psalms of instruction, see the Introduction, sec. 5.6.

2. The problem the teacher addresses is set by wealth and the way people orient their lives to its acquisition and possession. The wrong is not in wealth itself but in the way people

191

allow riches to disorient their living in relation to God (I Tim. 6:10). Wealth takes the place that God alone should and can have. People trust in wealth; they worship it (v. 6). They make it the substance of happiness, satisfy the life hunger with it, find in its possession the justification and approbation of their existence (vv. 13, 18). The teacher uses an idiom from Israel's legal life to make a revealing analysis of what is going on in such conduct. Such conduct is an attempt to use wealth as a "ransom of life" (see the term in vv. 7–8, 15). In certain cases before the court where the penalty of death was stipulated, a "ransom of life" could be paid as punishment; the life of the guilty party was purchased by the payment of a ransom (Exod. 21:28–32). The teacher uses this idiom because he perceived the profound truth that behind the human fascination of wealth is a denial of death. The fascination is based on a deep and powerful presentiment that life can be secured against death by wealth. It is an immortality strategy.

3. The teacher takes up this problem not to denounce the rich but to instruct and comfort the faithful. His purpose is pastoral. In hard times when the rich take advantage of their wealth and use it to take advantage of others, the faithful are tempted to "fear" (vv. 5, 16). "Fear" means far more, as the teacher uses the term, than simple reaction to danger. He speaks of a fear that is a deep apprehensive anxiety about the meaning and destiny of life, a worry in the face of the faith of the rich in their wealth that one has failed and missed it all. That is a fear that disorients one from the only fear that belongs to faith, the fear of the LORD (Prov. 1:7).

4. The teacher's first and primary counter against such fear is stated in the refrain and reiterated in both parts of the speech. Trust in riches as an immortality strategy doesn't work (vv. 7–9). Human beings die, just as do animals (vv. 12, 20). Death is inexorable and inevitable for all (vv. 10–11). Those who thought they needed no divine shepherd end up with a shepherd whose name is death, who herds them into the grave and Sheol, there to dwell forever (vv. 13–14). There is nothing available to mortals that will serve as a ransom of life from death. Death is the great negation. The very wealth thought to be a ransom is lost in death (v. 17). The pomp and honor that wealth brought is lost in death (vv. 11, 18). Death is the great equalizer. The teacher is relentless in driving this gloomy lesson home. It

192

is bitter counsel to his audience, but it does deflate and debunk those who live by and for riches as the real and significant clue to life and its destiny. It does uncover the ultimate emptiness of an immortality strategy that disturbs the faithful. Psalms 37 and 73 also deal with the problem of the prosperous powerful wicked, but in those psalms teachers assure the faithful that the wicked will be undone in the midst of life, while the righteous will be vindicated. Here the resolution is universal death. The argument that all inexorably die is more certain for experience than the contention that the wicked perish in contrast to the righteous. But the argument could replace one fear with another in the souls of the teacher's audience.

5. So the teacher has another surprising word for the congregation (v. 15). It is given in the confessional first person style of a thanksgiving psalm, but it is offered to the audience as a salvation word. In the Old Testament context, it is an unexpected word, and it is put in cryptic terms. Essentially it is a statement of confidence in God, a declaration of trust that God will not let death cancel the relation to him that the faithful have in life. There is no valid immortality strategy for mortals, but with God it is a different matter. God is more powerful than the power of Sheol. God will pay the ransom that liberates the teacher and those who identify with him from the death penalty. Here the legal idiom is a metaphor: There is no payment and no court; the focus is on the actor and the result. How the deliverance will take place is said only in the mysterious "he will take me" (NRSV, "receive me"). The expression points to the reception of Enoch and Elijah from life into the divine presence as analogies (Gen. 5:24; II Kings 2:3, 5; see the comment on Pss. 16:10–11 and 73:24). In many psalmic contexts, the divine rescue from death is help that delivers from the dangers of death. But in the context of this psalm, with its emphasis on the eventual death of all, such a salvation word would mean little. Here the hope is that God, not Sheol, will be the final hope of the souls who trust in him (vv. 14–15).

6. When Christians read and hear this psalm, they will recognize the polemic against wealth turned into a surrogate for God (Matt. 6:21, 24; Mark 10:23). They will remember that Jesus said, "The Son of Man came . . . to give his life a ransom for many" (Mark 10:45; see I Tim. 2:6), and the cryptic language of verse 15 will be enfolded in the mysterious power of the death

193

and resurrection of Jesus and in the faith that "those who believe in Jesus can no longer look at their death as though it were in front of them. It is behind them" (Barth, III/2, p. 621).

Psalm 50: That He May Judge His People

The reading of Psalm 50 creates the liturgical time "for judgment to begin with the household of God" (I Peter 4:17). Some psalms praise the LORD as judge of all the earth (e.g., 96; 98). Here the LORD is presented as judge of the people of God, who holds them accountable for their worship and conduct. The psalm is not a hymn or prayer or song of thanksgiving. It is composed on the model of a speech for trial proceedings. It begins with an introduction (vv. 1–6) in which the LORD appears, convenes a court, and summons his covenant people as defendants. The body of the psalm is a speech made by the LORD to put the worship (vv. 7–15) and the conduct (vv. 16–22) of the covenant people under judgment. The speech ends with a summary statement on worship and conduct, a sort of instructive finding of the court (v. 23).

1. *Introduction (vv. 1–6).* The psalm lets us envision the convening of a trial whose proceedings can be seen only by the eye of faith. The convocation is depicted as already in process. The LORD has already spoken and appeared (vv. 1–2) and, as the psalm is read, is organizing the trial. The judge is introduced in ways that emphasize his deity, power, and authority. A trinity of names identify the judge; he is El, Elohim, and YHWH, whose authority reaches from one horizon of earth to the other (v. 1). His seat of government is Zion, the perfection of beauty (on Zion, its beauty and significance as city of God, see the comment on Psalms 48; 84). He appears in shining radiance of light (*hopia'*; see Deut. 33:2; Pss. 80:1; 94:1) in the form of a theophany whose elements are fire and storm (vv. 2–3). He is the God who appeared at Sinai (Exodus 19) and afterward in the crises of need of his people (on the theophany description, see the comment on Psalm 18). The heavens announce "Here comes the judge" and present the LORD as the one who sets things right (v. 6).

As personnel and witnesses for the trial the LORD summons heaven and earth (vv. 4, 1, 6). In the ancient Near East, lists of gods were invoked as witnesses and enforcers of sworn agreements and treaties. In the theological dramatization of covenant proceedings between the Lord and Israel, heaven and earth as cosmic personifications replace the gods (Deut. 32:1; Isa. 1:2; Micah 6:1–2).

As defendants the LORD calls those "who made a covenant with me (confirmed) by sacrifice" (v. 5). The effect of this identification is to equate those to whom the psalm is being spoken with the congregation of Israel at Sinai (see Exod. 24:3–8). They are the *hasidim* of the LORD, the ones whose identity and life are determined by the covenant they have made with the LORD (NRSV, "faithful ones"; NJPS, "devotees"). To be a *hasid* is to hold oneself subject to the LORD under the claims of the covenant. The terms of the covenant are set out in statutes (v. 16) and words (v. 17, i.e., commandments; see Exod. 20:1). The covenant belongs to the liturgical life of *hasidim;* they recite its terms and pledge allegiance to its commitment (v. 16). By participation in the worship of Israel they have entered into the relation established at Sinai.

2. *The judgment speech (vv. 7–23).* The introduction has prepared for the speech of the LORD. The central act of his coming is speech; he comes to break the silence about what is wrong in the life of his people (vv. 1, 3, 21). The speech sets out the charge against the defendants; the judge is also the prosecutor. The terms describing the speech are "testify against" (v. 7) and "accuse and arraign you" (v. 21). The theological and liturgical importance of the speech, and therefore of the whole psalm, is disclosed in verse 21. The patience of God with his people, the forbearance of the LORD in the face of misunderstanding and faithlessness, could lead to a terrible conclusion. The congregation could make the very worst mistake. They might think of the LORD, and may already think of the LORD, as one like themselves. To project themselves on God and take that for the ultimate reality in terms of which to live, instead of taking the revelation of God and the covenant to be the determination of life—what hideous error! For that reason God must break silence in the face of error. God must be judge. The righteousness of God is at stake. That is what happens, liturgically and theologically, through the psalm. Like the commandments, the speech is direct address to a simple "you" so that the people and each person in it is addressed as a person.

3. *The judgment of worship (vv. 7–15).* The indictment of worship is not a rejection of sacrifice as such. The use of sacrifice and burnt offering is explicitly excepted from the charge (v. 18).

195

The problem is a misunderstanding and misuse of sacrifice. If sacrifice is brought as a gift to God from "your house" and "your folds" and offered as something transferred from their ownership to God's possession, that sacrifice is rejected. Such a sacrifice denies that God is creator and owner of all (vv. 9–11; 24:1–2). If sacrifice is brought to God as something that God needs and is dependent upon the people to bring, that denies God's absolute sovereignty (vv. 12–13). The scornful questions about God's being hungry and eating the sacrifices are a vehement attack on worship that thinks of God as like the worshiper. Worship is to consist of two things. First, sacrifice is to be brought as an act of thankful praise; the praise may even serve as the sacrifice of thanksgiving, the *Todah*. Vows to God are to be fulfilled by thanksgiving, thanksgiving alone; there is to be no transference of property as payment (vv. 14, 23*a*). Second, in time of trouble prayers for help are to be made. The people are to depend on God and in no way pretend that God depends on them. It is prayer and thanksgiving that honor God (vv. 15, 23). "A thank-offering is dearer to God than all other offerings, for these are brought only because of transgressions" (Midrash Tehillim, I/470). For other qualifications and interpretations of sacrifice in the psalms, see Psalms 40:6–8; 51:16–19; and 69:30–31. For reflections on sacrifice in the Old Testament, see Barth, IV/1, pp. 277ff.

4. *The judgment of conduct (vv. 16–22).* The indictment of conduct begins with an introductory formula: "To the wicked, God has said" (many consider it an interpretive gloss). The formula does not mean that the following charges are addressed to a different group from the people or a special group within it. The style of direct address to the congregation as an individual continues. The category "wicked" is the appropriate one for a community in which the cited transgressions occur. There is a disparity, goes the accusation, between confession (v. 16) and conduct (v. 17). They recite the statutes and ignore the commandments. They confess the covenant and reject its discipline. But covenanters must conform to the covenant. Disciples must observe discipline. Servants of God must bring innate human willfulness and selfishness under the control of commitment. The charges list the transgression of the commandments against stealing, adultery, and false witness (vv. 18–20). The list is meant to be illustrative, not exhaustive. But the charges are serious enough. Perversion of the covenant ethos in the areas

of possessions, sex, and speech corrupt a society. For similar sayings by the prophets listing broken commandments as community indictments, see Hosea 4:1–3 and Jeremiah 7:1–15.

5. *Performance.* Psalm 50 represents a type and style of speech that the prophets employed (e.g., Isa. 4:13–15). But where the prophets would typically conclude an indictment with an announcement of punishment, this saying concludes with warning and instruction (vv. 22–23). It threatens punishment (compare v. 22*b* with Hos. 5:14) but offers another way. Understanding must replace misunderstanding. Conduct must take the right way. If the speech is heard, God will save instead of punish. The difference indicates the liturgical and sermonic character of the psalm. "Psalm 50 is an actualization of the *Sinai* theophany" (Keel, p. 225). It is the agenda for a prophet of the sanctuary to be used when the silence of God needs to be broken because worship is misunderstood and discipline rejected. Psalm 50 is the first of the psalms of Asaph, a collection that shows the influence of the theological tradition to which Hosea and Jeremiah and Deuteronomy belong. Its focus on the Sinai covenant, the covenant stipulations, corporate wrong and the way to restoration, and the prophetic style are typical of the collection (see Nasuti, pp. 127–135).

This psalm can and must be heard in the liturgy of the church because the Christian community has been incorporated into the people of the LORD by a covenant made through the sacrifice of Jesus Messiah (Mark 14:24). Where is there a congregation whose worship perfectly reflects the sovereignty and grace of God? Where is there a community of faith that loves the discipline of discipleship so much that the commandments are obeyed, and possessions and sex and speech sublimated to the love of God? If the judgment of God is not proclaimed in the church, then heaven will proclaim it (v. 6).

Psalm 51: I Have Sinned

The sentence that is basic to all penitential prayer in the Old Testament is the simple confession, "I have sinned" (Gerstenberger, 14/1, p. 213). Psalm 51 is the fullest exposition of that sentence in the Bible. Luther observed that whoever first called it a penitential psalm "knew what he was doing.... Here the doctrine of true repentance is set forth before us" (Luther, 12:304–5). The claim that Psalm 51 has been said in full or in

197

part more often in worship and devotion than any other Scripture is probably true. It has been used as a penitential prayer (it is the fourth of the traditional seven penitential psalms; see Psalm 6), as the proper psalm to introduce the season of Lent, as a hymn in metrical version, as a regular prayer of confession, as a source for liturgical sentences, and as a text for reflection on Christian doctrine (see Luther, 12:303ff.; Calvin, 2:281ff.; and Barth, IV/1, pp. 578ff.). Because of this varied and continuous use, the psalm has had an incalculable influence on the theology and practice of the Christian faith.

1. In its formal characteristics Psalm 51 is an individual prayer for help, but it is a very developed and unusual case of the type (Introduction, sec. 5.2). Clearly the prayer is written for a person in trouble, but the description of trouble does not appear as a separate component. Nor is there any complaint against others or against God. The trouble is wholly the sinful self.

Petitions are in control of the structure throughout; the prayer begins, continues, and concludes in the asking mode. Other components of the type that are used in the psalm are attached to petitions. The petitions in verses 1–2 are supported by verses 3–6, which offer reasons for the prayer and motives for God's response; it is in these motives that the trouble of the self is fully described (v. 6 is quite obscure). Petitions resume in verse 7 and continue through verse 12, to be concluded in verse 13 by a promise to witness to the ways of God. Verses 14 and 15 plead for a deliverance that restores the praise of God, and the reason for the petition is given in verses 16–17. A request on behalf of Zion concludes the sequence (v. 18) supported by the anticipation of the resumption of acceptable sacrifices (v. 19).

As a whole, the psalm is a prayer of unrelieved intensity and eloquence. Its theme is stated in the opening words, "Be gracious to me, O God," and the rest of the psalm unfolds that basic appeal.

2. The superscription identifies the psalm as a prayer made by David after the prophet Nathan had confronted him with his sin in the affair with Bathsheba (II Samuel 11—12). The learned scribe who found a setting for the psalm in the story of David saw a verbal connection between verse 4 and II Samuel 11:27 and 12:13 (see Introduction, sec. 3.5; and Psalm 3, sec. 4). The superscription has been the basis for the interpretation of the

psalm as the expression of David's individual experience and penitence. This approach has produced moving and profound readings of the psalm, but it has always, especially in the modern period, stood in a certain tension with the liturgical use of the psalm for general, corporate, and individual penance.

There are many features in the psalm that suggest it was composed during or after the exile and was used in Israel as a general penitential prayer. The psalm may be the product of considerable development; verses 16–17 and 18–19 are often thought to be expansions of an individual prayer for help. But its history may even be more complex than that of two expansions. In its present form, its language and thought are connected with that of Jeremiah, Ezekiel, and Isaiah 40—66. It reads like an anticipation of or response to the promises of a new heart and spirit in Jeremiah (Jer. 24:7; 31:33; 32:39–40) and Ezekiel (Ezek. 36:25ff.). Interpreted in this context, some of the prayer's difficult points will make better theological sense, and verses 18–19 form an appropriate conclusion rather than a contradictory addition. The prayer seeks a cleansing and purification from all transgressions, iniquities, and sins (vv. 1–2, 9). It may have been composed for use by the congregation, and individuals as part of it, in connection with the Day of Atonement (see Lev. 16:30). Understanding the psalm as a prayer composed for the community and for individuals in their identity with the community has important consequences for its interpretation and liturgical use.

3. The confession of sin is based on the grace of God. "Be gracious" (NRSV, "have mercy") is the first word of the psalm. The plea appeals to God's steadfast love and abundant mercy (v. 1). The prayer is not merely an expression of human remorse or preoccupation with failure and guilt; it looks beyond self to God and lays hold on the marvelous possibilities of God's grace. Confession of sin is already on the way to justification because it is first of all a response to grace. It is the act in which we humans acknowledge what we are before God and what God is for us. We are sinners; God is gracious. Jesus told of a man who went down to his house justified, whose prayer was, "LORD, be merciful to me, a sinner" (Luke 18:13). That man's prayer was in effect the opening words of Psalm 51.

4. Those who confess their sin know and believe that their life is judged by God. This is the point of verses 3–4. The psalmist is a penitent, not only a person who has sinned, but one who

199

acknowledges and confronts the sin that his life has produced (v. 3). And he understands that the meaning and reality of sin is that it puts one's life in question before God. That is what the astonishing absolute declaration of verse 4 says.

Verse 4 may seem to confess an act that offends God but affects no human being. But the notion that a person could sin without injuring others is inconceivable in the Old Testament. Even idolatry, which might be thought to concern only one's relation to the LORD, was understood to damage one's community severely. The Old Testament knows of hidden sins and unintended sins but not of private sins that neither concern nor affect others. When David recognized his wrong in the matter of Bathsheba, he said, "I have sinned against the LORD" (II Sam. 12:13). In speaking thus, he did not mean that he saw no wrong against Uriah and Bathsheba. His adultery and murder had been his sin against the LORD. He spoke as he did because it was the LORD who called him into question. Psalm 51 addresses the LORD and concerns the relation to God. Verse 4 with its emphatic and exclusive expression is a way of saying that apart from God's relation to all human acts, there would be no sin. Sin is essentially a theological category. It is God and God alone whose way and will as criteria for human acts reveal them as sin. The parallel measure (v. 4b) points clearly toward such an understanding; it is a kind of definition of sin as "that which is evil in thy sight." It is the divine oversight of human life that makes talk about sin meaningful and necessary. When there is no reckoning with the oversight of God, the vocabulary of sin becomes meaningless and atrophies.

Through the preaching of the prophets and the exilic experience Israel came to know in an intenser, profounder way that they stood under God's judgment. It is the voice of that knowledge that says, "So you are just in your sentence, and right in your judgment" (NJPS). Christians know the truth of that admission also through the cross. The beginning of salvation from sin is God's judgment upon the sinner.

5. The prayer confesses sinfulness, not simply one or several sins. It concerns the condition of the self, not just responsibility for a particular transgression. In its first petition, the entire Old Testament vocabulary of sin (transgression, iniquity, sin) is used; and the words appear as plurals as well as in the singular (vv. 1–2, 3, 9), as though the confession were a general

one intended to be comprehensive. "Deliver me from blood-shed" (v. 14, NRSV) seems to name a particular sin, but the Hebrew word *dammim* in this context is a comprehensive term for guilt (cf. Isa. 4:4; Ezek. 18:13; 22:1–16; Hos. 12:14; note that all of these refer to corporate Israel). It is in this context that the perplexing verse 5 with its reference to a sinful conception and birth is to be read. The verse has been taken in the history of Christian morality and doctrine as a general statement about sex and the human condition rather than as a specific confes-sion. It has been used to support theories about sin as a biologi-cal and causal inheritance and human procreation as a necessarily sinful act. These are views which also seem incon-ceivable for Old Testament thought. Genesis 2—3 does teach that human beings were sinful from their beginnings. There is a scattering of texts in the Old Testament that say that all do sin (Gen. 6:5, 12), and none are righteous before God (Ps. 143:2; Job 14:4; 15:14–16; 25:4). Verse 5 is surely a way of confessing, not a particular transgression, but a whole life conditioned by sin from its beginning, a way of saying not just that I have sinned but that I am in my existence a sinner. My problem is not just the need of pardon for a particular wrong but deliverance from the predicament of my self. Such a confession prepares for the petitions in verses 10 and 14.

The closest parallels to verse 5 and its references to mother and birth as the beginning of sin are found in the exilic proph-ets. Three times Ezekiel told a version of Israel's career that began with sin (Ezekiel 16; 20; 23) and accusingly said, "Your origin and your birth are of the land of the Canaanites; your father was an Amorite and your mother a Hittite" (Ezek. 16:3). Second Isaiah said of Israel, "Your first father sinned" (Isa. 43:27) and "from birth you were called a rebel" (Isa. 48:8); and he used "mother" as metaphor for Israel (Isa. 50:1). These exilic prophets seemed to have realized that the problem of Israel's relation to the LORD was not an aberration of the time just before the exile or a problem of the conduct of its kings. The problem reached back to the very beginning of the LORD's way with them. The people of the LORD were from their birth sinful. Verse 5 could well be a confession tutored by that prophetic insight, a statement about the community and based on the community's experience with the LORD. It is a clue to how the biblical witness came to its realization about the human condition—not through general human experience or the autonomous conclusions of reason, but by the self-knowledge that comes from the judgment and salvation of God.

The confession of sin is first of all the act of the people of God, and its doctrine of the human condition is a reflection on all humanity from that perspective. At this point the psalm leads away from an individualistic and episodic understanding of the content of penitence. Repentance concerns what I am, not just something I have done that is an expression of what I am. The confession of sin always has a corporate dimension. When a person says "I" in the confession, the pronoun is used in identity with the congregation and with all humanity. In confession, I am Israel and Adam. The sins of all concern me because they are the expression of the sinfulness that conditions me. To be actual, the congregational confession of sin needs to be based in its character as a unity and in its representative connectedness with all humanity.

6. The confession of sin seeks renewal as well as forgiveness. The psalm leads the penitent to seek both justification and sanctification. This purpose of the prayer corresponds to its confession of sinfulness and comes to its central expression in verse 10: "Create a clean heart for me, O God, and renew a steadfast spirit within me." It is important to understand just what is being asked here and how it is related to other parts of the psalm.

a. Many of the prayers for help say, "Change my situation so I may praise you." This one says, "Change me; I am the problem." "Create" (bara') is a verb of which God alone is subject in the language of the Old Testament. It means to bring into existence what was not there before. The prophecy in Isaiah 40—66 uses "create" to speak of God's saving action of transforming what is already there so that what comes to be is different (Isa. 41:20; 45:8; 65:17, 18). "Renew," as the synonym of "create," confirms that meaning here. The synonyms "heart" and "spirit" do not merely designate parts of a person; rather, they stand for that through which the self is expressed. In biblical vocabulary, what is said of heart and spirit characterizes the condition and direction of a person's life. What the prayer seeks is a *clean* heart and a *steady* spirit. The terminology of purification is being used here and in the entire prayer as the prophets used it, in a personal and spiritual rather than a ritual and physical sense. What is unclean is inimical to God. A clean heart would be a mind and will open to God, oriented to God. A steadfast spirit would be a mind and will fixed and steady toward God—ready to praise (57:8), true to God's covenant (78:37), and trusting during evil times (112:7).

b. The petition in verse 10 illuminates the heavy use of ritual language in the prayer. If God were to deal only with the psalmist's sin (blot it out, hide his face from it, deliver him from his guilt), that would leave the person/self untouched. The ritual verbs (wash, cleanse, purge) provide a way of speaking of God's direct action on the person and prepare for create/renew. They may indicate that the psalm regards the ministry of the temple as the means through which God works to create the clean heart. But only if God acts in and through them! The use of God as subject of wash/cleanse/purge is striking; comparable texts occur in the exilic prophets and refer to God's salvific action on the community (Jer. 33:8; Ezek. 24:13; 36:25, 33; 37:23; cf. Mal. 3:3). It is even more surprising that God's Holy Spirit is still with the sinner; unclean and holy are mutually exclusive. Yet the Holy Spirit remains with the sinner and must be regarded as the presence and power of God acting already to create the clean heart that the prayer seeks. Note that the only other occurrence of "Holy Spirit" in the Old Testament is in Isaiah 63:10f.

c. Heart/spirit figure in the prayer in another way. In verse 17, the psalm states that God accepts the broken spirit and contrite heart as a sacrifice. Broken spirit and crushed heart are metaphors for the mind and will made humble by God's judgment upon the sinner. Note "the bones that you have crushed" in verse 8; "bones" is another physical metaphor for self and its consciousness. The broken heart says to God, "I am yours, not my own; mind and will are yours." The psalm itself is the liturgy of the broken heart. Verse 16 is probably not a rejection of sacrifice as such; rather, it is a way of saying that sacrifice is not what God wants from the sinner (see Psalm 50). Sacrifice of animals as the essential way to deal with one's sinfulness is, however, relativized. That God turns to and accepts the broken and contrite heart/spirit rather than sacrifice is announced by the prophet who speaks in Isaiah 66:1–4; see also Isaiah 57:15–21 and 61:1.

d. The petition that God show his royal goodwill toward Jerusalem by rebuilding its walls (v. 18) corresponds to the petition that God create a clean heart and renew a steadfast spirit.

203

The restoration of the city of God completes the renewal of the people of God. Both are to be works of God by which God brings the people out of sin through judgment to renewal. It is in the restored city inhabited by the pure in heart that right sacrifices, the ritual worship of God, can be resumed.

The psalm in all these respects holds together what must be held together. It instructs and guides repentance toward the fullness of justification and sanctification. It wants us to realize the deep connection between our sins and our sinfulness. It discloses our identity with congregation and world under the judgment of God. It teaches us to find our renewal in the renewal of the church and the church's renewal in our sanctification. Because the psalm instructs us in these ways, its use as introduction to the meaning and practice of repentance is profoundly justified.

Psalm 52: The One Who Would Not Take Refuge in God

What is the strength that sustains life? Is it the power of the lie and riches, or is it the strength of the steadfast love of God? What makes life endure? That is the question on which Psalm 52 turns.

1. The psalm has three sections. The first section (vv. 1–4) is the descriptive denunciation of a destructive person in the style of direct address. The second (vv. 5–7) warns the addressee that God will destroy him in a way that instructs the righteous in the fear of the LORD. In the third, the psalmist confesses his trust in God (v. 8) and offers God thankful praise for vindicating the trust of the righteous (v. 9). The confession is made and the praise offered before the faithful (v. 9) for their instruction and encouragement. The style of direct address seems to suggest the setting of confrontation between the psalmist and someone who has injured him. But the style is rhetorical, a dramatic way of personalizing a warning against the character and conduct described. If such people are present in the congregation, let them take heed and consider the destiny that God has in store for them. The faithful are assured that they will see the downfall of the wicked as confirmation that the righteousness of God does prevail (v. 8).

204

2. The vocative "mighty man" (*gibbor*) is certainly derisive. The term often refers to a warrior. Here it comes across
as "big shot," "big operator," or "tycoon" would in our vocabulary. The characterization of the "mighty man" is conventional:
boasting, having deceptive injurious intent and speech, loving
evil instead of good, trusting in riches instead of taking refuge
in God. The portrait is that of a person who turns human capacities and possession into the basis of his existence. The psalm was
composed for a time when power joined to wealth was destructive of the social order and a tribulation and scandal for those
who loved good and trusted in God. Its basic theme is the
conflict between the wicked and the righteous in a world governed by God. See Psalms 11; 12; 14; 37; 49; 73; and Introduction, sec. 5.6. The basic confidence of Psalm 52 is that God will
overrule the way of the wicked. The psalmist commends the
way of trust in God with a testimony that compares his own life
to "a green olive tree in the house of God." The simile of the
flourishing tree represents an existence rooted in a relation to
God that draws on all the resources of worship and instruction
provided in the temple (1:3; 92:12–15; Jer. 17:7–8).

3. The superscription attributes the psalm to an incident in
David's life when Doeg the Edomite told Saul that David had
gone to the priest Ahimelek at Nob for help when David was
fleeing from Saul (I Samuel 21—22; note 21:7 and 22:9). This
information resulted in the murder of many of the priests at
Nob. The scribe who searched out the scriptural setting for the
psalm took Doeg as a character who exemplified the "mighty
man" addressed in verse 1 (see Psalm 3, sec. 4). His words
"devoured" an entire cadre of priests of the LORD (v. 3).

Psalm 53: There Is No One Who Does Good

Psalms 53 and 14 are slightly different versions of the same
poem. In Psalm 53 the superscription contains two additional
items. "God" is used instead of "LORD" in conformity with the
practice in Psalms 42—83, a group in which "God" as name
occurs where "LORD" would be expected elsewhere in the
Psalter. The most noticeable difference is found in verse 5 (cf.
14:5–6), which describes God's terror as it falls on the evildoers
(the text is uncertain). In Psalm 14, the corresponding lines
describe the terror of God as God's action to protect the poor.

The two versions were in different smaller collections of psalms that were later incorporated into the emerging Book of Psalms. See the comment on Psalm 14.

Psalm 54: The Ruthless Seek My Life

1. Psalm 54 is a brief individual prayer for help (Introduction, sec. 5.2.1). It is so terse and typical in its use of the elements of the genre that it can serve with Psalm 13 as an illustrative example of such prayers. It begins with a vocative and a petition to be helped (v. 1) and heard (v. 2). A concise description of trouble (v. 3) supports the petition. Then a declaration of confidence in God (vv. 4–5a) is rounded off with a petition for God to act against the enemy (v. 5b). The prayer concludes with a vow of sacrifice and thanks that makes a transition into the praise that will accompany the sacrifice and expresses its meaning as thanksgiving (vv. 6–7).

2. The petition asks that God save "by your name" and "by your might" (v. 1). The poetic synonymity between the name of God and the might of God shows that the name is understood as the power of the person of God. It is not merely an identification; the name is the identity of God (on the importance of the name of the LORD in the theology of the Psalms, see Kraus, *Theology*, pp. 17–31). The trouble from which the prayer seeks deliverance is created by enemies who are described in two ways (v. 3). They are ruthless in seeking the life of the one who prays and insolent in not setting God before them. Their disdain for God's judgment leaves them free to be ruthless with others (cf. 10:3–4, 10–11; 14:4; 53:4). Threatened by faithless foes, the psalmist appeals to the faithfulness of God (v. 5). In such a situation Jeremiah appealed to the LORD and was promised, "I will deliver you out of the hand of the wicked, and redeem you from the grasp of the ruthless" (Jer. 15:21).

3. The superscription gives this prayer a narrative setting in the story of David, "when the Ziphites went and told Saul, 'David is hiding among us.'" The reference is to I Samuel 23:19 (see also I Sam. 26:1). The learned scribe who was searching the text of Samuel for connections to David's prayers found a correspondence between "The ruthless seek my life" in verse 3 and "Saul had come out to seek his life" in I Samuel 23:15 (see Introduction, sec. 3.5; and the comment on Psalm 3, sec. 4).

forsaken by trusted friends + partners (handwritten)

Psalm 55: Betrayal by Friends

Psalm 55 is a prayer for help in first person singular style (Introduction, sec. 5.2). Its text is uncertain at several places, as comparison of current translations will show. Its unity has been questioned. Petitions for help against enemies (vv. 1–2, 9, 15) are supported by laments over hostility (vv. 9*b*–14, 20–21) and the suffering caused by it (vv. 2*b*–8) and by assertions of trust in God (vv. 16–19, 23) and an exhortation to others to depend on God (v. 22). On enemies in the prayer, see Introduction, sec. 6.17.

p. 35 (handwritten)

The psalmist describes the hostility that afflicts him in terms of general urban lawlessness (vv. 9–11) and betrayal by a covenant partner of his intimate circle (vv. 12–14, 20–21). The violence and strife of his city and the scorn of his closest friends are experienced as the very terrors of death (vv. 4–5). Jeremiah once spoke of a wish to flee to the wilderness to escape a collapsing society in which even neighbors were dangerous (Jer. 9:2–9). There is a similar lament over social chaos in Micah 7:1–6 that probably reflects postexilic conditions. Perhaps these are hints of the circumstances for which the prayer was composed.

Gen 11⁹ "confuse their speech" vs 9a (handwritten)

Jesus knew the anguish of betrayal by one who belonged to his own circle (Luke 22:47f.), and the anguish in the language of this psalm tells us how the betrayal hurt. Life is so inextricably connected with friends and society for support and confidence that the betrayal of the one and the unreliability of the other are threatening to life. "Cast your burden on the LORD" in such times, the psalmist urges (v. 22). First Peter repeats that exhortation for a congregation of early Christians (I Peter 5:7). They may have found in the psalm a prayer through which to respond.

Psalm 56: In God I Trust

1. Psalm 56 is a prayer for help in which statements of trust dominate. It opens with the basic petition "Be gracious to me" (v. 1) and asks that God frustrate the intention of enemies (v. 7) who are described as fighters that plot against the one who prays and lie in ambush to take his life (vv. 1–2, 5–6). The situation would naturally bring fear, but the psalm majors in assertions of trust (vv. 3–4, 8–11). The prayer concludes with a

promise to perform the rituals of thanksgiving in response to God's deliverance (vv. 12–13).

2. Repetition makes the statements of trust the theme of the psalm. In their similarity the confident confessions in verses 3–4 and 10–11 sound like a refrain or antiphon. The statements employ two sets of antonyms whose contrasts and relations tell us something about the way the psalmists thought about trust. The antonyms are the verbs "trust/fear" and the nouns "God/man-flesh." In the biblical vocabulary, to trust is to rely on someone or something for security, to put one's life in someone's hand, or to depend on things one has or controls to sustain life against threats to it. Deciding about trust is deciding about the existential basis of living. Trust belongs to situations in which fear as anxiety or terror is possible. Fear is the reaction of insecurity in the face of threats. Fear is always a possibility where trust is called for. "Fear and hope may seem opposite and incompatible affections, yet . . . the latter never comes into full sway unless there exists some measure of the former" (Calvin, 2:349).

3. The second set of antonyms is "God/man-flesh." In the formulaic pattern in which the two sets are related in the prophets and the psalms, man-flesh is the cause of fear. It is human beings as enemies, accusers, persecutors, slanderers of the servants of God and the people of the LORD. They raise the question about the reality on which life in history and society is truly based. In the face of such threats, trust in the LORD is to say "You are my God" (31:14), to believe that "God is my salvation" (Isa. 12:2; Ps. 27:1), rather than taking anything at human disposal as security and refuge (52:7–8). The polarity in this pattern (trusting God/fearing man) is used in prophetic and psalmic texts to speak of the basic choice that the people of God have to make in the crises of corporate and personal life (see the discussion of the theme in Ps. 118:5–9; cf. Isa. 31:3; 51:7–12; Jer. 17:5–8; II Chron. 14:11; Pss. 9:19–20; 124:2; 146:3–4).

4. Trust is not an independent act of human will. In Israel it was a response to salvation and to the promise of salvation. This explains the unusual formulation, "God, whose *word* I praise" (vv. 4, 10). The word here is the Old Testament gospel, the answer to laments given by a representative of God, "Fear not, I am with you" (Isa. 41:10, 13, 14; 43:1–5). This is the word behind the confident claim, "This I know, that God is for me" (v. 9; see the discussion of the claim in Ps. 118:6). The claim is

208

a response to the word of salvation; the word gives the knowledge of faith (119:42). Note the apostle's rehearsal of this claim: "If God is for us, who can be against us?" (Rom. 8:31). See also Jesus' discourse on the theme "Fear not" in Luke 12:4–7.

5. The psalm closes with some words of thanksgiving found in Psalm 116:8–9, thanksgiving for a salvation that brings the soul from death to live in the presence of God (see the comment there). The phrase "the light of life" recalls the saying of Jesus, "I am the light of the world; he who follows me will not walk in darkness, but have the light of life" (John 8:12).

6. The title connects the psalm with I Samuel 21:13 when David was "in the hands" of the servants of the king of Gath. The Septuagint translated the mysterious words "according to The Dove on Far-off Terebinths" (so NRSV) as "for the people far removed from the Sanctuary," thus designating the psalm for corporate use (so also the title of the psalm in the Targum). The request that God should "cast down the *peoples*" (v. 7) may indicate that the psalm was composed for congregational use in first person style or was revised for corporate use. Psalm 56 has connections with Psalm 116 and 118, and, like them, its content is appropriate in the mouth of the community as well as of an individual.

Psalm 57: Your Glory Over All the Earth

1. A refrain (vv. 5, 11) divides Psalm 57 into two parts. The first part opens with a double petition for God to be gracious (v. 1*a*). The petition is supported by an extended statement of confidence that God will provide refuge and help from danger (vv. 1*b*–3; on the motif of taking refuge with God in the Psalms, see the discussion of Ps. 7:1). The danger comes from adversaries portrayed as carnivorous lions (v. 4). The second part begins with a statement that anticipates the downfall of the adversaries as already come to pass; they, themselves, have fallen into the very pit they dug for the psalmist (v. 6; cf. 7:15–16; 9:15–16). Certain of God's help (v. 7*a*), the psalmist rouses self and instruments to begin each day with music (vv. 7*b*–8) and promises to praise the LORD in a worldwide setting (vv. 9–10). Verses 7–11 are used for the first part of Psalm 108.

2. The opening appeal to the grace of God identifies this psalm as a prayer for help, but it majors in trust and praise. The reason lies in the vision of God that permeates the prayer and

diminishes the reality of danger. The prayer is a cry to "God Most High" (v. 2). The title "Most High" belongs to Israel's God as the one who, enthroned in the heavens, rules over the nations and peoples of earth, the God portrayed in the hymns of the LORD's kingship and songs of Zion (e.g., 47:2; 46:4; see Introduction, sec. 6.3, 10). His glory is the manifestation of his sovereign rule (8:1; 113:4; Num. 14:21). In his vision the prophet Isaiah heard the seraphim chant "The whole earth is full of his glory" (Isa. 6:3) as the central truth about the world. The exalted God exalts himself in the world in the events of salvation by which his city and messiah and people are saved from the threats of world history (46:10; 18:46; 21:13).

3. So in times of trouble, when the distance between the transcendental truth of God's rule and the actuality of present history is experienced, it is possible and necessary to pray for the exalted God to exalt himself, as the psalmist does in the refrain. He believes that God's steadfast love and faithfulness, the characteristics of God as savior, are as great as the universe itself (v. 10; cf. 36:5). He trusts that the God throned in heaven will send his steadfast love and faithfulness out like agents of a king to do his will (v. 3; cf. 43:3; 85:11–13). God rules. But it is still possible and necessary as individuals and as the church to pray "Thy kingdom come, thy will be done, on earth as it is in heaven." The experiences of God's saving grace that come to us are anticipations and signs of the consummation of God's reign. Our thankful praise is testimony to the nations (v. 9).

4. Who is it that presumes to pray like this, assuming that the God who rules the universe would demonstrate the glory that belongs to God's rule in his salvation? The scholarly scribe who completed the psalm's title answers, "David, when he fled from Saul (and hid) in a cave" (did he have I Sam. 22:1 or 24:3 in mind?). Because the Davidic king represented the kingship of the LORD to the nations, his deliverance by the LORD was a vindication of his rule to the king's enemies. Another Old Testament witness says that it is the chosen people whose salvation reveals the glory of the LORD to all flesh (Isa. 40:5). For Christians, the resurrection of the Messiah Jesus is the consummate manifestation of God's reign in history. It is in union with him that the church gives thanks and praise to God in the midst of the nations.

Psalm 58: There Is a God Who Judges

There is violence on the earth; there is no justice for human-kind. That is the painful dilemma with which Psalm 58 begins (vv. 1–2). At its conclusion, it makes the confession that enables the faithful to live with the dilemma in hope; there is a God who judges on the earth (v. 11). The psalm is one of the many in the Psalter concerned with the problem that the power and success of the wicked set for the life of the righteous who live in trust and obedience. See Psalms 9—10; 11; 12; 14; 37; 49; 73; 91; 94; and Introduction, sec. 6.18.

1. At the center of the psalm is a prayer for the justice of the LORD (v. 6), but the psalm begins with an accusing rebuke addressed to the powerful who are responsible for righteous-ness and justice but instead conduct an administration of wrong and violence (vv. 1–2). The purpose of the rebuke is to personify and locate the source of the trouble that afflicts the community for whom the prayer is composed. The lack of justice in the world is not some impersonal natural inevitable condition of human life. It is the intended work of the hearts and hands of responsible powers (see the use of direct address in 52:1–5). The rebuke is supported by a description of wicked people (vv. 3–5) who are birthed into an environment of falsehood and condi-tioned by it all their lives. The lie is the belief that their heritage of privilege is theirs to use in selfish destructiveness of the society in which they hold power. The description compares them to a poisonous snake that cannot be controlled by a snake charmer; they are so enchanted with the lie of their life that they are deaf and blind to any other influence. The prayer begins with a petition that the LORD "defang these young lions" (v. 6) and continues with a series of wish petitions composed of similes that invoke images of disappearance. The prayer is a vehement passionate plea by the powerless for God's powerful help against the powers of wrong and violence. The psalm con-cludes with an assurance for the congregation about the future (vv. 10–11). The faith and life of the righteous will be vindicated by the God who judges on earth.

2. The identity of those addressed by the vocative in verse 1 is a perennial question, because the meaning of the Hebrew word is uncertain. If "you gods" is correct (so NRSV), then the psalm addresses the minor deities of the ancient Near Eastern

211

pantheon who were thought of as intermediate officials in the divine administration of the world (see the comment on Psalm 82). The wicked would be the human instruments of their injustice. It seems better to translate "O mighty ones" (NJPS) or "you rulers" (REB), understanding the vocative as a derisive appellation like "O mighty man" at the beginning of Psalm 52. Then the reference to the birth of the wicked would stand in direct continuity with the opening verses.

3. The psalm as a whole is an expression of the faith common to the psalms and prophets that the God who is sovereign of the world inevitably and inexorably acts as judge in the world. The role of judge belongs to the kingship of God (e.g., 7:11; 9:7–12; 11:4–7; and 96—99; Luke 18:7–8). To believe in the reign of God is to reckon with and hope for the judgment of God. The notion of "vengeance" (v. 10) is a feature of the vision of God as ruler. The term does not mean vindictive revenge; it refers to an action to do justice and restore order where the regular and responsible institutions of justice have failed. "Vengeance is mine," says the LORD of Israel and the God of nations (see the comment on Ps. 94:1). The harsh petitions in verses 6–9 use poetic rhetorical similes based on the conviction that the unrepentant wicked have no lasting place or future in God's world (Psalms 1; 4—6; and many other texts). The righteous rejoice when they see the vengeance of the LORD, because it is a sign of the reign of God (52:6–7). The cruel idiom of the righteous bathing their feet in the blood of the wicked belongs to language adopted from military rhetoric used to describe the utter defeat of enemies in warfare (68:23; Deut. 32:42–43) and is a symbol of participation in the victory of God. That is the reward of the righteous, not some sort of earned payoff, but the knowledge of the vindication of God's reign in spite of the power and arrogance of injustice. For the New Testament, see the description of the eschatological day of the LORD in II Thessalonians 1:5–12 and the prayer of the martyrs who were slain for faithfulness in Revelation 6:9–11.

Psalm 59: Deliver Me from My Enemies

1. Psalm 59 is a prayer in which the use of an individual prayer for help for corporate petition is particularly evident. It is composed in the form of a prayer for help in first person singular style (see Introduction, sec. 5.2). A person whose life is

threatened by powerful enemies appeals in trust to the LORD. The principal elements of the type appear: petition (vv. 1–2, 4b–5, 11–13), description of trouble (vv. 3a, 6–7, 14–15), professions of innocence (vv. 3b–4a) and of trust (vv. 8–10), and promises of praise (vv. 16–17). The whole is divided into two parts by a set of repetitions that function in a refrain-like manner at the conclusion of each part. Each set is composed of a characterization of the adversaries as wild dogs (vv. 6–7 and 14–15), followed by assertions of trust (vv. 8 and 16) and promises of praise (vv. 9–10 and 17). Verses 6 and 14 and verses 9 and 17 are exact equivalents.

2. But the psalm contains recurring features that indicate that the "I" who prays is, or represents, the community. The LORD is addressed as "God of hosts (see Psalm 24) and "God of Israel" (v. 5). Petitions seek action against "all the nations" (v. 5) at whose pretensions the LORD laughs in derision (v. 8; see Psalm 2). God is to intervene in a way that has a twofold result. First, the punishment is to be extended over a period of time so that the community will realize that God is at work and not "forget" God (v. 11). Second, God's intervention is to be a revelation to the ends of the earth that God is ruler in and over Israel (v. 13).

3. The prayer seems to express the anxieties and needs of the postexilic religious community seeking to maintain its trust in the face of surrounding nations whose cultures and religions are viewed as hostile to the community's faith. The prayer is the voice of the congregation that has no refuge in the midst of history other than the LORD of hosts. The scholarly scribe who completed the title found a clue to the psalm's setting in the story of David (I Sam. 19:11).

Psalm 60: With God We Shall Do Valiantly

Psalm 60 is a corporate prayer for help (Introduction, sec. 5.4). It begins with a complaint that the LORD's anger has visited disaster upon the land and its population; the people of God are suffering hardship (vv. 1–3). The disaster is described in cosmic terms and metaphors, but it is apparent from the entire psalm that the hosts of Israel have failed in battle (especially v. 10). Petitions are made for help for those who fear God, the beloved ones (vv. 4–5; translating v. 4 as a petition with NJPS).

In response to the plea for an answer (v. 5), a saying of God

213

is delivered (vv. 6–8). The oracle lays claim to territory identified by a series of names arranged to move from places to tribal regions to nations. The territory marked off by the names is more or less the central territory of David's kingdom. The oracle comes in the midst of the prayer song and gives the impression that it is being quoted from a tradition of prophetic sayings belonging to the sanctuary (Nasuti, p. 129; and Kraus, *Psalms 60—150*, p. 3). Verse 9 may belong to the oracle and be a challenge to a king or military leader to lead the army accompanied by God to Edom, the possible source of the trouble. The function of the oracle as a whole is to furnish a contrast with the present and bring encouragement to the one who prays.

The psalm concludes with a complaint about the rejection of God (v. 10), a petition for help against the foe because human strength is not enough (v. 11), and an assertion of confidence (v. 12).

The psalm is based on the old theology of holy war, validated by narratives from Israel's past, according to which military ventures were successful only if God accompanied the hosts of Israel into battle (e.g., Numbers 13—14; Judg. 4:14–15).

Verses 5–12 are used also in Psalm 108:6–13, a further clue that traditional material has been employed in composing both psalms. The learned scribe who searched for narrative settings in the story of David saw the connection between the nations named in the psalm and those named in the account of the expansion of David's kingdom in II Samuel 8 (see Psalm 3, sec. 4).

Psalm 61: Lead Me to the Rock

"O, lead me to the rock that is higher than I," prays this psalm; that is, "Help me reach safety that I cannot find on my own." The psalm is a prayer for help in first person style. It is predominantly petition (vv. 1, 4, 6–7) supported by assertions of confidence (vv. 3, 5) and concluding with a promise of praise (v. 8). The psalmist is at "the end of the earth," a metaphor for being at the end of one's resources, and his resolution and courage are exhausted (v. 2); reference to "the enemy" rounds out the formulaic description of trouble.

214   The central notion is that of God as refuge from trouble. On the notion, see the comment on Psalm 7:1. To dwell in God's tent draws on the image of the protection afforded a guest (see

23:6). The "sheltering wings of God" is another image of divine protection (see 17:8).

In verses 6–7 there is a petition for the king, that he have a long life in the presence and under the protection of God (so 72:5, 15, 17). At other places in the Psalms, third person statements about the king (28:8; 63:11) and petition for him (84:9) appear in the midst of first person style. Psalm 84 is a corporate hymn; in it the congregation prays for the messiah-king because he is their shield and their well-being is identified with his. Perhaps here and in the other cases the king is mentioned for the same reason. Or it is possible that these psalms were composed for royal recitation, with the king referring to himself in the third person. In either case, all these instances witness to the importance of the Davidic king as one in and through whom God bestowed protection and blessing on the community and individuals in it. See the Introduction, sec. 6.11.

Psalm 62: My Soul Waits for God Alone

1. Psalm 62 is a sustained declaration of trust in God. Its rhetoric and arrangement are designed to serve its purpose. Six of its poetic lines begin with a Hebrew word that introduces an emphatic assertion (vv. 1, 2, 4, 5, 6, 9; Heb. *'ak*: NRSV, "alone"; NJPS, better "truly"). The reiteration of this introductory emphatic sustains the declaratory character of the whole. The psalm is arranged in three sections. The first section begins with a confessional declaration of the psalmist's relation to God (vv. 1–2) followed by a depiction of hostility in the social setting (vv. 3–4). Unidentified figures of a typical character are addressed and described as a rhetorical device to evoke the threatening context in which trust is practiced. The second section begins with a modified repetition and expansion of the first confessional declaration (vv. 5–7) followed by an exhortation to the congregation to put their trust in God (v. 8) rather than in mere human beings (v. 9) or in violent attempts to make life secure (v. 10). The third section gives the reason for trust by reporting the revelation of statements about God's character and way (vv. 11–12).

2. The first measures of verses 1 and 5 are difficult to put in English. The Hebrew does not mean verbal silence, as some translations suggest; verse 8 commends pouring out one's heart in prayer as an act of trust. Nor is waiting implied; the state of

215

soul described is already consummated. The measures speak rather of a quietness of soul, an inner stillness that comes with yielding all fears and anxieties and insecurities to God in an act of trust. In Hebrew, verse 1 is a declaration, while verse 5 is a self-exhortation (see NJPS). Something like "Truly, my soul is at rest in God; from him is my salvation. . . . Truly, O my soul, rest in God, for from him is my hope." The variation speaks of a trust that is present now in the gift of salvation but must be maintained in life as the practice of hope. This stillness is like the peace of God which passes all understanding that will keep your hearts and minds in Christ Jesus (Phil. 4:7).

3. The substance of trust is set forth in confessional statements (vv. 2, 6–7). A series of predicates are acknowledged as the truth about God and are claimed by the psalmist with the possessive pronoun. "He is my rock, salvation, fortress, honor, refuge." These predicates are the traditional attributes of God that Israel came to know through its history with the LORD (e.g., Deut. 32:4; Exod. 15:2). They belong to the community's confession of faith made in hymns and prayers (compare v. 8, "God is our refuge," with Ps. 46:1). The individual receives and enters into this confessional life as a member of the people of God and practices it in liturgy and faithfulness as one of the congregation. And the individual gives testimony to the confirmation of the confession in his own life, as is happening in this psalm. The various predicates are all language that identifies the LORD as the source and foundation and future of life.

The two descriptions of human beings and their conduct (vv. 3–4, 9–10) are introduced to enhance the confessions. In human society there is hostility and deceit. Human beings are in the long last insignificant and transient. Efforts to secure life by gaining things, even when violent or successful, are futile. For collateral teaching from the New Testament, see Luke 12:15, 22–34; Mark 4:19; and I Tim. 6:7–10. There is one source and foundation and future for life—one alone. "Trust in him at all times, O people."

4. Using a numerical formula ("Once . . . twice" equals two times), the psalm makes a theological statement based on revelation. Just how God spoke is not said. What was heard was twofold: "Power belongs to God, and to you, my lord, belongs loyal love." These characteristics are so frequently attributed to the LORD in the praise at the temple that it is possible that the experience of worship became the medium of the speech of

216

God (e.g., "power," 93:1; 96:6; loyal love, 136. On the revelation in the sanctuary, see Kraus, *Theology,* pp. 33f.). These attributes are important here because they validate trust. Power means that God can, and loyal love means that God will, "requite a man according to what he does." God will vindicate those who trust him and shatter the illusions of those who trust human strength and violence (Matt. 16:27; Rom. 2:6ff.; II Tim. 4:14).

5. Through most of its lines, Psalm 62 is composed in the style appropriate for a person's own confession of faith and for a testimony of witness and instruction to others. But in its closing line (v. 12) the style shifts to direct address to "my Lord," showing that it is also composed to be said in the presence of God as a declaration of commitment. It is thus a psalm that guides our own confession, instructs the congregation in trust, and makes a commitment to our Lord.

Psalm 63: Your Steadfast Love Is Better Than Life

Psalm 63 was greatly valued in the early church. It was selected as the morning psalm to introduce the singing of the psalms in the Sunday service (Delitzsch, 2:212f.). It speaks of the thirst of the soul for God, the quenching of that thirst through the presence of God in the sanctuary, and the response of praise as the expression of life itself.

1. The psalm is a prayer for help in first person style (see Introduction, sec. 5.2). It is composed as the prayer of a person who comes to the sanctuary (v. 2) from a dangerous world where there are people who seek his life (v. 9; the expression is a formulaic identification of adversaries in prayers for help: 35:4; 38:12; 40:14; etc.). In that dangerous world the psalmist has experienced the absence of God as the thirst and hunger of soul, a need for the presence of God without which his soul cannot live. On the powerful metaphor of thirst for the soul's need of God's presence, see the comment on Psalm 42.

The need has been met by encounter with the Presence in the sanctuary. There the psalmist has beheld the power and glory of God in a vision. On the temple as the place where God's presence is real and available for the faithful, see the comment on Psalms 36 and 42—43. The encounter with the Presence has met his need and satisfied his soul as if he had fed on the richest food (v. 5); in response, he promises to live in praise, day and night, all his life (vv. 3–7).

217

The prayer concludes with a twofold petition in verses 9–11. These verses can be translated as statements of confidence but are more likely requests (so NJPS). Using a series of images of final disempowerment, the psalmist asks that the dangers to his life no longer exist. Then, as one who has sworn an oath of fealty to the king, he prays also for his human ruler upon whom the welfare of the people so much depends (cf. Ps. 61:6).

2. The present title locates the psalm in David's life when he had to live in the wilderness (see Psalm 3, sec. 4). A scholarly scribe has connected the dry and weary land of verse 1 with the wilderness of Judah and thought of texts that report that Saul sought David's life there (I Sam. 23:14; 24:2).

3. The prayer contains a truly remarkable confession of faith: "Your steadfast love (*hesed*) is better than life" (v. 3; on *hesed* in the psalms, see Introduction, sec. 6.8). The statement is astounding. The psalmist seems to say that God's faithfulness to him is more valuable than his own life. But *hesed* is a characteristic of God that is known in God's preservation of the life of those who call him "my God." It is God's *hesed* in which the psalms put their trust and hope for the salvation of life. How can prayer separate God's faithfulness from the life that depends on it and hold it up for praise as more valuable than that life? It seems that the vision of God and the praise of God carry the psalmist to a point at which prayer transcends the soul and its need to contemplate God alone. Trust becomes for a moment pure adoration that leaves the self behind as any participant in the reason for adoration. In the interpretation of patristic times this confession was associated with martyrs who valued God more than life and gave up their lives rather than deny their testimony. But in a salvation religion there is always the danger for all believers to take the value of their own lives as the primary reason to trust God. This verse leads us in prayer to the point of devotion to God alone that must be the goal of all true faith.

Psalm 64: Hide Me from the Wicked

218

Psalm 64 is a prayer for help in first person singular style (Introduction, sec. 5.2). It begins with a petition to be heard and helped; the psalmist seeks divine protection from the hostility of evil persons (vv. 1–2). Enemies attack him verbally and use words like arrows to wound him (vv. 3–6). The description of the enemy's conduct points to the damage done to a person's standing and security in Israel's society by hostile talk. But the one who prays is "blameless" with respect to this vicious assault (v. 4).

Verses 7–10 function as an assertion of confidence made in a near instructional style. The psalmist describes what God will do and what the consequences of the divine intervention will be. God also has arrows to shoot. God will make the talk of the wicked the instrument of their downfall. The fate they sought for their victims will be theirs. This outcome will be recognized as the work of God. All will fear God and report what has happened in testimony. The righteous will rejoice and be taught anew to take refuge in God when in need.

At the beginning of the Psalms, the speech of wicked men; at the end, the speech of witnesses to the salvation of God.

Psalm 65: A Psalm for Thanksgiving

Psalm 65 is a song of joyful praise. From beginning to end, it does not cease its grateful recital of God's works and their benefits. It praises God as God of the temple (vv. 1–4), God of the world (vv. 5–8), and God of the earth (vv. 9–13). Each of these three parts of the psalm is concluded by a description of the effect of God's works (on the congregation, v. 4; on the world, v. 8; on the earth, vv. 12–13). Throughout, God is directly addressed. The congregation stands in the presence of God in gratitude, awe, and joy.

1. *God of the temple.* The song begins with a declaration that praise is the right and fitting offering to God. God is the one who answers prayer, and those whose prayers have been answered keep their vows of gratitude with praise (vv. 1–2; vows are the anticipation of answer to prayer). God is the one who himself propitiates (NRSV, "forgives") the sins of those overwhelmed by guilt (v. 3). God whose holy temple is in Zion is the one on whom the congregation depends in its need and guilt, its finitude and failure. God present for them and merciful toward them satisfies the needs of their mortality. They are but flesh; they must come to God. With a beatitude (v. 4) they acknowledge that even their presence in the courts of God is his work; they are there because God chose and drew them to the satisfaction of their needs with the goodness given in his

219

temple. On dwelling in the courts of the temple as an expression for the occasion and experience of worship, see Psalms 15:1; 23:6; and 27:4.

2. *God of the world.* The awesome deeds of God as the savior of his people have revealed that Israel's God is the hope of the whole world (v. 5). Why Israel's salvation should establish its God as the one in whom the ends of earth and farthest seas should trust is not immediately apparent. The connection lies in the way Israel saw God's deeds of deliverance as an exercise of his power as cosmic ruler. (See the comment on Psalms 68; 114.) That is why the psalm goes on to celebrate God's strength in creating mountains and mastering the unruly seas (vv. 6–7). Israel's God disclosed himself as cosmic ruler in the deliverance of his people. Their savior is the creator; his saving power is the power of creation. So the marvels of the created world are his "signs," the evidence of his power as God of the world. When people all over the world are awed by the magnificence of morning and evening, they are responding to the awesome deeds of the God whom the congregation praises (v. 8).

3. *God of the earth.* In language rich in imagery and poetic exuberance, the psalm praises God as the cosmic farmer. God, says the psalm, "takes care of the earth" (*paqad*; NRSV, "visit"). The description of God's provision concentrates on water; it represents an understanding of fertility and productivity that depend on seasonal rain. Grain grows, meadows and wilderness pastures flourish, the flocks scatter and feed when the rains come. Their coming "crowns the year." Their source is "the river of God," a mythical, inexhaustible flow of water thought to issue from the mount of God's heavenly dwelling (see the comment on Ps. 46:4). This imaginative portrayal of God as provider of fertility is somewhat similar to descriptions of the Canaanite storm-god, Baal, whose victory over chaotic powers was followed by rains that revived fertility (Keel, pp. 212f.). There is probably a connection in the mentality of the psalm between God's power over mountains and seas (vv. 6–7) and his role as the giver of fertility. In Israel's faith, the God whose holy temple is in Zion is the one and only God from whom all goodness comes.

4. Psalm 65 is often used in services at harvesttime and on the American day of Thanksgiving. Read and sung on such occasions, it furnishes the right agenda. The psalm directs attention first of all to God, away from any preoccupation with secu-

lar good fortune. It insists that thanksgiving is a theological work whose subject is God, not ourselves. It sets the priorities in the right order and begins with God, who answers our prayers and forgives our sins. It leads the congregation to come to God first of all in its neediness and failure. It is an antidote to self-satisfaction and self-congratulation. The psalm sets thanksgiving in a universal context and breaks open the proclivity to celebrate our national identity. It binds the congregation to people in the most distant places who also rejoice at the signs of the creation's beauty and goodness. The psalm gives us language to celebrate our dependence on the good earth and its produce in a poetic and personal way. It transcends our growing habit of thinking of productivity in a technological fashion and allows us to speak to the one upon whose gift of a fertile earth all our science and economies depend. That all together is thanksgiving as it should be.

[handwritten marginal note: only "healthy" in the perspective of the larger world]

Psalm 66: How Awesome Are Your Deeds

Psalm 66 is a song that celebrates the deeds of God for the people of God. That is the theme and purpose that unites it. The psalm is composed of two genres, a hymn of praise (vv. 1–12) and a song of thanksgiving (vv. 13–20; see Introduction, sec. 5.5 and 5.3). The hymn is congregational in style and the song individual. The psalm is generally treated as a composite of two distinct pieces. But as in the case of Psalm 118, the combination of group and individual praise seems to reflect the service of thanksgiving as a general institution in the postexilic period. The hymn is a processional for the congregation preceding the presentation of offerings by a representative person whose thanksgiving is made in identity with and on behalf of the congregation.

1. The processional hymn has three stanzas, each introduced by an imperative summons to praise. The first stanza (vv. 1–4) begins with the same line that opens Psalm 100, a call to all the earth to acclaim God as king. The universal dimension of the praise is reiterated here (v. 4) and in the next two stanzas, nations in verse 7 and peoples in verse 8. Verse 3 gives instruction about the basis and content for the praise: "Say to God, 'How awesome (*nora'*) your deeds.'" What deeds are in mind will be said in the second and third stanzas. Here, and in verse 5, the accent is on their awesome character. They are events

numinous with the glory of God, causing the awe that grips people in the presence of divine power (Luke 5:1–11). God is to be praised, not only because "he is good" but also because of the majestic deity in which that goodness and loyal love (v. 20) are based. His deeds display a power that causes those who oppose his reign to pay him homage (Kraus, *Psalms 60—150*, ad loc.; NRSV, "cringe") in worship. The assertion that "all the earth worships you" (v. 4) has a prophetic dimension, for it states what should be and will be in light of the revelation of the glory of God. Compare this opening stanza to Revelation 15:3–4 with its hymn on the great and wonderful deeds of God to whom all the nations shall come and worship. There is a sense in which the praise of God as king always has a prophetic reach. God's rule is eternal (v. 7), but his kingdom is coming.

The second stanza (vv. 5–7) invites the nations to "Come and see the works of God." The challenge is like that of Psalm 46:8, where the works of God are visible in the self-destructiveness and futility of war as a manifestation of human power. Here it is the exodus and the wonder at the sea: "He turned sea (*yam*) into dry land; the river (*nahar*) they crossed on foot." The event was not just a miracle. Yam and Nahar are the names of the personalized cosmic powers whom the Canaanite god Baal overthrows in the ancient myth of Baal's ascent to kingship over nature. The psalmist draws on that myth to speak of the primal saving event in Israel's story as the revelation of the LORD's rule over the nations. The hymn recalls (vv. 6–7) the rejoicing that broke out "there" among the people in the song of Exodus 15 over the revelation that it is the LORD who reigns forever over the gods and the nations (cf. vv. 11, 14, 17–18). The congregation recalls that rejoicing as a celebration in which they participated. Worship transcends time, and the congregation that sings the psalm becomes part of the astonished joyous people of exodus. In the same way, Christians sing, "Were you there when they crucified my Lord?" This must be the answer to how the nations are to come and see the works of God; the works are rendered by the congregation's praise, made perceivable in their re-presentation in liturgy.

In the third stanza (vv. 8–12), the congregation tells the peoples of the world directly what God has done for them. God has put them through a time when they were subjected to mere human beings (*'enosh*, v. 12), a time when they were proved and refined like silver in a smelter (v. 10). The language describ-

222

ing their suffering is similar to that by which the prophets describe the afflictions of the exile (the figure of testing and smelting in Isa. 48:10; Jer. 9:7; Zech. 13:9; Mal. 3:3; the net in Ezek. 12:13; 17:20; and passing through water and fire in Isa. 43:2). The corporate travail of the congregation is described in this way to make it very clear that their humiliation was no contradiction of the reign of "our God." Quite the opposite, it was, itself, God's work. And now he has brought them through and given them life abundant (vv. 9 and 12*b*). "You brought us forth" (v. 12) is exodus language used to say that the first exodus has happened again, but in a different and unexpected way. Human and cosmic powers sought their death, but God brought them to a new life. Noting this, the Greek version named this psalm "a song of the resurrection."

2. After the procession, the representative liturgist enters the area of the altar in the temple to present the offerings of the people to acknowledge the saving work of God (vv. 13–15). The offerings are the Old Testament sacrament that goes with the offering of praise (vv. 1–12) and testimony (vv. 16–19). The list of sacrificial animals presented as burnt offerings is so long that it sounds like poetic hyperbole for complete and consummate sacrifice (v. 15). The offerings are presented to keep the promises made in prayers for help in times of trouble. They are not to be thought of as ways to pay God back but rather as ritual acts of acknowledgment and confession.

Then the leader calls on the congregation of God-fearers, the people in whose lives the awe of God has lodged, to hear his account of God's deed for him (vv. 16–19). The deed is the gift of life described in the hymn. The leader speaks in first person to identify himself personally as a recipient of the gift. His testimony to the congregation opens the way for each of them to identify themselves in the same way. The leader's account is the simple formulaic story of answered prayer from the ritual of thanksgiving: I cried to him—he heard my prayer. It is expanded only by the statement that God's answer confirmed his innocence of intending wrong (v. 18). The statement is more one of witness to the way of God who listens to those who fear him (34:19, 15–18) than it is a claim of self-righteousness.

The psalm closes with an exclamation of praise to God for showing his loyal love in the answered prayer (v. 20).

3. When the church uses this psalm, it recognizes its continuity with the community of those whose story is made up of

exodus and return and confesses that it is a shoot grafted into the olive tree of Israel. And it has a new witness to God's awesome deeds of salvation to add to the old, a story of death and resurrection that is the gospel of the kingdom of God to the nations, an answer to the cry for life that lies in the heart of everyone.

Psalm 67: That Your Way May Be Known

Numbers 6:24–26 records the blessing to be used by Aaron and his sons, the priests, when they bless the congregation of Israel. The first verse of Psalm 67 is a creative reuse of the first two sentences of the priestly blessing: "The LORD bless you and keep you; the LORD make his face to shine upon you and be gracious to you." In the psalm, the priestly blessing is used to introduce a congregational prayer for a blessing that will make the LORD's way known among all the peoples of the earth.

universal reach

1. The theme of the psalm is stated in its first two lines, a blessing for the people of the LORD that leads to praise of the LORD. The literary structure of the psalm develops the theme. The psalm begins with a focus on the blessing of the congregation (v. 1), moves to the praise of the LORD by the nations (vv. 2–5), returns to the topic of blessing for the LORD's people (v. 6), and concludes with a line that combines the two (v. 7). The style of the psalm is predominantly that of a bidding prayer with an alternation between indirect and direct address. The form of the Hebrew verbs allows for a different decision about their function, whether they express statements or requests; NJPS, for instance, translates verses 3–5 as statements about the future.

2. In its theme of a blessing that will make the nations know the LORD, the psalm can be related to two great theological traditions of the Old Testament. The first is the LORD's promise to Abraham of a blessing by which all the families of the earth shall be blessed (Gen. 12:1–4). The psalm sees God's favor to Israel as that which will bring the nations to fear the LORD. Notice how the motif "earth" is used in verses 6–7; the earth gives a harvest as the blessing of the LORD, and all ends of earth come to fear the LORD. The second tradition is the prophecy of Isaiah 40—55 and its proclamation that the LORD's salvation of Israel will be a revelation to the nations that the LORD reigns and leads the ends of the earth to praise the LORD (e.g., Isa.

224

40:1–5; 45:20–25; 49:22–26). In the psalm, what the nations are to come to know is the LORD's way as savior (v. 2). His salvation of Israel will reveal his identity as judge and shepherd of the nations (v. 4). The blessing of Israel will gain the attention of the nations, and they will see in Israel's story the revelation of the reign of the LORD. The blessing of the church is for the salvation of the nations.

Psalm 68: The Victory of God

"Let God arise!" Psalm 68 begins with this invocation of God as the divine warrior whose victory established his reign in the world and whose strength is the salvation of his people (Introduction, sec. 6.6). The victory and the reign of the divine warrior are its underlying theme. In this and other respects the psalm is similar to Exodus 15, the great song that praises the LORD for the deliverance of Israel from Pharaoh's army. That song focuses on the battle at the Red Sea as the victory that led to God's establishment of his people and his sanctuary "on the mountain of his own possession." Psalm 68 focuses on the march from Sinai through the wilderness and the battles with the nations who opposed the progress of God and Israel to the sanctuary that represents God's rule over Israel and the kingdoms of the world.

Though its theme is certain, the analysis and the interpretation are particularly difficult. It has an unusual density of uncertain texts, rare words, allusive language, and shifting styles. Remarks on the problems the psalm poses for translators and exegetes appear like a litany in their work. A large part of the psalm seems to belong to the earliest poetry in the Psalter. Its present form may be the result of a process of compilation and expansion. The power and the effect of the song are nevertheless compelling. Whatever its uncertainties, to read it or to hear it read is to experience something of the awesome, wonderful majesty of the warrior God who saves his people and brings in his kingdom.

1. In spite of the psalm's shifting styles and allusive language, an analysis of its literary structure is possible. It has an introduction (vv. 1–3) and a body of various styles of praise and prayer (vv. 4–35). The body is bracketed at beginning and end by a summons to sing praises to God, the LORD, who is rider upon the clouds in the heavens (vv. 4 and 32–33). The body has

225

two parts. The first is based on a narrative scenario that tells about the savior God who led his people through the wilderness, defeated kings and armies, and proceeded as victor to the mount he had chosen as his royal residence (vv. 4–18). This first part closes with a recollection of God's victory parade ascending the mount where he reigns as God and king (v. 18). The second part is composed of praise and prayer to the LORD resident in his sanctuary, whose salvation is the power and strength of his people in their life in the midst of the nations (vv. 19–35). This part is marked off by the doxological cry, "Blessed be the LORD" (vv. 19, 35; notice the summons to "bless God" in v. 26). Each part has four sections or strophes, whose contributions to the whole, along with the introduction, can be described in the following way.

Introduction (vv. 1–3). The opening invocation seeks a theophany of God in the world, an appearance of divine power that will defeat God's enemies and a victory that brings the wicked to an end and evokes joyful praise from the righteous.

The identity of God (vv. 4–6). God is the "rider upon the clouds" whose name is the LORD, the one who comes from his holy habitation to give help to the helpless.

The original theophany (vv. 7–10). The psalm recalls how God's identity was made known. Once, when Israel was helpless and needy, God led them like a flock through the wilderness to the place where they dwell. They were led by the God of Sinai, appearing as the storm-God, whose presence shook the earth and brought reviving rain to the land that God claimed for his flock.

The victory (vv. 11–14). The psalm recalls the battle in which the land was gained. The recollection is evoked in allusive language that speaks of the flight of kings and their armies, women who brought the tidings of victory and shared in the spoils when the Almighty scattered kings.

The victory procession (vv. 15–18). The psalm recalls God's arrival to claim the place that is now the royal residence of the victor. The place is a mountain that even Mount Bashan must envy because it has been chosen by the victorious God as the place of his abode and so made the location of the reign of God. The arrival is portrayed as a victory procession accompanied by thousands of heavenly chariots and the captives and booty won in the battle.

The savior God (vv. 19–23). The LORD is praised as the

savior of his people. God's victorious saving rule is their daily support and deliverance from death. God can and will defeat his enemies whether they flee to the heights of Mount Bashan or to the depths of the sea; God will give his people participation in his victory.

The procession of God (vv. 24–27). The psalm describes a festive procession in which God as king enters the sanctuary accompanied by a great congregation led by representatives of the tribes of Israel. The procession corresponds to and dramatizes the victory parade in which God took possession of the holy mount (vv. 17–18).

The power of God (vv. 28–31). The congregation prays that God manifest the strength revealed in his deeds done in their behalf and bring kings and nations to acknowledge his divine royal presence in the temple at Jerusalem.

The reign of God (vv. 32–35). The psalm summons the kingdoms of the earth to acknowledge the kingship of the divine warrior who rules over Israel and the universe.

2. The psalm has a clear epic-historical subject. At the core of the psalm is the memory of foundational events that are crucial in the story of Israel's relation to its God. The narrative span reaches from Sinai to Jerusalem. The psalm remembers that the God of Israel is the God of Sinai (v. 8). It recalls the journey through the wilderness (v. 7), the battles with the kingdoms that stood in the way of Israel's entry into the land (vv. 11–14), the settlement in the land (v. 10), and the establishment of Jerusalem as the sanctuary of Israel's God (vv. 15–18).

The psalm's subject is given a mythopoeic dimension. It portrays the movement from Sinai to Jerusalem in poetry that employs the language and narrative motifs belonging to the religious world of the ancient Near East. The LORD is called "rider upon the clouds" (vv. 4, 33; cf. 18:10; Deut. 33:26–29). The title in Ugaritic sources belongs to Baal, the storm-god, who does battle with primeval forces to restore the fertility of the earth and gains victory and the right to kingship and royal residence. Images and motifs from this mythic background are used to clothe the LORD's action with features of the divine warrior, whose theophany is manifest in thunder and rain (vv. 8–9) and whose armies are thousands upon thousands of heavenly chariots (v. 17). His enemies are of cosmic proportion (v. 22) and include death itself (v. 20; the god Death was the chief adversary of Baal). The effect of this mythopoeic rendition of

227

the epic-historical subject is an evocation of its revelatory significance. In the wilderness march, the battles with Canaanite kings, the settlement in the land, and the establishment of the temple in Jerusalem, Israel's God, the one of Sinai, is disclosing his identity as sovereign of the universe. His coming from Sinai to his holy place (vv. 17–18) is the coming of the reign of God in time and space. His warfare in the history of his people is his campaign to bring the kingdoms of the world into his reign. For other instances of this hermeneutic, see Psalms 18:7–15; 29; 114; and 77:16–20. On the mythopoeic background, see Cross, chaps. 2 and 3; and Miller, *The Divine Warrior*, pp. 101–113.

Elements in the psalm seem to reflect a liturgical agenda. Repeatedly the focus is on God's presence and rule in his holy habitation, the mount of his abode, the sanctuary in Jerusalem (vv. 5, 16–18, 24, 29, 35). The opening invocation is a version of the ancient liturgical cry, "Arise, O LORD, let your enemies be scattered" (Num. 10:35). The cry belonged to the ceremonies of taking the ark of the LORD with Israel's armies when they went out to battle. In the narrative in Numbers, the ark was the sacred symbol of God's guidance and protection on the march through the wilderness, a role that is reflected in this psalm (v. 7). Processions of the LORD as God and king into the sanctuary (vv. 24–27) were probably centered on the ark and dramatized the LORD's victorious arrival from Sinai at the mount of the sanctuary (see the comment on Ps. 24:7–10). The psalm could well have been assembled for performance at various celebrations of the kingship of the LORD.

3. The confessional purpose of the psalm is to remember and represent the LORD as the power and strength of his people (v. 35). During much of its history, Israel lived with and through warfare. Its corporate existence as a people was threatened and conditioned by the military power of surrounding peoples and kingdoms. The military imagery of the psalm's theology reflects the conditions that were common to its time. Israel existed both as a national state and as people of the LORD. Their corporate security was a religious as well as a political issue. The psalm could be read as an expression of military hubris, the voice of a conquering imperialistic élan. But in spite of its militant character and victorious confidence, such is not its spirit. There is a self-understanding and self-description in the psalm's measures that belies such a reading. The uses assigned to the power of the LORD as divine warrior are crucial. The God who dwells

228

in his holy habitation as victor is father of orphans and protector of widows, who gives the desolate a home and liberates prisoners (vv. 5–6). Israel remembers itself as the lowly, the needy flock for whom God provided a dwelling. The power of God opposes those who lust after tribute and scatters the peoples who delight in war (v. 30). It is as savior that the psalm praises the divine warrior. The congregation confesses that it depends daily upon the victory of God for its salvation. It is God alone, they say, who provides escape from death (vv. 19–20).

The abiding setting of this exuberant praise of the victorious God is, then, a beleaguered piety. The song belongs to the lowly, who in the midst of the powers of this world remember and hope for the victory of God. Long after the ark was lost and Israel was no longer a national state, the psalm provided a liturgy of dependence on the power of God for the faithful righteous. The early Christian community found in Jesus Christ a new meaning for the confession, "To God, the LORD, belongs escape from death" (v. 20). The apostle Paul, knowing that sin and death are the ultimate enemies of God's reign in the world, gave thanks to God "who gives us the victory through our Lord Jesus Christ" (I Cor. 15:54–56). John Knox understood the warfare of God in a profound way when he concluded the Scots Confession with this prayer: "Arise, O Lord, and let thine enemies be confounded; let them flee from thy presence that hate thy godly name. Give thy servants strength to speak thy word with boldness, and let all nations cleave to the true knowledge of thee. Amen."

Psalm 69: For Your Sake I Have Borne Reproach

Psalm 69 is a prayer for help in first person singular style (see Introduction, 5.2). It is like Psalm 22 in some of its features, in the form of its composition, and in the important ways in which it is used in the New Testament (read the comment on Psalm 22). Understandably, it has been reread as a passion psalm of Christ and used in the services of Holy Week.

1. *The psalm has two parts.* The first part (vv. 1–29) is opened and concluded by pleas for salvation (vv. 1 and 29) and is composed of alternating petitions (vv. 1a, 6, 13–18, 22–28) and descriptions of trouble that serve as motivations for the petitions to be answered (vv. 1b–5, 7–12, 19–21, 26). The trouble is twofold. The psalmist is helplessly in the grip of a trouble

229

depicted only in metaphors for the power and sphere of death (vv. 1–2, 14–15), and in his trouble he is derided and insulted by those who shame him without cause (vv. 4, 6–12, 19–21). The petitions seek deliverance from both forms of trouble; verses 22–28 are a particularly vehement invocation of God's wrath on those who shame him. The theme of reproach (shame, insult, dishonor) is strikingly prominent (vv. 6, 7, 9, 10–12, 19–21). The second part of the psalm is quite like the second part of Psalm 22. There is the promise of praise to be offered in response to salvation, a praise that will encourage the oppressed because it will be a witness that the LORD hears the needy (vv. 30–33). Then there is a prophetic hymn in praise of the LORD who will restore Zion and Judah as an inheritance for the servants of the LORD (vv. 34–36).

2. Typically the prayer gives no unmistakable clues to the identity of some one historical person for whom it was written. But in its self-descriptions are features that together sketch a liturgical-theological profile of an identity. It is this composite that has been so provocative and stimulating to reflection and interpretation. The identifying features of the figure are these.

a. The psalmist confesses that he is a servant of the LORD (v. 17) and a lowly one (v. 29; Heb. *'ani*); he is therefore one of the servants of the LORD (v. 35) and the lowly (v. 32) whose future is at stake in his salvation.

b. He is one of a group who have been smitten by God (v. 26, which in the Hebrew contains both a singular "him you have smitten" and "those you have wounded"). Is the reason for the affliction given in verses 4*b* and 5? Verse 4*b* is hardly a literal denial that the psalmist is a thief; rather, it is an idiomatic claim of innocence with respect to injury of others. Verse 5 can be read two ways. It is either a further claim of innocence ("If I had committed folly, you, God, would know") or it is a statement that what folly he has done is known by God and not a cause for those who hate him and seek to destroy him (v. 4).

c. In his affliction the figure waits on the help of God (v. 3). The trust of those who hope in God and seek him is at issue in his predicament (v. 6). If he gives up hope and is not finally vindicated, those who hope in the God of Israel will be humiliated and undone.

230

d. As he waits on God he fasts and wears sackcloth (vv. 10, 11), the garb of mourning and lamentation to God. It is in this connection that the famous line "Zeal for your house has eaten me up" (v. 9) can be understood. "Zeal for your house" must mean fervent devotion to the temple. The only really analogous phrase in the Old Testament is "My zeal consumes me because my foes forget your words" (Ps. 119:139). There the fervent devotion is to the words of the LORD, his instruction, the medium of relation to the LORD. Here the devotion is to the temple, the focus of the figure's relation to his God. The phrase reflects a piety like that expressed in Psalms 42—43; 84; and 137 that has transformed the role of Zion and its temple in the national religion into a faith in which they are the focus of personal devotion. Notice the role of Zion in the promise of verse 35. Perseverance in that faith has eaten him up, worn him out, and exhausted his vital energies (v. 3).

e. The figure is the target of disabling scorn (vv. 19–20) directed at his fervent lamentation of his affliction to the LORD (vv. 10–11). The verbal abuse and humiliation take place within his own social group. He is alienated from his own family (v. 8). His conduct has been turned into a local proverb (v. 11). He is the subject of a speculation in the gathering of elders in the gate, the butt of drinking songs (v. 12). The scope of this scornful attention suggests that the figure's affliction and faith are important to his social community. He looked to it for support (v. 20), but instead he was given "gall for food and vinegar for drink" (v. 21, a metaphor for inflicting extreme pain and anguish; cf. Jer. 8:14; 9:15; 23:15).

f. Because the figure suffers in faith, he bears reproach because of this faith. "For your sake I have borne reproach. . . . The reproaches of those reproaching you have fallen on me" (vv. 7, 9). The basic form of the reproach of God in the Old Testament is the scornful question, "Where is your/their God?" (Joel 2:17; Micah 7:10; Pss. 42:3, 10; 79:10; 115:2). The question is a rhetorical way in which one group derides the power of the god of another group to help them. It is usually heard from the enemies of the people, but it also appears in Psalms 42—43 directed at an individual (see the comment). The reproach is against the god of the nation or group, but it is directed at the one or ones trusting in the god in a time of need. So the reproaches of those reproaching their God fall, as verse 9 says, on them (notice that the figure in Ps. 22:6–8 is derided because of trusting God).

231

g. The salvation of the figure will be significant for others. He represents the affliction and the trust of a group identified as the lowly, God-seekers, the needy, the prisoners who belong to the LORD (vv. 32–33; the last term refers to liberated exiles in Zech. 9:11; see also Lam. 3:34). When they see his deliverance and hear his song of praise for it, they will be glad and their hearts revived (cf. 22:27). His salvation will also be a promise to the servants of the LORD who hope for the salvation of Zion and the restoration of Judah, a sign that the scenario of salvation proclaimed by the prophets of the exile will be completed (vv. 35–36). That will be significant for the entire universe (v. 34) because it will mean the coming of the kingdom of God (cf. 22:27–28).

3. Because the profile of the identity of the psalmist is drawn in liturgical and theological terms we cannot assign it to a particular historical person. We have to ask, rather, for what kind of person it was composed. Clearly it belongs to the exilic/postexilic period (vv. 35–36) and comes from circles who in the hardships of those times persisted in "waiting for God" and were treated with scorn. In the history of the psalm's interpretation, Jeremiah has often been identified with the figure. The Jeremiah of "the confessions" suffered reproach for the sake of the LORD, was alienated from family and peers, cried out to God about his affliction, and prayed for God to vindicate him and punish his persecutors (Jer. 11:18–20; 15:15–18; 17:14–18). He was zealous for the integrity of the LORD's house (Jer. 7:1–15) and was literally thrown into "deep mire" at the bottom of a cistern (Jer. 38:6). But there are other good candidates for comparison with the figure in the psalm. The lament of the figure who prays in Lamentations 3 shares even more of the features of the psalm. So does the corporate prayer in Psalm 44 that laments the suffering caused by God's wrath (note especially Ps. 44:13–16, 22). And there is the servant of the LORD of Isaiah 53 whose affliction was not his punishment but his vocation to carry out the purpose of God. Out of the anguish of the exile and its aftermath an understanding of affliction that goes beyond punishment and fits into the saving purpose of the LORD began to emerge. Psalm 69 is one piece of the pattern.

4. Because of its relation to the pattern and the correspondence of the life of Jesus to it, Psalm 69 was used repeatedly in the New Testament for christological and theological purposes (Kraus, *Theology*, pp. 101–193). It furnished a context for reflection on Jesus' rejection by his own people (John 15:25), on his motive in driving traders from the temple (John 3:17), on the

bitter treatment he was given instead of pity at the time of his death (Matt. 27:34; Mark 15:23; Luke 23:36; John 19:19–30), and on the meaning of his suffering (Rom. 15:3). Even the harsh prayer against the persecutors (Ps. 69:22–28), which seemed appropriate in the mouth of Jeremiah but not for Jesus, took on meaning. Luke saw in it the prayer for vindication answered in the fate of Judas (Acts 1:20); Paul found here a clue to the hardening of those in Israel who rejected Jesus (Rom. 11:9–10). For the prophet of Revelation, it pointed to the eschatological outpouring of wrath against the foes of the coming kingdom of God (Rev. 16:1). Psalm 69 cannot be read directly as the prayer of Jesus or as an intentional prophecy of his suffering. But it does provide a context for reflection on the passion of one who bore reproach for the sake of his God and by the way he bore it and by the vindication of his resurrection gave hope to the lowly and promise that God's saving will for his servants will be completed. Jesus is the consummate and correcting example of the kind of person for whom the psalm was composed.

Psalm 70: Make Haste to Help Me

1. Psalm 70 is an individual prayer for help (Introduction, sec. 5.2.1). It is composed almost entirely of petitions. The psalm begins with vocatives and imperatives asking for the LORD's help (v. 1). Then petitions for the failure and disgrace of enemies (vv. 2–3) are balanced by pleas on behalf of those who seek God (v. 4). The prayer concludes with a twofold declaration of dependence on the LORD combined with imperatives asking for help (v. 5). The motifs of "haste" and "help for me" form an inclusion around the whole (vv. 1, 5). "I am poor and needy" is a declaration of dependence on the LORD, a confession that one has no resources to cope with the demands made by trouble. It is a theological, not an economic statement (Introduction, sec. 6.18). All the petitions in the prayer are the expressions of the confessed neediness.

2. Psalm 70, with a few variations in text, composes the conclusion of Psalm 40 (cf. 40:13–17 and the comment on Psalm 40). Whether Psalm 70 is a fragment of Psalm 40 or a composition used in Psalm 40 is difficult to determine with certainty. The literary completeness of Psalm 70 favors the latter possibility. Psalm 70 has its own designation of use in its superscription, "For the memorial offering," a designation it shares with Psalm

233

38. The term may refer to the memorial portion of a sacrifice prescribed in Leviticus 2:5; 5:12.

3. The psalm's first verse has been used traditionally as a litany introducing corporate prayer. Currently the psalm is appointed in the Common Lectionary as the psalm for Wednesday of Holy Week. When read in this context, the psalm in verse 3 echoes the scornful "Aha!" addressed to the crucified Jesus (Mark 15:29). It is reread, as it has been for centuries, as the prayer of Jesus in his passion and of the church in its neediness.

Psalm 71: Like a Portent to Many

Psalm 71 repeats sentences and motifs that appear in Psalms 22 and 31 (compare vv. 1–3 with 31:1–3; v. 6 with 22:10; v. 12 with 22:11). Because both are used in telling the passion story, Psalm 71 has also been associated with the passion of Jesus and the services of Holy Week. In the Common Lectionary and others it is the psalm set for Tuesday of Holy Week.

1. The psalm is a prayer for help prayed as a way of seeking refuge with the LORD (v. 1; on the formula "I take refuge with you," see the comment on Ps. 7:1). It is composed of repeated petitions interwoven with declarations of trust and descriptions of trouble. It begins with petitions for deliverance from the power of the wicked (vv. 1–4) followed by declarations of a trust and dependence that have lasted throughout life and are publicly known (vv. 5–8). A second petition for deliverance, confessing the infirmity of old age (v. 9), is followed by an account of the hostility of those who think the psalmist has been deserted by God (vv. 10–11). From these adversaries a third petition asks deliverance (vv. 12–13). Again the psalmist declares his trust in the LORD by describing how praise occupies all of his life (vv. 14–16) and prays not to be forsaken (v. 18a), that he may continue to praise God as he has been taught, even to coming generations (vv. 17–19). The psalm concludes with a declaration of confidence that the prayer will be heard (vv. 20–21) and a promise of praise (vv. 22–24).

More than most, this psalm is composed using familiar formulaic phrases and motifs. But several distinctive features claim attention.

2. Though a prayer for help, the psalm majors in assertions of trust, so much so that confidence in God outweighs the con-

cern with trouble. The theme is struck in verse 5: "You, LORD, are my hope, my trust." This form of sentence, making "my hope" the predicate of a sentence whose subject is LORD, means that LORD is one in whom the psalmist trusts. But the effect of the form is not to be missed. It says that the LORD not only is an other who is out there but has reality and power in my hope and trust, is present to me in and through hope.

3. The psalmist speaks as one who is elderly (vv. 9, 18) and looks back on a long life (vv. 6, 17). So the psalm has been a favorite of the old through the centuries. But we must not overlook how plastic the idioms of psalmic language are. The prayers for help use every resource to describe trouble. Old age means declining powers and can be read as a metaphor for neediness. Let the young be reminded that they will be old and in times of weakness are infirm like the old. In the Old Testament the community can be viewed as old in times of decline and young in times of renewal (Hos. 2:17; 7:9; Jer. 2:2; Isa. 46:4). The psalm has been read corporately by the community of faith aware of its need of regeneration (the Masoretic text preserves a first person plural reading of v. 20).

4. More than most prayers for help, this one is focused on praise. The psalmist describes his life as occupied with praise and looks to a future whose days are full of praise (vv. 6, 8, 14–19, 22–24). When the psalmist speaks of singing praise to harp and lyre, a skill belonging to a special group (v. 22), and looks back on a divinely given teaching to proclaim the wondrous deeds of Israel's salvation history (v. 17), the possibility is raised that the psalm is written as a prayer of one of the guild of temple singers. A psalmist whose work was to compose prayers for others and perform them for others here prays for himself.

5. The psalmist says he has been "like a portent to many" (v. 7). The expression could mean a sign of God's favor (so NJPS and others) or a manifestation of divine wrath (so NRSV). The latter is probably right. Adversaries discuss the psalmist's suffering and conclude that he is God-forsaken (vv. 10–11). In Israel's religious community, suffering always posed a question about the relation of the afflicted one to God, and the question became a major theological theme (e.g., Job, the servant of the LORD in Isaiah 40—55). When Psalm 71 is read during Holy Week the line "I have been like a portent to many" announces

that the suffering of Jesus calls for understanding and response. A portent of what? Faith must say.

It should be noted that we are all portents for someone.

Psalm 72: May God's Reign Come Through the King

Psalm 72 is a prayer for the anointed king asking that God bring about his rule on earth through the reign of the king. It looks and hopes for a new era created by God through the person of the king. The agenda of intercession includes all that belongs to the ideal ruler: justice, prosperity, long life, universal dominion with power over his enemies and submission from other kings and their nations, the prayers of his people, fame, and admiration. The prayer is composed almost entirely of intercessions, the first in imperative style (v. 1) and the rest in the form of wishes (vv. 2–11, 15–17); a statement of the responsibilities of the king is given as the basis of the intercessions in verses 12–14.

1. This prayer poem was probably composed for the inauguration of a Davidic king in Jerusalem. It is appropriate for such an occasion and has a general character that would allow it to be used repeatedly. It is not about any particular king; rather, it is concerned with the office and vocation of kingship (see Psalm 2; and Introduction, sec. 6.11). The belief and hope that rulers were the medium and agent through whom the gods dealt with their people was a common feature of the monarchical cultures surrounding Israel. The administration of justice, the conduct of warfare, and the provision of well-being belonged to the office of a king, and he was believed capable of these responsibilities because power flowed to the people from deity through the king (see Keel, pp. 280–306).

2. Psalm 72 is a particularly clear example of Israel's appropriation of this view. Repeatedly the poem connects what God is asked to do for the king with the hoped-for acts of the king for the people (v. 1 and vv. 2–4, v. 5 and vv. 6–7, vv. 8–11 and vv. 12–14, v. 15 and v. 16). In the social psychology of ancient peoples a connection had been made between power and possibility. The possibility of ordering, protecting, and supporting a social unit depended on the use of power for the corporate group. In selecting a leader, they brought all their hopes for

justice, security, and well-being to one who possessed charisma that was a gift of their gods. Israel entered and took up that hope with the establishment of monarchy and began to nurture and modulate the belief that there was one among the many who could make it possible for the rest to live in the kingdom of God.

In Judah's modulation of royal theology a priority emerges that is characteristic of Israel's understanding of the God of Israel. Justice and righteousness became the first and organizing responsibility of the king upon which all else depended. They are not one item in a list but the foundation on which the other possibilities rest. That can be seen in the compositional arrangement of the poem. The opening petition, the only imperative prayer, asks for the gift that enables the entire royal vocation, the judgments (plural in the Masoretic text, singular in the versions) and righteousness of the LORD. The one other variation from the style of the third person wishes delineates the saving effect of the king's performance of justice; by his judgments he delivers the needy and saves the life of the poor (vv. 12–14). That is why kings should bow before him and nations serve him (v. 11)! Saving justice for the helpless is the definitive mark of the reign of God, the sign of the one who represents the lord of all the world. Read Psalm 82. Of course, this conviction is central to the theology of the eighth-century prophets for whom justice and righteousness are the primary criteria for the use of power in their society.

3. The correlation in this psalm between the place and way of God and that of human kingship is unmistakable. The king himself is to be the source of righteousness, well-being *(shalom)*, fertility, and victory, the one who saves the helpless when they call, the one served by nations, and the one whose name endures forever. All these things are said first of all of God in the psalms. Though prayers were to be made for the king continually (v. 15), he clearly has a vocation that is an extension of the character of Israel's God. He is believed to be the one through whom God's promise to Abraham is being worked out, the one in whom the nations perceive such blessedness that they seek and pray for it themselves (compare v. 17 and Gen. 12:1–3). The chasm between calling and capacity yawns under the feet of every king for whom this prayer was made. The prayer calls for divine government to inhabit human rulers. The model of kingship is far more than a challenge and goal; it

237

is, if taken in ultimate seriousness, as the prophets surely did, a prescription for failure. It creates a tension out of which come prophecies of "one to come," as in Isaiah 11:1–9. By the time Psalm 72 became part of Scripture it was probably being understood by some as a prayer for the coming of the Messiah.

4. The title connects the psalm with Solomon and so points to another way of understanding it. The scribe who so entitled it doubtless found a number of connections between the prayer and the account of Solomon in I Kings (e.g., the reference to the gold of Sheba in verse 15 and the Queen of Sheba's gift of gold, I Kings 10:10). But the most compelling connection was probably Solomon's choice to pray for wisdom to judge his people with justice (I Kings 3:3–14) with the priority given justice in the psalm. In the attribution to Solomon the psalm is read as Scripture in the context of other Scripture, a record of the past for instruction of the present. The account of Solomon in I Kings comes closer to fulfilling the model of the true king sketched in this psalm than that of any other king of Judah. But the Scripture also records his failure and judges him a flawed example of the model.

5. Such seems the best we can hope for in any ruler, leader, or governor—partial success and eventual failure at fulfilling the ideal of his vocation. The New Testament exhorts us to pray "for kings and all who are in high positions" in a keen awareness of their need and the consequences for the welfare of all in the way they use power (I Tim. 2:1–4). We do pray for leaders because we want them to be drawn by divine help as close as possible to the model of God's rule.

But Christians have always known that they can pray this psalm in its fullness only for the heir of David who was Jesus of Nazareth. Through him the God of the universe has already bestowed righteousness, peace, and victory upon those who find in him the nearness of the reign of God. For them, the prayer is a form of petition for the consummation of the kingdom of God.

6. The doxology in verses 18–19 is the liturgical marker of the conclusion of book II of the Psalms (see Introduction, secs. 3.6; 4.1). As the conclusion of Psalm 72 it turns attention to the One who alone does marvelous things. It reminds the reader that it is the God of Israel who alone will be forever praised and whose glory will fill the whole earth. The sovereignty belongs to the LORD, and all that is wished and claimed for the king is

238

but a reflection of the heavenly reign (cf. vv. 18–19 and vv. 17 and 8). According to verse 20, Psalm 72 is the last of David's prayers. The verse is an endnote to a collection of David psalms that constituted the basic material of the Psalter and now in a revised form makes up the first two books of the Psalms (Introduction, sec. 3.6).

BOOK THREE
Psalms 73—89

Psalm 73: Blessed Are the Pure in Heart

"Naught be all else to me, save that Thou art... Thou and Thou only, first in my heart... I ever with Thee and Thou with me, Lord." These phrases from the beloved hymn "Be Thou My Vision" are echoes of the final verses of Psalm 73. They point to lines of devotional intensity (vv. 23–28) that have made the psalm a classic of prayer and contemplation. In the psalm, the pure devotion to God at the psalm's conclusion replaces bitterness and estrangement at its beginning (vv. 2–3). The meaning and the mystery of the psalm lie in its transition from one to the other.

1. The literary structure of the psalm is marked by a Hebrew emphatic particle that stands at the beginning of verses 1, 13, and 18, dividing the psalm into three major sections. The particle can be translated "indeed" (so REB) or "truly" (so NRSV, which does not render it at verse 13). The first and third sections are composed as contrasting statements. Verses 1–12 lay out the problem: the predicament of the psalmist (vv. 1–3) caused by the success of the wicked (vv. 4–12). Verses 18–28 describe the problem's resolution: the divine undoing of the wicked (vv. 18–20) and the well-being that has come to the psalmist (vv. 21–28). The central section (vv. 13–17) tells about the transition from one to the other. (On this analysis and its implications, see McCann, "Psalm 73," pp. 249ff.) The entire psalm is written in first person style as an account of what happened to the psalmist. Direct address to God begins in verse 15; the whole psalm may be intended as a confessional address to God. The account has a narrative movement somewhat like that of a song of thanksgiving, in which a person reports past troubles, makes an

240

appeal to God, tells of deliverance, and asserts consequent trust and praise (see Introduction, sec. 5.3). But here the trouble is not so much a question of survival as a problem of faith. The resolution is not deliverance from danger but a new and solving understanding of God's way. The psalm is the voice of a teacher of the faithful. The first person style is a convention of instruction. The narrated experience is surely real and personal, but the poem is not a piece of private reflection. Its purpose is to provide others in the psalmist's community with guidance and insight that will help them with the problem of disparity between faith and experience. Psalms 37 and 49 take up the same problem in somewhat different ways (see Introduction, sec. 5.6).

2. The psalm begins and ends with statements about the goodness of God (vv. 1, 28), but how that goodness is experienced and understood undergoes a profound recasting in the course of the psalm. Verse 1 is a proverbial statement of the teaching that is basic to the faith of the psalmist. "Truly God is good to Israel, to those who are pure in heart" (so NJPS; NRSV, with most contemporary versions, adjusts the Hebrew text to create a better poetic line and translates "the upright" instead of "Israel," though the Hebrew text is supported by all the ancient witnesses). God's goodness is a sure blessing for the pure in heart among God's chosen people because they are the ones who respond to the election of God with a singleness of devotion (24:4; Matt. 5:8). Purity of heart is to will one thing, the love of God (Kierkegaard). It is the love of God that answers the free choice of God to have a people and opens the self to the will of God to be with them. Hidden in the proverb is the implication that it is God himself who is the goodness given those he chooses to be "with." But that marvelous implication is not explicit in the proverb and waits to be disclosed at the end of the psalm.

3. The teacher admits that the ignorance of the implication almost undermined his life (v. 2) and turned him into a stupid beast oblivious of God's presence for him (vv. 21–22). The problem that nearly undid him was the untroubled, successful life of the boastful wicked. "I saw," he confesses, "the *shalom* of the wicked" (v. 3). His portrayal of their abundant life and arrogant self-confidence and social influence is a verbal cartoon of people whose existence is a refutation of the belief that "God knows the way of the righteous, but the way of the wicked shall perish" (vv. 4–13; cf. v. 11 and 1:6). What he saw bid fair to become reality for him, the truth about the way things are. It drove him

241

to envy. It called his own faithfulness into question (v. 13). He was afflicted while the wicked enjoyed life (v. 14). Was their good life the only goodness there was? Was their prosperity the true and only *shalom?* Did their living denial of God's goodness to the pure in heart even call God into question? Job wrestled with the problem of the affliction of the righteous. This teacher struggles with the question of the *shalom* of the wicked.

4. The predicament of the teacher's quandary of soul was twofold. First, if he turned his questions into affirmations and conceded in public lament that his faithfulness was in vain and his afflictions a denial of the goodness of God, he would have betrayed "the circle of your children" (v. 15). "Children of God," a rare expression in the Old Testament, is a metaphor for Israel as people of God who look to and depend on God as children do to their parent (Deut. 14:1; Wisd. Sol. 2:18; 5:5; see Matt. 5:9, 45). The teacher knows and belongs to a circle of faithful who think of themselves in this way. His identity with them and responsibility to them is his first restraint against public cynicism. Probably they are the community for whom his confession was composed. In this restraint he teaches all who teach the faithful that personal doubts, however anguished and authentic, must not be turned quickly into lessons for their community. The teacher's bonds to his community closed that door to him. Second, he could not rescue himself from his perplexity and its accompanying bitterness and envy by the effort of his own reasoning (v. 16). He tried to think it out, but the effort only brought troubled weariness. That door was closed to him also. With his concession of failure, he warns against trying to find the truth of faith in the independent work of the human intellect. Reason cannot unravel experience to supply the ground for faith.

5. Constrained by responsibility to the children of God and discouraged by his failure to explain his experience in the light of his doctrine, the teacher entered the sanctuary of God and brought his problem with him. There he considered and meditated on the destiny of the wicked (v. 17). In verses 18–20, he describes what he perceived: The wicked have no permanent place in the world of which God is sovereign. Viewed from the perspective of their end, they are unreal, as a bad dream. It must be apparent that this conviction that the wicked had no future was not new to this psalmist. It was a structural element in the tradition of theological wisdom (e.g., 1:4–6; 11:4–7; 37:9,

242

20). But on his own, overwhelmed by what he saw and experienced, he could not "understand" it (v. 16). When his heart was sour and his emotions transfixed, he could not "understand" it (vv. 21–22). "Understand" here means nothing less than the knowledge of faith. The mystery of how his unknowing was changed to knowing lay in what he found in the sanctuary of God. Its sign is the confessional style of his description of the end of the wicked. God is subject; God is actor (v. 18).

6. On entering the sanctuary, the teacher entered the sphere of the powerful presence of God. The possibility of the Presence was the ministry and mystery of the sanctuary, the place where God chose to be for the pure in heart of Israel. (On the importance of the Presence in psalmic belief about the temple, see 26:8; 27:4; 43:3; 65:4; and Psalm 84.) The reality of God flooded his heart and became the consciousness by which he understood himself and his experience. The uncertainty of experience became the certainty of faith. The certainty he was given was not merely belief in the doctrine that the wicked perish; it was more the certainty of God as his God. The presence of God transcended the moment of his visit to the sanctuary to become the truth of his entire existence. The teacher speaks of this knowledge in a litany of sentences that repeat the phrase "with you" (only partially visible in English translation). Even in his ignorance he was "with God" (v. 22; NRSV, "toward you"). Through all his turmoil, he had been continually "with God," who had grasped his right hand in support (v. 23, past tenses with Hebrew for NRSV's present tenses). "With God" he desires nothing else (v. 25; NRSV, "other than you"). His course of life is guided by God; his future is in the care of God. At the end of his life God will "receive" him with glory (v. 24; on "you will receive me," see the comment on Ps. 49:15). He does not have to depend on body and mind; he has learned that they may fail him. He gives himself up completely to trust. God is the rock of his mind and his portion in life forever (v. 26). He desires and needs nothing else but God (v. 25). "Let goods and kindred go, This mortal life also; The body they may kill: God's truth abideth still" (Luther).

7. The proverb of verse 1, then, is true. God is good to the pure in heart. But by the testimony of his confession to God, the teacher provides a different way to grasp its truth. The goodness of God is not defined by the *shalom* the wicked enjoy, nor is it denied by the affliction suffered by the pure in heart. The ulti-

243

mate misery is to be "far from God" (v. 27). The everlasting *shalom* is to be "near God" (v. 28). The goodness of God is the self of God. God is good to the pure in heart precisely in being their God. Read Romans 8:18–39.

Psalm 74: Remember Your Congregation!

1. Psalm 74 is a corporate prayer for help (see Introduction, sec. 5.4). It was likely composed for performance at services of mourning over the destroyed temple in Jerusalem during the exilic period. Such services appear to have been held recurrently at the ruined sanctuary (Jer. 41:4–5; Zech. 7:1–3; 8:18–19) whose razing is reflected in verses 3–7.

The psalm has three sections. The first (vv. 1–11) opens and closes with laments over the rejection of God (vv. 1, 10–11); petitions for God to remember his congregation and temple (vv. 2–3) are followed by a description of the destruction of the temple (vv. 3b–8) and the absence of any communication with God (v. 9). The second section is hymnic praise (vv. 12–17) based on the confession of God's ancient kingship manifested in deeds of salvation in the world (v. 12); the deeds are rehearsed in verses 13–17. The third section is an insistent series of petitions (vv. 18–23) for God to act to vindicate his name against the taunts and insults of the enemy and to deliver his covenant people from their oppression.

2. The psalm gives an intensely theological interpretation of the desperate straits in which Israel was left after the fall of Jerusalem. The foundations and institutions of Israel's religion had been demolished. Any further exercise of Israel's traditional religion must have seemed without basis or purpose. But this psalm is a prayer that speaks of God and the community and its central religious institution in a way that shows the fierce vitality of Israel's faith in the LORD in the midst of the worst of times.

The God to whom the prayer is made is identified and evoked in the confession (v. 12) and its hymnic exposition (vv. 13–17). The confession uses the only first person singular in the psalm in the predicate "my *king*" to show the intimate direct and personal relation of those who pray to the one who is and has been king "from olden times." The content of the title "king" is given in the appositional phrase "the one who does

244

saving deeds in the world." They are the revelation and the reality of the kingship that belongs to God. The exposition of the confession is composed with the emphatic repetition of "you" as pronoun and verbal subject so that the identity of the one addressed is insistently and progressively portrayed. God's kingship in its fullness of action must be evoked so that the addressee is there in the reality of his person. God is told who he is in terms of title and its reality, not only to hold his identity before the consciousness of those who pray but to remind God himself of his identity which from the human perspective of the congregation is not evident in the world.

The recital of saving deeds conflates myth and history. It draws on a narrative pattern widespread in ancient Near Eastern myth and on Israel's experience with the LORD in their early history. The interweaving speaks of the victory over primeval chaos and establishment of the world order and of Israel's passage through the sea and wilderness in the same breath. In the myth a god becomes king by achieving mastery over primeval chaos in the form of water (sea, rivers). The water is dramatized as seven-headed Leviathan, as dragons. When the chaos water is mastered, its bounds are set, order is established, creation in its ancient Near Eastern sense takes place. The god establishes his kingship with the establishment of world order and builds a palace as royal site and residence. The story is one of the basic ways in which the ancients understood the world. Israel used motifs and sequences and figures from the story in a variety of modulations for its own liturgical and theological purposes. For other uses in the Psalms, see Psalms 77:17; 89:9–11; 93; 104:5–11; and 114; for the prophets, Isa. 51:9–11. God's making a way for Israel through the sea, providing water in the wilderness, and perhaps drying up the Jordan River for the people to cross is spoken of in the language of verses 13a and 15. The recitation goes directly into the ordering activity by which day and night, sun and moon, dry land and sea, summer and winter are bounded and distinguished. Salvation history and creation process are not thought of separately. All these actions are "saving deeds." It is not correct to say that myth has been historicized or that history has been turned into myth. Both dimensions are necessary. Myth elicits the cosmic dimensions of certain historic events. Historical reference furnishes concretions and revelations of universal and eternal

245

depth. (On the battle with chaos, see Keel, pp. 47ff.; on Psalm 74, Levenson, *Creation,* pp. 7–25; and on the symbol of chaos and water in the Bible, Barth, III/1, pp. 147ff.)

3. The point of this particular recitation of "saving deeds" is evident when we look at the way the congregation describes itself and at the content of its lament. Those who pray call themselves "the congregation which you created *(qanah)* in olden times" (v. 2), a clear allusion also to the traditions of the nation's beginnings in the creative redemptive work of God at the sea and in the wilderness (see the corresponding phrase in Exod. 15:16; Deut. 32:6). The other identifications also emphasize the relation of the congregation as the particular domain of the LORD's royal mastery; they are the "flock of his pasturing" (79:13; 95:7; 100:3; Jer. 23:1; Ezek. 34:31) and the "tribe of his possession" (note the context of the phrase in Jer. 10:16; Isa. 63:17). The congregation confesses itself to be the creation and special possession of the LORD's kingly work in the world. What touches them touches his rule.

More particularly, the destruction of the temple puts a question against the rule of God. The temple on Mount Zion is the institutional sign of God's mastery of creation and history. The prayer uses the entire vocabulary of reverence for the site in speaking of it: Mount Zion on which you dwell, dwelling place for your name, sanctuary *(qodesh* and *miqdash),* meeting place. The enemy's purpose in destroying the sanctuary was clear; it was a way of taking over mastery of the flock of God (v. 8). They set up their own military standards in the holy place as signs of the real power that ruled the world (v. 4). The prophets of the temple have been discredited; there is no one to interpret any signs as promises of favor (Ps. 86:17; see Lam. 2:9, 14; 4:13 on the failure of institutional prophecy after the fall of Jerusalem). The destruction of the divine king's palace, the silence of his royal messengers, and the taunts of the victorious enemy (vv. 10, 18, 22, 23) all combine to deny the reign of God.

4. The petitions show that the congregation does not yield its faith to experience but instead shapes its bitter experience by faith into poignant urgent prayer. In the petitions the congregation admits and recognizes that they are truly and only the lowly, the downtrodden, the poor and needy. They find themselves as a group in the place of those in the social order who have a special claim on the justice and help of the king (on

the significance of the role of the *'ani* in prayers for help, see Introduction, sec. 6.18). So they appeal to "the covenant" under whose terms the poor and needy are to be protected from violence (v. 20). What those in power in the nation were obligated to do for the needy, God must do now for his flock. "Arise, O God; plead your own case" (on the petition "Arise, LORD, see Pss. 3:7; 68:1).

5. If we come to this psalm from the preexilic prophets, its assumptions and purpose may make us uneasy. The congregation identifies itself and its central sanctuary completely with God's way in the world. They present themselves to God in terms of election and salvation history as though there were nothing to say from their side about their way in the world. They believe that the anger of God is the cause of their suffering (v. 1). But there is no express penitence. They even appeal to God to see to the covenant (v. 20), which the prophets said they had betrayed. The prayer seeks relief from the disaster that Jeremiah had proclaimed as the judgment of God.

The prayer does not, however, seem to protest the anger of God as unjust. Rather, its focus is on the question of God's kingship. Will God's mastery of chaos, begun in creation and initiated in history through the creation of his own people and the election of Zion, be frustrated? Are the taunts and the signs of the enemies the truth? Is the humiliating present the shape of the future? How long? Forever? (vv. 1, 9–10, 23). The psalm testifies that there are times when it is right for prayer to be made on the basis of the honor of God that is at stake in the plight of the elect and redeemed people. A prophet did arise during the exile who proclaimed the very vindication of God's kingship in the salvation of his flock (Isaiah 40—55; see 40:1–12) for which this prayer pleads. Centuries later, the Huguenots in France and the Covenanters in Scotland under fearful persecution sang this psalm as the voice of their suffering faith (Prothero, pp. 212, 163). The psalm reveals the connection between creation and salvation history and the history of the people of God. The church must never lose sight of that connection (Rom. 8:18–25, 28–32; Phil. 1:6).

As for the self-understanding of the congregation in this prayer, is it of no importance that they have learned to think of themselves as the lowly? This may be a form of the transformation worked in the character of the congregation by judgment for which Jeremiah and Ezekiel looked (Jer. 31:33; Ezek. 36:26). "Blessed are the poor in spirit . . . the meek . . ." (Matt. 5:3, 5).

Psalm 75: Do Not Boast

A conviction runs through all of Scripture that boasting is an offense to the divine majesty, that the arrogance of self-importance and autonomous power stands under the judgment of God. Psalm 75 is a song to praise God who judges the boastful wicked.

1. The song is composed of a variety of literary types. It begins with congregational praise, thanking God who is near through the presence of his name, for his wondrous deeds (v. 1). The singer who performs the psalm (see v. 9) then speaks on behalf of God (vv. 2–4). God has set an appointed time for judgment. Though the earth and its inhabitants dissolve in disorder, God maintains its stability. Because time and world, history and cosmos, are subject to God's sovereignty, God warns the boastful wicked not to exalt their own power and importance. The singer repeats God's warning (v. 5) and reiterates the theology on which it is based (vv. 6–8). The boastful wicked should not lift themselves up, because "putting down and lifting up" belong alone to God, and God will surely make the wicked drain the cup of judgment to its dregs. The singer vows to declare this truth always in praises of Israel's God (v. 9). The song concludes with a declaration of the truth again in the form of a divine saying (v. 10). God will bring the power of the wicked to an end and vindicate the righteous.

2. In the psalm, God is portrayed as judge of all the earth. The role of judge and the work of judging with equity belong to God's kingship (9:8; 98:9). God's rule over chaos by which the world is established and his reign over the inhabitants are closely connected (v. 3; 24:1–2). God's judgment of societies and nations corresponds to his work to create and maintain the world. The one extends and completes the other. Creation and judgment cohere in the reign of God (see the comment on Pss. 82:5; 11:3). God rights and rules human affairs by "putting down one and lifting up another" (v. 7). The boastful wicked are brought low and the lowly righteous are exalted (v. 10). This reordering of the human situation is the equity of God's judgment. This corrective interference in society and history is

248

God's way of bringing affairs in line with his policy of opposing the arrogant wicked and favoring the lowly righteous. On this conception of God's royal judgment, see Psalm 113 and Hannah's Song, which is similar to Psalm 75 at numerous points (I Sam. 2:3, 6–8, 10). The psalm uses a metaphor that was a favorite of the seventh- and sixth-century prophets to personalize and dramatize judgment. God has a cup whose content is his decreed destiny for those under judgment, and he will pour a draught from it for all the wicked of the earth to drink (Jer. 25:15; 49:12; Ezek. 23:32–34; Isa. 51:17; Hab. 2:15–16). When that will happen is a matter of God's choice, but the divine saying in verse 2 makes it very clear that God will set an appointed time for this judgment. In the prophecy of Habakkuk, the "appointed time" is the terminus of the current dominance of Babylonian violence (Hab. 2:1–3). But the psalm has an eschatological reach in its expectation that the cup of judgment will be poured for "all the wicked of the earth" (v. 8). In the eschatology of Revelation, the cup of wrath is a feature of the final judgment (Rev. 14:10; 16:19; 18:6).

3. The warning of the psalm is directed at the boastful wicked, who lift up their horn on high (vv. 4–5, 10). "Horn" is an ideogram for power. The motif of "lifting up" is fixed as the focus of the psalm by its insistent repetition. The motif is the only characterization of the wicked (vv. 4–5). It designates a power and prerogative that belong to God alone (v. 7) and can be derived from no other source (v. 6). When the wicked lift their horn, they presume to preempt the very right and power of God, who will vindicate his reign by lifting up the righteous (v. 10; NRSV, "exalt"). The psalm typically gives no decisive clue to the identity of the wicked. If the psalm is read in the context of Habakkuk, who wrestled with the problem of the power of wicked Babylon in a world ruled by God, then the wicked are the arrogant nations who think of themselves as the true powers of history (connections between the psalm and Habakkuk are often noted; e.g., Hab. 1:4, 12–13; 2:3–5, 15–16). The term "boastful" *(hollelim)*, on the other hand, is a category used for the arrogant powerful in the community in the only other uses of the term (Pss. 5:5; 73:3). As a psalm, the song is open to both international and social reference. It teaches the congregation that in the coming kingdom of God, "all who exalt themselves will be humbled, and all who humble themselves will be exalted" (Matt. 23:12).

249

Psalm 76: You Are Awesome

Psalm 76 praises the LORD for his awesome power over kings and princes and their weaponry. The armaments of nations are useless against the majestic wrath of God at human pretensions to power. Psalm 76 is usually grouped with the songs of Zion because it features a divine victory against forces threatening Zion (cf. vv. 2–6 and 46:8–9 and 48:3–8). But the psalm is more about the resident of Zion than about Zion itself.

1. God is portrayed as the divine warrior who has established his residence by a decisive victory over his adversaries (see the comment on Psalms 24 and 29). The psalm can be divided into four parts. The first part (vv. 1–3) states the theme. The God whose greatness is known in Judah and Israel established his dwelling in Zion by shattering the weapons of war. The second part (vv. 4–6) describes how the very glorious majesty of the divine warrior paralyzed his adversaries. The third part (vv. 7–9) states the purpose of the victory; it was the intervention of God's justice to save the lowly. The fourth part (vv. 10–12) draws the implications of God's power. Human wrath is useless; the only response is to acknowledge the kingship of the LORD with fealty and tributes.

2. In portraying the disaster that befell warriors and weapons around Salem (an ancient name of Jerusalem), the psalm draws on the mythic notion of the divine warrior whose kingship was established and whose capital was gained by victory over other gods. But the notion is informed and transformed by memories of the victories by which the land was gained and David's kingdom and capital won. In the psalm it is kings and princes and the human powers that make history who are the foil. The myth has become the language of Israel's confidence that the dangers of history do not endanger the purpose and policy of the LORD. The description of God's victory is general and formulaic. The identification of specific battles is not the point. The language is suited to liturgy and confession, and its purpose is to evoke the character and power of the divine warrior.

3. Verses 8–9 give an important interpretation of what the LORD is about in the use of his irresistible power against the political powers of the world. These interventions of divine power are actions of the heavenly king who pronounces sen-

tence in the cosmic court and then brings judgment. The point of this judicial intervention is "to save all the lowly of the earth" (NRSV, "oppressed"). In the language of the psalms, the lowly are those who base their life on trust in God rather than on their own strength. God judges to save them. The LORD has taken residence on Zion as a counterforce to the powers that, unopposed, threaten and oppress those without power to resist them.

The congregation that worships on Zion sees itself as the lowly surrounded by the threats of history and takes hope in the vision of the divine warrior who judges to save. Their hope is the promise to all the lowly of the world. The theology of this psalm is precisely that of the eighth-century prophets who saw the divine warrior acting in judgment against those who oppress the lowly within their own nations. Christians using this psalm will think of Christus Victor, whose defeat of the powers of sin and death deepens hope in their sovereign God.

Psalm 77: Your Footprints Were Unseen

Psalm 77 turns on the pivot of a series of anguished questions that begin, "Will my Lord reject forever, and never again show favor?" The questions express the most fearful anxiety that can come upon the soul, the apprehension that God has abandoned his own once and for all. They have often been the liturgy of those on the edge of despair. These questions came rolling into John Bunyan's mind when he was in his own personal "slough of despond" (Prothero, p. 240).

1. The psalm begins and proceeds in the style of an individual prayer for help (vv. 1–12; see Introduction, sec. 5.2). But the form of the prayer is changed in important ways. God is spoken of in third person. The prayer never reaches a petition. It is composed only of a description of trouble, with God interspersed with concentrations of verbs of reflection—remember, meditate, consider, inquire, muse (vv. 3, 5–6, 11–12). There is no mention of an enemy, no assessment of self.

Instead, the psalm is composed as a report of prayer that, unsatisfied, turned into reflection on God. The cry to God has brought no comfort (vv. 1–2), so the psalmist turns to thinking of God, his spirit fainting, so troubled he cannot continue to pray aloud (vv. 3–4). There is no purchase for hope in the present, so the psalmist turns to the ancient past (v. 5) and searches

251

there for an answer (v. 6) to a series of questions (vv. 7–9) that are in truth only one: Is the LORD's rejection final? The one question is elaborated by using the list of the attributes that have characterized the LORD's way with Israel: favor, covenant loyalty *(hesed)*, promise, graciousness, compassion. The series of questions reaches its climax in a conclusion that confesses the distress driving his reflection: "It makes me sick [NRSV, "is my grief"; NJPS, "is my fault"] that the right hand of the Most High has changed" (v. 10). Here the psalmist holds to the idiom of prayers by those who are ill and uses sickness as a very realistic metaphor for the effect of his conclusion on his entire being. The "right hand of the LORD" is the term for God's power and readiness to deliver his people from distress. It was by the right hand of the LORD that Israel had been saved from the Egyptians (Exod. 15:6, 12) and had been protected and preserved as a people. The psalmist puts in words the awful reality that God's way with his people has changed and raises the awful question whether that means that God has changed.

2. Instead of making a petition for help or a vow of praise, the psalmist resolves to deal with his distress by recalling the marvelous deeds of the olden original times of Israel's relation to the LORD (vv. 11–12). The resolution brings to a climax the theme of remembering, of thinking the past into the present, that is woven into the psalm (*zkr* in vv. 4, 7, and now twice in v. 12). It is as if there is a reality of God in the past that, if re-presented in the present, will cope with the awful question. The re-presentation takes the form of hymnic address; now God is spoken to directly. The very shift in style gives the effect of presence.

The hymnic address confesses what God is like (v. 13) and rehearses the wonder of his deeds (vv. 14–20). The theme is the "way" of the LORD (vv. 13, 19). The LORD's way is "in holiness." Holiness is the basic attribute of deity; it is all that contrasts with and transcends the human, the marvelous, the mysterious, the incomprehensible. In holiness the LORD is incomparable. The LORD's way was through the sea (v. 19). The entire rehearsal describes the one primal originating saving event that brought Israel into existence, the wonder at the sea. The rehearsal contains many echoes of the Song of the Sea (Exod. 15:1–18); compare "incomparable in holiness" (v. 13) with Exodus 15:11; the "power" (v. 14) by which God "redeemed his people" (v. 15) and "led" them (v. 20), with Exodus 15:13. Like the Song of the

252

Sea, this hymnic recital combines the myth of the chaos battle
by which creation was established and kingship achieved with
the historical memory of crossing the Red Sea (see the comment
on Psalms 93; 74; 114; and Cross, p. 136). God's way through the
sea leading his people like a flock corresponds to and enacts the
mastery of the chaotic waters by which the world is established.

3. When the psalm as a whole is considered, it is evident
that the individual style is being used to speak of a dilemma that
is corporate. Either the speaker's problem with God is situated
completely in the distress of the whole people of God or he
speaks as their representative and recapitulates their experience in his account. Because it is composed in the style of an
account of experience, it is suitable as a liturgical text to lead
others to articulate their distress and bring it to confrontation
with the God evoked in the hymnic address. Though engaged
with a somewhat different problem, it is like Psalm 73 in this
respect. The character of the questions in verses 7–9 and the
hypothesis of verse 10 suggest that the psalm was composed for
use during the exilic or the postexilic period. The hymnic address may well have been quoted in whole or in part from a
repertoire known to the psalmist (Fritz Stolz, *Psalmen im nachkultischen Raum* [Zurich: Theologischer Verlag, 1983], pp. 31–
34, on the character of this psalm).

4. The hymnic address serves as a resolution to the anguished questions in several ways. The presence of God is
evoked. The God of incomparable holiness is spoken to and is
there in the portrayal drawn in the speaking. The divine
"Thou" is called forth, the God of revelation, who is who and
what he has revealed himself to be in creative and salvific
deeds. The LORD is there in the recital as the God whose right
hand has not changed. The hymn does what praise and confession are meant to do—to represent the God of revelation as the
reality and subject of truth in the face of all circumstances and
contrary experience.

The hymn also functions in place of the missing petition. It
plays the role that the "recollections of past" play as a frequent
feature of corporate prayers for help. The hymn is a way of
"seeking" the God of revelation in a time of need (*darash* in
v. 2). Motifs of the hymn are relevant to the need. The chaos
waters are a historical as well as a cosmic symbol; they represent
the unruly threatening nations. The hymn portrays the LORD
as the God who defeats the waters (v. 16) and leads his people

historical
78, 105, 106; 136

like a flock through the sea (v. 20). That is what the congregation needs and yearns for. One notes the relation to the salvation prophecies of Isaiah 40—55 and the proclamation of the new exodus theme. The recital of salvation history is always relevant because salvation history is not yet over (e.g., I Cor. 15:20–28).

The recital contains one line that is unique to this account of the wonder at the sea. Though described in verses 16–18 as a theophany similar to Psalms 18:7–15 and 114:3–5, God's way through the sea is said to be invisible. "Your footprints were not seen" (v. 19; literally, "not known"). "The waters saw you, O God" (v. 16), but no human being beheld that wondrous passage! Is this quite special remark the psalmist's way of observing that the marvelous work made visible in the hymn may be invisible in its occurrence? God may be at work, but beyond our ken (cf. Job 37:5, where the great deeds of theophany are said to be "not known," i.e., incomprehensible). That needs also to be remembered and believed when hymns are sung and confession is made.

Psalm 78: That the Next Generation Might Know

1–8

Deuteronomy
6:1–9
26:5–11

Psalm 78 is the voice of a teacher. It is largely composed of narrative, a telling of the story of the LORD's way with Israel. In this respect it is similar to Psalms 105, 106, and 136. Because of this common dominant feature, this group of psalms is often classified as "historical psalms."

1. The so-called historical psalms all recite a version of the foundational narrative of Israel found in Genesis—Samuel, from Abraham to David. Though the psalms seem based on the narrative as it is recorded in these books, each version is selective and distinctive in the way it tells the story. The different versions illustrate the creative ingenuity employed in shaping the material of Israel's traditions about its past. The distinctiveness of each emerges from the purpose of its recital. Each recital is composed to elicit a lesson from the tradition. These psalms are instructional in the broadest sense of that term. The styles of presentation vary from *torah* to hymn and prayer, but their central purpose is to inform, correct, and nurture the faith of the congregation in whose midst they were performed. Obviously, calling them historical psalms can be misleading. Their composers did not practice or present "history" in the sense

254

that term has for modern historians. These psalms are concerned with the past and its bearing on present and future. The past is the past remembered, not researched. It is a past of traditions about events with a very prominent confessional dimension—events experienced and reported as interactions of Israel's God with Israel's will and way. For these psalmists, God's way and will are essential elements of reality. Any account of past experience that excluded God as a principal participant would have been reductionist and meaningless. (On the "historical psalms," see Brueggemann, *Abiding Astonishment.*)

2. Psalm 78 is obviously composed as a speech. It is the address by a speaker to his people for their instruction (v. 1). The speaker is performing a divinely constituted duty that Israel's God has ordained as the responsibility of every generation of the people of the LORD (vv. 5–6). Speech though it is, the psalm is poetry designed to be recited or chanted as part of the liturgical agenda of religious assembly. In style and form, it has no close analogies in the Psalter; it does resemble the poetic speech of Moses in Deuteronomy 32 in significant ways, a relationship that is suggestive of the psalm's genesis and original function. The psalm does for those who hear it what Moses is portrayed as doing for Israel before they entered the land; it instructs Israel about the peril and promise of being the people of the LORD.

The speech has a long introduction and two parts. The introduction explains at some length what the speech is about and what its purpose is (vv. 1–11). It is identified as a "parable" *(mashal)* and "riddles *(hidot)* from the past" (v. 2). The psalm is a *mashal* because it deals in comparisons. The audience will be instructed not to be "like their ancestors" (v. 8) or "like the Ephraimite bowman who played false in the day of battle" (so NJPS, v. 9). The two principal parts then correspond to these two comparisons. The first turns on the failure of the ancestors of the wilderness generation (vv. 12–39). The second turns on the failure of the ancestors that happened in Ephraimite territory (vv. 40–72). The psalm contains *hidot* in the recitals of things that happened in the past from which meanings in the present are to be inferred. Each of the principal parts follows the same pattern: recitation of the LORD's marvelous deeds for Israel, an instance of failure, the responding divine wrath, a concluding account of how the LORD maintained the relation with his sinful people. (See the analysis of Clifford, pp. 127–129.)

The two narrative sequences tell about God and people; both are protagonists in every stage of the pattern. Those who hear the speech are given *torah* about the power and compassion of God and about the possibilities created for them by God's power and compassion. The first sequence reviews the marvels in Egypt—the wonder at the sea, the leading by fire and cloud—and comes to focus on the provision of water from rock in the wilderness (vv. 12–16). The stories of God's provision of water and food in the wilderness (Exod. 15:22—17:7) are used in a rather free way to tell about Israel's failure (vv. 17–20) and God's anger and punishment (vv. 21–31). The sequence concludes with a summary account of continuing failure, punishment, false repentance, and forgiveness coupled with divine restraint because of the people's finitude and transience (vv. 32–39). The second sequence begins with a lamenting transition over the failure of the wilderness generation to respond to the power of the LORD shown by his signs and marvels in Egypt and then reviews God's guidance in the wilderness and the rescue at the sea; it finally comes to focus on the settlement of the land in God's holy territory won by displacing others to make a place for Israel (vv. 40–55). Then it tells of Israel's betrayal of the LORD in the very land given to them (vv. 56–58) and draws on the story of the loss of the ark (I Samuel 4) to tell how the LORD rejected Israel by deserting to the enemy the sanctuary of his presence at Shiloh, the ark as the symbol of his power, and the people who were his heritage (vv. 59–64). This impasse was resolved, says the psalm, by the reappearance of the LORD as divine warrior to defeat his foes, by the replacement of Shiloh with Jerusalem and its temple as the divine residence among human beings, and by the election of David to be the shepherd of Israel (vv. 65–72).

3. The speech is an eloquent testimony to the crucial importance of tradition in biblical religion. Its basic assumption is that remembering and telling are essential to the existence of the people of God. The speaker views the people of God as a family whose identity and ethos are maintained across generations because parents tell children the story of how they came to be the people of the LORD. The psalmist names his tradition "the praises of the LORD and his might, and the wonders he performed" (v. 4, NJPS). Inseparably associated with God's mighty acts are the responsibilities they entail, the commandments and decrees (vv. 7, 56). Together the two comprise the

256

covenant or decree and the *torah* that it provides (vv. 5, 10). The purpose of the tradition is to nurture a community who put their confidence in God and observe his commandments (v. 7). That is why the psalm must be more than simple storytelling; this remembering by the parents for the sake of the children leads to praises that disclose the reliance of the heart and obedience that displays the commitment of the soul.

4. This teaching does recite the mighty works of God (vv. 12–16, 43–55), but each recital leads up to a specific case of Israel's failure, and the instruction turns on these cases as negative examples of what the audience should not be like. The speaker's *torah,* just like the canonical form of Israel's foundation story, includes the response of the people. The way of God and the way of the ancestors (Hebrew "fathers") are woven together. The people of God are instructed, not only by what God has done and said, but also by what the fathers and mothers in the faith have done and said. The biblical *torah* of the first five books and the four Gospels is composed in that way. The speaker uses examples of failure by the ancestors. There is irony here; those who passed on the tradition also failed it. Every generation will have to reckon with the fact that the story tells of failure as well as faithfulness.

5. The two cases of failure illustrate dangers that always threaten the people of the LORD. The psalmist may have selected them because they were particularly relevant to his audience and their situation. But they are mistakes of faith that endanger every generation. The first mistake was to crave and demand more than they were given. The ancestors in the wilderness made their desire the measure of their need and wondered whether the LORD could indeed "spread a table in the wilderness" (vv. 18–20). The second mistake was to worship at high places, the shrines of the Canaanite gods. Once in the land, the ancestors sought salvation and blessing from other gods besides the LORD. The speaker uses a rich vocabulary to evaluate both mistakes as at root the same. Such conduct is sin: falling short of the mark (vv. 17–32). It is rebellion: recalcitrance toward those to whom one is responsible (vv. 17, 40, 56). It is testing God: putting God's power in question (vv. 18, 41, 56). It is not believing in the LORD: not relying on the LORD alone and completely to be God for them (vv. 8, 22, 32, 37, 42). It is not observing the covenant and its instruction (vv. 10, 37, 56). It is forgetting the LORD: not remembering his mighty works for

257

them (vv. 7, 11, 35). The speaker uses this vocabulary to hammer home the lesson that wanting more than the salvation and blessing God provides and seeking salvation and blessing from another source are both failures to trust themselves to the Redeemer and his redemption.

6. The speaker also tells about the wrath of God in a way that gives instruction. In both cases, the punishment corresponds to the crime. In both cases, but in quite different ways, the power of the LORD as their God is vindicated. For the wilderness generation, the giving of the very blessing they craved and demanded became the moment and the means of God's anger against them. When the generation that settled in the land were faithless to God, whose power had redeemed them from their foe, the LORD abandoned them to the power of their enemies. The lesson of the second account of God's wrath is especially ominous. By utterly rejecting Israel, the LORD cancels and dissolves the very manifestation of his sovereignty in the world achieved in redeeming a people as his possession, settling them as his people in his holy mountain and dwelling in their midst through the representation of his power in the ark at the sanctuary of Shiloh. The sovereign LORD is free to abandon the very achievements and institutions of his sovereignty. The LORD is not identical with his holy hill, his dwelling in the midst of mortals, his ark of power and glory, even his people. Some prophets in the eighth and seventh centuries had to preach that lesson to Israel and Judah.

7. The final point of the speaker's instruction, however, is not about wrath. Judgment is the word, but it is not the last word. The last word is the triumph of grace. The people fail, but the failure of the people is not the failure of God. God prevails against faithlessness. In the first instance, it is by forgiveness. Punishment does not cure sinfulness; it only brings a temporary and transient repentance. Israel sinned repeatedly, but the compassion of God sets a limit to the wrath of God. His forgiveness creates room for Israel to exist before him as sinners—not because they are the people of the LORD but simply because their mortality evokes the divine compassion (v. 39). Forgiveness because of mercy is what keeps the story of God and human beings going. Know that, and one knows that there is no place for presumption or pride before God. Human beings stand before him as "flesh." In the second instance, the LORD

258

deals with his rebellious and punished people by a recapitulation and extension of the original saving drama. The LORD appears once again as the divine warrior to defeat his foes who afflict his people. But things are not simply restored. Ephraim is passed over as the place where the divine sovereignty is manifested, and Judah is now chosen. Mount Zion becomes the site of a new sanctuary that represents the victory of the LORD over opposition to his deity and rule in the same way that heavens and earth are the work of the LORD's victory over chaos. In a second sovereign choice, the LORD makes the shepherd David the shepherd of the people of the LORD. The divine shepherd who led Israel in the wilderness chooses a human being as undershepherd to lead his people in the land. This servant David has, says the last line of the psalm, what Israel lacked—integrity of heart and wise judgment. Because of his character he can and will shepherd and guide Israel. Along with forgiveness, the election of Zion as sanctuary and of David as shepherd king are the provisions of grace to keep the story of the LORD and his people going.

8. Clearly the teacher who speaks in the psalm attributes immense importance to the temple in Jerusalem and the Davidic king. Zion and David are institutions of the divine sovereignty to deal with Israel's faithlessness toward their Rock and Redeemer. In the sanctuary's worship, Israel will remember the marvelous works of their God. In David's rule, Israel will be led in the ways of trust and obedience. The lesson taught in the language the speaker employs could have had an appropriate historical setting during the reform of Josiah (II Kings 22—23), or more likely the reform of Hezekiah (II Kings 18), both periods of crucial emphasis on the importance of Zion and the Davidic king as institutions for the renewal of Israel's relation to the LORD. The prophets of Israel raised searching questions about the temple and its worship and about the character of the Davidic kings they knew. Within the Old Testament, the quest for a Zion that truly remembers the Rock and Redeemer of Israel and a Davidic king whose character makes him a faithful guide of the flock finds no final resolution.

Psalm 79: Where Is Your God?

Psalm 79 is a prayer of the people of the LORD in a time of grievous trouble. It is quite similar to Psalm 74, and the comment on that psalm should be consulted. On the type of corporate prayers for help, see the Introduction, sec. 5.4.

1. The psalm is largely composed of lamenting descriptions of trouble and petitions for help. It begins with a sequence of laments following the "they, we, you" pattern. The sequence describes how the nations (they) have dishonored God and afflicted the people of God (vv. 1–3), the humiliation of the people of God (we, v. 4), and the enduring anger of God toward his people (you, v. 5). The laments are followed by a sequence of corresponding petitions supported by reasons why the petitions should be answered. The petitions plead with God to turn his anger from his people to the nations (they, vv. 6–7), to deal with the iniquity of his people in compassion (we, v. 8), and to save his people in an act of forgiveness (you, v. 9). The cry, "Why should the nations say, Where is their God?" (v. 10a) is the climax and theological theme of the psalm. The cry leads to another threefold sequence of petitions that God make the nations know the vindication of his people (v. 10b), that God respond to the affliction of the afflicted (v. 11), and that God deal with the taunts of others against him (v. 12). This sequence concludes with a promise that the people of God will answer his answer of their prayers with everlasting praise (v. 13). Throughout, the motifs of nations, people, and God are interwoven in a way that keeps the focus on the painful problem of this three-sided relationship.

2. The scope of the disaster sketched in verses 1–4, 7, and 11 points to the fall of Jerusalem to the Babylonians in 587 B.C. (II Kings 25). The holy temple has been defiled by the intrusion and uses of foreigners. Jerusalem is in ruins. The population has been slaughtered, its land devastated. The remaining population lives in weakness and shame in the midst of its neighbors. The psalm is composed of an unusually high incidence of language conventional in descriptions of disaster, so it is impossible to be certain. But the Babylonian destruction of Jerusalem fits the picture best of the disasters known from Old Testament times. There might have been and there would be other such occasions. This prayer was probably used first in ceremonies of

grief and lament in the long years of the sixth century. It is liturgy for a time of the wrath of God.

3. The purpose of the psalm is to keep the community's tribulation in the context of its faith in God. If one goes through the psalm and marks every "you" and "your" addressed to God, the intention and effect of the prayer is clear. Jerusalem and its temple are the inheritance of God, the territory that belongs in a special way to the LORD. The worshiping congregation calls itself God's servants, his faithful, his people, the flock of his pasture. The nations are the human historical agent of the disaster, but what the congregation experiences as its greatest desolation is the wrath of its God. God's "jealous wrath" (v. 5) is his zeal for Israel's exclusive relation to him and is the term used for God's response to Israel's commerce with other gods (Exod. 20:5; 34:14; Deut. 5:9; 32:16, 19; Josh. 24:19; Ps. 78:58). The term's appearance in the psalm may be an acknowledgment of apostasy. The reference to "the iniquities of our ancestors" (v. 8) recalls the warning of the second commandment that the apostasy of parents would lead to the punishment of the children to the third and fourth generations. Psalm 79 is the only corporate prayer for help that includes a confession of sin. If the connection with the commandments is correct, that would explain why it is the iniquities of the community's history that are confessed.

4. The psalm does not stay with sin and punishment as the meaning of Israel's desolation. It appeals to the glory of the name of God. It expressed the marvelous presumption of faith that the honor of God's name in the world is more important than even the sin and punishment of his people (v. 9). When city and temple that belong to God and the people who call on the name of God are pushed to the edge of extinction, then the nations and kingdoms who do not acknowledge that the LORD is God and do not call on his name (v. 6) are in a position to taunt the flock of God with the scornful, derisive question, "Where is your God?" (v. 10). The taunts of neighboring folk over the humiliation of God's people (v. 4) are really directed at the LORD (v. 12). On the taunt question, see Psalms 42—43, sec. 2, and 115:2; for a narrative setting, read II Kings 18:13-37. Ezekiel announced to the exiles that the LORD would restore Israel, not for their sake, but for the sake of his own holy name among the nations (Ezek. 36:16-37). The purpose of God in the world is the glory of God in the world. Even the salvation of the

261

people of God serves the glory of God. This prayer believes that. Its appeal is the hope that God would not leave the taunt question unanswered. The people of God cannot answer it. Only God in his own way and time answers that question. In I Maccabees 7:17, verses 2–3 of the psalm are quoted as a scriptural lament over the murder of Hasideans whose trust was betrayed by rulers who used power as the rulers of nations do (cf. Mark 10:42). Revelation 16:6 echoes verse 3 to speak of the shed blood of the saints and prophets. The psalm is recited as a lection in synagogues on the ninth of Ab. In all these ways the psalm continues to voice the prayer of those who raise the question, "Why should the nations say, Where is your God?"

Psalm 80: Restore Us, O God

Psalm 80 is punctuated by a refrain that carries its theme: "Restore us, O God (of hosts), let your face shine, that we may be saved" (vv. 3, 7, 19). The psalm is a corporate prayer appealing to God to resume the favor bestowed on Israel in the past, restoring all that had been lost because of his anger (vv. 4, 12). On the type, see Introduction, sec. 5.4.

1. The opening petitions for God to hear (v. 1) and help (v. 2) are accompanied by vocatives invoking God as the shepherd-king of Israel who occupies a throne supported by cherubs and who appears in flashing theophany when his people-flock are threatened. All these appellations are related to the ark and its role in Israel's history and faith. The top of the ark was decorated with hybrid creatures associated with deity in the ancient Near East; these cherubs represented the base of the LORD's invisible throne, the place on earth of the royal presence of the one who reigns from heaven. The ark led Israel through the wilderness like a flock. It manifested the appearance of God when it was taken out with the armies of Israel (I Sam. 4:4; II Sam. 6:2) and symbolized his presence when it rested in the temple (II Kings 19:15; see Ps. 99:1). Shepherd is the title for God as king who leads, protects, and provides for his people (see the comment on Psalm 23). God of hosts, the title used in the refrain and elsewhere, is the name particularly associated with the ark (vv. 4, 7, 14, 19; see the comment on Ps. 24:10). It is to the way of God represented by this cluster of identifications that the prayer appeals, to the God who leads his people through the perils of history and saves them from its dangers.

262

Verses 4–6 describe in succinct formulaic fashion the distress of the flock of the LORD. The LORD God of hosts has been angry for a long time with his people, even though they pray to him (v. 4; not "angry with his people's prayers," as NRSV suggests). There is nothing wrong with the prayers; they just don't help. Mourning (v. 5) and humiliation (v. 6) continue to be the lot of the people of God.

2. The rest of the psalm develops the image of a vine; the congregation speaks of itself as a grapevine planted by the LORD. The closest analogy is found in Jeremiah (Jer. 2:21; see 6:9; 8:13), though he probably reflects the use of the image in Hosea (Hos. 10:1; 14:5–7; see also Gen. 49:22). Ezekiel also employed the image in a variety of ways (Ezekiel 15; 17; 19:10–14). Like the flock, the vine and vineyard represented a basic and familiar possession that was owned, cared for, and prized as a primary good of life. Here God is portrayed as the owner who secured a vine, planted it, and cleared space for its growth. The portrayal covers the story of Israel from exodus and conquest (v. 8) through possession of the land (v. 9) up to the Davidic empire whose boundaries reached from sea to river (vv. 10–11). Like the Song of the Vineyard in Isaiah 5:1–7, this parable interprets the history of Israel as the work of the LORD. All that has happened has been God's work and the outcome of his labor. The parable functions as the "recollection of the past," a regular feature of the corporate prayer. Isaiah told his parable to express the disappointment of God. The psalm's parable introduces the anguish and bewilderment of the people over the contrast and contradiction between what God began and what he now has done, leaving it exposed for strangers to gather the fruit of the vine and for wild animals to ravage the vine (vv. 12–13).

The psalm concludes with a series of petitions (vv. 14–17) and a promise of faithfulness and praise if the congregation is granted life (v. 18). The prayer calls on God to repent, to return (*shub;* NRSV, "turn again") to his former ways with Israel and take responsibility for the vine whose stock was planted by his right hand. As further ways of identifying itself as the possession of the LORD, the congregation calls itself (v. 17) "the man of your right hand" (a synonym for "the stock your right hand planted") and "the son of man [i.e., human being] you have taken as your own" (so NJPS). The Hebrew text of verse 15 contains an appositional phrase omitted by NRSV ("and upon

263

the son you have taken as your own") that was appended by a scribe to make sure the terms "man of your right hand" and "son of man" were not understood to refer to the king (cf. 110:1). The theology upon which the prayer bases its appeal is the identity of the congregation as the work of the LORD's right hand.

3. Like most of the other psalms of Asaph, this one contains connections with the tradition that appears in Hosea, Jeremiah, and Deuteronomy, the Ephraimite or northern tradition (see Introduction, sec. 3.6). It also calls Israel "Joseph" (v. 1) and lists the tribes of Ephraim, Benjamin, and Manasseh. What this means for the historical context in which the prayer was composed has been the subject of a long and inconclusive discussion. Does the use of these names and the distress described in verses 5–6, 12–13, and 16 reflect the disasters of the northern kingdom in the late eighth century or concern for its state in the seventh or for the loss of its population in the sixth? Whatever the original historical setting, the psalm in its continued use belongs to the repertoire of the afflicted people of God on their way through the troubles of history.

4. The psalm prays for the restoration of the vine from the very judgment upon the vineyard announced by Isaiah (compare vv. 12–13 with Isa. 5:5–6). That poses the theological question raised by the prayer. It contains no expression of penitence, no assessment by the congregation of its own past or present conduct. The prayer does acknowledge that the congregation's distress is the work of divine wrath; it does not complain that God's anger is unjust. The congregation does pledge its faithfulness to God (v. 18). Does the pledge imply an admission that they have not been faithful in the past? Yet these are only marginal notes in the psalm.

The prayer concentrates with a single focus on one thing and one thing alone—the divine Thou. It addresses the God identified in the invocations as the actor in the congregation's experience of salvation and suffering and seeks God's resumption of his earlier work as the means of restoration. The psalm is a witness that the congregation must in the long last and in its extremity look away from its own repentance to a kind of repentance in God—his turning away from wrath and returning to grace. The trust that God will in the end do so is based on nothing in the congregation. It is based on the self-understanding that the congregation is the work of God, there in existence, wholly and only as the act of God. Believing that, the congregation can hope that God will not abandon what he has begun. Paul spoke of that confidence to the infant church when he wrote, "I am sure that he who began a good work in you will bring it to completion at the day of Jesus Christ" (Phil. 1:6). Sharing that confidence, the church sings a paraphrase of the psalm's refrain on its way through history. "Revive us, revive us; restore to Thy grace, And then we shall live in the light of Thy face" (A. J. Gordon).

Psalm 81: Listen to Me!

Psalm 81 begins with the praise of God and then turns quickly to preaching. The sermon is delivered as the voice of God! Its text is the first commandment. The pathos of the sermon is the yearning of God for a people whose faithfulness answers his choice of them.

1. The psalm's literary structure has two parts, a summons to the celebration of a festival (vv. 1–5) and an address to the people of God composed in divine first person style (vv. 6–16). The summons follows the pattern of the imperative hymn of praise (Introduction, sec. 5.5.4). It begins with a call for music and praise of God on the day of Israel's festival (vv. 1–3) and then cites the divine authorization for observing the festival (vv. 4–5ab). Verse 5c seems to be a transitional introduction to the speech of God. The speech has two sections. The first reviews the relationship that God had established with Israel (vv. 6–10) and the second lays out the situation created by Israel's unfaithfulness (vv. 11–16). But neither part is simply narrative recollection. At the center of each stands an appeal of God to the people of God to listen to God (vv. 8, 13). The first appeal is followed by a declaration of the central word that Israel should hear (v. 9) and a self-identification of the God whose word it is (v. 10). The second appeal is followed by the promise of the protection (vv. 14–15) and provision (v. 16) that God will give if Israel would listen to God. The conditional promise to fill Israel's mouth (with food?) at the end of the first appeal (v. 10c) seems to anticipate and correspond to the promise of the finest wheat and honey from the rock that concludes the second appeal (v. 16). The unifying theme of the speech is clearly "Listen to me/to my voice." God in his deeds for Israel sought to create a listening people; that Israel should listen to

265

God is the essential of their identity as the people of God (v. 8). But Israel did not listen (v. 11). In the encounter created by the address, everything depends on Israel's listening (v. 13).

2. The psalm convokes a festival whose observance, it claims, was established by divine decree in the era of the exodus (vv. 4–6). The citation of sacral law probably refers to the tradition recorded in Numbers 29 and Leviticus 23:23ff. concerning the institution of the Festival of Booths or Tabernacles. This festival was one of the three annual festivals celebrated by all Israel. Its duration of two weeks would account for the psalm's reference to both new moon and full moon (v. 3; Lev. 23:23, 34). The psalm could well have been composed for performance at the opening convocation of the festival (Lev. 23:24). The speech confronts the assembling people with an address from the God who founded the festival by his work and ordinance. The third measure of verse 5 is enigmatic. Most contemporary scholars interpret the sentence as an introduction to the divine saying by one who receives and delivers it. The performer of the speech points to the superhuman source of what he will say and characterizes it as unrecognizable as ordinary speech (see I Sam. 3:7; Job 4:12–16; Num. 24:4–16). Probably the sentence represents more a liturgical than a prophetic phenomenon. The divine speech would be repeated every time the psalm was performed. The introduction invites the congregation to hear it as the message of God. A term is used in verse 8 and also in the similar divine speech in Psalm 50 (50:7) that indicates what kind of speech it is. The term is "admonish" *(ha'id);* it marks the address as a warning witness that calls on those to whom it is addressed to right a relationship that has gone wrong (see the use of the term in II Kings 17:13, 15; Jer. 11:7–8; Neh. 9:29, 30, 34; compare the prose saying of Jer. 7:16–29, where the important motifs of Psalm 81 also appear). The speech tells the congregation what the true significance of the festival is. It is not mere celebration, not simply music and liturgy; it is an occasion when the congregation can become again a listening people of God. In its structure of liturgical introduction and divine saying and in many of its features, Psalm 81 is similar to Psalms 50 and 95; they must have all been composed for the same kind of use and setting.

266

3. In the first section, the speech confronts the congregation with God's true identity. God recalls what he has done (vv. 6–7) and what he requires (v. 9) and therefore who he is

(v. 10). He delivered Israel from the oppressive labors of Egypt in answer to their prayers of distress. He listened when they cried out (Exod. 3:7). The "secret place of thunder" is a reference to God's theophany as the storm-god at the Red Sea (Exodus 15; Psalm 68). Strangely, Meribah is remembered as a place where God tested Israel, reversing the usual tradition that the people tested God there (95:8–9; Exod. 17:7; Num. 20:13). By his salvation the LORD claimed and took Israel as his people and revealed himself as "the LORD your God." He gave Israel an identity and existence that excluded any relation to other gods. Henceforth all other gods should be strange and foreign to Israel. The first commandment is the true meaning of the exodus. Any commerce with other gods meant that Israel had not listened to the God who listened to their cry of distress. The concluding self-presentation of God says it all: "I am the LORD your God, who brought you up out of the land of Egypt." That was God's word at Sinai; that is the word which introduces and founds the ten words of the covenant of Israel. With that word the confrontation between God and people at Sinai is reenacted (Exod. 20:1–3).

4. In its second part, the speech turns from the theme of the LORD as Israel's God to Israel as the people of the LORD. God recalls Israel's unresponsiveness (v. 11) and how he dealt with it (v. 12) and then utters a fervent wish that Israel would respond (v. 13) so that the blessings of covenant obedience could be theirs (vv. 14–16). It is significant that the speech does not charge the present congregation with failure; instead, it talks about Israel's refusal to hear and respond willingly as a continuation of the story about the past. Israel's not listening is a permanent part of their story, and the story reminds them who they really are as they assemble for the festival. They are people with a record of not listening. God's punishment is also part of the story. God did not compel his people to listen. Instead, he left them on their own because they stubbornly wanted to be on their own following their own advice. The diagnosis of the "stubborn heart" appears elsewhere in Jeremiah, where there are helpful contexts for considering its character (Jer. 7:24; 9:14; 11:8; 13:10; the only instance outside Jeremiah is Deut. 29:19). God consigned them to the consequences of their willfulness. This way of punishment sounds very much like the pattern that is repeated in the Book of Judges, where Israel turned to other gods, forgetting the LORD,

267

who consigned them to the power of their enemies until they cried out to the LORD for deliverance. Notice the similar notion of the way of divine wrath in Romans 1:24, 26; Acts 7:42. In Judges, the Jeremiah contexts, and also the New Testament references, the problem is always the integrity of the people's relation to the self-revelation of God as the LORD. The classic failure of the people of God is not a lack of religiosity or fascination with the divine. It is instead a failure of faithful and discerning responsiveness to the LORD's self-revelation. To put it in the psalm's idiom, the people of the LORD do not *hear* the word, "I am the LORD your God."

5. The effect of the speech is to constitute the festival as a time of decision that is like the time Israel stood at the foot of Sinai to hear the voice of God and like the time beyond the Jordan when Israel listened to the preaching of Moses (Exod. 19:4–5; 20:1–3; Deut. 5:1–6). The festival is a time to decide anew whether they will continue the story of their past recalcitrance or will listen to the LORD and walk in his ways (note "today" in 95:7). If they will listen to the LORD, he will give them protection and provender, the yet unrealized blessings of covenant faithfulness (vv. 4–16; on finest wheat and honey from the rock, see Deut. 32:13–14). Psalm 81 is thus a paradigm for what should happen in every religious festival. Festivals are times when the people of God consider the story of God's way with them and their way with God, times to face the appeal of the LORD, "O that my people would listen to me."

Psalm 82: The Trial of the Gods

1. Psalm 82 is surprising in content and character. It speaks of God presiding over a court where gods are on trial. Instead of praise of God or prayer to God, most of it is a quotation of what God said. Verse 1 sets the scene; God has taken the central—that is, the preeminent—position in the midst of an assembly of gods to officiate as judge. Acting in this capacity, God, in rhetorical questions and exhortations, accuses the gods of failure in their role of bringing justice to the earth (vv. 2–4), finds them guilty of destabilizing the earth by their incompetence (v. 5), and sentences them to loss of office and death (vv. 6–7). The psalm concludes with a petition to God to take over as judge of the earth in place of the gods who were supposed to judge the nations.

268

2. What God does and says in verses 1–7 reflects the proceedings of a court. Sayings modeled on arguments made in legal proceedings in Israel were used by prophets to speak of God's judgments against Israel and its leaders. Isaiah 3:13–15 is quite similar; see also Isaiah 1:18–20; Micah 6:1–5; and Hosea 4:1–3. But the trial saying in Psalm 82 was composed for performance in liturgy; its report of what God is doing and saying would have been repeated every time the psalm was used. God's reported deed and word form the basis and background of the liturgy. The purpose of the trial saying is to prepare for the final petition for God to rise up and judge the earth. The psalm is a prayer that calls on God to do what the trial scene portrays: dispense with the gods and take over the judgment of earth as its rightful supreme sovereign.

3. Psalm 82 is in fact one of the songs in the Psalter that celebrates the reign of the LORD. It portrays God's reign, not as a state or condition of things, but as something that is happening, an unfinished story. The ideas and notions used in the portrayal come from the intellectual world of the ancient Near East, and it helps us grasp the theology of the psalm to be aware of them. Israel lived in the midst of cultures with ancient and imposing religions that dealt with pantheons of gods. These gods were thought to meet in a divine assembly under the presiding authority of the first or father deity, a notion that turns up in a number of places in the Old Testament (I Kings 22:19–20; Isaiah 6; 40:1–8; Job 1—2). How the gods got along and what they decided and did were fateful for nature and human society. Psalm 82 takes up that worldview and gives it a particular Israelite expression. The LORD is the central authoritative deity, presiding over the council. The other deities are subordinate; indeed, their status as deities rests on the LORD's decree as the highest of gods, Elyon (v. 6). All the nations are under the sovereignty of the LORD, and the gods are assigned to the nations to bring justice to those who need it (v. 8; see Deut. 32:8–9). The charge against the gods is not that they are idols or nonexistent but that they have failed to put down wickedness and bring justice. Their failure, says the psalm, makes the foundations of the world unstable, a mythopoeic way of saying that their failure threatens the creation, the achievement on which the LORD's rule is based (see 24:1–2). So the LORD as reigning deity removes them from office and condemns them to death. This portrayal of the assembly of the

P. 120

269

gods is unlike any other because it announces the permanent adjournment of the assembly and the execution of its constituency: the psalm announces the death of the gods. It is a way of saying in the face of a polytheistic worldview, "I believe in God the Father Almighty." The notion of the council is used to dramatize a profound shift in understanding reality. The context for human life is not the careers of the gods of the nations but the reign of the LORD.

An observation must be added at this point about a rather puzzling use of verse 6 made by Jesus in chapter 10 of the Gospel of John. In the Gospel, the fellow countrymen of Jesus were about to stone him because they perceived that he was claiming to be divine. He quoted Psalm 82:6 in response and asked, If those to whom the word of God came were called "gods," could the one whom the Father has sanctified and sent into the world be condemned for blasphemy because he said, "I am God's son"? (John 10:34–36). The cogency of Jesus' argument depends on an interpretation traditional among the Jews that understood "gods" in Psalm 82:6 to refer to the Israelites who had received the word of God. If they, Jesus reasoned, could be called "gods," surely the one sanctified and sent into the world by God could be called "son of God" without blasphemy. This use of verse 6 sheds light on Jewish debates about the meaning of Scripture and their extreme caution concerning divinity claims for any other than the LORD God of Israel.

4. In the trial, the gods are judged by a clear and simple norm: whether the rights of the weak are protected in human society. This criterion is not peculiar to Israel. It was believed to be a feature of authentic authority and expected of all who exercised power over others in the ancient Near East. Both gods and monarchs were expected to provide justice for the weak. One can view this conviction as a general knowledge of God known broadly in the culture. In this psalm the provision of delivering justice is made the decisive criterion for the authenticity of deity! It is not one feature among others; it is the sole issue. In the background is a severe concentration of the LORD's revelation of his way and will through the law and the prophets. It is through law and prophecy, supported by historic interventions against the wicked, that this God manifests identity and rule. It becomes an axiom of Old Testament theology that the worship of the LORD must and shall bring justice to the weak. On the other hand, the forces and powers that control a society

270

in which rights of the needy are violated and neglected are unmasked as failed gods.

5. The concluding prayer is important. It calls on God to replace the false gods and set things right in the world by his rule. The court saying provides a revelation of what is happening in history; the false gods are being uncovered and condemned. But the congregation worships in the midst of a world where nations and societies are still ruled by false gods. The wicked still have power and the weak are deprived of justice. So the congregation prays the ancient prayer that Israel addressed to the LORD when the ark was moved as a symbol of the LORD's intervention in the affairs of earth: "Arise, O God" (see Num. 10:35; Pss. 132:8; 74:22). The liturgical movement of the psalm's recitation holds the "already" and the "not yet" of the LORD's rule in tension. Faith knows that the LORD rules over all the powers and forces that compel the hearts and lives of nations and societies. Living in the midst of history, faith can and must pray for the LORD's saving judgment upon all that denies the reality of the reign of God. The psalm helps the Christian congregation understand better what it means to pray, "Thy kingdom come, thy will be done, on earth as it is in heaven." As long as nations and their peoples do not see the reign of God as the reality that determines their way and destiny, there will be other gods who play that role. Faith must always see the LORD standing in the midst of the gods of the nations and know that to say "Thy kingdom come" is to pray for the death of our gods.

Psalm 83: The Enemies of God

Psalm 83 is a prayer of the people of God when enemies plot their liquidation. The prayer sees the plot as a conspiracy to usurp the place on earth that belongs in a special way to the LORD of all the earth. On the corporate prayer for help, see Introduction, sec. 5.4.

1. The psalm is composed simply of petitions and a description of the trouble that is the occasion of the petitions. It opens with a threefold plea that God not be uninvolved in the present crisis (v. 1). Then the crisis is sketched. The description reports to God what his enemies are doing (vv. 2–5) and who they are (vv. 6–8). God must not remain inactive, because his enemies are astir, preparing an assault against his people, and the

271

enemies are many. A series of petitions calls for the divine action that will resolve the crisis. The first set calls on God to do now what he had done in comparable situations in the past (vv. 9–12). The second set appeals for a divine victory portrayed in similes of destruction (vv. 13–14), motifs of the divine warrior's power as storm-god (v. 15), and images of defeat (vv. 16–17). The concluding and climactic petition says what the victory will mean. By it, God will make known that the One whose name is the LORD is the Most High over all the earth (v. 18).

2. The list of nations and peoples in verses 6–8 calls the roll of a covenant league of enemies united against Israel (v. 5). Giving names to enemies is not the usual practice in psalmic prayer. The list is made up of small states and tribal groups on the boundaries of Israel and concludes with the great imperial state of Assyria. When were these kingdoms and tribes, supported by Assyria, in league against Israel? Scholars have given answers that ranged from the period of Assyria's dominance in the Near East down to times very late in Judah's history. Even the name of Assyria is not a decisive clue, since the name came to be used, like that of Babylon, as a cipher for the great enemy who wields power in the world (examples are Ezra 6:22; Lam. 5:6; Zech. 10:10). The roll call is more likely a summarizing combination of names for liturgical purposes than historical data. To speak of a typical and recurring crisis that belongs to Israel's history, the danger of being overrun and wiped out by other peoples, is poetic rhetoric. Portrayal of enemies seething in tumult (v. 2) and plotting together against the LORD's people (v. 3) is quite similar to the description of general hostility with which Psalm 2 begins (2:1–3).

3. The purpose of the prayer is to invoke the LORD's intervention to protect the existence of Israel. It holds the nation's danger up to the LORD as a crisis to which the LORD must respond. The nation Israel is the LORD's own people, his "treasured ones" among the peoples of the earth (v. 3; NRSV, "those you protect"). So the conspiracy to eliminate them from history and their name from memory is an assault on the LORD's way and work in the world. Their plan makes these nations the enemies of God. The prayer recalls what God had done in the past when other generals and rulers planned to take possession of "the pastures of God" (vv. 9–12; the literary record of the recollection appears in Judges 4—8). In those ancient classic battles, God defended the land that he had claimed for his

people from others who tried to take it for their own. Israel's existence and place in geography and history was and is the LORD's revelation that he is the Most High over all the earth (vv. 16, 18). The LORD's name and claim on history are at stake. In faith and hope that this is all true, the prayer pleads for the LORD to vindicate his work in the past and his rule in the present.

4. Talk about the "enemies of God" belongs to the vision of the LORD as the divine warrior who wins the battle of creation against the primeval forces of chaos and the battle of salvation to deliver his people. The extra-psalmic sources for this vocabulary are Exodus 15 and Deuteronomy 32. In the Psalms, see 66:3; 68:1, 21; 74:4, 18, 23; and 89:10. In all these contexts, the theological issue is the vindication of the LORD as sovereign of the universe and earth. It is of course venturesome and dangerous for the people of God to see those who threaten them as the enemies of God and to invoke God's vengeance against them. Such prayers can easily become the language of a self-serving, blind ideology. The prophets insistently reminded Israel that they could and did become the ones who obstructed the coming of God's kingdom in the world. The integrity of such a prayer for Israel depended on the integrity of their life as the people of the LORD. The apostle Paul reminded the early church that "while we were yet enemies, we were reconciled to God through the death of his Son" (Rom. 5:10). But the scandal of God's election of a particular people and his involvement with a particular story inevitably mean that the way of God in the world confronts opposing hostile forces. For the early church, the enemies were "the cosmic powers of the present darkness, the spiritual forces of evil in heavenly places" (Eph. 6:12). The prophet John saw the enemy incarnate in the imperial forces of persecution (Revelation 17—18). It takes no imagination to guess the horror that Jews feel on reading the declaration of the covenant of hate: "Come, let us wipe them out as a nation; let the name of Israel be remembered no more." Modern history is punctuated with attempts by secularized powers to dispossess the people of the LORD in both synagogue and church. Psalm 83 is in the Psalter as the prayer of his people whose existence is the work of his reign and who leave the vengeance to God (see Psalm 94).

Psalm 84: How Lovely Your Dwelling Place

Of all the psalms that celebrate Zion and its temple as God's dwelling place, the eighty-fourth has been the favorite. Its joy in the place where God dwells and the comparisons and experiences used to illustrate that joy make it a highly expressive poem. It has been particularly open to reinterpretation through the ages. The exuberant anticipation of coming to God's presence and the references to traveling (vv. 5–7) and to entering God's house (v. 10) suggest that the psalm was used in processions by pilgrims to Jerusalem. The prayer that the king be accepted (vv. 8–9) is evidence that the royal figure was part of the procession and the ceremonies of its approach to the courts of the temple.

1. From its opening exclamation to its concluding beatitude, the psalm celebrates the joys afforded by the dwelling of God with mortals. Because the temple on Zion's mount was a place of God's presence, longing for God took the historic form of pilgrimage. The dwelling place of God is beloved and sought out because the soul yearns for God. The appeal of the holy place is first of all religious, not aesthetic. Even birds find the sanctuary a desirable place to nest, says the psalm (v. 3). Pilgrims with their minds set on the highways to Zion seem to bring the early rains with them as they go from strength to strength on their way to appear before God in Zion (vv. 5–7, whose text is notoriously obscure). One day in the temple courts is better than a thousand elsewhere. It is better to stand at the threshold of the house of God than to be a resident with the wicked (v. 10). The psalm sets incomparable value on being present in the place of presence for the shortest time and in the most minimal way.

2. The way the psalm speaks about God gives at least a partial clue to why God's particular place is the object of such desire. Four times God is called by the title "LORD of hosts." The title is especially associated with the ark, which is the symbol of the LORD's will to be present and with his people (see the comment on Psalm 24). The LORD is the living God, a title that means "lively," as the giver of life, rather than "alive," as opposite of dead. God is sun, the source of life, and shield, the protector of life (v. 11). God gives grace and glory; the good in life comes from the LORD. He is, says the psalm, "my king and my

God," a double title that means something like "the sovereign power of the universe and the center of my personal life, the one who makes all things cohere for the life I have to live." To draw near to such a God is the summum bonum. Pilgrimage to God's place is a profound symbol of the centering and direction of all of life (Levenson, *Sinai and Zion,* pp. 176–178).

3. There are three Old Testament beatitudes in the psalm (vv. 4, 5, 12). They also show us the reason why God is sought with such desire. Like their New Testament counterparts, the sentences beginning with "Blessed is" or "Happy is" declare that those lives centered in and ordered by the kingdom of God are those who have chosen the way of life and good. In the psalm the beatitudes are spoken as direct address to God so as to take the form of praise. "You are the one," these beatitudes say, "who orders the world in such a way that blessedness comes to those who dwell in your dwelling in unbroken praise of you (v. 4), to those who find in you the strength to travel the highways to you (v. 5), and to those whose life is an expression of trust in you (v. 12)." Pilgrimage to God's place is a ritual of entry into God's ordering of reality and the conditions of human life.

4. Like Psalms 42—43, this one holds together yearning for God and the longing to be at a place because God has made it a place of Presence. The two mean that faith must take the form of movement, that one must go toward God. For Christians, the era when ark and temple were visible signs of an invisible presence of God in Jerusalem belongs to the time of the Old Testament, but that does not mean for us that God is placeless. We exist in space and time. How could God deal with us if not through space and time made holy by divine claim? God is everlasting, but he has his appointed times. God dwells in heaven, but he has place on earth. We "go" to God. Every visit to a temple or church or meeting of believers is in a profound sense a pilgrimage. We "go," not just for practical or personal reasons; we go theologically. Christians have read and sung Psalm 84 and through it praised the God to whom we "go" in different ways. The psalm has interpreted churches and chapels as "dwelling places of God's love, the abode to which our hearts aspire with warm desire to see our God" (Paraphrase from Isaac Watts, "Lord of the Worlds Above"). It has been sung also of life as a pilgrimage that leads to a final being with God.

Psalm 85: He Will Speak Peace to His People

1. The last part of Psalm 85 (vv. 8–13) has often been used as a psalm for the season of Advent. It is a poetic and dramatic promise that "God's salvation is at hand" (v. 9), an Old Testament form of the announcement "on earth peace among those with whom God is well pleased" (Luke 2:14). As a whole the psalm is a corporate prayer for help (see Introduction, sec. 5.4). It begins in the style of hymnic address and praises the LORD for his favor to his land and people in the past (vv. 1–3). Then it asks that the LORD turn again, as he did in the past, from anger to favor and manifest his covenant faithfulness (*hesed*) in the salvation of his people (vv. 4–8). An individual voice, responding to the petition, announces that he will listen on behalf of the congregation to what God says and bring them God's message of *shalom* (v. 8). A thematic sentence (v. 9) introduces the message, which takes the form of a portrayal of the powers of salvation at work creating *shalom* (vv. 10–13).

2. The first part and the second part seem contradictory. The first says that God has withdrawn his anger, forgiven his people, and restored their fortune. The second laments that God's anger goes on and on and asks that God turn from wrath to restore his people. Some propose to relieve the contradiction by translating the verbs of verses 1–3 as future to make the first part read as a statement of trust (e.g., NJPS). But the recollection of the past is a frequent feature of corporate prayers; God's past activity is contrasted with the present as both lament and appeal. What is somewhat unusual about Psalm 85 is the symmetry between past salvation and present need. In this respect, Psalm 85 is a mate to Psalm 126.

One way to account for this is to locate the psalm in the postexilic period when the community could look back on their amazing deliverance as a real "restoration of fortune" and yet had to live with such failure, frustration, and conflict that they cried out for salvation, the situation assumed by the restoration prophets (Isaiah 59; Hag. 1:5–11; Zech. 1:12). The great prophet of the exile had announced a change in the times bringing God's forgiveness and deliverance, culminating in the revelation of his glory (Isa. 40:1–11; 45:8; 46:13; 51:5; 52:7–10; 54:8). Deliverance did happen; the exiles returned. But "glory" did not dwell in the land and the powers of salvation did not prevail (Isa. 60:2;

276

62:2). Salvation had come; but the need for salvation remained. As is typical of the psalms, however, this prayer is composed in general and formulaic language that can be located in other times and circumstances. It is part of the liturgy of the saved community who must live in awareness that its salvation is not yet consummated.

3. The individual whose voice is heard in verse 8 does not use the divine first person style in assuring the congregation of salvation. He does not speak as one who has himself received an oracle by revelation. The promise of salvation is, rather, a reiteration of the salvation prophecy of Isaiah 40—55 (compare v. 9 with Isa. 51:5; 55:6; note 56:1). The singer, whatever office he holds, prophet or Levitical priest, rehearses the promises of God before the congregation as reassurance in their time of distress. He asks them to trust in the word of God that he has received by oral tradition.

The promise is addressed to those faithful to the covenant (v. 8) who fear the LORD (v. 9). The promise is a word of *shalom* (v. 8; NRSV, "peace"; NJPS, "well-being") that will be brought about by the LORD's salvation that is near (v. 9). Salvation is portrayed as the dynamic activity of a quartet of attributes characteristic of the way of the LORD: covenant loyalty *(hesed)*, faithfulness *('emet)*, righteousness *(sedeq)*, and peace *(shalom)*. These four salvation powers unite and make common cause (v. 10) to dominate and prevail in the land from earth to sky (v. 11) and create the condition in which God bestows the good and makes the land productive (v. 12). The optimum conditions for human life will exist (on the productive land as a feature of salvation prophecies, see Amos 9:13; Hos. 2:21–23; Isa. 30:23–25; Jer. 21:12; Lev. 26:3–6). The point of this way of describing a time of salvation is to interpret salvation as a dynamic process in which the character of God in all its fullness is at work. Salvation is happening when the *hesed* and *'emet* and *sedeq* and *shalom* of God are active in and through the community of the God-fearing faithful. For similar portrayals of divine attributes, see Isaiah 32:15–18; 45:8; 58:8; 59:14–15; Pss. 43:3; 89:14; 96:6.

4. This vision of salvation as the conformation of life to the character of God always transcends the life of the people of God. The vision has an eschatological reach. It needs the coming of God himself to realize it fully (vv. 9, 13). The psalm therefore is a judgment on any easy satisfaction with life under the conditions created by human character and a summons to

look for and pray for the time and life created by the character of God. That does make the psalm a good song for the season of Advent. The church believes that the attributes of God were present and active in Jesus Christ; in and through him were and are grace and truth and righteousness (John 1:17; Rom. 1:16–17). In him the fullness of God was pleased to dwell (Col. 1:19). Believers know that salvation is happening when the characteristics of Christ prevail in human life and the peace of God rules in their hearts (Col. 3:12–17). Living between "already" and "not yet," they join with Israel in taking heart at the promise, "Surely his salvation is near!" (v. 9).

Personal

Psalm 86: Save Your Servant

Psalm 86 is a prayer for help in first person singular style. Studies of this psalm always observe that it is largely composed of phrases and expressions found in other psalms and texts (e.g., compare v. 1b and 40:17; v. 4b and 25:1; v. 11a and 27:11; v. 14 and 54:3; vv. 15, 5 and Exod. 34:6). The composer appears to have used, not just the material for psalmic composition, but other psalms as well. This reuse of material in an "anthological style" has been judged imitative and inferior, but that is to mistake the genius of liturgical writing whose principal characteristic should not be originality. One has only to remember the Lord's Prayer to be reminded what power and possibilities lie in a liturgical text composed of traditional and formulaic material.

In fact, the composer has created a quite individual prayer out of his resources. It has been written so that whoever uses the psalm prays with a sustained concentration on the character of God and the identity of the one who prays. The prayer begins with a long series of petitions and associated vocatives supported by statements about self and God (vv. 1–7). A section of hymnic praise expands and develops the characterization of God (vv. 8–10). Then there is a petition to be given a life adequate for keeping a promise of praise with the whole heart (vv. 11–13). Only then is there a brief description of trouble (v. 14). The prayer resumes the praise of God (v. 15) and concludes with petitions for God's grace given in the form of a sign of God's favor (vv. 16–17).

278

The very formulaic character of the whole and its sustained

concentration on the One to whom prayer is made and the one who prays make the psalm a paradigm of the theology of the prayers for help. It illustrates in an almost summary way the theological setting of these prayers and so offers an agenda to guide reflection in prayer. The psalm guides thought about supplicatory prayer (v. 6) in the following ways.

1. Prayer is the cry of a *servant* to his or her *lord.* Servant (*'ebed*) and lord (*'adon*) were paired roles in Israel's culture. An *'ebed* was a person who belonged to an *'adon,* who lived and worked in the sphere of the purposes and decision of the *'adon,* and who had the right to the support and protection of the *'adon.* The last is especially important here. The psalm calls God "my lord" (so NJPS with the possessive pronoun) seven times; and the one who prays names himself "thy servant" three times and strengthens the self-designation finally with "son of thy handmaid," that is, servant all my life, born to it (v. 16). The use of these titles establishes the basic relation in which the human being stands to God.

2. Prayer is made in confidence that God *will* respond.

a. God is known as a lord who does answer when his servants call on him (v. 7).

b. Confidence in God is based on what Israel has known about God from earliest times, so the prayer praises God with an old liturgical confession: "Thou, Lord, are a God merciful and gracious, slow to anger and abounding in steadfast love and faithfulness" (vv. 15, 5; see Exod. 34:6 and discussion of the confession in Ps. 103:8). Prayer is not based on one's personal faith alone but on the ancient and continuing confessions of the whole community.

c. The servant can speak in confidence because the servant has been spoken to. When the prayer makes the confession "You are my God" (v. 2), it is an answer to the divine word to Israel "I am the LORD your God" (Exod. 20:2). Only in answer to this electing word could one dare to say "my God." But having heard it, one can say nothing else.

3. Prayer is made in confidence that God *can* help. The section of praise in verses 8–10 establishes that confidence. The servant's lord is incomparable in deity and works, indeed the only God, creator of the nations and the one whose reign is the final consummation of history (see the comment on Ps. 113:5). The personal god of prayer is also the universal and only God.

"Deliver us from evil" is said along with "Thy kingdom come, on earth as in heaven." The possibility that prayer can be answered rests on the reality that the kingdom of God is coming.

4. Prayer is the utterance of an identity that is lived out. It is not mere language but brings to expression the role of servant adopted in existence. That is the force of all the self-descriptions in the psalm.

a. *"I am poor and needy" (v. 1)*. In liturgical use these adjectives identify a suppliant as dependent for life on the help of God. They disavow all self-sufficiency and claim the right to help that belongs to the helpless. With them, prayer admits that life is dependent on God whose deliverance alone keeps the soul from the depths of Sheol (v. 13). Prayer is the voice of dependence.

b. *"I am* hasid" *(v. 2;* NRSV, "devoted"; NJPS, "steadfast"). The *hasid* is one who lives in and by the covenant, who trusts in his lord and calls on him when in trouble (vv. 2, 7). Prayer is the voice of trust.

c. *"Unite my heart to fear thy name" (v. 11,* RSV). The prayer seeks not only deliverance from trouble but as well help in the formation of the self. The one who prays acknowledges that even his faith and faithfulness depend on the instruction and integration of his soul. The people of God are commanded, "You shall love the LORD your God with all your heart" (Deut. 6:5). This prayer answers with a plea for a heart undivided so that thanks may be given "with my whole heart." "Unite my heart" is a petition that reaches out for the salvation promised by Jeremiah to the redeemed Israel: "I will give them one heart and one way" (Jer. 32:39). Prayer is not only a plea for life, it is a submission of life. The servant can serve only one master (see Matt. 6:19–34). Prayer is the voice of commitment.

Psalm 87: Born in Zion

Psalm 87 is a song about Zion and its role in the LORD's rule of the world (Introduction, sec. 6.10). Verse 7 suggests a possible liturgical use, a procession of worshipers led by singers and dancers who rejoice in Zion as source of their blessedness and joy. The psalm expresses two basic ideas. The first is the central premise of the songs of Zion: Zion is the city of God. The second is the particular elaboration of that premise that gives Psalm 87 its theological distinctiveness. The city of God is the spiritual

Spiritual veality for all who acknowledge God. 280

home for people who live in all the nations. The combination of the two has made the song a text through which the people of God in many times and places have been able to say: We have a "city that has foundations, whose builder and maker is God" (Heb. 11:10).

1. Verses 1 and 2 set out the basic premise tersely. The LORD founded his city in Zion and made the mountain on which it stands "holy" by his act. Zion, the human city built by men, *became* the city of God. It acquired a specific role in God's way with the world (see Psalms 48 and 132). The reason for the choice of Zion is "not the worth of the place, but the free love of God" (Calvin, 3:398). God preferred Zion to all the other sanctuaries (NRSV, "dwellings") in the territory of Jacob-Israel. It is God's inexplicable love, which has no basis beyond its own existence, that led to the election of Israel (Deut. 7:8) and to the choice of Zion (Ps. 78:68–69), and will be expressed in the election of all people, the world, in Jesus Christ (John 3:16). Faith sees the earthly things God has chosen, not in terms of themselves alone, but in the light of what God's love has made them. That is the reason glorifying songs are sung about Zion (v. 3).

2. Verses 4–7 reveal that there are citizens of the city of God resident in all the nations of the world. The sequence is a prophetic report of the vision of the LORD as he keeps the register of the peoples (v. 6). In verse 4, the LORD speaks and calls the roll of all those who know him as sovereign of the universe. Surprisingly, the roll begins with the two classic foes of Judah, Rahab (a mythical name for Egypt) and Babylon. The theme repeated three times is "born there." The theme is a theological metaphor that means that those who acknowledge the LORD have birthright status in Zion, no matter where they live. Their true home is the place toward which their spirits turn in yearning for God, and God declares that they were "born there" and makes it official by writing them in the book (69:28).

3. This vision of the LORD making distant and scattered people citizens of Zion is theologically powerful. Having Zion as religious home becomes thereby a spiritual reality rather than an accident of historical exigencies. Exiles from Judah and the Jews among the dispersion could know that by the grace of God they were "born there." The psalm can be read as a dramatic portrayal of the Old Testament hope that all nations would be drawn to the kingship of the LORD (e.g., Isa. 2:2–4;

45:22; Zech. 2:10–11; Pss. 22:27; 48:8–9). Christians read and sing it in the light of Philippians 3:20; Galatians 4:26; Hebrews 12:22–24; and Revelation 21.

Psalm 88: The Depths of the Pit

Psalm 88 is a very unusual prayer for help in first person singular style (on the type, see Introduction, sec. 5.2). There are no confessions of trust and no vows or expressions of praise. Only one petition is made (v. 2). The rest is all lament over the psalmist's condition, his relation to others, and the silence of God. The psalmist suffers from an affliction of long duration (v. 15). In his affliction he has become abhorrent to friends and neighbors (vv. 8, 18). The LORD has rejected him, and the psalmist understands all his suffering to be the effect of the wrath of the LORD (vv. 6–8, 14, 16, 18; on the connection made between sickness and sin, see the excursus to Psalm 38). These features of the lament are common to many prayers for help. What is remarkable here is the prominence of death. The lament speaks not only of an affliction that leads to death but of death itself. Death is so near and so real that it becomes the subject of the lament.

Because this is so, Psalm 88 is one of the texts where the view of dying and death assumed by the psalms comes more distinctly into focus.

1. Death is displacement from the realm of life and the world of the living. The dead have a place. No one knows what lies on the other side of death. In Israel the principal source of imagination about the state of the dead was the grave. The realm of the dead was thought of as an extension of the grave. Its name was Sheol, the Pit, Abbadon. It was deep and dark and silent. Notice in the psalm how language about the grave and Sheol merges. In Sheol one continued to exist as one of the shades (v. 11) in a way that was the opposite and negation of every characteristic of the living. The psalm reminds us how sad our understanding of death must be when imagination has only the end of life as its subject. It stands in contrast to the picture of the state of the dead who have died in the Lord drawn in the New Testament, where imagination has been given eschatological hope (see Revelation 14).

2. Death is present in life in everything that weakens it. For the psalmist, death is not just an event and state at the end of

life. In his affliction and loss of strength, he is already at the threshold of Sheol. He is like the dead. He already experiences the darkness and depths of the Pit. Because death marks him, his companions treat him with abhorrence, as if he were dead. The psalm reminds us that every sign and experience of our finitude and transience tells us that we have an end. Death has ways of putting us in question in the midst of life.

3. The realm of the dead is beneath and outside the world of the living where the LORD's works of salvation occur. The dead are not remembered by the LORD; they are separated from his power. The answer to the bitter questions in verses 10–12 is no. The LORD does not work his wonders for the dead, so there is in the grave no responding praise of his steadfast love and faithfulness. See the comment on Psalms 6:6; 30:10; and 115:7. The psalm reminds us of the limits set for praying that is not based on the knowledge that God raised Messiah Jesus from the grave. This Old Testament prayer sounds like a cry to hear that good news as its answer. For theological reflection on Old Testament texts on death and dying, see Barth, III/4, pp. 588ff.

Psalm 89: The Rejected Messiah

This long psalm begins with the praise of the LORD's everlasting faithfulness to his covenant with David and ends with a lament of bewildered anguish over the suffering and humiliation the LORD has brought on his anointed. The chosen one has become the rejected one. That reversal is the plot of the psalm and the problem with which it wrestles.

1. The psalm reaches its climax in verse 49, which sums up the whole: "Where are your former deeds of loyalty which you swore to David in your faithfulness?" Most of the psalm is devoted to an evocation of those former deeds of loyalty (vv. 1–37). The introduction announces the two related themes, the faithfulness that belongs to the heavenly king (vv. 1–2) and the covenant promise made to David (vv. 3–4). The first theme is developed in praise of the LORD as sovereign of the universe, who in faithfulness has founded the world and is worshiped by his people as the one who gives them strength through their king (vv. 5–18). The second theme is developed by the quoting of an oracle in which God announced his selection of David to be the anointed king and promised faithfulness to him and his

283

descendants forever (vv. 19–37). Then the present situation is described as an incredible contradiction of the LORD's faithfulness to the covenant with David. The anointed has been defeated and humiliated by his enemies; wrath and rejection have replaced steadfast love and faithfulness; the covenant has been canceled (vv. 38–45). The psalm concludes with an appeal to the LORD to respond to the mortality and humiliation of the one who prays (vv. 46–51).

2. It is important to see the purpose of the particular way in which the psalm declares the faithfulness of the LORD. Since the humiliation of the anointed is the concern of the lament, it would seem that the citation of the LORD's sworn covenant with David would be enough. Instead, there is a long section (vv. 5–18) declaring that "steadfast love is established forever; you confirm your faithfulness in the heavens" (v. 2). This section has three parts. The first part (vv. 5–8) calls up the scene of the divine council assembled in heaven (see the comment on Psalms 29; 82). There the LORD reigns as the incomparable God of hosts surrounded by the holy ones and divine beings who praise his marvelous deed of faithfulness. In the intellectual world of the ancient Near East, the assembly of the high gods represented the ultimate location of authority and power. Israel used the notion to portray the LORD as God of gods, the ruler of the universe.

The second part (vv. 9–14) rehearses the marvelous deed for which the LORD is acclaimed supreme in the divine council. The LORD is ruler of the raging sea, the elemental chaos (v. 9), because he crushed Rahab, the chaos dragon, in a battle against the cosmic enemies of his kingship (v. 10; on the chaos monster, see Ps. 74:13–14; Isa. 51:9; Job 9:13; 26:12). The victory over chaos created the universe (vv. 11–12) and established the LORD's universal kingship (vv. 13–14). In this rehearsal the psalm is drawing on the scheme of the combat myth of creation that was widespread in the ancient Near East. According to its plot, the deity who prevailed over the forces of chaos created or restored the world by his victory and established his right to rule as king among the gods (for other uses of the myth, see Psalms 93; 29; 82; 47). The myth is used to portray the LORD as the warrior God upon whose victory over his enemies the very existence of the world depends. Creation and kingship are inseparably connected. This second part concludes with an important theological declaration (v. 14). The two pairs of attrib-

284

utes that characterize the LORD, righteousness/justice and steadfast love/faithfulness, are represented as aspects of his kingship. The first pair of attributes constitutes the pediment or foundation on which his throne rests; the second pair goes before him as the principal ministers precede a king on state occasions. These characteristics are objectified and personalized as a way of emphasizing and visualizing their distinct reality as structural elements of the divine reign. Attributes that are usually spoken of in connection with the LORD's way with Israel are portrayed as inherent in the LORD's cosmic rule. The divine righteousness and justice are manifest in the victory over chaos, and steadfast love and faithfulness in the trustworthy and reliable rule over chaos. That is why the faithfulness of the LORD especially is praised in the divine council (vv. 5, 8). What this vision of the LORD does is to anchor the faithfulness of the LORD in the foreverness of the LORD's cosmic rule above the vicissitudes of time and history; note the repetition of the theme "forever" in verses 1–4.

The third part (vv. 15–18) turns from the divine council in heaven to earth, and from the primeval past of creation to the present. Its focus is the congregation of the LORD's people who praise him because their human king, their strength and horn and shield, belongs to the LORD and receives glory and favor from him. The human king represents and mediates the glory and favor of heaven's rule to them. The praise of the congregation reflects and corresponds to the praise of the divine council, and a vital connection is made between the heavenly and the earthly king.

3. The second section of the psalm (vv. 19–37) deals with the origin and terms of the connection between the king of heaven and the king in the congregation. Resuming verses 3–4, it takes the form of a divine word given in a vision to God's faithful ones, presumably the prophet Nathan and his successors in the prophetic office in the royal court (v. 19; the Hebrew has a plural for NRSV's singular "faithful one"). The oracle is similar in content to Nathan's oracle to David recorded in II Samuel 7:4–17. First, David's kingship was created by God's choice of him from among his people; it is wholly a work of the LORD (vv. 19–20 and II Sam. 7:8). Second, the LORD promised to be with him to give him victory over his enemies and establish his kingship against all opposition (vv. 21–27 and II Sam. 7:9–11). Third, David's kingship will be conferred on David's

descendants permanently (vv. 28–37 and II Sam. 7:11–16). The third point is guaranteed by a sworn covenant of grant (a term not used in II Samuel 7) by God to his servant David. The LORD takes it upon himself, apart from any conditions on the human side, to make David's kingship through his descendants a permanent part of reality (vv. 3–4, 28–29, 36–37). The threefold repetition of this covenant oath shows that it is the issue between those who say the psalm and God.

The quoted oracle does not say why the LORD chose David and swore a covenant oath of faithfulness to his kingship. What the oracle does do is depict David's kingship as a reflection of the LORD's kingship. The language and features used to describe God's sovereignty reappear in the oracle on David's kingship. The divine warrior chose a warrior (NRSV, "one who is mighty") from among the people to be his anointed servant (vv. 19–20). The right hand and mighty arm of God will empower the hand and arm of David (vv. 13, 21). As God defeated and crushed his enemies, so David will defeat and crush his (vv. 10, 22–23). David will even share in the power of God over the cosmic chaos (vv 9–10, 25)! Just as the LORD, because of his dominion over chaos, is supreme in the heavens, David will be highest among the kings on earth (vv. 6–8, 27). The firm establishment of the LORD's steadfast love and faithfulness in the heaven guarantees the firm establishment of David's kingship in his descendants (vv. 1–2, 5, 14, 28–29, 36–37).

The point of this carefully drawn parallel between the kingship of God and that of David is to claim that the latter is integral to the former. It actualizes in the world what is reality in heaven. David's kingship is the agency through which the LORD's rule is extended from heaven to earth, and his dominion over cosmic chaos expanded over historical confusion (see the comment on Psalms 2 and 18). David is the human being on earth who cries out, "My father and my God" to the LORD (v. 26; see the comment on Ps. 2:7). Just as sun and moon are in the heavens, so David's line will be the enduring witness on earth to the reign of the LORD. The typological relation between the theology of the Davidic kingship and the Christology of the New Testament is apparent (e.g., Col. 1:15–20; Eph. 3:8–12).

This version of God's promise to David reckons with the failure of David's descendants (vv. 30–32, also II Sam. 7:14–15; cf. Ps. 132:11–12). They are subject to the conditional covenant made at Sinai between God and people. The laws of God apply

286

to them. They are subject to judgment and punishment without reservation. But their faithlessness does not cancel the faithfulness of God. They may violate the people's covenant with God, but God will not violate his covenant with David (vv. 33–35). The repeated assertions about the permanence of David's kingship through his descendants form an inclusion around the statements about the disobedience of David's line (vv. 28–29 and 36–37) to make it absolutely clear that the promise is founded on divine, not human, faithfulness.

4. *"But now . . ."* (v. 38)! The psalm turns to the painful present (vv. 38–45). God's everlasting reign and the oracle concerning David have been introduced to form a precise and unbearable contrast to the present. The defeat, humiliation, deposition, and death (possibly the inference of v. 45) of the LORD's anointed are understood as God's renunciation of the covenant with David. What has befallen the king goes beyond punishment for disobedience. The catastrophic circumstances seem to allow no future for the line itself. The psalm describes the disaster as the work of the LORD. It does not question his power but his promise.

5. Because it is the LORD's sworn covenant that is in doubt, the psalm concludes with two sets of grieving, protesting questions combined with a plea to "remember" (vv. 46–48 and 49–51). The first question is about time. "How long" will time mean the absence and wrath of God? If God's steadfast love is forever, can wrath last forever? The accompanying plea is for God to remember the mortality of the psalmist and his community; there is not much time available for God to keep his promise; death sets limits for all humankind (see the appeal to mortality in 144:3–4; 90:5–6, 10). The second question is about space. "Where" are the LORD's former deeds of loving-kindness promised to David's descendants? The accompanying plea is for God to remember what does fill the scene—the demeaning scornful taunts of God's anointed from God's enemies. The enemies of the anointed king are the enemies of the kingdom of God. Will the God whose faithfulness establishes the universe fail to establish the throne of David?

6. The psalm is a community lament composed for an occasion when the continuity of the Davidic kingship was in direct doubt. The individual who performed the lament represented the community and voiced its appeal (vv. 15–18; see Introduction, sec. 5.4). The future of the community was at stake in the

287

fate of its king. In a way, the psalm locates the people of God where the Books of Kings leave them—with their king and their future in the power of their enemies. In the arrangement of the Book of Psalms, this lament is placed at the conclusion of book III (see Introduction, sec. 4.5). It stands as the counterpart to Psalm 2 with its divine decree that the anointed is God's answer to the hostile turmoil of the nations, and it voices the anguish of faith over the disparity between the reign of God and the destiny of the Messiah. The covenant with David incorporated the Davidic kingship into the eternal structure of God's reign, but the temporal career of the people subjected it to all the vicissitudes and uncertainties of human history. The psalm contains no resolution of the dilemma, save appeal to the faithfulness of God.

Maundy Thurs The scene evoked by verses 38–45, the portrayal of the messiah in the power of his enemies, rejected and scorned, his life cut short, has another counterpart in the passion narrative of the Gospels. The psalm read as Scripture on Maundy Thursday is a powerful witness that the very cosmic reign of God is involved in what is happening on that day; and it makes it very clear how much the outcome depends on and reveals the faithfulness of God.

BOOK FOUR

Psalms 90—106

Psalm 90: Teach Us to Number Our Days

Psalm 90 has unusual liturgical and theological significance. It is a traditional reading at funerals, so it is heard regularly on an occasion when our minds are particularly open and sensitive because of grief and memory, perhaps guilt and regret. More than at any other service we are likely to reflect then on our own condition and destiny. The psalm is concerned with the relation between God and time and mortals and time and what that portends for the relation between God and mortals. Because of its concern with time and God and mortals, it has played an important role in the reflection of theologians. It is regularly compared to Ecclesiastes 3 and 5 in this respect, a comparison that can disorient interpretation of the psalm.

1. The psalm has three parts, with a transition between the second and third. It begins with two lines of hymnic address praising Israel's LORD for his protection of his people in one generation after another (v. 1) and acclaiming him as creator whose being preceded the existence of the world (v. 2). Then the psalm confesses that the transience of human life and the trouble in the lives of those who say the psalm are the work of God's wrath (vv. 3–6 and 7–10; this section is more cumulative in effect than logical in arrangement, and we would do well to take the "for" at the beginning of vv. 4, 7, and 9 as emphatic in function rather than as conjunctions). As a transition from this confession to supplications, a rhetorical question asserts that only the fear of God recognizes that this transience and trouble is the effect of God's anger (v. 11), and God is asked to make the specific limits set for life a source of wisdom (v. 12). A series of petitions for God to turn from anger to deal in

289

covenant love with those who pray concludes the psalm (vv. 13–17).

Though the structure of the psalm is clear enough, one has difficulty following its thought from beginning to end and making out its inner coherence. Briefly put, verses 3–12 deal with the tragic predicament of human life in general and ask for wisdom to live life under the conditions set for it. Verses 13–17 are concerned with Israel's history with the LORD and seek a change from a time of affliction and mourning to one of satisfaction and joy. With one we seem to be with Ecclesiastes; with the other we seem to be with Isaiah 40—55. How does a change of eras for the people of God deal with the fact of general experience that life is troubled and transient? The apparent disjuncture in the psalm's thought has raised questions about its unity, coherence, and compositional history.

The psalm, however, has been composed as a unit and has features that direct us to understand it as such. Its style is consistent throughout. The voice is that of the congregation speaking in direct address to its LORD. The psalm is composed as a corporate prayer for help, and its parts seem to function as elements of that type (see Introduction, sec. 5.4). The hymnic introduction serves as a recollection of God's way in the past; it asserts confidence in God and is a motive for God to hear the congregation's lament over its painful present. The confession of transience and trouble is the description of distress from which the supplications seek deliverance. The transitional verses (vv. 11–12) are the unusual element in the genre. Phrases and motifs are repeated in different parts of the psalm. For instance, the supplications appeal to God to be the refuge for present and future generations (v. 16) that he had been for past generations (v. 1). The verb "return" *(shub)* is used for God's command to mortals to die (v. 3) and for the congregation's petition for God to change (v. 13). "In the morning" is used in the lament (vv. 5–6) and in the petitions (v. 14). Other correlations are to be found. The theme of time is woven through the whole in a way that identifies time as the problem of faith with which the psalm's theology is concerned (vv. 1, 2, 4, 5, 6, 9, 10, 13, 14, 15). All these unifying features direct the interpreter to seek the coherence and meaning in the way the psalm leads those who use it to speak to God about themselves.

290

2. The hymnic introduction identifies the God to whom the prayer is addressed. It calls on God by the title *'adonay* (v. 1),

the title for God as Lord of a servant people (see v. 16). The introduction describes Israel's Lord as the one who acts and the one who is. It holds together two roles. God is the LORD of Israel's history. In every generation, God has been the "dwelling place" of his people; that is, his care and protection have preserved them. This the congregation knows from its own story; they would not be there as a congregation to pray in trouble except for his help. God is Lord of the universe. He is the "everlasting Thou" who was there when the primeval mountains emerged and earth-world was brought forth to rest on them. The being of God precedes all that exists and is the precondition of and sovereign over all that exists. The congregation as human beings would not be there apart from God's creation. These two roles are directly relevant to the two identities in which the congregation prays. They pray as mortals (vv. 3–12) and as servants of God (vv. 13–17). So the psalm's introduction brings together the eternal whose concern is universe and humanity and the LORD whose concern is with a particular people in a special history. The tension in the psalm appears in its opening theological statement. Faith often has to believe and think and worship in the tension between the universal and the particular, between Creator and Savior, between humanity and congregation.

3. The congregation's confession of its distress begins (vv. 3–6) as a lament over the tragic lot of the human being (v. 3) as individual *('enosh)* and species *(bene 'adam)* and continues (vv. 7–10) as the congregation speaks of itself as mortal humanity. We die, they say. Our life is so evanescent that it is like grass that flourishes in the morning and withers during the heat of the day. Even if they are fortunate enough to reach the ripe age of seventy, or the unusual age of eighty, the years they are given are full of toil and trouble. The years slip by quickly and life is over. Such laments are based on the experience of life and on the observation of the lives of others. They come spontaneously to expression in bad times and are not far from awareness at all times. No revelation is necessary to learn their truth. The psalm in speaking in this way is open to all who realize the tragic character of life, and it undertakes to speak for them. It is apparent that the congregation speaks not only as and in their general humanity but as well in their individuality. The members united by their mortality are in focus rather than the congregation in its corporate identity. Nothing is heard in the

291

lament about foes who humiliate and oppress the whole community or about a disaster that unites them in suffering. What they lament is mortality that is experienced as affliction.

While the topic of the lament belongs to the congregation's identity as human beings, the way they speak of it does not. In their understanding of their mortality they are definitely the people of the LORD. God is the subject of their description of distress. They speak of their mortality by speaking of God. Death is not viewed as natural, the end that must come for all living things. Death is the work of God, it happens to the children of men at the command of God. The toil and trouble of life is not mere misfortune, something accidental; it is the effect of the wrath of God. General human life in its course and end is lived under the sign of God's anger. God has resolved to look at the guilt of human beings and to deal with them as sinners (v. 8). The lament is based on a view of the human predicament like that in the story told in Genesis 3. "You return man to the dust" sounds like Genesis 3:19. This way of understanding the tragic predicament of life comes from the congregation's history with the LORD. From their experience of living under the kingship and covenant of the LORD, they have learned about his judgment. In the usual corporate prayer the lament over God's anger refers to some disaster that has fallen on the people of God. Here the lament is extended and applied to the whole human race.

So the theological account of the human predicament offered by the psalm is the wrath of God at human sinfulness. The lament uses a whole vocabulary to make the point: anger, fury, wrath. The wrath of God is a linguistic symbol for the divine limits and pressure placed against human resistance to his sovereignty. Here perhaps lies the explanation for the relation of verses 3 and 4. Eternity belongs to the sovereign deity of the LORD as God (Heb. *'el*, v. 2). Death is the final and ultimate "no" that cancels any pretension to autonomy from the human side. The mortal is returned to the dust *(dakka')*, which elsewhere means "contrition," a probably double entendre in the psalm. The psalm has an interpretation of the human predicament that belongs to biblical faith. It does not leave misery and death meaningless. In seeing human finitude under the sign of God's wrath, the psalm stands with Genesis 3 and Romans 1—2.

292

4. The transitional verses conclude the lament (v. 11) and prepare for the supplications (v. 12). Verse 11 poses a question

about the lament. "Who knows/recognizes/understands the
power of God's wrath according to the fear of God?" The fear
of God is that awe and reverence before the sovereign deity of
God which leads to understanding the course of life in terms of
the way of God and to ordering life according to the will of God.
The fear of the LORD is the theological basis for the interpretation of life's trouble and transience given in the lament. Only
the fear of the LORD will recognize the power of God's wrath
at work. The question is rhetorical; it has a critical and instructional function. It recognizes that it is hard to view life and
death as the lament does. The psalmist puts the question in the
mouth of the congregation as warning and instruction that
without the fear of the LORD they will not see their situation
seriously and authentically in terms of God's wrath. That is the
reason for the petition in verse 12. Question and answer are
directly connected. The question asks, "Who knows . . . ?"; the
petition says, "Make us know." The psalmist has the congregation pray for the wisdom of heart/mind that comes from considering the finitude of human existence, its frustration and
brevity. The first principle of wisdom is the fear of the LORD
(Prov. 1:7). This petition is preparation for the concluding
supplications, because only those who understand that the
wrath of God is their problem will and can pray as the supplications do.

5. The supplications plead with God to turn back from his
wrath and relent concerning his servants (see these verbs in
Jonah 3:9; Jer. 4:28). The prayer for God to "repent" is formally
similar to petitions in the corporate prayers for help. But since
the wrath of God is not manifested here through enemy or
disaster, the content of the change prayed for differs. Essentially the prayer seeks a change in time, in the character of the
time in which life is spent. "All our days . . . our years" spent
under wrath are to be exchanged for "as many days . . . as many
years" (v. 15) spent under "the favor of the LORD our God"
(v. 17). It will be a time of satisfaction instead of frustration, of
joy instead of toil and trouble. It will be a time that lasts and
makes it possible for their own work to last. It will endure
through their generation to include their children's generation.
The basis and reality of the change will be simply the *hesed* of
the LORD, his covenant loyalty to his servants (v. 14). The
change will be brought about by a revelation of a work of the
LORD, an appearance of his sovereign majesty (v. 16). The

293

V) aging + dying

psalmist leads the congregation to pray for the new era promised by the great prophets. For the psalmist, the primary significance of the new era is that it will be a time when human life in its uncertainty and brevity can be lived under the sign of God's favor (v. 17) instead of God's wrath. The psalmist does not say, or even hint, what the work of the LORD will be that brings the change about. He does not know. But he believes in the LORD of the congregation's history as the God who is sovereign over time. He leads the congregation to pray for God to change the sign of the time under which life is lived.

6. The psalmist is a pastor, theologian, and liturgist all at once. He and the congregation live in a time when the congregation's faith and hope are thin, and they can see and think no further than their own human limitations and mortality. Resignation, cynicism, and nihilism beckon. The psalmist gives the congregation a prayer that includes and gathers up their human lament and leads them to understand it in relation to God. He teaches them the fear of the LORD through the prayer, so that having understood that they live under the sign of God's wrath, they can pray for God to change the time in which they live as the resolution of their predicament. There is a similar pattern of lament over human transience to be resolved by a change of eras from divine wrath to covenant loyalty in Isaiah 40 (note vv. 6–7 and 1–5, 6–11). But the psalmist lives in a later time and offers the prophetic pattern to the congregation as prayer rather than promise. In it he gives them the voice of a people reaching out for a promise not yet fulfilled.

In a sense, Psalm 90 is instruction, *torah*. It belongs to the period of psalmody in which those who composed liturgy for the community had to lead the congregation in understanding as well as worship. It is appropriate that the psalm is attributed to Moses. The attribution probably is based on the relation between verses 1–2 and Deuteronomy 33:27. (For a complete list of relations to the Book of Deuteronomy, see Delitzsch's comment on Psalm 90.)

7. The richness, profundity, and faith of this pastor/theologian/liturgist inform the use of the psalm as Scripture, liturgy, and hymn.

When we are made aware that all around us changes, and that those we cherish most pass away, the human spirit yearns for the constant and the lasting. Then more than ever we need to find a relation to something reliable and enduring as a refuge

294

wisdom of the elderly from the perspective of lived experience from all that is not. The psalm's introduction lets us speak directly, personally, to the one who alone is constant and eternal, and leads us to say, "Our God." To speak so to the faithful and eternal one is solace to the soul. It is this comfort of the psalm that Isaac Watts's great hymn expresses so beautifully: "O God our help in ages past, our hope for years to come." The caring and eternal God as contrast and comfort for time-bound humanity—it is this dimension of the psalm that Watts develops in his entire hymn.

The church reads the supplications in verses 13–17 in the light of God's revelation in Jesus Christ. He is the work of God that has decisively once for all changed the sign under which we live and die from wrath to grace. That is theological fact. Those in Christ use the troubles of life as chastisement and discipline. They face death in the trust that God's judgment on their sinfulness has fallen on Jesus Christ. Troubles come. Life ends. But the character of the time through which life runs to its end has been qualitatively changed. The supplications guide us to realize and be grateful for and to ask to receive what we are given already in Jesus Christ. When the psalm is used as a lection, the reading often omits verses 13–17. Care must be taken not to leave the congregation with Ecclesiastes. The psalmist gathers the human predicament up into prayer for the fulfillment of the prophetic promise.

The lament gives voice to the "not yet" in the believer. Mortality and sin remain an existential, physical, and moral fact. Adam lives on in those who are in Christ, the "old human, in the new." The lament leads us to speak of our toil and trouble and death and to speak of them in the way it does. The psalm stands against all shallowness and flippancy, all false bravery and empty optimism. In this way it leads to realism and honesty about the human predicament. It teaches us how truly desperate is the human need and opens our minds to what is given in Christ. On the psalm as the rejection of every false understanding of mortality, see Luther, 13:76–79.

The prayer for a heart of wisdom that comes from considering the specifically limited time given our lives remains crucial. Time is the medium of our mortality and so the favorite focus of our folly. We do not concentrate on the fact that we are given only a limited, though unknown, number of days and years and undertake to live them with wisdom. The young think they are immortal, the old despair because their time is over. Time is a

295

burden when we have to wait, a scarcity when we are busy. It is the source of anxiety, illusion, remorse. Wisdom, in contrast, sees the time given us as "the unique opportunity" (Barth), the chance to be and do in the fear of the LORD. On the importance of considering that we shall die, see Barth, III/4, pp. 569ff.

Psalm 91: My Refuge and My Fortress

"If you desire," writes Athanasius to Marcellinus, "to establish yourself and others in devotion, to know what confidence is to be reposed in God, and what makes the mind fearless, you will praise God by reciting the ninetieth (ninety-first) Psalm" (from Neale and Littledale, 3:103). That experience and commendation of Psalm 91 is repeated again and again in the history of its use and interpretation. It is a classic on the sure providence of God as the citadel of faith. The hymn "Sing Praise to God, Who Reigns Above" echoes its confidence in God and is a good companion to the study of it.

1. The literary structure of the psalm has two major parts, distinguished by the style of direct address to an individual "you" (vv. 1–13) and by that of a declaration in the divine first person (vv. 14–16). The theme and those to whom the psalm is addressed are identified at the beginning: those who trust themselves to the protection of the LORD (vv. 1–2). A description of the LORD's protection from many dangers follows (vv. 3–13). The declaration lets hearers and readers of the psalm know that God confirms the trust of those who are committed to him (vv. 14–16). The psalm seems to be the work of a teacher who seeks to nurture the trust of the faithful by encouraging each of them to take the LORD as their refuge from all the troubles of life. (The Hebrew text allows for different readings of the style of verses 1–2 and 9. Compare NRSV, REB, and NJPS. The above analysis is based on NRSV.)

2. "Refuge" used as a metaphor for God's care and protection is a pervasive theme in the Psalter. It is frequently employed in prayers and confessions of confidence in God as a noun (e.g., 14:6; 46:1; 61:3) and as a verb ("take refuge," e.g., 2:11; 5:11; 11:1). In general secular use, the verb means to seek protected space (Judg. 9:15). In its liturgical context, it means to look to the LORD for security from threatening dangers. Verb and noun belong to the psalmic vocabulary of trust in God (note the parallel in v. 2). They are primarily items in a word field

296

used to speak of the LORD as protector of those who hold to him: fortress, stronghold, dwelling place, shelter. The idiom "shadow/shade of the wings of the LORD" belongs to the vocabulary (see v. 4; 17:8; 36:7; 57:1; 63:7). The life of the faithful in Israel was set in an environment of threatening dangers. This vocabulary and its frequency in the Psalms brings out the important role of trust in coping with the anxieties that beset their life.

3. The dangers listed in verses 3–13 do not seem to reflect any particular historical or social setting. They are, rather, a catena of the more drastic anxieties to which individual life in Israel was subject. They are named—some with idiomatic hyperbole (e.g., "snare of the fowler," "dash your foot against a stone"), some in general terms (e.g., "evil," "scourge"), and some directly (pestilence, lion, and adder). The pairs of diurnal and nocturnal dangers (vv. 5–6) may be demons of types known from ancient Near Eastern sources. In these other cultures, procedures that used charms and magic and ceremonies of exorcism were employed to counter supernatural dangers. In Israel, as this psalm shows, trust in the LORD and only that became the one religious resource on which the faithful depended. One of the potential dangers feared by the pious in Israel was "the punishment of the wicked." Using exaggerated numbers, verses 7–8 promise that, should such a punishment strike thousands, the faithful will only see it happen but not be harmed by it. The entire list is composed as a poetic survey that is a spiritual antidote to the range of anxieties that could afflict the lives of Israelites. Though its items are strange to other and later times, it still does its work of anchoring the soul in the midst of anxieties with different names.

4. The psalm itself poses a danger. Because its assurance of security is so comprehensive and confident, it is especially subject to the misuse that is a possibility for all religious claims, that of turning faith into superstition. In Judaism and Christianity, bits of the text have been worn in amulets that were believed to be a kind of magical protection for those who wore them. The promise that the ministering angels would guard the way of the pious (v. 11) was one of the bases of a belief that God assigns individual believers a personal angel to watch over them, and the angel easily became the focus of concern and piety. In an infamous use of Scripture, Satan employed verses 11–12 in his attempt to corrupt Jesus (Matt. 4:5–7; Luke 4:10–11). The psalm

[handwritten margin note: not to be used to force God's hand ~ this demonic]

must always be read and understood in the light of that encounter. Satan placed Jesus on the pinnacle of the temple and challenged him to jump off to test God's promise that the angels would bear him up. The temptation was to take the promised protection of God into the control of his own will and act. That would have shifted the power of the promise from the free sovereignty of God to individual willfulness. Jesus saw that as a way to test God, not as the way of trust. Real trust does not seek to test God or to prove his faithfulness. These matters have been the subject of constant discussion in the interpretation of Psalm 91 (e.g., Luther, 11:210–211; Calvin, 3:486; and Barth, III/3, pp. 517–518).

Psalm 92: The Wicked and the Righteous in the Reign of God

The creation of the world and the salvation of the people of the LORD are, together, assurance that life belongs to the righteous, not to the wicked. The sovereignty of the LORD will be vindicated in human life just as it has been in cosmos and history. This is the lesson of Psalm 92.

1. Psalm 92 belongs to the phase in the history of psalmody when the styles and functions of different types were being combined in compositions informed by a concern to nurture and develop the faithfulness of the congregation. The psalm, like a song of thanksgiving, for the most part addresses the LORD directly in individual voice (vv. 1–5, 8–11, 15b) and includes a report of what the LORD has done (NRSV) or will do (NJPS) for the psalmist (vv. 10–11). There are also panels of instruction about the wicked (vv. 6–7) and the righteous (vv. 12–15). The psalm begins with a general commendation of grateful praise for the LORD's steadfast love and faithfulness shown in his works (vv. 1–4). Then it observes that the meaning of the LORD's works is hidden to the wicked, who do not understand that their prosperity has no future (vv. 5–7). The reason is given in the declaration standing at the very center of the psalm: The LORD is on high forever (v. 8). The everlasting reign of the LORD means that the LORD's enemies will perish, and with them the enemies of the psalmist will fail (vv. 9–11). It is the righteous whose lives will endure and be fulfilled as vindication of the LORD's uprightness (vv. 12–15a). The song concludes

with a confession of confidence in the LORD as refuge (v. 15*b*). Corresponding motifs emphasize certain points. The enemies of the psalmist fail because the enemies of the LORD will perish (vv. 9 and 11). The wicked flourish like grass, but the righteous flourish like the palm and cedar (vv. 7 and 12). The wicked are doomed forever, because the LORD is on high forever (vv. 7–8). Praise declares the steadfast love of the LORD, and the lives of the righteous declare that the LORD is upright (vv. 2, 15; the verb in both verses is *higgid*). The central concern of the psalm is the contrast between the destiny of the wicked and that of the righteous. In this respect it is like Psalms 1; 37; 49; 73; and 94, among others. Psalm 92 puts the problem in the context of faith in the sovereignty of the LORD.

2. The psalm is based on a three-dimensional theology of the sovereignty of the LORD. In the psalmic vocabulary, "works" is used as a summary term for God's deeds in creation (8:6; 103:22; 104:24, 31) and in the history of salvation (74:12; 77:14; 90:16). The LORD's work in both spheres, the cosmic and the historical, is understood as a combat in which opposition was overcome. In creation the LORD established kingship by superior power over the primeval waters (e.g., the comment on Psalm 93). In the LORD's way with Israel he established kingship by victory over nations and peoples (e.g., the comment on Psalms 47 and 68). This is why the LORD's supremacy (v. 8) means that the LORD's enemies will be scattered (v. 9). Overcoming the world is inherent in the reign of God. (On the combat theme behind Psalm 92, see Levenson, *Creation,* pp. 1–50.) What the psalm does is to invite those who hear and sing it to extend this understanding of the LORD's work into the sphere of personal existence. "All evildoers shall be scattered." Moral life, like cosmos and history, involves combat. Loyalty to the reign of God exposes the righteous to the opposition of the wicked. The wicked are dull at this one point; they do not grasp the wholeness of moral life with history and creation (vv. 6–7; 73:3–9; 94:8–11). But the victory of the LORD over evildoers is just as certain as the works of the LORD in creation and history. The psalmist confesses that this certainty sustains his own life (vv. 10–11), and through the psalm he teaches that it is in the enduring fruitful life of the righteous (1:3) that the LORD's uprightness as ruler of the world will be vindicated (vv. 12–15).

3. Psalm 92 is one of the few psalms in the Hebrew Psalter assigned to a particular occasion, and the only one assigned to

299

a specific day. Its title says it is the psalm for the Sabbath. Its selection for this day poses an interesting interpretive question about the reason for its choice. Was a reference to completed creation recognized in verses 4 and 9? Was it because the name of the LORD appears in the psalm seven times? Commenting on the title, the *mishna Tamid* (7:4) says, "It is a psalm and a song for the era to come, for the day that will be entirely Sabbath, for eternal life." This rabbinical observation recognizes that creation will not be completed in the LORD's victory over all enemies until the end of the age. Then there will be a final Sabbath rest for God and the righteous. The Sabbaths in time are a foretaste of this eschatological consummation. When the psalm is sung in this light, it brings the end time into the present and gives a marvelous interpretation of Sabbath worship and rest (Levenson, *Creation,* p. 123).

Psalm 93: The LORD Reigns

Psalm 93 declares its theme at its beginning. It is praise that portrays and proclaims the reign of the LORD. "The LORD reigns" (RSV; "The LORD is king," NRSV; on this formulaic sentence, see Introduction, sec. 6.1, 3). This psalm gives those who sing it a way to imagine the kingship of God and to understand its meaning.

1. The lines of the hymn evoke for the imagination a word picture of the One who cannot be represented by images. This king is clothed, not with garments, but with majesty and power (v. 1); his attributes are for him what splendid royal robes are for an earthly king. His reign is not measured in years but spans all of time. "You are from everlasting," says the psalm; a time cannot be thought when the king was not and his government not in control (v. 2). His place is "on high," in the heights of heaven above and beyond all place as human beings know space (v. 4c). His house expresses in its architecture the very quality of divine holiness (v. 5). The hymn portrays "what eye hath not seen." The features are part visual and part conceptual; the two merge in poetry that both conceal and reveal what the mind cannot know directly—the divine sovereignty.

2. Notice that the same thing is said about the world and the throne of the LORD (vv. 1*b* and 2*a*). When a king had gained firm control of his subjects and his rule was secure against external threat, it would be said in a figure that "his throne is estab-

300

lished." When the psalm says that the world is established and cannot be shaken, it means that the stability and continuity of the human home is secure against unstable chaos, from which it was created by the LORD. The two are coordinate because in the way the psalm thinks about reality, the establishment of the world was the deed by which the LORD gained kingship, and his kingship is guarantee of the stability of the ordered, inhabitable world. The floods, the primeval currents of verses 3 and 4, are compared to the majestic power of the LORD because they represent the uncreated chaos out of which the world was brought forth and established (see 24:1-2). The psalm is drawing on the mythopoeic tradition about the god who wins a victory over the chaotic sea to gain kingship (see Psalm 29). Through its use the psalmist portrays the stability of the world as a manifestation of his theme, "The LORD reigns." In turn, the psalm teaches that belief in the reign of God is a way of rejoicing in the existence and continuity of the world. The meaning of the world is, "The LORD reigns." The Septuagint and the Talmud both see this psalm as holding creation and reign of God together. In the Septuagint the psalm has a title that designates it as the hymn for the day before Sabbath when the world was inhabited, that is, Friday. The Talmud (*Rosh ha-Shanah*, 31*a*) says that having completed his work on that day, God ruled over them (his creatures). The reign began when the world was peopled with subjects; by creation, God provided himself with a kingdom.

3. In verse 5, a further statement about the meaning of the theme is made: The decrees (*'edot*) of the LORD are very sure, reliable, trustworthy. In this context, decrees might refer to commands by which the LORD governs the natural world, a notion present in places like Psalms 104 and 74:12-17. But every use of this particular term in the Old Testament, and there are many, refers to the laws and ordinances by which the LORD governs and orders the religious and social life of his servants and subjects. In our view of the world, there is no direct continuity between creation and society. What we call natural laws and moral laws seem to be quite different things. But in the view of the psalmist, the commandments that order human life are the decrees of the sovereign of the universe. The ordering of the world and the ordering of society are expressions of one and the same rule. The decrees are just as sure as the establishment of the throne of God and the world are

301

certain and continuous. To confess that the LORD reigns is to believe that the decrees of God are as given a part of reality as the very continuity and stability of the world. It is this way of thinking about the connection between creation and law that holds the two themes together in texts like Psalm 19.

Psalm 94: Vengeance Is Mine

"Though the wrong seems oft so strong, God is the ruler yet." That line from the hymn "This Is My Father's World" (Maltbie D. Babcock) is the theme of Psalm 94.

1. The literary structure of the psalm has three principal parts. The first part is composed of an appeal to God to judge the wicked (vv. 1–2) and a lament over their arrogance and wrongdoing (vv. 3–7). The second part pairs the rebuke to the foolish who do not reckon with God's judgment (vv. 8–11) with a commendation of those who hold to God's instruction in bad times out of trust in God's eventual justice (vv. 12–15). The third part is a confession of confidence in God as the help of the psalmist and judge of the wicked (vv. 16–23). The prevalent style is direct address to God with an intermingling of statements about God in instructional and confessional mode (vv. 8–11, 14–15, 17, 22–23). The psalmist has set a rebuke to the foolish and a beatitude commending faithfulness in the center of the elements of a prayer for help. The purpose of the psalm is to encourage the people of God to trust in God's righteous judgment and to give them a prayer to appeal to God to vindicate God's rule. Compare Psalms 9—10; 11; 12; and 92, among others (Introduction, sec. 5.6).

2. The initial double vocative names the LORD as "God of vengeance," a title unique to this psalm. The title sets the theological theme of prayer. Though the title itself is unique, the understanding that the LORD acts to "avenge" the oppression of his people by their enemies, the wrongs by the powerful within the community of Israel, and the breach of covenant by his people is a feature of Israel's belief in the justice of the LORD, especially among the prophets (e.g., Deut. 32:36; Isa. 34:8; Jer. 46:10; Jer. 11:20; Ps. 99:8; Jer. 5:5, 29; Ezek. 24:8). The background of the theological use of "avenge/vengeance" in Israel is not in the emotion of a hate reaction but in the sphere of legal custom. "Vengeance" was an act to enforce or restore justice where the regular legal processes were not competent or had

failed. As an activity of the LORD, it was understood as a function of God's rule as the king who has right and responsibility to restore the order of things and to vindicate his authority. The function is an aspect of the LORD's rule as judge of all the earth (v. 2; cf. 7:8; 9:8, 19; 50:6; 58:11). The psalm's appeal to the "God of vengeance" is a plea for the LORD to vindicate his reign by intervening in the human situation in a time when wrong was rampant (50:1–4; 80:1–3).

3. The psalmist prays because the power of wrong contradicts the reign of the LORD. The trouble described in his prayer is not individual; it afflicts the LORD's own people (vv. 5, 14). The trouble is created by the wicked, whose conduct is a challenge to "the judge of the earth." The wicked do not praise God but exult in their own success and power (vv. 3–4). In their arrogance they dismiss the justice of Israel's God as nonexistent (v. 7). Free of any accountability to the LORD, they prey on the weak, the widow and stranger and orphan, the very people whom the LORD's justice was concerned to protect (v. 6). The righteous and the innocent are condemned instead of vindicated (v. 21). It is as if the requirement of God's law and the words of the LORD's prophets had never been spoken (Exod. 22:21–24; Deut. 24:17; Isa. 1:17; Jer. 7:6; Zech. 7:10). Wrong sits in the seat of power, and the statutes that should provide justice have been perverted to the service of evil (v. 20). The description points to a time when the offices and courts of the society were controlled by a class for whom the sovereignty of Israel's God was irrelevant. Passages from postexilic prophets may point to the psalm's social setting (e.g., Isaiah 58—59; Mal. 3:5, 13–15).

4. The psalmist is confident that his prayer conforms to the will of God. What he prays for is anchored in the very character of the LORD. It is impossible that the judge of the earth should be in league with the earthly throne of injustice (v. 20). The wicked have no future except the consequences of their own evil. God will see to it that they are eliminated through their own wickedness (v. 23, NJPS). It is just a matter of time, because "the LORD is coming to judge the earth" (96:13; 98:9). So the prayer is both petition for the community that suffers injustice and assurance to them in their tribulation. Notice the corporate "our God" at the end (v. 23). In praying within and for his community, the psalmist finds ways in his prayer to instruct and nurture the faithful while "the days of trouble" go on (v. 13).

303

The psalmist is teacher as well as intercessor for the people of God.

5. First, the teacher points to the dull foolishness of thinking that "the LORD does not see" (vv. 8–11 as answer to v. 7). Wisdom understands that the LORD who created ear and eye and disciplines nations observes what people do and will chastise them for their wickedness. To think otherwise is to think thoughts that are empty of the reality of God (v. 11). The rebuke addressed to "fools" is meant for the ears of his community to debunk any standing that such folly may have with them. The rebuke is the counterpart to the following beatitude.

6. Second, the teacher, with a beatitude saying, points to the way of faith's wisdom (vv. 12–15; on the beatitude saying, see Psalm 1, sec. 1). The way of life that has a good future is the life that is disciplined and instructed by the law of the LORD. The discipline and teaching of the law of the LORD provides a calm endurance in the time of trouble. The law keeps the soul safe from the foolishness of the wicked and nurtures confidence in the faithfulness of the LORD to his people and the eventual restoration of justice. On the law as a source of help in times of trouble, see, above all else, the great Psalm 119.

7. Third, the teacher gives a testimony to his own faith and experience (vv. 10–22; on the reflective confessional style as a means of teaching, see Psalms 49 and 73). The teacher himself has no other than the LORD upon whom to depend. He himself has been in danger of falling from faithfulness and overwhelmed by cares. He can testify that the steadfast love and comfort of the LORD brought support and calmness to him. The LORD has become his stronghold and refuge, the protection of his soul in the presence of cruel injustice all around him. On the LORD as refuge, see Psalm 91.

8. This intercessor and teacher had a ministry different from that of the prophets who spoke the LORD's message of judgment upon the officials and rich who oppressed the lowly and helpless. The problem of prophet and psalmist was the same: injustice that afflicted the people of the LORD. But the psalmist had a pastoral calling to encourage and support the discouraged and hurt in their life as the people of God. He did not summon them to hatred and violent revenge. Instead, he prayed for the vengeance of the LORD, and in his prayer he taught them that vengeance belongs to the LORD. He must have known the divine word given in Deuteronomy 32:34–36.

In a different later situation, he turned that word into petition and instruction for the people of God. Consider the uses of the divine word, "Vengeance is mine," in Romans 12:19 and Hebrews 10:30.

Psalm 95: Do Not Harden Your Hearts

1. Psalm 95 combines a hymn and a word from God. It begins with praise (vv. 1–7a) and concludes with a warning exhortation (vv. 7b–11). The basic hymn form is used twice: summons to praise (vv. 1–2) and the content or reasons for praise (vv. 3–5); summons (v. 6) and reason (v. 7a). Then an appeal to listen to the voice of God (v. 7b) introduces a warning in divine first person style not to repeat the conduct of the wilderness generation (vv. 8–11). The first part of the hymn reflects a joyous processional into the presence of God (v. 2); the second, the act of prostration (v. 6). The divine word then addresses the bowing congregation. The liturgical sequence represents the movement of subjects into the presence of their sovereign, there to bow in submission awaiting a royal declaration from the throne. So the psalm is another that depicts and interprets the reign of the LORD. The theology is clear: The LORD is "the great king" because he is maker and ruler of the universe and maker and shepherd of his people; therefore his people should heed his voice. In its literary structure and in other features, Psalm 95 is similar to Psalms 50 and 81, especially the latter. See the comment on each of the psalms.

2. The hymn sets forth two basic theological statements about the LORD. The first is that the LORD is a great God and a great king over all gods (v. 3). The doctrine that the god of the Old Testament is great and king among gods may seem inconsistent with the belief that there is only one God. But this way of speaking about a god belonged to the polytheistic culture in which Israel existed, and it was adopted as one way for faith to reason in that culture (see Exod. 15:11; Pss. 96:4; 97:9; 136:2). In the pantheons of the ancient Near East, one god was believed to be supreme and to rule over others. His superiority and kingship were based on his action as creator (see 24:1–2). Verses 4 and 5 are total and inclusive statements about the LORD's relation to the world. As maker of sea and dry land, the LORD owns it all and it is still in his power from deepest depths to highest peaks. There is no sphere of the cosmos left for any

305

independent divine powers. For those who live in the world, there is no need to think about or worship any other God. This way of thinking about the reign of the LORD is not anachronistic. We human beings are incurably polytheistic. So the psalm's theology is a theology that has to be reckoned with in a religiously pluralistic world.

3. The second basic theological statement about the LORD is simply that "he is our God" (v. 7). The worshiping congregation know they belong to the LORD because he is "our maker." The LORD brought them into existence, created them as a social group by election and covenant and by deeds of salvation. The shepherd image used to interpret the relation of God to people is far more than a lovely pastoral metaphor. It is a royal image of the relation of a king to those he rules and portrays his role as leader, provider, and protector (see 77:20; 78:52; 80:1; 100:3 and the comment on Psalm 23) and so is a way of talking about the LORD as king of his people. The LORD rules this people, not only because they live in his world, but even more because they owe him their existence.

4. What a people owe their king is "to heed his voice." Verse 7b points out that singing this hymn and praising the LORD as "our God" raises this issue. It is possible that in the liturgy for which this psalm was composed, the first commandment, the preeminent word of the LORD, was read at the conclusion of the hymn: "I am the LORD your God, who brought you up out of the land of Egypt, out of the house of bondage. You shall have no other gods beside me." When that word is spoken, it turns the time into "today," the present opportunity to hear the LORD's voice. The right response is trust in "the rock of our salvation" (v. 1), not doubt and anxiety. It is exclusive fealty that recognizes no other divine powers. The LORD's way is that of shepherd and suzerain; failure to trust oneself wholly to the LORD as king is, in the language of verse 10, to be "a people who err in heart and do not acknowledge (in life) my ways."

5. The conduct of Israel at Massah-Meribah (Exod. 17:1–7; see Num. 20:1–13) is cited as a warning that such failure is a real possibility for people of the LORD. What happened there was a "testing . . . putting to proof" of the LORD (v. 9). Testing the LORD is conduct that raises the question of whether the LORD is in fact here and now the God of exodus who provides for his people and lays exclusive claim on them. At Massah the Israel-

ites demanded water and laid down the presumptuous challenge, "Is the LORD among us or not?" Putting God to the test is a self-centered demand for signs and wonders for me and us in the present, as though the signs and wonders of God's creation and salvation were not enough reason to trust him, and him alone. Look at the context of Numbers 14:22; Deuteronomy 6:16; and Psalms 78:18, 41, 56; 106:14. The LORD was provoked by such conduct by the wilderness generation, and he is provoked by it in all times. It is a particular danger for the people of God. God's angry resolve that the wilderness generation should not enter his rest refers to his decision not to allow them to enter the promised land as the goal and conclusion of their wandering. The past is warning to the present. The fact that the congregation who sing this psalm are in the land physically does not mean they have entered the rest of God theologically and existentially. If they do not heed his voice today, they are still wandering in the wilderness, erring in their hearts and not knowing the ways of the LORD.

6. Jesus understood this very well, and it is this understanding with which he overcomes the devil (Matt. 4:1–11). He turned aside from wonders, relying instead on the word of God. He refused to test God or to worship any other. In his time in the wilderness, he "knew the ways of the LORD." Hebrews 3:7—4:13 uses Psalm 95 as a text for a sermon exhorting the early church not "to fall away from the living God," so that they may complete their wandering in the wilderness of this world by entering into the rest of God. In Christian liturgies, Psalm 95 has been used as an invitatory, a psalm to summon the congregation to authentic worship; as such, it serves admirably. The hymn identifies God as sovereign of all and as shepherd of the church, and then teaches that true worship is the devotion of life, trust, and obedience to this God and to God alone.

Psalm 96: Say Among the Nations, "The LORD Reigns"

1. Psalm 96 proclaims the reign of the LORD to the nations. It is another of the hymns whose subject is the proclamation: "The LORD reigns" (v. 10; see Introduction, sec. 6.1, 3). The familiar form of the hymn, summons to praise followed by the reason or content of praise, is used twice (vv. 1–3 plus 4–6 and

307

vv. 7–12 plus 13). The psalm has a definite evangelical cast. The singing to the LORD (three times) is to be "a telling his salvation" (v. 2b; the Hebrew word is the verb for the duty of the herald who precedes a victor to bring a report to those who wait for good news from the battle), a declaring his glory and marvelous works (v. 3a), a saying "The LORD reigns" (v. 10). The audience of this gospel is the nations and peoples of all the earth. Its purpose is to turn them from their gods to the God whose reign means stability for the world and equity for its peoples (v. 10).

2. The psalm envisions the LORD as a divine presence in his sanctuary-palace. The presence is mediated through the attributes of glory and majesty, strength and beauty. These attributes are said to be before him, where he is (vv. 6, 7, 9). The king cannot be visualized directly; one must imagine him by thinking of these attributes. The response for which the hymn calls is a procession of the nations into the courts of the LORD to bring tribute (NJPS; "offering," NRSV) and do homage, all as a ritual of fealty to the LORD as the true king of the world (vv. 8, 9).

3. Part one of the psalm contrasts the gods of the nations with the sovereign identity of the LORD. To say "The LORD rules" is to say that the gods whom other nations worship do not. In the thought world of the ancient Near East, nations were thought of as religious as well as political communities; each had its particular god for whom it made claims. The claim to kingship for a god was per se universal and preemptive of the claims for the rule of other gods (see Psalm 82). The god question took two basic forms in the ancient world: Which god is your god? and Which god rules the others? Israel answered the first with the covenant theology of Sinai and the second with the royal theology of Jerusalem. In Israel's faith and hymnology, the two answers influenced and amplified each other, as they do in this hymn, which states two bases for the LORD's claim to rule. The first is the salvation that Israel has experienced in the mighty deeds of the LORD in its behalf (vv. 2–3), marvelous works that typically demonstrated the LORD's power against other nations. The second is that the LORD is creator; he made the heavens (v. 5), and the very stability of the world is a manifestation of his continuing rule (v. 10). In comparison with the LORD, the gods of the nations are ineffective, incompetent (NRSV, "idols," but the emphasis of the text is on function rather than on form).

4. Part two describes the prospect of the world and its peoples because the LORD reigns. Verse 10 states the twofold significance of the central declaration for cosmos and society. First, the world is reliable, the earth is stable, the human home is dependable. Life does not need to be lived in anxiety. So the very elements of the world itself are summoned to rejoice before the LORD because of the stability his power establishes (vv. 11–12). Second, the affairs of people will be ordered according to equity. History and society are not left to the capriciousness of fickle gods or the arbitrary decisions of human rulers. Instead, the LORD will rule with righteousness and faithfulness. There is a power that sets things right, a might that can be trusted. The ancient longing that stirred in human beings when they first thought of order and power in world and society, the longing for reliability in nature and justice in life, will be answered in the reign of the LORD.

5. When verse 13 says "he *comes* to rule [NRSV, "judge"] the earth," to what does it refer? To a historical or a liturgical or an eschatological event? The language of the psalm and its connections with other texts in the Old Testament argue that these alternatives are not mutually exclusive for Old Testament faith. According to I Chronicles 16:23–33, Psalm 96 is one of the hymns of praise sung by Asaph and his choral guild before the ark after David brought it to Jerusalem. The procession bringing the ark of the LORD represented in liturgical drama his coming to his palace-temple as king (see Ps. 24:7–10). The reality behind the liturgical act was the marvelous works of salvation, the historical occasions when Israel had experienced the intervention of the LORD, moments Israel remembered in epic story (Exodus, Joshua, Judges, Samuel) and in poetry celebrating the LORD's coming in theophany (Psalm 18; note the repetition of Ps. 29:1–2 in 98:7–9). Phrases and clauses from Psalm 96 and from Psalms 97 and 98 appear in the prophecy of the exilic Isaiah (compare vv. 11–13 with Isa. 40:10; 44:23; 49:13; 55:12; also 59:19f.; 60:1; 62:11). Isaiah saw the return of the exiles from Babylon as a revelation of the LORD as king and as a demonstration of his rule that proved that the gods of the nations were nothing. The past "comings" of the LORD have a future. The liturgy remembers and anticipates. The psalm always places those who sing it in the presence of the LORD who has come and will rule the earth in righteousness and faithfulness.

309

6. Christians have traditionally used Psalm 96 on Christmas

Eve and Christmas Day. In that liturgical context, the hymn looks back to the nativity and forward to the second coming; Christ has come, and will come again. The psalm puts the Christ event in the sequence of the Old Testament marvelous works by which the LORD manifested his rule. It interprets the Christ as the LORD's demonstration that other gods are mere nothings. Through the Christ, the LORD is working out his rule of righteousness and faithfulness among the nations (see the comment on Psalm 98).

Psalm 97: The Reign of God and the Righteous

Psalm 97 belongs to the group of hymns that praise the LORD by offering an exposition of the proclamation, "The LORD reigns" (see Introduction, sec. 6.1, 3). It is a companion of Psalms 47; 93; and 95—99.

1. As in Psalms 93 and 99, the thematic proclamation is the song's first sentence. The psalm has three parts; each develops the significance of the opening proclamation. The first part (vv. 1–5) gives a verbal portrait of "the LORD of all the earth," taking singers and hearers imaginatively into the royal presence. The second part (vv. 6–9) describes the response to the proclamation (repeated in verse 9). Heaven is claimed as herald and all peoples as witness of a rule that has inescapable consequences for all. The third part (vv. 10–12) tells the righteous what the proclamation means for them. The motif "rejoice/joy" links the three parts. The opening invocation calls on earth to its farthest reaches to rejoice at the proclamation of the LORD's reign (v. 1), but the only part of earth that does rejoice on hearing the proclamation is Zion and the surrounding towns of Judah (v. 8). In the time of the psalm, only the people who know the LORD as their God can rejoice. In contrast, all who worship idols are put to shame, because all other gods are subordinate to the LORD's kingship (vv. 7, 9). The faithful righteous receive joy (v. 11) and may rejoice (v. 12) because the LORD's rule means protection and help against the wicked (v. 10). The introduction of the threat and problem of the wicked in the third part of the psalm means that the psalm recognizes that even the population of Zion and Judah is split in the matter of devotion to the rule of the LORD. Other motifs are distributed in the psalm to elaborate crucial emphases (earth, all, righteousness, justice).

2. Earth is the recurrent motif in the first part of the psalm

310

as it seeks to evoke the power and majesty of "the LORD of all the earth" (vv. 1, 4, 5, and repeated in v. 9). The imagery of the description is largely drawn from the theophany of the divine warrior who as the storm-god in the religions of Canaan and Mesopotamia defeated his opponents to gain kingship over other gods and the cosmos (see the comment on Pss. 18:7–15 and 89:5–14). The psalmist used features from that tradition to claim and proclaim Israel's God as the awesome ruler of the earth. His person is hidden in the mystery of clouds and thick darkness; irresistible fire proceeds him; lightning and thunder manifest his power (50:3, 6; 77:16, 18). At the sight, earth trembles and mountains dissolve. Israel used this dramatic and poetic language of its culture to affirm what we speak about with conceptual abstract terms like omnipotence, the absolute unqualified sovereignty of God. In Israel's polytheistic world, the language had the advantage of serving as a polemic against other gods (vv. 7, 9; see 95:3; 96:4–5) and in Israel's creative use of it, led to the monotheistic reduction of other gods to idols (v. 7; see 115:3-8; Isa. 42:17).

3. Among the descriptive features used to evoke the LORD's rule, only the word pair "righteousness/justice" occurs in all three parts of the psalm, an indication of its importance in the psalm's understanding of the kingship of the LORD. A king's throne was the central symbol of his kingship, and, by implication, its base represented that on which his rule was founded. The foundation of the LORD's throne, says the psalm, is not built of attributes of pure power but of qualities of ethical conduct. In naming righteousness and justice as the symbolic base of the LORD's throne (v. 2; 89:14), the psalm puts the focus on the attributes that lay at the center of the prophetic understanding of the LORD's reign. The LORD's reign is power devoted to righteousness and justice. Righteousness is the rightness that makes for life and *shalom;* justice is found in decisions and actions according to righteousness. Both, in the vocabulary of the psalms and the prophets, are qualities and events belonging to the LORD's reign. The righteousness proclaimed by the heavens (v. 6) is the LORD's identity and character as divine judge (50:6), who through his judgments (v. 8) acts to maintain and reveal his rule by intervening in the history of his people (see the comment on Ps. 98:1–3). The psalm is very near the vocabulary and message of the exilic Isaiah here (Isa. 40:5, 9–10; 42:17; 52:7–10). The faithful righteous are those who

311

are right in relation to the LORD's reign because they reject evil, whatever diminishes life and *shalom.* The righteousness of God is light and joy for them because they find help and protection from the wicked in the judgments of the LORD. The real message of the psalm is heard at this point in its third part. The psalm's proclamation of God's reign offers the righteous hope in their opposition to evil. When the kingdom of God is proclaimed, the righteous take courage. A connection that is important for the interpretation of many other psalms is made here, because the opposition between the righteous and the wicked, so frequent a feature in them, is clearly related to faith that "the LORD reigns."

Psalm 98: Joy to the World

Psalm 98 is the Old Testament text for Isaac Watts's Christmas hymn, "Joy to the World!" The hymn celebrates the birth of Jesus as the coming of the LORD to rule the world with truth and grace. It uses the language and themes of the psalm in order to say that the nativity is an event of the kind and significance proclaimed in the psalm. The psalm announces the coming of the Savior God as king of the world. It is a companion to the similar Psalm 96 (compare 98:1a and 96:1a; 98:7–9 and 96:11–13; and consult the comment on Psalm 96).

1. Psalm 98 is an imperative hymn of praise composed of three parts, each preparing for the next. The first part (vv. 1–3) begins with a general call to praise the LORD in song because the LORD has done marvelous things (v. 1a). The marvelous things are then summarized; the LORD has won a victory that showed his faithfulness to Israel and revealed his righteousness to all the earth (vv. 1b–3). The second part (vv. 4–6) invites all the earth, because of what they have seen, to join in the music that acclaims the LORD as king. The third part (vv. 7–9) intensifies the invitation by including all that is, sea and world, hills and floods. Nothing is to fail at praise, because the LORD comes as the king who will judge the earth with the same righteousness that he has shown toward Israel, a saving righteousness. The psalm lifts up the prospect of a coming kingdom where power and policy make for salvation. That is indeed reason for joy in the world!

2. The theme of the first part of the psalm is the LORD's salvation. The Hebrew word for save/salvation occurs in each

of the first parts' three verses (NRSV, "victory"). Clearly, Israel was the beneficiary; the psalm recalls the LORD's enactment of steadfast love and faithfulness in their behalf. But that is not the primary emphasis here. The psalm employs a vocabulary and an idiom that emphasize the Savior and his salvation more than the saved. Salvation was composed of "marvelous deeds," divine interventions that transcended human expectations, to open up new possibilities. A "new song" was called for, one that celebrated the new situation created by these marvelous deeds (see the context of Pss. 40:3; 144:9; and especially Isa. 42:10). The salvation was the exclusive work of the LORD's right hand and holy arm, expressions that evoke the identity of the divine warrior, whose victory over his foes manifested his kingship (see Ps. 89:10, 13, and the comment on their context). The purpose and the promise of this victory were revelation to all the world. The psalm makes no reference to enemies; the vanquished have dropped out of the picture. What matters is the meaning of the LORD's marvelous deeds for the whole world.

3. Isaiah 52:7–10 is the prophetic counterpart of the psalm. The prophecy uses the same vocabulary and idiom to announce that the return of Israel's exiled from Babylon would be a public display of the LORD's reign. "All the ends of the earth shall see the salvation of our God." What the prophecy foresaw, the psalm declares. On the basis of the declaration, it calls on the whole earth to join in Israel's joyous acclamation of the LORD as king. The psalm believes and claims that Israel's God had been shaping Israel's particular history to establish and reveal his rule over universal history. The belief is astonishing and the claim appears to be theological bravado. But the basic conviction was as old in Israel as hymns like Exodus 15 and Psalm 68 that celebrated the exodus and possession of the land as the manifestation of the LORD's everlasting reign. Long before the rescue of the exiles from Babylon, some in Israel had been given the insight that the LORD's victories in Israel's history were the work of the God whose victory over primeval chaos had brought forth the world. Salvation corresponded to and continued creation. Both were the royal work of the one who rules over all. That is why the psalm includes sea and world and floods and hills in the summons to praise (vv. 7–8). The savior of Israel is the creator of the world.

4. Psalmists and prophets saw the exodus and the return as a "coming" of the LORD into the affairs of human beings (see

313

the comment on Ps. 96:13; and see Isa. 40:10). They believed that the mystery of that coming was the meaning of history. The kingdom of God was coming through salvation. The righteousness of the LORD shown in the salvation of Israel was the clue to the future of the world. There is, then, a prophetic tension in the psalm itself. Its time is in the midst of a history punctuated with manifestations of the LORD's kingship that portend a reign of righteousness and equity. The New Testament witnesses saw in Jesus a continuation and climax of these salvific comings. In an echo of verse 3, Mary called her unborn child a marvelous deed in which the LORD "remembered his mercy to Israel" (Luke 1:54). Paul saw in the gospel of Jesus Christ the salvation of God that reveals God's righteousness to the nations (Rom. 1:15–17). The early Christians chanted the psalm as a hymn about the Christ to express their joy at having found a king who brought salvation instead of oppression and misery. When Isaac Watts transformed the psalm into a hymn for Christmas, he was tutored by Scripture and tradition—and he got it right. "Joy to the World!" as hymn reflects and renews what the psalm has always meant as Christmas liturgy. It catches and repeats the exuberance of humankind and nature in recognition of what is happening. It interprets Christmas as decisive event in the reign of God, something that changes history for the nations. It maintains the connection between salvation and rule: "The Savior reigns."

Psalm 99: Holy Is He

Psalm 99 is a hymn praising the LORD as king. Like Psalms 93 and 97, it opens with its theme, the proclamation, "The LORD reigns," and then unfolds an interpretation of the meaning of the proclamation (see Introduction, sec. 6.1, 3).

1. The psalm has a complex structure created by interlocking refrains. A summons to magnify Israel's God by worship at the place of his presence on earth (vv. 5, 9) divides the psalm into two parts. Each summons is concluded by a declaration of the holiness of the LORD that occurs also at the end of verse 3, dividing the first part into two sections with distinct subjects. The subject of the first section (vv. 1–3) is the kingship of the LORD over Zion and all the peoples of earth. It concludes with a general call for praise of the LORD's name, which represents his great and awesome identity. The subject of the second sec-

314

tion (vv. 4–5) is the LORD's love for and performance of justice and righteousness in Israel. The last part (vv. 6–9) praises the LORD as a God who answers those who call on his name. Though verses 1–3 portray the LORD as sovereign over earth and all its peoples, the rest of the hymn concerns the LORD's relation to Jacob/Israel. The whole seems a wondering, awed exclamation that the God of all peoples works justice and answers prayers for this particular people who are permitted to call him "our God" (vv. 5, 8, 9).

2. The kingship of the LORD is evoked by language that points to Jerusalem as the earthly capital and to the ark as the throne. The locale of the LORD's kingship is Zion (v. 2), the city of God set on his holy mountain (v. 9). These designations identify Jerusalem as the center of all the earth from which divine kingship is exercised (see the comment on Psalm 48). The symbol of the LORD's kingship is the ark of the LORD. The psalm calls it the LORD's cherubim-throne (v. 1; see the comment on Ps. 80:1) and footstool (v. 5; see 132:7; I Chron. 28:2). The ark represented the LORD's presence with Israel as the divine warrior at whose theophany earth shook and peoples trembled (v. 1; cf. 97:3–5). Because of its role in Israel's earliest religious history, this emphasis on the ark anticipates the designation of the LORD as "our God" in the major refrains (vv. 5–9) and the LORD's way with Israel as subject of the psalm's praise.

3. As the first way in which the LORD had exercised kingship in Jacob (an alternate name for Israel), the psalm points to the LORD's support of justice and his execution of justice and righteousness. Elsewhere justice and righteousness are said to be the very foundation of the LORD's throne (97:2; 89:14). In the vocabulary of the psalms, righteousness and justice are the attributes and acts of God in his ruling and judging to enforce his rule. Whether his judgments were salvific or punitive with respect to Israel depended on the case at hand, but the emphasis is on their restorative and redemptive effect (see the comments on Pss. 97:2; 98:1–3). God's royal exercise of judgment in Israel was prophetic of his coming rule over the world (96:13; 98:9). It is in texts like these that we can see the basis of the prophets' proclamation of justice and righteousness in a theology of the LORD's kingship.

4. As the second way in which the LORD had exercised kingship in Israel, the psalm points to his answering the cry of those who represented his people. In the royal ideal of the

315

ancient Near East, it belonged to the ethics of kingship that a king should respond to the petitions of the helpless. If the king heard their cry, he should answer. Of course, ideal and performance were not the same. But the psalm praises the LORD as a ruler who does answer. The psalmist reaches back into Israel's historic tradition to prototypical cases of cry and answer. Moses and Samuel, along with the priest Aaron, were the original intercessors for Israel on classic occasions of corporate guilt (Jer. 15:1; Exod. 17:1–11; 32:7–14; I Sam. 7:5–9; Num. 16:20–22). It is forgiveness as answer for which the LORD is praised, not just help in time of need. Forgiveness of guilt is a special exercise of the sovereign freedom of God (see 103:10–19; 130:4; Hos. 11:8–9). It should be noted that here all prayers and songs of gratitude for their answer in the Psalter are connected with the theology of God's kingship. Cry and answer are the rubrics of prayer in the psalms (e.g., 3:4; 4:1; 5:2) and belong to the setting in life of servants appealing to their king. For the pillar of cloud as oracular locus, see Exodus 33:7–11; Numbers 12:5; and Deuteronomy 31:15. Verses 7b and 8b are qualifications that instruct and warn against presuming on God's forgiveness as easy and routine. God's freedom to forgive does not negate the importance of obedience to God's requirements (v. 7b) or excuse individuals from the consequences of doing wrong (v. 8b). The prospect of forgiveness is held together with the place of obedience and responsibility in a way similar to the LORD's great self-proclamation in Exodus 34:6–7 (see 103:8–18).

5. The triple refrain suggests that the entire psalm is meant to be an exposition of the holiness of the LORD. "Holy" is the word for the numinous, the *mysterium tremendum* that belongs to deity as such. It is the dynamic quality that infuses persons and things specifically claimed and used by a deity; notice "holy hill" in verse 9. In its three parts, the psalm defines and modifies the basic meaning of "holy." The LORD is thrice holy: in supreme majesty, in justice, and in responsibility. "Holy" becomes a notion that means more than the fearful and fascinating divine; used to praise the LORD, it takes on connotations that the people of the LORD have come to know in their experience of his rule. The hymn is a liturgy for the vision that Isaiah saw in the temple when he felt the foundations tremble and heard the threefold "holy" sung in praise (Isaiah 6). He never viewed life and world in the same way after he said "my eyes have seen the king." The psalm still has the power to evoke

the vision of the thrice-holy king when read and sung with openness and imagination. It may also be thought of as a way to enact the adoration of "Hallowed (holy) be thy name."

Psalm 100: The LORD Is God

Psalm 100 is an *introductory* hymn in two ways, liturgical and theological. Its liturgical subject is the movement into the presence of God, the first and fundamental human act that constitutes worship. Its theological purpose is to incorporate into a hymn to accompany that movement the first and fundamental characteristics of the worship of the LORD. Psalm 100 initiates worship *and* sets forth a theology of worship.

The psalm is composed on the pattern of the imperative hymn (see Introduction, sec. 5.5.4). There are four poetic lines of three measures each. The first three give a call to praise (vv. 1–4), and the fourth (v. 5) states the basis and content of the praise. The second line (v. 3) is a significant variation of the pattern. It continues the imperatives of the previous line with its opening "know," which controls the function of the whole, but the clauses that are the object of "know" are statements about the LORD, the kind of material usually found in the second part of the pattern. This "irregularity" moves agenda from the basis to the summons, with an effect that will be examined below.

The liturgical role of the psalm in Israel's worship is apparent in a number of ways. It is a processional song for movement through the gates of the temple into its courts (v. 4) where the LORD is present (v. 2). There the procession is to offer the LORD thanksgiving *(todah)* and praise *(tehillah)*. The superscription says the psalm is for the *todah,* a word that means both the sacrifice of thanksgiving and the act of praising thanks. Probably the psalm itself is the text of the act of praise. Verses 4 and 5 incorporate the elements of the praise formula, "Praise [usually "thank"] the LORD, for he is good, for his steadfast love endures forever" (see Introduction, sec. 5.5.3). The result is a psalm that itself moves those who sing or read it into the presence of the LORD for praise.

1. The psalm characterizes the praise to be offered the LORD in three important ways. The worship that this psalm inaugurates is theopolitical in character. The imperatives in the first line all call for actions that belong to the approach to a king.

317

One "came into the presence" of a king by entering his precincts; note verses 2 and 4. The subjects and court greeted the appearance of the king with a shout of acclamation. "Serve" denotes the conduct appropriate in relation to a royal figure. To serve the LORD is to have him as sovereign, as king. To call oneself a "servant of the LORD" is to acknowledge dependence upon and subjection to him. Two concentrations of the verb "serve" are relevant to the point. In the exodus story, "serving the LORD" is the alternative to continuing as the servants of Pharaoh (Exod. 3:12; 4:23; 7:16; 8:1; 10:26). Deuteronomic exhortations call for Israel to serve the LORD instead of other gods (Deut. 7:4; 8:19; 11:16; etc.). Both clusters involve alternatives: the first between the LORD and a human ruler, and the second between the LORD and other gods. To serve the LORD is to live in a rule that excludes slavery to human governments and subjection to the power of the "gods."

So the call to worship is at the same time a summons to assemble as the realm of the LORD. The assembly can be called religious because its focus is god; but its symbols and rituals come from political life. So the assembly convenes to recognize the locus of the power that rules. By their rituals they point to the power to whom they entrust and submit their lives. Worship means opting for one "power structure" as decisive. It is, therefore, the most significant social action that people can take.

In Jerusalem, there were two buildings side by side. One was the palace/house of the human king; the other was the palace/house that represented the divine king. The question in Israel's history often was: whose will really rules? The prophets represented the heavenly ruler to the Davidic king, and the resistance they met shows that the worship at the temple did not always give the actual answer. In Roman times the early Christians said, "Jesus is lord," in their worship in an empire that required people to say "Caesar is lord," and they paid for the choice. Because worship is the direction of trust and obedience to a power whose will and way make a difference in life, it is always an activity with political consequences. If it makes no difference in the way those who worship set themselves in relation to other powers, it is not the worship that Psalm 100 inaugurates.

2. The worship that the psalm inaugurates is confessional in purpose. It is a way of enacting the call to "acknowledge [see

NJPS] that the LORD is god." Verse 3 states in confessional terms what it means to assemble as the people who have the LORD as king. Worship is a public declaration that the one whose name is the LORD (Heb. YHWH) is indeed god, the only god, the one to whom the predicate "god" belongs exclusively. In Israel's world such a declaration was polemical; it means that claims of the predicate "god" for others are denied. The polemical edge of the declaration is evident in the story of Elijah's contest with the prophets of Baal on Mount Carmel. When Baal failed to answer his prophets and the LORD responded to Elijah's prayer by consuming the sacrifice, the watching assembly began to shout, "The Lord is god" (I Kings 18:39). In Israel's day the question was not, "Is there a god?" but "Who is god?" In a profound though culturally different way, that is still the real question. Human beings are intrinsically polytheistic. Worship that names god is the confession of *one* god.

In the Old Testament, the knowing recognition of LORD occurs as response to an action of the LORD. The second and third measures of verse 3 state in familiar metaphors what action is in mind here. "He made us" is an abbreviation of the salvation history of election, deliverance, and covenant by which Israel was brought into existence as the people of the LORD, the flock that he tends as shepherd. This reference to the LORD's creation of Israel also makes clear how the term "god" in the declaration is understood—not by an abstract merely conceptual definition but by reference to the reality of experience. "God" means the one who creates and cares for the congregation, the one upon whom we depend for our existence and life as the people of God.

This is the place to note that the psalm without any embarrassment calls the whole earth to recognize as King and God the LORD who creates and cares for his people. That is because the revelation of the LORD's identity (as distinct from an awareness of god) occurs in his deeds and words for Israel. "The LORD is god" is based on salvation history, not on natural revelation. But it is also to be noted that the invitation to the world to join the people of God in worship and confession shows that the psalmist knows that God's way with Israel *is* his way to *the whole world* (see the discussion of particular history and universal claims in the comment on Psalm 117).

319

3. The worship that the psalm initiates is joyful. All who study Psalm 100 note the exuberance, enthusiasm, and mirth

that its language represents and invokes; and they yearn for such qualities in their own worship. The call for joy is not hype; it is based on the God to whom the psalm directs its praise. First, God is present, and it is possible to enter the very presence of the LORD through *his* gates and into *his* courts. In the view of the psalm, the LORD by his own choice and condescension is "there" in the most real way. The psalm testifies to the importance of "presence" for authentic and enthusiastic worship. It is the exciting anticipation of being in the presence that funds the joy of praise.

Second, the God who is present is the shepherd of his people. The LORD is savior. The situation of worship is evangelical. The congregation moves into the presence of the one who is "for us."

Third, the God who is present is "good" (v. 5). The adjective "good" is what the psalm offers as the sole basis for its call to worship. The word seems too simple and general to serve such a purpose. But it is precisely this common character that makes it appropriate here. In all their languages, human beings organize their discriminating responses to what they experience in every sphere of life by the word pair "good/bad," calling "good" that which enhances existence within any particular sphere. Israel came to know its god as good in an absolute sense in every sphere—in all his ways and words. Psalm 34:8 even says, "O taste and see that the LORD is good!" Here the following measures of verse 5 specify the goodness the psalm has in mind. It is the everlasting loving-kindness and enduring faithfulness of the LORD, the vocabulary of *hesed* and *'emunah* by which the hymns so often speak of the character of the LORD made known in his way with Israel (see Introduction, sec. 6.8). Worship is joy because, as far as time runs, the future is ruled by the loving-kindness and faithfulness of the LORD.

The two great mottoes of radical monotheism are: "I am the LORD thy God; thou shalt have no other gods before me" and "Whatever is, is good." The second can be said because the source of all things and the power by which they exist is good (H. Richard Niebuhr, pp. 37–38). Psalm 100 is a hymnic expression of these two great mottoes as praise. It creates a worship that knows who God is and why he is praised.

320

Psalm 101: The Way of Integrity

Martin Luther called Psalm 101 "David's mirror of a monarch." It is the song of one whose sphere of responsibility extends beyond his own "house" (i.e., palace and its occupants, vv. 2, 7) to include "the city of the LORD" and the land (v. 8). The psalm was composed for use at the inaugural of the king or a celebration of his kingship (see Introduction, sec. 6.11). It is a declaration of commitment to the righteous conduct that belonged to the ideal of a king (see the comment on Pss. 72:1–4, 12–14; 45:4–7; 18:20–30).

1. The song begins with a statement of its subject, praise of the loyalty *(hesed)* and justice of the LORD (v. 1). God's loyalty to the house of David is the basis and support of the very existence of the king (21:7; 18:50), and it is through the gift of divine justice that the king is able to rule (72:1). His righteousness comes from the LORD, so he must begin with praise that confesses that dependence as the foundation of his own commitment. Only in that dependence can and does he promise to practice the way of the blameless. He does not even make the promise without adding the appeal, "When will you come to me," that is, be present with him in loyalty and justice (v. 2a; NRSV, "When shall I attain it?"). The rest of the psalm develops the promise with commitments by the king to practice the way of the blameless himself (vv. 2b–4) and to support those in his realm who do and to oppose those who do not (vv. 5–8).

2. The organizing moral term in the litany of commitments is the Hebrew notion translated "blameless" in verses 2 and 6 *(tamim)* and "integrity" in verse 2 *(tom)*. The notion refers to what is whole, complete, finished; in reference to conduct, the word group describes acts that are coherent and consistent in relation to some foundational value. Here it would be the loyalty and justice of the LORD; the way of the blameless is the characteristic conduct of those whose motives and choices and acts are consistent with their dependence on the LORD. They are the faithful (to the LORD) in the land (v. 6). *Tom* and *tamim* are also the primary terms in the description of the king's righteousness in Psalms 18:20–30 and 78:72.

3. The principal antonym in the recitation to "integrity of heart" is "perverseness of heart" (v. 4; cf. Prov. 11:20; 10:9). It means conduct that is twisted, inconsistent, and lacking in

321

coherence with any inner commitment. Here it is expounded by both general (evil, wicked, base) and specific terms (falling away, secret slander, haughty arrogance, deceit, lies). The emphasis on heart makes it clear that the litany amounts to more than a specific list of wrongs; it is concerned with character itself, "the habits of the heart" out of which conduct emerges.

4. In its concern with character the psalm reaches for the ideal. The king's commitment is not simply to do what is legal and to oppose those who do what is unlawful. The psalm is a vow to develop a character and to practice a life that is coherent with a theological morality. It undertakes responsibility not just for law and order; it promises through the influence of the king's own life and use of his authority to nurture character itself. The psalm teaches that it is not enough for those who lead to live by the legalities and govern by codes. It is the character of the governor and the character of those in his government that really determine what the effect of their governing is on the governed. In this the psalm is radical, but history is replete with examples that prove it is right. The psalm also teaches that conduct depends on character and character is shaped by ultimate commitments. It would insist that "you cannot be good without God," a lesson for more than rulers.

Delitzsch reports that Ernest the Pious, Duke of Saxe-Gotha in the early seventeenth century, "sent an unfaithful minister a copy of the 101st Psalm, and that it became a proverb in the country, when an official had done anything wrong: He will certainly soon receive the prince's Psalm to read" (Delitzsch, 3:107). Because they saw in Jesus one whose life was perfectly coherent with his commitment to the loyalty and justice of God, early Christian interpreters read this psalm as a charge from him to all who would belong to the faithful.

Psalm 102: A Prayer of the Lowly

Psalm 102 is the fifth of the church's seven penitential prayers (see Psalm 6). Its unique superscription tells us the kind and condition of the person for whom it was written. It is a plea to be used by an 'ani (NRSV, "afflicted"; NJPS, "lowly"; on the importance of the identity of the 'ani, see Introduction, sec. 6.18) when faint, that is, without strength. There is no direct mention of sin or forgiveness in the prayer. The question of

what happens in the psalm to make it useful as a penitential
prayer is raised.

1. The psalm is composed of two strands. The first is a
prayer for help in first person style. The psalm begins with
petitions to be heard and helped (vv. 1–2), followed by a description of distress that involves personal suffering (vv. 3–7, 11)
the scorn of enemies (v. 8), and rejection by God (vv. 9–10). The
reference to affliction by God and a petition for God to relent
recur in verses 23–24*a*. This strand reads like an individual
prayer for help, possibly composed for one who is ill. The second strand concerns the restoration of Zion. It praises the LORD
as the everlasting king (v. 12) who will rebuild Zion as a revelation of his rule to all the nations and as an answer to the prayer
of the destitute (vv. 13–17). It calls for Zion's deliverance to be
recorded in writing so that the LORD will be praised in Zion by
future generations (vv. 18–22). Finally, it praises the creator
God whose eternal being assures the future of the children of
his servants (vv. 25–28).

The question of the relation between these strands has been
given different answers: two distinct psalms have been combined; or, an individual prayer has been expanded and adapted
for corporate use; or, the corporate group is represented as or
by an individual; or, an individual prays in identity with the
plight and prospects of the people as a whole. Formally speaking, the second strand can be read as an assertion of trust
(vv. 12–17), a vow of praise (vv. 18–22) and concluding praise
(vv. 25–28) and so as parts of the regular prayer for help.

The compositional unity is impressive. A motif of time runs
through the whole. The theme of days that vanish opens and
closes the description of trouble (vv. 3, 11) and is resumed in
verses 23–24. God's everlasting reign is set in direct contrast to
the ephemeral time of the psalmist twice (vv. 12, 24*b*–27), as if
in that contrast lay some resolution for the distress. The psalm
asserts that the time has come for the LORD to have compassion
on Zion (v. 13). And the psalm looks forward to a future time
when coming generations, a people not yet created, composed
of the descendants of the servants of the LORD, will praise him
and dwell in security (vv. 18–20, 28). Further, the prayer of the
destitute in strand two (v. 17) corresponds to the prayer of the
afflicted one in strand one (v. 1); and those doomed to die (v. 20)
correspond to the one about to die in the midst of his days

323

(v. 24). Clearly the afflicted one of strand one corresponds in some way to the destitute population of Zion of strand two.

2. The central theological question of the psalm is the salvific significance of the LORD's everlasting time for the incomplete time of the lowly. The lowly one exemplifies the human predicament of time. We live in time; our lives are timed; we need time to live. There is a tragic poignancy in the way the lowly one speaks of "my days" in verse 24. The life of human beings has an expected course, and they assume they possess the strength and own the days to live out that course. But human control of time is an illusion. Two devastating similes disclose the truth. "My days vanish like smoke" (NJPS). We think we have all the days we need, when suddenly something happens that makes controlling time like grasping smoke. "My days are like an evening shadow." We think we are in the midst of our days, and suddenly we are at the end of them. In one way or another all human beings come to see the illusion. But the psalmist knows more than this general tragic truth about human existence. He knows that the LORD disposes of his days. Time and its insecurity are the instrument of God's wrath for him (vv. 10, 23). The psalm does not give any reason for God's anger or make any confession of sin. It concentrates simply on the wrath itself—and prays to the God of everlasting time. Note the similar juxtaposition of God's wrath and human transience with God's everlastingness in Psalm 90.

With the LORD time is a matter, not of days, but of years, and generations, and forever (vv. 12, 18, 24, 27). The absolute contrast between the lowly one who is losing what time he thought he had and the LORD who has all the time there is would be discouraging and depressing if the psalmist thought only of God as infinite, eternal, and unchangeable being. Of course, it is comforting for transient mortals to say "my God" to the eternal (v. 24). In the midst of a world in which everything changes and passes away, including even heaven and earth, saying "my God" lays hold on the one who is ever the same and whose years are without end (vv. 25–27). The creature can bear its finitude in the knowledge that it is known by the creator. But the lowly one does not think of God as absolute being; the lowly pray to the LORD as absolute sovereign, the one who is enthroned forever (v. 12). The creation of heaven and earth was the work of a kingship that already existed and will be there when heaven and earth are worn out like a garment

324

(see Psalm 24). It is in the everlasting time of the LORD's reign that the lowly one seeks the answer to his incomplete time.

3. That is why the lowly one anticipates the restoration and renewal of Zion as the answer to prayer (vv. 13, 16). Zion and the kingship of the LORD go together; the entire theology of Zion as the chosen "city of God" is assumed in the psalm's turn to the theme of Zion (see Introduction, sec. 6.10). Zion is the place in human time and space where the LORD has chosen to be present as king for his people and to manifest the glory of his kingship to the nations. So his servants cherish the very stones and dirt of Zion (v. 14). Zion is God's provision for them to locate their finitude and fallibility in the reign of the LORD. If God's only action in time were his work of wrath in limiting the time of the lowly, there would be nothing left in human time to praise his name and testify to the kingdoms of earth about the king.

So there has to be an appointed time in human time, a time for compassion and favor for Zion (v. 13). The necessity is set in the kingship of God who chooses in sovereign freedom to be king over Israel as a way of bringing in his kingdom over the entire world. Zion may die in the wrath of God, and God will be justified; but only if Zion lives in the grace of God will the kingdom come and the glory be revealed.

The restoration of Zion will answer the prayer of the destitute (v. 17), relieve the groans of prisoners, and liberate the children of death (v. 20). Therefore there will be a future time for the servants of the LORD. Through the continuing renewal of Zion the children of the LORD's servants will be given life in the presence of the LORD (v. 28). An enduring community of the servants of the LORD will correspond to the kingship of the LORD that endures through all generations.

4. The psalm, then, is the prayer of one who finds hope for existence under the wrath of God in the kingdom of God. The affliction of the lowly will be relieved in the renewal of Zion. Is the lowly one the personification of Zion's destitute population during the exile or during the hard times of the restoration, as in Lamentations 3 and in the personification of the exiles in Isaiah 40—55? The psalm is replete with themes that occur in the sayings of the exilic prophet; perhaps his prophecy prompted the hopes of the second strand. If so, the psalm is the prayer of the people of God who believe and hope that the reign of God can and will rule over and overrule even their

325

failure. The church, ever under the wrath of God in its sinfulness, can use the prayer to turn to the necessity of grace that lies in the kingdom of God. Or, is the psalm the prayer of an individual who is so completely a servant of the LORD that he can only think of his deliverance from wrath as happening in and through the restoration of Zion? Then Christians can say the prayer to learn and confess that their renewal comes through and with God's revival of the church. The psalm, in its penitential use, has been and can be read both ways.

Psalm 103: Abounding in Steadfast Love

Psalm 103 is a profoundly evangelical hymn. It gives voice to the thankfulness of sinners that the LORD is a God of mercy and grace. It recites in a concentrated way what Israel learned about the ways of God; the LORD had not dealt with them according to their sins. Because of its subject and the way that subject is developed in a poem of subtle allusions and aesthetic power, Psalm 103 has been the favored praise of sinners. In every age, in liturgical contexts from Communion service to graveside, in the prayers of the simple and the sophisticated, the words of the psalm have been the means of remembering that the LORD is gracious.

1. The psalm has an intricate plan that is designed in every detail to serve its purpose. It opens and closes with the same measure, an inclusio that defines the whole as praising thanks. The imperative "bless" introduces two lines at the beginning and the four lines at the end to emphasize the psalm's function as a rehearsal of declarations that exalt the LORD. The psalm has twenty-two lines, the number of letters in the Hebrew alphabet, another clue to the poet's attempt to be comprehensive. In the second line there is a warning negative imperative that tells how the psalm executes its purpose. The psalm is a liturgical "not forgetting" of all the LORD's dealing; the body of the psalm is a recollecting, remembering, reminding.

The remembering praise can be divided by style and content into four parts, in each of which the attribute of steadfast love is featured, accompanied in the first three by that of compassion (vv. 4, 8, 11, and 13, 17). By this repetition and by the citation of Scripture in verse 8, the psalm names steadfast love (*hesed*) as the attribute of the LORD expressed in all the LORD's dealings and ways (vv. 2, 7). The first part (vv. 1–5) is held

326

together by the style of self-address and a list of dealings that belong to the LORD's relation to an individual. In the second part (vv. 6–10) the style shifts to indicative sentences and the focus to the LORD's ways with corporate Israel. In the third part (vv. 11–14) the poet has composed a chiasmus of "for, as, as, for" sentences, each of which in Hebrew begins with a K sound. In them, three comparisons and an assertion support and elaborate the claims of the first two parts. The fourth part (vv. 15–18) picks up the motif of human transience from verse 14 and contrasts the temporality of human existence with the everlasting steadfast love of the LORD. In what seems to be an abrupt shift in subject (vv. 19–22), the psalm concludes with a declaration of the unlimited sovereignty of the LORD as cosmic ruler and calls on the officials of the heavenly court and all the works of the LORD to join in the blessing of the LORD. Besides the divine attributes of "steadfast love and mercy," there are three other motifs whose repetition indicates something important about the meaning of the psalm. "All" occurs five times in the first six verses, and then four times in the last four, giving a sweeping and inclusive tone to the whole. The topic of sin appears in verses 3, 10, 12, and by implication in verse 9; all three sin words in the Old Testament vocabulary are used (iniquity, sin, transgression). Clearly the relation of the LORD to sinners is a thread running through the whole. "Those who fear him" is used twice as an identification of the corporate "us" who sing the psalm (vv. 10–11 and 12–13) and appears a third time in an important context (v. 17). The identification confers a particular theological identity on the psalmist and those who sing the psalm.

2. The twofold theme of steadfast love *(hesed)* and compassion (NRSV, "mercy") is rooted in a biblical text. "The LORD is compassionate [NRSV, "merciful"] and gracious, slow to anger and abounding in steadfast love" (v. 8) is a quotation from the LORD's proclamation of his name and character to Moses when the Israelites in the wilderness had committed the unthinkable sin of making and worshiping the golden calf (see Exod. 34:6–7 and the narrative context). The proclamation also describes the LORD as a God who "forgives iniquity and transgression and sin." This "attribute formula," as the proclamation is sometimes called, is one of the most important theological statements in the Bible. The influence of its language and content is apparent at many points in the law and the prophets. In the psalms it is

327

quoted in 86:15 (see v. 5) and 145:8 (see v. 9) and used in 78:38–39; 99:8; 111:4 (see the discussion in Fishbane, pp. 347–350). Psalm 103 reads like a hymn based on study and reflection on the proclamation in its primary context. The proclamation's theology is what the psalm is about: the LORD's abounding steadfast love, so much greater and more lasting than his anger at sin, as the ground and hope of forgiveness for sinners.

Steadfast love *(hesed)* is, of course, the attribute and activity of the LORD celebrated in the psalms as the LORD's essential goodness beyond all others (Introduction, secs. 5.5.3; 6.8). Steadfast love is both character and act. One can attempt to define it as helpfulness toward those with whom one stands in relationship. To do *hesed* is to do the best in and make the best of a relationship. That is why, in a theology that thinks of God's way with human beings in terms of creation, election, promise, and covenant, *hesed* is immensely important. The LORD's steadfast love, says the psalm, is so abounding that it fills all time and space. It is as great as the heavens are high above the earth (v. 11); it is lasting as everlasting lasts (v. 17).

The attribute usually paired with steadfast love in the psalms is faithfulness (see the comment on Ps. 100:5), but in Exodus 34:6 and in some other psalms, as here, the complementary term is compassion, which occurs in the psalm as noun, adjective, and verb (Hebrew root *rhm*). In secular usage, the term refers to the attitude and conduct of one who restrains anger and acts kindly (e.g., a military conqueror, I Kings 8:50; Jer. 42:12). In the psalms the compassion of the LORD, often in association with steadfast love, appears in contexts that involve human sin and divine anger and the resolution of God's forgiveness (51:1; 77:7–10; 78:38–39; 102:13). The comparison that is used here to elucidate compassion is that of a father's way with children (v. 13). A parent's anger at a child's failures occurs but does not last or prevail (Isa. 49:15). Compassion is a caring that prevails over anger. As a complement to steadfast love, compassion emphasizes and heightens the dominant inclination to forgiveness in the face of sin that belongs to God's abounding steadfast love.

3. The psalm testifies to the LORD's work of steadfast love and compassion in two ways. The first is a recitation of benefits for the soul (vv. 2–5). The benefits are not separate items but belong together as aspects of one redemptive process. In order, the list outlines the course of a forgiveness that heals, redeems

life from threatening death, so adorning life with steadfast love
and compassion, and making it possible to experience life as
good, with the result that life is renewed. The list summarizes
what Israel prayed for in their prayers for help. The items in the
list are the agenda of a song of thanksgiving. It all begins with
and is based on forgiveness. On the relation between forgiveness and healing, see the excursus on Psalm 38. This recitation
of the LORD's benefits to the soul is not composed as the report
of a particular individual. The style of relative clauses and the
recurrent "all" make it a characterization of the LORD. The
prophets used the vocabulary of sickness and healing to interpret the LORD's way with sinful Israel (e.g., Isa. 57:14–21; Jer.
16:4; 14:18). The soul called to praise the LORD is that of everyone in the nation, and that of the corporate people.

The second testimony speaks of the ways of the LORD made
known to Moses and the people of Israel (v. 7). When Israel was
"oppressed" in Egypt, the LORD by righteous acts of judgment
freed them from their oppressors (v. 6) and so revealed for all
times his ways with the oppressed. When Israel sinned in the
wilderness in the matter of the golden calf, the Israelites
learned that God's ways with them as sinners were based on
steadfast love and compassion (v. 8). The LORD did not keep his
anger, else they would not have survived (v. 9). They can truly
say, "He has not dealt with us according to our sins" (translating
the verbs in v. 10 with NJPS as past). The story of the wilderness
way of the people of the LORD is a story of the LORD's steadfast
love and compassion. The language used by the psalmist suggests that more is in mind than Israel's foundation story. At a
number of points, the language corresponds to that of the
prophecy in Isaiah 40—66. (Compare v. 5 with Isa. 40:31; v. 9
with Isa. 57:16; v. 11 with Isa. 55:9; vv. 15–16 with Isa. 40:6–8.)
In the psalm, the ways of the LORD revealed to Moses are
understood as confirmed and renewed in the restoration from
the exile. Not only the exodus but the return from exile is
reflected in the psalm's praise.

4. Three times the psalm says that the steadfast love and
compassion of God are for "those who fear him" (vv. 11, 13, 17).
"Those who fear the LORD" is a designation used in the psalms
along with the righteous, the faithful, and the servants of the
LORD for those who seek to make the LORD the decisive orient-
ing center of their lives (e.g., 25:12, 14; 31:19; 34:9; 85:9; and
Introduction, sec. 6.17). The fear of the LORD is simply rever-

329

ence practiced in trust and obedience. Does the psalm's connection between God's steadfast love and those who fear the LORD imply that they deserve and earn it by their piety? The psalm gives a twofold answer. Those who sing this psalm know themselves to be forgiven sinners. They do not receive steadfast love because they fear the LORD; they fear the LORD because they have been forgiven. See the comment on "there is forgiveness with you so that you are feared" (130:4). The only claim they make for themselves is the very humblest. "We are dust," they say (an allusion to Gen. 2:7; see Ps. 90:3–6), "and God remembers that in dealing with us" (v. 14). But as forgiven sinners, they also know that the reality of their fear of the LORD matters. They are not to sin so that grace may abound (the argument of Paul in Rom. 5:18—6:23 is helpful here). Rather, they are to observe the covenant of the LORD by remembering to do what his commandments require (vv. 17–18). They are to remember the steadfast love *and* the covenant, the gospel *and* the law. Both are essential to the life of faith.

5. Why does the psalm conclude with the proclamation of the cosmic universal reign of the LORD (v. 19) and summon all the heavenly court and all the works of the LORD to join the human praise of those who fear the LORD (vv. 20–22)? There are connections within the psalm that point to the reasons. The LORD's steadfast love can be as great as the heavens are high above the earth, because the LORD's throne is established in the heavens (vv. 11, 19). The LORD can remove our transgressions from us as far as the east is from the west because his kingdom rules over all (vv. 12, 19). These are poetic ways of stating one of the fundamental points of psalmic theology: The salvation of the LORD is the manifestation of the reign of the LORD in the world (Introduction, sec. 6.5; note the way the theme of the LORD's kingship is connected with the salvation of Zion in 102: 12–22). The grace of the LORD is a sovereignty of grace. The angels and hosts and works of the LORD are connected with the fearers of the LORD by the repetition of the verb "do/make" (the same word in Hebrew). The angels and hosts who *do* the word and will of the LORD join the earthly chorus of those who *do* the LORD's commandments. There should be and is joyous praise in heaven among the doers in the kingdom of the LORD that there are doers on earth who confirm the love of the LORD by their obedience.

6. "Why should the wonders he hath wrought / Be lost in

330

silence and forgot?" (Isaac Watts). The exhortation of the soul
with which this hymn begins warns against the danger of forgetting. The psalm is a marvelous way to remember, and there
is nothing more important for sinners to remember in life and
in death than the sovereignty of divine grace.

Psalm 104: The LORD God Made Them All

Psalm 104 praises the LORD as the one who created the
world and provides for all creatures that live in it. The psalm
is a poetic vision of the world and of what we moderns call
"nature" as the work of the LORD. Contemporary people have
a variety of ways of viewing and speaking about the world and
the forms of life it sustains—scientific, economic, aesthetic, recreational. This psalm offers the view and language that is appropriate for faith. For those who live by faith, its view and
language qualify and define the other ways of thinking and
speaking. Indeed, when understood in terms of its own culture,
the psalm includes the scientific and economic and aesthetic—
even the recreational; the word "play" appears in verse 26
(NRSV, "sport").

1. Psalm 104 begins and ends with the same self-exhortation
that opens and closes Psalm 103: "Bless the LORD, O my soul."
The sentence appears only in these two psalms; its repetition
holds them together as a pair. The first speaks of the abounding
steadfast love of the LORD; the second, of the innumerable
creatures made and sustained by the wisdom of the LORD.
Together the pair praise the LORD as the savior who forgives
and the creator who provides. Both see their themes as expressions of the LORD's kingship (103:19–21 and 104:1–4).

A traditional and favorite approach to Psalm 104 has been
to interpret it as a poetic version of Genesis 1. There are indeed
many connections of vocabulary and thought between the two.
Both are surely expressions of the same theology of creator and
creation. But attempts to analyze the psalm in terms of the
seven-day structure of Genesis 1 are forced. The psalm is lyrical
and exuberant. It reads as if it were a poetic version of God's
repeated appraisal of his work in Genesis 1: "And God saw that
it was good." The psalm is so full of wonder and joy at what God
has made—the joy of the psalmist and the joy of God.

331

There are interesting similarities between this psalm and
ancient Egyptian sources. The poet may have known about and

drawn on *onomastica* (cosmological lists) and traditions of praise of creator gods from Egyptian sources. In some of its features the psalm resembles the hymn of Amenhotep IV in praise of Aten, the sun disk (*ANET,* pp. 370–371). In verses 1–9 the psalmist also uses an ancient mythic cosmogonic pattern to describe the LORD's creating action. Such materials represented the learning of his culture. In his psalm he has adapted and converted all his sources to a praise controlled by Israel's knowledge of the LORD. (On these matters, see Levenson, *Creation,* pp. 53–65.)

2. The psalm follows the hymnic form. It begins and ends with a summons to praise. Between, in the body of the hymn, the praise occurs (vv. 1*b*–30). The body may be divided into three parts according to content (vv. 1*b*–9, 10–23, 24–30). The praise is composed in the style of direct address into which are woven sentences in the third person about the LORD. Before the concluding call to praise, the poet lists a series of responses to the God described in the praise (vv. 31–35). In form, the responses are wish prayers (vv. 31–32, 35), a vow of praise (v. 33), and the presentation of the psalm as an offering to the LORD (v. 34). Such elements belong properly, not to the hymnic genre, but to prayers for help and thanksgiving for help. In these responses the psalmist speaks of himself; here the personal dimension of the psalm is apparent. He calls the creator "my God" twice (vv. 1, 33), and verse 33 names the psalm "my meditation." These and other features of the psalm indicate that it is the composition of a poet who is working eclectically with styles and themes to express his own vision of God. Yet his materials are those which belong to the common tradition, and the form of the psalm and its presence in the Psalter show it was designed for the praise and the study of the larger community.

3. The first part of the body of the hymn (vv. 1*b*–9) portrays the LORD as sovereign creator. It begins with an acclamation of his greatness (v. 1*b*), and the rest expounds that greatness. Verses 1*c*–9 are composed on a mythic pattern of divine activity that was old and well known in the ancient Near East. The myth in various expressions told how the world came to be when gods were in conflict and one god won kingship over the others and by his victory established the stability and order of the world. The vocabulary and elements of the myth were the way in which ancient peoples in the general culture in which Israel lived comprehended and understood the existence of the

world—as brought about by the achievement of kingship by one god (see the comment on Psalms 93 and 29).

In verses 1c–9, there is an adaptation of the pattern to Israel's theological purposes. It is the pattern that lies behind the sequence in this part of the psalm. The LORD is portrayed as a royal deity (v. 1b) clothed in light itself (v. 2a) who builds his royal residence on the waters as a manifestation of his kingship over them (vv. 2b, 3a) and then goes forth as a warrior using the thunderstorm as chariot (v. 3bc) and its winds and lightning as his cohorts (v. 4) to triumph over the primeval ocean (NRSV, "deep") over which he shows his power by establishing the earth and banishing the waters (vv. 5, 7) that covered the earth (v. 6) so that the mountains and valleys would emerge (v. 8) and the waters be confined to an appointed place from which they would not return to cover the earth (v. 9). The pattern is more evident in NJPS.

In the adaptation, the other gods are eliminated; the victory establishing the reliability of earth is permanent and need not be repeated in annual cycle or crisis times; and resulting creation is unified ontologically with no remnant of cosmic dualism. Even Leviathan, the chaos monster of the mythic tradition, becomes a tamed creature of the LORD! The imagery of the myth is employed to connect creation with the kingship of the LORD. "The LORD reigns" and "the earth is secure" are collateral truths. Those who see the world through the lens of this vision behold and experience the rule of God in the reliable consistency of the world. And in the steadiness of the world—its processes, seasons, and productivity—they find assurance of the reign of God (see Introduction, sec. 6.1–4).

In this way of thinking, the creation of the world is less an act of producing its material reality and more an achievement of control to produce order and function. It recognizes a dynamic in reality. The world always depends on the authority of God. The bounds are set against the chaotic waters (v. 9), but the limits hold because the LORD reigns. Life in the world depends on the reign of God. That leads to the next section.

4. Verses 10–23 describe in a reflective wondering review the providence of the LORD for his creatures. Overall, the review tells how the LORD uses his control of the world to provide for the life of things. The categories of provision, interrelated and overlapping, seem to be water (vv. 10–11, 13, 16), food (vv. 10–15, also v. 27), habitat (vv. 12, 17–18), and times (vv. 19–23).

333

These are all the result of the LORD's intentional "making" to give the creatures what is needful and good for their life.

The review draws on a kind of knowledge that is based on observing where and how creatures live, a knowledge that represents the empirical learning practiced in the culture of the ancient Near East. It is informed by a basic ecological sense of the interdependence of things. Water, topology, and the change of seasons and day and night form an intricate system in which creatures live. But in the psalm the knowledge is not simply secular or technical. It is theological and given the form of wondering praise of God. What has been rent asunder in the modern view of the world, with consequences for motivation and conduct only recently grasped, is held together here—knowledge of the world and knowledge of God. To intervene in the flow of water, the habitat of birds and animals, the topography of the earth, is to breach an intricate divine ecology into which human life itself is integrated.

It is remarkable with what unqualified directness the human species is considered as simply one of the creatures dependent on the providing of God. Homo sapiens appears in the review (vv. 14–15, 23) as simply one more kind of creature that lives on the earth in the environment it provides. Psalm 8 gives another though not contradictory view. But there is not a hint of anthropocentric claim here. In the praise of the creator, the human being sees itself simply as one of the creatures sustained by the providence of God. Faith in the creator teaches that with respect to existence in the world and dependence on it for life, we are one among many. "The LORD God made them all."

5. The third section (vv. 24–30) makes two observations about the creatures that seem to sum up the preceding review. The first is an exclamation of amazement at how many creatures the LORD in wisdom has made (v. 24). The list of creatures in verses 10–23 is only a beginning that cannot be completed. The emphasis is on "all." Many as they are, the LORD God made them all. It is to insist on this point that even the creatures of the sea, that realm of ships where the great sea monster Leviathan plays, are mentioned (vv. 25–26). The LORD even formed that mysterious mighty denizen of the deep called Leviathan (see Job 3:8; 41:25; Isa. 27:1). The poet means to bring every living thing, no matter how strange or terrible some of them appeared to the mind of his day, within the defining compass

of one category—the "works of the LORD." His vision is the achievement of monotheistic creation theology in Israel. His category involves a viewing and valuing of living things that our category "nature" does not usually imply. For him, the world of nature in its variety and complexity is a display of the wisdom of the LORD. Wisdom belongs to the skill of the artisan and administrator. In the existence and behavior of all living things, the psalmist beholds the work of the LORD creating life and providing for life. Nature is for this faith first of all a reason for joyous praise, a praise that teaches that every use of nature should be informed with reverence before the creator.

The second observation is a recognition of the absolute dependence of all creatures upon the LORD for food (vv. 27–28) and for life itself (vv. 29–30). Nourishment by the products of the environment is the gift of God. The rhythm of life and death and the appearance of new life is the effect of the relation between the "breath" *(ruach)* of creatures and the "breath" *(ruach)* of the LORD. The notion that what animates creatures is the life-bringing breath of God is behind these verses (see Gen. 2:7). But the poet is careful not to identify the creaturely with the divine *ruach*. The creature's breath is given and taken away by God. On the other hand, the breath of God is sent by God to create living creatures and to renew the earth with life. When new creation occurs and life appears, the *ruach* of the LORD is at work.

6. The psalm concludes with a series of wishes and vows. They are all ways in which the poet responds and commits himself to the God addressed and described in the hymn. He wants the glory of the LORD to last forever (v. 31). The hymnic motif attached to the wish (v. 32) is a reference back to the theophany of the divine warrior who sets the earth on its foundation so that it will never totter (vv. 3–8). He wishes that the LORD himself will rejoice in his works (v. 31*b*) so that his own lifelong praise will be in concert with the divine joy. He wishes that this psalm, his meditation, will be a pleasing offering to the LORD (v. 34) serving in the stead of sacrifice (see Psalm 19, sec. 4).

The wish that the wicked vanish from the earth (v. 35) seems to conclude the lovely hymn with a jarring discord. But the wish is utterly consistent with the psalm's vision of the world because the wicked do not fit into that vision. Yet they are there in the world. They live in the LORD's world and benefit from his providence as do all other creatures. God sends his rain on the just and on the unjust (Matt. 5:45). But in their lives the wicked defy the sovereignty of God, deny their dependence on him, and offend and afflict those who praise the LORD. So the psalm wishes they were not there so that the response of the creatures to their creator would be unbroken. Note that the psalm does not say how this might happen. That leaves quite a problem—and several possibilities. The psalm only expresses the conviction, indigenous to biblical faith, that those who see the world as creation and themselves as creatures cannot praise the creator and make peace with wickedness, their own or anyone else's.

The psalm concludes with the first Hallelujah found in the Psalter. Could a more appropriate place be found?

7. The psalm gives us a way to talk to God about the world, to speak of it as creation and as providence for all living things. It puts us in the presence of the One to whom we must speak if we are to realize in heart and language the profoundest truth about the world. It also puts us in our place as one of many living things made by the LORD and utterly dependent on him for life.

When we talk to one another about the world, our usual perspective is different. We view it in the different identities we assume—scientists, developers, economists, artists, sportsmen, and others. We think of it in terms of the values and purposes that belong to these identities. So we see it in fragments. We imagine ourselves autonomous, distinct from the world and different from its creatures, disposing of it and them, not accountable to any transcendent person. We are learning slowly that we damage ourselves, live in alienation from that to which we belong, and threaten the future of life. But we cannot break out of the perspective of our current identities unless we also learn to speak to God about the world. That can be done only in the language of praise. Praise of God puts us with our assumed identities in a quite different place and opens up perspectives possible only from its vantage.

Psalm 104 is traditionally the psalm used on Pentecost and has been from the earliest Christian history. That seems something of an anomaly. The Christian Pentecost is the celebration of the gift of the Holy Spirit to the church in fulfillment of the prophecy of Joel 2:28–32 (Acts 2). Psalm 104 is about creation and providence, whereas Pentecost is about the eschatological endowment of the church with the power of the risen Christ.

The connection was made primarily because verse 30 of the psalm speaks of God's sending his *ruah,* which was translated into Greek by *pneuma* ("spirit"). The antiphon used during the reading of the psalm on Pentecost, "LORD, send out your Spirit and renew the face of the earth," focuses interpretive attention on that verse. The apparent anomaly makes a powerful and important theological connection. The psalm, read on Pentecost, places God's gift of our physical life alongside the gift of our spiritual life. Both are the work of the Spirit of God. The connection between psalm and occasion teaches that the inspiration of the Holy Spirit consummates our life as creatures and brings us to the true existence for which we are created. We are the creation of God twice over. Note that Psalm 51:10 uses the verbs of verse 30, "create/renew," to speak of God's regeneration of the sinner. In Ezekiel's vision of the valley of dry bones the restoration of the people of God is portrayed as a re-creation by the Spirit of God (Ezek. 37:1–14). The Spirit of God is the source of life in every sense that the word "life" can have.

Psalm 105: The Power of the Promise

Psalm 105 advances a single explanation for Israel's foundational story. The whole story from the wandering of Abraham to the settlement of Israel in the land of Canaan is based on the LORD's promise of the land to Abraham. The psalm praises the LORD, whose power was manifest in the wonderful works and acts of judgment of which the story is composed.

1. A long version of the foundational story makes up the principal content of the psalm (vv. 12–44). In this respect, the psalm is like Psalms 78; 106; and 136. (On the so-called historical psalms, see the comment on Psalm 78, sec. 2.) The version is dependent on the narratives in Genesis and Exodus, but it typically selects and shapes the material into a recital that serves its own purposes. In this telling, the LORD is exclusively the actor; it displays his power at work to save and preserve Israel. The actions and reactions of Israel are not, as in Psalms 78 or 106, included. In the arrangement of the Psalter, Psalms 105 and 106 form, like Psalms 103 and 104, a thematic pair. Psalm 105 tells how God remembered his promise to Abraham by his mighty works. Psalm 106 tells how Israel failed to remember the LORD's mighty works in its continual sinning. The first calls for trust, the second for repentance.

2. In form and function, Psalm 105 is a hymn of praise. Its first fifteen verses appear in the anthology of hymns that represent the praises assigned to the Asaphites by David (so I Chronicles 16). Verses 1–6 are an extended summons to praise, and verses 12–45 compose the content of praise. Within the body of praise, verses 7–11 state the introductory theme, a theme that is stated as a quotation of God's promise of the land to Abraham in verse 11. The following recitation of the ancestors' wandering in the land (vv. 12–15), Joseph in Egypt (vv. 16–22), Israel's sojourn (vv. 23–25), the signs and wonders against Egypt (vv. 26–36), the exodus and provisions in the wilderness (vv. 39–41), and the concluding summary account of the joyous singing departure and the gift of the land (vv. 43–45) is an account of how the LORD remembered the promise to Abraham (vv. 42, 8–11). The final verse, verse 45, discloses that the LORD had a purpose for his kept commitment all along—the creation of a people obedient to his statutes and laws. The position of this final statement at the end of the psalm gives it significant importance in the theology of the psalm in spite of its brevity.

3. The psalm views Israel as a people whose identity and destiny come to them from their forefathers, Abraham, Isaac, and Jacob. It addresses the congregation as offspring of Abraham and children of Jacob (v. 6). Their identity as people of the LORD (vv. 24, 25, 43) is rooted in God's relation to these ancestors. The relationship with the forefathers and the people is repeatedly named by a pair of terms, "servant" and "chosen," that are mutually explanatory (vv. 6, 20, 25, 26, 42, 43). In Israel's culture, servant was a term for a person who belonged to another, was identified, supported, and protected by that other, and did what he did in the context of that belonging. The pairing of servant and chosen means that the ancestors and their descendants came into such a relation to the LORD by the LORD's sovereign initiative. They became servants because the LORD chose them in the election of Abraham. It was not separate individuals that God chose in the election of Abraham and Isaac and Jacob but a people through its generations. The choice was not an episode; it was the opening of an epic that would run through all of time. "Servants" is so important as the term for the identity of the people of the LORD that the psalmist even lets the LORD call them "my anointed ones" and "my prophets" because kings and prophets were the offices beyond all others in Israel who were known as servant of the LORD (v.

338

15; the psalmist is probably drawing on Gen. 20:7 and 17:6; 35:11).

4. Israel was chosen as servant by the LORD's promise to Abraham, Isaac, and Jacob (vv. 7–11). The promise is given in the narratives of Genesis in different forms, but the psalmist focuses on one, the promise of the land of Canaan as Israel's assigned inheritance (v. 11). The psalm views the gift of the land in analogy to the grant of territory by human suzerain to a king who thereby becomes his vassal. It is the basis of all that follows in the LORD's way with Israel, and the most solemn vocabulary available in the tradition is used to speak of it. The psalm calls the promise everlasting covenant, oath, word of command, statute, and, coining a unique phrase, "holy word." The psalmist is drawing on passages in Genesis like 15:18–21 and 17:8; and on Exodus 6:4. (That the sworn promise of the land to the forefathers was the basis of the story of Israel from Egypt to Canaan was an essential tenet of the Deuteronomist; see Deut. 1:8; 4:31; 8:1; etc.) This concentration reflects the importance that life in the land assumed during and after the Babylonian exile. The psalmist describes the exodus in the colors that the exilic prophet of Isaiah 40—55 uses to portray the return to Judah (compare v. 43 with Isa. 55:12). Israel is to experience life in its land as a life lived out of the promise of God. Having their own land and means in the midst of the nations is a sacrament of God's faithfulness to his covenant with Abraham.

5. There was purpose to the promise and the history that unfolded out of it. The LORD wanted a people in the midst of all the other peoples of the world who "keep his statutes and observe his laws" (v. 45). The sovereign of the universe sought to establish a colony of obedience, an enclave of those who represented and displayed his reign. This psalm has not a word to say about how God's purpose fared in Israel's history. The psalmist, writing after the exile in all probability, knew the painful story of Israel's repeated failures that is rehearsed in Psalms 78 and 106. But he also knew from the restoration of the people and the promised land about the power of the LORD to work out the covenant with the ancestors. So he composed a psalm that speaks only of the promise and the purpose. By it the descendants of Abraham are summoned to seek the power and the presence of their God (v. 4) because trust is the first act of obedience. The lesson for the church is clear. There is a time and need for the church to hear the pristine word of God's

339

power and promise revealed in Jesus Christ (Mark 12:18–27). The church has no promise apart from its election in him and its identity as Abraham's spiritual seed through him (Gal. 3:29). God's purpose to have a people who live by his rule in the midst of the nations persists through all times (Matthew 5—7).

Psalm 106: We Sinned with Our Ancestors

Psalm 106 is the counterpart of Psalm 105 and stands in a relation of dialectical contrast to it. Psalm 105 concentrates on the marvelous works of the LORD; Psalm 106 focuses on Israel's failure to trust themselves to the LORD in spite of his saving wonders. In the first, Israel possesses the land of Canaan because the LORD has kept his holy promise to Abraham; in the second, Israel has lost the land because it failed to trust and obey. Read together, the two psalms constitute a study in the tension between the promise and the purpose of God on the one hand and the perversity of the people of God on the other as the *logos* of Israel's story. Psalm 106 is similar in theme and thought to Psalm 78, and the comment on Psalm 78 should be considered.

1. The body of Psalm 106 is composed of a recitation of incidents taken from Israel's foundation story, beginning with the exodus and concluding with Israel's life in Canaan (vv. 6–46). The recitation begins with an introductory confession that the present Israel and its ancestors have sinned (v. 6). Examples of the sins of the ancestors follow. The examples come from the tradition recorded in the books of Exodus, Numbers, and Judges, though the canonical order of the material is not followed in all cases. The composer selects and shapes the material to serve the purpose of the psalm. The tradition is remembered and recited, not as mere information, but as instruction. On the historical psalms, see the comment on Psalm 78, sec. 2. After accounts of what happened at the Red Sea (vv. 7–12) and in the wilderness (vv. 13–33), the recitation tells about Israel's life in the land (vv. 34–46). This confession of sin is set within a complex introduction and conclusion that combine a variety of forms with different functions. It begins and ends with the Hallelujah formula, marking it as a piece that belongs to the praise of the LORD. Verse 1 is a basic formulaic hymn of praise for use in thanking the LORD for the steadfast love manifest in the salvation of Israel (see the comment on

340

Psalm 136, sec. 1). Verse 2 raises a question about who is qualified to offer the praise called for in verse 1. The beatitude at verse 3 answers that those who always do justice and righteousness are qualified. Thus preparation is made for the praise of God's mighty works that is in substance a confession of sin. Before the confession begins, the composer-performer offers a prayer to be allowed to experience himself the salvation of the LORD's people and participate then in their joyous praise (vv. 4–5). This prayer, with its assumption of a present national tribulation and a certain salvation to come, anticipates and prepares for the corporate prayer for deliverance from subjection to the nations that concludes the psalm (v. 47). This complexity of form and function results from a combination of different types of speech to serve the liturgical needs of the time and situation for which the psalm was composed. The psalmist writes for a congregation whose vocation to praise the LORD is put in question by their sin and its consequences, so he provides a recital of God's deeds that features the failures of the fathers as a confession of sin and instruction about God's way with sinners. The recital teaches that God's wrath is followed by his salvation when his people cry out to him (v. 44). So the basis is laid in the recital for the concluding prayer for salvation. The final doxology (v. 48) marks the end of book IV of the Psalter (see Introduction, sec. 3.6).

2. The basic confession of sin (v. 6) with its three verbs may be a liturgical sentence for corporate penitence. Its vocabulary and style appear in other penitential sentences (I Kings 8:47; Dan. 9:5; Lam. 3:42). What is different here is the close connection made between the sin of those who say the psalm and that of their ancestors, though notice Daniel 9:7. The Hebrew of verse 6 says, "We have sinned with our fathers." The sentence could mean, "Both we and our ancestors have sinned" (NRSV), or "We have sinned like our forefathers" (NJPS). Could it also mean, "We sinned in the sinning of our ancestors"? That would explain why the recital of failures speaks only of the sins of the ancestors and stays in the narrative mode throughout. Both of the exilic prophets, Jeremiah and Ezekiel, said that the guilty character of their contemporaries was rooted in the character and conduct of Israel's earlier generations (e.g., Ezekiel 16; Jeremiah 2). At the very least, the psalm shows how Israel had come to use the traditions about their beginnings. Everything about their life and God's way with them is viewed through the

341

lens of the traditions of the ancestors. The stories about the ancestors are also about contemporary Israel. The final section of the recital about early Israel's corruption by the nations with whom they mingled is told in terms that reflect the conduct of Israel in the period before the exile (vv. 34–46). The stories about the ancestors blend into language about the time in which the psalm was written, and verse 46 is clearly speaking about the exile and dispersion. Israel had learned that sin is intergenerational and social. If any penitence does not comprehend that, it fails to grasp the profundity and tragedy of the sinful predicament. Paul found in verse 20 the clue to the fundamental error that underlies all sin in the human race (Rom. 1:23), and he seems to have drawn broadly on the language of Psalm 106 in his depiction of universal sin (Rom. 1:18–32; Allen, p. 43).

3. The psalm begins with a summons to praise (v. 1) and ends with a prayer for the restoration of praise (v. 47) because it understands praise to be the crucial factor in Israel's relation to its God. Praise is the joyful, thankful rehearsal of the LORD's promises and deeds to re-present the words and acts as the reality in terms of which the congregation lives. The basic failure underlying all particular sins is the failure to take the words and the deeds as the basis of life (vv. 7, 13, 21–22, 24). The voice of trusting praise is the sound and sign of a people restored by the LORD's salvation (vv. 12, 47). The litmus test for the spiritual health of the people of the LORD is the integrity and actuality of their praise, whether they "remember the abundance of the LORD's steadfast love" (v. 7) or forget his deed and let themselves be determined by dangers or desires or the ways of the nations.

4. Though the focus of the psalm is on case studies of Israel's failure, it never loses confidence that the determining factor of God's way with sinful Israel is the relationship that God has initiated. Israel is the people of the LORD, his chosen ones, his heritage (vv. 4–5, 40) to whom belongs the sworn covenant (v. 45). Because of the abundance of his steadfast everlasting love he saved them, in spite of their sin, again and again (v. 43). But the psalm has an important understanding of how God's just wrath is restrained from the destruction of his people. Deliverance from punishment does not come automatically. At the Red Sea the LORD acted because his name and power were at issue (v. 8). But when Israel itself rejected the name and power by

342

gratitude is always nourished in praise

idolatry (vv. 19–20) and apostasy (v. 28), only the intercession of Moses and Phinehas turned away the wrath. It is idolatry and apostasy that have corrupted Israel's life in the land and created the distress that is the burden of this psalm (vv. 34–39). The psalm gives the office of the intercessor a significant place in God's relation to his sinful people. God answers when he hears the cry that they lift up on behalf of sinners (v. 44). The psalm itself in its closing petition is such a cry of an intercessor on behalf of his congregation and people.

BOOK FIVE

Psalms 107—150

Psalm 107: Consider the *Hesed* of the LORD

Psalm 107 is a song that praises the loyal love *(hesed)* of the LORD shown in marvelous works of deliverance performed in answer to the cry of those in distress. (On *hesed,* see Introduction, sec. 5.5.3.) Martin Rinkart's great hymn, "Now Thank We All Our God," captures its spirit. Verses 23–32 are the biblical basis for the mariner's hymn, "Eternal Father, Strong to Save."

1. The psalm has a very clear arrangement, with a liturgical quality in its repetitions. There is an introduction that begins with the basic hymn sung in services of thanksgiving for salvation (v. 1; see Jer. 33:11 and the comment on Psalm 136). Then the celebrants are identified as all whom the LORD has redeemed from adversity and gathered from the four points of the compass (vv. 2–3). The redeemed are divided into four groups in terms of kinds of adversity, and a stanza is devoted to each: those who were perishing from hunger and thirst (vv. 4–9), those who were in prison (vv. 10–16), those who were sick unto death (vv. 17–22), and those who were in a storm at sea (vv. 23–32). Each stanza is shaped in a similar way: an account of their adversity, their cry to the LORD, and his deliverance; then a summons to praise the LORD for his *hesed.* The report of the cry and deliverance (vv. 6, 13, 19, 28) and the summons to praise (vv. 8, 15, 21, 31) are identical in each stanza. In verses 33–41 the theme of the "wonderful works" in the summons is taken up in a hymnic recitation of ways in which the LORD reverses the conditions of human beings so as to gladden the upright and silence wickedness (v. 42; I Sam. 2:4–8; Job 5:11–16). A concluding admonition com-

344

mends all that has been said about God and human beings as evidence of the LORD's loyal love (v. 43).

Two patterns unite the psalm. The first is that of the imperative hymn in verse 1 with its summons to thankful praise supported by a statement of the basis and content of the praise (God's goodness, loyal love). The complete pattern is repeated in verses 8 and 15, giving concrete instances of the LORD's loyal love. The imperative element is extended in verse 22 to say *how* thanks is to be made (with sacrifices of thanksgiving and the recitation of the LORD's deeds in song) and in verse 32 to say *where* the ritual is to be observed (in the assembly of people and elders). Verses 33–41 "tell of his deeds in joyful song." This pattern maintains the purpose and function of thankful praise throughout. The imperative is both a call to praise and a way to praise. All the redeemed are to hear the call and join in the song to exalt the redeemer whose loyal love has saved them.

The second pattern is that of the narrative of deliverance from the prayer of thanksgiving (see Introduction, sec. 5.3). Its report of past trouble, of the cry to the LORD and of the LORD's deliverance, is used to identify each of the four groups of the redeemed. It tells what redemption is and how the group came to be the redeemed. The worshipers are those who have lived through a story of salvation. Motifs from these narratives reappear in the hymnic recitation (vv. 33–41) to connect it with the reports and to identify the deeds recited in verses 33–41 as also saving acts for which thankful praise is to be given (compare vv. 4 and 33, vv. 5 and 36, vv. 4 and 40, and vv. 7 and 36). This second pattern maintains the focus on what kind of praise is intended—not just the exaltation of what God is like and typically does—but thanksgiving for what he has specifically done for those who are gathered.

2. The four groups of the redeemed are doubtless intended to represent by illustration all those who have experienced the redemption of the LORD. They add to the force of the psalm as a general summons to and offering of thanksgiving. They do give a brief catalog of the kinds of adversity in which prayer for help would be made. It is interesting that among the prayers for help in the psalms are a number appropriate for sickness unto death (e.g., Pss. 6; 38; 88), perhaps one for the imprisoned (Ps. 142?), none for hunger and thirst except the hunger and thirst for God (e.g., Psalms 42—43), and none for peril at sea (see

Jonah 2). The list seems to be one that suits the experiences of the exiles and the dispersion. The language of God the redeemer and the returnees as the redeemed is characteristic of Isaiah 40—66 (e.g., Isa. 51:10; 62:12; 63:4; 35:9). The redeemed have been assembled from the dispersion (v. 2). The types of adversity must symbolize the corporate experience of the people who had wandered hungry and thirsty for the salvation of God "in the great desert of the world"; had been imprisoned in the exile, had been terminally ill because of their transgressions, and "had been all but swallowed up in the vast sea of the nations" (Kirkpatrick, pp. 637f.). Thus the psalm can be understood as praise for Israel's second salvation history. In the Gospels, Jesus feeds the hungry in the wilderness, frees those possessed from the bonds of demons, heals and forgives the sick, and quiets the storms (Mark 6:30–44; 3:20–27; 2:1–12; 6:45–52). His wonders correspond to those of the Old Testament salvation history and so extend it and identify with it. The four cases are really open paradigms of deliverance into which any and all who have benefited from God's saving work can enter. Hunger and thirst, darkness and gloom, sin and affliction, storm and sea all belong to the general symbolic vocabulary with which the redeemed portray the trouble from which they have been saved. The psalm as a whole is the great summary song of thanksgiving for salvation by all the redeemed.

3. Liturgically and theologically, the psalm is an exaltation of the *hesed* of the LORD. *Hesed* is the obvious theme named in the opening summons as the content of praise (v. 1), reiterated in the repetition of the summons as the reason for praise (vv. 8, 15, 21, 31), and proposed at the conclusion as the subject for thought by the wise (v. 43). The conclusion makes it clear that the psalm is not only exaltation but as well exposition of *hesed*. It is praise that is to be thought about, reflected on; it is a text from which the wise can learn about the *hesed* of the LORD. Its performance has an instructional effect; through it the upright "see" the *hesed* of the LORD and rejoice, while the voice of wrong is silenced (v. 42).

a. Hesed is the goodness of the LORD as redeemer. It is at once an everlasting attribute of the character of God and occasional in its manifestation in saving actions. The psalm uses the singular (v. 1) and the plural (v. 43) of *hesed* as a way of indicating that the eternal reality of God is revealed and can be known in specific temporal acts of salvation.

b. The psalm uses the term "wonderful works" for these acts of *hesed,* the term that is generally used as the summary term for God's saving acts on behalf of the whole people. This is one of the ways in which the psalm teaches that God's *hesed* is present in the deliverance of individuals as well as in the salvation history of the people. The one is an event that is part of and like the larger history. Individual salvation and corporate salvation are held together as the wonderful work of the LORD's *hesed.*

c. In Psalm 107 the *hesed* of the LORD is a matter of his relation to those who cry out to him. No other basis is mentioned than the goodness of the LORD and the cry of those in trouble. The beneficiaries of the wonderful works are "the sons of men" (vv. 8, 15, 21, 31). No special relation between Israel and the LORD is cited. Twice those in trouble suffer as sinners (vv. 11, 17), but in the other two cases they come into trouble inadvertently. What sets the *hesed* of the LORD in motion in every case is the cry to the LORD in trouble. The psalm sees the *hesed* of the LORD manifest in salvation completely in this way. It elevates the prayer for help, the voice of dependence on God, to the central place in the relation to God. Even in the hymnic section (vv. 33–41), where the cry is not mentioned, God's way with human beings is described in terms of his help for the hungry and needy (vv. 35–39, 41) and by contrast his action against the wicked and against princes (vv. 33–34, 40). The wicked and the strong do not depend on God.

In all these ways the psalm teaches the congregation and its members to understand themselves as the redeemed. Most of all and first of all they are the sinners and the helpless whose cry to God has been answered by his *hesed.* Most of all and first of all they are to thank the LORD with praise of his *hesed.* We are the hungry and thirsty who have been fed. We are the bound who have been liberated. We are the sinners deserving death who have been given life. We are the fearful before the terrors of existence who have been given hope.

Psalm 108: On Edom I Cast My Shoe

1. Psalm 108 is composed of material found in two other psalms. Verses 1–5 correspond to Psalm 57:7–11 and verses 6–13 to Psalm 60:5–12. Psalms 57 and 60 appear to be the earlier contexts for the material. The portion from Psalm 57 is

347

a section from the second part of that psalm, and the portion from Psalm 60 includes the last verse of its first part and its entire second part. See the comment on Psalms 57 and 60.

2. The psalm composed by combining the two portions of material has a literary structure with divisions that obscure the seam between the two sources. It begins as an individual hymn of praise sung in the midst of the nations exalting the LORD as the God whose steadfast love is higher than the heavens (vv. 1–4). Then a petition appeals to God to manifest that exaltation and answer with the salvation of his beloved (vv. 5–6). At this point it is obvious that the individual is representative and speaks with and for the national community. The answer sought in the petition is given in the form of a divine oracle in which the LORD declares his dominion over the territory and peoples that largely composed the old Davidic kingdom. The psalm concludes as a corporate prayer for help, with a lament over the inability to turn the claim of the oracle into actuality (vv. 10–11), a petition for help from God (v. 12), and an assertion of confidence in God (v. 13).

3. The psalm is a prayer of the people of God at one time in their historical career when they understood that only God can establish the reign of God in the world. Human help is worthless; God alone can bring his promises to fulfillment. Verse 10 is probably the clue to the interest and purpose of the psalm. It may reflect the unresolved conflict of the postexilic community with Edom, whose treachery contributed to the fall of Jerusalem. See Obadiah and the comment on Psalm 137.

Psalm 109: They Curse but You Bless

1. Psalm 109 contains the most vehement of the imprecations in the Psalter. This prayer for help in first person style opens with a plea for an answer from God (v. 1a) and a supporting account of the activity of accusers who attack the psalmist without cause (vv. 1b–5). A long curse occupies the center of the prayer (vv. 6–20). It is composed of an invocation of a narrative of disaster that begins with a hopeless trial, runs through total ruin, and reaches its climax with the eradication of the very family of the one who fails to do *hesed* and drives the poor and needy toward death; so should curse become the destiny of the one who loves to curse instead of bless. After the long curse, there is a second petition (v. 21), supported by a description of

348

the psalmist as "poor and needy" (vv. 22–25), and a third petition (vv. 26–29), followed by a concluding promise of praise
(vv. 30–31).

2. The situation assumed by the prayer is that of an innocent person on trial for his life, literally or socially (vv. 6, 31; see
Introduction, sec. 5.2.2). He is surrounded by "accusers" (vv. 20,
25, 29); the term means hostile witnesses rather than plaintiff
or prosecutor. In the process of the trial they lie about him and
voice wishes for his doom rather than his welfare (vv. 2–3, 17,
28). The prayer seeks a saving answer of blessing from the LORD
that will establish innocence and turn the curse of the accusers
back on them (vv. 20, 28). Because the curse is spoken against
an individual rather than a group ("he," not "they"), some interpreters take verses 6–19 as the quotation of the curse that the
accusers invoke against the psalmist (so NRSV). It is understood
here as a formulaic curse against each of the accusers, a case of
the typical prayer against the enemy that they themselves be
caught in the trap they have laid (e.g., 10:2). The other opinion
does not, in any case, relieve the theological problem of the
curse; the psalmist prays that it fall upon the accusers, whoever
says it in the psalm (v. 20).

The use of a countercurse by those who pray in the psalm
is a part of the larger problem of the enemies and the prayers
against them.

3. This psalm is based squarely on the theology of the LORD
as one who shows *hesed* to his servant (v. 28) when he is "poor
and needy" (vv. 16, 22, 31; see Introduction, sec. 6.16). The
psalmist has done *hesed* to his accusers by acting in love for
their good (vv. 4–5). But there is no *hesed* from them (v. 16) in
return. He must depend on the *hesed* of the LORD to whose
character it belongs to show *hesed* to the poor and needy
(vv. 21–26). Threatened by the curses of men, the psalmist seeks
the blessing of God. The one who prays believes also that cursing and blessing are finally in the power of the LORD. Foes may
curse, but God decides upon whom the word of disaster will fall.
The LORD can bless in the place of human cursing. See the story
of Balaam in Numbers 22–24.

Perhaps this is where the psalm touches a profound theological theme of Scripture most clearly; in the face of the human
proclivity to bring about a curse, the LORD wills blessing (see
Gen. 12:1–3 and related texts).

Judas opposed the one through whom God blesses all the

349

world, and for that reason Acts 1:20 sees the fulfillment of the psalm's curse in his fate (compare v. 8 with Acts 1:20).

Psalm 110: Sit at My Right Hand

In using the Apostles' Creed to declare its faith, the church says over and over again, "I believe in Jesus Christ . . . who sits at the right hand of God." In this declaration a spatial metaphor is used to speak about the identity and role of Jesus in relation to God. The statement is the nearest approximation the church has to an answer to the question of where Jesus is now. The place of this phrase in the confessions is based on the repeated citation of Psalm 110:1 in the New Testament (Matt. 22:44; Mark 14:62; 16:19; Luke 22:69; Acts 2:34–35; 7:55; Rom. 8:34; Eph. 1:20; Col. 3:1; Heb. 1:3, 13; 8:1; 10:12; I Peter 3:22). These citations together with other references and quotations make it the psalm most used in the New Testament. All of them put the psalm to christological use. In the early church it was regarded as the messianic text above all others. Luther called it "the main one [psalm] to deal with our dear Lord Jesus Christ" (Luther, 13:228). The prominence of Psalm 110 in traditional Christology raises the question of what there is in the psalm as an Old Testament text that makes it so significant.

1. Reading the psalm as prophecy about the messiah is an approach based on the purpose for which the poem was written. In style and content it is similar to sayings of the prophets. The psalm has two parts, each opened by a formula for introducing oracular sayings by prophets and seers: "The LORD says" in verse 1 and "The LORD has sworn" in verse 4. Each formula is followed by a saying spoken in divine first person style, a style characteristic of prophetic speech. Each divine saying is followed by a declaration of the LORD's policy with respect to the addressee (vv. 2 and 5–6); style and content again are characteristic of prophecy. (Verses 3 and 7 are obscure, verse 3 because its text and meaning are uncertain and verse 7 because who and what are spoken about are unclear.) The title calls the poem "a psalm," and it may well have been a piece sung in liturgical ceremony by one of the prophetic singers who were part of the professional personnel at the temple.

350   The psalm is "messianic" in one of the senses that that term can have in relation to Old Testament texts. The addressee is a Davidic king whom the prophet calls "my lord" because the

prophet is the king's servant, a subject and an official in the royal retinue. Psalm 110 shares a number of features with Psalm 2 and is one of the several psalms composed for use in rituals concerning the kings of Judah (the comment on Psalm 2 is assumed in the following discussion of Psalm 110). In the Old Testament the Davidic king was the primary figure who was called "the messiah," that is, the one whose investiture in office involved anointing. The first divine saying (v. 1) is an instruction to assume the throne, and the whole was probably composed to be used in inaugural ceremonies for the king at the point of his enthronement.

2. The psalm, then, served as a text for the installation of a king in office. In the culture in which it was used, the office was far more than a position; it was a status in the very order of things that endowed a person with identity and powers. The person was endowed with the identity of the office. The esoteric and sometimes violent things said in the psalm are traditional cultic speech and express the ways kingship was understood in Judah. It is an Israelite adaptation of what was said to kings in the nations round about in the conduct of inaugural rituals. The divine sayings in verses 1 and 4 are the crucial words by which God through the prophet bestows office. Whoever sat at the right hand of a king on formal occasions was next to him in rank and identified as the official empowered to represent the king and carry out his policy. Verse 1 is authorization for a Davidide to assume that position in relation to the divine sovereignty. Perhaps he was invited in the ritual to a throne to the right of the ark, the sacred symbol of the divine king himself. The appointment to priestly status in verse 4 is part of the royal installation. In the traditions of kingship observed in Canaan, the king was the principal mediator between God and people. Melchizedek, the ancient predecessor of the Davidides in the kingship of Salem (old name for Jerusalem), was such a king (Gen. 14:18–20). This second saying is a permanent and irrevocable ordination to be the one who draws near to God on behalf of the people as a function of the royal office.

The declarations in verses 2, 5–6 are promises that develop the theme "until I make your enemies your footstool," a metaphor for subjecting them to the Davidic king's rule. (On the promise of rule over kings and nations, see the comment on Psalm 2, sec. 3.) The metaphor even found visual expression in thrones of the period in the use of carved figures representing

351

defeated foes in pediments and supports for the thrones (Keel, pp. 254–255). The enemies and foes of verses 1–2 are the kings and nations of verses 5–6, and "until" of verse 1 looks forward to "the day of his wrath," the time when the LORD acts to quell resistance to his sovereignty. Kings and nations are considered foes, not because of some specific quarrel or conflict with Israel, but for the very fundamental reason that their rulers were not appointed by the LORD, owe fealty to other gods, and institutionalize in their government an exception to the LORD's worldwide dominion. For that reason they will be judged and defeated by God. The brutal description of slaughter by the LORD on "his day" is the same visionary tradition of the LORD as warrior (see Exodus 15) that is heard often in the prophetic declarations about the LORD's way with rebellious nations (Isa. 5:15; Jer. 9:21; Ezek. 32:5–6).

Verses 3 and 7 fit into these promises and rituals in some way, but their meaning is uncertain. Recent versions of the Bible translate verse 3 differently and add disclaimers of uncertainty about its meaning. Is verse 5 a picture of a victorious warrior, pausing to drink and rising in confidence, or does it refer to some unknown ritual drink of sacred water? For the purposes of preaching and teaching, it is best to admit that the perspicuity of Scripture is missing here.

The psalm, then, is a prophetic text for an event—the incorporation of a person into a primary role in the order of God's way with the world. The event took place in the sacred proceedings of enthronement; the oracle gave the event the reality of God's authorization and purpose. The language of the oracle is symbolic and ideal because it speaks about the merging of a human political office and divine sovereignty. What is said to the Davidide transcends the actualities of Judah's international relations because it is visionary language about the LORD's purpose to use this kingship as an instrument of his sovereignty over the kings and nations of the world. In their every claim to autonomous significance and power, they are in the prophetic vision "enemies." For the religion of Judah, the recurrent enthronement of a Davidic king was the answer to the question of meaning in history, to the question about what power is in control and what is to come of the disastrous hostility among the powers of the world.

Taken by itself, a text like this can be seen as a claim to the divine right of a king, a political ideology that has troubled so much of history, and as a use of religion by politics as its own propaganda. In the context of the Old Testament, however, the psalm is qualified in two important ways. First, there is the prophetic critique of the kings of Israel and Judah that says essentially that royal politics must serve and be judged by the policy of God that they announce and that the person of the king and his relation to God are as important as the office in which he is installed. For the prophets the conduct and character of the king were evaluated by the ideal of the office that God had given him.

Second, there is the eschatological reservation. Prophets, in the light of the failures of contemporary kings, began to speak of an ideal king of the future who would fill the messianic office. The apocalyptic movement saw the victory of the LORD over kings and nations as the climax of a drama played out in a cosmic and universal context. The day of the LORD's wrath became the climax to world history. By the time Psalm 110 was incorporated in the Book of Psalms, it no longer represented a cultic actualization of Israel's faith in the relation between God's sovereignty and the nation but instead an eschatological vision of God's coming kingdom. The location of Psalm 110 in the last third of the Book of Psalms may point to the way it was understood by those who gave the Psalter its final arrangement. It is a sequel to Psalm 89 and its lament over the rejected Messiah. It is a prophetic voice repeating and affirming the promises of Psalm 2 that the LORD will claim the nations through the Messiah. Until God has defeated his enemies, the Messiah is "seated on the right hand" (see Mays, " 'In a Vision': The Portrayal of the Messiah in the Psalms," p. 6).

3. It is against this background that the christological use of the psalm in the New Testament is to be understood. In a story told in the Synoptic Gospels (Matt. 22:41–45 and parallels), Jesus uses verse 1 in a way that assumes that he and his contemporaries understand that the oracles in Psalm 110 concern the Messiah. The references to Jesus' session at the right hand of God (listed above in the introductory paragraph) use the psalmic phrase, "Sit at my right hand," as a kind of code to speak about the outcome of the career of Jesus. The phrase draws on the cosmic and eschatological understanding of the psalm to define the christological "now." While Jesus' words and deeds, his life and death and resurrection, belong to the past, his session belongs to the present. It is this present "location" of Jesus

that holds his past in relation to the believer's ongoing life. In I Corinthians 15:25, Paul uses "until I make your enemies your footstool" to set the eschatological horizon of the christological present. Paul identifies the "enemies" as "every rule and every authority and power" and last of all "death." Hebrews is right on target in its use of verse 4 when it differentiates the priesthood of Aaron from that of Jesus because the priesthood of Jesus is a messianic, a royal priesthood, the priesthood of the Son (Heb. 1:3; 5:6; 7:17, 21). The priest on whom believers depend is the Messiah at the right hand of God. The New Testament uses the psalm as language to speak about the true identity and role of Jesus in the coming kingdom of God. It is using the psalm in the way the church will later use philosophical ontological language. It is no surprise that Psalm 110 was debated on such occasions as the Arian controversy.

4. Psalm 110 has come to be used widely in the liturgy on the day of our LORD's ascension. It puts that celebration, and every confession of faith in the ascension and session of our Lord, in the perspective of the Old Testament witness to the office that Jesus occupies. The poetic and prophetic vision of the psalm lets us see the enthronement of Jesus at the right hand of God as the great theological reality of the christological present. The crucified and risen Jesus has been "installed" as the one for whom and through whom God is working out his purpose in the world.

The psalm holds the enthronement of Jesus in relation to the question of political power in the world. It insists that the office of Jesus concerns nations and rulers. The office of regent of God has been filled and fulfilled by a person who was not a ruler and had no national constituency. In the Old Testament the messianic king had his first context in the LORD's use of Israel's national history as a declaration of his sovereignty. In Jesus the messianic office completes the prophetic and apocalyptic direction and is consummated in the context of cosmic and universal history. But that is not an abdication of any claim on the nations and rulers of this world. Instead, it is an assertion that every nation and ruler is subject to the royal judgment of Messiah Jesus. His ways and values are final. No claims to "divine right" or any semblance of it by rulers, dictators, presidents, and so forth, are valid. The goal of world history is not to be found in the destiny of any people or nation, nor is the governance of any leader the way to it. Indeed, all the nations who think and dream of autonomous dominance and destiny are in that way enemies of the coming kingdom of God and its Messiah, including the one in which we happen to live. The psalm is a repeated invitation to think that way about the question of power in the world.

The psalm is also a declaration to the church about its relation to the Jesus whose session at the right hand of God it confesses. Jesus is King! The meaning of that symbolic word makes absolute claims on the obedience of the community and its members. His instructions and commands are not subject to approval and revision. They are, rather, provisions for us to acknowledge the coming kingdom of God in living. The psalm, with its focus on the relation between Messiah and nations, puts special emphasis on the command of Jesus to the church to make disciples of the nations (Matt. 28:20). That mission is the action assigned to the church in relation to these "enemies" of the Christ. Faithfulness to that assignment is the way the church shows it believes its confession and knows that all power in heaven and earth is given to Jesus. The meaning of the symbol "King" also makes an absolute claim on our trust. Because it is Jesus who is divine King of the universe, we may take hope. After all, the King is the eternal priest. God turns no other face to his people than the visage of mercy and grace and love known through the person Jesus. That person in all the particularity known through the Gospels is at God's right hand. "We have this as a sure and steadfast anchor of the soul" (Heb. 6:19).

Psalm 111: Delight in the Works of the LORD

Psalms 111 and 112 belong together. They are a pair, a kind of diptych. They correspond in form and language and deal with complementary topics. Psalm 111 is praise of the works of the LORD by those who fear him. Indeed, it teaches that fear of the LORD is a work of the LORD. Psalm 112 is a commendation of the way and life of those who fear the LORD. The theme of Psalm 112 is set by the last verse of Psalm 111. The close relation between the two is discussed in the comment on Psalm 112.

1. Psalm 111 is a song of praise introduced as the hymn of an individual. Like other hymns composed as the voice of an individual (8; 103; 104; 145; 146), it deals with a subject that is

355

the concern of the community. The psalm begins with an introductory declaration of thankful praise (v. 1), and the rest of its lines delineate that for which the LORD is to be praised. The concluding measure (v. 10c) emphasizes the song's function as praise; the psalm is composed and said as participation in praise that lasts forever. The external form of the hymn is set by the Hebrew alphabet (Introduction, sec. 5.6.2). The first word in each measure begins with the next letter of the Hebrew alphabet, twenty-two measures for twenty-two letters. In the Hebrew text each measure is composed of three words or bound expressions. The scheme obviously imposed constraints on the choices of words used in the psalm's composition.

2. The psalm nevertheless has an internal design. After the introductory verse 1 announces what is happening in the psalm, verse 2 establishes the theme of the whole; its subject is the great works of the LORD. Thematic words of the subject are repeated in verses 3, 4, 6, and 7 (work, wonderful deeds, works, works of his hands). The psalm describes the works of the LORD as twofold, keeping the covenant of promise (v. 5) and establishing the covenant of commandments (v. 9).

Verses 3–6 give a terse, allusive rehearsal of Israel's foundation story from Egypt to the promised land, drawing on the story as it is told in Genesis through Joshua. "Wonderful deeds" (v. 4) is a code word for God's marvelous acts in delivering and establishing his people (Exod. 3:20; 34:10). "Gracious and merciful" (v. 4) are the attributes the LORD gave himself in the wilderness when Israel made the golden calf (Exod. 34:6; see the comment on Ps. 103:8). The provision of food recalls the gift of manna and quails in the wilderness (Exodus 16; Numbers 11). The gift of the nations as Israel's heritage (v. 6) refers to the settlement in the land (e.g., Deut. 4:21; cf. Ps. 2:8!). The covenant mentioned in verse 5 is the LORD's covenant promise of a future existence as the people of the LORD in the land of Canaan (105:8–11; 106:45); in all the divine works that compose Israel's story the LORD was "remembering his covenant."

Verses 7–10 turn to the LORD's work of establishing a covenant of commandments. According to verse 7, faithfulness and justice are also the work of the LORD (see NJPS, REB; NRSV translates the nouns as adjectives, faithful and just, and makes them attributes of the LORD's work). The LORD provides for faithfulness and justice through the precepts given as terms of his covenant. The covenant of verse 9 is the covenant of Exodus

356

19—24 and Deuteronomy, whose content is the law (cf. Pss. 25:10; 103:18). Just as the LORD sent redemption to his people, he also commanded his covenant forever (v. 9). Salvation and law are together the works of the LORD, and the psalmist wants them kept inseparably related. Israel's life in the land is the reality of redemption. Faithfulness and justice are also objective realities, works of the LORD, in the faithful precepts. The faithfulness and justice in the faithful precepts are to be performed with faithfulness and uprightness (v. 8). In this way the works of the LORD are to become the work of his people. We note here that this idea that the people of the LORD enter and participate in the works of the LORD through the performance of the commandments is central for Psalm 112.

3. Up through verse 9 the psalm carries out the intent declared in verse 1; it is thankful praise for the works of the LORD and does not cease even in dealing with the precepts of the LORD to tell of what the LORD has done. But at the end, just before the final statement, "His praise endures forever," there is a plain didactic statement about human life that seems at first reading out of place. "The beginning [point of departure, basis, first principle] of wisdom is the fear of the LORD." This thesis about wisdom appears elsewhere in the Old Testament three times, always in the literature of instruction classified itself as wisdom (Prov. 1:7; 9:10; Job 28:28). The psalmist knew the principle and cited it here. One might suppose that the psalmist needed a word that starts with the letter R, and the Hebrew word "beginning" is *re'shit.* The formal and substantive connections of the statement with its contexts, however, argue against such a loose relationship. The preceding clause says of the LORD, "Holy and awesome is his name" (v. 9c). In Hebrew, "awesome" and "fear" are forms of the same root; fear of the LORD corresponds to the fearsome reality of God. The following clause says, "All who do *them* have a good understanding." The plural pronoun "them" is a synonym for "fear of the LORD," but it is plural because its antecedent is the "precepts" that express faithfulness and justice (v. 7). For this psalmist, fear of the LORD is the precepts, the motive to do them, and their performance (see "fear of the LORD" in 19:9). The psalmist belongs to the circle of those who believe that wisdom comes from learning and living *torah,* the instruction of the LORD (see the comment on Psalms 1 and 19). Wisdom for this circle goes beyond the distillation of experience into guidance about the prudent way

357

to conduct life. It begins with knowing and obeying the LORD. It is the instruction of the LORD, not the teaching of the sages, that produces a "good understanding." Verse 1 of Psalm 112 is a direct sequel to the conclusion of Psalm 111. So in the context in which it stands, the didactic principle in a quite profound way speaks of the works of the LORD. For this psalmist, wisdom is not mere prudence, however sagacious and useful, nor is it a theory about the meaning of the world, an explanation of what is and how it works. Wisdom rises out of and is given through the twofold works of God.

4. The term "fear of the LORD" does not appear until the end of the psalm, but the term is, in fact, the name of the piety whose praise the psalm is. This praise is offered "with the whole heart" (v. 1) because it is only the undivided heart that truly fears the LORD (86:11–12). The psalm's setting is the congregation who are the company of the upright, who as those who fear the LORD still receive their daily bread as the manna given Israel in the wilderness (vv. 1–5). Their chief delight in life is the works of the LORD, and they "study" them. "Study" is a translation of *darash* ("seek, search out"); for *darash* with statutes, laws, and precepts, as object, see Psalms 119:45, 94, 155; I Chronicles 28:8; and Ezra 7:10. Compare Psalm 1 with its commendation of those who delight in the *torah* of the LORD and meditate on it day and night (v. 2). The psalmist seems to know the works of the LORD through Scripture that can be studied. What is to be learned forms an important dimension of the psalm itself. The work of the LORD is honor and majesty, the attributes of a sovereign (45:3; 96:6; 145:5). The LORD is gracious and merciful (v. 4). The LORD remembers his covenant of promise forever and commands his covenant of precepts forever (vv. 5, 9). His name is holy and awesome (v. 9). The study of the works of the LORD nurtures the fear of the LORD in the heart. In this piety, Scripture study and praise inform and strengthen each other. Such praise, like the righteousness of the LORD, endures forever (vv. 3, 10).

Psalm 112: Delight in the Commandments of the LORD

358

Psalm 112 opens with a "Hallelujah" and a beatitude, thus combining at its beginning genres of praise and instruction.

That is one important clue to its character and meaning. It corresponds to Psalm 111 in ways that identify it as a companion and sequel, another directive to its interpreters. The comment on Psalm 111 is assumed in the following discussion.

1. The relationship between Psalm 112 and Psalm 111 is obvious and close. Their external forms are similar. Psalm 112, like Psalm 111, is an acrostic poem of twenty-two measures, each measure beginning with the next letter of the Hebrew alphabet. The measures tend to be composed of three Hebrew words or bound expressions. Words, phrases, and even an entire clause from Psalm 111 are repeated in Psalm 112. "His righteousness endures forever" from Psalm 111:3 occurs twice in Psalm 112 (vv. 3, 9), in Psalm 111 said about the LORD and in Psalm 112 about the one who fears the LORD, a major clue to what is going on in the repetitions. Compare 112:1a with 111:5a, 10a; 112:1b with 111:2b; 112:2b, 4a with 111:1b; 112:4b with 111:4b; 112:5b with 111:7a; 112:6b with 111:4a; 112:7b with 111:1a; 112:8a with 111:8a; and 112:9a with 111:5a.

2. Psalm 112 takes its subject from its companion. Psalm 111 ends with the statement, "The beginning of wisdom is the fear of the LORD," and Psalm 112 begins with a responding, "Happy is the one who fears the LORD." Psalm 111 is praise by the upright who fear the LORD, and Psalm 112 describes how the fear of the LORD works out in the life of the upright. The description is cast in a form appropriate to the subject; the psalm is composed as an expanded beatitude, the "happy is the one who . . ." saying, whose typical purpose is to commend and encourage a kind of conduct. On the beatitude as a type, see the comment on Psalm 1, sec. 1. The introductory beatitude (v. 1) characterizes those who fear the LORD as those who delight in his commandments; these are the same upright who in Psalm 111 delight in the works of the LORD (v. 2) and do his precepts (v. 10). The rest of Psalm 112 expounds the congratulatory word "happy" by listing ways in which the life of the upright is blessed. Even where the psalm seems to speak of conduct that deserves the blessing rather than of the blessing itself, the conduct is meant by the psalm to be a blessing that comes from delight in the commandments. That the upright are gracious and merciful (v. 4), are generous lenders and deal justly (v. 5), and are generous with the poor are all characteristics and actions that come with delight in the

359

commandments, blessings that enrich life because of that on which life is centered. The concluding verse 10 contrasts the conduct and fate of the wicked with that of the righteous. The wicked see in the blessing of the righteous a rebuke to their own folly and failure to live in the fear of the LORD. Psalm 112 shares fundamental features with Psalm 1. Both are expanded beatitudes, commend delight in the law, describe the blessing of the righteous, and contrast the transience of the wicked with their secure permanence.

3. The dependence of Psalm 112 on Psalm 111 is a literary signal that the second is meant to be read, interpreted, and used in relation to the first. The relationship guides the interpretation of Psalm 112 in important ways.

a. From Psalm 111 we know that the delight in the LORD's commandments is a dimension of delight in the works of the LORD. Psalm 111 holds the LORD's work of establishing his people and his work of establishing his precepts in unity. So the commandments are not viewed as legalistic requirements. They are the word of Israel's savior. That is why the righteous can and do delight in them. They are a medium of the LORD's relation to the upright. Through them the LORD reveals and bestows the gift of the wisdom that makes for life. The commandments are grace, not a burden.

b. Psalm 112 makes an astonishing list of claims for the well-being and well-doing of those who delight in the commandments. The claims are even more astonishing when they are compared to what is said about the LORD in Psalm 111. The righteous are described in Psalm 112 in terms of the praise of the LORD in Psalm 111. The righteousness of both endures forever. Both are said to be gracious and merciful, to do justice, to give. Both have created a memorial by their works and way. As the work of the LORD is honor and majesty, so is the horn of the righteous exalted in honor. See the list of repetitions in section 1 above. This correlation between the praise of the LORD and the commendation of the upright is the psalm's way of teaching that the works of the LORD can and should shape the life of the righteous. The correlation is not a presumptuous claim that the upright independently and autonomously realize goodness. Rather, by their fear of the LORD, they enter into the works of the LORD, who works on and in and through their lives. Their goodness is godliness.

c. Taken on its own and out of its present context, Psalm 112

360

is a wisdom poem whose purpose is instruction. It could well be located in the Book of Proverbs. But clearly it was composed by the same psalmist as Psalm 111, or at least as a companion to it. It is paired with a hymn of praise and equipped with an introductory "Hallelujah." Its genre and purpose are thereby revised. Its composer believes so profoundly that the works of God take shape in the life of the righteous that for the psalmist the commendation of the latter becomes also the praise of God. This theological conviction is an important reason for the inclusion of psalms of instruction in the Psalter and the basis of their use as praise (Introduction, sec. 5.6.)

Psalm 113: Who Is Like the LORD Our God!

Psalm 113 is a hymn of praise composed as a symmetric statement of the majesty and mercy of the LORD. After a call to praise (vv. 1–3), the body of the hymn describes the exaltation (vv. 4–6) and the condescension (7–9) of "the LORD our God." In the Hebrew text it opens and closes with a "Hallelujah."

1. The summons contains elements of a theology of praise. First, it is the servants of the LORD who are to praise. "Servants of the LORD" are those who have been claimed by his choice of them and who respond by calling the LORD "our God." Their chief service is to praise the LORD, and their worship is therefore called "service." Second, the name of the LORD is the mode of God's presence for the congregation. The god who cannot be comprehended in space or seen by human eye is graciously available in the name that bears his identity and all that goes with it. The name is the way the transcendent god who is not "there" in any ordinary sense is nonetheless present for those who worship. They praise the name by making it the subject of praiseful sentences. Third, the one who knows no limits must be offered a praise unlimited by time or space. Each act of praise must be understood as participation in a universal and everlasting activity.

2. Verses 4–6 declare the incomparability of the LORD, a theme focused in the rhetorical question in verse 5a (cf. Exod. 15:11; Micah 7:18). The theme appears always in hymnic contexts and frequently in the Psalms (see 18:31 and texts cited there). Other peoples in the ancient Near East claimed incomparability for their gods, so in the praise of Israel the attribution of uniqueness to the LORD has a polemical and confessional

tone. The claim serves its true purpose only as a statement of faith that no other power ranks with the LORD as that to which obedience and trust are offered. The theme is used in the Old Testament to evoke various divine excellencies of the LORD. Here it points to the LORD as the incomparable sovereign who is above the nations and above the heavens, beyond and superior to every sphere of power. Yet the one who is beyond all is concerned with all below. The LORD is a god who is capable of both transcendence and immanence, free to make himself high and low. No human power can do that. No other god does that. The combination of opposites is beautifully depicted in the portrait of the victorious warrior who comes as gentle shepherd in Isaiah 40:9–12. The combination into one personality is a hallmark of the God of the Bible.

3. Verses 7–9 cite two illustrations of what happens when the Incomparable acts upon closed continuities of finite human life. Each case shows both the compassion of the LORD for the helpless and the change that occurs in human arrangements because of his mercy. In the larger society the underclass of poor and weak are raised to rank with the preeminent of the upper class. In the nuclear unit of the larger family the wife who has no status because she is barren is made the joyous mother of children. Israel knew about the LORD's concern for the helpless from its history with the LORD and from his instructions given in law and prophecy. They knew stories of his help to barren women whose children played crucial roles in the nation's past—Sarah (Gen. 11:30, 17), Rebekah (25:21), Rachel (29:31), Samson's mother (Judg. 13:2–3), and Hannah (I Samuel 1—2). And they marveled at the surprising reversal of extremes that God's intervention brought about in the circumstances of life (I Sam. 2:4–8; Pss. 18:27; 107:39–41; Job 5:11–16). The sovereign of the universe interfering in and setting right the societies and families of human beings—that is, says the psalm, the incomparability of the LORD.

4. Psalm 113 is the first in the cycle of psalms called the Hallel (Psalms 113—118), which were sung at all the joyous festivals celebrated in early Judaism. The cycle found a special place in the liturgy of Passover, and one can see why Psalm 113 makes an appropriate overture to the celebration of Exodus. In that context, it is Israel who are poor and weak and prompted by the prophets; they can think of Zion as the barren woman who needs the help of the LORD (Isa. 54:1). The God who uses

his superiority to help the inferior, who interferes in the settled circumstances of society and family to create new and surprising possibilities, is precisely the God praised at Passover. The psalm would have been the first sung by Jesus and the disciples in the celebration of their last supper, with profound implications for the occasion and its consequences.

5. In traditional commentary the psalm has been interpreted as a connecting link between Hannah and the Virgin Mary, with good intratextual reason. The psalm contains both phrases and motifs that appear in I Samuel 2 (compare especially vv. 2, 4–8). Mary's Magnificat does the same; in joy over the child in her womb she praises the God whose power is expressed in a compassion that reverses the fixed extremes of the human order (Luke 1:46–55). For the apostle Paul it is clear that this incomparable God is at work in the incarnation (Phil. 2:6–8) and the creation of the church (I Cor. 1:26–29).

Psalm 114: The Past and the Presence

Psalm 114 tells how the LORD came to be the holy Presence in the midst of Israel and, at the same time, how the God who is sovereign of the whole earth came to have this particular people as his dominion. It is thus a kind of poetic etiology of the situation assumed by all the psalms.

1. The psalm accomplishes all of this in only eight lines with measures composed in a nearly perfect synonymity. The lines come in pairs. The first pair (vv. 1–2) connects Israel's exodus from Egypt with Judah's becoming the place where Israel's God has the sanctuary that represents his dominion over Israel. The portrayal of the one as procession constitutes the other as culmination. The second pair of lines (vv. 3–4) reports the effect of Israel's going out on the very structures of the world. Sea and River Jordan fled as if defeated in battle; mountains and hills jittered like startled sheep. The third pair of lines (vv. 5–6) turns the report into questions that ask why this happened. What was it in Israel's going out that provoked such reaction? The questions are a foil for a final pair of lines (vv. 7–8) where an answer is given in the form of a summons to the world itself. The LORD, the God of Jacob who turns rock into water, was present in Israel's exodus. It was that Presence that sea and river, mountains and hills, "saw." So, let the very earth tremble before the Presence that owns Judah's sanctuary!

363

In spite of the gravity of its subject, the tone of the poem is exuberant, almost playful. There is a mood of celebration and victory in it. In style and format it is not like the usual hymn of praise. The summons to react to the LORD's presence is its only hymnlike feature. The first six lines tell only what Israel did and became and what sea/river and mountains/hills did. No wondrous works of God are reported. The pronouns in verse 2 even lack an antecedent, unless the "Hallelujah" at the end of Psalm 113 goes with Psalm 114, which is a likely possibility. The psalm is composed to build suspense over the meaning of what it tells about until the suspense is resolved at the conclusion. The compositional strategy argues that what is told and the Presence belong together inseparably. Verse 8, with its reference to marvelous deeds in the exodus story, even returns to the memory evoked by the telling. The psalm is designed for occasions when the connection between story and Presence is crucially important. The psalm evokes that connection with allusions and motifs and rhetoric in a way that poetry alone can achieve.

2. The psalm's reference to Israel's foundational story is unmistakable. The departure from Egypt and the settlement in the land mark its beginning and its conclusion (vv. 1–2). The recession of the waters of the Red Sea and those of the Jordan are paired as corresponding events (vv. 3, 5; cf. Josh. 4:23–24). The provision of water in the wilderness is remembered as illustration of divine providence when the people were on the way (v. 8 and Exod. 17:6; Num. 20:10). But the story of the foundational events is sketched in a way that evokes also another scenario, the basic pattern of the cosmogonic myth of the ancient Near East. In its various versions, the divine warrior enters into combat with primeval hostile forces (sometimes "sea and river"), wins a victory, and gains possession of the holy mount where he builds a sanctuary to represent his dominion. The psalm sketches Israel's foundational epic as a version of the scenario. (For other uses of the scenario, compare Ps. 77:11–20; Exod. 15:1–18; Hab. 3:2–15; see Introduction, sec. 6.2). Allusions to the scenario disclose the revelatory significance of the story. Its events constituted a theophany, a manifestation of the God of the cosmos doing battle in the world to establish the people and place that represent his dominion. It was the presence of the divine warrior that sea and river "saw." The reaction of mountains and hills is a standard feature of theophany reports

364

(18:7; 29:6; Judg. 5:5). The Presence in the sanctuary in Judah is that of the sovereign God of the universe. The God of Jacob is ruler of the world (compare the presence of the sovereign deity as focus of the world's praise in 96:11–13; 97:4; 98:4; 29:1–11).

3. As the second in the Hallel sequence of psalms sung at the joyous festivals of Judaism and at Passover (see Psalm 113), Psalm 114 had a crucial role to play in connecting place and people with meaning and hope. The celebrants are reminded that they have come to be where and who they are by the self-manifestation of the God who rules all peoples and times. Their story belongs to the plot line of the coming kingdom of God. The church has read and sung the psalm in the light of what happened in Judah and Israel through Jesus Christ. It sees in his death and resurrection yet another and a climactic theophany of the divine rule in which the Presence assumes a new relation to people and place.

Psalm 115: Where Is Their God?

Psalm 115 is a psalm for the congregation in the midst of a world of nations who trust the gods they have made.

1. Though the psalm contains different styles and forms, it has a clear literary and theological unity. It begins as a prayer composed of petition (v. 1), complaint (v. 2), and an assertion of confidence in the God of Israel (v. 3). In a time when the nations scorned the competence of their God, the congregation implores the LORD to glorify himself and they confess their faith in his unqualified sovereignty. They counter with a polemic against the idols that the nations make and trust (vv. 4–8). In a threefold exhortation Israel and the Aaronic priests and all who fear the LORD (the categories are not mutually exclusive) are instructed to trust the LORD as their help and shield (vv. 9–11). Blessing upon Israel's priests and the pious is promised (vv. 12–13) and invoked from the LORD, maker of heaven and earth (vv. 14–15). Concluding praise of the LORD as sovereign over heaven and earth (v. 16) is offered by the congregation, who contrast themselves in their unending lively praise (v. 18) with the dead, who do not praise the LORD (v. 17). The changes in style of discourse may indicate that the psalm was composed as a liturgy, but the whole could

365

be recited by a voice speaking for and to the congregation. The concluding "Hallelujah" shows that the psalm has been included in the Psalter as a psalm of praise.

2. The entire psalm is concerned with the problem of faith identified in verse 2. The nations say, "Where is their God?" "The nations" are the peoples whose power and plan seem to determine history; they are forms of human social organization that do not serve the LORD. Sometimes by their stratagems and always by their very existence they put in question trust in Israel's God. On "the nations" as an adversarial context for faith, see the comment on Psalms 2 and 9—10. The nations' scornful question is a taunt that belongs to the rhetoric of war and social conflict in which adversaries try to undercut their opponent's confidence in their god (see 79:10 and 42:3, 10; and the comment on Psalm 42, sec. 2). The form of the lament in verse 2 gives the impression that it speaks of a continuous predicament for the congregation. Their apparent insignificance as players in the world of nations prompts doubts. They are tempted to measure their God by their sense of insignificance and inadequacy. If they do, they become people who in a sense make their own god, the great danger of religion that this psalm addresses. That is why the opening petition appeals to God to act for God's own sake. "We are a people," the congregation says, "whose identity and destiny are defined by our trust in you, and you are called in question! As an activity of your steadfast love and faithfulness to care for us, give yourself glory, reveal yourself as sovereign. Not for us, but for your own sake!" This psalm knows that the glory of its God is its first and profoundest need.

3. The psalm leads the congregation in a liturgy of speaking and listening that addresses its predicament in three ways. First, the psalm is a polemic against "their idols" (vv. 4–8). The derisive listing of organs that don't work is simply a satirical comment on the obvious. Their idol can't do anything; he is impotent, a fraud. The polemic views the idols as the very deities that the nations trust (v. 8). The view belongs to the strategies of polemic; it is hardly an accurate and fair description of the religions of the nations around Israel who made images to be representations and symbols of the person and presence of their deities (see Levenson, *Sinai and Zion,* pp. 109f.; Von Rad, 2:219). The caricature is really based on the uncompromising bias of Israel's religion against the use of anything made by human work (v. 4) as a medium of mind and

366

spirit in relating to God. How can what human beings *make* rightly represent "the *maker* of heaven and earth"? The polemic, moreover, believes that the gods represented by the images are as impotent and unreal as their copies (note the point of the polemic in Isaiah 40—55, e.g., 44:9–20; 45:16–17). The claim that those who trust what they made become like what they trust (v. 8) does touch on a profound truth. If human work sets the boundaries for the reach of trust, then those who trust are limited to possibilities of their own making and the power of their own potential. Finally, it is important to remember that the polemic in the psalm is liturgy meant for the ears of the congregation (note the use of this polemic in 135:15–18). Its purpose is to chasten and correct the congregation itself in support of the first and second commandments. The temptation to forms of faith that fashion their own representations of God is never absent from religion, even that of the congregation. The congregation needs to be taught in its liturgy a language that debunks the gods we make.

4. Second, the psalm leads the congregation to speak of their God in a way that expresses the LORD's absolute difference from gods made by human powers. The psalm uses the term "heavens" in a symbolic way that turns the spatial sense into theological meaning. In response to the taunt of the nations, the psalm teaches the congregation to say, "Our God is in the heavens; all that he wills he does *('asah)."* The sentence (v. 3) verges on a doctrinal statement in which heaven is not so much a matter of above in contrast to below as the sphere of absolute sovereignty. Place means power. The LORD's doing/making is purely a matter of will, a total contrast to idols made *('asah)* by human hands who can do nothing. Lest it be imagined that "the heavens" represent some reality alongside God, the psalm uses the famous phrase "maker"*/'asah)* of heaven and earth" (also in Pss. 121:2; 124:8; 134:3; see also Gen. 14:19, 22). The phrase is one of the fundamental titles by which the God in whom the church believes is identified in the Apostles' Creed, and in saying the creed we need to be reminded of the function of the title in its psalmic context. For the reader of Scripture, the phrase is a reference to Genesis 1:1 and its "in the beginning" before anything called heaven and earth existed. "Heaven and earth" forms a word pair that comprehends all reality. Nothing exists that the LORD did not make *('asah).* Even the heavens, the realm "where" God is, was made by God.

367

The LORD is related to but transcends all that exists; the LORD transcends even the work of his sovereignty in the world. Verse 16 continues the line of thought. The heavens are the LORD's heavens because he made them. The LORD's gift of the earth to human beings is a disposition of the LORD's sovereignty. The earth as the realm in which human beings will and act is an institution of the LORD's rule in the sense that Psalm 8 speaks about. The psalm thus prompts those who say it to grasp the great irony of any derogation of their God; the very capacity of the nations to make gods and discount the congregation's God is a potential bestowed by the maker of heaven and earth. Whether in faith or unfaith, all exist and act within the realm of the LORD.

5. Third, the psalm summons the congregation to live by the knowledge of God given in the history of salvation. It exhorts the congregation to trust the LORD who has always been "their help and shield" in the long story of their life in the midst of the nations (vv. 9–11; "help and shield" belong to the protection vocabulary of the psalm; on shield, see Ps. 3:3 and on help, Psalm 121). The congregation is to remember that the LORD has always "remembered" Israel, and they can be confident in praise and prayer that the LORD will bless the congregation with "increase" (vv. 12–15). The promise to Abraham stands! The power that the congregation must and may live by in the midst of the nations is the power of the promise. By its blessing they will be sustained.

Psalm 115 belongs to the cycle of psalms used in the liturgy of the joyous festivals and Passover. See the comment on Psalm 113, sec. 4. It will prompt the interpreter's imagination to think of the psalm being sung as part of the sequence of Psalms 113—118 by Jesus and the disciples in their observance of Passover.

Psalm 116: What Shall I Return to the LORD?

1. Psalm 116 is a song of thanksgiving (Introduction, sec. 5.3). It is the praise of one whose prayer for help has been answered. The heart of the song is a narrative of salvation. In a past predicament of life-threatening trouble (vv. 3, 10, 11), prayer was made (v. 4); the LORD heard and helped (vv. 1, 2, 6, 8, 16). In the prayer, vows of sacrifice and praise were made. Now the one who has been saved comes to the temple bringing

sacrifice (vv. 13–14, 17–19) and singing this song as thanksgiving to the LORD (vv. 8, 16) and as testimony about the goodness of the LORD (vv. 5, 6, 9, 15) to the people of the LORD.

2. In the Greek and Latin Bibles, Psalm 116 is divided into two psalms. Verses 1–9 appear as Psalm 114 and verses 10–19 as Psalm 115. In liturgical practice also, parts of the psalm have been used separately. There is, however, a literary design that unifies the song. Something essential is missing when its performance begins, for instance, with the question, "What shall I return to the LORD for all his bounty to me?" (v. 12). The song is composed of three parts (so L. C. Allen and others). The refrain-like repetition of vv. 13b–14 and vv. 17b–18 marks the end of the second and third parts. Verse 7 is a corresponding conclusion to the first part. This rare exhortation of the self to return to its rest is probably a rhetorical statement of an intention to visit the temple as the sphere where God's presence provides relief and security. Each part thus concludes with a performance statement: going to the house of the LORD (v. 7); offering of libation, the cup of salvation (v. 13; cf. the "drink offering" in Numbers 28); offering of thanksgiving sacrifice (v. 17). Each part is introduced by a report of salvation combined in chiastic arrangements with statements of praise. In verses 1–2, that pattern is praise, report, report, praise; in verses 8–9, the pattern is evident in the motifs of death, stumbling feet, walk, and life; in verses 15–16, the pattern of motifs is death, servant, servant, deliverance. This design emphasizes the reports of salvation (vv. 1b–2a, 8, 16b). All the elements of the narrative of salvation (trouble, prayer, answer, result) are present only in the first part, thus its importance for the other two parts.

3. The affliction that was the occasion of prayers for God's help is not identified. Instead, it is characterized. For the purposes of the song of thanksgiving, it does not much matter what the clinical or social particulars were. The song does not diagnose or record; it interprets and gives meaning. It uses a vocabulary that renders experience in terms of the soul's relation to God. The thematic word is "death." This terrible, final word is used in all three parts of the psalm (vv. 3, 8, 15). The psalm speaks of death in a special way that is found in a number of prayers for help and thanksgiving psalms. This way of speaking of death has two aspects, both of which are present in this song. First, death and Sheol are equated; the phenomenon and

369

the place are used as synonyms (vv. 3, 8, 16b). Together the condition of being dead and the location of the dead are conceived as a sphere of power that invades the realm of the living and entangles life. Where distress and its tears, and anguish and its stumbling, grasp the living, one is already in the sphere and power of death. The living are not dead, but death conditions their living. By speaking of death in this way, the psalms give expression to the mortality that is unveiled by serious trouble. They assign the ultimate category of death to affliction to reveal the possibility it evokes, the possibility of not being there. The psalms then can speak of God's help as deliverance from death, salvation from its sphere and power, the liberation of life. (See 30:3; 33:19; 49:15; 56:13; 86:13; 89:48.) There is a telling illustration of the interpretive use of death language in Psalm 88:3-7. Consult the comment on Psalms 30 and 88. By casting neediness and divine help in the categories of death and life, the prayers reveal what is always at stake in human dependence on God.

Second, death and Sheol are viewed as a condition and place that is beyond any possible relation to God. The dead are not reached by God's steadfast love, nor are songs of thanksgiving heard in Sheol. Death and Sheol are used phenomenologically to describe the final helplessness of the dead rather than interpretively of the living (see 6:5; 30:9; 115:17; and the comment on Ps. 88:10–13). This way of speaking about death is present in verse 15. The death of the faithful is "costly," or "grievous" to the LORD, because when they die their praise is silenced and their witness in the land of the living is lost to God. There is an evident tension between these two ways of viewing and speaking about death. If God rescues his faithful from the power of death, how can the realm of death lie beyond the help of God? The psalm as a song of the Old Testament celebrates the deliverance of life from the snares of death, but it is subject to another reading that will emerge in time, a reading in which it speaks of salvation from the final death.

4. The song opens with a declaration of love for the LORD (v. 1). The declaration attracts attention because of its uniqueness in the Psalter; there is only one direct parallel, the opening of the great thanksgiving Psalm 18, where a different verb is used. But no other declaration so rightly responds to salvation from death! Indeed, "I love the LORD," as introductory theme, defines the whole song as a declaration of love. The psalm says

[handwritten: Lord's supper]

what form thankful love takes. First, love "calls on the name of the LORD." The lover calls out to the beloved by name. The set expression is used for prayer (v. 4) and praise (vv. 13, 17). The name invokes the person and the presence of the other; its use is a confession of belonging (cf. 79:6; 80:18). Second, love finds rest in the beloved (v. 7). The soul freed from distress and anguish goes where the beloved is to shelter thenceforth in God's keeping. Third, love lives always as if in the presence of the beloved (v. 9). It keeps the LORD always present to memory and will (cf. 16:8). Fourth, love fulfills its vows to the beloved (vv. 14, 18). Promises made are promises kept. Faithfulness in the keeping of promises binds the saved to the savior. The promises are kept in public, "before all the people of the LORD," as a witness of love to the one who is loved. (On vows and their role in praise, see the discussion in Westermann, *Praise and Lament,* pp. 75–78.) Fifth, love serves the beloved. A servant is one whose life is defined by belonging to another (see Introduction, sec. 6.16). "LORD, I am your servant, the child of your serving girl" (v. 16; cf. 86:16) is a declaration of unconditional, everlasting fealty and devotion.

5. Though Psalm 116 was composed for use by an individual in a service of thanksgiving, it came in time to play a liturgical role in celebrations of the larger community. The text of the psalm required an occasion when a cup and a sacrifice figured in the rituals of celebration. It found two closely connected occasions. The first was the celebration of Passover. Psalm 116 is the fourth in the sequence of psalms, "the Egyptian Hallel," that were read during the course of the Passover meal (see Psalm 113, sec. 4). According to the Mishna (*Pesachim* 10:1–9), reporting on the way the meal was ordered, four cups were raised and blessed in its progress. Psalms 115—118 were recited in connection with the fourth cup, which supplied a ritual reference for "the cup of salvation." The recitation of the psalms was introduced by a thanksgiving to the LORD, who "brought us from bondage to freedom, from sorrow to gladness, and from mourning to a Festival-day, and from darkness to great light, and from servitude to redemption" (*Pesachim* 10:5). Introduced in this way, the psalm's language is turned into thanksgiving for the salvation celebrated at Passover. The psalm becomes the thanksgiving of every participant in Passover who thereby acknowledges that each was delivered in the salvation of Exodus.

[handwritten margin notes: 8 then / 4 cups]

371

The second occasion was the Lord's Supper. In the development of Christian liturgical practice, Psalm 116 came to be used in the celebration of eucharist, in particular and always as the psalm connected with the Communion observed on Holy Thursday. Paul called the Communion cup "the cup of blessing that we bless," an expression associated with the Passover cup in Jewish tradition (I Cor. 10:16). Through the death and resurrection of Jesus Christ, Passover was transformed into eucharist, and Psalm 116 was reread as a thanksgiving for the promise of life given in Jesus' salvation from death. The psalm becomes the voice of Jesus and the congregation, the one providing the cup and sacrifice, the other united by them with him in his death and resurrection.

Psalm 117: All You Nations

1. This is the littlest psalm of all, but it thinks on a grand scale. The little hymn has hardly graduated from the class of the one word "Hallelujah," but it takes a giant step in its development. A worship that includes the world's population is envisioned. The nations and their many peoples are called to praise the LORD. The hymn is composed in the pattern of the imperative hymn of praise (Introduction, sec. 5.5.2). It is just long enough to use both elements of the pattern; verse 1 is the call to praise and verse 2 is the reason for and content of the praise.

2. We expect the praise of the LORD to be the concern of God's people. But in the psalms the call to praise the LORD is addressed to a whole list of possible participants. Psalm 148 puts virtually the whole list together in one psalm and the list includes literally the world and those who live in it. Here it is the nations and peoples of world history who are invited. That says something fundamental about the praise of the LORD. It is not complete, not what it should and must be, until all are drawn into its faith and joy. Until the answer of praise arises from every people on the globe, the LORD is not recognized as one and only God. The speech of the world does not correspond to the reality of the world. Moreover, the nations of the world will not have found the center that holds, the centering focus of values and life. They will remain, as now, chaotic, warring, disastrous, confused, working their own destruction, until they hear the call and find beyond themselves the power that unites in truth and joy. The call to the nations reaches toward an eschatological

horizon when nationality and race shall be comprehended and healed in a larger unity that can be constituted only by the faith spoken in praise of God.

3. Why should the nations praise the LORD? This psalm and those who sing it give a surprising answer that hardly seems an appropriate reason for those invited. Other psalms give other reasons; Psalm 86:9, for instance, says the LORD is maker of the nations. But here the theological basis of the call is salvation, not creation. The steadfast love *(hesed)* and faithfulness *('emet)* of the LORD are the vocabulary with which the people of God speak about the salvation of the past and the hope of the future. In his way with us God's fidelity to his election and covenant has prevailed over our frailty and failure. His *hesed* has triumphed. The triumph of the LORD's fealty to us is the truth about our future because the faithfulness of the LORD is everlasting truth about him. In that salvation and hope the nations may see the revelation of God. This triumph of God in the salvation of his people is the same reason given the world in psalms like Psalm 98 and in the prophecy of Isaiah 40—55 and in the missionary gospel of Paul. In Romans 15:11 the apostle quotes Psalm 117 as scriptural testimony to expound God's purpose in Jesus Christ (note vv. 8–9).

4. When Christians say and sing this psalm they remind themselves that the praise of God is complete only when they intend to praise in concert with all people. And they bear witness to the world of the triumph of grace over them in fervent hope that the nations—their own as well as others—will find in that triumph the work of the one whose being is the center that heals and holds. It is a psalm for any LORD's day, but it is especially appropriate for the celebration of Worldwide Communion Sunday.

Psalm 118: The One Who Comes in the Name of the LORD

Psalm 118 concerns the coming of One who comes in the name of the LORD. The One who comes makes the most marvelous statement: "I shall not die but live." The celebration that the LORD did not give him over to death is hailed as the day the LORD made. Because of his deliverance, the people of the LORD renew their confession that the LORD is God. Who is this? The psalm itself gives us his identity only as a question. Interpretation must press on through the text to occasions of the use of the psalm to find a name.

1. The psalm is composed of two sections (vv. 5–18 and 19–28) set within a framework of hymnic praise (vv. 1–4 and 29). It begins with a formulaic imperative hymn used for general thankful praise of the LORD (v. 1; see Introduction, sec. 5.5.3 and the comment on Psalm 136). The imperative of the hymn is continued in a threefold litany of invitation to Israel, priests, and God-fearers to say, "His steadfast love endures forever" (vv. 2–4; the list of the three groups comprehends the worshiping community as in Pss. 115:9–13 and 135:19–20). The psalm ends by repeating the opening formula of praise (v. 28). This framework gives a first definition of the whole. It is a "giving thanks" to the LORD for the goodness of his steadfast love *(hesed)*. The term "steadfast love" is not used in the body of the psalm, but what is reported there is introduced by the framework as a demonstration of the LORD's *hesed* that calls for the thanksgiving of the entire community.

In the first section, an individual praises the LORD by testifying to the community. The theme of the testimony is stated in verse 5: The singer was in distress and called on the LORD for help; the LORD answered and rescued him. This brief narrative of salvation is the hallmark of the individual song of thanksgiving (Introduction, sec. 5.3.1). Elements of the narrative recur in verses 13 and 18. The section has three parts; each bears witness to the significance and effect of the LORD's salvation. The parts are held together by repetitions and by an interweaving of motifs. The pair of doublets in verses 6–9 contrast reliance on the LORD with either threat or help from human sources; the motif "mortals" (Hebrew man) connects the two. The name of the LORD links verse 5 to the doublets, appearing in each poetic line. The second part (vv. 10–14) begins with three similar lines, featuring the motif of "the name of the LORD." The motif identifies the real source of strength that enables the celebrant to resist the power of surrounding nations, a motif that continues the emphasis on human powers in contrast to the LORD. Verses 13–14 assert further that the celebrant's survival and strength came from the LORD, who in his deliverance became his salvation. The third part (vv. 15–18) picks up the motif "salvation" from verse 14 in "songs of salvation" (NRSV, "victory") and repeats the song three times. The motif of the song is "the right hand of the LORD," another expression for the LORD's power exercised among human beings and nations. The motif "die/death" appears in verses 17–18 to describe the true measure of the salvation. It means life and the praise of the LORD in contrast to death.

The second section (vv. 19–28) is composed of an alternation of voices between the individual and the community and a succession of different types of speech. It begins with a request for entrance (v. 19) that finally introduces the motif "give thanks" from the framework; the motif then occurs in verses 21 and 28 as an inclusion that says what is going on in this section of the psalm; the celebrant is now with the community performing the ritual of thanks. After permission to enter (v. 20), the celebrant twice addresses thanks directly to the LORD (vv. 21, 28). Between these thanksgivings the community acknowledges the salvation as a wondrous act of the LORD by its own praise (vv. 22–24) and prays for its own salvation (v. 25). The One who comes in the name of the LORD (cf. vv. 10–12) is blessed (v. 26). Corporate confession (v. 27a) is made, and ritual instruction (v. 27b) is given.

2. The psalm seems to have been composed for a service of thanksgiving. The service has its center in a person who has survived a dangerous crisis. This celebrant stands at the gates of the temple courts accompanied by a congregation of worshipers. There he gives testimony of his escape. After a ritual of admission, he enters with the company of worshipers and gives thanks to the LORD in a liturgy in which congregation and ministers of the sanctuary participate. The parts of the liturgy can be assigned in this way: the request for entry and the thanksgivings, to the celebrant (vv. 19, 21, 28); the admission, the blessing, the confessional declaration, and ritual instruction, to ministers of "the house of the LORD" (vv. 20, 26–27); and the corporate praise and prayer, to the congregation (vv. 22–25). Other guesses about the distribution of parts are possible. What is clear is that the celebrant speaks, is addressed, and is spoken about. Verse 27b seems to refer to some ritual in connection with the altar; just what is not known.

3. Who the person was who "comes in the name of the LORD" and from what particular crisis he had escaped is left as open and indefinite, as is usually the case with individual prayers for help and songs of thanksgiving. The language used in verses 10–12 and 15–16 suggests the military threat of

375

surrounding nations. But the way such language is employed generally in liturgical settings raises a caution about drawing confident conclusions from it. The psalm was not composed to answer historical questions; instead, it is wholly concentrated on portraying what happened to the celebrant as the work of the LORD. That is the significant identity of the celebrant; he is one who comes in the name of the LORD.

Everything the celebrant says about himself is a way of saying that "the LORD has become my salvation" (vv. 14 and 21). He does describe himself as actor in verses 10–12; he resisted all the surrounding nations ("resist" instead of "cut off" as in NRSV depends on the Septuagint's translation of a verb of uncertain meaning). But what he achieved was done "in the name of the LORD," that is, as the representative of the LORD and by the power of the LORD (see 54:1; 20:5, 7; and David's declaration in his fight with Goliath, I Sam. 17:45). Indeed, he was hard pushed and would have fallen without the LORD's help (v. 13). The deliverance in reality was gained by "the right hand of the LORD" (vv. 15–16; cf. 20:6; 60:5; 98:1; 108:13). "The right hand of the LORD" is a figure for the intervening action of God in human affairs. The circles of the righteous understand what happened in the celebrant's rescue and they themselves celebrate it in a song of salvation. The celebrant even takes his own salvation as the occasion for giving testimony and instruction by contrasting the power of God with human power. The most wonderful truth a person can know is: "The LORD is for me." The cry of the celebrant was an expression of that knowledge, and the LORD's answer its vindication (cf. 56:9). That knowledge opened up the marvelous possibility of living by faith instead of fear. Human strength is vulnerable to the power and threat of adversaries. It is better not to rely on it, even if it belongs to princes. The LORD's help is a power in which one can take refuge from both human weakness and human threats. "If God is for us, who is against us?" (Rom. 8:31). On this contrast between the power of God as the possibility of faith and the power of man as the cause of fear, see the comment on Psalm 56 and the other texts cited there.

The use of this contrast between the LORD and the human being as introduction to the celebrant's testimony puts an interpretive perspective on two other important items. "All nations" (v. 10) as a term for the celebrant's adversaries continues the human pole of the contrast. The term does not refer to some specific international coalition. It is, rather, a collective category for the history that human beings make in opposition to the role of the LORD manifested in the history of the people of God. See the equation of mortals with nations as opposition to God's reign in Psalm 9:17, 19–20, and "all nations" in Psalm 59:5, 8. The second item is the righteous who rejoice over the LORD's salvation (v. 15) and are qualified to come through the gates of righteousness (vv. 19–20). As is usually the case in the psalms, the rightness of the righteous is a matter of relation to the LORD. The morality involved is a morality of trust. The righteous are right in knowing that it is better to take refuge in the LORD than trust in mortals. They fear the LORD (v. 4), rejoice over his victories (vv. 15–16), and cry out to him for salvation (v. 25). As a group, they are the opposite of the wicked nations that do not fear God (9:17).

4. Everything the congregation says also portrays the celebrant's deliverance as the work of the LORD. "This is from the Lord," they say, because they view it as "marvelous," the unexpected, wonderful kind of happening that could only be the LORD's doing (v. 23). A proverbial saying is used to evoke the marvelous character of what happened: "The stone that the builders rejected has become the chief cornerstone" (v. 22). The saying may be a proverb with a single, simple point, the reversal of what was expected. The deliverance of the celebrant was as much a surprise as finding that a stone cast aside by builders as useless turned out to fit exactly as the cornerstone, the most important component of the building. But the sentence must have been chosen or coined to characterize the deliverance in more than its element of the unexpected. The celebrant was surrounded by those who hate and reject him (v. 7). Why was he rejected? In the theological reasoning of psalmic theology, it was because he was there in the world in history "in the name of the LORD," as one who came as representative of the LORD and in the power of the LORD. Clearly the deliverance of the celebrant is of the greatest importance to the congregation. By it the LORD has "made a day," created a special time and occasion whose content and character are determined by what happened (v. 24). It is a time for the community to rejoice and be glad. It is a reason for the community to pray and hope for its own salvation (v. 25). It is a day when the congregation can renew its central confession of faith: "The LORD is God." In the blessed one who comes in the name of the LORD,

377

the LORD has given light in the darkness of the world and its history (v. 27).

5. The more one ponders this complex psalm, the more insistent the question about the identity of the celebrant becomes. Who is the one who comes in the name of the LORD and, with a congregation of the people of the LORD, observes a thanksgiving on the day the LORD made by turning the rejected one into the chief cornerstone? Attempts to answer the question in terms of the original occasion for which the psalm was composed result in a variety of answers. The psalm sketches a theological and liturgical role; it does not name a name. It is only when the psalm is read in connection with some known use that the role can be related to a name.

Psalm 118 is the concluding psalm in the group known as "the Egyptian Hallel," customarily used at the joyous annual festivals and especially in the observance of the Passover meal (Psalms 113—118; see the comment on Psalms 113 and 116). The cycle begins with Psalm 113 and its praise of the LORD as the God who reverses the fixed arrangements of human affairs by lifting up the lowly, needy, and helpless. Psalm 114 tells the story of the exodus as the manifestation of the LORD's rule in the world. Psalm 115 contrasts the LORD as Israel's help to the nations and their gods. Psalm 116 thanks the LORD for deliverance from death, and Psalm 117 calls on all the nations to praise the LORD. Every one of the first five psalms in the cycle anticipates themes and motifs of Psalm 118. The cycle and the occasion provide a combined literary and liturgical context for understanding the psalm as Israel's thanksgiving for the steadfast love of the LORD shown in their deliverance from death. The tradition of the exodus informs and construes the psalm's language. The context also calls attention to a crucial intrascriptural connection with the exodus. Sentences and motifs of the Song of the Sea (Exod. 15:1–18) appear in Psalm 118. The pivotal declaration, "The LORD is my strength and my might; he has become my salvation" (v. 14; see v. 21), is the theme of the Song of the Sea (Exod. 15:2). The song also features motifs of the psalm: the right hand of the LORD (vv. 15–16 and Exod. 15:6, 12), exaltation of the LORD as "my God" (v. 28 and Exod. 15:2*b*), and steadfast love as the specific motivation of the LORD (vv. 1–4, 29 and Exod. 15:13).

But more than the moment of the exodus is remembered in the way the psalm speaks of the LORD's salvation. The psalm's language can include the whole history of the LORD's preservation of Israel in the midst of all the nations, especially the exile and return. When the psalm says, "The LORD punished me severely, but he did not give me over to death," it views the distress caused by all the nations as divine chastisement, a view characteristic of Jeremiah (especially Jer. 30:11; 10:24; 31:18; also 2:30; 5:3; 32:33). The prophets had announced the death of Israel as the LORD's judgment (e.g., Amos 5:2; Hos. 13:1; Ezek. 18:31). But the LORD did not give Israel over to death. At every festival they can praise the steadfast love of the LORD in the faith that "I shall not die, but I shall live, and recount the deeds of the LORD" (v. 17). In trust that the LORD's steadfast love is indeed everlasting, they can pray, "Save us, we beseech you, O LORD" (v. 25) and so commit their future to the LORD's salvation. On Psalm 118 in canonical context, see Mays, "Psalm 118 in the Light of Canonical Analysis."

6. In the New Testament, Jesus is identified as "the one who comes in the name of the LORD." In all four Gospels, Psalm 118:26*a* is used by the crowds to praise and acclaim Jesus on his entry into Jerusalem. As the one who comes in the name of the LORD, he is recognized as "Son of David" (Matt. 21:9), the one in whose coming "the coming kingdom of our ancestor David" is present (Mark 11:9–10), "the king" (Luke 19:38), "the king of Israel" (John 12:13). Clearly the acclamation is understood in the Gospels to be a messianic identification. Jesus is the king in the Davidic succession who comes as representative and in the power of the kingdom of the LORD. This messianic use of verse 26 calls attention to the messianic dimensions of the figure in the psalm. In his conflict with all the nations and in the significance of his salvation for the people of the LORD, the celebrant in Psalm 118 resembles the anointed king of Psalms 2; 18; 20; 21; and 89.

The messianic reading of the psalm not only supplied an identification of Jesus; it offered in verses 22–23 an interpretive allegory of his destiny. In his crucifixion and resurrection, Jesus is the rejected stone that has become the chief cornerstone (Acts 4:11). The verses are cited by Jesus as a Scripture that discloses what was happening in his treatment by the official religious leaders. The judgment they exercised in rejecting Jesus invoked God's judgment against themselves because "the stone" they rejected was the one chosen to become the chief cornerstone (Matt. 21:33–46; Mark 12:1–12; Luke 20:9–19). The way verse 22 is used in I Peter 2:4–8 shows that "stone" has become a messianic cipher in Scripture interpretation; stone texts have been assembled from the Old Testament (Isa. 28:16; Ps. 118:22; Isa. 8:14–15) to testify to what God was doing through Jesus as messiah. Jesus is "a living stone, though rejected by mortals, yet chosen and precious in God's sight." Psalm 118 furnishes a scriptural warrant for taking the very rejection of Jesus as a moment in messianic disclosure. "The stone that the builders rejected has become the chief cornerstone. This is the LORD's doing; it is marvelous in our eyes."

7. In the church's liturgical use of Psalm 118, "the day that the LORD has made" (v. 24) has become the day of rejoicing and gladness over the resurrection of Jesus. In practice, the psalm was associated first with Sunday as the special day of the week for Christians and then, as the observance of the Christian year developed, with Easter as the special Sunday of the year. Used in this liturgical context, the psalm celebrates Easter as the day the LORD has made, and the resurrection of Jesus is hailed as the LORD's doing, marvelous in our eyes. The salvation of Jesus from death becomes the great event by which transformations are worked in those whose lives are centered in him. Read, sung, and heard this way, the psalm becomes the language of the risen Jesus and of his community, celebrating the wonder that God himself has become our salvation through the resurrection.

8. Through the centuries of Scripture interpretation in the church, two points in the psalm have received repeated emphasis. The first is the grateful cry in verse 17, "I shall not die, but live." That is just the reverse of the natural human condition. The normal human predicament is that, because we must die, the expectation of our final negation infects our living in all kinds of conscious and subliminal ways. The church has found in verse 17 the expression of the transformation worked by the resurrection in one's fundamental stance in life. The way in which believers face every threat and crisis and need is colored by the knowledge that God has not given us over to death. "We whose life is hid with Christ in God ought to meditate on this psalm all the days of our lives, Col. 3:3" (Calvin, 4:325).

The second point of repeated emphasis has been verses 22–24, which portray Easter as the day for celebrating God's deed in making the rejected stone the chief cornerstone. These verses teach the church that the risen Christ is the crucified

380

Jesus and warn us against separating Easter from its context in the passion of our Lord. It was not the free choice and approval of the human community that established the crucified as foundation and keystone of God's coming kingdom but God's raising him from the dead (Acts 4:11). He is present in the world as the one contradicted and rejected by every way that human beings go about building their world. The risen Christ is not the acceptable Christ; rather, it is in all the ways that he differs from us that he calls us to the transformations of repentance that answer God's deed in him. Luther, in commenting on verse 22, observed that in the Gospel story, people became angry and condemned Jesus because they did not know how to use him, and then wrote: "It is no different today. The stone is rejected and stays rejected. . . . The builders do it *ex officio,* for they must see to it that their building has no crack, rent, or disfiguration" (Luther, 14:97). The marvelous thing is that the one whom our human instincts and wisdom reject, God has nonetheless, in spite of us and for our salvation, made the chief cornerstone.

Psalm 119: Your Word in My Heart

God is the teacher (vv. 33–39). Creation is the classroom (vv. 89–91, 73). The students are the servants of God (vv. 17, 23, 124f.). The lesson is the "law" of God (vv. 97–100). Learning is the way of life (vv. 9–16). Such is the faith and vision of this longest of the psalms. Psalm 119 is the sequel to Psalms 1 and 19 in topic and outlook. Like the first, it knows the delight of the law of the LORD and the importance of the constant study of it. Like the nineteenth, it knows the inestimable value of the law in all its forms as a life-enhancing power. But in its design it has taken the topic to the limits of literary expression.

1. Psalm 119 is shaped by a formal plan composed of the twenty-two letters of the Hebrew alphabet and a thematic vocabulary of eight terms. The poem has twenty-two sections, one for each letter of the alphabet. Each section is composed of eight lines, whose first words always have the same first letter, that is, eight *aleph* lines and eight *beth* lines, and so on. Each line has one of the terms in the thematic vocabulary; a few variations show a certain freedom in composing the lines (there are two terms in vv. 15, 16, 48, 160, and none in v. 122). The eight terms are "law," "decrees," "statutes," "commandments," "ordinance(s)," "word," "precepts," and "promise" (as

381

translated in NRSV). Again, there are a few variations ("ways" in vv. 3, 37; "paths" in v. 15; "faithfulness" in v. 90). Apparently the poet knew of eight principal terms in the authoritative tradition that named the subject about which he wanted to write. So he used the alphabet to signal completeness and the whole vocabulary to represent comprehensiveness.

The resulting poem of 167 lines has an impressive literary structure that combines a sharp simplicity with constant variation. Within the control of the formal structure, the same thing is said in 167 different ways, in a progression that moves through the alphabet without ever moving from its single subject. The psalm has been called artificial and boring. Such comments are blind to the aesthetic and psychological effect of this combination of repetition and variation. The poem is meant to be read aloud to others or to oneself so that the repetitions guide the hearing and the variations enchant the imagination. It establishes a focus of contemplation and evokes the mood of concentration and submission in which meditation occurs. In liturgical and devotional use, only a part of the psalm, often one eight-line section, is read. Because of the way the parts are composed, each part can stand for the whole, but the whole is needed to reach the effect of fulfillment.

2. The thematic vocabulary is used in a deliberately abstract manner. We are not told specifically to what the terms refer or what their content involves or requires. The first and most frequent term in the psalm is "law" (Heb. *torah*), better translated "instruction" or "teaching." *Torah* is used in the Old Testament vocabulary for sayings and literature that give direction from God (see Psalm 1, sec. 2). It is the comprehensive term; the other terms all name sentences or sayings of various kinds that give instruction. "Decrees," "statutes," "commandments," and "ordinances" usually refer to the requirements and prohibitions found in Exodus—Deuteronomy as the LORD's instruction to the people of the LORD (see Psalm 19, sec. 2). "Precepts" is a specialty of psalmic language with a similar meaning. "Word" as a term for a saying from God is most frequently associated with prophetic material. "Promise" is simply a saying (Heb. *'imrah*), a synonym of "word." The occasional use of ways and paths shows that the list of terms points, not to some one genre of material, but to a function. The list covers whatever functions as instruction from the LORD. *Torah*

could replace the other terms in every line. One and all they refer to the same thing.

There are some variations on the thematic vocabulary scattered through the psalm that are significant for the question of what *torah* includes. In several lines the content of the thematic term refers to what God does for the psalmist rather than what God requires of the faithful. In verse 41 the content of God's promise saying is the saving work of his steadfast love (see also vv. 76, 81, 107, 116, 123). Once, the faithfulness of God is itself the term (v. 90). Several times, the plural noun "ordinances" is used in the singular with a shift in meaning to God's saving justice (vv. 132, 149; cf. v. 156). There is a telling phrase in verse 13 where the psalm speaks of reciting "all the ordinances of your mouth" (also v. 88). The phrase could refer specifically to sentences recorded in the tradition revered by the psalmist as spoken by God. But likely the phrase refers more broadly to what had the status of divine origin and so to what was reckoned as revelation. That is really what is at stake in the thematic vocabulary. All the terms turn on divine communication. The unfailing repetition of the possessive pronoun "your" with every occurrence of the terms emphasizes with an unwearied insistence that what matters is God's use of these modes of language as divine communication. It is with respect to that meaning of the thematic vocabulary that verse 96 makes the amazing statement that while every perfection has its limits, the commandment of the LORD is broad beyond measure. Clearly it is not the limitedness but the inclusiveness of the LORD's instruction that the psalm celebrates.

3. *Torah,* then, is the central theologumenon. It is valued beyond all else because in all its forms *torah* is the medium of the LORD. In the psalm's understanding of God's way, *torah* is the means by which the LORD deals with human beings and they with the LORD. What the hymns and prayers in the Psalter usually say about the LORD is said here about all forms of *torah.* The wondrous works of the LORD are to be found in them (vv. 18, 27). They are the reason and content of praise (vv. 62, 164, 171), and learning them is a means of praise (v. 7). They are the source of comfort in trouble and protection from being put to shame (vv. 50, 31). The psalmist loves the LORD'S commandments (vv. 47, 113), hopes in his ordinances (vv. 43, 49), and longs for his commandments (v. 131). He trusts in God's word

383

(v. 42) and believes in his commandments (v. 66). The enduring word corresponds to the everlasting LORD (v. 89). All that the LORD is and has done is present in and through *torah.* One seeks him with a whole heart by keeping his decrees (v. 2). The psalmist's exaltation of *torah* is in fact his exaltation of the LORD. What he has come to know is that in dealing with the teaching one deals with the teacher.

4. The voice speaking in the psalm is that of a consciousness shaped by many influences, all of them scriptural. The psalmist knows and thinks with the theology and vocabulary of Deuteronomy. The great exhortation of Deuteronomy 6:1–9 to love the LORD by keeping and teaching his words is the central impulse of the psalmist's religion. Jeremiah, Isaiah, and Proverbs are other books that affect his composition. Reflections of their features appear in lines of the psalm (e.g., compare v. 84 and Jer. 15:15; v. 176 and Isa. 53:6; v. 4 and Prov. 3:13–18). All the styles of the principal types of psalms appear in this psalm. The elements of the individual prayer for help predominate; petitions, descriptions of trouble with self and others, assertions of trust, and vows of praise compose most of the psalm. But it begins with beatitudes and employs didactic sentences, thanksgiving testimonies, and hymnic praise as well. In type, the psalm is a montage of other types. The result is not a pale imitation of what is used. The psalmist does not merely copy. His sources have been absorbed by a profound and authentic piety, a devotion to Scripture into whose creativity they have entered. That piety so occupies his mind, leads his thinking, and guides his life that he can speak of himself only in terms of it. The psalm is the voice of a suppliant, a witness, and a teacher. One may pray with it, be converted by it, and learn from it.

5. As prayer, testimony, and lesson, Psalm 119 is the classic text of faith for which Scripture is a form of the word of God. It establishes certain points that are crucial for Scripture piety. Among them are the following:

a. God's instruction in all its forms is important because it is God's, and only because and insofar as God's word is given through the forms. The instruction never has any independent reality, any existence on its own. It is never in the psalm a separate subject. The psalm speaks to God about the psalmist's relation to God and God's way with his servants, and the word of God is spoken about only in that context. The psalm excludes both a Scripture idolatry and a faith that does not depend on the word of God.

b. The word of God calls for both obedience and faith. The right hearing is a faith that obeys and an obedience that believes, both together, as if one response. To hear is to choose the way of faithfulness (v. 30). To hear is also to have a reason for trust and hope (vv. 41, 42). The word commands (v. 4) and the word promises (vv. 81, 82). It allows no piety that takes the form of legalism, nor any that takes the form of fideism.

c. The word of God is given but never possessed. Because it is God's instruction, it is not owned apart from the teaching of God. It is there, objectively available in all the forms of God's communication. But it must be sought and constantly studied in prayer in order to be taught, to learn with the help of God, to receive the gift of understanding (e.g., vv. 12, 18, 26, 125). Scripture piety is faith seeking understanding (v. 66). Every line of the psalm assumes the givenness of the word without ever making anything of the human security of having it in written or fixed form.

d. The instruction comes from God, but it must become part of the servant of God. It must be gathered into the store of the heart, the mind and mentality with which one thinks and wills (v. 11). The heart itself must be converted from all else (v. 36). The word is reason and opportunity for the human heart to be whole (vv. 2, 10, 34, 58, 69, 145).

Psalms 120—134: The Songs of Ascents

1. Psalms 120—134 all bear the superscription "A Song of Ascents." This identification of these fifteen psalms distinguishes them as a collection within the Book of Psalms. The existence of the group as an apparent collection raises a question about its character and purpose. Do the psalms contain common features that unify the group? Are there signs of a meaningful arrangement in their order? Do they as a group combine to serve some religious purpose? Does the superscription offer any guidance for their interpretation?

2. The most likely and widely held theory about the superscription is that "ascents" refers to the journeys made by pilgrims to the three annual festivals observed in Jerusalem (Deut. 16:16). The verb "go up, ascend" is used to speak of the journey

to Jerusalem in one of these psalms (122:4) and elsewhere (24:3; I Kings 12:28; Isa. 2:3; Matt. 20:17; Luke 2:42). The psalms on this theory are a collection for use by pilgrims either in their journey or in processionals during a festival.

3. The collection is unified by some recurring features that are consistent with their use by pilgrims. (*a*) They are as a group shorter than the typical psalm, with the exception of Psalm 132, which seems to play a special role in the collection. (*b*) The names Jerusalem and Zion occur in an unusual density, twelve times in eight of the psalms, and "house of the LORD" in two of the eight, with a possible allusion in another (127:1). (*c*) The name Israel is used in a frequency untypical of the psalms, nine times for the company the songs concern. A number of them alternate between individual and corporate style, so that the song is suitable for individuals as part of a company and a company made up of persons who assemble also as individuals (121; 122; 123; 129; 130; 131). (*d*) Liturgical phrases are frequent: benedictions of blessing and peace (125:5; 128:5, 6; 134:3); summons to confess and hope (124:1; 129:1; 130:7; 131:3); confessional terms (121:2; 124:8; 134:3). (*e*) There is a pronounced interest in the topic of blessing and its vocabulary ("bless," "blessing" in 128:4, 5; 129:8; 132:15; 133:3; 134:3; "peace" in 120:6, 7; 122:6–8; 125:5; 128:6; "good" in 122:9; 125:4; 128:5; 133:1).

4. The collection contains a variety of literary types. There is no generic consistency or dominance in the group. See the comment on the individual psalms. The collection gives the impression that it is made up of existing pieces assembled and sometimes adapted for its purpose. It does seem to reflect the concerns and interests of everyday life that might occupy the minds of lay pilgrims (e.g., neighborhoods, 120:5; daily routine, 121:8; relatives and friends, 122:8; successful work and fruitful families, 127 and 128; kindred living together, 133:1).

5. There is no obvious pattern in the order of the collection, and perhaps none was intended. It is possible to think of Psalm 120 as a song of longing for Jerusalem's peace, Psalm 121 as an approach song, and Psalm 122 as a song on arrival, while Psalm 134 serves nicely as a concluding piece. Within the collection, pairs of psalms seem to be related by common features (121 and 124; 124 and 129; 127 and 128; 130 and 131).

6. The songs do reflect a pattern of convictions and concerns that would be appropriate for a pilgrim piety. Jerusalem

is destination and goal because it is the place where God is present for his people (Psalm 132). Tribes of the LORD go up there to give thanks to the LORD as provided in the covenant order (Psalm 122). They come with two primary concerns, protection and blessing. Their coming is a confession of their dependence on the LORD for the salvation and support of their lives in the past and for the future. Jerusalem is symbol and residence of the One who keeps Israel (122:3; 125:1–2). Jerusalem is the place where the LORD has ordained and promised blessing (132:15–16; 133:3). The pilgrims thank the LORD for protection in the past and pray for and trust themselves to his help in the present and the future (124; 126; 129; and 121; 123; 125; 130; 131). They come from a world that afflicts the faithful (120; 123), seeking the peace that Jerusalem represents (122:6–9). In Zion they hear the call to hope (130; 131) and experience the delight of the family of God assembling in its unity (133). There they bless and are blessed (134).

Psalm 120: I Am for Peace

Psalm 120 is the first in the collection of songs of ascents (see Psalms 120—134). On first reading, it seems an unlikely selection to serve as an introduction of the collection, a strange and difficult little poem. But the declaration, "I am for peace," uses the theme that is repeated in the following songs in the collection (Psalms 120—134, sec. 3). The connection is an important clue to the role of the psalm and its meaning.

1. Short as Psalm 120 is, it contains a variety of kinds of material. Verses 1–2 are a report of an answer to prayer, the kind of report typical of thanksgiving songs (Introduction, sec. 5.3). The verbs in verse 1 should be translated in the past tense (with NJPS, RNAB, REB) instead of the present (NRSV). Verse 2 quotes the prayer. Verse 3 uses the conventional form of a curse ("May God do so to . . . and more also . . ."; e.g., I Sam. 3:17; 14:44) framed as a rhetorical question with an answer in verse 4. Verse 5 is a cry of lament, the traditional sentence expressing distress (Isa. 6:5; Jer. 10:19; Lam. 5:16). The motif whose repetition binds this variety together is "deceitful tongue." It appears in verses 2 and 3 and is implied by the description of neighbors as those who hate peace (v. 6; see the portrayal of enemies as those who betray and oppose peace by their speech in 28:3; 35:20). The report, the curse,

387

and the lament with the repeated motif mark the three parts of the psalm, verses 1-2, 3-4, and 5-6.

2. The designation of the psalm as a pilgrims' song provides a context for its interpretation. It is a poignant expression of pilgrims' pain over the world from which they come. It puts that world in sharpest contrast to the peace they desire and seek in coming to Zion. The distress that forms the background of the pilgrimage is featured in all three parts of the psalm. The first part (vv. 1-2) recalls that distress drove the pilgrim to prayer. It could be endured and surmounted only by dependence on the LORD. The movement to prayer was indeed the first movement of the pilgrimage. The journey to Zion enacts in space the verbal move toward the LORD made in prayer. Lying, deceitful speech is often cited in the psalms as a powerful weapon of social hostility (e.g., 5:9; 10:7; 12:1-4; 31:18; etc.). Lies subvert life; deceit undermines it; the soul is left insecure and damaged. In part two (vv. 3-4) the curse turned into a rhetorical question reflects the depth of the pain caused by the distress. What did such hostility deserve? Would it not be only right that those who were so much "for war" (v. 7) should undergo its pain, the arrows and fire of attack on a city? For those who want war, the reward of war! In an extended lament cry, the third part of the psalm (vv. 5-7) describes the distress as a sojourn among people who hate peace and love war. War is here a metaphor for the hostility of personal adversaries, as in Psalm 27:3. Meshech and Kedar are also used metaphorically; they are the names of alien distant places associated with wars and warring people (see Ezek. 38:2 and Isa. 21:13-17). One could say, "Alas, I live in Meshech and dwell in the midst of Kedar" as a way of characterizing any residence beset with social strife.

3. The pilgrim says who he is and why he is a pilgrim with the declaration, "I am for peace." Peace (Heb. *shalom*) is the central issue of the psalm. *Shalom* in the psalmic vocabulary is the hopefulness and wholesomeness of life when living is knit into the fabric of relatedness to God and others and world. It is the at-one-ness that makes for goodness. The pilgrim's distress comes from having to live without *shalom*. The pain of its lack shows in his all too human invocation of the wages of war on his mean neighbors (v. 4). But the pilgrim is a pilgrim because he is committed to *shalom*. The pilgrim comes to Jerusalem as one who seeks *shalom*. It is the connection between this need and

388

quest and the various ways that *shalom* features in the following psalms that uncovers the introductory role of this first one.
Note the place of peace, its constituent elements and blessing
as its source in the following songs (see 122:6–9).

Psalm 121: Help from the Maker of Heaven and Earth

1. Psalm 121 is the second in the sequence of Songs of
Ascents (see Psalms 120—134). It speaks of a trust that can
sustain the journeys of life and the journey that life is.

The psalm states its theme in an introduction (vv. 1–2) and
then develops the theme (vv. 3–8). Introduction and its exposition are distinguished in two ways: style and controlling motif.
The two poetic lines of the introduction are composed in first
person style, and the motif "my help" appears in both. The rest
of the psalm uses the style of direct address (the second personal
pronouns are all singular), and the motif "keep" is repeated six
times. The theme, a declaration of trust that "my help comes
from the LORD," is thus developed by a series of assurances that
"the LORD is your keeper." Uncertainty about the meaning of
looking to the hills raises a question about the relationship between the two lines of the introduction. Are the hills a region
of danger, perhaps the territory of brigands, and the gesture of
raising the eyes to them an expression of anxiety? Then verse
1 acknowledges a need for which verse 2 gives a resolution.
Another more likely interpretation takes the hills to be the hills
around Jerusalem (125:2), the hilly location of Zion (133:3; cf.
87:1). In Psalm 123:1 the gesture of lifting up the eyes is a
movement of appeal and trust that the LORD is said to answer
with help from the sanctuary on Zion, his holy mount (e.g., 3:5;
20:3). Because of the emphasis on Zion and the use of equivalent repetition in the Songs of Ascents, it is preferable to read
both verses of the introduction as statements of trust; the question in verse 1*b* is a rhetorical foil for the following declaration.
The body of the psalm can be divided into sections of two lines
each. Verses 2–4 share the motif "slumber." Verses 5–6 employ
the image of shade from sun and moon. Verses 7 and 8 deal in
summary terms (all evil, life, going out and coming in, now and
always) and so provide a conclusion for the whole.

2. Does the shift in style indicate that the psalm was com-

posed as a litany performed by two persons, a departing pilgrim and a neighbor or a returning worshiper and a priest? Both settings can be imagined. The psalm does evoke the sense of a journey. The idioms of the foot that does not slip (v. 3) and departing and returning (v. 8) form an interpretive inclusion around the main part of the psalm, with the image of being abroad day and night in the center (v. 6). In its position as the second in the sequence of Songs of Ascents, it can serve as a psalm of approach to Jerusalem when the pilgrim's eyes are lifted up to see the distant hills around Jerusalem. The whole could be recited by a pilgrim or a group achieving a dialogical effect in the performance. In any case, the psalm as Scripture has come to be used as a whole to speak of the larger movement of life itself.

3. The psalm is an unqualified song of trust in the LORD's help. The introduction is a declaration of reliance on the LORD's help, and the rest of the song is composed of promises of help. Israel customarily spoke of the LORD's help in connection with crises of danger for the community (e.g., Deut. 33:7; 26:29; Gen. 49:25; I Sam. 7:12). The help took the form of protection and preservation in the face of overpowering adversaries. The LORD is called Israel's "help and shield" in a compound predicate that emphasizes protection (33:20; 115:9–11). Psalm 124 recalls the LORD's help in times of peril and concludes with a corporate version of the declaration of trust (v. 8) with which Psalm 121 begins. The theme of dependence on the LORD in a hostile world is a recurring feature of the Songs of Ascents (Psalms 120—134, sec. 6). Psalm 121 is like Psalm 23 in many ways. One way is the individual form given to a corporate relation: "my help" as well as "our help." The keeper of Israel (v. 4) is the help of each pilgrim in Israel. But this individualization of the LORD's role as protector does not create an independent individual. It is only as one who says "our help" that the pilgrim can say "my help."

The promises or assurances of help in verses 3–8 do not cite specific dangers or give details of divine assistance. Instead, images, general statements, and the repetition of the verb "keep" (NRSV) in the sense of "guard," "protect" (NJPS, REB) are used to compose a litany of assurance that says no more and no less than that "the LORD will protect your soul everywhere always from every danger." In this, Psalm 121 is a counterpart to Psalm 91, where several of its images of danger and protection are used (shade in v. 1, danger at day and night in vv. 5–6, all evil in v. 10). On the slipping foot as idiom of the trouble of helplessness, see Psalms 38:16 and 94:18.

4. The opening declaration of trust contains a confessional formula that was made especially significant by its use in the Apostles' Creed: "maker of heaven and earth." The formula appears three times in the Songs of Ascents and then in the hymn of Psalm 146. Its first appearance in the Bible is in Melchizedek's blessing of Abraham as an epithet of "God Most High" (Gen. 14:19), a telling clue to its function. "Heaven and earth" is used as in Genesis 1:1 to refer to all that exists. The formula reinforces either the LORD's help (121:2; 124:8; 146:6; see also its use in Hezekiah's prayer when the Assyrians threatened Jerusalem, Isa. 37:17, and in Jeremiah's prayer during the Babylonian siege of Jerusalem, Jer. 32:17) or the LORD's blessing (134:3; Gen. 14:19). It identifies the LORD as one whose power in help and in blessing is unlimited by anything that is. It points to the maker rather than to what is made. In the creeds, the formula is an appropriate explanatory synonym for "almighty." In the Songs of Ascents, the use of "the LORD, maker of heaven and earth" says that pilgrim Israel and every pilgrim in Israel can depend on the sovereign of the universe for help and blessing. As an introductory declaration, Psalm 121:2 says that it is the assurance of the help of the maker of heaven and earth that gives the pilgrim courage to undertake the journey.

5. Because of Jesus' role in God's way with us, the New Testament emphasizes the assurance of the help and protection afforded in Jesus to those who belong to him. He is the good shepherd who protects the sheep given him: "No one will snatch them out of my hand" (John 10; see v. 28). He will be shepherd and guardian of all the souls who trust themselves to him (I Peter 2:25; also Phil. 4:7). The church, in its use of Psalm 121, came to understand the psalm as a testimony to God's providence in the life of believers through Jesus Christ. The Heidelberg Catechism makes a marvelous statement about trust in the providence of God that provides a nice confessional commentary on Psalm 121. To believe in God the Father Almighty, maker of heaven and earth, is, the catechism teaches, to "trust in him so completely that I have no doubt that he will provide me with all things necessary for body and soul. Moreover, whatever evil he sends upon me in this troubled life he will turn to my good, for he is able to do it, being almighty God,

391

and is determined to do it, being a faithful Father. . . . We are to be patient in adversity, grateful in the midst of blessing, and to trust our faithful God and Father for the future" (Questions 26 and 28). Psalm 121 voices and teaches a trust like that for pilgrims in their going out and coming in during life and at the beginning and the ending of life.

Psalm 122: The Peace of Jerusalem

Psalm 122 is the third in the series of Songs of Ascents (see Psalms 120—134). Its first word in Hebrew is the verb for rejoicing. The entire song overflows with joy over Jerusalem—being there, contemplating its significance, and praying for its peace.

1. Jerusalem as site of the house of the LORD is the theme. "House of the LORD," appearing in the first and last lines (vv. 1, 9), forms an inclusion around the whole. The city's name appears in each of the song's three parts. Verses 1–2 compose an introductory statement of joy over being in Jerusalem. Verses 3–5 praise the security of Jerusalem and its central place in Israel's life. Verses 6–9 pray for the peace of Jerusalem. Jerusalem is even addressed directly as if the city were greeting the singers and receiving their benediction (vv. 2, 6–9). First person singular and plural styles alternate, as in several of the other songs, making them suitable for performance by an individual as part of a company.

2. In the sequence of these pilgrimage songs, Psalm 122 serves as a song of arrival. Verse 2 locates the company of pilgrims within the gates of the city. Each of them remembers their gladness as they exchange the mutual invitation to make pilgrimage to the house of the LORD (v. 1; for the conventional form of invitation to visit a shrine, see I Sam. 11:14; Isa. 2:3; Jer. 31:6). The anticipation of a spatial and liturgical nearness to the Presence of God makes pilgrimage a way of joy from its very beginning (84:5–7).

3. The second part of the psalm is a panel of praise of Jerusalem composed of statements about the city of the kind found in the songs of Zion (46; 48; 76; 84; 87). Jerusalem is praised for three reasons. First, it is a place of refuge, "a city built compactly and solidly" (v. 3, REB). Its walls and towers (v. 7) are a promise of protection and stand as visible symbols of the refuge afforded those who trust the LORD (cf. 125:1–2). Praise of Zion as a refuge that stands secure against hostile

powers, cosmic and national, is a feature of the songs of Zion
(46:5–6; 48:4–8; 76:1–6). Second, Jerusalem is a place of praise.
The tribes of the LORD have always gone up on pilgrimage for
the annual festivals, "to give thanks to the name of the LORD"
(v. 4). Indeed, the practice was authorized and required by
covenant law (e.g., Exod. 23:14–17). The requirement of praise
at a common place brought the tribes together in a congregation, in which all knew themselves as sisters and brothers and
as neighbors (v. 8). Pilgrimage is a journey to unity in the LORD
(133:1). Third, Jerusalem is a place of justice (v. 5, taking "for"
as an emphatic rather than a subordinating conjunction, so that
the line is an independent statement with its "there" coordinate with "there" at the beginning of verse 4). The thrones for
judgment were the legal institutions, seats of justice, that had
been established by the Davidic monarchy in Jerusalem (II Sam.
8:15; 15:2–6); the prophets held the city to be especially responsible for the provision of justice in Israel (Micah 3:9–12; Isa.
1:21–23). Pilgrimage season was likely a time when conflicts and
disputes unsettled in the country courts were brought to the
royal officials and their successors in the postexilic period. The
peace of the community depended on the establishment of
justice. Pilgrimage is a journey in search of justice.

4. In the third section, the singer bids the company of pilgrims to invoke peace upon Jerusalem. They are to ask after the
peace of Jerusalem (v. 6a) as if Jerusalem were a person being
greeted by each pilgrim with the traditional question of greeting: "Is it well *(shalom)* with you [name]?" (as in Jer. 15:5; for
the greeting form used much like our "How are you [name]?"
see, e.g., Gen. 43:27; Exod. 18:7). The greeting of peace extends
from verse 6b through verse 9; its repetition in several forms
elaborates what and whom the peace of Jerusalem involves.
Aspects of *shalom* are introduced that will occupy most of the
other songs. The peace the pilgrims wish for Jerusalem is calm
undisturbed by social conflict within and dread of enemies
without (see the Hebrew *shalah* in Prov. 17:1; Job 3:26; NRSV,
"prosper" and "security" in vv. 6b, 7b). It is the well-being that
is composed of both well-doing and doing well (see "good" in
v. 9). This peace involves those who love Jerusalem (v. 6)
enough to make the pilgrimage to seek their peace and its
peace (see the comment on Psalm 120:5–7). It involves the
protected space within the walls of the city (v. 7) where security
is afforded (see 125; 126; 129). It involves sisters and brothers,

393

neighbors and friends (v. 8) who come to Jerusalem to find a harmonious unity they have lost in their ordinary life (Psalm 133). It involves the very house of the LORD, for unless Jerusalem knows peace, the place of the Presence is set in an environment that ignores and denies the purpose of the LORD (35:27).

5. The joy of this psalm and its concern for the peace of Jerusalem stand in tragic contrast with the arrival of the pilgrim who, when he "saw the city, wept over it" (Luke 19:41–44). He too greeted the city, but his greeting was a lament. "If you, even you, had only recognized on this day the things that make for peace! But now they are hidden from your eyes . . . because you did not recognize the time of your visitation from God." Tears and lament disclose how deeply Jesus cared and shared the psalm's concern for the peace of Jerusalem. That his rejection was blindness to the things that make for peace only deepened his sorrow. When we return to the psalm from this scene in Luke we have to read it and sing it tutored by his questions. As we pray for the peace of church and city, have we recognized the things that make for peace? Do we know that unless we go with him, the pilgrimage toward peace will find no Jerusalem?

Psalm 123: The King of Grace

Psalm 123 is the fourth in the sequence of songs of ascents (see Psalms 120—134). For the first time in the sequence the pilgrim speaks directly to the LORD. The song is a prayer.

1. The prayer is composed of two parts. The first is an affirmation of trust (vv. 1–2). The second is a petition (v. 3a) supported by a description of trouble (vv. 3b–4). These elements identify the psalm as a prayer for help (Introduction, sec. 5.2). It combines first person singular and plural styles so that it is appropriate for use by an individual who speaks as a member of a company. In the first part the basic affirmation of trust (v. 1) is elaborated by a double simile (v. 2). The whole is connected by the motif "eyes toward," which appears in each poetic line. The final clause uses the verb "be gracious" (NRSV, "have mercy"), which then becomes the double petition that opens the second part. The theme of the supporting description of trouble is "contempt, scorn."

394   2. In the context of the songs of ascents this prayer serves as a statement of the meaning of pilgrimage. The pilgrims stand within the gates (122:2) and their first word to the LORD is a

prayer for grace. The pilgrimage is a turning from the world's words of contempt for trust and obedience to the one whose ways are gracious. The pilgrims lament that they have had their full of scorn from the arrogant and comfortable. The language used in verses 3–4 is general and does not identify the social and historical circumstances in which the pilgrims lived. Does it speak of derision of the faithful for their trust (31:18) or of the scorn a humiliated and weakened Israel endured from its conquerors (44:13–16)? The language could refer to either or both. Either way, the scorn was a challenge to their faith that had the form of the taunt, "Where is your God?" (See the comment on the pilgrim songs, Psalms 42—43 and 115:2.) The gesture of raising the eyes to the One enthroned in heaven is the pilgrims' answer to that derisive question. The gesture is at once one of entreaty and dependence. The pilgrims look from a world that questions their god to the God who rules the world. The heavenly throne is a spatial image that represents the LORD's transcendent unlimited sovereignty over earth and all that is in it (2:4; 11:4; 115:3; Matt. 6:9).

3. The psalm's petition is a simple "Be gracious to us, LORD, be gracious." It is one of the basic petitions heard often in the prayer psalms (e.g., 4:1; 6:2; 9:13; 27:7). Translating the petition "have mercy" (NRSV) may suggest that the petitioners are undeserving or guilty; most contemporary versions prefer "show favor" for the Hebrew verb *hanan* (NJPS, REB, RNAB). The verb, along with its nominal and adjectival forms, expresses the disposition and action of a superior to be for those who are related as dependents. The idea fits the opening image of the heavenly sovereign. It is illustrated by the similes that compare the pilgrims looking to the LORD to servants looking to master and mistress. The comparisons work because embedded in the notion of "servant" is the responsibility of master and mistress to and for their servants. Just as servants can depend on their master, so pilgrims expect and pray for the "LORD our God" to show them favor. That the LORD is gracious, inclined to show favor to those who belong to him, is a characteristic featured in the famous attribute formula of Exodus 34:6 (see the comment on Ps. 103:8) and in the blessing said by the Aaronic priests (Num. 6:25). The pilgrims look to the heavenly king to find what they do not find in the world, graciousness. Their prayer does not say what help is requested or what need is to be met. In this song the simple contrast of contempt and grace is the concern.

395

When pilgrims from the world's contempt lift their eyes to behold the one who rules the world, they find the grace that overcomes the world.

Psalm 124: Our Help Is in the Name of the LORD

The fifth song of ascents begins, "If it had not been the LORD who was for us . . ." and then recalls a past the pilgrims would not have survived without the LORD's help. The song's concluding declaration is a corporate form of the personal confession of trust in Psalm 121:2, and the whole is a counterpart to the earlier song (see Psalms 120—134).

1. The song is a poem of liturgical quality composed of an artful use of repetitions and images. The liturgical quality is apparent in the invocation "Let Israel say" (cf. 129:1), the formula of praise "Blessed be the LORD" (v. 6), and the concluding confessional sentence (v. 8). The psalm has three parts, a recollection of past deliverance (vv. 1–5), praise for deliverance (vv. 6–7), and a corporate declaration of trust (v. 8). The first part uses the repetition of the syntactic elements of a conditional sentence: a protasis with "if" (2 times), an apodosis with "then" (3 times), and a "when" clause in protasis and apodosis. "Escaped, snare, snare, escaped" forms a chiasmus in verse 7. Images are the overwhelming waters (vv. 4–5, 3 times) and the bird that escapes the fowler's snare (v. 7).

2. The danger from which Israel had escaped is depicted only with images and a simile. Waters that engulf or sweep away are a frequent image for personal and corporate danger; the image evokes the sense of a power before which one is helpless (18:16; 69:1–2; 144:7; Isa. 8:7–8). Does the figure of a broken snare (v. 7) represent defeated Babylon, from which the exiles returned? The recollection is not composed to tell what happened but to dramatize how great was the danger and narrow the escape. A phrase in verse 2 gives an important clue to the character of the danger: "When man (*'adam*) rose against us" (NRSV, "when our enemies attacked us"). The word *'adam* is used here as in Psalm 10:19–20; it is a collective noun for Israel's enemy, the nations in their humanness. The enemies are "man" in contrast to the LORD. The danger was of the quality and kind that posed the basic choice of existence in history, the choice between trusting God or man as the decisive power. "If it had not been the LORD who was for us . . . !" That

return of chaos

396

is what the pilgrims must and may say as the truth about themselves. They have learned and here confess that the people of God cannot live merely as "man," because the human powers around them will engulf them in the history that "man" makes. That is the negative truth the pilgrims know. See the comment on Psalms 118:6–9 and 56:2–3, 10–11.

3. Therefore the pilgrims declare: "Our help is in the name of the LORD, who made heaven and earth." That is the positive truth they know, the confessional meaning of their choral recollection. In prayer they had called on the name of the LORD, and the one whose name they called had helped them. The epithet "maker of heaven and earth" emphasizes the absolute distinction between the LORD and the forces of human society and history named "man." The people of the LORD are a community chosen and constituted by the LORD, and they live in the history that "man" makes by the help of the "maker of heaven and earth." In the liturgy designed by John Calvin for use at Strassburg and Geneva, the service began with the sentence, "Our help is in the name of the LORD, who made heaven and earth." Calvin chose it because he understood that this declaration said the truth about the congregation gathered for worship as well as any one sentence could. On verse 8, see the comment on Psalm 121, secs. 3 and 4.

Psalm 125: Like Mount Zion

Psalm 125 is the sixth in the collection of songs of ascents. On the collection, see Psalms 120—134. In this song, Jerusalem, the destination of pilgrims, becomes a symbol for the LORD's way with the faithful.

1. The song begins with a double positive statement composed in the form of a chiasmus about the LORD's protection of those who trust him (vv. 1–2). The pattern is: relation to the LORD, simile, simile, relation to the LORD. The statement uses the place (Mount Zion, Jerusalem) to teach the protection the LORD gives Israel. Then the danger from which protection is needed is identified in a negative statement of assurance that the power of wickedness would not prevail over the righteous (v. 3, translating Hebrew *ki* as "surely" with REB instead of "for" with NRSV). A double petition, one on behalf of the good (v. 4) and one against the wicked (v. 5), corresponds to the preceding statements about the righteous and the wicked. The

397

song prays for what it first teaches. It teaches trust and prays for those whose trust is heart-true. A liturgical invitation of peace upon Israel concludes the whole (see 128:6).

2. The topic of the psalm is the LORD's way with the righteous and the wicked. It is one of the many and various expressions in the psalms of the basic belief that the destiny and welfare of the righteous depend on the reign of the LORD (Introduction, sec. 6.17). In the psalm, those who trust in the LORD, the people of the LORD, the righteous, the good, the upright in heart, and Israel are designations used as equivalents. They establish the theme and unity of the psalm. Their use as equivalent designations also expresses a conviction about Israel. The list says that the Israel who is truly the people of the LORD consists of those who are righteous, upright of heart, and good in trusting their lives to the LORD in faith and obedience. The character of the psalm as a pilgrims' song is evident in its use of Mount Zion and the geographic setting of Jerusalem as images of the LORD as refuge of those who trust him. Just as Zion cannot be shaken because of its relation to the LORD, so the righteous will not be shaken because of their relation to the LORD (46:5; 16:8; 21:7; 62:2, 6; 112:6; see the comment on Psalm 15, sec. 3). The pilgrimage is an enactment of trust. The song thinks of Israel in this way as a pilgrim people.

3. Verse 3 is concerned with a danger to pilgrim Israel that "the scepter of wickedness" should "rest on the allotment of the righteous" and cause the righteous to do wrong. The language here is tantalizing in its allusiveness. Does "the scepter of wickedness" refer to the rule of foreigners or to a prevalence of deceit and injustice in the society? Is "the allotment of the righteous" the land (see the use of *goral* as the term for the portion allotted to each tribe when Israel settled in the land, Josh. 15:1; 17:1)? Or does it mean the conditions of life given to the righteous in the providence of God? Hidden in this opaqueness is the awareness of the corrupting effect of dominant evil. In the living of life, the rightness of the righteous depends on the goodness of the LORD. The double prayer asks that the LORD confirm and implement the choices that human beings make, good for the good, and that those who choose crooked ways be made to walk with evildoers. The concluding benediction says what the entire psalm is about, the *shalom* of Israel. The *shalom* of the people of God is both well-doing and doing

well, united in their interdependence. Both depend on the
LORD.

Psalm 126: Restore Us

Psalm 126 is the seventh in the collection of songs of ascents
(see Psalms 120—134). It is the voice of pilgrims to Jerusalem
who have come to remember the restoration of Zion and seek
the renewal of the people of the LORD.

1. The psalm's literary structure is marked out by the use
of the interrelated repetitions. It has two parts, each introduced
by a line that employs the phrase "restore the fortunes" and a
simile (vv. 1, 4). In the first part, "then" (2 times) connects the
lines of verse 2 with the introductory "when" of the first line.
"The LORD has done great things" (2 times) holds verse 3 to the
end of verse 2. In the second part, weeping and joy are correlated with sowing and reaping twice (vv. 5–6). Words for
laughter/joy occur five times in the whole, giving the song its
dominant emotional tone. The song is about joy remembered
and joy anticipated. In both cases the joy is the work of the
LORD, in the first through the restoration of Zion and in the
second through the renewal of those who sing the song.

2. "Restore the fortunes" is a translation of the Hebrew
idiom that is difficult to replicate in English. It is a fixed expression found primarily in prophetic sayings, where it is used for
the radical change from the conditions brought about by divine
wrath to those which result from divine favor. It means restoration of an earlier situation between God and people (e.g., Amos
9:14; Joel 3:1; Jer. 29:14; Zeph. 2:7). The formula is used in the
psalms with the same meaning (14:7; 85:1; the comment on
Psalm 85 should be consulted). The recollection of the restoration of Zion could refer to its rebuilding and return to a central
role in Israel's life after the return from the exile. The description of the restoration of Zion as a great work of the LORD that
brought joy to Israel and caught the attention of the nation
sounds like an echo of the prophecies in Isaiah 40—55 (e.g.,
52:1–10; 49:8–26). The pilgrims remember it as a time when
they were "like those who dream," that is, experiencing the
opposite of the actual (see Isa. 29:7–8; REB, "like people renewed in health," is a possible alternate translation). It may be
noted that NJPS translates all the verbs in verses 1–3 as futures,

399

making the two parts of the song a consistent reference to what is not yet.

3. What the pilgrims remember about the past they pray for in the present. The restoration of Zion needs completion in the restoration of the people; the memory of its restoration gives hope for their own renewal. In the memory they remember what the LORD can do. They need ever-recurring rhythms of renewal that come like the seasonal freshets that make the dry watercourses of the Negeb run with water. The prayer for that renewal uses a contrasting correlation between weeping/sowing and reaping/laughing. The contrast between tears and laughter represents the change sought (e.g., 30:5). In the old religious myths of Ugarit and Egypt, seedtime was associated with the death of the god of fertility, and harvest was associated with his revival. The ancient tradition seems to have created an association of sowing with grief and of joy with harvest. The song uses the association as a cultural idiom. Perhaps it intends that the sowers represent the going out of the pilgrims and that those who come carrying the sheaves of harvest represent their return.

4. Because of its reference to reaping and harvest, Psalm 126 has been used as a lection for Thanksgiving Day. In that liturgical context the psalm teaches the church that it should give thanks for and seek God's work in its own restoration. In the Common Lectionary, this psalm is also designated for Sundays in Advent and Lent. Heard in those seasons, it speaks of the great change that occurs in the birth and resurrection of Jesus Christ, and it teaches that only those who move toward Christmas and Easter with the "tears" of repentance and need may enter into the joy of "the great thing God does for us."

Psalm 127: Unless the LORD Builds the House

Psalm 127 is the eighth in the collection of songs of ascents (see Psalms 120—134). It is composed of sayings that teach how dependent we mortals are on the LORD in the basic areas of ordinary life. Used as a song for pilgrims, the psalm acknowledges that dependence and discloses an important reason why the pilgrims make the journey to give thanks to the LORD (122:4). The following draws broadly on Miller, *Interpreting the Psalms*, pp. 131–137.

1. The psalm contains two quite distinct parts. The motif of

400

the first is "in vain" (3 times in vv. 1–2); of the second, "sons" (2 times plus a synonym, "fruit of the womb," and pronouns in vv. 3–5). The first part is composed of three sayings. The first two sayings are similar in form; the third shifts to direct address. They teach that such endeavors as building a house, guarding a city, and daily toil are futile unless the work corresponds to the work of the LORD. The second part is composed of two sayings. The first saying is a proverb supported by a simile (vv. 3–4); the second is a beatitude elaborated by an illustration (v. 5). The relation between "arrows" (v. 4) and "quiver" (v. 5) connects the two. Both concern sons as divine blessing. Sons bring security; the larger the family, the less vulnerable it is, an emphasis that reflects Israel's culture. When a man had to face his adversaries in a legal conflict that ended up in the court convened in the gates of the city, it helped greatly to appear accompanied by a platoon of strapping boys.

2. The theological subject that unites the topics of work and children is the blessing of the LORD, a subject characteristic of the collection (see Psalms 120—134, sec. 3). Fruitful work and fruitful family as the blessing of the LORD are topic and subject of the following song, Psalm 128. The two psalms should be read together as a mutually interpretive context. Work and family were the two constitutive dimensions of ordinary life in Israel. Life was set in the social unit of the family and supported by work. But both involved a mysterious uncertainty; work and family were human endeavors, but human action was not ultimately determinative in them. Work did not always come to fruition; marriage did not always produce children. The psalm is grounded in fundamental trust in the providence of God as the decisive factor in all of human life. Children are a heritage from the LORD as the land is a heritage given to Israel by the LORD. No projects are completed unless they are embedded in the larger purpose of God. The anxious toil of those who believe that it all depends on them is in vain. Work should be an endeavor of trust, not anxiety or arrogance. One of the proverbs says, "The blessing of the LORD enriches, and toil adds nothing to it" (Prov. 10:22; alternate reading in NRSV). Perhaps in "the bread of anxious toil" of verse 2 there is an echo of the frustrating labor to which the autonomous human being is condemned (Gen. 3:16–17). The precise sense of verse 2*b* is uncertain. Alternate meanings have been proposed for the Hebrew word translated "sleep" in most versions (e.g., REB, "he supplies the

401

need of those he loves"). If "sleep" is correct, does the clause mean that God gives the weary and anxious sleep as relief? Or more likely, that God gives while those who labor sleep (NRSV alternate reading; cf. Mark 4:26–29; Matt. 6:25–34)?

3. Psalm 127 serves as a pilgrim song because its subject is blessing, and the LORD blesses from Zion (128:5; 133:3; 134:3). When it is read in the context of the entire group, its principal terms are interpreted by the interest of the collection: "house," by house of the LORD (122:1; 134:1) and house of David (122:5); "city," by Jerusalem (122:3); and "sons," by David's sons (132:11–12). When the terms are read in the light of these associations, the whole question of the building (and rebuilding) of city and temple and the continuity of the Davidic kingship looms as a setting in which to read the psalm. Then the attribution of this one song to David's son Solomon becomes a major clue to how the psalm was understood when included in the collection. Solomon was a builder of the temple (I Kings 3:1–2) and cities (II Chron. 8:1–6). God is also one who builds: his sanctuary (78:69), Zion (102:16; 147:2), people (28:5), David's dynasty (89:4). In the LORD's covenant with David, the promise was that the LORD would build David's house, and David's successor would build the LORD's house (II Sam. 7:27, 13). It may be important also that the term "beloved" is regularly used for corporate Israel or a tribe (60:5; 108:6; Jer. 11:15; Deut. 33:12). It is Israel that is called "you" (v. 2, plural) that labors anxiously to build the house and keep the city. Informed by these associations, the psalm reminds the pilgrims that the human work of building and protecting Jerusalem and installing kings always depends on God's work. It can teach the church the same. Unless the LORD builds the church, they labor in vain who build it.

Psalm 128: The Blessing of Those Who Fear the LORD

Psalm 128 is the ninth in the collection of songs of ascents (see Psalms 120—134). It is a companion of the preceding Psalm 127. The subject of both is the blessing of fruitful labor and fruitful family. It can serve as a song for pilgrims because of its orientation toward Zion in its final lines.

1. The psalm is composed of two parts. The first part (vv.

402

1–4) is enclosed by general statements in impersonal style about the person who fears the LORD. Within the statements are assurances of fruitful labor (v. 2) and fruitful family (v. 3) in direct address style (the "you" is singular). Verses 1 and 2 are bound together as a subgrouping by the "happy the one who" form that opens one and concludes the other. Verse 3 is composed of two similarly composed sentences using similes. Verse 4, with its introductory "thus," identifies the good fortune of verses 1–3 as the blessing of the LORD. Whereas the first part begins with a beatitude (see Psalm 1, sec. 3), the second opens with a benediction (v. 5*a*) in which the blessing that comes to the one who fears the LORD (v. 4) is pronounced over each pilgrim. The benediction is elaborated with wishes that use terms from the first part of the song ("good" and "children"). The song concludes with a benediction on all Israel (see 125:5).

2. God's blessing is the enhancement of life that brings it to fulfillment. That understanding is apparent in the way this psalm speaks of the two basic areas of human life. Mortals work, but it is the blessing of God that brings work to completion and makes the labor satisfying. Mortals marry, but the birth and growth of children is the blessing of God. By putting the formulas for the beatitude (vv. 1*a* and 2*b*) and the blessing (vv. 4, 5*a*) in parallel, the psalm assumes that whatever makes life good is the effect of blessing. Without blessing, life is incomplete, frustrated (see 129:5–8).

3. Because Zion is the place of the Presence, the pilgrims bring the needs and hopes of everyday life with them. Jerusalem plays a central role in the understanding of blessing in the songs. God blessed Zion as the place in the world representative of his reign (132:15); it is the place of blessing by the LORD's sovereign decree (133:3). The LORD blesses from Zion (v. 5; 134:3). As they come to receive the blessing of the LORD, the pilgrims are not independent autonomous individuals. Their lives are bound into Zion, and their hope for blessing is bound up with the good of Jerusalem (v. 5; see the prayer for the good and peace of Jerusalem in 122:6–9). In a similar way, the lives of Christians are bound up with Christ, through whom God bestows spiritual blessings (Eph. 1:3).

4. This song, like all the psalms, speaks about the LORD's blessing in a way that makes clear it is not simply a matter of a ritual of place and ceremony. The LORD's blessing is for those who fear the LORD (vv. 1, 4). There is a concurrence between

403

the way life is lived and the way life is enhanced. Well-doing and doing well are interdependent. Walking in the ways of the LORD is a receptivity to the blessing of the LORD (see 125:4; 115:13; 24:5; and I Peter 3:8–12). The spirit of pilgrimage always incorporates walking in the ways of the LORD.

Psalm 129: Often They Assailed Me

Psalm 129 is the tenth in the collection of songs of ascents (see Psalms 120—134). The song recalls the peril of the past in which the people of God have been preserved and prays for the failure of present and future hostility.

1. The song is composed in first person style as the voice of an individual. A liturgical summons in the first line identifies the individual as a personification of Israel (v. 1*b;* cf. 124:1; 118:2–4). The people of the LORD on pilgrimage to Zion are called on to remember the course of their corporate life (vv. 1–4) and to pray for the city to which they have come (vv. 5–8). The repetition of the opening clause in the first two lines (vv. 1–2) emphasizes the conflicted character of Israel's story. Even before Israel reached the adulthood of a nation, it was beset. From the time of Abraham and Moses down to that of Ezra and Nehemiah, Israel suffered assault. The figure of a plow cutting furrows evokes the wounds suffered by the corporate person (v. 3; cf. Isa. 1:6; 51:23). "The history of Israel is one single passion narrative" (Kraus, *Psalms 60—150,* p. 462). Yet, they have survived, and now in this song they remember the fact (v. 2*b*) and the author (v. 4) of their preservation. The LORD is called righteous because his action opposed the wicked. The image of the "cords of the wicked" may continue that of the plowers in the previous line. For "cords" as a figure for political control by rulers not ruled by the LORD, see Psalm 2:3, and for their designation as wicked, see Psalm 9:15–17. In form, topic, and purpose this first part is a counterpart to Psalm 124.

2. The wicked are those who hate Zion. Zion is the LORD's chosen residence, the place that represents the LORD's reign in the world (Psalms 122; 48). The peace and blessing of the pilgrims is bound up with the good of Jerusalem (122:6–9; 126:1–3; 128:5). So they pray for the failure of Zion's foes (v. 5). The prayer employs the simile of grass that takes root on the earthen roofs only to wither without producing enough growth to fill a reaper's hand (vv. 6–7). The reaper would receive no greeting

from passing folk to congratulate him, saying, "The LORD's blessing be yours" (v. 8*a*, see Ruth 2:4). The final blessing (v. 8*b*) may simply be parallel to the preceding one (so the punctuation in NRSV), or more likely it is a liturgical conclusion to the psalm, a mutual invocation of blessing on the pilgrims (see NJPS and 118:26).

3. The pilgrimage of the people of the LORD is sustained by memory of the LORD's help and continues in prayer for the victory of the LORD's reign.

Psalm 130: Out of the Depths

Psalm 130 is the eleventh in the collection of songs of ascents (see Psalms 120—134). The psalm has a remarkable history in the spiritual life of the church. It came to be known as *De Profundis,* the opening words of its Latin version; the title pointed to its usefulness for all who found themselves in the depths of existence. It is one of the seven penitential psalms that were used in the services and disciplines of repentance. Luther called it "a proper master and doctor of Scripture," by which he meant that the psalm teaches the basic truth of the gospel. John Wesley had heard the psalm sung on the afternoon before his transforming experience at Aldersgate. This record commends the psalm as a succinct but powerful expression of the theme that is the heart of Scripture: the human predicament and its dependence on divine grace.

1. The psalm is composed in the form of an individual prayer for help (Introduction, sec. 5.2.1). The form is revised in significant ways to create a prayer song suitable for an occasion when individuals and their religious community merge in one identity. An individual voice speaks with, for, and to the community. The song has four parts that are unified by connecting elements. Petitions to be heard open the song (vv. 1–2). Then a statement about the relation in which sinful human beings stand to the forgiving LORD follows, instead of a particular personal account of trouble (vv. 3–4). A confession of faith that takes the form of waiting in hope for the LORD is made (vv. 5–6). The waiting is compared to that of watchmen for the morning, a simile that repeats the first verb of verse 3; the pilgrims "watch" for the LORD, who does not "watch" (so the Hebrew; NRSV, "mark") for iniquities. At its conclusion, the song shifts from address to the LORD to exhortation to the religious

405

community to hope for the LORD's redemption (vv. 7–8). The theme of iniquities in verse 3 returns in the form of all the iniquities of Israel (v. 8). "The forgiveness is with you" (v. 4) is resumed and expounded by "The steadfast love is with the LORD" and "Full redemption is with him" of verse 7. These connections show that the theme of the song is hope for forgiveness that the LORD will bestow by showing steadfast love in the redemption of Israel from all its iniquities.

2. The song discerns the human situation. Life is lived in danger of, and also in the experiences of, "the depths." The term is a metaphor, an abbreviation of the expression "the depths of the sea" (Isa. 51:10; Ezek. 27:34). It represents drowning in distress, being overwhelmed and sucked down by the bottomless waters of troubles (cf. the context in Ps. 69:2, 15 and Jonah 2:2–3, 5–6). To be in the depths is to be where death prevails instead of life as prospect and power, where the authentic word about existence is "I am lost" (Lam. 3:54–55). In this song, being in the depths is clearly connected with iniquities, those which belong to every human life (v. 3) and specifically all those of which the community of faith is guilty (v. 8). The predicament is the complex, multifaceted condition created by iniquity in individual and corporate life. It is not just guilt; it is the flood of wrong and its consequences that sweeps life along and from which there is no escape apart from a liberating, rescuing redemption.

3. The song is based on a fundamental theology. The theology is stated by contrasting an erroneous hypothesis about God and its consequences for the human situation (v. 3) with the truth about the LORD and its consequences for the community of faith (v. 4). The error is to understand the LORD as a god whose principal way with human beings is to watch for iniquities. If that were the case, there would be no hope for anyone. Even those who are reckoned righteous because of faith and faithfulness would be caught. None could survive if such were God's way. The "depths" would be the only possibility (on the confession that none are righteous before the LORD, see the comment on Ps. 143:2). The truth that the song knows and teaches is that "the forgiveness is with the LORD" (forgiveness has the definite article in Hebrew, as does steadfast love in v.

406 7). The sentence means that the authority to forgive and the disposition to forgive belong to the LORD. Sin is essentially a matter of relation to the LORD who alone in his sovereign deity

has the right to forgive, choosing to deal with sinners by grace (see Exod. 33:19; Mark 2:1–12). That much of the truth is inherent in the nature of iniquity and the sovereignty of God. Dependence on the LORD's disposition to forgive was learned from God's way with Israel, especially in the exilic experience (see the comment on Psalm 103). The consequence of this truth for those who believe it is that they "fear the LORD." They can live as "God-fearers," that is, as people who take the authority and disposition of the LORD as the greatest reality of all and base their living on God without reservation.

4. The song provides a stance for those in the depths who fear the LORD. The stance is waiting for and hoping in the LORD, one of the ways in which fearing the LORD takes the form of conduct (Ps. 33:18–22). The theological use of the word pair (wait/hope) is a specialty of the books of Isaiah and the Psalms. The two verbs are synonyms (Isa. 51:5) used to speak of trust as an activity that must and does reckon with time, a stance of enduring the present in anticipation of vindication in the future. "Waiting for the LORD" belongs to a time of trouble when a prophetic word of salvation (Isa. 8:17; 25:9; 26:8; 33:2; 40:31; 49:23; 60:90; Lam. 3:24–26) or a divine promise of steadfast love (Pss. 25:3, 5, 21; 119:43, 74, 81, 114, 147) has been given. It is trust that finds strength and courage from the certainty of what is yet to be (31:24; 27:14). It finds voice in prayer that will not be discouraged (40:1; 69:3, 6; Jer. 14:22). Psalm 130 is a waiting on the LORD.

5. The psalm declares the certainty of a comprehensive and final redemption. The LORD who has the authority and power to show steadfast love *(hesed)* in the work of redemption will consummate his sovereignty by redeeming Israel from all its iniquities. The declaration has an eschatological reach unusual in the Old Testament. Psalm 25:22 prays for the LORD "to redeem Israel from all its troubles," a prayer that in its similarity with the declaration reminds us that redemption includes liberation not only from guilt but also from the whole imprisoning network of sin's effects on life. Divine forgiveness will be fulfilled in the freedom that belongs to the children of God. How and when that full and final redemption will come, the Old Testament song does not say. But it is in the hope of it that every pilgrimage in the depths is made.

[handwritten margin note: "They also serve who only stand and wait" — John Milton]

Psalm 131: Like a Child My Soul

Psalm 131 is the twelfth in the collection of songs of ascents (see Psalms 120—134). Its subject is confidence in the LORD, and it concludes with the exhortation, "O Israel, hope in the LORD." In both respects it is similar to its preceding and companion psalm, Psalm 130.

1. The song is composed as the voice of an individual in a corporate setting. Its principal part is the testimony to the religious stance of one person (vv. 1–2), but its conclusion is an exhortation that commends that stance to Israel (v. 3). The confidence in the LORD of one pilgrim is offered to the company of pilgrims. The first two verses contrast the self that is proud and arrogant with the soul that is patient and composed. The simile of a weaned child with its mother illustrates the patient soul. Verse 2 prepares for and interprets verse 3. The genius of this brief, simple song is its use of the poignant picture of child and mother to evoke the personal and psychological reality of the theological expression "hope in the LORD."

2. The heart that is lifted up and eyes raised high are figures for pride, arrogance, and self-assertion. These are attitudes about which the ethical traditions of Israel give warning (Prov. 6:17; 18:12; 30:13). The narrative and prophetic traditions see them as presumption against God (II Chron. 25:16; 32:25) or even as presumption to act as if one were as God (Ezek. 28:2, 5, 17). Great things and marvelous things are performed by God; in Daniel, "great things" are the boasts of the fourth beast (Dan. 7:8, 11, 20; cf. Rev. 13:5). The attitudes and ways rejected by the psalm are the sum of autonomous pride. The stance adopted is that of the calm and patient soul, calm because ultimately it does not have to depend on itself and patient because it does not believe that the present time is a prison. The simile of the weaned child with its mother gives the stance human and emotional depth. The translation of NRSV brings out the possibility in the Hebrew text that a mother speaks: "My soul is like the weaned child that is with me" (v. 2*b;* see Seybold, pp. 149–150).

3. At its end, the song bids Israel to hope in the LORD. Hope in the LORD is like a child with its mother. Living in hope is having One with you who takes the terror out of need and time.

408

The simile may reflect the occasional use of parent and child as an image of the relation between God and people (Deut. 1:31; Isa. 46:3–4; Hos. 11:4 as usually emended). On waiting and hoping for the LORD, see Psalm 130, sec. 4. At this point it helps to remember that Jesus taught that we must become like children to enter the kingdom of God (Matt. 18:1–4) and that Paul rejected every "confidence in the flesh" in order to be found in Christ (Phil. 3:4–11).

Psalm 132: David and Zion

Psalm 132 is the thirteenth in the collection of songs of ascents (see Psalms 120—134). It is different from the other songs in two important ways. It is much too long to fit in with the characteristic brevity of the rest of the songs. It has Zion and David as a double topic. Zion is a regular concern of the songs, but there is only one hint of an interest in David in the text of the other songs. Psalm 122 refers to "the thrones of the house of David" (v. 5) as an important institution of Jerusalem. Three of the songs (122; 124; and 131) are attributed to David and provide an anticipation in the sequence of the concentration on his figure in Psalm 132. The psalm balances what David had done for the LORD with what the LORD will do for David. A coordination between Zion as the LORD's habitation and David as the LORD's anointed is the basis of the structure and purpose of the song.

1. The psalm is composed of various materials. It uses quotations extensively: a vow of David (vv. 3–5), an oath of the LORD concerning the Davidic succession (vv. 11b–12), a word of the LORD about the election of Zion (vv. 14–16), and another joined to it about the future of David's dynasty (vv. 17–18). There is a narrational recollection in verse 6 accompanied by a summons to visit the sanctuary in verse 7. Verses 8–9 seem to be part of a liturgy for a procession with the ark. It is likely that some of this material comes from old sources drawn on in the composition of the psalm (see Allen, pp. 204—209, for a review and evaluation of possibilities). The background of verses 2–9 is certainly David's introduction of the ark into Jerusalem recounted in I Sam. 7:1–2 and II Sam. 6:1–19. Though there is some uncertainty about the location of Ephrathah and Jaar (v. 6), the first could refer to the district in which Bethlehem lay

and the second to the region where Kiriath-jearim was. Verses 6–9 then dramatize a group who go from central Judah to its western borders to move the ark in a sacral procession.

2. These various materials have been crafted into a psalm of corresponding sections and integrating repetitions. The narrative theme of the whole is "find a place for the LORD" (v. 5). The vocabulary of the theme punctuates the composition (place or dwelling place, v. 5; dwelling place, v. 7; resting place, v. 8; habitation, v. 13; resting place, reside, v. 14; and significantly, "there" in v. 17). There are two major sections, verses 1–10 and 11–18, each introduced by the recall of an oath and its citation (vv. 2–5 and 11–12). The first section concerns David's role in finding a resting place for the LORD, and the second concerns the LORD's role in maintaining David's throne in that place. David's vow to find a place for the LORD has its counterpart in the LORD's oath to maintain David's line. Verses 6–9 tell how David carried out his vow, and verses 13–18 say how the LORD will keep his oath. Note the correspondence in language between verses 8–9 and verses 14, 16. The first section opens and closes with petitions to the LORD on behalf of David (vv. 1, 10). The closing petition is bound to the citation of the LORD's oath to David by the repetition of the verb "turn" (Heb. *sub*). The petition asks the LORD not to *turn* away the face of the LORD's anointed, and the citation gives assurance that the LORD will not *turn* back from his sure oath to David (vv. 10 and 11). So the psalm is composed as a prayer and its answer. That is the decisive literary feature of this rather complex composition. It is an appeal to the LORD not to turn away from the Davidic kingship because of David's role in finding a "place" for the LORD, followed by a response to the appeal that says the LORD will not turn back from his path to maintain David's kingship, because the LORD has chosen Zion and "there" will provide "horn" and "lamp" for his anointed.

3. Zion and the anointed king are topics of central importance in the psalmic theology of the reign of God. There are psalms devoted to Zion and to the messiah. (See Introduction, sec. 6.10, 11 and the comment on the psalms cited there.) Psalm 89 is the only other one that delineates the terms of the LORD's choice of David; it contains a section on the permanent establishment of David's line and the conditions set by the law for it (89:29–37; see also II Sam. 7:4–17 and comments on Psalm 89, sec. 3). In Psalm 89 and II Samuel 7, God's commitment to

410

David's line is irrevocable; Davidic kings will be punished if
they do not keep the covenant, but God's steadfast love will not
be rejected. Here keeping the covenant is a condition of the
permanence of David's throne (v. 12). Of the psalms about Zion
as the dwelling place of the LORD, this is the only one that even
hints at the historical events that led to its role in the LORD's
relation to Israel and the world. Its first part is a liturgical version of the narrative of David's movement of the ark of the
LORD from Kiriath-jearim to Jerusalem. "We found it in the
fields of Jaar" (v. 6) is very much like the LORD's statement in
Psalm 89:20: "I found my servant David"; both indicate a historical point of beginning. The only other place in the Psalms that
coordinates the LORD's election of David and Zion is the long
lesson taught in Psalm 78; at its conclusion, the dual choice of
Zion and David is said to be the salvific institution by which the
LORD overcomes the sinful history of his people (78:67–72). But
it is only in Psalm 132 that David is actor in the way he is in the
Samuel narrative. Here David takes initiative and makes the
vow. Yet what David did is reported as the LORD's desire and
choice. The human initiative is mysteriously concurrent with
the divine pleasure. The human commitment to finding a place
for the Presence takes the form of the divine choice of a place
for the Presence.

4. In the context of the songs of ascents, Psalm 132 can have
two functions. First, it states the theological reason why Zion is
the city "to which the tribes of the LORD go up" (122:4). The
LORD rose up and went to this city as his "resting place" (v. 8).
The pilgrims follow where their LORD has gone. "Resting
place" is a term distinctive to this psalm as a designation of Zion.
It means destination, goal of journey. "Finding a resting place"
is coming home (84:3; Lam. 1:3). Because Zion is all that for the
LORD, for the pilgrims it is also destination, culmination, coming home (see Psalm 84). Because the LORD has made Zion the
place of blessing (vv. 15–16; see 133:3), the pilgrims come seeking the provisions and bread and salvation and joy to be found
in the Presence. The psalm says that blessing is the gift of God;
they come to receive.

Second, the psalm serves the pilgrims as a liturgy of prayer
and promise. It gives the clear impression that it belongs to a
time when there was no successor to David on the throne of
Judah. Zion is there, but the anointed one of the LORD is not.
Yet Zion is there as place of the Presence because of David's

411

unstinting commitment. It is interesting to note that the version of Solomon's inaugural prayer for the temple in II Chronicles 6 closes with a quotation of Psalm 132:8–11; the prayer pleads that the temple be a place of efficacious prayer, and the quotation bases the plea on the movement of the ark and David's role in it. Again, place and person. Zion without a messiah denies the indissoluble connection between David and Jerusalem. Place and person go together as representation and manifestation of the reign of God (see 2:6). The psalm assumes and reasons with that connection. The LORD, it says, will not turn back from his oath to David *because* the LORD has chosen and desired Zion (vv. 10, 13). The concurrence between David's service and the LORD's desire means that Zion is forever a claim on the LORD on behalf of David. So the psalm is, in its two parts, the voice of prayer and the proclamation of hope. In it, pilgrims hear that there will be—it is the word of the LORD—a horn and a lamp for David, there, in Zion.

5. When the psalm is read in the context of the canon of Scripture, the opening petition arrests attention. It appeals to the *'unnot* of David. The Hebrew word means "his being afflicted, humbled." The NJPS, with an eye on the context in verses 3–5, translates "his great self-denial." David denied himself place and rest to find the LORD a dwelling place and resting place. He humbled himself in order to be a servant of the LORD. His self-denial served the dwelling of the LORD in the midst of his people. A resonance sets in with another poem that speaks of one who took the form of a servant, and, being found in human form, humbled himself, and in his obedience unto death (Phil. 2:6–8) has become God with us and God for us, the presence and the power of the kingdom of God. The need for a Messiah who keeps the covenant and promise of horn and lamp for David to appear in Zion are fulfilled in him.

Psalm 133: When Sisters and Brothers Sit in Unity

Psalm 133 is the fourteenth in the collection of songs of ascents (see Psalms 120—134). It shares the motif of "Zion as a place of blessing" with the preceding and following songs (v. 3, with 132:13–15 and 134:3). The psalm is an exclamation of delight at the goodness the pilgrims experience in assembling as one family in Zion.

1. The first verse is the main clause of the whole, to which

412

all the other clauses in the psalm are attached. The clause attributes the compound predicate, "good and pleasant," to a social situation of unity. Two similes (vv. 2*a*, 3*a*) follow to add the reality of specific experience to the general adjectives of the predicate. The similes say just how good the achievement of unity is: as pleasant as the best oil poured on the head until it runs down the beard; as delightful as when dew as heavy as that which falls on Mount Hermon falls on the mountains of Zion (125:2). Verse 2*b* is an appositional phrase identifying the beard of the first simile as the beard of Aaron. Verse 3*b* is an explanatory subordinate clause that makes a specific theological assertion; the LORD has commanded "there" his blessing of everlasting life. All three of the clauses in verses 2–3*a* contain the participle "going/coming/falling down"; it links them to blessing in the final clause as that which comes down from God. "There" in the final clause points back, first to Zion as the place of blessing, and beyond Zion to the achievement of unity as what is blessed. This brief little psalm has a complex compositional structure that renders its various parts mutually defining. The appositional phrase in verse 2*b* and the ambiguity of "there" in verse 3*b* indicate that the psalm has a history of development.

2. The phrase "when brothers live together" occurs elsewhere in the Old Testament only in Deuteronomy 25:5 in the law regulating the practice of levirate marriage. It reflects a social custom in which sons continue to live together in the father's household. Taken on its own, the exclamation and first simile could comprise a folk saying recognizing and commending the richness and strength of life in the extended family, the joy and satisfaction of parents and children in one another. The translation "when kindred live together" (NRSV) understands the exclamation in this way. When, however, the psalm is read in its present form and location, the phrase refers to the pilgrimage practices of people who were kin through the LORD's covenant, sitting together at festival meals and dwelling together during a festival such as Tabernacles (NJPS translates "that brothers sit together"). The festival transformed the pilgrims into a family that for a holy time ate and dwelt together. The covenant bound them together, and the Presence brought them together. Both the appositional phrase (v. 2*b*) and the theological assertion (v. 3*b*) reinforce this reading of the psalm. Good oil poured on the head so liberally that it runs down on

413

the beard refers to hospitality customs that honor a guest (23:5; 82:10; 141:5). But when the apposition is added, a picture of the ordination of the Aaronic priest who presides at the Jerusalem temple emerges (Exod. 29:7; 30:22–32; Lev. 29:7). Zion is the place of ordained blessing, the place where the people of the LORD in their unity receive everlasting life. It is this abundant life, which Israel can receive only in its unity, and only from the Presence at this place that is the *summum bonum*. The life that the LORD gives his people in their unity is the supreme family value.

3. The psalm, then, celebrates the goodness of the life with which the LORD blesses those who are assembled by his Presence. It has often been used as a lection for the observance of the Lord's Supper, a liturgical setting with which it resonates wondrously well. Augustine claimed that the psalm gave birth to the monasteries; at the least, it was an important text for these brotherhoods assembled by the vocation of God. In services of Christian unity, the psalm is a witness that God is at work building a family that transcends all the given and instituted barriers that separate and diminish life.

Psalm 134: Blessed Be the LORD and You

Psalm 134 is the fifteenth and final unit in the collection of songs of ascents (see Psalms 120—134). It coordinates as if in reciprocal relation the blessing of the LORD by the congregation and the LORD's blessing upon the people.

1. Psalm 134 is the shortest of a collection of brief psalms. Its theme, bless, appears in three of its four poetic lines. It is composed of two liturgical movements. The first is a summons to praise addressed to the servants of the LORD and enclosed by the imperative sentence, "Bless the LORD" (vv. 1–2). The second is a blessing upon an individual (v. 3). It is impossible to assign the summons and blessing to specific groups or offices with certainty. The servants of the LORD who stand in the house of the LORD may be Levites (Deut. 10:8). Psalm 135:1–2 contains similar but undefined language. "Servants of the LORD" are addressed in general calls to praise (113:1), and the term is used for faithful Israel in the psalms (e.g., 135:14; 90:13; 102:14). Some translations favor professional temple personnel who are performing regular services ("nightly," NJPS; "night after night," REB). The blessing in verse 3 may be a priestly

414

[handwritten at top: ᵥ mortals to "bless the Lord" is to praise & thank]

benediction (Lev. 6:22–27; but cf. 128:5). Psalm 129:8 implies that passers-by say blessings on others, but perhaps the phrase "from Zion" favors the priestly identity. The psalm now stands in a literary rather than a liturgical location. In that context it serves well as a conclusion of the songs of ascents. It sums up the major concerns of the collection and states the purpose of pilgrimage to Zion: to praise the LORD and receive blessing from the LORD (122:4 and 133:3).

2. In the vocabulary of worship, "bless" with the LORD as object is an established synonym for "praise" and "thank." The verb praises the LORD as the one with whom alone there is the power that creates and sustains life. He is the source of all blessing. Human living is dependent on blessing in its personal, social, and national dimensions. Blessing is the LORD at work in human work (Psalm 127). The family, the community, and the world are brought to life-supporting and life-fulfilling completeness and rightness by the LORD's blessing. The final word of the songs is a benediction upon "you," the reader of Scripture, an invocation of the LORD's life-fulfilling power on your life.

Psalm 135: The People God Makes

Psalm 135 is a hymn of praise that has clear verbal connections with its literary context. Like Psalm 134, it addresses "the servants of the LORD who stand in the house of the LORD" (vv. 1–2; 134:1); both feature the theme of blessing in and from Zion (vv. 19–21 and 134:3). Psalm 135 praises the LORD as the God above all gods (v. 5), a note that is heard in Psalm 136 (vv. 2–3), where a summary of Israel's story used in Psalm 135:8–12 is repeated (136:10–22). As a pair, Psalms 135 and 136 stand as partners in praise to resume the "praise the LORD" and "O give thanks to the LORD" psalms in Psalms 111—118, after the interval of prayer for the law of the LORD (Psalm 119) and the pilgrim voices of the songs of ascents (Psalms 120—134).

1. Psalm 135 is not only a hymn of praise in form; its composer equipped it liberally with expressions of praise. It is enclosed by the liturgical cry "Hallelujah" (Introduction, sec. 5.5.2). It opens as an imperative hymn (Introduction, sec. 5.5.4) with a summons to the servants of the LORD to praise his name because the LORD is good and his name delightful (vv. 1–3). In the midst of the psalm the LORD's name is praised in direct

address (v. 13). At its conclusion, there is a call to Israel, its priests, and all who fear the LORD to bless the LORD (vv. 19–20) and a final shout of blessing on the resident of Jerusalem from the congregation in Zion (v. 21). The body or content of praise stands within the imperative sections and is divided into two panels by the praise of the LORD's name in the style of direct address in verse 13. The arrangement and the thought of this central part are rather complex. Two distinct themes appear in the coordinated clauses (vv. 4–5) attached to the opening imperative section. The first theme is the LORD's special relation to Israel; the second is the LORD's superiority over all the gods. The first theme seems to be developed by the summary recitation of Israel's foundation story (vv. 8–12) and by the clause attached to the central praise (v. 14). The second theme is developed by assertions about the LORD's unconditional sovereignty (v. 6) and supervision of storms (v. 7) and resumed by the polemic against idols and those who trust them (vv. 15–18). The material of the two themes is interwoven so that together it all serves one point: a contrast between the LORD and his people and the nations and their gods. Verse 6 opens up the motif of what the LORD does; verse 7 says what he does in the heavens, and verses 8–12 what he has done on the earth. Then verses 15–18 tell in contrast what the gods of the nations cannot do. The LORD has chosen Israel as his own people (v. 4) and established them in the world of nations (v. 12); in the process, the LORD overwhelmed many nations and their mighty rulers (vv. 8–11). The LORD made Israel, but the nations make their gods (v. 15). Note the way the terms "servants," "people," and "nations" and proper names are employed to emphasize the basic contrast.

2. To carry out his purpose, the psalm's composer used some classic texts drawn from significant contexts. The praise of the LORD's name as everlasting (v. 13) is a restatement of the LORD's comment on his own name in Exodus 3:15. The attached assurance that the LORD will vindicate his people quotes the climax of Moses' song, where he speaks of how the LORD will maintain his relation to Israel in the midst of the nations and their gods (Deut. 32:36). Verse 4 employs the vocabulary of Moses' identification of Israel as the chosen people of the LORD, his treasured possession, in a context that speaks of the LORD's clearing away the nations whose gods Israel is to avoid (Deuteronomy 7; see v. 6; cf. Exod. 19:5). The personal confession of the

416

LORD's greatness above all gods and idols (v. 5; "know" in the sense of acknowledge) invokes the psalms that celebrate the reign of the LORD (see 95:3; 96:4, 5; 97:7, 9). Verse 7*b* appears elsewhere in the context of a contrast between Israel's God and the gods of the nations (Jer. 10:13; 51:16). For the polemic against the gods of the nations, the composer used Psalm 115:3–8 and set its thematic phrase on the sovereignty of the LORD at verse 6, and the rest in verses 15–18, as a way of putting both parts of the body of the psalm under the rubric of "the gods of the nations" (see the comment on Psalm 115). For his account of what the LORD had done in the world, the composer used a version of Psalm 136:10–22 that selectively emphasizes the LORD's victory over other nations; their specific names are played against the theme of the name of the LORD. So not only in the literary structure but also in the use of other texts, the interest of the psalm in contrasting the LORD and Israel with the nations and their gods is evident. The psalm recalls and evokes all these contexts; their significance and power flow into its language and performance.

3. The LORD's election of Israel is the demonstration that all the gods are idols. That is the theology of the hymn. The LORD chose a people to be his own special possession, defended them from the powers of the world, and gave them their land as a heritage. The LORD rules over all and performs his sovereign will, but his people are his special possession. Their story is the clue to the basic truth about the universe, the clue to who reigns in heaven and on earth. Behind the praise of the God whose intervention to liberate and establish his people is manifest in the thunderstorm (vv. 7–12) is the tradition of the LORD as the divine warrior (see the comment on Psalms 68; 114) whose victory is the revelation that "the LORD reigns." Such is the greatness of the LORD praised in this hymn, and it is on that greatness alone that the people of the LORD rely. In the center of the hymn is a statement about the present and the future. "The LORD will vindicate his people" (v. 14). The statement admits that the people of the LORD still worship in the midst of powerful governments and in contradiction to gods that are the product of human capacities. Not only their past but their future must be the LORD's work. Christians say and sing the psalm in awareness that God's choice of a people to be his own special possession in the world illumines the meaning of their calling through Jesus Christ (I Peter 2:9; Titus 2:14). The con-

417

trast between the people God makes and the gods the nations make is no dead issue for us.

Psalm 136: His Steadfast Love Is Forever

Psalm 136 is a companion of Psalm 135. Both are hymns that praise the LORD with a recitation of the deeds of the LORD. Psalm 135 uses the recital to contrast the LORD and his people with the nations and their idols. Psalm 136 uses the recital to expound the steadfast love of the LORD. On the verbal connections between the two psalms, see the introductory paragraph of comment on Psalm 135. Because the recital forms the content of praise in Psalm 136, it is often classified as a historical psalm along with Psalms 78; 105; and 106 (see Brueggemann's treatment of these psalms in *Abiding Astonishment*). But history as it appears in these psalms is not a critical reconstruction of the past. Psalm 136 is a liturgical use of tradition whose interest is the way the past impinges on the present and shapes the future. The events recalled outrun those which find their way into the usual historical records because they bear forth the identity of the LORD whose steadfast love comprehends all time.

1. The psalm begins with a brief formula of praise: "Give thanks to the LORD, for he is good, for his steadfast love endures forever" (v. 1). The verse can be called a formula because it clearly existed independently in Israel's liturgical repertoire as a fixed expression of thanksgiving. In Chronicles, its use is associated with the Levitical guilds of singers who apparently sang it as their primary sentence of praise on various occasions, and it could be used in a litany in which the people participated (I Chron. 16:34; II Chron. 5:11–14; 7:1–3; 20:21; Ezra 3:11). The formula was used in the composition of psalms as introductory and concluding framework and as an element of composition (106:1; 107:1; 118:1–4, 29; 100:4–5). The formula follows the pattern of the imperative hymn of praise (Introduction, sec. 5.5.3, 4). The pattern consists of a plural imperative call to worship supported by a "for" clause that states the basis and content of the praise. In the formula, the basis consists simply of the predicate "good," amplified in a coordinate clause by the assertion that the LORD's steadfast love *(hesed)* is everlasting. The coordinate clause appears to have been used as an antiphon, as it is in Psalm 136.

418

2. The composer of Psalm 136 used the formulaic hymn to compose a litany on the wonderful works of the LORD. In each of the psalm's twenty-six lines, the second measure is "for his steadfast love endures forever." The first three lines are an extended summons to give thanks to the LORD (vv. 1–3), with the name of the LORD replaced by titles in the second and third. The final line (v. 26) is the concluding summons to praise, with yet another title. Verse 4 states the subject of the body of the hymn, "the great wonders" of the LORD. Verses 5–25 are a recitation of the wonders. The recitation is divided into unequal parts by lines that begin with "to the one who" (in Hebrew, an l preposition with a participle); the effect is to replace the name of the LORD with an action, one of the great wonders. The wonders are: making the heavens (v. 5), spreading earth over the waters (v. 6), making the great lights (vv. 7–9), smiting Egypt and bringing Israel out (vv. 10–12), the wonder at the Red Sea (vv. 13–15), leading his people through the wilderness (v. 16), and conquest of land for his servant Israel (vv. 17–22). The final two wonders are marked by a change in syntax in the Hebrew text. A relative particle begins the lines about the rescue of Israel from its low estate (vv. 23–24), and a simple participle opens the line on the gift of food to all flesh (v. 25). This shift seems intended to separate these two lines as different from the preceding wonders, all of which use familiar language from the traditions about creation and Israel's foundation story.

3. "Wonders" is the collective term used here (v. 4) and in the other historical psalms (78:4; 105:2, 5; 106:2, "mighty doings") for the items that compose the recitations. It is a liturgical and confessional term for the recognition and claim that certain events are so marvelous and extraordinary as to transcend the normal and the usual. Wonders are special happenings enacted by the divine power and purpose. In the other historical psalms, the wonders are all occurrences in the story of the LORD's way with Israel, and the items are selected and their telling shaped to suit the purpose of the psalm. Here the wonders are recited as an exposition of the name of the LORD. The liturgical logic is not so much to thank the LORD for doing all these things, but rather to thank the one whose identity is constituted and known in and through these wonders. The titles give first and final emphasis to this process of liturgical identification. The LORD is God of gods; Lord of lords; God of heaven. All three titles are superlatives that attribute incomparable and universal power

419

to the LORD. The selection of wonders then implements this emphasis. Unlike the other historical psalms, this one includes the wonders of creation. The items from Israel's story are chosen and worded so as to illumine the sovereignty of the one "who alone does great wonders" (v. 4). The person of God is rendered in the recitation of the works of God. The name takes on content and actuality in being connected with world and Israel's story, and the world and the story of the people become marvelous as they are envisioned as the work of the LORD.

4. The hymn is constructed so that the recitation is also an exposition of the refrain, "for his steadfast love *(hesed)* endures forever." *Hesed* is the characteristic and activity of reliable helpfulness, the attribute of the LORD most often praised and appealed to in the Psalms (Introduction, secs. 5.5.3; 6.8; see the comment on Psalm 103, sec. 2.) The coordination of the items in the recitation with the refrain makes it clear that *hesed* is action; the wonders are a performance of *hesed.* The sections that tell Israel's story in every case say how God's power was helpful to Israel; for example, the LORD struck Egypt to bring Israel out (see vv. 11, 14, 16, 21). Israel's story is a witness to the LORD's *hesed* saving "his servant Israel" (v. 22). But, says the recital, even creation displays the steadfast love of the LORD. Heaven and earth and day and night are the work of the LORD's steadfast love; all life is lived and supported by the LORD's helpfulness (see Psalm 104). The making of the universe and the salvation of the people of God are together a history of *hesed.* The LORD's *hesed* is everlasting and fills all time (see 36:5–9; 57:10; 119:64).

5. The distinctive section that concludes the recitation extends its telling beyond the classic sequence of creation and salvation story, but its two items parallel them in reverse. Verses 23–24 continue Israel's story, and here the congregation who say the psalm refer to themselves for the first time. The record of the LORD's steadfast love extends into their life. They testify that the LORD remembered them when they were "down and out" and rescued them from their foes (the verb "rescue" occurs elsewhere only in Lam. 5:8). These items appear to be the voice of the postexilic community confessing that they are the beneficiaries of the LORD's *hesed* in their time. The classical story is always being brought up to date by the congregation. The church of the New Testament will add its own testimony to the work of God's steadfast love. His steadfast love

is indeed everlasting. Verse 25 corresponds to God's work in creation. The LORD gives food to all flesh (see 104:14–15, 27–28; 145:15–16; 146:7; 147:9). That brings the story down to every meal and makes the recitation of the LORD's mighty works a preface to every blessing said over the food we eat. It becomes apparent here why our LORD taught us to pray for the coming of the reign of God and the gift of daily bread in one short prayer. They are both part of the continuum of God's mighty works. All of history and each day of living are contained in the story of the LORD's steadfast love.

Psalm 137: A Song of Two Cities

Psalm 137 is a song about Zion, but it is not one of the "songs of Zion." The songs of Zion are hymns full of joy and confidence. In them, Jerusalem is majestic and invincible, secure against the threats of hostile armies (read Psalms 46 and 48). In this psalm, Jerusalem has been razed to its foundations, and the psalm is full of bitter memories and vehement pain.

1. Unlike all the other psalms, this one refers to particular times, places, and events. It identifies a specific historical setting. It looks back on the fall of Jerusalem to Babylon and its Edomite allies, on a time of residence in the foreign territory of Babylon, and on the experiences of a captive, deported people. The psalm seems to be the voice of exiles who have returned to live in the ruins of a Jerusalem not yet rebuilt. The memories of their humiliation by and in Babylon are fresh, and the account with the treacherous Edomites still unsettled. The composer may have been one of the temple musicians carried into exile with harp and repertoire of temple music. He and his guild of Levitical singers would have been the special targets of their captor's cruel humor.

2. The theme is "remember Zion-Jerusalem." The theme states the central action of the three parts of the song. The singers remembered Zion when they were in Babylon (v. 1, past); they vow not to forget but to remember Jerusalem now (vv. 5–6, present); they appeal to the LORD to remember the day of Jerusalem (v. 7, future). In the first two cases, "remember" is used as part of the vocabulary of lamentation (cf. 42:4–5; Lam. 3:19–21; Num. 11:4–6); in the third, it is a verb of petition for the appropriate action by God (e.g., 25:7; 74:2; 109:14). The singers remembered Zion in Babylon; they vow to remember

421

and not to forget now, and they ask the LORD to remember. In the first part (vv. 1–4), the singers in corporate style tell about their faithfulness in the face of humiliation when they were in Zion. In the second part (vv. 5–6), they individually vow faithfulness in the present. The vow ("if so and so, then so and so") is made in the form of the invocation of a curse upon the one who vows, the most vehement expression of commitment possible. The third part (vv. 7–9) is composed of a petition to the LORD to deal with the Edomites and two beatitudes in the style of direct address to Babylon wishing for retribution against that capital city. Though it does not conform to the type of the corporate prayer for help, the psalm with its description of trouble, vow of faithfulness, and petition could have served the function of that genre among the returned exiles (Introduction, sec. 5.4). The combination of formal elements, corporate and individual styles, and concern with Zion give the psalm a resemblance to the songs of ascents (see Psalms 120—134). Perhaps that is why it concludes the three psalms (Psalms 135—136) attached to the collection of the songs.

3. The psalm is a song of two cities. It sings of resistance against one and devotion to another. The soul of the singers moves between Babylon and Jerusalem. First there is a focus on Babylon, its streams and trees and officers. In the first three lines, "there" is repeated as if to point a verbal finger at that place of "alien soil" (v. 4, NJPS). It was a place where Zion was remembered in services of communal lamentation and weeping. The exiles kept their relation to Jerusalem alive in liturgies of lament. Their remembering was not just personal homesickness, longing for familiar scenes and accustomed places. It was disciplined devotion, devotion at a price. Their Babylonian captors taunted the singers with a request for one of "the songs of Zion." The expression is likely a general one referring to hymns of praise to the LORD sung in the temple at Jerusalem, not to a specialized genre. The request was intended as an insult to the exiles' God, similar to the derogatory question, "Where is your God?" (see the comment on Psalms 42—43, sec. 2). Captors and captives alike were very clear that the issue was not music; it was faith. There could be no hymns of joy in Babylon. That would have been betrayal, singing joyous songs of the sovereignty of the LORD in a territory that represented another sovereignty. The voice of faith "there" was the voice of prayer

with tears. Note Nehemiah's response to the news about Jerusalem's condition (Neh. 1:4).

4. In the second part, the psalm puts the focus on Jerusalem. The city is addressed directly. An oath is made that forswears hands that play the harp and tongues that sing the LORD's song should the oath not be kept. The singers promise Jerusalem that they will not forget; they will remember. They remembered in Babylon and they will remember Zion, in Zion. They will allow no happiness of life and circumstance, even that of being in their own land again, to take priority over their tears and prayers for the city whose place in the reign of the LORD is not vindicated. Zion is not simply a place where they are at home; it is "the city of the great king" (48:1). The singers are very clear that the issue is not where they are but whether the LORD rules in the world in which they live.

5. In the psalm's third part, the focus is on the LORD. The LORD's name is called and prayer is made. The singers remember Jerusalem by appealing to the LORD to remember Jerusalem by vindicating the destruction against the partners in its fall, Edom and Babylon. The beatitudes in verses 8–9, with their harsh contents, serve as wish prayers. In sum, the prayers are a naked appeal for retribution. Slaughter of children (v. 9) was an occasional military policy where the purpose was to eliminate a population (cf. II Kings 8:12; Hos. 10:14; Nahum 3:10). There is no evading the passionate pain and anger that animates these prayers. They call for the accounts in the books of history to be balanced. But they are not to be reduced to a personal desire for savage revenge. The singers pray out of a zeal for the LORD and the place of the LORD's habitation. They pray with an understanding of the reign of the LORD that looks for its manifestation in the affairs of peoples and nations. In this they have a context in the chorus of prophecies that look for the punishment of Edom and Babylon (on Babylon, Isa. 47:1–15; Jer. 51:1–58; on Edom, Isa. 34:1–17; Jer. 49:7–22; Ezek. 35:1–15; Obadiah). Whatever justifiable reservations may lead us to omit their prayers from our lections and prayers must not obscure the question their passion and understanding places against ours.

6. As their song was preserved and used as a psalm, the names of Babylon and Jerusalem were on the way to becoming symbols—Babylon of the civilization of this world that does not

423

know the LORD reigns, and Jerusalem of the city of God that is and is coming (cf. Revelation 18; 21). The song can quicken our awareness of the anomaly involved in singing the LORD's song in an alien culture without any sense of the contradiction between our words and our world. Faith can never "forget Jerusalem." Faithfulness will remember in pain and prayer.

Psalm 138: With My Whole Heart

1. Psalm 138 is a song of whole-hearted thanksgiving for salvation. It employs the form of an individual thanksgiving song, beginning with the basic sentence of the genre, "I give you thanks, LORD," expanded by a poignant phrase from Deuteronomic rhetoric "with my whole heart" (Introduction, sec. 5.3). Rather than sacrifice, the singer offers this song after bowing down in worship toward the temple, holy because it is the place of the Presence (v. 2). The basic report of deliverance, "I called—you answered," declares the reason for the praise (v. 3). Then a hymnic section announces the expectation that all the kings of the earth shall join the praise because they have come to know the ways of the LORD (vv. 4–6). The final section is an affirmation of trust in the LORD's continuing deliverance concluded by a petition that the trust be vindicated (vv. 7–8).

2. Though composed in first person style, the psalm can be understood as a general song of praise by the restored community in the postexilic period, written under the influence of the prophets whose words are gathered in Isaiah 48—66 (Kirkpatrick, Kraus). The psalm is the song of a person who speaks in identity with the community or is the personified community (Isa. 12:1–6; 25:1). The salvation and restoration of the community exalted the LORD's name and word by fulfilling the prophecies of salvation made in the LORD's name (v. 2; Isa. 12:4; 41:26; 42:8; 45:23; 48:11). In this psalm the redeemed are carrying out their vocation to be witnesses before the gods and nations to the sovereignty of the LORD revealed in his salvation (vv. 1b–2; Isa. 43:9–10; 44:8; 41:21–24). That revelation should command the recognition of kings of the nations because they heard the words spoken by prophets that now are fulfilled (v. 4; Isa. 49:7; 52:15). The glory of the LORD has been revealed to all (v. 5; Isa. 40:5) through his surprising ways with the world. His salvation is the act of the high for the lowly, of the powerful for the weak (v. 6; Isa. 40:9–11; 57:15; 66:1–2; see the comment on Ps.

424

113:5–9). The redeemed community confesses to the LORD that
it is "the work of thy hands" (v. 8; Isa. 60:21; 64:8). In that
self-understanding they undertake to live a life of trust in the
midst of the dangers of history (v. 7), knowing that what the
LORD had begun in them he will surely bring to completion
(v. 8).

3. The psalm is, then, a sound guide to the meaning and
practice of thanksgiving by the redeemed. It reminds us that
salvation comes to us as individuals in community and creates
a community that can speak as one in unity. It teaches that our
salvation is not first of all and only for our sake but is also and
foremost the revelation of the coming kingdom of God. Of that
we are to be witnesses to the "gods" and rulers of the world.
The outcome of salvation is a life of trust and prayer. Life with
all its uncertainties and dangers goes on for the redeemed;
God's salvation gives them reason to hope that what God has
begun with them he will surely bring to completion. "I am sure
that he who began a good work in you will bring it to completion at the day of Jesus Christ (Phil. 1:6).

Psalm 139: You Know Me

Psalm 139 is the most personal expression in Scripture of
the Old Testament's radical monotheism. It is a doctrinal classic
because it portrays human existence in all its dimensions in
terms of God's knowledge, presence, and power. It reflects an
understanding of the human as enclosed in divine reality. The
psalm is even more a devotional classic, because used as prayer
it bestows and nurtures an awareness of the LORD as the total
environment of life. It teaches and confesses in the fullest way
that "my times are in your hand" (31:15).

1. The psalm is composed of two unequal parts. There is a
sharp break in tone, content, and function between verses 18
and 19. The function of verses 1–18 is praise; the purpose of this
longer part is indicated by the specific declaration, "I praise
you" (v. 14a), by the characterization of the LORD's ways and
works as "wonderful" (vv. 16, 14) and in general as unlimited.
Three sections tell how the psalmist's existence is totally comprehended by God. The LORD knows whatever the psalmist
thinks and does (vv. 1–6); the LORD is present to him wherever
he is (vv. 7–12); the LORD was even present to him when he
began to be (vv. 13–16). Verses 17–18 round out part one with

a wondering summation and awed declaration; no inventory of life can outrun the truth that at its end "I am still with you." The function of the second part, verses 19–24, is prayer that concerns the wicked in the world (vv. 19–22) and the possibility of wrong in the self (vv. 23–24). The two parts are held together by an inclusion formed by the repetition of the opening declaration, "LORD, you have searched me and known me," as a petition, "Search me, God, and know my heart" (vv. 2, 23). In spite of this stark transition between the parts, the psalm is a unit.

2. The principal clue for the interpretation of Psalm 139 is given in the relationship of its opening declaration and concluding prayer. What the psalm confesses to be the case at the beginning is sought in an appeal at the end. The initial address and concluding request form a parenthesis around the whole psalm to indicate that the whole is a continuous unfolding of their one theme and concern. The prayer does not wander away from its beginning subject only to return to it at the end. The psalm is speech addressed to the God who searches and knows the human being.

The inclusion within which the whole is set establishes two things about the psalm. First, the concern of the psalm is the relationship between the psalmist and God. The opening sentence speaks of the self as the object of God's action, and so does the rest. From the opening vocative to the final word, the prayer confesses an existence described in terms of the activity of God. It portrays the self in the light of the work of God and God's work and person as the context of the self. Even where others finally enter the picture being drawn (vv. 19–22), they are introduced into the prayer only as a way of speaking of the psalmist's relation to God. Of course it could be said that the concern of all psalms is the relation between God and those who use them as praise and prayer. But here that relation is the single unrelieved concern. It is explored and unfolded with an intensity and development that transcends any of the others.

Second, the psalm concentrates on one dimension of God's relation to human beings. "You know me"—that is the theme of the whole all the way to the plea, "Know me so that you can lead me." The verb and its synonyms recur in verses 2–4 to fix the theme. "Know," together with "search" and "test," belongs to the vocabulary used to describe the LORD's activity as a divine judge who discerns and assesses the human heart (e.g., 11:4–7; Jer. 9:7; 17:10; Job 7:17–18; 13:9). Reference to this

426

divine activity has a variety of functions in prayer in the Old
Testament: as a motive for God's intervention in prayers for
help (Ps. 69:19; Jer. 11:20; 15:15; 18:23) and as a statement about
the self in confessions of innocence (Pss. 17:3; 26:2; 44:21; Jer.
12:3) and sin (Ps. 69:5; Exod. 32:22) and trust (Ps. 142:4). No one
of these functions seems an adequate account of what is happening in Psalm 139. The prayer of the second part certainly
is related to the praise of the first part. The petition and accompanying declarations of identification with God in verses 19–22
seem calculated to put as much distance as possible between
the psalmist and the wicked; the declarations depend on the
confession of God's total knowledge of the psalmist's existence.
The whole has the cadence of a faith that trusts itself to a being
known by the LORD that includes discernment of the self, presence to the self, and creation of the self. The psalm is a spiritual
achievement that transcends the limits and functions of the
usual types.

3. The three sections of the psalm's first part are a literary
fabric woven of first and second personal pronouns. Virtually
every line's syntax contains a "you" or "your" and an "I" or
"me" or "my." God is thou to the psalmist's I. The psalmist
speaks about self by speaking to God and speaks about God by
speaking as a self. God and self are inextricably the subject of
the psalm's language. What is said about God is not abstract,
conceptual, about God in and of himself. It is not neutral ontological language about the being of God as ultimate reality. It
is relational, deals with thou and I, God in relation to psalmist.
What he does, *where* he goes, *that* he is are all comprehended
by the knowledge, presence, and power of God. God is not a
passive sphere of existence "in which he lives and moves and
has his being" (Paul's mistake at Athens), but knower, presence,
actor—a personal vis-à-vis to every dimension of the psalmist's
existence as person. Omniscience, omnipresence, and omnipotence are often used as expository language for the three sections of part one. But it must be done with care lest this
conceptualization becomes a knowing about God without a
being known, accompanied, created, and sustained by God.
Devotion and confession must not be reduced to metaphysics.

The psalmist confesses that he is never *free* of God in his
total existence, but the relation is described in such a way that
neither is a prisoner of or mere function of the other. The
psalmist is free for and to God. God is the limit of his existence,

427

yet he is himself a real person to God—accountable, confronted, known. God is free for and to the psalmist. The motions of God's relation to the psalmist transcend the psalmist's understanding. What he knows, he knows he does not know. His knowing is an unknowing; its achievement is wonder, and its only certainty is "I am with you" (vv. 18, 6, 14). The prayer in the second part of the psalm must not be forgotten; in the prayer, the psalmist appeals to God's freedom for decision and confesses his own accountability. There is some risk in using only verses 1–18. The psalm as a whole is not a text for any kind of divine determinism and resists any theology that compromises the freedom of God or the responsibility of the human being.

4. The second part of the psalm (vv. 19–24) has always posed the sharpest problems for interpreters. After eighteen verses of profound reflection on God as the ground of existence, the psalm abruptly calls for the death of the wicked and avows hatred in return for those who hate God! The vehement sentiments in verses 19–22 seem so inconsistent that some have suggested that they are a crude addition, and so unacceptable to religious sensibility that they are customarily omitted in liturgical and theological use. But in the thought world of the psalms, this section is not incoherent at all, no more, for instance, than the wish for the elimination of the wicked at the end of Psalm 104 or the references to the enemies in the midst of Psalm 23's calm expression of trust. In the worldview of the psalms, the wicked and their dangerous threats to those who base life on God are an important part of the reality in the midst of which faith must live. To speak of them in speaking of one's relation to God was completely consistent, especially where the relation was to God in his judging discernment of one's life.

It is probably a mistake to take verse 19 as a real petition directed against some particular identifiable threat. The style of the wish is, rather, to be read as a form of the description of the self in relationship to God, and so in continuity with the rest of the psalm. The language used to describe the wicked is composed of terms and characterizations that are common in the psalms for those who threaten the righteous and their relation to God. The psalm makes no petition for help; the wicked do not seem a personal threat to the psalmist's life. They are described rather as the enemies of God. That is their danger! They are part of the society in which the psalmist lives who by their moral and religious conduct oppose and ignore God. To be

428

willfully an enemy of God is unthinkable to the psalmist, but there the wicked are, the embodiment of another way than the fear of the LORD, conditioning and endangering the whole society by their character. So the psalmist at the conclusion of speaking to God about his relationship to God puts himself at all possible distance from them. Verses 19–22 are a rhetorical identification of self with God in the matter of the wicked. The topic of the wicked offers yet one more way in which the psalmist describes his life as an existence that is completely within the sphere of God's knowledge, work, and ways.

5. The first real petition comes at the very end, in verses 23–24. It is only two poetic lines long, but it gives theological balance to the whole as the counterpart of all the rest. The petition asks God to do now and in the future what God has done in the past, to examine and test the psalmist's heart and thoughts to uncover any way that troubles his relation to God so that God may lead him in another way, the way everlasting. The way everlasting is the existence that is not shaken or brought to an end as the way of the wicked will be. The psalmist wants God to be his judge so that God may be his shepherd. Such is his experience of God and confidence in God that he does not fear a judgment that leads to punishment but prays for a searching and testing that lead to pastoral care. This final prayer is reason to recognize that the foregoing confession contains no murmur of self-righteousness. It does not protest innocence or admit guilt. It is, rather, the voice of a person who has come to know the judge and the shepherd so much as one that he can wish nought else than to be known by God.

6. How did the psalmist come to the understanding of the self expressed in the prayer? The composer of Psalm 8 looked to God the creator and found one answer to the question, "What are human beings, that you are mindful of them?" The composer of this psalm seems to have meditated on the vision of the LORD as the righteous judge who knows, searches, and tests the hearts of human beings. The psalm is composed of the implications of that vision for the existence of the psalmist, voiced as praise and prayer. The vision of God to whom every aspect of one's life from conception is present can be terrifying (e.g., Job). The psalm shows that the vision inspires wisdom and trust for those who want nothing else than to be led in the way everlasting. The apostle Paul once said of himself, "Now I know only in part; then I will fully know even as I have been fully

429

1 Cor 13^12

known." Perhaps this psalm is a knowing only in part, but it is a knowing that knows already that it is fully known by God. It is a prayer that will lead all who make it their own into that knowing.

Psalm 140: Preserve Me from Violent Men

Psalm 140 is a prayer for help in first person style (Introduction, sec. 5.2). It is composed of petitions supported by descriptions of trouble (vv. 1–5), more petitions supported by confessions of confidence (vv. 6–8), wishes of disaster upon adversaries (vv. 9–11), and a concluding confession of confidence (vv. 12–13).

The repeated petition, "Preserve me from violent men" (vv. 1, 4) identifies the general situation. The violence is verbal (vv. 3, 11). The hostility is characterized with metaphors of war (v. 2), snakes (v. 3), and hunting (v. 5). The basic theology is stated in verse 12: The LORD preserves justice for the "poor and needy." The prayer is an appeal to God as the judge whose justice protects the weak from the violent (see Introduction, sec. 6.7, 18).

Paul used verse 3 in a catena of quotations from the Old Testament (Rom. 3:13) composed to show that all are under sin. The use indicates that the descriptions of wickedness in the psalms and similar texts had come to be read as descriptions of the human condition.

Psalm 141: My Prayer as Incense

Psalm 141 is a prayer composed for those who take refuge in the LORD (v. 8) in flight from the words and deeds of the wicked in their world (vv. 3–4). It is composed largely in the idiom of petitions (a comparison of translations will show how uncertain the text of verses 5–7 is). The trouble that occasions the prayer is not described as a personal threat to the one who prays, as in many prayers for help; the danger lies, rather, in the general power and pervasiveness of wickedness that entices and entraps the faithful. Against that danger the psalmist prays for divine help. Here is honest confession that the faithful life depends on the faithfulness of God.

430

The psalmist asks the LORD to accept his prayer and its

accompanying gesture of petition (hands lifted up toward heaven) as incense and evening sacrifice (v. 2). Does the request imply a belief that prayer can replace sacrifice in the worship of the LORD? The precise implication of the request cannot be determined, but it probably does not involve a spiritualization of sacrifice. Rather, the request may express confidence in the offering by asking that God accept the prayer just as God accepts sacrifice. Word and sacrament are not at odds here.

Psalm 142: Bring Me out of Prison

1. The learned scribe who searched out the relation between the story of David and the psalm found a biographical setting for it in David's predicament "when he was in the cave" (Introduction, sec. 3.5). Perhaps the reference is to the cave of Adullam, where David fled from Gath to find refuge and was alone for a time with none to care but his God (cf. vv. 4–5 and I Sam. 22:1; others suggest the cave of Engedi, I Sam. 24:3–4). The psalm is a prayer for help (Introduction, sec. 5.2) that begins with an appeal to be heard (vv. 1–2) and a statement of confidence that the LORD knows the need (v. 3*a*). It continues with a description of danger and helplessness (vv. 3*b*–4), another confession of confidence (v. 5), and concludes with pleas for help supported by reference to need and anticipation of deliverance and praise (vv. 6–7).

2. The one who prays is beset by persecutors, and in his danger he is alone. No human being offers a refuge of concern and care. The reference to prison or confinement in verse 7 is ambiguous. In the Old Testament context, it could mean the custody in which one was held before trial (Num. 15:34), or being shut up in the exilic situation (Isa. 42:7), or it could serve as a metaphor for distress (Ps. 88:8; Lam. 3:6–9), or as a metaphor for the bonds of death. The ambiguity may be intentional. It has certainly rendered the psalm open to use by people who are bound and shut up in all sorts of ways. The need for liberation takes many forms.

3. The faith on which the prayer is based is stated in the confession: "You are my refuge, my portion in the land of the living" (v. 5). The prayer declares that the attention and care and help of God will suffice where human beings fail. On the prayers for help as a way to take "refuge" with the LORD, see

431

the comment on Psalm 7:2. "When other helpers fail and com-
forts flee, Help of the helpless, O abide with me" (Henry F.
Lyte).

4. Calling the LORD "my portion in the land of the living"
is an adaptation of an ancient tradition about the Levites. When
the land was apportioned to the tribes, the tribe of Levi was not
given a share; instead, they were to serve the ark and tabernacle and be supported by a portion of the offerings at the shrine.
The LORD said to them, "I am your portion" (Num. 18:20; Deut.
10:9; Josh. 13:4). Here, and in other prayers, that tradition has
been turned into a confession that the LORD is the basis of
existence (16:5; 73:25; 119:57; Lam. 3:24). The land of Israel
becomes "the land of the living" and the material support of the
Levites is transformed into the liberating deliverance of the
LORD. The confession says, "I have no other support for my
existence but the help that comes from you, O God."

Psalm 143: None Righteous Before You

Psalm 143 is the seventh and last of the penitential psalms,
the traditional list of psalms to be used as scriptural and liturgical texts to inform and guide the practice of repentance (see the
comment on Psalm 6, sec. 4). It was composed as an individual's
prayer for deliverance from enemies (v. 9; Introduction, sec.
5.2). That raises an interesting question about just how it expresses repentance.

1. The prayer begins with petitions to be heard (v. 1) rather
than be put on trial before the LORD (v. 2). The trouble is
pursuit by an enemy who has driven the psalmist into the
sphere of death (vv. 3–4). The memory of God's saving work for
and among his people leaves the psalmist longing for God as
parched land needs rain (vv. 5–6; see 63:1). Then an intense
sustained series of pleas for God's answering help, supported by
descriptions of trouble and confessions of confidence, express
the longing and need for God (vv. 6–12). Is that the form and
movement of a prayer for repentance?

2. Undoubtedly, the feature of the psalm that led to its
selection is verse 2, with its plea to be spared the judgment of
God, for the reason that no living person is in the right before
God. The plea with its reason is quite unexpected in a prayer
for help. In other similar prayers, the plea is "Judge me according to my righteousness" (see 7:8; 26:1; 35:24; and the comment

on Psalms 7 and 26). It is possible that the setting of those prayers to be judged or vindicated was an institutional arrangement in Israel that provided at a shrine for an accused person to plead innocence of accusations in hope of an acquittal delivered by an official of the shrine as a representative of God. The innocence claimed by the petitioner was not an absolute righteousness but a rightness with respect to the charges. Even there the primary basis of the appeal was the righteousness of God testified to in the trust of the petitioner.

But here something has changed; instead of citing a specific innocence, the prayer appeals to the general predicament in which all mortals stand. It must be because the judgment is thought of here as a judgment with respect to God rather than with respect to human accusations. "Before you" no one is in the right (qal of *sdq;* the only other cases of the verb in the Psalms, 51:4 and 19:9, have God and his ordinances as subject!). It is interesting that the only other occurrences of the sentence, "The LORD enters into judgment with a person," are in Job 9:32; 14:3; 22:4; cf. Eccles. 11:9; 12:14). It is also in Job that a cluster of statements that no human being is righteous before God appear (Job 9:2; 15:14; 25:4; see also the late psalms 14:3; 130:3). Behind Job and these psalms is a deepening awareness of the human predicament before God. Job nonetheless holds on to the claim of personal integrity and stays with the stance of Psalms 7 and 26. In Psalms 143 and 130, the confession of general unrightness takes the place of any claims of rightness or integrity. Not "on account of my integrity" or "I have sinned," but "all are sinners." That is why these texts are so important for Paul's argument that there is no justification based on human righteousness (Rom. 3:20; Gal. 2:16).

3. Psalms 7 and 26 are there in the Psalter along with Psalms 143 and 130, the prayers to be judged along with the prayers not to be judged, the profession of righteousness and the confession of sinfulness. One stance does not succeed the other, replacing it. Altogether they represent refractions of Scripture's testimony to divine and human righteousness, *simul justus et peccator.* "There is . . . only an apparent contradiction between the prayer of Psalm 143:2 . . . and that of Ps. 7:8. . . . If Ps. 7 expresses the confidence of the man whom God has justified and who has in this way established his case in the teeth of all his accusers and adversaries, Ps. 143 shows how he attains this confidence—namely, by allowing that God is in the right

against him, and accepting God as his only righteousness, his own but his real righteousness" (Barth, II/1, pp. 387–388).

4. If verse 2 led to the selection of Psalm 143 as a penitential psalm, how then does the whole function as a text for repentance?

a. The psalmist says to the LORD, "You are my God" (v. 10) and "I am your servant" (vv. 2, 12). These confessions are not based on human initiative. They speak of identities created by the election and the covenant. Repentance situates itself in the relationship God has created. It is from its beginning the response to grace.

b. The prayer appeals to the faithfulness and righteousness of God (v. 1). The righteousness of God is his will and work to set things right according to his election and covenant in spite of all that denies and perverts them. This is the righteousness of God of which Isaiah 40—55 (45:22–25) and Paul (Rom. 1:17) speak. "He is faithful and righteous to forgive our sins" (I John 1:9). Repentance looks to the righteousness of God, to his righteousness alone.

c. The psalm prays not to be brought to judgment, because no human being will be found in the right before God. The psalm knows the truth of the human condition and does not talk about this and that sin but about sinfulness. Repentance is in order because of what we are, not just because of what we have done. But the psalm does not yet know the truth that God in his righteousness brought Jesus Christ into judgment in our place. We can now say verse 2 knowing that we have another great reason to plead to be spared judgment.

d. The danger and need in which the psalm is said arises because of an enemy, a mortal foe whose work is darkness and death (vv. 3, 7). The psalm does not name this enemy; he is not someone, but a certain hostility and work, and he is also many (v. 12). The prayer is not made because of some sin but because the assault of the enemy and the prospect of death bring to light human unrighteousness before God. Repentance is turning to God for salvation from the darkness and death that is our lot. It is a move of hope, a stretching out of the hands, the thirst of the soul (v. 6).

434

e. The prayer asks, "Let me hear your covenant love *(hesed)* in the morning" (v. 8). This unusual formulation is a request to be given a salvation oracle, a word of the LORD's solidarity with the sinner who trusts in him. Repentance is a fresh turning to the gospel as the answer to the danger and darkness of our world.

f. The prayer asks, "Teach me to do your will" (vv. 10, 8). The prayer assumes an understanding of salvation that includes divine help to instruct, guide, and direct the living of life according to the good pleasure of God. Repentance hopes for sanctification as well as forgiveness (25:4–5; 40:8; I Thess. 2:1–8).

Psalm 144: As David Prayed

Psalm 144 appears to be designed for use by a king (see v. 10). It has often been identified as one of the royal songs composed for use in ceremonies involving a Davidic king (Introduction, secs. 3.3; 6.11). But its combination of different kinds of material and its relation to other psalms point to different conclusions concerning its composition and character.

1. The psalm is divided into two parts by style and subject. The first part (vv. 1–11) is composed in first person singular style, and its concern is rescue from the power of aliens. The second part (vv. 12–15) uses first person plurals, and its subject is the blessings of a people whose God is the LORD. Part one begins with a liturgical exclamation of praise blessing the LORD as patron in warfare and refuge from trouble (vv. 1–2). The following reflection on the LORD's attention to transient humankind (vv. 3–4) seems to support the opening praise by confessing unworthiness to be the recipient of the help reported in verses 1–2 (see the use of the reflection in 8:4 and Job 7:17). An extended petition appeals to the LORD to come from on high and deliver the one who prays from the power of aliens (vv. 5–8). The offer of praise to the God who rescues Davidic kings (vv. 9–10) may function as a vow of praise supporting the petition. Then the petition is repeated in a shorter form (v. 11). Part two of the psalm is a list of blessings: healthy sons and lovely daughters (v. 12), fertility in fields and flocks (vv. 13, 14*a*), security for the population (v. 14*b*). The list is concluded by a double beatitude on people so blessed because their God is the LORD (v. 15). This second part is awkwardly attached to the first by a Hebrew relative particle at the beginning of verse 12, which may imply that the list is to be read as a prayer (so NRSV). But the sentences in verses 12–14 are nonverbal and could be a description of present blessing (NJPS) or a statement of hope (REB). The two petitions dominate the center of the psalm and

435

give it the appearance of an individual prayer for help. But the presence and the employment of the elements of praise and blessing make the psalm difficult to classify as one of the standard types.

2. Psalm 144 bears an obvious resemblance to Psalm 18, the long psalm of thanksgiving for deliverance composed for use by Davidic kings. Verses 1–7 are woven of material that also appears in Psalm 8. The correspondences of Psalm 144 to Psalm 18 are: 144:1 to 18:1, 34; 144:2 to 18:2, 47; 144:5 to 18:9; 144:6 to 18:14; and 144:7 to 18:16, 44, 45. "His servant David" in 144:10 may reflect the superscription of Psalm 18. Lines from Psalm 33 also appear in Psalm 144: 144:9 is like 33:2b, 3a; and 144:15b is like 33:12a. The composer of Psalm 144 was obviously drawing on Psalms 18 and 33 to compose one for his own time and situation. A clue to his situation and reason for drawing on Psalm 18 may be found in the repeated petitions that are unique to Psalm 144. "Mighty waters" in the first petition (v. 7), which does come from Psalm 18, is replaced in the second (v. 11) by "the evil sword," an expression found only in this psalm. "Sword," however, is used as a figure for the words that the wicked employ as weapons (57:4; 59:7; 64:3), a meaning supported by the repeated "the hand of aliens whose mouths speak lies and whose right hands are false" (vv. 8, 11). The psalmist wrote in a time when the welfare of his community, its enjoyment of the blessings the LORD bestows on his people (Deut. 28:1–14), was threatened by the treacherous reports and actions of aliens (Heb. *bene nekar*). The plural and the singular of the term occur elsewhere in material that reflects the relationship of the exilic and early postexilic community to the aliens who where their constant problem (plural: Ezek. 44:7; Isa. 56:6; 60: 10; 61:5; 62:8; and singular: Gen. 17:12; Exod. 12:43; Lev. 22:25; Ezek. 44:9; Neh. 9:2; and Isa. 56:3). A likely setting for the psalm is the time of Nehemiah. The one other place where "aliens" appears is in Psalm 18:44, 45. These verses tell of a David whom the LORD empowered against foreigners. The composer of Psalm 144 must have found in these verses a promise for his own time. So he composed a psalm of praise and prayer to the God "who gives salvation to kings and rescues his servant David" (v. 10) as a context for petitions for deliverance from the aliens of his time. By re-praying Psalm 18 in a new version, he appealed to the LORD to do for his people what the LORD had done for his servant David.

3. This psalm, then, is an illustration of the practice of using psalms to compose hymns and prayers, combining earlier material into new compositions for new needs. In the process, the formal limits of the traditional types are transcended, and the employed material is put to different purposes. Revising the material of psalms for new hymns and prayers is a practice that continues to this day. By it the power and beauty of psalmic material continuously make a canonical contribution to worship. This psalm is also evidence of the influence of the use of psalms attributed to David as the praise and prayer of the people. By the time of its composition, using David's prayers as their prayers was already a tradition among the fearers of the LORD. The tradition made it possible to compose a psalm for the community in the form of a psalm of David. Psalm 144 is a prayer in which the community prays as David. "The future mystery of praying 'in the name of Jesus' and of being 'in Christ' is here foreshadowed in Old Testament contexts and presuppositions" (Kraus, *Psalms 60—150*, p. 544).

Psalm 145: Great Is the LORD, and Greatly to Be Praised

In its superscription, Psalm 145 is introduced as a song of praise (Heb. *tehillah*) by David. It is the only psalm identified in that way. The Talmud showed its estimate of the psalm's worth by saying, "Every one who repeats the *Tehillah* of David thrice a day may be sure that he is a child of the world to come" (*Berakot, 4b*). The psalm has always had a prominent place in the liturgy of the church. It is used four times in the current Common Lectionary as the psalm for the Sunday service. The high regard for the psalm is based on the comprehensive range of its praise of the LORD.

1. The psalm is an acrostic poem, and acrostics aim at comprehensiveness. In the Hebrew text, there are twenty-one lines, each beginning with the next letter of the alphabet. The line beginning with a *nun* is missing from the Masoretic tradition but is included in most English versions as verse 13*b*, with the support of an array of witnesses. The alphabetic pattern obviously forces certain constraints on the author's choice of words and the composition of lines, but within those constraints, the composer of Psalm 145 has created a hymn with a literary structure not determined simply by the order of letters.

437

An inclusion formed by the repetition of "bless your/his name forever and ever" (vv. 1, 21) states the purpose of the psalm. It praises the name of the LORD by reciting the attributes and actions that comprise the character of the LORD. The hymn tells the content of the name of the LORD, and its text is the means by which "David," through the mouth of all who use it, will continue to praise the LORD forever and ever.

The praise proceeds from *aleph* to *taw* in panels composed of an alternation of statements of praise and attribute declarations. The statements of praise are addressed directly to the LORD, and the attribute declarations speak about the LORD, so there is also an alternation of style. The first three panels are verses 1–2 plus verse 3, verses 4–7 plus verses 8–9, and verses 10–13a plus verse 13b. In the fourth panel, the components are reversed, so that the psalm ends with a statement of praise, verses 14–20 plus verse 21. In the fourth, the attribute declaration itself is found in verse 17. It stands in the center between a description of the LORD's providence to all (vv. 14–16) and the LORD's help to those who belong to him in contrast to the wicked (vv. 18–20). The statements of praise refer to characteristics and actions of the LORD as well as the attribute formulae, so there is a content of praise distributed throughout the entire psalm. The word "every/all" is repeated sixteen times throughout the hymn, emphasizing the unlimited comprehensiveness of the praise of the LORD and of that for which the LORD is praised. The LORD is praised every day forever and ever, from one generation to another by all his works and all his faithful for all his words and deeds. The repetition comes to a climax with the prophetic praise of the final line: "All flesh will bless his holy name forever and ever."

2. In its opening vocative, the psalm identifies the role in which the LORD is praised. The psalm calls the LORD "My God, the King" (unique to this psalm, not "my God and King," as NRSV). The theme is the greatness of the LORD as king. "Great is the LORD, and greatly to be praised" appears also in Psalms 48:1 and 96:4 in hymns whose subject is the LORD's kingship. The theme is restated in verses 11–13, where the glory and power and splendor of the LORD's kingdom is praised. It is interesting that an Aramaic version of "your kingdom is an everlasting kingdom, and your dominion endures throughout all generations" turns up in Daniel 4:3 and 4:34 as Nebuchadnezzar's praise of the God of heaven. God's greatness as king is

unsearchable, beyond all knowing and telling (v. 3b), but the psalm does its inspired best to find the words for human worship. The LORD is great, says the hymn, in power and works of power and in goodness and works of goodness. Though power and goodness as topics cannot be assigned to distinct sections of the psalm, the statements of praise feature power and the attribute declarations, goodness. The sequence in verses 4–7 from acts of power to abundant goodness implies that the two are essentially inseparable. God's power is good and God's goodness is powerful. Verses 14–20 ascribe the LORD's powerful goodness to "all his ways and all his doings" (v. 17), first in his way with the needs of all (vv. 14–16) and then in answering the cry and desire of all who call upon him. The king of heaven is a God of "the open hand" (v. 16) and "the available presence" (v. 18). Like the composer of Psalm 103, the author of Psalm 145 has used the famous self-declaration by the LORD from Exodus 34:6 as a source for theological work (v. 8; see the comment on Psalm 103, sec. 2). In contrast to its use there as a word for sinful Israel, he draws out its relevance here to "all that he has made" (v. 9) and to all that the LORD does (v. 13b). Calvin called verse 8 "as clear and satisfactory a description of the nature of God . . . as can anywhere be found" (Calvin, 5:275).

3. Psalm 145 is the overture to the final movement of the Psalter. It is followed by five hymns, all of which are opened and concluded by the liturgical cry "Hallelujah!" All five echo features and language of Psalm 145. At its end, the David of the psalms promises, "My mouth will speak the praise of the LORD" (v. 21a). The following psalms, all without attribution, are a literary fulfillment of that promise. The declaration that "all flesh will bless his holy name forever" anticipates the last line of Psalm 150, where a final summons to praise is sounded: "Let everything that breathes praise the LORD." Psalm 145:21 and Psalm 150:6 stand as an inclusion around the paean of praise that concludes the book.

Psalm 146: The LORD Keeps Faith Forever

Psalm 146 is the first of five Hallelujah psalms that conclude the Psalter. Its opening summons to the soul to praise the LORD (v. 1) and promise to praise throughout life (v. 2) are a response to the commitment to lifelong praise at the end of Psalm 145.

1. The psalm is an adaptation of forms of instruction to the

439

purpose of praise. It is undoubtedly composed as a hymn. It is set within the parentheses of the liturgical cry "Hallelujah" (Introduction, sec. 5.5.2). It has the introduction of an individual hymn of praise. Like Psalms 103 and 104, it begins with a self-invocation addressed to the soul (v. 1) and then vows praise that lasts as long as life (v. 2; cf. 104:33). But the body of the hymn is composed of instruction. There is a warning exhortation not to put trust in human leaders because of their transient mortality (vv. 3–4). Then there is a beatitude commending reliance on the LORD (v. 5). The beatitude is expanded by a series of praising predications attached to the divine name. First there are five poetic measures with hymnic participles as predicates (vv. 6–7a) and then five in which the name of the LORD is subject of the participles (vv. 7b–9a). The portrayal of the character of the LORD is rounded off by a saying contrasting the LORD's support of widow and orphan with the fate of the wicked (v. 9b). The body of the hymn thus gives instruction about the wrong and right way (cf. Psalm 1). The wrong way is putting trust in human leaders; the right way is to trust the LORD for help and hope. The series of predications contrasts the reliable helpfulness of the LORD with the transient incompetence of human governors. The psalm concludes with a proclamation of the everlasting reign of the LORD (Introduction, sec. 6.3) addressed to Zion (122:2; 137:5; 147:12). The hymn is composed as a sung lesson. Those who sing and hear and read it will be taught as they praise.

2. The contrast between God and humankind is often used in psalms as a way of dealing with the problem of fear before human threats: Trust God and be unafraid of mortals (118; 9—10; 56; 124; cf. Isa. 51:12–13). Here the contrast is used to address the problem of trusting in leaders (NRSV, "princes"; NJPS, "the great") to save from the predicaments of human and historical existence. The problem with human leaders is that they don't "keep faith forever"; their plans and projects die with them. With their death the hopes of those who trusted in them are dashed. Perhaps Israel's experience with its leaders is reflected in this wisdom. Their kings and officials were unable to deliver them from the dangers of existence and history. The exile set its seal on their ultimate inability. The hymn does not say that leaders are unnecessary or not useful. It does warn against trusting them for salvation. Hope based on what passes away is doomed to disappointment.

3. In contrast, "the LORD will reign forever" (v. 10). The God of Jacob and Zion is a leader whose tenure is not temporary. Hope attached to his reign is founded on a reality that does not pass away. The God of Israel is king of the universe; "maker of heaven and earth" is a title of the God who rules all (see the comment on Psalm 121, sec. 4). But permanence and power alone are not the grounds for trust. Trust is also founded on character, so the LORD's character is epitomized in a phrase (v. 6*c*): Not only does the LORD rule forever but in his rule he keeps the faith forever. Then verses 7–9 render the LORD's character by reciting the characteristic activities by which the LORD keeps faith.

The recitation portrays the LORD as Israel has come to know him through his acts as interpreted by prophets and *torah*. Each item cites how the LORD is "help" (v. 5; see Psalm 121) for a particular category of need: the oppressed, the hungry, prisoners, and so on. In the Old Testament vocabulary, these terms stand for individuals and for the corporate group of the people of the LORD in their need. The terms are used for both physical and spiritual need (for instance, the use of hunger and blindness for the condition of the exiles in Isaiah 40—55). In the list of groups in need, the categories of the "righteous" with its antonym the "wicked" may seem out of place. Their inclusion is an excellent illustration of the way the righteous and the wicked are thought about in the psalms. The pair is viewed more in salvific than in strictly moral terms. If the LORD did not vindicate the righteous and frustrate the wicked, he would not be keeping the faith. In a world where right and wrong have no meaningful place in the order of the universe, nothing at all could be trusted (cf. 145:20; 139:19; 104:35).

The temptation to put ultimate trust for salvation in human leaders and institutions is perennial. In Psalm 146, praise becomes a critique of such misplaced trust and a proclamation of the only right use of trust—in God who keeps faith!

Psalm 147: God of Cosmos, Congregation, and City

Is 61
Lk 4 vs 7b-9a

Psalm 147 begins with the praise of praise itself (so NRSV, NJPS; the text is uncertain and the adjectives "good" and "delightful" may be predicates of the LORD instead of praise; see

441

33:1; 135:3). The LORD is so much the content of praise that praise begins to reflect his attributes. In it his goodness is apparent. Through it the singers experience pleasure over the delightfulness of the LORD. The psalm can be read as a verbal portrait of that delightfulness.

1. The psalm has three distinct parts. Each part is composed on the pattern of the imperative hymn with an opening summons to praise followed by the praise itself (Introduction, sec. 5.5.4). The first part praises the LORD because he restores Israel (vv. 2–3), controls the stars with power and wisdom (vv. 4–5), and reorders the conditions of human beings. The second part thanks the LORD because he provides food for his creatures (vv. 8–9) and prefers from his people dependence on him rather than trust in military strength (vv. 10–11). The third part exalts the LORD because he provides security and well-being for his people (vv. 13–14), controls the coming and passing of winter (vv. 15–18), and reveals his statutes and ordinances to Israel alone (vv. 19–20).

2. As one reviews the items of praise, it becomes immediately apparent that each part of the hymn combines activities that concern the community of the LORD's people and deeds that concern the world at large. The LORD restores city and people after the exile, and he numbers and names the stars. The two kinds of actions are ranged alongside each other to create what seems to be an indiscriminate montage. But there is a theological purpose behind this mingling. Two kinds of experience are being brought together: experience of the way the world works and the way the religious community's history has run. The purpose is not to reduce both to a general providence. The purpose is the same as that so powerfully executed in the prophecy of Isaiah 40—55: to see both as the exercise of one sovereignty and to create a unified view of all reality (e.g., note how the prophet correlates governance of world and salvation history in passages like Isa. 40:12–31; 45:18–25).

In this unified view, the two areas inform and interpret each other. The history of the community of faith is a small part of reality, but the power that moves its course is the same that governs the stars. On the other hand, the processes of the world are vast, impersonal, and uncaring, but the sovereignty at work in the world is the saving, caring God whom Israel has come to know in its history. Notice that the cry of the young ravens is seen in analogy to the cry of Israel for help, and see Luke 12:24.

442

When beheld as the vision of the one sovereignty, both the course of the world and the life of faith are experienced differently.

3. The psalm was written for the Jerusalem congregation (v. 12) in the period of the restoration after the exile (vv. 2–3, 13–14). The way that particular experience of the LORD's help is expressed is one example of the way hymnic theology in Israel's praise turns a specific deed of the LORD into a general confession. The hymn does not say in narrative mode that the LORD rebuilt Zion and gathered the outcasts, but using participles it makes the deed a typical activity, a feature of the character of the LORD. The deed becomes a symbol, a means of knowledge of God and a guide to what to expect from him. So Israel, and later the church, can say through the years in its praise, "The LORD builds Jerusalem," and state its confidence that the LORD not only founded the church but restores and gathers it when it passes through tribulation.

4. In the third part of the psalm, the poet uses the notion of the "word of the LORD" to describe the exercise of God's sovereignty. As the prophets used the term, "word of the LORD" means the communication of the LORD's thought, will, and decision. The psalmist speaks of it as an agent of God's rule set to do his bidding (vv. 15, 18). The word is an active force by which the LORD deals with the world. Here the notion is carried a short distance toward thinking of the word as the personified agent of God so important in the New Testament. Again the poet reflects Isaiah 40—55 (Isa. 40:8; 55:10–11).

The word of the LORD takes different forms and has different functions. In verse 19, "word" is the summary concept for statutes and ordinances. The laws given to Israel as revelation of the will of the LORD are altogether the word by which he orders their life. The psalmist views the law as the gift of God that distinguishes his people from all others. What marks the people of God is the gift of the word (see 1; 19; 119). For Israel, the law became the most significant form of the word. The vocabulary and thinking echo that of Deuteronomy 4:1–8. For the church, the Christ and the gospel that proclaims him be- John 1 1–3
came the most significant form. Both communities of faith praise and thank God for the gift of his word because it is the word that makes it possible for them to live as the people of the LORD.

443

Psalm 148: All Creatures of Our God and King

Psalm 148 is third in the group of five Hallelujah psalms that conclude the book (Introduction, sec. 5.5.2). Indeed, the psalm not only opens and closes with a "Praise the LORD," but once having uttered this cry of praise, the psalm repeats the cry over and over. The reason seems to lie in the purpose of the psalm. It is a hymn composed as an invitation to all creation and creatures to join in the praise of the LORD.

1. There are two parts, each arranged in the same way (vv. 1–6 and 7–14). The arrangement follows the form of the imperative hymn, a summons to praise and a basis or content of praise (Introduction, sec. 5.5.4). The psalm is distinctive in the proportion of the summons to the content. In the first part, the summons runs from verse 1 through 5a, and the basis is stated in verses 5b and 6. In the second part, the summons covers verses 7 through 13a, and the reason is stated in verse 13b and 14. Each section of summons is concluded by a summary jussive sentence: "Let them praise the name of the LORD" (vv. 5a, 13a). The first part is dominated by the repetition of "Praise him," accompanied by adverbial phrases and vocatives. The second shifts to repeated vocatives alone. In its first part, Psalm 148 is well on the way to the form of Psalm 150, where the imperative call to praise occupies the whole. The Book of Psalms draws to its close, and the call to praise rises toward its final crescendo.

2. The parts of the psalm are based on the theme "heavens and earth." The first part concerns the praise of the LORD "from the heavens" (v. 1) and the second "from the earth" (v. 7). The heavenly choir is to include angels and host (cf. 103:19–22), sun and moon and stars, even the highest heavens and the cosmic waters above them. The earthly choir includes the sea monsters and the deeps they inhabit, weather, mountains, trees, animals, rulers and nations, all sexes and ages. The motif "all" punctuates the roll call to insist that the list is inclusive, representative of everything that is. The psalm intends to recruit the entire realm of being for the praise of the LORD. The call to the whole world to recognize the reign of the LORD in joyous praise in Psalms 96 and 98 is here extended to the universe. The royal majesty of the LORD is "above earth and heaven" (v. 13), and only the praise of all in both realms can respond and correspond to the

LORD's exalted name. "All creatures of our God and King, Lift up your voice and with us sing, Alleluia!" (Francis of Assisi).

3. The LORD is praised as the sovereign who by the authority and power of his commanding word made all that is and orders all according to his purpose (vv. 5, 8). The psalm thinks of creation as bringing what is into existence and maintaining it in its place and purpose (compare vv. 5–6 and 8 with 33:6–9 and 104:5–9). The entire list is apparently included in the category of creation. Echoes of Genesis 1:1—2:4 are scattered through the psalm. It could be sung as a hymnic response after the first chapter of the Bible is read. We human beings who are addressed in verses 11–12 should recognize that we are in the list with all the creation and creatures as creature and creation ourselves. We are in our obligation to praise no different from and no more than all the rest. Everything and everyone is identical in being addressed by the psalm. We human beings are one with all being in our relation to One whose name alone is exalted and whose majesty is above earth and heaven.

4. How are sun and moon, heavens and waters, storms and mountains, animals and birds to answer the call to praise? How can they fulfill their obligation? One might attribute the call to them to poetic license, but that would miss the theological seriousness behind the hymnic joy. Perhaps there is the hint of an answer in verses 5–6 and 8. The celestial lights and firmament and waters are the work of the LORD's command, and they are maintained in their place and purpose by his power. The stormy wind fulfills his command by being a stormy wind. The creation and the creatures praise in their very being and doing, by existing and filling their assigned place. But verse 14 says something more about Israel as the faithful people of the LORD. For them, the LORD "has raised up a horn"; the expression is an idiom for the bestowal of dignity and fame (75:10; 92:10; 112:9). The LORD has given his faithful praise as their dignity and power. They are the ones who are "near" to him, know and can speak his exalted name. They are given the praise with which to voice the unspoken praise of all creation. Praise is their place and purpose. In the praise of the people of the LORD, the name that is the truth about the entire universe is spoken on behalf of all the rest of creation.

445

Psalm 149: Praise in Their Throats and a Sword in Their Hands

Psalm 149 is the fourth in the group of five Hallelujah psalms that conclude the book (Introduction, sec. 5.5.2). Like the others, it begins and ends with the liturgical cry, "Praise the LORD." The distinctive feature of the psalm is surprising; it seems to be a hymn of preparation for holy war waged by the people of God against the nations.

1. The psalm is an imperative hymn of praise (Introduction, sec. 5.5.4) composed of two parts. The first part follows the hymnic pattern of a summons to praise (vv. 1–3) supported by a statement of the basis or content of praise (v. 4). When the summons resumes in the second part, it is phrased in jussive sentences (vv. 5–6), which are followed by infinitives of purpose stating a course of action for the faithful to complete their praise (vv. 7–9a). The second part concludes with a declaration about the meaning of the action (v. 9b). The term "glory" *(hadar)* in the declaration corresponds to the "glory" *(kabod)* in verse 5, forming an inclusion around the second part and defining its topic, the glory of the faithful ones. Whereas the LORD by name, title, or pronoun is present in every clause of part one, it is the faithful who occupy the measures of the second part. Part two is a very unusual section for a hymn of praise.

2. The hymn praises the LORD as king (v. 2), and its first part resembles in many ways the hymns whose subject is the reign of the LORD (Introduction, sec. 6.3). Like Psalms 96 and 98, it begins with a call for a new song to the LORD. As in Psalm 95:6–7, the LORD is Israel's God because he is its maker (also 100:3), in accord with the ancient logic that the creator is ruler (see the comment on Psalm 24, sec. 1). It is this relation of the LORD's kingship to Israel in which the psalm is interested. Even in its first part, Israel is featured and given a series of identifications: the assembly of the faithful, children of Zion, his people, the humble. The LORD is identified without exception in relation to Israel; the LORD is maker and king of Israel, who takes pleasure in his people and adorns the humble with victory. Verse 4 is the transition that unites the two parts of the psalm. The LORD is praised in part one because the pleasure of his royal purpose is vested in his people, these lowly ones whom he

will adorn with a saving victory that manifests his reign. Part two then says that the faithful are to be actors in the saving victory. They are called to praise the LORD and arm themselves in preparation for combat that serves the LORD's vengeance on the nations. The victory that the LORD will give them in that warfare will be their adornment, their glory and honor.

3. Note that it is by the combination of praise and sword that the faithful serve the vengeance of the LORD. Sword without praise would not serve; only the sword that can be drawn in praise of the LORD can serve. The vengeance is not theirs; they are to carry out the judgment decreed, "the written sentence," as the Hebrew puts it. The vengeance of the LORD is the action the LORD takes to maintain and enforce his reign against his adversaries (see the comment on Psalm 94, sec. 2). In the Psalms, the vengeance of the LORD is his vindication of his relation to his people, who suffer under the assault of the nations (Psalm 79, see vv. 9–10), and his vindication of those who trust him against the threat and oppression of the wicked (Psalm 94). Here it is the vengeance against the nations and their rulers that is the concern. In the rhetoric and theology of the Psalms, nations and their rulers are typically the opposition to the reign of the LORD. They are systems of rule in history that threaten to dissolve and overwhelm the story of the LORD's people, who represent and make known his reign (see the comment on Psalms 9—10). We cannot be certain to what particular source, if any, the reference to "the written verdict" refers. A likely source is the prophetic oracles against the nations, which speak more often than any other written tradition of the LORD's vengeance. If that is right, the psalm is calling the faithful to prepare for service when the prophetic words are being fulfilled.

4. Like some of the other hymns about the reign of the LORD, this one has some illuminating connections with the prophecies in Isaiah 40—66. These are the prophecies that speak overall of the LORD's revelation of his kingship in the world through the victorious salvation of his people (e.g., 40:1–11; 41:21–29; 52:7–10). Specifically, the LORD in these prophecies promises to make Israel a *two-edged* instrument to crush those who war against them (41:11–16) and to *adorn* his people with a saving victory (55:5; 60:9). In assigning to the faithful the role of warriors who carry out the LORD's judgment on the nations, the hymn can be grouped with prophecies in

447

Micah 4:13 and Zechariah 10:5; 12:6. There is an eschatological, almost apocalyptic, dimension to the psalm's anticipation of a warfare of the faithful that will settle the conflict between the kingdoms of this world and the kingdom of God. The expectation of a victory over nations and peoples that leaves kings and princes in chains as subdued captives is a vision that transcends local conflicts and specific wars. Inspired by psalms and prophecies of the coming kingdom, this psalmist has composed a hymn that calls the faithful to a praise and militancy that serves its coming. It is important to note that the faithful are the humble, the lowly (v. 4), the type who will be called in the New Testament the poor in spirit, the meek (Matt. 5:3, 5). Something wonderful and strange is afoot here, the lowly becoming the warriors who fight for the kingdom and inherit the earth.

5. The location of Psalm 149 in the book adds two perspectives on its interpretation. It clearly continues the preceding hymn. Psalm 148:14 already speaks of Israel as the LORD's people, his faithful ones, and says that the LORD has raised up praise for them that will be their fame and power. Psalm 149 as sequel is that praise and discloses how praise can be glory and honor for the faithful ones. In Psalm 148, the kings and princes and all peoples are part of the universal choir that praises the LORD (v. 11), while in Psalm 149 they are the powers to be overthrown in praise of the LORD. The two psalms juxtapose the two unreconciled pictures of the LORD's rule and the nations found in both testaments, one of inclusion and one of conflict. Both pictures cast the light of revelation on the purpose and way of God. As the next to the last psalm in the book, Psalm 149 corresponds to the location of Psalm 2 as the second. Psalm 2 announces that it is through his anointed king that the LORD will claim kings and nations for his rule. In Psalm 149, the human instrument is the assembly of the faithful, who seem in their service to be a messianic community through whom the LORD achieves what was assigned the vocation of the Davidic king (see the comment on Psalm 2, sec. 4; and see Dan. 7:18, 21). In the Old Testament, the relation between the roles of messiah and people in the coming of the kingdom is also not reconciled but left to cast light on things to come.

6. Used as hymn and Scripture, Psalm 149 also provokes two unreconciled responses. Its call to eschatological war is of course the provocation. The call is heard, and must be heard, with an apprehension, because wars launched in the name of

God and attempts to force the coming of the kingdom have brought cruel disaster. It is interesting that the term "assembly of the faithful" turns up in I Maccabees 2:42 as a designation of certain "mighty warriors of Israel," who made cause with Mattathias and his sons. The psalm was used by Caspar Scloppius to inflame the Roman Catholic princes to the Thirty Years' religious war, and by Thomas Müntzer to stir up the War of the Peasants (Prothero, pp. 152–153). The warning of Jesus stands: "Put your sword back into its place; for all who take the sword will perish by the sword" (Matt. 26:52). On the other hand, the psalm asks whether attempts to banish the stance and metaphors of militancy from the conduct and language of the faithful mistake the world in which faithfulness exists. The mode of the militancy has been transformed by the death and resurrection of Jesus and his instruction to claim the nations for him by conversion and baptism (Matt. 28:19). But faithfulness is placed in conflict with the purposes of nations and their rulers. The faithful may hear in the psalm the call to draw "the sword of the Spirit" in the praise of the LORD (Eph. 6:10–17). "For the weapons of our warfare are not worldly, but have divine power to destroy strongholds" (II Cor. 10:4, RSV).

Psalm 150: The Final Hallelujah

Psalm 150 is the fifth in the group of Hallelujah psalms that conclude the Book of Psalms. It is, in fact, the liturgical cry, "Hallelujah," turned into an entire psalm. Its vigorous and enthusiastic repetition of the call to praise forms an inspiring and instructive conclusion to the sequence of hymns and to the book.

1. Like its four predecessors in this final sequence of hymns of praise, Psalm 150 is enclosed by the defining liturgical cry, "Praise the LORD" (Introduction, sec. 5.5.2). Its composer followed literary strategy used in Psalm 148 by expanding the role of the first part of the imperative hymn (Introduction, sec. 5.5.4). In Psalm 150 the strategy is taken to its limits. The psalm stays with the imperative mode. It is composed simply of ten imperative sentences and a concluding jussive, each of them a summons to praise the LORD. The usual basis or content of praise is incorporated in the imperative sentences of verse 2. The expected vocative identifying those to whom the summons is addressed is delayed until the final line (v. 6), where the

449

transition from imperative to jussive mode gives the vocative a special emphasis. This compositional strategy achieves two effects. The act of praising the LORD is lifted up as possibility and responsibility. The responsibility is given to all for whom it is a possibility, all who have breath.

2. The content as well as the structure of the psalm seems to depend on the liturgical form. The psalm is a hymnic exposition of "Praise the LORD." Its sentences say *who* is praised (v. 1), *why* he is praised (v. 2), *how* he is to be praised (vv. 3–5), and finally, *who* is to praise him (v. 6). The One praised is God (*'el*), whose sanctuary is above the vault of the heavens. Title and location identify the LORD as the supreme sovereign who rules over all (cf. 29:10; 96:6; Ezek. 10:1). The LORD is to be praised as the one who reigns. He is to be praised for his mighty deeds that manifest his immeasurable greatness, his works of creation and salvation. Verse 2 summarizes in a poetic line what is said in all of Psalms 145 and 147. The LORD is to be praised in music. The list in verses 3–5 seems intended to include all the instruments that could be used in the performance of worship (cf. 98:5–6). Tambourine and dance are there! This emphasis on music in the final psalm reminds us of all the introductory notations concerned with musical performance and the fact that even prayers adopted as psalms were set to music. It is a witness to the power of music, its amazing potential for evoking beauty and feeling and for carrying vision beyond the range of words into the realm of imagination. That we sing the praise of God is no accidental custom. Music performed, sung, enacted is so much a dimension of praise that words of praise without music need to be musical in rhythm and elegance if they are to serve as praise. The very poetry of the psalms is musical in quality and has been easily set to music of every age and culture. The name of the LORD set to music or voiced in language that is musical—that is praise.

3. The final line calls upon everything that has breath to praise the LORD. In the Old Testament vocabulary, "breath" (*neshama*) more than any other term designates the vitality of the physical life of the human being that comes from God. The term is not a common one and is used in a significant pattern of contexts. The original human being received the breath of life from God (Gen. 2:7). All human beings have life by God's gift of breath that brings vitality and reason (Job 32:8; 33:4; Isa. 42:5). If God should withdraw his breath, all would return to the

450

dust (Job 34:14–15). The breath of life is, in the long last, the human being's only possession, and in this the human being is dependent upon the LORD (Isa. 2:22). No other use of breath could be more right and true to life than praise of the LORD. No other sound could better speak the gratitude of life than praise of the LORD. So the psalm concludes with a vocative addressed to all of humanity calling for a simultaneity of praise with life. This final call echoes the promise that "all flesh will bless his holy name forever and ever" at the end of Psalm 145; the promise and the call form a significant inclusion around the fivefold "Hallelujah" that concludes the Psalter.

4. As the final psalm in the Psalter, the 150th tells us something about the book. It brings to a resounding climax the increasing dominance by hymns of praise that sets in with the hymns to the LORD's reign in the 1990s (Introduction, sec. 4.4). The book that began with a commendation of Torah of the LORD as the way of life ends here with an invitation to praise of the LORD as the use of life. The correspondence between the repeated verb "praise" *(hillel)* and the title of the book in Hebrew, "Praises" *(tehillim)*, argues that those who gave the book its name understood the book itself to contain the praises of the LORD offered to all that have breath. The book is the language by which life can say its dependence and obligation and gratitude to the LORD. Hallelujah!

SELECTED BIBLIOGRAPHY

1. For Further Study

BRUEGGEMANN, WALTER. *The Message of the Psalms.* Minneapolis: Augsburg Publishing House, 1984.

————. *Israel's Praise.* Philadelphia: Fortress Press, 1988.

CALVIN, JOHN. *Commentary on the Book of Psalms.* 5 vols. Edinburgh: Printed for the Calvin Translation Society, M.DCCC.XLV.

DELITZSCH, FRANZ. *Psalms.* Three volumes in one: C. F. Keil and F. Delitzsch, *Commentary on the Old Testament,* vol. 5. Repr. Grand Rapids: Wm. B. Eerdmans Publishing Co., 1980.

HOLLADAY, WILLIAM L. *The Psalms through Three Thousand Years.* Minneapolis: Fortress Press, 1993.

INTERPRETATION: A JOURNAL OF BIBLE AND THEOLOGY. Articles on the Psalms in 28/1 (1974), 39/1 (1985), and 46/2 (1992).

KRAUS, HANS-JOACHIM. *Psalms 1—59: A Commentary* and *Psalms 60—150: A Commentary.* Minneapolis: Augsburg Publishing House, 1988 and 1989.

————. *Theology of the Psalms.* Minneapolis: Augsburg Publishing House, 1986.

LUTHER'S WORKS. Edited by Jaroslav Pelikan. Vols. 12, 13, 14, 15, 16. St. Louis: Concordia Publishing House, 1955.

McCANN, J. CLINTON, JR. *A Theological Introduction to the Book of Psalms.* Nashville: Abingdon Press, 1993.

MILLER, PATRICK D., Jr. *Interpreting the Psalms.* Philadelphia: Fortress Press, 1986.

MOWINCKEL, SIGMUND. *The Psalms in Israel's Worship.* Oxford: Basil Blackwell, 1962.

NEALE, J. M., and R. F. LITTLEDALE. *A Commentary on the Psalms: From Primitive and Mediaeval Writers.* 4 vols. London: Joseph Masters & Co., 1884.

SEYBOLD, KLAUS. *Introducing the Psalms.* Edinburgh: T. & T. Clark, 1990.

STUHLMUELLER, CARROLL. *Psalms 1 and Psalms 2.* OLD TESTAMENT MESSAGE 21 and 22. Wilmington: Michael Glazier, 1983.

WEISER, ARTUR. *The Psalms, A Commentary.* OLD TESTAMENT LIBRARY. Philadelphia: Westminster Press, 1962.

453

WESTERMANN, CLAUS. *Praise and Lament in the Psalms.* Atlanta: John Knox Press, 1981.

———. *The Psalms: Structure, Content and Message.* Minneapolis: Augsburg Publishing House, 1980.

WORD BIBLICAL COMMENTARY. Waco, Tex.: Word Books. Vol. 19, *Psalms 1—50,* by Peter C. Craigie, 1983. Vol. 20, *Psalms 51—100,* by Marvin E. Tate, 1990. Vol. 21, *Psalms 101–150,* by Leslie C. Allen, 1983.

2. Literature Cited

ALLEN, LESLIE C. *Psalms 101—150.* WORD BIBLICAL COMMENTARY, vol. 21. Waco, Tex.: Word Books, 1983.

ANCIENT NEAR EASTERN TEXTS RELATING TO THE OLD TESTAMENT. Edited by James B. Pritchard. 2nd ed. Princeton: Priceton University Press, 1955.

BARTH, KARL. *Church Dogmatics.* 4 vols. Edinburgh: T. & T. Clark, 1936–1962.

BONHOEFFER, DIETRICH. *Life Together.* New York: Harper & Brothers, 1954.

BRAUDE, WILLIAM G. *The Midrash on Psalms.* YALE JUDAICA SERIES XIII. New Haven: Yale University Press, 1959.

BRUEGGEMANN, WALTER. *Abiding Astonishment: Psalms, Modernity, and the Making of History.* Louisville, Ky.: Westminster/John Knox Press, 1991.

CALVIN, JOHN. *Commentary on the Book of Psalms.* Translated by James Anderson. 5 vols. Edinburgh: Printed for the Calvin Translation Society, M.DCCC.XLV.

CHILDS, BREVARD S. "Psalm Titles and Midrashic Exegesis." *Journal of Semitic Studies* 16:137–150 (1971).

CLIFFORD, R. J. "In Zion and David a New Beginning: An Interpretation of Psalm 78." In *Traditions in Transformation,* ed. B. Halpern and J. D. Levenson, pp. 121–141. Winona Lake, Ind.: Eisenbrauns, 1981.

CRAIGIE, PETER C. *Psalms 1—50.* WORD BIBLICAL COMMENTARY, vol. 19. Waco, Tex.: Word Books, 1983.

CROSS, FRANK MOORE. *Canaanite Myth and Hebrew Epic: Essays in the History of the Religion of Israel.* Cambridge, Mass.: Harvard University Press, 1973.

454

DAY, JOHN. *God's Conflict with the Dragon and the Sea.* Cambridge: Cambridge University Press, 1985.

———. *Psalms.* OLD TESTAMENT GUIDES. Sheffield: JSOT Press, 1990.

DELITZSCH, FRANZ. *Psalms.* Three volumes in one: C. F. Keil and F. Delitzsch, *Commentary on the Old Testament,* vol. 5. Repr. Grand Rapids: Wm. B. Eerdmans Publishing Co., 1980.

FISHBANE, MICHAEL. *Biblical Interpretation in Ancient Israel.* New York: Oxford University Press, 1988.

GERSTENBERGER, ERHARD S. *Psalms: With Introduction to Cultic Poetry, Part 1.* THE FORMS OF THE OLD TESTAMENT LITERATURE, vol. 14. Grand Rapids: Wm. B. Eerdmans Publishing Co., 1988.

KEEL, OTHMAR. *The Symbolism of the Biblical World: Ancient Near Eastern Iconography and the Book of Psalms.* New York: Crossroad, 1985.

KIRKPATRICK, A. F. *The Book of Psalms.* CAMBRIDGE BIBLE FOR SCHOOLS AND COLLEGES. Cambridge: Cambridge University Press, 1930.

KRAUS, HANS-JOACHIM. *Psalms 1—59: A Commentary.* Minneapolis: Augsburg Publishing House, 1988.

———. *Psalms 60—150: A Commentary.* Minneapolis: Augsburg Publishing House, 1989.

———. *Theology of the Psalms.* Minneapolis: Augsburg Publishing House, 1986.

LEVENSON, JON D. *Creation and the Persistence of Evil.* San Francisco: Harper & Row, 1988.

———. *Sinai and Zion.* Minneapolis: Winston Press, 1985.

LUTHER'S WORKS. Edited by Jaroslav Pelikan. Vols. 12, 13, 14, 15, 16. St. Louis: Concordia Publishing House, 1955.

McCANN, J. CLINTON, JR. "Psalm 73: A Microcosm of Old Testament Theology." In *The Listening Heart: Essays in Wisdom and the Psalms,* pp. 247–257. JOURNAL FOR THE STUDY OF OLD TESTAMENT, SUPPLEMENT SERIES 58. Sheffield: JSOT Press, 1987.

———. *A Theological Introduction to the Book of Psalms: The Psalms as Torah.* Nashville: Abingdon Press, 1993.

MAYS, JAMES L. "The Center of the Psalms," *Festschrift for James Barr.* Oxford: Oxford University Press (forthcoming).

p. 87 ———. "The David of the Psalms." *Interpretation* 40:143–155 (1986).

p. 89 ———. " 'In a Vision': The Portrayal of the Messiah in the Psalms." *Ex Auditu* 7:1–8 (1991).

———. "The Language of the Reign of God." *Interpretation* 47:117–126 (1993).

p. 128 ———. "The Place of the Torah Psalms in the Psalter." *Journal of Biblical Literature* 106:3–12 (1987).

p. 136 ———. "Psalm 118 in the Light of Canonical Analysis." In *Canon, Theology, and Old Testament Interpretation,* Gene M. Tucker et al, eds. Philadelphia: Fortress Press, 1988.

p. 46 ———. "A Question of Identity: The Threefold Hermeneutic of Psalmody." *The Asbury Theological Journal* 46:87–94 (1991).

METTINGER, T. N. D. *In Search of God: The Meaning and Message of the Everlasting Names.* Philadelphia: Fortress Press, 1988.

MILLER, P. D., JR. *The Divine Warrior in Early Israel.* Cambridge: Harvard University Press, 1973.

———. *Interpreting the Psalms.* Philadelphia: Fortress Press, 1986.

NASUTI, H. P. *Tradition History and the Psalms of Asaph.* SBL DISSERTATION SERIES 88. Atlanta: Scholars Press, 1988.

NEALE, J. M., and R. F. LITTLEDALE. *A Commentary on the Psalms: From Primitive and Mediaeval Writers.* Vols. 1, 2, 3, 4. 4th ed. London: Joseph Masters & Co., 1884.

NIEBUHR, H. RICHARD. *Radical Monotheism and Western Culture.* New York: Harper & Row, 1970.

PEROWNE, J. J. STEWART. *The Book of Psalms.* Vols. 1 and 2. Andover: Warren F. Draper, 1898.

PETERSEN, DAVID L., and KENT HAROLD RICHARDS. *Interpreting Hebrew Poetry.* Minneapolis: Fortress Press, 1992.

PROTHERO, ROWLAND E. *The Psalms in Human Life.* London: John Murray, 1903.

SEYBOLD, K., and V. B. MUELLER. *Sickness and Healing.* BIBLICAL ENCOUNTER SERIES. Nashville: Abingdon Press, 1981.

ST. AUGUSTINE ON THE PSALMS. Translated and annotated by Scholastica Helyn and Felicitas Corrigan. 2 vols. Westminster, Md.: Newman Press, 1960.

STOLZ, FRITZ. *Psalmen im nachkultischen Raum.* THEOLO-
GISCHE STUDIEN 129. Zurich: Theologischer Verlag, 1983.

VON RAD, GERHARD. *Old Testament Theology.* 2 vols. New
York: Harper & Row. Vol. 1: *The Theology of Israel in
Historical Traditions,* 1962; vol. 2: *The Theology of Israel's
Prophetic Traditions,* 1965.

WESTERMANN, CLAUS. *Praise and Lament in the Psalms.*
Atlanta: John Knox Press, 1981.

WILSON, GERALD HENRY. *The Editing of the Hebrew
Psalter.* SBL DISSERTATION SERIES 76. Chico, Calif.: Scholars Press, 1985.